THE COMPLETE
WOODHOUSE
GUIDE TO
DOG TRAINING

BARBARA WOODHOUSE

RINGPRESS

An imprint of Ringpress Ltd.,
Spirella House, Letchworth, Hertfordshire SG6 4ET

Text © Michael Claydon Woodhouse
and Ringpress Books 1990

First published 1990.
Some of the material contained in this book
has previously been published in the
United Kingdom under the titles
No Bad Dogs and Dog Training My Way.

ISBN No 0948955 95 3

Production consultants: Landmark Ltd.
Typeset by Ringpress Books.
New photography by Sally Shore.
Printed and bound in Great Britain by The Bath Press

CONTENTS

FOREWORD

BY PATRICK WOODHOUSE

My mother was born in Ireland in 1910 at a boys' public school where her father was headmaster. Both her family and the boys at the school had a great many different animals and thus she grew up surrounded by them from a very early age. Dogs and other animals became so much a part of her life that it was obvious from the start that she would have animals around her all her life.

One of my earliest recollections of my mother was that she was always with one or other of her two dogs. In the early Fifties she had a Great Dane which responded so perfectly to her training that it won numerous prizes for obedience work. She realised that she really did have a gift for training dogs and she decided that she must use this gift to help others train their dogs.

She started professionally in 1951 with a dog training club meeting on Croxley Green, just a few yards from our house, which was called Campions. She soon had a class of 25-30 dogs and their owners every Sunday and this led to the founding of four other training clubs, in nearby towns, which were always full of dog owners wishing to learn. Her weekends and evenings were thus spent doing the thing she enjoyed most, the training of dogs.

Her own Great Danes, Juno and Junia, were trained to such a high standard that they could work in films and on TV programmes by just being shown the action. Then by simply giving them a command or signal, they would act out the part to perfection. Juno, mother's best known Great Dane, became known as " Take 1 Juno" on the sets of the studios where she worked with famous actors like Sir Alec Guinness,

Clark Gable, Roger Moore, Eric Morecambe, and many others. Her Great Danes acted in more than eighty TV and movie productions in their careers, and many of the films were produced by my mother and often directed by her as well.

Her career really started to take off when she was invited to do a TV series about dog training for the BBC and the series was to be called: Training Dogs The Woodhouse Way. This series became such a success that it was repeated three times during its first year and led to two more series and a host of appearances on other programmes in which she was interviewed and in which she demonstrated her methods of dog training to TV stars such as Terry Wogan and Michael Parkinson. In the United States the programmes of her dog training became so popular that they are still being shown to this very day. She became known as the "Dog Lady" and her books became some of the best-sellers ever known in America.

In 1980 she won the cherished TV award presented by the Pye Corporation as the Female TV Personality Of The Year and went on to win the title of the World's Best Dog Trainer. Since those hectic days she has travelled the world demonstrating her methods to countless dog owners and visiting numerous countries, including the United States of America, Canada, Australia, New Zealand, Singapore and many parts of Europe.

This book is a completely new edition and compilation of two of her best-selling books on dog training. It includes many new photographs and much of the text has been rewritten to bring it right up to date. I hope that you, the reader, will get a great deal of help from this book and that it will answer all your questions about the difficulties many people experience when training their dogs. I am sure that the sense of achievement you will experience when you have successfully trained your dog to do even the simplest of exercises will give you a sense of oneness with your dog that cannot be bettered by a relationship with any other animal.

May I wish you every success with your training and hope that your dog will become, to quote my mother:

"A DOG THAT IS A PLEASURE TO ALL AND A NUISANCE TO NO ONE."

CHAPTER ONE

THE OWNER

There must be few people who have never owned a dog at some time or other in their lives, not necessarily a dog belonging exclusively to themselves, but one shared with the family. The main reasons for owning or sharing a dog come under these three headings in my opinion: for pleasure, profit or protection. I believe by far the greatest number are owned purely and simply for the joy of having a dog either to play with if you are young, or to take for walks and keep you fit if you are not so young, or just for the sheer delight of having a lovely creature round the house to be admired, to admire you, and to keep you company. In this book we are going to exclude those dogs that are kept for profit, as stock-in-trade of a business which must succeed or fail through the amount of money made; the business man or woman presumably sees to it that their dogs are made as attractive as possible to would-be purchasers. If the animals are fierce or unkempt they will not find buyers easily. So we will presume that they are sold before the disobedience, if it exists, has had time to develop or show itself. We are solely concerned with the training and therefore the health of the dog that belongs to the ordinary man in the street.

I wonder how many of these ordinary men in the street give much thought to this matter of owning a dog, before they are attracted by a cuddly puppy, with liquid brown eyes, that begs to join you by your fireside? Very few, I am sure. I am therefore going to try to point out the snags that exist and should be considered before any attempt is made to get a dog. First of all, before you buy a dog, decide whether you can afford to give it the home this wonderful friend of man deserves. I don't mean by this that you must be well-off financially to keep a dog. As long as the dog is properly fed, and properly exercised, he is willing to share the humblest abode with his owner. But a dog cannot be kept for nothing. A small dog needs approximately half a pound of meat a day in some form or other, and dog biscuits or brown bread according to its appetite. Therefore I believe that the very lowest sum for which one can keep a dog is about £3 a week. I know that in some households the dog costs nothing, as there are sufficient scraps from the table to give the dog an adequate and balanced diet, but this is the exception rather than the rule. Occasionally the dog becomes ill, and there are charities like the P.D.S.A. who will treat animals free if the owner cannot afford to pay. If every owner depended on this service, the cost of drugs alone would be impossible to meet. So we will conclude that the dog owner should support his own dog.

One must be prepared, too, to spend a small amount on tonics and flea powders, and soaps for washing the dog. No dog that is kept in the house should escape a bath or dry clean less than once a month. A good many people say to me, 'How dogs smell! We'd never keep them in the house!' If a dog smells, it is the owner's fault. He wouldn't keep his children unwashed and expect them to remain pleasant companions, yet the dog in some households is expected to keep clean with no help from outside. Have you considered how often the dog dips his mouth into gravy, and milk, into meat or fish, and that some of it is bound to adhere to his lips; yet how many people wash their dog's muzzle occasionally? I clean my dog's muzzle often. But then my dog gets a frequent bath with a really easy-lathering soap. The soap not only cleanses her but protects her from any infestation by insects. However dean you keep your dog, if she goes out for walks in the country she is liable to pick up insects. Bathing also helps to get the old coat out, and the rubbing one gives one's dog in lathering the soap acts as a tonic to the skin.

Another frequent complaint is: 'My dog's breath smells.' Of course it may do, unless you take care to see that your dog eats the right food, that his digestion is in good order, and that his teeth are clean. When one opens some dogs' mouths one is shocked by the state of their teeth. We know such illness as distemper makes the teeth a bad colour, but a lot of this deposit can be removed if, when the dog is ill, its teeth are kept clean with a piece of rag dipped in salt or some toothpaste. At once we hear cries 'My of dog wouldn't let me open his mouth

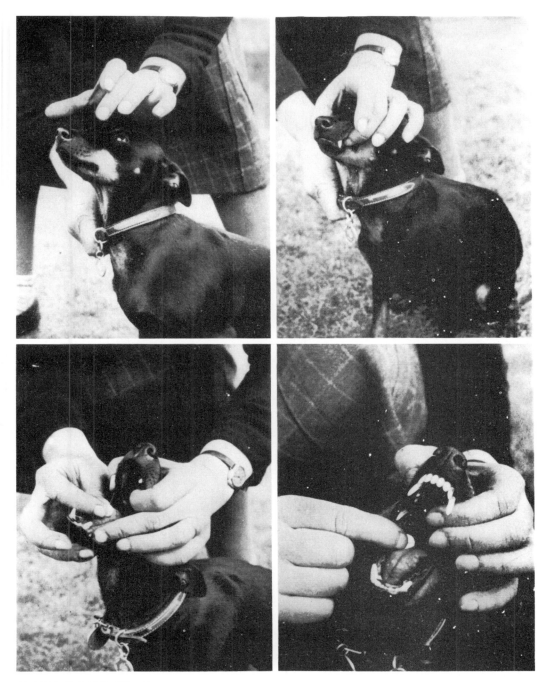

EASY DOES IT: The correct way to give your dog a pill.

DOWN SHE GOES: How to give liquid medicine

and do that! He'd bite me!' My answer to that is, 'Why haven't you trained your dog better? What happens when you wish to give your dog medicine?' I suppose there is an awful fuss, much growling, and probably spilling of the medicine all over the owner's clothes, with the dog breaking away, and much more friction between dog and owner. I believe that dogs should be trained from early days to sit quietly and have their mouths examined, and their teeth rubbed over; and that if any medicine has to be taken, the dog should be told that he must 'come for his medicine'. Then, in spite of the fact that the draught is nasty, he must learn to take it without biting or struggling. With liquid medicine it is easy, as there is a convenient pouch at the side of the dog's mouth; the liquid can be poured into this, and the dog's head tipped gently and down it goes. But with pills it is different. With hungry dogs that bolt their food it is easy to wrap a pill in a piece of meat, and down it all goes without the dog knowing it has taken anything; but with a sick dog who doesn't want to eat anyway, one must know the procedure to follow. I always open the dog's mouth and pop the pill right on the back of the tongue. The dog will move its tongue backwards and forwards in an effort to bring the pill back, but if one tilts the head slightly, down goes the pill. In no circumstances should you push the pill down its throat, or one day you will push it down the windpipe, and choke your dog.

If your vet wishes to give an injection the safest thing to do, if your dog is likely to turn round and bite either you or the vet, is to get a handkerchief and tie it round the dog's mouth. Then you should sit on a sofa or the floor and get the dog to lie down with its head in your lap and your arm over its neck. In this manner the dog cannot see what is going on and all is over before he has had time to resent it.

The mental outlook of the owner towards these operations is very important, for the dog at once picks up its owner's nervous reactions; and people who turn a ghastly white when anything has to be done to their dogs are not the ones to hold them for the vet. The dog senses their nervousness and becomes terrified at once. They should try to get a less squeamish member of the family to help. With a very tiny dog, of course, the previous hints do not apply, since one can manage to hold it for an injection with its head turned away from the vet. I never allow my dogs to be injected on the shoulder. If it has previously hurt, the dog fears that everyone who is going to stroke it may be going to give it another prick. If the injection is made in the loose skin just in front of the flank the dog doesn't seem to mind so much, or to have that same desire to bite when being stroked. Fear is one of the most difficult things to overcome in dogs, and that is why we should do everything in our power to prevent anything happening that is likely to leave fear behind. Never let anyone bend down and stroke your dog when it is asleep. It may wake up in a fright and snap without thinking, then it gets a scolding and your dog has a new problem to overcome.

I find one of the most troublesome things to persuade your dog to accept is that he may be caressed in the street by all and sundry. My dog, being a Great Dane, attracts attention wherever she goes. She is just the right height for everyone to stroke without bending down. Therefore, as one cannot stop dog lovers caressing dogs (or baby lovers kissing babies) one has to train the dog to put up with it without showing annoyance or trying to be too friendly. It is always extremely annoying when you have a trained dog, and have put it down to the 'sit' or 'down' outside a shop, to come and find a crowd round it trying to make it get up and talk to them, or trying to feed it on everything from a lollipop to a mince pie. When one's dog is trained fully, it must of course refuse food of all sorts from anyone but its owner or owners. Otherwise there is always the risk that a burglar or some malicious person may poison it. On the other hand there is the risk that a dog so trained, on going to kennels while its owner is away, may refuse food. This has happened and has been extremely worrying for the people concerned. I think if you are likely to leave your dog a lot with strangers, it is best not to teach it to refuse food from other people. I have found occasionally that my dog has had to take food whilst acting in a film, from people other than myself, and I have only had to introduce the person who is to give her food, and tell her it's all right, for her to take the food willingly. But I do not think many of my readers will at this stage have achieved, or perhaps ever will, such perfect communication as I have with my dog. For if they have reached that stage of training they will probably not have bought this book.

One of the vices we are going to tackle is the bad manners of boisterous dogs who jump up on greeting their owners, or visitors to the house, or even people in the street. Other suggestions concern dogs that chew up everything in the house, and which one daren't leave alone a minute in a room without finding there is no longer a newspaper to read, or your slippers to wear. Then there are the dogs who bark incessantly at everyone or anything, or the dogs that welcome everyone as though he were a long-lost friend, and won't bark at all (such a one was the dog mentioned in the newspapers recently, who made a bosom pal of the burglar). There are dogs that chase cats or other livestock; dogs that chase cars and bite postmen; horrid dogs that bite their owners; dogs that are only seen at mealtimes or when they want to be let into the house to sleep. There are the dogs that soil the whole house when they feel like it, and who have therefore to be kept outside for health reasons, as no one should tolerate in the house a dog that is not house-trained. Then there are the dogs that are so clean and well trained that they will not relieve themselves when away from home. I once had a Great Dane like that, and it worried me terribly. I spent one day at the seaside taking her for miles trying to find a suitable piece of grass which she would use. There are the dogs that jump on all the furniture, and refuse to come off. And there are the dogs that steal food, so that one has to be always on the alert not to put a bit of food within their reach. Lastly there are the dogs that won't come when they are called and the dogs that fight all other dogs, so that it is a misery to take them out. We are going to deal with all these misdemeanours of dogs in separate chapters and if in so doing I find myself able to give hints on other problems that crop up as an outcome of these, I shall do so incidentally.

I would like to say that in my opinion if, by the time you have owned a dog six months he has any of the faults I have listed, except nerves, it is in practically every case your own fault. You have not really persisted in training your dog in the right way. I meet an enormous number of dog owners in a year at my courses, and hundreds of others whom I never meet write to me from all over the country for help or advice with the training of their dogs. I am always ready to admit there may be a dog somewhere that is untrainable, but it is a rare exception.

But that is more than I can say of dog owners. There are hundreds of dog owners everywhere who ought never to keep a dog. These are some of the reasons why. They believe that by giving a dog everything it wants it will repay their kindness by implicit obedience and love. That is nonsense. A dog must respect its owner from the day it joins the household. Occasionally in every dog's life there comes a time when firmness is a necessity. If at that time the owner only tries coaxing, the dog will become the master, and the true understanding which exists between the master and dog has been lost. There are plenty of owners who think that it is cruel to control their dog in any way. They really believe that for a dog to be happy it must have complete freedom to go where it will when it will. I have even heard dog owners tell me, not very logically, that it is my duty to put my beloved bitch into kennels when she is on heat so that their dog will not be attracted round to my home when fights and other troubles might develop. The idea that they might control their own dog's movements, and leave my bitch safely in my own home and garden, never enters their heads. To impress their duty on them I have often taken their dogs, unwelcome on my premises, to the police station, and they have had to fetch them and pay for their keep. Another erroneous notion is that a dog is only happy when racing over the countryside chasing rabbits or livestock, and that it must not be thwarted by being called home. The numbers of times I have heard owners telling me it took two hours to catch their dog is unbelievable. These dogs neither love nor respect their owners. A dog that loves its owner cannot bear him or her out of sight or hearing, and will not run off for hours on its own private concerns.

Many owners think a dog should eat until it can eat no more and that it is cruel to give their dogs only the correct amount of food, however much those lovely eyes plead. There are excellent books dealing with the nutrition of dogs, and most dog biscuit manufacturers are only too pleased to tell owners about feeding, so I shall not enlarge on the theme beyond saying that it is not cruel to diet your dog. He will not be too fat, and therefore lazy, when you wish to take him for a long ramble, and lastly he will cost less to keep when given his suitable rations. I do believe that dogs need extra vitamins and that the ordinary diet they get does not always provide all they need. Vitamins A and B are, in my opinion, the ones they seem to need, in most cases, as supplement.

There are thousands of dog owners whose lives are made a misery by their male dogs' insistence on stopping at every lamppost. This is a thing I never allow. A dog of mine would get his freedom whenever possible and at this time he relieves himself as often as he wishes, but I should get extremely annoyed if I were forcibly stopped by my dog in a walk through the streets, and I should be tempted to commit murder if my dog attempted to relieve himself on a shop front or near anyone's front door. I am revolted by the way dog owners allow this disgusting behaviour. I have dogs brought to my classes who try this on. They are only warned twice and then they are removed from the class. This does not mean that I cannot forgive a puppy or a nervous dog for forgetting himself, it means that an adult dog whose owner is not attending properly to its behaviour, and allows it to soil our hall, will be sent out. Each session only lasts two and a half hours, and any dog can behave itself for that time. If not, the owner is at liberty to take it out for exercise.

Most owners think this lamp post stopping is natural and must be allowed. I wonder whether they do or do not train their children? I look upon dogs as having the same mental capacity as children of five years old, and I think a dog or a child of that age should be trained to cleanliness. And as for dog owners who say that they must put everything out of reach of their dogs, so that it shall not be torn up, and who blame themselves if something does get destroyed because they didn't remember to put it away, I can only assume that they have little else to do.

In my busy life, I certainly haven't time to be so careful. Before going into the handling of 'difficult dogs' let us for a few moments analyse the owners of these misfits, and see if we can tackle the problem by re-educating the owners. Without a moment's hesitation I say: 'Yes we can'. If the owners are interested enough and fond enough of their dogs to read training books or to attend training schools or courses, they are well worth the time spent in helping them. For the most part those who seek my help and advice are women. The female of the species undoubtedly not only wields the rolling pin, but holds the dog's lead as well. Older children I find make excellent handlers of dogs, but owing to school they seldom have sufficient time to be entrusted with the entire training of the dog, so it naturally falls to Mother.

The worst dog trainers are undoubtedly mothers with young children; they simply haven't time or energy to give to an animal. The result is the dog becomes a nuisance. It is regarded as the plaything of the children, and seldom have the children been taught to respect the privacy of the dog. It amazes me what patience most dogs show towards children. They suffer being dressed up and put in a pram, they endure their ears being pulled, and being hugged too tightly, and they endure being woken up when they want to sleep in the gentle manner of nice dogs. But I am definitely not in agreement with people who buy puppies for small children, and then abandon the puppy to the mercy of the children and feel angry if the puppy bites the children or tears up their things. Few children would stand what many puppies have to put up with, and if in time the puppy grows adult and no longer wishes to be the target for little Willie's tantrums, and answers back with a bite, it is always the dog that is to blame, never the child. I can quite honestly say that when my children were tiny I never left my dogs to play with them unsupervised in case, without meaning to be unkind, the child did something that hurt or annoyed the dog. The children were trained to 'let sleeping dogs lie', and that they must not approach a dog that was not wagging its tail happily.

Most dogs seem to put up with the rough handling children give them in the same way as they put up with the nips from their own puppies. But without growling, how can a dog show it has had enough? That is why I think all small irresponsible children should be supervised in their play with dogs. Once the dog has learnt that only by growling can it check the children and their unwanted attentions, it is a short step to the quick irritable bite, and a very short step to becoming a problem dog or one on its last walk to the vet's. Children must be trained if they are to be good companions to dogs, and that is the way round I think it should be, for the human being always has the advantage over the dog, as it is the human being who decides its destiny. I have with my own eyes seen boys and girls send their dogs after livestock. How then is the dog to know that to chase cats and chickens, not to mention sheep, is a crime? Children can quickly learn to train their small dog to quite a high standard of obedience, and love doing it. If they have a pride and personal interest in the dog they will not teach it bad ways. It is up to the parents to see this interest is cultivated.

How many grown-ups make suitable handlers? I regretfully say good handlers are few and far between, the main reason being lack of light and shade in their personal character and make-up. Every day of my life I am astounded at the amount of annoyance and inconvenience owners put up with on account of their dogs. And by this I do not mean having holidays restricted by not being able to take their dog along, nor the work resulting from polished floors being covered with paw marks. I mean real good cases of having their new linoleum torn to shreds, or the baker refusing to call because the dog bites him, or not being able to turn over in bed at night because the dog bites if disturbed from his position in the centre of the bed; or not being able to knit one's husband a pullover, because the dog dislikes his mistress knitting and bites her as soon as the knitting is picked up! Or having to watch a dog chew something up because he won't let go. Or having to stay rigid in the garage because your guard dog has misunderstood whom to guard! These and countless other faults are borne by countless owners for no other reason than that they love their dogs. I feel very humble when I read their letters, for I doubt whether I would tolerate these faults so easily.

On the other hand I get irritable with the people who try to persuade me to take their dogs from them and train them myself, for I explain that if I trained their dog it would probably take me half a day to get it trained to quite a high standard; but that the dog would return to them just as bad as ever, because they themselves would not be trained in controlling it, and that it is their voice and their manner of working the dog that matters. I explain that I worship dogs, that I have no inhibitions when I work dogs. I say silly, lovely things to them, I love them so much I can hardly keep my hands or face away from them in caress, and the problem of training them hardly ever arises for more than a few moments when we decide between ourselves who is to be master - and it most certainly is going to be me. After that it is purely a matter of showing the dog what is wanted in order to get loving and instant obedience from it. But if the owner likes to come with the dog, and honestly wishes to train it, then by copying everything I do, however silly they may think it, they have reasonable hope of having a good dog in a very short time.

I always hope that people bringing their dog for training will do so in the same frame of mind as they bring their children to the dentist or doctor, realising that to train a dog well and quickly needs one hundred per cent co-operation between dog owner and trainer. There may be a few bad trainers to whom training is only exploiting their ego or their business acumen but most trainers are real dog lovers to whom training is a calling. Few owners realise that the training of dogs, if done conscientiously, is quite a dangerous occupation for the trainer and that, if they are bitten badly many times, it could lead to a lack of confidence in dogs which would be fatal for any trainer's work. Therefore the owner should want the dog to like the trainer and not be cross if it shows pleasure on being handled by the trainer. The owner should realise the association is only for a very short time and for the sole object of making owner and dog happy together. If this work can be done with the dog supremely happy in learning its lessons, it is nicer for the dog, although the owner naturally doesn't like sharing her dog's affection with a stranger.

Sometimes harsh things have to be done with dogs who are out of control. At these times the mind of the owner should try not to send out waves of horror, nor to think, 'I can't stand this, I shall take my dog home,' for soon the stormy scene will become a placid one and the dog taught for life that respect is necessary for true happiness. Rushing from one training school to another only bewilders the dog, for every trainer has his own tried methods and is unlikely to be impressed or influenced by other ways that the owner may have been taught. Most trainers recognise that their pupils have been to another school so they shouldn't try and deny it, for dog trainers have long ago learnt that absolute honesty in dealing with dogs is essential; if the owner is a bit of a 'story-teller', her dog will not be the easiest to train.

Some years ago I tried out an experiment. I asked through the Press for twenty-five of the worst dogs in Britain to take part in the first residential course for dogs and owners ever to be held in Britain. I wanted to prove myself right or wrong in the assumption that dogs can be trained to a high standard of obedience in a few hours. The dogs turned up with their owners; they were not all bad dogs, but a large majority were fighters, biters, pullers, won't come when called, etc. The owners hadn't all the right voices, or temperaments. Many of them found the strenuous work almost beyond them; all admitted they had no idea there was so much to learn. At the end of three days when there was nothing more I could teach them, dogs and owners passed a stiff test. There was only one failure, an

Alsatian who behaved perfectly without his owner, but who would go for people if they went too near his mistress when they were together. This guarding instinct in dogs can be dangerous, and no amount of training will stop it, unless the owner really wants to stop it, and shows great displeasure when the dog attacks. Most owners of this type of dog had grown to like being well protected. But once the instinct has been developed to this extent, the dog, in my opinion, is unreliable and therefore dangerous. Away from its owner the Alsatian was trained to a high standard and was sweet-tempered.

I spend many hours teaching TONE OF VOICE to the owners, and we had a film made at a course which clearly shows the response by the dogs to the owners' tone of voice, and then my voice. Inevitably some of the dogs came to me, not the owners, but it was fascinating to watch the steady improvement in the owners; to see them learn to let themselves go with praise when the dogs obeyed, and steadily learn to use the right firm tone in giving commands, and thus getting instant obedience. Bit by bit they got accustomed to the fact that to give a dog a very sharp jerk on a choke chain is not cruel. In fact the dogs who were depressed cheered up as soon as I jerked them firmly and confidently, secure in the knowledge that the right choke chain could not hurt them. This I demonstrated on my own wrist. Whilst I am on the subject of choke chains, far, far too many people have the wrong type. They buy the thin ones in the mistaken idea that they are kinder than the thick ones. I refuse to work a dog on a thin one, as I know it hurts the dog. I feel quite sure that the wrong chain retards the dog's progress.

What do I do if the owner cannot get the right tone of voice? That is one of my big problems; it is a physical impossibility for many women to have a wide range of tone. If they try to get the right tone it often ends up as a squeak. This makes training doubly difficult for those people. All they can do is to train their dogs by voice and signal, and eventually work almost entirely on signal. The tone of voice coupled with sending out the right telepathic thought is most important. You would be surprised how dogs pick up thought before you have ever said a word. It is useless giving commands without willing them to obey with your mind as well.

Most women, to begin with, think the training is harsh, and find it difficult to jerk their dogs, or put them to the 'down' position. Unless they can master this over-sentimental feeling they will fail. If you learn the correct way of doing these things it is akin to jujitsu and in no way hurts or upsets the dog. The slow way on the other hand annoys the dog and often leads to bites. The best dog handler is the quick-minded type of person who wants to learn it all in a day. To those who say you must walk before you run in dog training, I say: 'Nonsense': if you can keep up with your dog's brain there is no need to worry. I have no hesitation in saying it is inevitably the owner who is much slower to learn than the dog; and they admit it.

Very often one has to train the dog who in turn trains the owner. I have often seen a dog, on my command: 'Halt', sit, whilst the owner has absentmindedly walked on, only to be brought to a standstill by the dog.

The question of age of the dog constantly crops up. Are there limits as to when one can train a dog? My answer is: any age between three months and eight years old, providing the dog is fit. After that the dog in my opinion should not be bothered by training; before that the puppy gets tired too quickly. The age of the owner matters far more. Training a dog is almost a gymnastic feat in my classes. The owner has to bend down quickly to push her dog to the sit many times in an hour. Speed in working is essential if you want your dog to work happily. Dawdlers make bad handlers. If you want your dog to walk well to heel don't wait for it; stride out, and if it doesn't keep up, jerk it quickly on and up to you using an excited tone of voice and lots of praise. The slower you go the slower the dog will go, and the more bored you both will be. Running and stopping suddenly teaches a dog to sit like lightning and becomes quite a game. No room here for twenty stone of fat. Dog training revitalizes owners, if done in the right spirit with others in a class, and it can be wonderful fun at home when you feel like making progress. If you feel irritable or worried don't train your dog. Train him when you and he are in a happy mood; get quick results; give quick praise, and then leave him in peace. Never nag. What can't be achieved in ten minutes will seldom be achieved in ten hours of boredom for the dog.

Some owners choose big dogs and haven't the physical strength to control them or train them. Unless these breeds are trained young few women can do anything with them. Breeds like Pyrenean Mountain Dogs and Boxers come into this category, for they have enormous strength and will-power when adult.

Providing they get the right type of owners there are few dogs which cannot be made into reasonable companions. But I regret to say that there are a vast number of misfits in this dog-owner partnership. With some I believe it is a sheer waste of time attempting to train them. The most difficult to help are the elderly owners, either man or woman, who for purely physical reasons cannot carry out the necessary corrections. Many of them have arthritis in their joints, which makes them weak in the wrists, or makes bending down to put the dog to the sit almost an impossibility. Yet they love their dogs and are often the keenest of learners. Is it fair that they should have to put up with disobedient dogs, or is there some way of helping them train their dogs? Yes, there is. For example, when teaching a dog to lie down I usually use two methods. In one I put the dog to the sit, and standing in front of it, I lift one leg and push the opposite shoulder, which puts the dog off its balance and down it goes without fuss. Or when walking I catch hold of the running end of the choke chain underneath the chin and pull it quickly to the ground slightly ahead of the dog's chin. Then a quick press on the dog's flank with the other hand completes the movement and down goes the dog, again without fuss if done swiftly enough. Now it is quite obvious that these exercises could not be easily carried out by elderly or infirm people. Yet this 'down' exercise is wanted for the cure of almost every vice, for at the 'down' you have your dog under your control. Well, this exercise can be done just as easily by placing the left foot over the lead when you are standing up so that the lead runs under the arch of your shoe. Then pull quickly and strongly on the lead, and the dog's head is pulled to the down, and it quickly lies down to get more comfortable.

To teach a dog to sit on command it is not necessary to use the left hand to push the dog down. It can just as well be done by working the dog against a wall on the left-hand side so that it cannot sidle away from you, and then with the firm command: 'Sit' give the dog's rump a tap with a rolled-up newspaper or the end of another leather lead which you have in your hand. It is the noise that makes the dog sit, not any pain caused by the tap. If the dog shows signs of biting, as some nasty dogs do when put to the down, muzzle them for one or two minutes; they will soon find out that they cannot bite and must go down, and that directly they have gone into the down position they get praise, and then all idea of biting in retaliation will be given up. Be sure when making a dog sit that the lead, which is always held in the right hand for training purposes, is raised tightly over the right hip, for that almost puts a dog in the sitting position without further help.

Pulling on the lead can seldom be cured by infirm people because the dog needs a really quick sharp jerk to correct it. It is for this reason that I do not recommend big dogs or heavy boisterous dogs for old people. Even if they get some young person, or the trainer at a club, to do the initial pulling, the dog will soon realize it has its elderly owner at its mercy and start pulling again. One thing can be done, however. Take the dog's lead in your left hand and whilst walking with it, turn sharply, throwing the right leg in front of the dog's nose and turning to the left all the time. The dog is checked quickly because otherwise it would bump into that right leg and it won't bump into the leg more than once or twice before it realizes it is safer to keep back. Always use the word 'heel' as you turn. Association of ideas lies beneath the whole system of training: that, and the praise the dog gets when it does right.

I cannot stress too strongly that an owner who is frightened of his dog must protect himself if he wishes to train it. If you know your dog will bite when you try to make it lie down, naturally you are sending out fear waves, and the dog knows you are beaten and will bite all the more. If however you have protected your hands by thick leather gloves, you can with confidence ignore the efforts of the dog to bite, and what is better retaliate with two or three good jerks on its choke chain. Unfortunately nobody can teach your dog to respect you. They can teach the dog the exercise, so that it knows what to do, but you yourself must carry out that exercise with confidence, secure in the knowledge that the dog cannot hurt you. Then and only then will the dog obey you happily. As soon as the dog obeys, cast away your protection, and have confidence that you will not be bitten. Directly the dog has been put down, scratch its chest, for no dog will bite when you are scratching its chest, it is a movement that calms the fiercest breast.

I don't believe timid people make good trainers. I don't believe over-sentimental people make good trainers, as with any problem dog there is bound to be friction at one time or another until the dog recognises who is master. If you feel quite sick at having to jerk a dog on its choke chain you will not do it with vigour, you will therefore nag at the dog with ineffectual jerks which would never train a dog, and both you and it are getting nowhere. If you take a dog to a training school undoubtedly you get help. I do all the initial jerks necessary to save the owner and the dog from misunderstandings, but the owner must keep up to the high standard reached in class when the class is over. If you do not, the dog becomes cunning and behaves like a lamb in class, only to throw off the cloak of goodness later on.

I well remember a lady who had just won the obedience certificate at a dog show being pulled like nothing on earth down the street, shouting at me as she passed at her dog's speed, 'What price my future obedience champion?' Personally I wouldn't have tolerated such behaviour, but she thought it funny. And that brings me to another aspect of training dogs. So many people think their naughty dogs are really rather funny. If they think that, there is no hope for them or their dogs, as they do not really object to the dog's faults. You must really want to make your dog good, you must put everything you have got into teaching him kindly but quickly to obey. If one day you rock with laughter at his having eaten your knitting, and roar with rage the next day when it is your Sunday hat, how is the dog to know what you will tolerate and what you won't? I don't tolerate destruction of any kind; if one day you allow him to play with your old gloves how is he to know the difference when he finds your new gloves and tears them up?

Quite the most difficult thing to teach owners is enthusiasm. How dry and dull I find lots of them; they don't seem to be terribly pleased when the dog does right, it doesn't seem to matter much when the dog does wrong, and the result is a sort of grey picture with no light or shade. The dog also becomes grey in nature, it does its training with its tail down, it yawns as it stays resignedly at the sit or down, and eventually it refuses to do anything well, it is happy in its mediocrity. I hate that; I like to appear very angry when the dog does wrong, although curiously enough I never feel angry with the dogs. I like to bubble over with joy when they do right. I know I must look a perfect ass when training dogs, a cross between a ballet dancer and a clown, for I am always on the move. I try not to let the dogs feel bored for a second whilst that particular exercise is being carried out, and I always have a quick romp with each one after every exercise. I shall be sorry when I become too old to feel like this, for in spite of the fact that one pupil remarked that my classes were more like the Palladium than a dog class, I do believe that enthusiasm in working both dogs and owners is essential for success.

How I hate to see dogs and owners ploughing round a hall with the trainer issuing orders which many owners don't comprehend or carry out. How I hate the idea that if a dog fails on something it cannot have another chance because of shortage of time. That is why I find my weekend courses so satisfying. I have all day to cure the dogs' and owners' faults, no one grumbles if I spend twenty minutes on one dog and then win, for that is what we are there for - to make sure no dog leaves with the faults it came with. I think they are as anxious as I am that the dog should be good. There is a great camaraderie amongst owners of difficult dogs, and if we all pull together we must win.

So often in the street I feel like snatching a pulling dog from its owner, correcting it, and giving it back. One day I was walking behind a very troublesome dog with its owner and heard her say to it, 'If you don't behave I shall take you to Mrs Woodhouse.' I never let on that the threat could easily have been carried out sooner than the dog anticipated! Sometimes the training or correction of the dog in the home is impossible because the husband or wife or some other relative doesn't approve of the training and deliberately spoils the dog or lets it get away with doing wrong because he thinks it cruel to train dogs, or rather enjoys seeing the dog do naughty things in the same way as: 'Boys will be boys'. Then there is the opposite type who imagines himself a smashing dog trainer. He doesn't need anyone to show him what to do, he thunders at the dog, gets poor results, then out of pique suggests the best cure for naughty dogs is to sell them, give them away or put them down. This causes great rifts in families, and I shudder to think of the number of divorces or quarrels dogs have caused in the past. I well remember the husband of one person I met who had shouted at her: 'Get rid of that dog or I go.' 'That is easily answered,' said the wife, 'go'. Many a quarrel is caused by differences of opinion as to whether the dog shall live in the house or a kennel. Whether the dog shall sleep on the bed or in its basket. Whether the wife can accompany the husband on an outing where dogs cannot go. All these rows could be avoided if the dog were trained, for a trained dog does not need a baby sitter, a trained dog sleeps in its own bed, a trained dog makes no mess or trouble in a house, so the kennel plan never comes into operation.

What a joy it is to meet some of the people who train their dogs intelligently and who endeavour, with help, to follow instructions; who practise their dogs at home, and are rewarded by owning a delightful and obedient pal who can be taken anywhere without a preliminary working-out of the snags. Man's life is made richer by owning a dog, but the enrichment is vastly increased if he owns a well-trained, healthy, clean and intelligent one.

CHAPTER TWO

THE MIND OF THE DOG

The thing that has always struck me forcibly is how awful it must be to be a dog. You don't choose the home you live in, nor the owner. If you want to leave it, you run away or commit crimes for which you get punished. If you run away you are either taken back to the same unsavoury home or given away to one that may prove just as horrid or, if not claimed or found another home, your short life on this earth may be ended for you by the police or a welfare society.

You can't argue with your owner except by refusing to carry out commands or, in worse cases, biting the person you disagree with. You can't speak, so a psychiatrist can't help you. The vet only examines you and gives an opinion as to your state of health. A trainer may or may not understand you and for brief moments give you supreme happiness or dejected hopelessness. Yet with all the troubles in the world you are always ready to give unbounding love and affection to those to whom you belong, if only they will understand you. You can read the mind of your owner and all with whom you come in contact, yet your simplest wants are often misunderstood by humans.

You are always interested in things like smells which human beings seem to totally disregard and, if a certain smell particularly interests you so that you don't even hear your owner calling, you will have a cross owner.

You often get left behind suddenly in a strange boarding kennel with people you may not know or like and a multitude of other dogs who are also bewildered by the action of their owners. You show how upset you were when they do eventually come and fetch you by an overpowering welcome, yet the same thing happens again and the owners seem to completely misunderstand your dread of being deserted. Weeks before they leave you, you have picked up by telepathy the unrest in the household as the time approaches for their departure, and you know you are to be left once more with strangers, with no assurance that you will ever see your owners again.

You are encouraged to defend your home, yet, if you defend it too well and bite that nasty-looking man in a black hat who swaggers up the drive, you are punished for biting and probably shut up somewhere. How were you to know which people needed biting and which people just needed frightening?

After all, dogs were really meant to live natural lives whereby they probably ran at least twenty miles per day in pursuit of food. Their instincts were highly developed to gauge by scent alone the approach of danger, and their lives were fraught with risk of sudden death.

Now most of that is passed. The sniffing of a lamp post by a male dog not inoculated against Leptospirosis is far more likely to cause quick death than murder by another animal or human being. No longer can a dog wander off and fight to annex a wife for himself by sheer force of superior masculinity. He is expected to behave at all times like a gentleman and ignore the calls of nature. Do you wonder sometimes his mind gets a bit disturbed? He doesn't always fit into flat life in Kensington.

I think dogs on the whole are very accommodating creatures. They love human companionship, and endure hours of boredom in the hope that a walk or a game will come their way. They endure beauty treatment that in the past no self-respecting dog would have endured. They have to eat what is given to them instead of pouncing on the nearest sheep and gorging their tummies. And cats mustn't be chased? In return for all this they get a warm comfortable home, vitaminised food of the right quality to ensure all their vital organs are sustained and nourished. They get as much exercise as the health and desire of their owner permits. They sometimes get unrestricted romps with interesting dogs and, if their owners are sensible, they learn their lessons like human children. Sometimes they get too little affection; often they get overwhelming affection which has exactly the opposite effect on a dog's mind to that the owner thinks it will have.

Occasionally unfortunate dogs get only hatred, misunderstanding and despair for a bedfellow. The mind of a dog is really very simple to understand. All it wants is someone to love and respect, a reasonable amount of fun, to be useful to its owner and to have a comfortable well-fed tummy. At certain times its mind runs almost exclusively on sex, then it is not easily controlled by the owner. On the whole, the life of the dog and owner have to be in tune to get perfection out of the partnership. Both must respect each others' likes and dislikes, and a deep understanding must exist between them.

What governs the behaviour of a dog? How far does its mind think? What can be put down to instinct? I think that, before the puppy is eight weeks old, instinct is nearly ninety-nine per cent of the dog's mind, and the control of its actions is almost entirely guided by the desire to eat, sleep, keep warm and play. After that the human contacts it makes, the discipline it receives, and the affection it develops for the person who nurtures it, begin to play an important part in the forming of the dog's mind and character.

No two people are alike, no two dogs are alike. We often see in the same litter an entirely different make-up in character and looks. Although it helps to study pedigrees and see the parents of the dog you are going to take into your home, it is no guarantee that the dog will be anything like the last dog you had with similar breeding, or even like the rest of the litter he was born into. This is where owners trip up badly. They feel 'done in the eye' if the breed that was previously a joy to them lets them down. They assume, for example, that all Border Collies are easily trained, affectionate and nice to own. They get extremely annoyed if their small puppy bites them, or won't come when called, and maybe is dirty in the house, when their previous one made none of these mistakes. From that moment the dog hasn't quite the same loving owner as he had when he was purchased and he subconsciously picks up the irritation of his owner by telepathy. He becomes aggressive because the owner is not feeling too well disposed towards him, and a vicious circle is started in more senses than one.

To train a dog with sympathy and understanding one must try to understand a dog's mind. That mind has several big thoughts, its body a few major requirements. Firstly, the body governs the mind to a great extent when the puppy is young. The need to eat, sleep, urinate and defecate are the main factors. It hasn't entered a dog's mind that it is wrong to puddle on the floor or soil its bed. Its reactions are entirely spontaneous. When scolded for these things it does not at first connect its action with the cross words and 'fear' enters its mind.

Nature's reactions to fear are many: some animals crouch and stay as still as if dead; others snarl and attack the thing or person that frightens them; others turn on their tummy believing this age old action of a baby animal will help them;

some urinate and open their bowels with seemingly no control whatsoever. Most young animals rush to drink from their mothers if frightened. In training dogs we must take all these things into consideration before we punish a dog and look upon it with disappointment or disgust.

Only by repetition do dogs know what is right or wrong when very tiny. Their minds cannot reason what is right or wrong. They learn from experience of the tone of voice of the owner, or the resulting jerk on a choke chain, or by being put into their kennels when naughty or any other punishment that the owner has thought to be suitable. But, whatever the punishment, it is not always effective, for one has to gauge the natural reaction of the dog's mind to the treatment it is receiving or is about to receive. In many instances this reaction is to bite the person that is reproving it, or to lick and jump up on the person who is praising it. That is why, in my school, I am very loathe to correct a keen and loving dog from jumping up in the early stage of training, for, if you repress its natural exuberance and show of affection in the only way the dog knows, you may also be inhibiting the dog's natural love for you.

I think this love is of paramount importance and I constantly hug, kiss and play joyfully with my pupils even if I have had to be extremely firm with them to achieve initial obedience. The result is that there enters the dog's mind a memory of affection and fun rather than fear of correction. For, make no mistake, dogs don't object to fair correction. In fact, if you face up to it, the most loving dogs often seem to belong to owners to whom I would hate to be related in any way. A dog longs for love and it thinks that by fawning on a horrid owner it may achieve its desire, and so keeps on fawning ad infinitum. But woe betide the owner who refuses to face up to the fact that a dog's mind is not a human mind, and firmly believes that any correction given to the dog will be remembered by that dog for ever and held against the owner.

The dog has an enviable mind; it remembers the nice things in life and quickly blots out the nasty. That is why, when people tell me their small puppy was attacked by a big dog and that in later life made him into a fighter, I say, 'Bunkum!' If your dog wasn't a fighter by nature, he wouldn't be one. Forget the past and deal with the present. Face up to the fact that his hormone balance or his hereditary characteristics are far more likely to make him into a fighter than having been attacked by another dog.

After all, in the wild state, dogs were always attacking each other, and even play amongst dogs consists of biting and knocking each other over. Lack of firmness and leadership by the owner is far more likely to cause emotional upsets in the dog than a previous attack by another dog. I get masses of letters from people who wish me to choose the breed or sort of dog they should have. They usually write me reams about what they don't want, instead of fully writing to me about their homes, their children, their relatives, their other animals, the amount of time they can give to their dog, etc. They may say they've heard all long-eared dogs get canker, that all Dachshunds get follicular mange, and class all dogs of those and other particular breeds under one heading as impossible.

Dogs are no different to human beings in the wide range of characteristics and temperaments they possess. Dogs can have nervous breakdowns the same as human beings but dogs get typed as bad-tempered or disobedient. Few people think of the stresses of modern life, the noise of the traffic, the perpetual human rat race which spills off on to the dog as its owner is forever dashing out of the front door leaving the dog behind bewildered. The slower ordered life of the past has almost disappeared for dogs and owners, and dogs get put to sleep for things which could easily be cured, if only the owners would understand them and give them time.

The first thing to understand about dogs is that any change of home is traumatic. I was watching a T.V. programme recently on disturbed children and the only thing that had apparently made these children disturbed was that their parents had split up and the children had been put 'in care'. Has it ever struck a new dog owner that exactly this has happened to a dog and that it takes time to readjust itself to a new home, new rules, new food, a new house, new people? Seldom is this given much thought. The new owners conclude that they are acceptable to a dog, in spite of the fact that to a dog they may not have the right scent. They may not handle him correctly; the voice may grate; they may have someone in the house who hates dogs; they may have an enemy cat which would willingly scratch out the new dog's eyes if he wasn't careful to avoid it.

People should understand life from a dog's point of view before blaming everything that goes wrong on the dog. Mothers-to-be buy every book they can on baby welfare, but hundreds of people buy dogs with very little knowledge of them and then blame the dog for its behaviour. I would suggest that before anyone gets a dog, he should examine his knowledge of the breed he is choosing. Talk to people who have owned these dogs, see them at a dog show. If the breed shows aggression towards other dogs in the ring, or extreme nerves when handled by the judge, think twice before buying one. Temperament faults are the most difficult to cure and it may cost a lot to have professional help in this matter. Think about how much exercise you are going to be able to give your dog; if it is somewhat restricted either due to your age, your work, or your health, don't go and buy a Great Dane or a Dobermann. Think about the dog's coat; have you time to brush it as often as it needs doing? There is nothing more horrible than an Old English Sheepdog or a Bearded Collie all matted. Make up your mind what role the dog has to play in your home. Is it just a pet? If so, you can often buy a puppy not up to show standard cheaper from a breeder than one with show potential, but don't rave if you take it to the local show and find it has an undershot jaw or other fault, for you must have known it had some fault to get it cheaper. Don't take it out on the dog, for dogs understand your moods, your thoughts, and if you are thinking unpleasant things about your dog, he will pick it up and be down-hearted. You must be prepared to get to know what your dog is feeling and thinking, if you are to get the best out of him. Telepathic communication with your dog is something everybody should try and achieve. I know few will reach this height of understanding, but it is worth striving for.

Try to understand when your dog doesn't perhaps feel one hundred per cent well and leave out the long walk or the training for that day. Usually the eye of a dog gives away his health and his mood. When I am training, my eyes are forever watching the eyes of the dog I am training. I then know whether he intends co-operating or whether his mind is on other things. If his mind is on other things, I become much firmer with him until he realises second best is not good enough for me or for his owner in due course. But the other side of the situation is the mind of the owner. Is he or she really concentrating on the dog's behaviour or is the mind also wandering? If so, give up training for that day, as one should do if not feeling well or in a bad mood. Dogs are very sympathetic animals if truly loved. They seem to sense when quiet sympathy is what is wanted from them and do not intrude on the owner's thoughts or actions when the owner is not in the mood. But this takes understanding from the owner and a lot of companionship with the dog, as well as talking to the dog. I wonder how many words in a day the average owner speaks to the dog. Usually it is very few. Amongst those few may be: 'Din dins, walkies, shut up, go to your bed, and good boy or girl,' but actual conversation is not all that common. I used to really talk to my dogs, whose understanding became 'almost human'.

Everyone who has a lot to do with the training of dogs can't help but notice that bitches are far easier to train than dogs. The reason is that, except when she is 'on heat' or in the throes of a 'pseudo pregnancy,' a bitch's attention is not disturbed by matters of sex - although Greyhounds are not raced within three months after being on heat, because they are supposed not to be at their best at those times. A bitch is better tempered than a male dog on the whole, for the fighting instinct for supremacy over other dogs is not so prevalent, although bitches do get extremely jealous, especially of their own offspring. I have known mother and daughter fight incessantly so that one has to be parted with. This often happens in the human race - mother and daughter don't get on - so it is nothing new to us to find it in the animal kingdom as well. Sex is a thing no so-called psychiatrist can fathom, for the dog again cannot answer questions as to whether his sex life is normal, or whether he had unpleasant sexual adventures when young. Therefore the dog owner must rely on experience of sexual behaviour in dogs and use that knowledge to make the dog's existence healthy and happy.

Many dogs literally seem to have minds that rely almost entirely on sex for most of their lives, and these oversexed dogs are a curse to themselves and their owners; they are abnormal and should not, in my opinion, perpetuate the race, for in these days of built-up areas and lack of free run for dogs an oversexed dog is a curse. You can't get through to their minds at all without intensive training for long periods and with a greater degree of firmness than, in my opinion, is kind. I say with all my heart that, unless the owner of this dog particularly requires it for show purposes, it should be 'doctored' to make its life happy and that of its owners equally trouble-free. Wild cries of: 'I shouldn't like to do that to my dog,' or, 'I would hate to take its nature away,' are bound to be heard from ignorant people who don't know enough about castration, whose vets have little or no personal experience of it or from people who know someone who knows someone who had their dog done and it got fat and dull. What they didn't bother to find out was, what was the owner of the castrated dog like? Did that owner feed the dog every time it asked for food? Did they reduce the food that they had been giving it, as it was no longer using up energy fussing over sex matters? Did they give it reasonable exercise and sufficient training to make its life interesting? These are the factors that make a castrated dog no different to any other dog except that it is happier in every way and a joy to own in town or country, with or without other dogs. Only when sex is a nuisance need this be done, and I heartily recommend it to everyone, whatever the age of the oversexed dog.

What goes on in the mind of the oversexed male dog? The answer is, nothing but the desire to copulate. It doesn't really matter whether the bitch it meets is on heat, it often doesn't matter whether the dog it meets is male or female, it is quite happy to carry out its sexual exercises on the leg of a child or even the furniture. It growls ferociously at other dogs, willing to fight any of them due to nervous sexual excitement; it often bites its owner in a fit of frustration. It barks or whines most of the day and cannot at any time be made to attend with proper concentration when there are other dogs about, whatever their sex. Many people think they will cure this oversexed menace by letting him 'have a bitch'. How sorry they will be if they do this! All the full flood of sexual fulfilment makes the dog after that a maniac, for now his instincts are more fully aroused than ever and discipline becomes more impossible than ever. Yet get this dog alone in some place where no dog has been, and no smells or dogs are about, and he will often be the nicest possible dog, gay, loving and obedient.

Why then are owners so queer about castrating dogs? I have had more than 400 dogs done on my advice, and in every case the owner and dog are happy where formerly the dog was impossible, the owner fed-up, and the partnership in grave danger of being ended. But these owners are taking my advice as to diet of a strict nature and are continuing the training of the dog, for castration takes time to work until all the hormones already manufactured in the dog's body are exhausted; but even after three weeks most owners note a difference. The normal male dog shows no interest in a bitch not on heat, and only cursory interest in a bitch on heat for her first week; he shows no interest in mounting other male dogs, furniture or people's legs and will leave smells and lamp posts alone when trained in obedience. He is seldom a fighter.

There have been dogs that are unstable because they are hermaphrodite, i.e. they have two sexes in one body. This causes dogs to be bad-tempered and unreliable, as are the male dogs known as monorchids or cryptorchids. This means they have only one or neither of their two testicles descended into the scrotum. Castration in these cases is difficult and a major operation. In normal cases it is a simple and uneventful operation done by an experienced vet; no stitches need be inserted and the dog can return home in under 24 hours.

The dog's mind is not adversely affected by castration. There must be no ideas in the owner's mind about denying the dog its natural pleasures; an ordinary dog doesn't get those 'natural pleasures' unless it is a stud dog or belongs to a bad owner who allows it to wander and have promiscuous relations with any bitch it meets. Dogs who have no desires don't fret because they have lost these desires; they love their owners more dearly; they are gay, happy dogs, not deluded miseries cursed by too many hormones.

After all, sex in a dog cannot be looked upon in the same way as sex in humans. Dogs don't have sex hormones for any other reason than to perpetuate the race and, with this object in mind, will get thin and miserable when a bitch is on heat in the neighbourhood; will travel miles, making their feet sore, in spite of hunger and thirst, to wait hopelessly outside a bitch's home; will take even a beating without noticing it in the attempt to attack or carry out sex impulses with other male dogs; and will destroy floors or furniture and fittings in sexual frustration. The mind of a dog doesn't look into the future if its sex organs are to be removed; it doesn't anticipate a loss of pleasure; it has a general anaesthetic so knows nothing about the operation. Three or four days later nobody would know the dog had had anything done to it except that it remains the same gay dog it always was and becomes more interested in the odd snack between meals!

With bitches this oversexed characteristic doesn't exist; the spaying of bitches, except in case of disease, is not to be lightly recommended from my experience. It is a more serious operation than castration; the bitch does become less lively, and there is a tendency to get fat. This does not mean that I think every bitch should breed a litter for her health. I think that utterly wrong. It has been proved in veterinary circles that bitches bred with are more susceptible to uterine disease than those not bred with. Many over-sentimental people worry when their pets, obviously keen to get with a dog, fret a bit and, although puppies are not wanted, they mate the bitch 'for her own sake, bless her.' I think they are wrong. There are too many unwanted dogs in this country today to warrant breeding for this reason.

Only bitches and dogs with some special points should be bred with and never if temperament is bad. Breeding will not make a bad-tempered or shy bitch or dog better tempered or non-shy; all that is being done is passing on to unfortunate dog owners a bad-tempered dog. This particularly applies to owners of breeds whose temperament is deteriorating in so many cases.

If a dog is mentally unhappy with its sex and shows it by fussing at all times about other dogs, castrate it. You are being kind, not cruel, to the dog and all who meet it.   No psychiatrist can help the dog by mind reading. Sex is above all that nonsense. Firm training can do a lot, but take an experienced trainer's advice. No dog-loving trainer will tell you your dog is oversexed if it only lacks training.

When I had written my first book on dog training, I sent it to my mother. Her remark after reading it was that although she had enjoyed it as a book, she felt certain no one would need it, as surely everyone knew how to train their dogs. Time has shown that not only do people not know how to train their dogs, but that in increasing numbers they own 'problem dogs' and are in need of specialized help and advice. In the hundreds of letters I receive the phrase 'difficult dog' occurs time and time again. Many of the writers tell me they have owned dogs for thirty years or more and have never come up against such stubborn, 'wilful, vicious', or such-like dogs before. They all, without exception, imagine that their dog stands out on its own as a unique example of canine wickedness. If only they could read my daily post they would know their letters are repeated almost word for word by many hundreds of dog owners all over the world. What they are unwilling to believe at first is that their dog is no worse than dozens of others, and that if it is 'difficult', the reason can often be placed on their own doorstep. I still maintain, and always shall maintain, that with the exception of dogs which have some physical or mental abnormality, there is not one that cannot be made a good companion by the right training—that is IF the owner can be trained. During the last ten years I have trained 15,000 dogs and owners, and my heart bleeds for the so-called problem dogs brought to me for correction. In most cases the dog can be taught all that is necessary in a very few minutes. When I work it, using a thrilling happy tone of voice, the dog works happily with tail wagging, and an expectant interested look on its face. When it errs I use the tone of voice that means: 'I win or else' and few dogs fail to recognize that voice and that look on my face. But hand this same dog back to its inexperienced owner and the picture changes. Why? Firstly because it is the nature of our people in recent years to put up with more from our children and our dogs. Next, kindness to animals has been drummed into us as a nation for a long time, and many owners mix up in their minds the true meaning of kindness. Is it kinder to allow a dog to make human lives and its own a misery, rather than to correct it firmly on a choke chain for a few minutes, thereby making it understand clearly who is boss?

I wouldn't hesitate to answer this question. I would say, 'Correct the dog quickly and firmly, and then love it with everything you possess, and the dog will worship you in return.' Dither weakly in the mistaken idea that all bad dogs can be trained by endearing words and you might just as well give up the idea of training a bad dog. Remember, writing this I am not dealing with the normal puppy or young dog, or with the experienced owner to whom training a dog is as easy as eating his breakfast.

There is no doubt in my mind that, due to the vast increase in the number of dogs kept in this country, and the conditions under which these dogs are housed, a type of dog that should never have been bred is being produced by breeders for sale to the public. The professional breeders cannot be excused for doing this. They should know better than to breed from bitches or dogs with bad temperaments, thus passing on trouble. The amateur breeders still believe the old wives' tale that to breed from a nervous or bad-tempered bitch improves its temperament. What they don't know or don't care about is that they are filling this country with unstable, neurotic and unreliable dogs which are causing thousands of dog lovers misery, and keeping me and others like me glued to our typewriters and our training classes, trying to right the wrongs that should never be met with in normal dogs. But in spite of what I say about the breeding of these dogs, I still believe that if the owners knew how to train them these faults could easily and quickly be eradicated. There is however one thing I cannot teach a dog, and that is to love its owner. I meet many hundreds of dogs in a year who seem to have no affection for their owner whatsoever. These dogs have to be taught to obey their owners more or less by fear—of the results of disobedience. How very sad it is to find such a relationship. It tears my heart strings when the dog's eyes light up when it meets me, and it shrieks with joy when I kneel down to caress and kiss it. How is it possible to feed and house a dog, and presumably to love it, and get no affection in return? The answer is respect. Without respect there is little love in the animal kingdom. An animal must always have a boss to love and respect. Some breeds of dog need to respect their owners more than others, some are naturally docile and obedient.

I am going to deal with the many types of problem that are presented to me by dog owners in person or by letter. On reading what I say many indignant owners will deny that they come under any of the categories I mention. Many more will insist that their dog is more wicked than any of those that I talk about, and that theirs could not be cured by the means I recommend. Some will write to me and say they have tried everything and are quite sure that their dog would be my Waterloo. I willingly accept such challenges, if the owners are willing to bring their dog to me for five minutes. For in those five minutes I will find out who is to blame for the 'problem dog', and if I think there is no future happiness for dog and owner in that particular partnership, I will admit it quite freely. For make no mistake, there is no future in many of these dog and owner relationships. The reasons are numerous; one of the most common is a fear of the dog, fear of the dog fighting, or biting, or both. Unless the owner can master his own fear there is no hope for the dog. To be a good trainer or handler of dogs you have to have overwhelming love for them, you have to have the patience of Job, but also that little spark of strong will that doesn't take defeat too easily. If you don't possess these qualifications, don't fret too much, you can soon develop them; if not, with reasonable luck your dog can be trained to train you.

CHAPTER THREE

HOUSE TRAINING

This is an extremely difficult subject to tackle, as I don't know in what circumstances many dogs have to be trained. But as far as general principles go, I think all dogs must be treated in the same way. First, the owner of a new puppy must realise that this puppy has been brought up in a kennel or shed where he has been able to run about and relieve himself at any time, day or night, and it is a great change for him to have to learn to do otherwise. But what does help is that in his new home he is fed at regular intervals, and can't just go and have a drink from his mother at any time. As it is a natural reflex for the puppy to wish to pass water after a feed, this is the first clue to a method of house-training. Always put your puppy out immediately after a meal, and give him the command you will use for ever after. I use the words: 'Hurry up', because then no one in the street knows what I am talking about; but it doesn't matter which words you use, so long as in the future your puppy is going to connect those words with his obligations. Immediately the puppy has obeyed your wishes, praise him for all you are worth, then take him in and have a game. Soon after a short gambol, he will feel tired and comfortable after his meal, and he may then safely be put in his basket or kennel, or whatever you are going to keep him in in the house.

I strongly recommend all puppy owners to buy an indoor kennel such as a welded wire folding indoor kennel. The details of where to obtain one are given in the Appendix at the back of the book. The use of the indoor kennel is very important, and the first step is to consider where to site it. I strongly recommend

HIGHLY RECOMMENDED: A folding kennel, ideal for puppy owners.

ARTIFICIAL TURF: Place mat in kennel for use in emergencies.

the kitchen as it will be both warm and have a floor which will not be damaged in the event of an accident. I would then put a nice, warm blanket or cushion in the bedroom end of the kennel and adapt the far end for house-training purposes. To do this, cover the sheet metal floor with a piece of real or plastic turf. The puppy then has an area to do his 'jobs' if he feels desperate and cannot wait for his master to take him out. The turf should be changed - or washed if it is plastic- every two days.

The next question in house training arises when your puppy wakes up after a long sleep; you must then be ready to rush him out of doors. Most puppies will whimper when they wake up, to show that they are ready for a playtime or a meal. (It is absolutely vital that a young puppy should be kept warm if you want him to become clean quickly; a cold puppy cannot control his bladder.)

Next comes the vexed question as to what one should do when a puppy makes a puddle on the floor. Some people advise rubbing his nose in it. What a wicked idea! Should the puppy make a puddle, catch him, show him what he has done, and scold him resoundingly by your tone of voice, then immediately take him out to his usual spot. This usual spot is another vital chain in the training link. The puppy quickly gets to connect that spot with his 'jobs' and associations are quickly made. If, after puddling the floor, you put him out and he does it again outside, praise him fervently, and with great love in your voice.

The most difficult thing to do is to train your dog to be clean the night through and I sometimes have had my puppy to sleep in my room so that immediately it wakes I rush downstairs with it, and out. I know it's as bad as having to attend to a baby, but I have always had my tiny puppies clean at about nine weeks; in fact, I have twice had six-week-old puppies quite safe to take into hotels with me, with never a mistake. But to achieve this one must always be watching the puppy, and at the slightest sign of sniffing around in an interested manner, must whip the puppy up in one's arms and put him out.

Then there is the problem of flat dwellers, probably unable to get up and down stairs quickly enough; the best thing for them to do is to have a large tray or flat box in one corner of the room or landing, filled with earth or whatever you wish to use, and to get the puppy used to going on to that. But of course that does not implant the idea in the puppy's mind that it is wrong to soil in a house. I really feel that if flat dwellers must have a young puppy, they should make the effort to take it out into the street. Should a puppy ever be smacked for being dirty? I think it should, after the age of six months, providing it has been given every chance to be clean. I have known puppies go out and have a good time and immediately come in and disgrace themselves in the house. That is the time to pick the puppy up and show it what you are smacking it for; give it two or three sound smacks on its rump and put it out again.

Now comes the question of how to keep a puppy warm at night so that it sleeps right through and therefore doesn't wet its box. I always recommend putting puppies in their indoor kennel in the hot cupboard at nights with the door ajar for air. Put a very warm cushion in the box so that when the puppy is lying down the pillow billows up round it much as a litter of other puppies would. A hot bottle is not a good idea. These get cold too soon, and there is always the risk of the bottle getting chewed and the contents soaking the box. If you put the puppy's box by a fire it gets cold towards morning, and a cold puppy is inevitably a dirty, wet puppy.

The other thing that helps a puppy to become clean quickly is to give it its milk or liquid feeds early in the day. Keep the meat or solid feed for the evening meal. I always give the last meal at ten o'clock at night, as dogs have very slow digestions and that meal lasts well round until the morning. I give the last sloppy meal at four o'clock. Be sure to take the puppy out to his favourite spot last thing before you go to bed. We have a tiny black and tan miniature terrier which we took on a tour, staying at different hotels each night, and we never had any mistakes with her. We had her blanket and wrapped her up in it at night and put her with the door very slightly ajar in the cupboard usually kept by the bed. It made a snug bed, and I could hear her immediately she woke. If there was a balcony I popped her out on that; if not I went downstairs to the garden. For all these reasons, it is always best to buy a puppy in the summer months: I have never had to house-train one in this way in midwinter.

The best chance of getting a clean puppy within reasonable time is never to allow him to be free in any room, when very tiny, unless you are there to watch him. Pop him back in his kennel when you have to go out of the room. It teaches him to lie quietly in the one place, and he comes to look upon it as his very own home. A dirty dog in the house is usually a consequence of the owner's just not taking enough trouble to watch the puppy and rush him out quickly. Mothers of children know how essential this watching is; so should dog owners.

Much the most difficult trouble to overcome is the reluctance of a bitch to relieve herself except in her accustomed spot at home. I have never known a dog suffer from this particular inhibition, so different is his nature. I have known bitches hold out for well over twelve hours, and it is extremely bad for them. This is where training helps, for if you always use one unvarying word, and expect the bitch to relieve herself when you employ it, she will then know it is not wrong to use the road wherever you and she happen to be. It is usually most difficult when you have a bitch used to using only grass - that is why I advocate also teaching her to use the road. It is all association of words and deed, and this association must be established at a very early age if you are to avoid snags like this. Other considerations apart, it is extremely annoying to have to walk your bitch for a long time, say in rainy or bitter weather, when, had she been taught to behave on command, time and temper could have been saved and the risk of catching cold obviated. I have never known this inhibition occur in kennel dogs, it is usually confined to very clean, house-trained animals.

My 'In' tray is full of letters from owners of dirty dogs. Dogs that are taken out for exercise and then return to the house and at once go to their favourite spot in the home and relieve themselves. The damage to carpets can be enormous as, unless one immediately neutralises the urine with some proprietary fluid such as No Stain, the carpet not only smells but eventually loses its colour, especially if the animal soiling it is a bitch. Not only that, this smell is the signal for the dog to relieve itself again and again on the same spot. The owner may think that by washing the place the dog has fouled with detergents or disinfectants, she has removed the scent for the dog, but in fact she hasn't. Therefore it is useless scolding the dog; he is only doing what nature prompted him to do, using only one chosen place for his toilet.

The cure is simple providing there is nothing physically wrong with the dog: change the site. This can be done by confining the dog in an indoor kennel for about three days, so that it is either carried or rushed out from the kennel to the spot the owner has chosen for its toilet. Otherwise take the dog away from home for a few days. It is most unlikely it will soil in a new home at first and can then easily be trained to relieve itself on command. Once this is learnt, house-training is easy.

The most important thing of all is to praise the dog enormously when eventually it does do right outside. It is amazing how quickly a dog picks up the happy praising tone of voice when he does perform on command. One eight week old Dalmatian, star of a dog food commercial, I house-trained in two hours, and from thenceforth he relieved himself on command wherever I told him to. When he was eventually sold to a very luxurious home at twelve weeks old he never made a mistake, his manners were impeccable. When I advocate keeping a puppy in an indoor kennel for three days, I do not mean it cannot go out for play and exercise. What I mean is, do not let it free in the home until the association of ideas as to where it may use for its functions has been clearly built up. This must be out of doors, that is why it is easier to house-train a puppy in summer. If, however, the weather is very bad the puppy can be free, say in the kitchen, after relieving itself outside, for about half an hour before being put back in its kennel. It is surprising how often a puppy can pass urine, and the owner must constantly watch it and pick it up and pop it out if it shows any signs of sniffing around. An adult dog must be taken outside for exercise and not allowed the freedom of the house at all for three days. If it doesn't relieve itself out of doors, put it back in its kennel and try again in an hour or so. Once you achieve what you wish outside you are on the way to a permanent cure.

By being confined in a kennel for three days the dog quickly enlarges the size of its bladder and obtains bladder control which is so necessary in a puppy. No animal willingly soils its bed. The regularity and number of times the puppy or dog can be taken out of course governs the speed with which the animal will learn to be clean.

So many owners these days are going to work leaving their dog at home alone for long periods. They leave newspapers for the dog's toilet, which I think a revolting idea. If they must have a dog under these unsuitable conditions, they must expect somewhat unstable behaviour. No one should leave a dog for more than three hours without taking it out. Small puppies could not last this time. I feel if owners have to inflict these conditions on a dog, it would be better to buy an older house-trained dog in the first place. Given a good run before the owner goes to work, the dog should be able to last out until lunch-time.

Another very trying misdemeanour owners write about in dogs, or rather bitches in particular, involves the involuntary passing of urine when excited or frightened. The answer to this is of course training the dog to lie down and stay down on command, so that the squatting and uncontrolled wetting does not occur. Remaining in the down for quite long periods teaches a dog calmness and control. It is particularly essential to insist on the down when visitors are arriving, for it is at this time dogs are particularly prone to disgrace themselves, especially if a visitor tries to talk to them.

Training to lie down and stay down should start at an early age. A trained dog is one that trusts its owner and the outside world. It is usually calm under all circumstances, is seldom car sick, is seldom a fighter, and takes in its stride any upheaval in the home. This trust only comes with daily training, with firm insistence on immediate obedience and then much praise. I think most of the mental upsets except schizophrenia are caused by owners. I think most puppies are born normal but some are made abnormal by their upbringing. Too many people are over-sentimental and lack clear firm commands. They end up with dirty dogs, biting dogs, disobedient dogs for several reasons. They think the dogs will grow out of their faults; this seldom happens. They think biting puppies are only biting because they are teething; this is wrong. Puppies bite because they want to be master. In sensible circles we don't allow puppies to teethe or bite on our fingers; a firm command: 'No bite' puts an end to this. One other reason for lack of correction is the owner's words: 'Oh, he's so sweet'. Sweet the puppy may be at ten weeks, but he may turn out to be a likely candidate for being put to sleep at twelve months if he is allowed to continue unchecked.

Fear can often be a cause of the problem. Dogs wet the carpets, just as children wet their beds, normal house training breaks down and desperate owners write to me for new training methods. All that is wanted to right the trouble is to give the dog confidence. Put it in the kitchen where the floor can be washed, praise the dog when you greet it in the morning, completely ignoring the puddle, give only one meal early in the day and restrict drinking after 5 p.m., and in most cases the trouble clears up. The poor dog knows it has done wrong to puddle, even the tiniest puppy learns quickly what is right or wrong. Add to the dog's fear when it has made a mistake and you will never cure the fault. I have known a night or two with the owner in their bedroom to cure this fault completely, for the dog rests peacefully.

Dogs undoubtedly suffer night terrors if they are highly strung, and develop all sorts of queer faults, yet these faults have been found to disappear on holiday when the dog has been with you day and night. I always believe dogs are like small children, and well I remember lying awake as a small child on Nanny's day out suffering tortures for fear she might get run over by a bus, and not until she came home did I fall asleep. I think the same thing happens with beloved highly strung dogs: the night is long for them, where they cannot hear their owner, and they sleep restlessly and then their bladder plays them up and a puddle results. Think before you punish a dog that has been perfectly clean in the past.

I believe the owner's voice is the thing that makes many dogs delinquent. The hopelessly inadequate tone of voice on giving a command. The lack of meaningful words, the dreadfully flat tone they use for praise and the laziness of their movement all go to make a dog bored and uncaring. For example, if the owner sees a puppy just about to soil the floor or actually in the act, she should leap to scold it and pick it up and put it out. That leap instils into the dog's mind that there is something wrong with what he was doing or was about to do. A loud:

'Naughty dog' completes the correction. Never rub a dog's nose in what it has done - that is useless and not understood by a dog, and it is unhygienic and unkind.

If a reasonably adult dog continues to have dirty habits, restrict its fluid intake after 4 p.m., and of course confine it in an indoor kennel. People often go on far too long giving their puppies milk. I think after six months old this is unnecessary and adds to the fluid intake because the puppy likes it, then it has to pass more urine. With correct feeding and adequate supplement of minerals and trace elements, the dog should not need milk.

CHAPTER FOUR

EARLY TRAINING

In the dog's mind, a master or a mistress to love, honour and obey is an absolute necessity. The love is dormant in the dog until brought into full bloom by an understanding owner. Thousands of dogs appear to love their owners, they welcome them home with enthusiastic wagging of the tail and jumping up, they follow them about their houses happily and, to the normal person seeing the dog, the affection is true and deep. But to the experienced dog trainer this outward show is not enough. The true test of real love is when the dog has got the opportunity to go out on its own as soon as a door is left open by mistake, and it goes off and often doesn't return for hours. That dog only loves its home comforts and the attention it gets from its family; it doesn't truly love the master or mistress as they fondly think. True love in dogs only comes when every door can be open and the dog will still stay happily within earshot of its owner. For the owner must be the be-all-and-end-all of a dog's life.

To achieve this the owner has to master the dog at some time or other as the leader of the pack did in bygone days. There must be no question as to who is the boss of the house; it must be the owner. Dogs not only love owners who have had at one time a battle of wills for supremacy, they adore them, for a dog is really a subservient creature by nature, longing to trust his true love to someone's heart.

Now we come to the word 'honour', or, as I prefer it, 'respect.' This respect in a dog's mind is paramount, and I can't repeat often enough that, without respect which includes a certain amount of 'righteous fear' as the Bible would say, the dog lacks something in his essential make-up which sentimentality cannot replace. When I use the words 'righteous fear' women in particular shrink with horror; they wouldn't like their dogs to be frightened of them. When I explain that righteous fear is not being frightened, they don't understand. The reason humans don't all steal, lie or what have you, is simply because in most of us there is a righteous fear of the results. In dogs it should be the same. If they run off or fight another dog, their minds must be educated to know that there will be a reprisal and, without this righteous fear, the dog will never be completely happy, for dogs love looking up to their owners or, as the case may be, their trainers.

It is indeed very sad for me to see the number of dogs whose minds are forever tuned-in to mine in a class when they should be tuned-in to their owners' thoughts and wishes. The reason is, I make them immediately do as I wish and then give abundant praise. Many owners, in a distorted sense of kindness, let the dogs get away with disobedience, or make them do it so slowly that there is no respect for the owner from the dog. In fact many dogs show this in no mean way by biting their owners. When a dog bites its owner I feel sure it is mostly done as a last desperate resort to rouse the owner into being someone the dog can respect. Once the owner has got that respect the dog can be taught everything with the least possible number of scoldings or corrections. A dog loves to learn things and adores to please. Once the hurdle of respect has been jumped, the continuation of training goes smoothly.

This sequence of events is very hard to teach the owners, for a vast number of dog owners have no idea what their dog prefers. They think dogs adore sentimentality. Dogs do up to a certain point, but even the tiniest of toy dogs wants a proper owner to love and respect; just because he only weighs 2 lbs that doesn't mean he has no character or that he should not be obedient. People are now finding out that the tiniest Yorkshire Terrier, for example, has a brain big enough to do first class obedience; its mind works the same as a Great Dane's mind; it also wants to respect its owner. There is no difference between men owners and women owners as regards over-sentimentality. In fact I have found some men to be more stupidly sentimental than women and when I have to be firm with their dogs they feel very badly about it. Yet the dogs show which they prefer and every time it is the strong-minded but loving handler who gets real love and implicit obedience from the dog.

If a dog is cringing and frightened I always know the owner has not been firm enough with it, for this type of dog needs someone to respect more than any

Be firm and decisive when giving a command.

other; it is weak-natured itself and likes to draw courage and strength from a firm owner. What do I mean by the word 'firm'? I use it so often that people may think I mean, 'Get a stick and beat the dog.' This is far from my mind. In fact I think owners should practically never smack a dog, for it is a sign of defeat on the owner's part. It means that the dog's progressive training and the development of its mind and intelligence has not been accomplished. It means the owner has to resort to something that may be beyond his own strength. It is degrading for both dog and owner, for a dog that has been firmly but kindly trained never needs a beating. No, firmness in my estimation means a firmness of purpose, a strength of will that doesn't take defeat however long it takes to succeed. A firmness that is gentle as well as strong, for, make no mistake, a disobedient and wilful dog needs prolonged patience and perseverance to win.

By being firm I mean setting the dog something to do and making him do it, knowing in your own mind that that which you wish him to do is fair and right and necessary for his and your happy co-existence. He may fight, scream as if being murdered, or just bite you in retaliation, or may just seem mortally afraid; all these ruses can be tried on by a dog when asked to obey. If you are not firm your inner heart revolts at making him obey and you are sorry for his whimperings or his apparent fear or defiance. You let up and let him get his own way. The seeds of disrespect are sown and will accordingly germinate, to the ultimate misery of both owner and dog.

Often in my class I meet these disrespectful dogs who don't truly love their owners. But the owners are mightily annoyed when I tell them their dogs don't really love them. They assure me the dog never leaves them in the house, etc; but it cuts no ice with me. I know that once I have shown the owners how much their dogs prefer me to them after I have made them carry out my wishes they will be converted. I think the old motto, 'You have to be cruel to be kind,' should be changed for dog owners to, 'You have to be firm to be kind.' Firmness only has to be continued until the right kind of respect enters the dog's mind. And, when being firm, unending praise and affection must be given to the dog.

This praise and affection is where a multitude of owners fail their dogs. A pat and a kind word are not enough in the initial training of dogs; the atmosphere must be charged with a certain excitement, for dogs are very sensitive to excitement; when they have done right, they love having the wildest show of affection and a good romp round. Dull owners make dull dogs, stony-faced owners, zip-lipped owners, and inhibited owners tend to have dull disobedient dogs, who take a long time to learn obedience. The dog's mind is only equal to a child's mind and, as comedy makes up a big part of a child's life, it should do the same in a dog's life. Dogs love laughter, clapping and jokes. I had a little dog who laughed when we laughed although she hadn't the slightest idea what she was laughing about. It was the happiness that pervaded the room when we were laughing that entered her brain and made her feel happy so she smiled too. Try smiling at everyone you meet down the street; you will be amazed how many complete strangers smile back before they zip up again realising they don't know you. It is the same with dogs even if they don't know you; they respond to a smile and a clap if they have done well. They watch your eyes and face for the happy sign that you are pleased. I am intensely sorry for the dogs who see no smiles on their owners' faces. You can't train a dog well if you are unhappy; your tenseness communicates itself to the dog, and the dog becomes depressed.

What a wonderful indicator of happiness is the dog's tail; the half-mast wag with the very tip of the tail, showing nervous expectation; the half-mast slow wag of the interested dog who wants to know what master is saying but doesn't quite pick it up; the full-mast wag of excitement and happiness when he is really happy; and, last but not least, the tail between the legs of the nervous, shy or unhappy dog who trusts no one and to whom life is a burden.

When a dog is happily learning, or happily obeying I like to see its tail at the medium sensible height; when having a game after lessons or when free I like the full mast. But what I like most is to change in a matter of minutes the tail between the legs to the half-mast by firm and sensible handling, for this can be done in minutes if you get through to the dog's mind and give strength to it by your own forceful happiness and strength of purpose. A dog that loves, honours and consequently obeys is a joy to himself and his owner.

'How soon shall I start training my puppy?' is a constant request that I get by letter. I think, contrary to some trainers' ideas, that a puppy is never too young, once it is weaned, to begin understanding small things. I put a very light cat's collar on a very small puppy so that it gets accustomed to wearing something round its neck. It will most likely sit down and scratch vigorously at first, and devote most of the first day to efforts to get rid of it, but harden your heart and pay no attention. If the puppy learns early that it must wear a collar there will be none of that fighting against it later on. Usually the owner gives up in despair and puts on dog braces. One cannot obedience-train a dog on braces, so that is a step backwards. If a dog arrives at my classes with braces I put on a choke chain collar and don't listen at all to the owner's assurance that: 'He won't wear a collar'. I don't believe that a dog in good hands should be allowed to have a say in what he will or won't do. The owner must be the judge in every case. If the owner is a fair-minded dog lover he will do nothing that is not right for the dog, unless he does so from ignorance. And there is absolutely no excuse for ignorance on dog management in these days.

Very well then. We have bought an extremely light collar and the puppy has got used to wearing it. What about a lead? A very young puppy should definitely not be taken for walks in the accepted sense of the word. There is a grave risk of infection in the streets, and the puppy gets easily tired; but from about three months old he should have a lead on and be walked about for a short time each day. He is never too young to know that he must come back to your side on the command: 'Heel!' But serious training in this heelwork should not commence until the puppy is about three and a half months old. It is most important not to allow the puppy to play with or chew his lead. This is an extremely bad habit which is very difficult to break. I had a dog arrive at my class one night that provides a good example of the folly of allowing the lead to become a plaything. Every time his master pulled on the lead, he stood up on his hindlegs and gripped the lead in a vice-like grip with his front paws. That meant one could not pull the lead at all to any good purpose. The only way to break this habit was to pull the dog sharply to the ground whenever he did it. If a puppy learns while walking to play with the lead he never recognizes its authority and just bites it when you wish to give him a jerk. I shall go into the correct methods of training a puppy to walk to heel later.

The puppy is never too young to be taught that when you say: 'Bed' or 'Box' or 'Basket' or the name of whatever else you may have as a home for him, you mean that puppy to go to its bed and stay there until you want it. If it gets up to go away it must be firmly put back with the command: 'Stay in your bed.' Give him a gentle pat to soothe him before you go away.

Naturally the puppy would rather be playing with you or dashing about than staying in his basket, but this training is so very important. All his life there will be times when he must stay quietly in a certain place when you can't have him with you, and it is his early training that matters. If he barks or howls, go back to him and scold him. Never think, 'Poor little puppy, I'll take him on my lap.' If you do, you've lost the first battle. But on the other hand, never leave a puppy too long. Once he has obeyed and stayed quietly in the box for some time, try, if you can manage it, to give him a romp. I cannot impress on my readers too strongly the necessity to be firm but kind to a puppy. His idea of your authority is forming, and if he knows you give in on the slightest whimper, you are whacked for life. To break him of habits formed when young is far more tiresome than training him in the right way at first. Barking is an inexcusable trick, and if the puppy continues to do it, make sure he is not wanting to go out, make sure he is comfortable and warm, and not hungry. If you're certain on all these points, leave him to yell, only coming back at intervals to speak to him firmly. Then settle him down again quietly and with gentle stroking and words of encouragement, leave him again. Under no circumstances take the dog out of his box when he is yelling, except to make certain all is well. If the puppy thinks he is going to be picked up or let out, you are lost. Usually a puppy will cry for two or three nights at first, on leaving his old home; he misses the warmth and comfort of the rest of the litter or his mother, and his box is a frightening thing to be left alone in. But harden your heart and just try not to listen. Warmth is the all-powerful cure for this sort of thing at night. No puppy can help becoming sleepy in a really warm bed.

The next thing we must stop is the impulse to chew up every thing he sees. This is, of course, a natural thing to do; he is cutting his teeth and he wants to gnaw everything in sight to help his troublesome little teeth through. The answer is, of course, to give him plenty of material that he is allowed to chew. My puppies always have bones in plenty, big marrow bones, not tiny ones that might splinter. A rubber bone is useful, or a hard old dog biscuit, or even an old slipper. Give the puppy plenty to play with, but as soon as he touches something that he mustn't, the firm command and the words: 'No, naughty!' must come in. Take the object away and then offer it to him again; if he goes to take it, scold him severely and give the command: 'Leave!'; offer it again, and repeat the word 'Leave!' He will soon know that he mustn't touch that article. The same applies to food stealing. If you can catch him stealing, take the food away and scold him with the same: 'Leave!' command. Offer it again, and so on.

When you give him his own dinner, give it to him with a lot of praise and always in his own dish. If you use several different plates it is difficult for the dog to know what he may and what he may not take. Teach him to have a piece of meat put between his feet with the command: 'Leave!' and then a second or two later pick it up and give it to him with much praise. Anything you give him is right, anything he just takes is wrong. That will help when people offer him things to eat in the street: he will await your permission before taking it. Do keep to very regular meal times for your puppy. My dogs know the time to a second and I make a point of feeding them (and, incidentally, all my animals) absolutely by the clock. If I happen to be out driving I stop and feed the dog at the right time. I always take their food with me. It keeps their digestions happy, as nature has a peculiar way of making the saliva run and the digestive juices flow ready to digest the meal at those times. I have often seen my dog dribbling at the right time for a meal.

Jumping up is, in my opinion, one of the greatest curses of owning an untrained dog. With a puppy, one is inclined to forgive it as just a show of exuberance, but later on, when the dog comes in with muddy paws and jumps up for play, or a kiss, it can be the ruination of a dress or suit. Therefore stop this trick in the beginning. I always kneel down when really praising a small dog, so that the inclination to jump up needn't arise. The dog only jumps up to be near your face. Faces have a fascination for dogs. A well-trained dog never takes his eyes off his master while working in a competition, and this eagerness to be near his master's face begins very early in life.

Quite often I am asked: 'Am I likely to catch any disease if I kiss my dog?' I always reply that only one ill is communicable to man from dogs and that is the tapeworm, so if you want to kiss your dog don't kiss his nose or muzzle. I always lay my face against a dog's cheek so that I can whisper sweet nothings into its ear. I have trained our little English Toy Terrier to wait for a kiss; she puts her head on one side and waits until I give her a kiss before showing terrific pleasure by really lifting up her upper lip in a toothy smile. Sometimes I have to give her five or six kisses before she is satisfied: I really have to love her a lot! Dogs adore affection. I know very few owners who really give their dogs all the affection they need. Of course there are cranks who overdo it but we are not concerned with such people, who probably lack love in their normal human relations and who therefore give exaggerated affection to their dogs and expect it to be returned. One must have a reasonable perspective in these matters.

I believe it is essential to talk to your dog as frequently as you would to a child. You will be amazed how much your dog understands, not only by the tone of your voice but from actual words. I save myself many an unnecessary journey by asking my dog to go and 'shut the door' or 'fetch the newspaper', etc. I have no trouble at all in teaching her a new thing to do, because she knows so many basic words, as for example, 'go', 'fetch', 'bring', 'put it over there', 'come', 'sit', 'stay', 'down', 'away', 'corner', 'go round', 'turn round', 'walk back', etc.; in fact, there are a vast number of combinations of words in a dog's dictionary. It is your business to help him build up this vocabulary, beginning with his name, then simple words like 'Box!' 'Leave!' and 'Naughty!' already mentioned, then perhaps 'Bone', 'Dinner', and the various names of objects or actions that fill

ONE DALMATIAN: Dogs, says Barbara, just adore affection.

him with pleasure or excitement. As his comprehension of single words grows, so does his power of understanding separate sounds strung together.

The mind of a dog is forever open to take in, by touch, by telepathy, and by talking, the feelings, ideas, emotions and wishes of its owner. That is, if the dog loves its owner. To get through to a dog's mind you don't need a couch and sweet music or probing questions from a psychiatrist. You need hands that on touching the dog send messages of love and sympathy to its brain. You need a voice with a wide range of tones to convey aurally your wishes and feelings towards the dog. You need eyes that tell the dog who watches them what you are feeling towards it, even though it may be hidden from the outside world, and above all you need telepathy so that the dog thinks with you.

These things are not always born in people. They can be developed as any sense or gift can be developed. That is, providing the person who wishes to develop them is honest in mind, because with animals you cannot cheat; it is useless watching a trainer handling your dog with hatred of her in your heart, or dislike of all the things she is doing which you think unnecessary or harsh, or both. If you give an order to your dog by word of mouth and are feeling sorry for it inside you are doomed to failure. Dogs above all creatures love honesty of purpose. If you pat a dog and your fingers are not carrying that loving message you don't deceive the dog.

No one knows why touch is so important. I think probably blind people know more than any of us about the sensitivity of touch; that is why guide dogs are usually so faithful. But the ordinary handler can develop this touch which calms the wild dog, which produces ecstasy in dogs when you caress them, but it has to come through the fingers or face direct from your heart. In every training school the words: 'Praise your dog' are heard constantly; by those words in my school I don't necessarily mean a big hearty pat. I mean a communion of brain and touch. I lay my face alongside that of the dog with its face cupped in my hands, and I sense that my deep love and admiration for it passes right through to its mind, often in silent communion, for I have already said: 'What a good dog' and clapped my hands to show approval at the end of the exercise.

But a dog needs more than that if you are to get its complete mind in tune with yours. Unhappy are the handlers who think this all stuff and nonsense. For it makes dogs truly happy. Lots of dogs have to put up with second-best praise but, if you can't let yourself go, you must at least mean what you say when praising. The tone of voice must convey great joy to the dog. It must convey to him that you think him the most wonderful dog on earth, and you must never mind what other people in the school are thinking. Half the trouble in training schools is the natural restraint and reserve that stifles people in public. They cannot forget themselves and abandon themselves to working and praising or correcting the dog.

In the same way, it is difficult for most of us to correct our dog in the street for fear of what people will do or say or think. If we truly loved our dog other people and their thoughts wouldn't matter, but it is easier to write this than to carry it out. The general public are so ill-informed on the training of dogs that I am certain the R.S.P.C.A. get a multitude of phone calls from over-sentimental ignoramuses who haven't the foggiest idea what goes on in a dog's mind, and who think it cruel to correct a dog firmly. They mix up discipline with cruelty, and would apparently rather see a dog run over or put to sleep than have it corrected in the street when it has done wrong. But the handler's life is almost in danger by correcting a dog in public in the effort to make it eligible for the praise to follow.

It is extraordinary how dogs pick up praise straight from your brain almost before you have had time to put it into words. A dog's mind is so quick in picking up your thoughts that, as you think them, they enter the dog's mind simultaneously. I have great difficulty in this matter in giving the owners commands in class for the dog obeys my thoughts before my mouth has had time to give the owner the command. I find it extremely difficult to correct a dog for this, although it shouldn't really be obeying me; it should be tuned into the owner who of course doesn't know what I am going to say until I have said it—that is unless the owner is also telepathic.

In the same way I know what the dog is thinking as it thinks it, and can often therefore stop it being naughty or disobedient before it has erred, which saves correcting it and helps quick training. But I find the chattering that goes on in class by those people who don't truly concentrate very hampering to this mind communication. It is like having constant interference on a wireless set. But then I don't suppose many people know what a thrill it is to be on the same wavelength as a dog.

Praise can be given in so many ways, by titbits for a puppy, by tone of voice, by scratching a dog's chest, by firm warm pats on the back, by kissing, which all dogs love, or by just looking straight into their eyes and smiling. You can't deceive dogs. It doesn't matter whether you say: 'Good dog' or 'Gadzooks'. The dog knows what you mean. We come now to the vexed question of how much encouragement he should get to bark at the telephone or at the doorbell, of how to teach him to stop barking or start barking. It is quite easy to teach him to bark by getting someone to bang on the door, whereupon you rush towards it with tremendous excitement, 'barking' yourself and getting terrifically worked up. The dog soon understands this game and should learn in under an hour what he is supposed to do. The greater trouble comes when you want to stop him. As he barks, you go to the door and open it. If it is a friend, you tell the dog: 'That will do' and if he doesn't stop barking immediately, scold him and straightaway put him, lying down, into his kennel. He will soon come to connect the words 'That will do' with being put in his kennel, or down, and as you say: 'That will do' he will soon learn to stop barking in anticipation of being put in his box. He also connects the words with a scolding. But always remember to praise him, when he barks at first with: 'Good boy!' then follow it by: 'That will do' and the command to go and lie down. Few dogs bark much when lying down.

Some dogs bark for hours if left alone in the house. The reason for this is loneliness, and the barking is really a compliment to the owner. But it is also a vice, and must be stopped. The only way to stop it is to train your dog while you are in the house to be put in another room with its blanket or basket, and to stay there quietly. At first it will bark very loudly. The owner must return very crossly and send him to his basket with extremely angry words. The dog will try to fawn over the owner, but under no circumstances must one give in. When you have got him lying down, change your tone of voice to a soft soothing one, and with plenty of praise tell him to: 'Stay, there's a good boy,' leaving him in a slow, comforting manner. If the dog is quiet for about half an hour go back and praise him with all the fervour you can muster, let him romp about, and take him with you to your sitting room or wherever you are; show him that you think he is the cleverest and most wonderful dog you know. If you do this daily your dog will learn that you are coming back and will eventually lie down quietly wherever you put him. But this is not taught in a day, and is never taught at all by a weak-willed owner. I maintain that to train a dog successfully the owner must be absolutely determined that with kindness and firmness he will make the dog do as it is told. The dog must get the impression that if he doesn't do right there is going to be real trouble with him, but if he does do right he's going to have a wonderful time.

I think you will find that a dog that has been trained to stay anywhere quietly in a house will also stay happily in the street in your car. I often think a dog is best left in a car rather than outside a shop, although I am often shocked by the way owners shut the windows up tight in hot weather until the dog is really suffering.

One's dog should be so trained that if the windows are all open a few inches he will not try to get out. At first, give him his own blanket or cushion on the back seat, so that he has the comfort of familiar things around him. He should bark if a stranger comes too close to the car he is guarding. It is natural for any dog to guard its owner's property. Should the dog lack the guarding instinct, it must be taught, with the help of a friend. Get the friend to approach the car and as she puts her hand on the door, tell your dog in a rousing voice to: 'See her off' or 'bite her.' This must be said with so much vehemence that the dog is egged on to such a state of excitement that he naturally barks. Directly he does so, praise him, and repeat this as often as is necessary for the dog to get to know that guarding is his job. To bite is only taught when the stranger has protective clothing on, and I think the average car and dog owner will be satisfied with a barking dog in a car. Training to bite is a risky undertaking; the training of guard dogs is a specialist job, and the ordinary dog owner should be wary of training his dog to do more than bark fiercely and agitatedly. Once a dog has been taught fierceness, the lessons are extremely difficult to unlearn.

I get many letters from dog owners whose dogs tear the edges of their husbands' trousers or overcoats; in fact they tear the clothing of anyone who comes to the house. The quickest cure I know for this is to arrive at the house and go straight to the kitchen, fill a small jug, walk on, and when the dog starts tearing, to pour some water over its head. The dog gets such a shock that it doesn't often do it again. This method is better than all the scolding in the world, for the dog doesn't know where the water comes from, he only comes to realize that cloth-tearing causes it to flow.

Dogs that kill chickens have so often been put to sleep as incurable that I hasten to tell readers of a cure I have never known to fail. It means slaughtering another chicken, but it is worth it. Get the dog on a very long cord, about twenty feet in length; if it is of string he won't notice he has it on. Then catch and kill a chicken, and while it is fluttering as they do after death, throw it down away from you. The dog will immediately rush in to the kill. Pull him sharply by the cord, pick up the chicken and hit the dog everywhere with it. The feathers will go all over his face, he will try to escape, but you have him on a cord. Keep on for about ten seconds, not hitting him hard enough to injure him, as the secret of the cure is the fright he gets when the chicken attacks him instead of letting him kill it. Next throw the chicken down away from him and loose the cord. If he shows the slightest indication of going after it, repeat the performance, but hit a good deal harder this time. I have never seen a dog need this treatment more than twice. The old trick of hanging a dead chicken round the dog's neck has no effect at all.

I had an urgent phone call from a lady the other day, telling me that her dog had taken possession of her bed, and neither she nor her husband could get it out, as it bit them on their approach. This is a common trouble; perhaps the dog may take the best chair and refuse to get off. The owner perhaps gives in the first time, from laziness or fear, so the dog does it again. But when you wish to go to bed and can't, because the dog says no, things have become serious. I went to the rescue of the couple I am talking about, and for me it was extremely annoying, for the dog immediately sensed that here was the sort of person who would tolerate no nonsense, and immediately came out of the bed wiggly-waggly fashion, doing his best to show me what a really delightful person he was by licking my face, and showing great friendliness. I told the owner to put him back in the bed while I went outside, but the dog knew that this was not the moment for repeating his act, and allowed his mistress to remove him from the bed without making any kind of protest. The cure which the owner should have adopted was to have put on thick gloves and an overcoat, grabbed the dog by the scruff of its neck, shaken it vigorously, and allowed any bite to come to nothing on thick cloth or leather. Always have a long piece of string on the dog collar so it can be pulled off the bed or chair by the string.

I asked what other tricks this delightful creature could produce, and was told that he was very fond of snatching and stealing food; and if anyone tried to take it away he would bite. So I got her to fetch a piece of meat and the dog promptly snatched some. I took the meat, and just as the animal was going to seize it I said: 'Leave!' in a thunderous tone. The dog sat back astonished, I offered it the meat again, and repeated: 'Leave!' in an ordinary tone; the dog did not attempt to touch it. Next I gave it to the dog with great praise and gentle coaxing. He enjoyed it. Now came the real test, which was to take the meat from the dog when actually in its mouth. I gave it a large lump which I knew it would have to chew, and directly it had the meat in its mouth I said: 'Leave!' again in a very fierce voice. The dog stopped chewing and I opened its mouth and took the meat away. I then gave it back, with much praise. I consider that a well-trained dog should drop what it is eating immediately on command. I have taught my dog, by these means, never to eat a rabbit bone. I take all the bones I can see out of the rabbit she has, but I do miss an occasional one. I always watch her eating and as soon as I hear a bone crunched, I tell her to drop it. The food is immediately dropped from her mouth and I remove the bone. After a short while she realized that it was the bone I wanted, not the food, and now if she cracks a bone she instantly drops it out on the plate and very carefully picks the food away from it. In the same way, I can give her a mutton bone and tell her to eat it as long as it doesn't splinter. Immediately it cracks she drops it and won't touch it again until I have examined it for safety.

The cure for all biting dogs that sharpen their teeth on their owners begins with protection for the owner; then, as he knows he is certain not to get his hand bitten, he can go over to the attack, and the biting dog gets what he didn't bargain for. I have advocated a loose muzzle before now and ordered the dog to do my bidding; he has at once gone to bite, forgetting he is muzzled, then I scold him very severely and force him to do what I want at least three or four times in succession, knowing he can't hurt me. I have never found this method to fail. Owners have found it to fail as they hate doing such things to their dog, but you are driven to use severe measures with a bad dog. It is probably the owner's fault in the first place for allowing the dog to begin a vicious trick. I have always found that men's thick leather gloves, and a man's overcoat that reaches over my hand a bit, give complete protection against any dog, although only about four dogs in my life experience have tried to bite me; they do what I want them to, 'or else,' as the saying goes, and well they know it. Yet the funny thing is that they love me for it. The naughtiest dogs and I have a great love for each other, and some of the cured ones won't rest in my class until I have loved and kissed them. To me they are the most precious of all. When I am brought really naughty dogs it is a challenge to my love for them, and I never feel happy until they are well behaved and have regained their faith in human nature; for that is what they have lost, or they wouldn't be so wicked.

The correcting of a dog inevitably gives more pain to the owner than it does to the dog; the resulting effect on the mind is far worse for the owner than for the dog. Dogs are the most wonderful creatures to own because they don't brood over the past, they don't hold a grudge against their owners, they seem to know when correction is fair and just, and they definitely have consciences, which to me proves they also have souls, although I am told this is not possible and in the next world we shall not see our dogs again!

This book is not to help those dogs for whom a pained look is enough to make them crawl in shame, nor those who listen for the sad tone of voice which denotes the owner's displeasure. Rather it is for those dogs whom the owners erroneously thought psychiatry could help. The dogs we are dealing with are problems in some way and the more gentle and persuasive treatment is unlikely to work on them. What can a handler do and what is the effect on a dog's mind? First of all I believe most correction can be done with a jerk on the choke chain providing the choke chain is the thick-linked variety, not the watch-chain type which is cruel. This sharp jerk has a wonderful effect on the dog; it does not pain him but it shocks his mind into thinking, and a shock, however caused, is much more likely to be remembered than a scolding. Everyone knows in medical practice these days shock treatment by electric impulses is given to nervously unstable patients. I believe the same sort of thing happens to nervously unstable dogs when jerked hard on a choke chain. I have cured the most cringing, terrified dogs in a matter of minutes, not days, with a few sharp jerks, the cupping of my hands round their faces and a lot of cheerful encouragement.

One Boxer got a First at Crufts with the report, 'What a wonderful temp-erament'; had the judge seen this dog three days previously she would have had to lie on the floor to inspect it. The owner was terrified when she saw me jerk her kennel hope, but was soon won over when she saw the almost instantaneous response. I have seen nervous Alsatians, terrified of everyone and dirty in the house because they were too nervous outside to perform their duties, become sound in mind and consequently immediately clean in the house when cured of nerves by this method.

After much thought I have decided that the effect of correction on a dog's mind is to give it confidence, a happy respect for its handler and a longing to be with the person who carries out the correction. No one quite knows why some dogs are excessively nervous. Even with faultless pedigrees showing no hereditary nerves or viciousness you get these pathetic creatures that many people despair of and put to sleep, when really there is absolutely no need for this if they can be cured in hours. They obviously have inner horrors such as fearing to jump into a car; they are terrified of going upstairs, horrified at the sight of a man or a child, neither of whom have ever done the dog harm. I get hundreds of letters from people who assume this fear is due to possible ill-treatment in the past, but this is most unlikely; few people really ill-treat a puppy. I know it to be mostly nervous instability, cause unknown.

Most people who have these nervous dogs coax them, sympathise with them, don't go in cars if the dog doesn't wish to accompany them, don't make the dog go upstairs if it is frightened, don't make it talk to men or children if frightened, and generally put up with a lot of unhappy inconvenience to, as they think, help the dog. This has a disastrous effect on the dog's mind, for he picks up the sad sympathy of the owner's mind, senses the gentle pull on the lead when he won't walk on it, and the nervous tension of the owner struggling to help him. The terror gets worse and worse, and the owner usually, on vet's or incompetent trainer's advice, puts the unhappy dog to sleep when it has often had under twelve months of life.

My heart bleeds for these misguided owners and their dogs. If only they knew how easy it is to change these nervous dogs, they would be happier. But first they must understand a dog's mind. They must harden their hearts and realise that what they are going to do to the dog is for its good, in the same way as a surgeon cuts off a limb to save a life; he doesn't squirm at the ghastly business of chopping off the limb, he looks forward to the regaining of health and life in the patient. I treat dogs in the same way. I know if I can shut my ears to the occasional terrified squeaks of the terrified dog and continue without emotion to jerk it on, that in about ten to fifteen minutes, I shall have won. The dog will stop being frightened, the cure will have begun. It is then only a matter of teaching a dog routine exercises to strengthen its sense of security.

But my greatest handicap is to get the owner in the right frame of mind. Some of them need shutting in somewhere away from the dog whilst the cure is going on; they should only be released when the dog is cured. But if you did this they would not see for themselves how the cure was carried out; they would not pick up the confident way the dog progressed, and above all, they would not see the loving way the dog responds to the correct handling. Definitely this cure must be with the co-operation of owner and absolute trust in the trainer, for sometimes it is necessary to muzzle a very nervous dog since otherwise, in their initial fear, they attempt to bite. This must never be allowed. The handler must be completely safe in carrying out this correction, for the slightest fear on the part of the handler will undo all the good the jerking has done.

Many dogs object at first to a muzzle and they struggle to get it off. The sentimental owner wrings her hands in suppressed sympathy. The atmosphere is charged with emotion, although really there is nothing cruel about a muzzle. Greyhounds wear them all the time when out. Dogs in Italy and other foreign countries wear them for protection against rabies. Many dogs with bad temperaments in this country would be far happier free with muzzles than kept snarling on a short lead. For, whilst the dog is muzzled, the owner need not fear a fight, for a dog can do no harm in a well-fitting muzzle. I have muzzles far too large for the dog so that drinking and panting is in no way stopped. After a few minutes the dog doesn't worry about a muzzle and usually under an hour later it can be discarded. Only for the initial safety of handler and dog is it occasionally necessary to use one. The next type of correction is a good shake. The dog needs grasping by his choke chain and scruff on both sides of his neck under his ears, and whilst looking the dog straight in the eyes scold in a thunderous tone and give three or four hard shakes. This will calm an hysterical dog and will make a 'don't care' one listen to you. It is a correction that makes the dog feel slightly silly, and he doesn't want it repeated, I have seldom had to shake a dog more than twice. It needs strength with a big dog, but it is of course a dog's own answer to unruliness in the pack. Dogs shake each other in play or fight and, when the handler does it, she is only being a better dog than the dog itself, which is an attitude all dogs respect.

Shutting a dog up and not speaking to it as a correction is quite stupid. The dog's mind doesn't understand this sort of correction at all. You can punish humans by sending them to Coventry; you can only lose a dog's deep affection by the same treatment. A dog's mind can't reason that, because he ate the Sunday joint, he is being shut in the outhouse or not being spoken to. His simple mind either frets for your companionship or goes off to find something interesting to amuse him and ends up by tearing up the floor or some other evil.

The dog's mind is not to be compared with even a child's mind. His conscience only acts when he knows from long contact with his owner that he has done wrong. By her attitude of mind he senses that he has done wrong, but unless correction is given at the moment of the wrong action, he won't remember what he has done. That is why smacking a dog when he comes back to you having run off for hours is useless. To him you are smacking him for coming to you - he doesn't remember he ran off hours ago. That is why in my school I personally try and catch dogs running away from their owners and give them a whack with the end of a soft leather lead on their backsides. It is being caught in the action that teaches a dog. I hate any owner to smack a dog. Let me be the horrid person that has to do it if all calling fails.

What a dog's mind can interpret is being put as a punishment into the 'down' position and being made to stay there until he feels more disposed to co-operate with his handler. This has a wonderful effect on hysterical dogs, barking dogs, fighting dogs and obstreperous dogs, and I strongly recommend anyone with a naughty dog to master the act of putting her dog into the down for short spells at a time. The dog is under control in the down and his mind recognises your mastery over him. Dogs like being mastered - it gives them a nice safe feeling and of course makes them respect the handler. Lastly, smacking a dog as a punishment is only to be used as a last resort and should be used if a dog without rhyme or reason attacks another dog or person. The inflicting of pain on him at these attacks is an 'eye for an eye' and is a quick and effective deterrent for a very serious crime. But the smacking should if possible be done with a leather lead over the dog's rump. Never hit a dog with a newspaper or on its face. No crime should ever involve a newspaper; it is ineffective and really annoys and hurts the dog's mind.

No dogs are permanently hurt in mind or body after three or four whacks with a leather lead, but I have known it cure a fighter caught in the act of aggression. The whacking of a dog inevitably hurts the handler more than the dog, and those in poor health cannot do it. In my school no pupil is ever allowed to smack a dog. If it has to be done I do it myself - without temper and sufficiently hard to make the dog feel it without harming it at all. All dog lovers hate doing it or watching it done, but in some cases dogs are so stubborn as to have no finer feelings, and this is the only effective treatment. It may save them from being put to sleep.

In all cases of correcting a dog the handler's character has to be taken into consideration, for most dogs' faults are really handlers' faults and the faults in handlers' temperaments are multitudinous. I think hundreds of them should never own a dog but, as there is no law that permits dogs to be taken away from stupid owners, the poor dog has to be made to conform to the owner whatever the state of mind or the condition of the owner and his home surrounding. I am often terribly, terribly sorry for dogs that come to me. I long to keep them and give them a sensible existence, but all I can do is to make misfits fit as far as is within my power. At the end of many of my training sessions I almost need a psychiatrist myself!

CHAPTER FIVE

HEEL WORK

Now I am going to suppose that you have acquired a completely untrained dog of three and a half months or over. The age doesn't matter. Time and time again I am asked, 'Is my dog too old to train at three years or more?' I answer: 'The age of the dog, providing it is not too young, does not matter. I have trained dogs at eight years old, and many times trained them at five and six years old.' Far more important than the age of the dog is the disposition of the owner. I am going to give a few examples of owners I have met and if you fall into one or another category I hope you are either duly proud or duly ashamed of yourself.

The first owner arrives usually with a medium-sized or small dog. The dog is shown to me as being quite impossible to train, as probably having been taken to the vet for pills to quieten it down, but all to no effect. I am, I am told, its owner's last hope. The owner is usually a very excitable person, as often as not a woman. Her nervous speech and movements and constant chatter make me realize at once that the dog is only copying its owner when it displays symptoms of hysteria. It fights other dogs because its owner inevitably gathers it up in her arms or shortens its lead to choking point on approaching another dog, so that the dog at once stiffens and expects a fuss when he sees another dog in the distance. This owner has got to learn that her dog is a good dog if only it is given the chance. I usually take it from her and demonstrate that the dog doesn't attempt to attack other dogs if I take it along with me. I have to make her understand that to train the dog she must believe that she can make it behave and that it is not witchcraft on my part when the dog behaves with me. The next type of owner is a very nervous type of man or woman, usually elderly, with a large animal that is far beyond their strength. He or she literally hasn't the physical power to give the dog the sharp jerks on his choke collar that are the preliminary to all good heel work. I tell them I think the dog is too much for them, but they insist that they adore big dogs, and 'he's such a darling' - if only he wouldn't pull them over, steal the joint, go off alone most of the day and chase everything that moves. Again it is usually I that have to give this dog its first lesson in the meaning of a choke chain collar, in fact I have nearly to choke him before he finally realizes that it is far more comfortable to keep to heel on a loose lead than to pull on a collar that tightens round his neck as he pulls.

The next type of owner is the one who arrives with the tiniest toy dog, complete with cushion, and does so want the dog to behave but it is so tiny to teach anything to. I adore training these mites, and have, in my time, spent many hours on the floor coaxing one of them to retrieve a dumb-bell. I have before now given a sharp slap to a tiny miniature Dachshund who with malice aforethought defied my every command. I have used two fingers only, and been most careful to smack in the right place. Some of these little mites can be extremely stubborn and no amount of coaxing will alter their behaviour.

Horror-struck onlookers have wondered how I could do such a thing, but I always maintain that I am the best judge of what to do with a dog. Had the owner been the best judge, it would not have been necessary to attend classes. In every case I punish a dog without feeling angry with it, and then only after every other means has been tried.

While I am on this matter of smacking dogs, I should like to pass on what I hear from many owners on their methods of punishing their dogs. When the dog is caught in the act of doing something dreadful the owners have several ways of showing their displeasure. Quite often, people tell me: 'Oh, I don't speak to my dog all day.' Can you imagine any dog seeing the point of this? If that is a sensible punishment, then I suppose we are to keep up a constant chatter to our dogs in order that they may understand that we are pleased with them! It sometimes happens that I do not speak much to my dogs in the course of a day; they quite understand, then, that I am very busy or worried. The other night I was both busy and worried and it wasn't until my husband said, 'Look at your dogs, Missis,' that I glanced at them and saw they were both lying gazing at me, their eyes full of urgent entreaties to go and get their dinner. Both tails were wagging and both heads were lying between their paws. They were relying on their beautiful eyes, that were fixing me with a stare, to make me understand what they wanted, without barking or disturbing my train of thought. Those dogs didn't take my silence as a punishment, but they knew I had temporarily forgotten them. I believe they thought that by concentration and telepathy they would attract my attention: as they would have, before long.

Another type of owner scolds her dog in the most gentle manner possible, being quite certain in her own mind that harsh words may cause severe and permanent injury to her dog. I fear that as a punishment for stealing or biting, or some such deed, this type of mild rebuke will get you nowhere. If your dog is as sensitive as this, one look from your displeased face will send him to the corner in a misery. I believe that if your dog really loves you, and you him, a bond exists between you, so that your merest hint of crossness is conveyed to him without words being said. But I maintain that if you have created that bond, you won't be at training classes.

The next type of owner gives a sound thrashing for whatever wrong the dog has done, believing the theory that 'the more you beat them the better they be.' This just gets a dog muddled and very unhappy. Some dogs cringe and show every kind of allegiance to this kind of behaviour, and I often think that the animals that do the best heel work, clinging to the sides of their handlers in obedience tests, have had one or two beatings before this level of obedience is attained. I would any day rather see an animal walk quietly to heel in an easy manner than cling in terror to the legs of its owner. But then I do not really approve of the artificial manner of working dogs in these tests. To my mind, it almost amounts to mental cruelty to expect it to work with certain dogs.

To resume: I think experience shows that if by a quick smack you can cut short the nagging necessary to make a dog do something which it is quite imperative he should do, then give a quick smack when you are not in a temper, and immediately show that you bear no malice. Recently it was so cold that instead of having a training class in our Nissen Hut I invited the handlers and dogs into my drawing-room and rolled back the carpets. This meant that we had a very confined space, and if we were to gain any benefit from a class under these circumstances the dogs not working at any given moment must be kept lying down and quiet. This was a good exercise in itself. One young Poodle would not lie down; he would sit, but while sitting kept up a ceaseless, stupid whimper.

I gave the owner instructions as to how to put him down, but the Poodle won every time by getting up again. The dog owner had had every chance to show how the dog should behave, and as the animal was spoiling the class for the rest of the handlers I went over, gave a firm command and the lightest of slaps on his lordship's posterior. He lay down at once, put his head between his paws, and went to sleep. He knew I meant what I said and certainly *felt* I meant it. When I was ready to have him work I went over to him in a very pleasant manner, and spoke to him amiably; he was delighted to see me, and we had both forgotten the former incident. I need not have slapped him. Had I had time to reason with him I could have made him do exactly what I wanted with nothing but my voice, but in class one hasn't always the time to give the necessary individual attention to each misbehaving dog. I believe the smacking of dogs should not, as a rule, be done by the owners. If the dog is behaving badly enough to require punishment the owner is probably in a temper, and I don't think anyone should hit in a temper. One inevitably regrets it. If a trainer does it in a calm way, without temper, the dog understands what it is all about.

In all future descriptions of how to train your dog I shall leave out all reference to corporal punishment. It is a very distasteful subject to all dog lovers. I have given my views as to the occasions on which it seems reasonable for a dog to be punished in that way, and I shall always think a dog caught in the act of doing something quite unpardonable is more quickly taught there and then by a sharp slap than by all the talking to in the world. If you need to smack your dog, in my opinion you have failed, as a trainer, to exert proper influence on him from the beginning. That is why your dog has to be broken of his bad habits the hard way.

Most people come to my courses in the right spirit, realizing that to train perhaps twelve dogs and handlers in a total of six and a half hours needs an almost super-human effort on my part; that is, if I am not content just to stand in the middle of a class and yell orders. My idea of training is that all the dogs should learn properly exactly what I set out to teach them, and I am afraid I spend a long time sometimes on a particularly difficult dog, trusting that the other members of my class will forgive the time filched from their own charges. I remember one day I was having tremendous trouble with a little toy dog and her dumb-bell; she just would not leave her mistress to go and pick it up, although if I took her and put it in her mouth she would run happily back with it. I sat on the floor and spoke to her in my 'little voice' and kissed her unashamedly; quite quietly I gave her confidence through my own love for her, and presently up she got and trotted off to fetch her dumb-bell. A few weeks after that she won a prize in a Special Novice obedience test at a championship show. Without that time spent on her, she would never have done it. It was typical of the spirit of the other dog handlers that immediately this little dog did the exercise in the class, there was a spontaneous outburst of applause. We all so want the dogs to work well, that you could hear a pin drop sometimes when I am having a particularly tough time with a dog. I often feel that everyone is willing me to win, and persuade the dog to behave well.

I find this training of dogs the most fascinating work possible. Sometimes it breaks my heart to see the utterly unsuitable owners that intelligent dogs have to put up with. Often I have to train the dog in spite of its owner. Some dogs I know will never be trained after they leave me. Whatever we do in the class is left unpractised directly the class is over. I think some members come for an entertaining weekend, but to those who come and really make progress I always feel extremely grateful. For by the mere fact of having a well-behaved dog on the streets they are helping to spread the gospel that training pays all along the line.

The first exercise must be to train a dog to walk nicely on and off the lead. First you require a choke chain of the required length and type. The thin small links on some that are on the market are quite useless for training a dog kindly. The broader the link the less likelihood of any damage to the dog's coat, and one can get more purchase on the dog with a broad chain than a narrow one. Lengths of these chains vary. Small dogs need sixteen to eighteen inch lengths. Bigger ones, up to twenty-eight inches. Tiny tots need the finer and smaller chains still, although I consider that a very small dog need not have a choke chain at all. Next, you take hold of both rings at each end in different hands, and with one hand held high above the other slowly drop through the lower ring, until both rings meet each other. I once sent a man a choke chain through the post and it came back twice with the remark that he was not a conjuror - the rings wouldn't go through themselves as they were both the same size. The rings do not thread through each other, but the chain is dropped back through one ring. Now that the chain is correctly threaded, put it on your dog so that the chain pulls in an upward direction when on the dog's neck; in this way the chain immediately loosens when you release the pull on the lead. If you put the chain on so that it pulls downwards when on the dog, it does not free itself but stays tight even though your lead is loose. This means that you are punishing your dog when he should not be punished, and spoils the whole idea of letting your dog realize that as soon as he stops pulling he is quickly comfortable again. This choke chain is in no way cruel; the only effect it has on the dog is it quickly gives up the idea of pulling and becomes a nicely behaved animal. Now that you have presumably attached your choke chain in the right manner, the correct length of chain should be such that when threaded through itself it has a couple of inches or so loose to

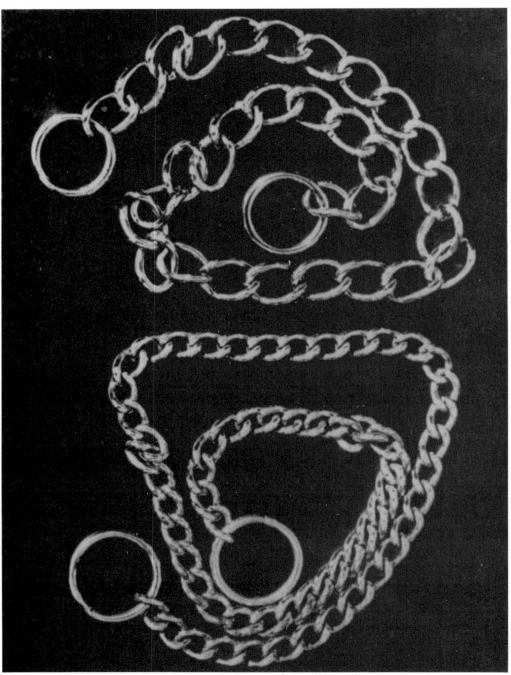

CHOKE CHAINS: The broader the link, the kinder to the dog.

TO USE: (1) Hold by both rings. (2) Drop chain through one ring. (3) Put on dog, pulling upwards. (4) Automatically loosens when used correctly.

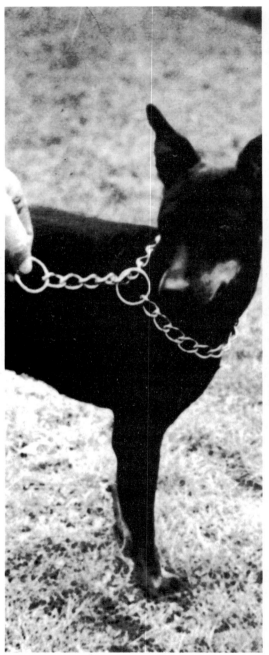

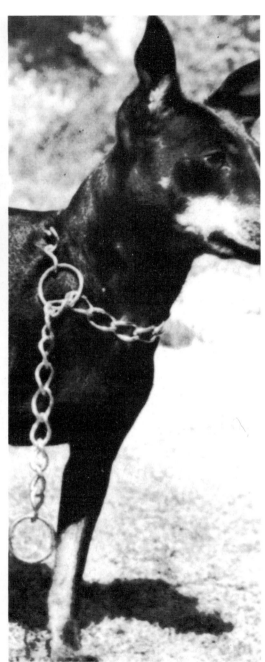

CORRECT: The proper way to use a choke chain.

WRONG: A chain incorrectly put on a dog.

Going to heel after recall: (1) Dog sits in front of you. (2) Pass lead to left hand. (3) Help dog to heel with right hand. (4) Pass lead over right hip and make dog sit.

spare; that means that it is easily put on over the dog's head. Never try to force on too small a choke chain for this could hurt or frighten the dog. Next, the lead must be fixed to that ring of the chain that is doing the pulling upwards. The lead must be approximately three to five feet long and of leather. Be sure not to have too wide a leather lead or the edges will cut your hand as you jerk the dog. The lead must have a strong clip, especially for big dogs. I have had little success with the convenient scissor-type of clip. They are inclined to break when you jerk your dog. The Trojan-type clip is the best. (See Appendix for availability of choke chains.)

The next step is to get your dog sitting on your left-hand side. Hold your lead in the right hand, over the two middle fingers only, and adjust the length so that when you are walking with your dog, and you are holding your hand slightly across your body, the lead hangs in a loop. It is vitally necessary to have the lead loose when held in the right hand. Now your left hand is free to do any correcting of the dog that is necessary. Should the dog pull on the lead, let him get nearly to the end of the lead and then put your left hand on the lead with your fingers facing the way you are going and your thumbs facing towards yourself, palm downwards; now with a firm command, 'Heel!' give your dog a very quick jerk back to your side. Take your left hand off the lead immediately; he will be almost certain to forge ahead again, so repeat the quick jerk with the short sharp command: 'Heel!' prefaced by the dog's name. Always preface any command with the dog's name, to attract its attention. Also try to keep the dog's attention on its work and position by cheerful encouraging word, such as: 'Good boy, close.'

Most owners do not jerk their dogs quickly enough, but give a few slow gentle pulls; this is useless, and will never train a dog. Slap your leg to attract the dog's attention, praise it when it comes near to your side, always try the encouraging word before the jerk. Stopping a really bad puller can only be achieved by the most peremptory kind of jerk. It may look rough, but it does not in any way hurt the dog. Most people forget to take their left hands off the lead immediately after the jerk, and therefore spoil the chance of the dog's lead being completely loose after he has been corrected. Always continue walking at a normal pace while jerking. *Never stop to jerk the dog*, or the lesson is spoilt. If the dog drags behind, jerk him forward in the same manner. If a dog lies on the ground when asked to walk, and no amount of encouraging words will make him stand up and come on, go on walking relentlessly, paying no attention to the dog. In no time he will get up and give up being dragged, and you will have defeated him in the first battle

HEEL WORK: (1) The correct length of lead. (2) Walking comfortably. (3) Right hand anchors over hip. (4) Pushing the dog to the sit.

of wills. I know it is easier to write about these things than to carry them out, but I am not keeping back any of the secrets of dog training just because some people think the procedure heartless. If you wish to take your dog out in the street on a loose lead you may have to achieve what you wish by a clash of wills. I recently dealt with a tiny three-pound Griffon whose owner had had to carry her in her arms for six months as she did this lying-down trick. I took her to a carpeted landing and dragged her; in a few seconds, she thought she might do well to mend her ways, and then I took her out for a walk. She has given no trouble ever since. I do not like these battles any more than the owners do, but I feel it my duty to help both owner and dog to live a happier life, and often one short, sharp engagement will do the trick.

There is never, in my opinion, any possible excuse for smacking a dog for bad heel work. If you continue to jerk in the right manner you must win. The time it takes depends on the sharpness of your jerks and your skill as a handler. Having got your dog walking better on the lead, you must now teach him to sit every time you stop. This obviates any chance of the dog causing you to be pulled into the road should you suddenly stop on seeing a vehicle coming, for as you stop, however suddenly, your dog sits. Eventually your dog becomes so well trained that he doesn't need the command: 'Sit' as you stop; he knows what to do. But this high degree of training will not be brought about in a week by the average dog owner without experience.

To get your dog to sit quickly and easily, your lead should be of just the right length, so that as you intend stopping you should place your lead, which is held in the right hand, up and over your right hip. This anchors the dog's head in an upward position and helps you to push him to the 'sit' with the free left hand. This movement is done in 'one-two' time. Up with the right hand on the *one,* and down with the left hand on the *two.* Now the correct position of the left hand should be thus: your four fingers are facing away from your leg, and should be placed over the dog's back so that the two middle fingers are in his flank just in front of the hind leg. The thumb should now be facing towards your own left leg and should also be placed lightly over the dog's back. On your command 'sit', you should, of course, raise your right hand over your right hip and smartly pull the dog down to the 'sit' with the left hand. If you are doing it correctly, the dog cannot do anything but sit. If you are too slow with the left-handed pull, your dog will have got ahead of you and will then be sitting in front of you; this is bad, because you would trip over him as you began to walk again. The secret of a tidy 'sit' beside you is speed; as you stop quickly, pull firmly with the left hand and the right hand goes to your hip. There are, of course, different methods of achieving this 'sit', but I have tried many others and have found the one described infallible for all types of dog and owner. It is just as easily performed by a child as an adult, as the dog is off its balance through having its head raised; and if the actions are done fast enough, it goes to the 'sit' almost before it realizes what it is doing. To get a dog to sit well in to your leg, do your practising with a wall on your left side, and walk fairly close to it. This can be done in the street.

We have got our dog to stop pulling or dragging by jerking the lead; we have got him to sit quickly by pushing him down. This is so far, so good, as long as your dog is on the lead, but how do we progress to getting the same results with the dog off the lead? That can only be done when the dog really walks well on lead, and by that I mean that the dog should have left the jerking stage well behind; on the command: 'Heel', you can count on his being close to your side, and when you about turn or left turn, or right turn, your dog should come with you. The next step is to remove the lead and place your dog on a very light long piece of string, so fine that he will not feel that he has any restraint at all. At first he will try to run away; call him in and if he doesn't come scold him sharply and repeat the command: 'Heel'. He will soon realize that there's no knowing whether he is on the lead or not. And rather than risk a scolding, he will stay to heel.

In all the above exercises, and after every exercise, please remember to give unlimited praise to your dog. I always tell my pupils to bring the right hand down and scratch the dog's chest after every exercise. Dogs love this, and stay still with a benign expression on their faces as long as you like to continue it.

The next step is to have no lead or string at all on your dog, and to walk about, calling him to stay to heel. If he does so, praise him at once. It is imperative that you never weary your dog of this heel work. Never practise it for more than ten minutes at home. In the street, do not allow your dog to pull you about; if he attempts it, correct him firmly. You are quite certain to have a few busybodies accost you and tell you how cruel you are, but their views are of no importance. I expect they think it kinder that the dog should be free to run across the road and kill himself or someone else.

We who really love dogs have to put up with a certain amount of ridicule and criticism from stupid so-called dog lovers who cannot bear even to see a dog corrected. Be comforted, for there are thousands of dogs who hardly need training, they are naturally obedient and well behaved. Their owners are lucky. I, and others like me, are here to deal with the not-so-fortunate owners of adorable but definitely badly behaved dogs. Do not at any time imagine that the training of a dog to absolute perfection is a matter of a weekend's work. It all depends on your dog's temperament, and your ability to absorb and carry out the instruction given to you.

The next most important task we have to tackle is to get your dog to come when you call him. This lesson is at first taught on a lead. Put your dog on his lead and tell him to stay; walk back to the full extent of his lead, and then call him up to sit in front of you. If he is unwilling to come a short quick jerk on the lead will pull him to his feet. Encourage him to come to you by putting all the love you can muster into your voice, coupled with a series of quick jerks and the word: 'Come', prefaced by his name. If he tries to bolt, jerk him sharply with the word: 'Come', changing to a warm, encouraging voice should he show any sign of coming to you. If you think it will help to give him a titbit on coming by all means give him one, but drop this habit as soon as is possible or the dog may get disgruntled later on with coming and not getting anything. This recall exercise must be treated as another lesson, not as a meal!

You have now got your dog to come to you on the lead. 'Sit' him in front so that his head touches your knees, or, according to his size, that part of your leg or body he can reach. My Great Dane touches my chest. Then with your lead still in your right hand, give the dog a cheerful command, 'Heel!' and help him to go round behind you and sit once more on your left-hand side, ready as usual to set off.

To get your dog to go round to this position the lead must be passed from the right hand, round the back of you to the left hand, and then back to the right hand so that you can as before push the dog down to the 'sit' with the left hand. If the dog is slow going round behind, you can help him to get there by gently pushing his rump. That means he is being pulled in the right direction with one hand and pushed as an aid with the other hand. I strongly recommend a titbit at first to supplement the reward of your enthusiastic praise when the dog gets to your left side. That left side of you must be the place that the dog comes to associate with love, praise, and the occasional little snack. To get a dog to do this going-to-heel easily, try doing it on a loose lead and flicking the fingers of your right hand as an encouragement, also patting the left thigh to induce him to come there. The less you pull tightly on the lead, the more easily your dog will learn this act. Now you are ready to put the dog on a ten-yard cord and make him come in to you in exactly the same way but from a greater distance. Most dogs find it difficult to

ABRACADABRA: And it works just like magic.

stay while their owners leave them to get to the end of the cord. Should the dog get up, go back to him and firmly push him to the 'sit' again. Walk backwards facing him all the time, keeping your arm raised and the fingers of the hand extended in a signal that I call the 'abracadabra'. It makes the dog sit very still and take notice, just as if it were under a spell. As you do this, gently repeat the command, accompanied by his name: 'Stay, Fido' or 'Fido, stay', whichever you like best. When you have at last got him to stay, get to the end of your cord and call him; should he run away, pull him in quickly on your cord and scold him. Then loose him again; at this stage I think he will hesitate, and this is the time to coax and praise him for all you are worth. He thinks this is just the life for him, and usually comes in. Give him a titbit if you want to. If he hesitates and tries to decamp, use his name firmly in a lowered voice, which means (to him) murder if he doesn't obey. At the slightest attempt to come to you, change at once to the loving tone.

I cannot stress too strongly that the tone of your voice is the secret to efficient training. Some people literally cannot alter their voices enough to make their dogs listen to them and perceive a change of mood. Such folk can register neither love nor displeasure. This is a great disadvantage in dog training and makes the handler's task a difficult one. I often say I would like my pupils to leave their dogs at home and come for a voice training lesson before attempting to teach their dogs. People have often asked why their dogs behave well with me and not with them, and I have explained that my tone range makes me sound exciting to the dog, or cross, or adoring, and in each case the dog responds accordingly. I have often demonstrated this by using the most hateful words to a dog in a loving voice, and the tail has wagged in the happiest manner. Alternatively I have said the most loving things in a stern voice, and the dog has cringed and been miserable. In dog training it is how you say things, not what you say, that matters.

Your final object is to make the dog come instantly, on command; not, as I have said elsewhere, when he feels he might as well come since there is no more attractive prospect; not simply because he is tired of what he is doing.

We now assume you have got your dog to come on the cord at all times. Next you must get him in an enclosed space and practise with the same tone of voice and commands with him off the lead. A landing is a good place for practice, or an enclosed yard. If he does it well, always take him for a walk in an open space. Practise on the cord first of all, and then without the cord. If the dog runs away go back to the cord and practise further. In a subsequent chapter on the question

USING THE CORD: Put your dog on a long cord and make him sit.

THE COMMAND: Gently, but firmly, pull the dog towards you.

of 'leaving other dogs alone', I shall mention means by which you may make your dog come to you without fuss. This business of making a dog come when it is called has two aspects. If the dog imagines he is going to get scolded when he does come, he naturally sees no point in coming. So many people, having chased their dogs for ages, at last capture the animals and proceed to beat them. That is fatal. If the dog comes to you, even after an hour, by himself, he must be praised, however evil you feel. If, however, you actually catch the dog as he is bolting away, then you must reprimand him. Most dogs adore being chased and, seeing a pursuer, run all the faster. A great many fall into the trap of hastily following you if, instead of chasing them, you turn round and run in the opposite direction. The dog races after you and a sudden turn round on your part makes a capture possible. I feel very strongly that any dog that runs away from its owner is not attached by that loving bond that should exist between owner and dog. I feel that this dog is one that has been turned or let out in the garden to amuse itself. This sort of treatment is not kindness, but is pure laziness on the part of the owner. The dog's place at all times should be with its owner; left to its own devices it gets into mischief and develops an independent set of habits through being forced to be by itself. I cannot believe that any dog that has the advantage of constantly being with its owner would enjoy running off. It has become used to being a constant friend and companion. We know many people who keep dogs say they are too busy to exercise them, and just turn them out, but I have proved that dogs need very little exercise. It is exercise even if they are merely following some member of the household from room to room as she goes about the usual household tasks.

Many dog owners see their dogs for only a short period each day. They are too busy to do otherwise. Are we, in spite of such a drawback, to deny these people the companionship of a dog when they come home in the evening? I think not, but I do think they cannot, on such terms, expect the dog to obey them instantly when so little of their lives is shared with the dog. It is particularly these people who should spend time in the evenings practising the art of training and getting to know their dogs better. Some dogs have the natural hunting instinct deeply ingrained and it is these dogs that are the most dangerous to domestic livestock, and the least to be relied upon without training, to return to the owner on command. Such dogs should be given a great deal of work of some kind to divert these natural instincts. A dog that does advanced obedience training, and receives much deserved praise, gets this joy and energy expenditure in such work, but other dogs just get into mischief. The trouble is that owners buy the wrong sort of dog for their circumstances. Often you see someone with a Greyhound, for example, a dog which everyone knows is not a quiet household pet but a breed with a job of work to do, and best kept for their work as a Foxhound is for his, whereas the owner, who wants a quiet steady house dog, should try another more placid type. I have not picked on Greyhounds for any particular reason except that they are so beautiful that many buyers cannot resist them, so that they are bought without any idea of their inheritance and requirements.

I expect a good many owners will be annoyed or distressed to read that I believe their dogs do not really love them enough if they prefer freedom to the owner's company; but they might reflect that our public houses are filled on most evenings with somewhat similar human beings, who prefer the company of acquaintances to that of their wives. Dogs can be 'almost human'!

CHAPTER SIX

IN COMMAND

By now, having got your dog to walk to heel on and off the lead, you can progress to one of the most difficult of exercises, that of teaching your dog to stay at the 'sit' or the 'down' when you go out of sight. This is essential with a town dog who likes to accompany his mistress shopping. Many shops nowadays, regardless of licked fingers and of hands unwashed after noseblowing and so forth, not to mention ash-dropping customers, pin up notices requesting that 'in the interests of health, will customers not bring their dogs into the shop'. So far as untrained dogs are concerned, I agree wholeheartedly. Some dog owners are indescribably lax in allowing their dogs to lift their legs and soil over shop doors, and even over vegetables in shops. It is thanks to this sort of owner that decent, right-minded owners must also keep their dogs outside.

As this exclusion is now general in many districts we should all endeavour to train our dogs so that they can accompany us so far, and yet comply with the shopkeeper's request. It is quite easy to train your dog to sit or lie down outside a shop; harder to train are the general public who cannot leave your dog in peace. It takes years of training to get a dog to that state where it will stay put under the most trying circumstances. In my classes I attempt to emulate the public. I bend down and stroke the dogs, I drop my handbag near them, I climb over them, I walk other dogs all round them, and generally do my best to upset them. But the trouble is that as they know me, the test is not strict enough. If it were possible to practise with strangers, the lesson would have more value. Here is the way to begin training your dog to wait outside for you. If you had him as a puppy, you would already, we hope, have carried out the instructions for making him stay alone in another room, but I am going to presume you have only just acquired an adult dog, and are about to train him to wait. Get out the familiar cord so useful in dog training. Put your dog again on to it, and as he has already learnt to 'stay' while you go to the end of the cord (in the recall) repeat this as the beginning of the exercise. Then return to him while he is still on the cord and immediately leave him again, at first giving him the command: 'Stay!' as you leave. Should he get up, push him down again, and leave him again. Get him thoroughly used to this, and then if you have a garden put him to 'sit' or 'down' in the garden and walk into the house. Watch him, and the moment he moves, shout: 'Down!' from your window without letting him see you. He will not know where the voice is coming from, but will probably drop again, comforted by the fact that you are about. Every time he moves repeat the command, then return to him, keeping him 'down' until you are right up to him, and then let him up and praise him for all you are worth.

Never leave a dog at the 'sit' for more than two minutes: it is a tiring performance. If you intend leaving the dog for longer than that, put him to the 'down'. This is easier to write than to accomplish. I am always surprised at the number of dogs who strenuously resist being made to lie down. Why, I can't imagine, for it is a natural and restful position. There are several ways, no doubt, of putting a dog 'down'. I use two. The first is a simple if rather slow method, and a good one to start on.

The second is a quicker but more difficult method, mostly used by those having to deal with very strong dogs. I use the command 'down', for I detest the word 'flat': it is a hard, uncomfortable word. 'Down' can be a caress and an assurance all in one, and if ever a dog needs assurance it is when a loved owner leaves him alone. I have seen owners in murderous temper with their dogs in the show ring obedience tests when the dog has got up when supposed to be lying down, but I believe that this happens because the dog has not trusted its owner enough. It is frightened lest maybe the owner should not come back. Do not we human beings feel worried enough to go a hundred times to the door when a loved one is late coming home? Such anxiety is quite understandable. Yet a dog must not have any such fears, and if he dares to get up and look around him, he is punished. I know he must learn this exercise for his safety's sake, but I wish owners would give more comforting words to their dogs as they leave them. I see owners

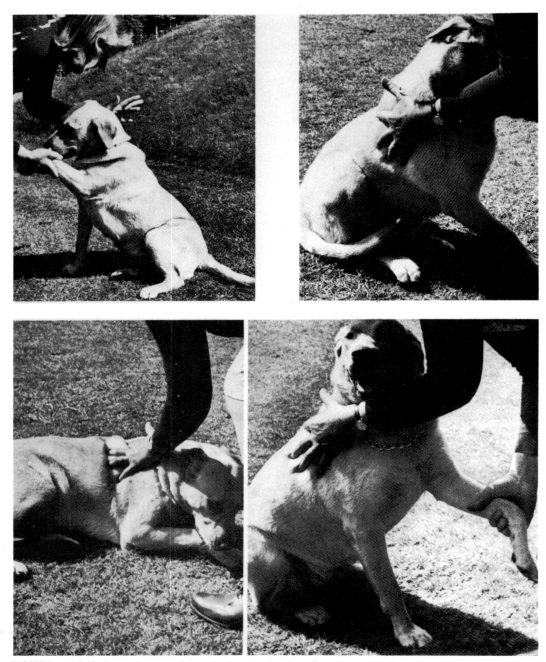

DOWN. (1) Lift front leg and push the opposite shoulder. (2) Push quickly with left hand. (3) Dog lies down. (4) Correct position of hand on the dog's shoulder.

leaving their dogs without a smile or a backward glance, and uttering the most aloof: 'Stay', yet they expect the dog to be happy while awaiting their return. Leave your dog with a pat and a kind word, give it a very slow firm command, 'Stay'. Don't leave it and go out of sight until it will stay for a long time when you are still in sight; then slowly go farther and farther away. Should the dog get up when you are still in sight, then is the time to be firm and rather cross. He has no excuse for anxiety when he can see you, and is showing disobedience that must be firmly checked. No soft: 'Do lie down for Mummy's sake' is any good in this case; a firm command and push down are indicated.

To get a dog to lie down without frightening or hurting himself or you in any way, put him at the 'sit', then lift one foreleg with one hand and gently push the opposite shoulder towards the leg you are raising. This puts the dog off its balance and it has to go down. As soon as it is down scratch its chest, and praise it. The second way to make a dog lie down if it is walking on your left side is to grasp the running end of the choke chain in the right hand still holding the lead, turn the hand until the palm faces ahead of the dog's nose, stand facing your dog's side with legs wide apart for balance; in this position, place your hand on the ground a few inches ahead of the dog and with the other hand press on its back; the pressure on the choke chain forces the dog's head down and the back pressure helps to overbalance it. Usually it only takes a minute or two to teach a dog this, if you use a firm command 'down' at the same time exerting the pressure on collar and back. I definitely prefer the first shoulder-pushing method for beginners, but the other method is quick and easy if you do it with lightning speed, and of course it does get your dog lying down directly beside you in a crouching position, whereas the shoulder-pushing method gets the dog down in a 'curled over' position. This latter position, incidentally, is quite essential if you intend leaving a dog for a long time. A crouching dog can get up quickly, but a dog in the 'curled' position has first to get into the crouching position before it can rise. If you use the lead method of dropping your dog, gradually get the lead longer and less tight. I find that after I have done this about six times, a dog will drop on my placing my hand on the ground in front of it, anticipating the tug on its collar which it finds unpleasant. The third method is to stand beside your dog raising the right hand holding the lead, and placing the left foot over the running end of the choke chain quickly pulling the dog to the ground.

In teaching your dog to stay outside shops it is essential to get the help of friends who will accustom the dog to having strangers walk near it, and perhaps bend down and touch it. That is one of the great advantages of a training class.

MAKING YOUR DOG GO DOWN:
(1) Place your left foot on the running end of the choke chain, keeping your right hand held high.
(2) Put on pressure with your left foot.
(3) Release pressure on the choke chain as soon as the dog is down.

So many people are rushing back to their dogs, or yelling at them, or falling over them, that the dogs get used to the most fantastic noise and disturbances. I have noticed in classes that no one thinks of the possibility of anyone else's dog getting upset by his sudden rush to reprimand his own dog. This, of course, certainly helps to train the other handlers' dogs, for there is no chance here for a nervous dog to show temperament. The extraordinary thing is that I have constantly found the most nervous dogs forgetting their nerves in this melee and becoming quite used to strangers jumping over them. Biting dogs no longer bite passers by; in fact, the relentless bustle and constant motion and uproar seem to help a nervous dog, rather than make it worse.

As I have said before, a good deal of patience will be required before you will be able safely to leave your dog outside a shop. You need to practise it by leaving it with its lead still attached at first, and keeping a watchful eye on it all the time. But with practice it will learn to ignore all passers-by.

In this book I have often used the words 'scold' or 'get cross with' your dog; this may mean just switching to a sad tone of voice while using his name, or even putting on a shocked look, or addressing him with a flood of cross words, or giving him a shaking. It all depends on the nature of the bond between you and your dog. If you are an owner who only talks to his dog when the rare mood takes you, you will probably have to use far harsher methods than someone who has a dog that is spoken to at every hour of the day and really understands change of tone and even expression. If I say 'Junia' in a sad voice and don't smile when I say it, my dog is sufficiently punished and slinks off in shame; but then she really understands my words and moods; we share our lives completely; she worries with me, she rejoices with me, and if she does wrong, she knows without my scolding that I am annoyed. Only a forgiving word will make her happy again, and I never prolong my disapproval for more than a minute or two, as she would be sick with sorrow if I did.

Many people complain that their dogs jump up, tear their clothes in so doing and are a menace to visitors, old people and children. What they don't seem to understand is that this jumping up is really a compliment. The dog only wishes to be near the face of its owner, which is a dog's way of showing affection. This of course differs from the jumping up and biting, which some dogs do. I remember a Pyrenean Mountain dog (Great Pyrenees) who arrived here with a tiny middle aged lady and proceeded to pin her against the wall, and go straight for her throat. I grabbed it from her and it tried to do the same thing to me. I had the worst few minutes of my life with this animal; it really meant to kill me, I think.

However, by tightening my hold on its choke chain I got the desired effect and it flopped to the ground beaten and winded. After that I kissed it and stroked it, and that dog became the gentlest animal imaginable. I have a lovely picture of it somewhere with its head on my shoulder. All this goes to show this terrible 'leader of the pack' syndrome still exists in the world of dogs if not curbed at an early age.

Dogs must be mastered at some time in their lives if respect is to be gained in the master/dog relationship. When this confrontation takes place (if it takes place) varies from dog to dog, but the dog must never be the winner. Bones are very often 'the bone of contention' and can lead to dangerous encounters. Unless the dog is taught to give up in its early days whatever is in its mouth, on command, confrontations may occur. The most dangerous side of this bone business is that the dog might get too near some small child when it has its bone, and could attack the child in the mistaken idea that the child wanted to take the bone. I don't believe in bones after the age of about three months. They are not necessary and the veterinary profession say that they can be positively harmful so why give bones? It is much better to keep the teeth clean by de-scaling.

If the dog jumps up in a nice friendly manner the correction is to teach the dog to sit on command and stay sitting. Then as it approaches it is given the command: 'Sit' in plenty of time for it to drop into that position, when the owner should of course get down on her knees and love the dog. At that height the dog can be near the owner's face and get loving hands to gently scratch its chest. Interaction of this kind is an essential part of the dog-owner relationship, but dogs that lick faces should be firmly stopped.

I know a dog caresses by licking; it is its way of showing love and appreciation of the person it does it to. But if it is stopped doing this as a small puppy it still learns to lay its face against the owner's cheek without the licking. Licking, after all, can be a cause of infection to owners in rare cases and not all dogs live a completely clean life. They eat manure, or lick their behinds - not only their own but those of other dogs who might not be so healthy as yours. Therefore I trained all my dogs on the command: 'No lick' to be kissed by me behind their ears and to have their chests very slowly and gently scratched. So many people rub their dogs when praising them and this I know for certain makes dogs bad tempered. At a class once I saw a boy rubbing his dog when I gave the command at the end of the exercise they were doing, 'Praise your dog'. I went up to him and rubbed his hair and asked him how he liked it. He went very red in the face and said he didn't like it at all, in fact he felt like 'bashing me one'. Well, if he felt like 'bashing me one' what does his dog feel like? Yet if his dog did anything like growling or biting, it would be severely reprimanded for no fault of its own. The rubbing of the hair the wrong way is particularly obnoxious to a dog, whereas the gentle smoothing of the hair on the chest or on the rumps particularly pleasing to the dog. They love being scratched on top of the tail; it is an area of pleasure. There are many areas of pleasure - behind the ear, under the lower jaw, on the ribs behind the front legs, on the tummy and especially between the front legs. Owners must find out which pleases each individual dog best and keep that pleasure for a reward, as well as to please the dog.

Excessive licking by dogs of their bodies may mean allergic reaction, may mean too full anal glands, may mean a skin disease. People sometimes imagine dogs wash themselves like cats; well, they don't do this like cats. Sometimes when they get their paws wet, you will see dogs licking them to dry them as does a bitch lick her puppies to dry and clean them. Dogs should be allowed to lick one's hand; one can easily wash one's hands before touching food, but generally licking should be avoided and stopped at an early age.

A dog's reaction to greeting strangers leads to the more serious aspect of how to teach a dog to guard the home and person of its owner. We must of course divide this question into two parts: the behaviour of puppies, and that of adult dogs. Dealing first of all with puppies, I would much rather see and meet an over-friendly puppy than one that slinks away shivering and shaking when strangers come to the house, for it is the shivery and shaky ones that may eventually be the cowardly biters of the future. How does the mind of a dog work in this matter of protecting the household it belongs to and their property? I believe under the age of twelve months old it hardly reasons it out at all. People who ring me up and tell me their five-months-old puppy is useless for guarding their house need to understand that, if a puppy barked and guarded at that age, in all probability it would be savage and a pest when adult. The development of the mind in different breeds of dogs varies vastly. A St Bernard might not be fully developed at two years old, while a Terrier may behave like a grown dog at twelve months. One cannot compare breeds or an individual dog's development as regards their protective instinct, or their desire to be a guard dog.

The upbringing of a dog counts for so much in these matters. Most puppies of up to say six months or over are boisterous and friendly to all, unless they have nervous temperaments, and that is how it should be. If they are put out into the garden for long periods to find their own amusement they will probably become scatty, and bark at everyone for a long time. The reason for this is that the early developing mind of a dog doesn't know who or what to guard. But when kept in the house with its owner the place to be guarded is quite plainly defined in the dog's brain. The garden however is a very different matter, especially in a built up area with lots of people passing by.

At first the dog is quite good, he only barks at people who enter the premises, then he finds to his delight that they pause when he barks, and he begins to feel superior and important; thus his lack of respect towards mankind commences. Next he tries barking at people walking down the road, and passing dogs, cars, bicycles, etc; perhaps even starts running up and down the fence with his hackles up, showing all and sundry what a brave dog he is.

He gets bolder and, as a tradesman enters the gate carrying something, he goes up to him barking. The tradesman automatically raises in the air whatever he is carrying to get it out of the way of the dog, and the dog interprets that as a sign of weakness, his ego grows, his fierceness increases and now people who enter the gate find quite a nasty dog barking at them, who refuses to go to the owner who is calling him or to stop barking when told. They back out of the gate and shut it in his face. That act alone annoys the dog and the result is, he bites the next tradesman who comes in. That is how a nasty-tempered dog takes his first bite at a human being.

In the dog's mind he is not only keeping strangers away from his home, but he is showing his superiority over man. Unless he can be quickly broken of this habit he will get worse. The owner is powerless to make him stop barking because he has probably not been trained to come when called, and therefore he wins all round. If however a dog is systematically trained to give warning of the approach of everyone to the house by barking when kept in the house, the owner can easily make him stop doing so by making him lie down with the command: 'Cease' followed by 'down'. If he doesn't stop, a sharp jerk on the choke chain will do the trick. The dog recognises authority, and quickly learns that to bark in the first place receives praise, but not to stop barking when told earns him a reprimand.

As with so many matters connected with dog-training, it is essential to start as you mean to go on. If you want your dog to act as a guard, I believe the correct attitude to take is this: when the bell rings at the front door the householder with a young dog should put on his most excited tone of voice and rush to the door saying, 'Who is it? See 'em off!' so that the dog barks in excitement. Next, as you approach the door to open it, give the command: 'Wait'. If you have trained your dog my way he will know that this means: 'Stand and stay standing where you are.' To teach this, put the dog on his lead attached to the end of which should be a seven-pound kitchen scales weight, and suddenly, when walking, give the command: 'Wait' and at the same time drop the lead to the ground. The dog quickly gets used to being checked by word and weight and soon learns what he must do to get the praise he waits for when he's done right. Now this lesson comes in useful, for he will not go further to greet the strangers or friends until released with the words: 'Good boy, or girl' as the case may be. If your friends are dog lovers your dog will probably come in for some friendly pats as he obediently stands there, and you will get the reputation of owning a well-trained dog. If this exercise presents difficulty to you, you haven't practised enough; if the dog drags the seven-pound weight after your leaving him at the stand, use the fourteen-pound one. Never allow a dog to defeat you in anything you wish to do.

Your dog must as far as possible always be with you in all you do, you must be indispensable to him. That is why two dogs together in one household are never so easy to train; they do not depend on their owner for everything, and may not care whether the owner comes or goes. These are the dogs most likely to greet everyone as friends as they have no real allegiance to anyone.

How, from a dog's point of view, is he to know who are your friends and who are unwanted intruders? Some dogs undoubtedly seem to sense this by instinct. Most judge people by their scent, and we suspect that fear in humans produces a strong scent perceptible to dogs. Therefore I think we can conclude that an intruder facing a dog feels fear and sends out this scent, but I think people may only just not like dogs and also send out this scent although they are welcome on the premises. And so it seems sensible to me to train dogs to give warning barks at the approach of foe and friend and to stop doing so when told.

Burglars have been known to be great dog lovers and have been welcomed by guard dogs, so I think it is difficult for a dog to know a burglar all by himself. Having trained your dog to bark, he should clearly understand his duty and beyond that we needn't go. Special guard dogs must receive specialised training for their work, and that training is not for the ordinary owner to teach. It is a very personal and rigid training only to be undertaken by experts for experienced handlers to work the dogs, never for the ordinary householder, for a guard dog is potentially dangerous and ordinary people couldn't manage them, and don't live under suitable conditions to keep one.

Some time back I got a letter from a farmer who complained that he had four or five Alsatians to guard his poultry farm and that they wouldn't guard, that they were unreliable with his wife, and didn't seem to care twopence whether he or his family existed or not. 'Yet,' he complained, 'I have one in my office on its lead when I am there.' He wanted to know how to train them really to guard and if necessary attack intruders. I think he expected me to write back with detailed instructions out of the Police Manual on Dog Training if there is such a book, but instead I asked him what affection he gave those dogs. Did he ever take them for lovely walks, or play with a ball with them? Why, I asked him, was the one in his office tied up on a lead? Surely if he loved and petted his dogs they would want to be near him and not have to be tied up near him. I assured him that guard dogs don't have to be taught to guard their owner and his property; if the dog loves you it is the most natural thing in the world for it to guard you.

I had no reply to my letter and as usual forgot what I thought was another ungrateful correspondent, but four months later I had one of the happiest possible letters from him enclosing some charming snaps of two of the dogs playing on the lawn with his wife, and two others sitting obediently in the background. His letter made me very happy, for it said the dogs were now completely different animals. He had taken my advice and given them much affection, he and his wife had taken them for walks, and trained them in obedience and above all played with them. Their suspicious natures had left them and he didn't think any thief or intruder would have a happy time. This man had the erroneous idea that you mustn't make a friend of a guard dog, that they must be more or less chained up, or left on their own, or they became soft and wouldn't do the job they were supposed to do. How wrong he was. Why, even the police dogs live at their handlers' homes and although they do not live in the house they are very much one of the family. And they are gentle creatures, not ferocious animals that in the interest of safety have to be kept away from human beings unless tracking and catching criminals.

Many people write to me to know, will I train their guard dog for them? Or where can they send it to be trained for such work? I assure them that they themselves must train the dog or it will guard the person who has trained it; dogs are not machines that can be switched over at will and know whom they have to guard. It is far more difficult to untrain a guard dog than to train it. Any handler of such a dog will tell you that the biggest problem is to teach a dog to stop attacking on command rather than to teach it to do so.

People want to know what breed of dog is best for this job, and when I tell them my little miniature English Toy Terrier weighing under ten pounds is a dog I would be perfectly safe with they think I am joking. It isn't always the biggest breed of dog that makes the best guard dog. Some of the small breeds, by their yapping alone would be adequate protection. Naturally a big dog frightens an intruder, and few unwanted visitors would face a Great Dane, purely and simply because of its size and tremendous bark. There is no special breed to choose for guarding your property and person: there are fool dogs in all breeds who would happily go off with the burglar and never look back at their homes. But that comes from lack of training by the owner. When a dog has been the constant companion of the family and has received adequate obedience training, it instinctively guards and stays at home.

If you wish to train your dog to attack on command and stop attacking on command you must do it in the right way. First, make up some padding for your right arm, and fix it on firmly. Then, in a very excited tone of voice, say: 'Attack' and have a terrific tussle with the dog pulling on the padded arm, turning the whole thing into a wonderful game. Next you make the dog sit and stay and run off a few yards, each time suddenly shouting: 'Attack'. The dog now knows what this means and races after you: you let him savage the padded arm for a while, then give him the command: 'Leave' and make him sit or lie down. Next you must have the help of a friend. The friend must run off wearing the padded sleeve, and you must give the command: 'Attack' to the dog. He must be allowed to reach the friend and have a real tussle for a few times to make him enjoy it and get really interested. Then you must put him on a cord and before he reaches the friend you must shout: 'Leave'. If the dog doesn't stop, give a terrific jerk on the cord, if possible facing the dog round to you, and repeat the command: 'Leave, sit', and when he does so, praise him. This training must not be overdone, it must be fun for the dog, but the dog must never become too ferocious. The idea is not to teach him to bite but to hold, therefore he must be taught 'to hold and to leave' on the padded arm as an exercise. Only in the very beginning should he be allowed to bite and pull at it to awaken his interest.

Next of course the dog must be taught to bark on command, as it is the barking that really frightens an intruder - few private owners' dogs ever get the chance of a real criminal chase. To teach a dog to bark you do several things. Get someone to knock on the door and rush to it barking yourself and using a very excited tone of voice. Then have a stick and threaten the dog, urging it to bark at you, and to cease barking as soon as you lower the stick. Next point a toy gun at it and fire the gun at the dog, also urging it to bark and later attack the hand that holds the toy gun. Running away and letting the dog chase you is the greatest fun for the dog, and that is a most important part of his training as a guard dog. As I have previously mentioned in this book the guarding instinct in some breeds can be a menace, and the dog becomes unsafe to take with you in public places. That is why I think an ordinary householder should not train his dog to be a guard dog: it takes an experienced handler to control a really trained guard dog, and an inexperienced handler will probably find himself in court, and his dog with an order against it to be kept under control.

If the right attitude has been trained into your dog it then it will guard.

The question of how to make it less friendly towards strangers is a difficult one, because in general people adore it when dogs run up to them and wag their tails and show pleasure at meeting them, when really they should give the dog a scolding and even possibly a quick slap and send it back to its owner. But one never gets the co-operation of the public. I find some of them a menace: if they see a trained dog standing outside a shop, they will not leave it alone, they allow their children to hug or pet it in spite of the fact that the dog shows no interest, and gives them no welcome, and, what is worse, if you ask them to leave the dog in peace they are rude or say: 'Why shouldn't we pet dogs if we love them?' My reply to that is, 'If you were a real dog lover you wouldn't torture strange dogs with your unwanted attentions.' I point out to them that my trained dogs have interest in only one person, their mistress, and they only tolerate without biting the unwanted stroking because they are polite well-trained dogs.

Very often these unwelcome attentions from the public will cause a nervous dog to get up and run away, and if it got killed or caused an accident those strangers would be responsible. But again you must have the help of friends if you wish to train your dogs not to welcome strangers. You must ask people to call at your house and when the dog rushes out to greet them they must give it a harsh word, or a quick slap if it really persists in forcing its attentions on them and send it off. I know it is a horrid thing to have to do with a friendly dog, but it is for its own sake.

Train your dog thoroughly in the two commands: 'Down' and 'Leave' and he will not annoy visitors. Teach him that the command: 'Talk' means that he should go up to strangers and allow himself to be petted, and then you will really have a nice well-behaved dog. Teaching a dog the command: 'Talk' simply means taking him up to people and asking them to caress and speak to him, whilst you are praising and reassuring him all the time. It is amazing how quickly they learn. Personally I do not wish my dogs to be friendly with all and sundry. They tolerate politely all advances made to them and on the command: 'Talk' will politely wag their tails, but that is as far as it goes, they are my dogs and mine alone. In the case of jealousy the mind of a dog works in almost an identical way to that of a human being. It wants the full attention and love of its owner. Whether jealousy only occurs when another dog enters the home or when the beloved owner talks to another dog outside or whether it be aimed towards another person in the home, the same driving force is at the root of the evil - the intention of the dog to reign alone and supreme in that household.

The guarding instinct so prevalent in some breeds has its roots in the same sort of thing - a desire to let no one enter the precincts of his master or mistress. Jealousy nearly always takes the form of a show of viciousness towards the dog or person the animal is jealous of. Quite often it is a mild form of jealousy and only involves its bone, toy or the piece of rug that it is fond of. It jealously guards them and woe betide anyone trying to take that object away.

This jealousy is particularly pronounced when puppies are reared and kept in the household. As the puppy reaches the age of about three months the mother will begin to feel jealous as her maternal instinct fades and the time draws near for another 'on heat' period. In spite of trying to treat both dogs equally and always talking to both at the same time, feeding both at the same time and exercising both together, the jealousy continues to grow.

Correction works at first and then bit by bit grows less effective. In the dog's mind a usurper has entered and, as in the wild state the young are turned out of the nest and abandoned, the dam is trying to do the same thing in the home. As she fails to get rid of the now grown-up pup her temper gets worse and worse in the effort to dislodge the now adult and unwanted member of the household. She becomes more and more thwarted as her owner attempts to make the newcomer as welcome as the old established member, and often she turns on her owner when that person is trying to make peace, as if she were trying to impress an ignorant person that it was time the youngster went out into the world to fend for itself.

If you are a really good handler your training methods will be good enough to make both dogs obey the command: 'Leave' when they are in your presence. The danger lies in the times you leave the dogs together on their own, for the slightest boldness on the part of the youngster in approaching the older one's basket or toy, etc, infuriates the older dog and she sets on the youngster tooth and nail. Sometimes the mother is a killer and, unless kept apart from her offspring, would no doubt have a go at killing it. Such is the age-old instinct to get rid of the young before it is time to breed again. Luckily this instinct is not very common. Generations of domesticity have dimmed it considerably, but I have met it, mostly in smaller dogs, and I am sorry to say that I have not been able to give much hope to the owner of curing it. Most dogs show a streak of jealousy at some time or other. When my own two dogs used to come to my bedroom, if I talked to the Dane the little English Toy Terrier would jump on the bed and have a go at nipping the Dane's nose in spite of the fact she was smiling all the time so that her own face would receive the pats and kisses the big one was getting, and she would also have got, but there was a streak of jealousy in her nature which did not appear in the Dane's. But then I think little dogs possess this factor in a more marked degree than big dogs, who are more placid.

Jealousy occurs when two terriers are hunting. If one catches a rat the other will often try and take it away, not because it wants it - most good ratters instantly leave their dead quarry to find other live ones - but simply because the dog is jealous, and wants to be equal with the killer.

Biting of husbands or wives is a very common form of jealousy. The dog senses that he is not the be-all-and-end-all of a beloved owner when the master of the house comes home, and therefore if the husband gets near his wife, he may get bitten. The answer to this one is for the husband to master the dog in no mean way by leaving a string on its choke chain and, when it attempts to be nasty, giving it an almighty jerk and a scolding, then petting and loving it. Then the dog will recognise he is the boss and all dogs are happy to submit to a real master.

Few men dare do this with their wives' dogs for fear of upsetting their wives or, in some cases, literally being attacked by their wives in defence of the dog, for some wives would rather have their husbands bitten than allow the husbands to correct the dog. How silly can some women be, for surely the life of the family depends on the happiness of all concerned and the dog is as much part of the family as a child. I encourage husbands to watch their wives training their dogs and sometimes to take over the training. It forms a happy camaraderie in the attempt to make the dog a 'joy to all and a nuisance to no one'.

In the curing of this husband-biting complex the wife must try and feel really annoyed if the dog attacks for, make no mistake, a dog picks up the thoughts of the wife without a word being spoken and, if it thinks the wife doesn't really disapprove of having her husband bitten, then the dog will continue to do so. But if she feels really angry about it and so does the husband, the combined waves of disapproval floating about for the dog's mind to pick up will be strong enough for the most insensitive dog.

Correction by the mistress of the dog in these cases seems to fail, the reason being that the dog doesn't respect the person it is jealous of. Otherwise it would live in a peaceful co-existence. The person of whom the dog is jealous must do the correcting and often this is an old grandmother or grandfather whose physical strength does not permit them to handle the dog in the right way. Then there is little hope of a cure and the dog must simply be kept out of the way of the person it is jealous of. It must not be the other way round, asking the person to keep out of the way. A human being must always come first in these matters or the dog will realise it is supreme and become worse and worse as its ego gets stronger support.

Dogs are seldom jealous of small children. The mind of a dog looks upon small children as it would look upon its own whelps. That is why even fierce dogs are seldom known to hurt children. The Alsatian that killed a child was obviously frightened by the tripping of the child who may even have caught its ear or something in falling. The immediate reaction to fear in a dog is to bite or kill your enemy and that dog in my view was temporarily deranged with fear. I do not believe it was a naturally savage dog.

A nervous dog is always a potentially dangerous dog. That is why I always curse the breeders who sell these creatures and who breed litters from problem dogs, hoping their traits won't come out in their offspring. This hope is not often fulfilled. Nervous parents teach their puppies fear by telepathy from an early age, and, if the bitch feels fear, the puppies automatically follow suit. Only with training, from an early age if possible, will the fear be eradicated.

Jealousy in kennelled dogs is particularly rife in stud dogs. Each stud dog wants to reign supreme over the kennel wives and, when there are a number of stud dogs there, it is wise to keep them apart. Although dogs are polygamous by nature, they often choose a favourite wife. I clearly remember my Alsatian choosing a wife and going off with her to our orchard and digging a fifteen foot underground passage and bedroom at the end for her to have her litter in; his other wives were just for business purposes only, this one was the true mate. She was allowed by us to have her nine puppies down there and to see Argus standing erect on top of the entrance the day she whelped was a thrilling sight, for we felt the true nature of the dogs had been allowed to develop by choosing their own home, and bringing up the babies in a homely atmosphere.

Only when the babies were fourteen days old and near to weaning time did we interfere. They were the most wonderful litter we had ever bred. But I have never seen or met with instinct like that before or since. When we opened up the nest it was beautifully made round a corner of the passage with straw and hay the bitch had picked up in her mouth, plus masses of her own hair she had plucked from her chest. The nest was scrupulously clean and dry; in fact she was a model many human mothers could have copied. I don't believe there is any cure for jealousy in stud dogs. I think, if some of them had the chance, they would fight to the finish and that is too near nature for the dog trainer to be able to do an efficient job, although I do recommend muzzling and exercising them together if the breed is not too big. Naturally if dogs are properly obedience-trained from the start these things seldom occur, but the average breeder has no time or wish to carry out obedience training for fear it may spoil the character of the show dogs. Most of us trainers know that, far from doing this, it enhances a dog's chance of winning by its perfect ring manners. I still hope the day will come when no working breed gets its championship title without also having obtained some simple obedience title.

A trained dog's mind is educated; the look on its face is quite different from the scatty brutes one often sees in the ring. It has an aura of warm friendly confidence sadly lacking in many show dogs. By having supreme confidence in its handler it rests quietly at a show if she has to be parted from it, and that counts for a lot when you require a dog on the peak of its form even after a tiring day. The mind of a dog can absorb so much that it is child's play for it to carry out obedience exercises when wanted and yet still remember to stand and be examined and to walk and run as required for the beauty ring. It only means that a few different commands are learnt, and that is no difficulty to an intelligent dog. If it is not intelligent it shouldn't win prizes, for who wants a stupid dog with no mind of its own?

Now that we are on the subject of jealousy I think some of my pupils are a bit jealous themselves when I work their dogs, and should realise that only by years of experience have I learnt anything about the training of dogs; they cannot expect to work a dog without learning the art the hard way, that is hard work, patience and the willingness to learn something new every day from someone. None of us know it all, and the pupil who rushes in here with a know-all attitude will not learn as quickly as those who watch and listen, eager to assimilate knowledge.

Every dog is different and, although they all undergo identical training, it is only by reading their minds and watching their reactions that progress is made. Most human pupils are wonderful the way they patiently try to follow suit in the training methods and I think some of their dogs are absolutely beastly to be uncooperative to such loving owners, but a dog's nature is governed by a multitude of instincts and reactions. I have tried castration for jealousy amongst male dogs not wanted for show or stud and it doesn't work. This is the one vice it doesn't touch, which proves that jealousy is a mental thing not a sexual one. If the dogs are both sent to boarding kennels or a trainer they will show no signs of jealousy and will live peacefully together again until such a time as they adopt that place as home, then the trouble starts all over again. All of which goes to prove it is true jealousy as suffered by the human race, not lack of training or an hereditary fault.

CHAPTER SEVEN

DOG FIGHTS

Fighting dogs are the ones that give most worry to owners. It is this vice which owners hope a psychiatrist will be able to probe and cure. But once again I stress that, since this is the process of investigating into the past of a dog's mind which cannot be probed as the dog cannot answer questions, one can't progress. That does not mean we cannot understand a dog's present state of mind. Although past events may have had disastrous effects on the dog and have affected his mind and make-up, it will have to be the owner who is psycho-analysed to find the answer to the dog's problems. But as few owners would have the nerve or sense to go to a human doctor to find out why her dog fights, I think we can leave out this subject too.

A dog fights for several reasons, usually the right to survive, whether this be taken as the right to eat and live peaceably or simply that the dog wants to live up to a certain standard whereby he has no enemies or neighbours that irritate him. We do not know which fits each individual case. What we do know is that dogs pretend to fight in play, mauling each other in a rough and tumble which nobody minds. Puppies have mock fights all the time to strengthen their limbs and develop their jaws and to wear off their superabundance of energy, but the subject we are looking at here is serious dog fighting, which is dangerous for dogs and humans, and has been known to end in death for the smaller and weaker dog. Even if the fight is not so bad as to end in death it can cause the owner of the dog to have a heart attack from fear, it can cause people to be bitten, and is most unpleasant and terrifying to say the least of it. Most people don't realise it takes quite a minute for two dogs to get really to grips. Before that they are playing for a hold, and therefore, when you go to separate a dog fight, there is no need to rush in and get bitten. It is far safer to watch at close range until you can safely get a hold of collar, or loose skin between the eyes of the dog. Once it has got a hold on the other dog it is unlikely to turn round and bite the person trying to release its hold, so you are reasonably safe when it has got a hold in slipping a lead on, or grabbing the choke chain or scruff.

It is useless beating the dog; they are mentally unaware of pain at that moment and unless you knocked the dog out you would not hurt them enough to separate them once they had a real hold. A mild dog fight, where death is not the object of the aggressor can sometimes be stopped by beating when the dog has no collar, but the best method if two people are about is for each on the word 'now' to grab their collars and hold them off their front legs so they begin to choke; it takes terrific strength to do this with big dogs, so I grab the flesh on the forehead between the eyes and they let go at once with this. Moreover they cannot bite you.

What is in the dog's mind when it attacks every dog it meets or just has one enemy round the corner? Most of it is show of strength, very often a cowardly show of strength aimed at other people's toy dogs who can't answer the bully back. Face that same bully with a big dog likely to answer back and it will disappear into the distance, for the dog knows who will be boss even in its own race and, if it senses superiority of physique or brain, it will automatically be subservient. That is why young dogs lie on their backs, all four feet in the air, when they meet an older or stronger dog; they know who is boss and are showing the other dog so by giving the 'pax' sign which is exposing the tummy to an enemy. That is why I tell pupils that this trick is not a nice one really and should be checked at an early age, for it is purely one of a weak animal giving in to a stronger one in mind and usually an enemy at that.

Few owners would like to think their dogs look upon them as enemies, but that is the case. When a dog no longer looks upon you as a potential enemy it stops this lying on its back as protection, though many dogs in later life do it because their owners have scratched their chests which they like, and they hope for it again. But primarily it belongs to the defence mechanism of the dog tribe. The mind of a dog that fights always has at the back of it the wish to be the boss of the tribe, and he fights other male dogs who are sexually mature to make sure there is no risk of his being questioned as 'lord of all he surveys'. Muzzle that dog and let him loose with the dog he has previously fought and nine times out of ten he will realise he is at a disadvantage and show no signs of aggression. That is why I muzzle fighters and free them with trained dogs or non-fighters. They then learn to enjoy themselves in a community and the wish to fight goes. Often, having muzzled, introduced and trained them for a short time together, I have formerly bad fighters lying side by side without muzzles after a few minutes.

It is much easier to teach a dog to ignore others in a training class, as we divide the class into two sections, one at each end of the room; and on the command: 'Forward' they walk forward and pass through the line of dogs opposite them, so that the dogs pass beside one another. We call this exercise 'countermarching'. As the dogs approach each other if one even looks at the other, a firm command: 'Leave' is given, and a sharp jerk on the offender's choke chain. If this exercise is repeated again and again, and the dog always receives a jerk just before he sniffs the other dog, he is left with the impression that it is rather unpleasant to talk to another dog in such circumstances.

I have cured fighters by this method in a very short time. But the real difficulty lies in knowing when your dog is going to fight; it is useless to take such steps once the dogs have come to grips with each other. How many people are sufficiently knowing with their dogs to sense the stiffening of the body which is preliminary to a fight? Too many owners usually wait until the fight has started before doing anything about it. That is why it is a good thing for an experienced trainer to have the first chance, especially in a class, to check this fighting tendency. But wherever they are, if owners really know their dogs they will sense the stiffening of the dog as he approaches another, the dog's way of sending out a warning to the other one that he is ready to hold his own against all comers. A dog that has no intention of fighting is relaxed. One that is not sure but wishes to be friendly keeps up a very fast but confined wagging of its tail as it approaches another dog; this will stop, and the dog will stiffen, if the enemy has evil ideas, and is not reciprocating the offer of friendship.

Most dogs approach a bitch in this way, hoping for friendship, and although it is unusual for a dog and bitch to fight, the bitch may attack first and then the dog will answer back, but usually not for very long. A growl, or course, must never be ignored. A fight inevitably follows unless checked, but an owner must be able to read far less obvious indications than the growl and the snarl if he is to stop fights at the right moment - that is, before they have begun. This business of making your dog ignore others needs constant vigilance; a second's carelessness,

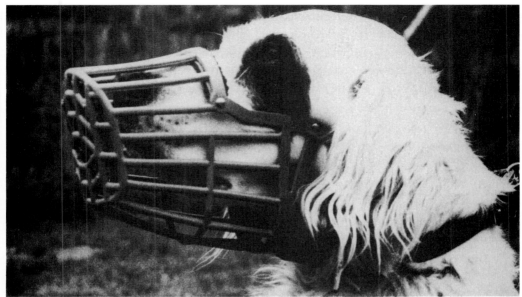

WRONG: An incorrect muzzle.

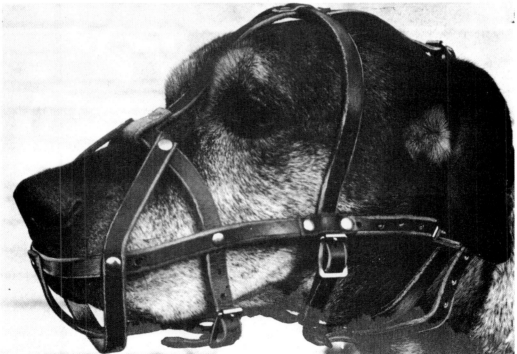

RIGHT: A correct muzzle.

and you are in a fight. I believe that if a dog does get involved in a fight he should be severely punished unless he was obviously attacked first. Therefore, as I hate to advocate punishing dogs, it is the owner's duty to see that no fight develops. It is a fatal move to tighten your lead as another dog approaches, and even worse to lift your dog up. Walk on quite naturally until reasonably near the other dog, then give a sharp jerk on your dog's collar to arrest his attention, and in a firm, low voice, command: 'Leave'. It is the most difffficult thing possible to impress on owners of fighting dogs that to cure them they must have long loose leads, that holding a dog on a short lead tends to make it want to fight more. A four-foot lead is essential, and a completely indestructible clip. The scissor hook and ordinary hook are dangerous, as both can open up with a sharp jerk. (For availability of training leads, see Appendix.)

For if a fighting dog did get free when jerked hard it would be twenty times worse than before, because the jerk would have sent it forward when the clip broke and would probably catapult it into the other dog. The jerks to cure fighting dogs must be hard and effective.

Quite a number of people want to know whether they can really cure a confirmed fighter so that it may safely be allowed to run freely with other dogs. I should say no. A dog can be so far cured as to be safe at all times when under the control of its owner. We have often trained fighters to be safely left in a hall with thirty or more other dogs lying all together, all the owners out of sight, but all the dogs in the room had had training, therefore the fighter was not getting challenges or rude remarks thrown at it by other dogs. However, I would not like to say that the former fighter, if attacked, would not fight to the finish. I think he would, and only a terrific amount of disciplinary training would make it safe at all times.

I have cured (to the point of their becoming very nice dogs to take out without a lead) dogs that were previously bad fighters; one had even killed another dog, but it had a sensible owner. It must depend to a great extent on the owner's temperament. If the owner is always nervous, the dog will always be on his guard against aggression; if the owner is confident that her dog is cured of its vice, the dog will gain assurance from that attitude, and be far less likely to want to fight. I think fighting, with biting of owners, postmen and visitors, are all attributable together to the one complaint: nerves and insecurity. The dog has probably not been taken out and about enough in its youth; to make a dog reliable, it should be taken into towns and crowds, shops and parks, and wherever you live, it must be allowed to meet other dogs. Let people caress it and talk to it. Be firm if it slinks away and won't talk to people; show it that human beings are its friends; if possible find a friendly neighbour's dog and let it have romps with it, making sure that on command it leaves off playing and comes back to you. Such a dog will never be a fighter: why should it be? Big dogs are often put on a very short lead and held in a vice-like grip in the street. Times without number I have shown owners that a fighter on a loose lead seldom attacks, but they are so scared that they daren't let up on the stranglehold. Naturally, if you get a big dog involved in a fight, it takes plenty of courage and strength to end the battle. I once separated two dogs, and then one got hold of my leg, thinking it was the other dog, and I couldn't let go of the second or the fight would have started all over again. Luckily someone took one dog from me while I prised the other off my leg, but I still bear the scar.

I think fighting is, to a certain extent, an inherited temperamental fault, and I strongly advise buyers of dogs to enquire about the parents' temperaments before buying a puppy. Fighters are always of a bullying nature, and therefore need from an early age a strict code of discipline. Any sign of rolling on their backs, and biting the owner or its lead when the lead has to go on, is often the prelude to serious biting or fighting later in life. I am always dead against allowing a dog to use its teeth on me even in play, and any attempt to answer back with its teeth when I give a command is instantly checked.

I often feel that dogs bite and fight to let off steam. Many live such restricted lives that they become psychological cases weighed down by repressions. In such circumstances, human beings lose their tempers or burst into tears, but dogs are allowed no such outlet. I feel that a dog that leads a fully occupied life as a complete member of the owner's family never gets these vices, having plenty of legitimate interests to keep it stable. I know of one household that owns two dogs, one a Staffordshire bull terrier, and one a charming old fox terrier. The two dogs belong respectively to the husband and wife, but never the twain shall meet, for the Staffordshire has only one idea in its head and that is to annihilate the old age pensioner and reign supreme alone in that household. He only developed this hatred for the fox terrier when he grew up. As a puppy he was all right. What should the owners do to make life liveable with two dogs, neither of which they wish to part with? I feel that as this situation has been allowed to develop over quite a long period of time, no very practical training has been carried out. The easiest way out has been taken by separating the dogs and dividing the household in two. I would give the bull terrier a course of obedience training, and take it out and about to meet other dogs as often as possible. I would fix up a very strong chain and collar near its bed or basket and make it lie down and stay down in that whenever the two members of the family wish to be in that room with the fox terrier. If the dog growled or showed signs of jealous temper I would jerk it hard on the choke chain giving simultaneously the command: 'Leave'. Then I would pet it. I would take the dogs out together on leads with the bull terrier wearing temporarily a Greyhound type of muzzle. No possible damage could then occur to the old dog, and I believe that by enjoying their walks together they would become friendly. I would never pet one in front of the other without speaking lovingly to them both.

One often hears of Spaniels, especially mother and daughter, who so hate each other that one has to be put to sleep to gain peace. This is terribly sad, and, on the part of the owner, an admission of failure to teach them obedience. You cannot make them love each other, any more than I can teach dogs to love their owners, but you can teach them to ignore each other by successful obedience training. The same sort of thing arises when people get a new kitten or puppy. How can they train the other animal to tolerate and accept it? This is not a very difficult problem if the newcomer is small enough to confine in an indoor kennel or cage at night, with the old dog chained to his bed near the newcomer, for I have found that when animals share the night in close proximity to each other they seldom are at war afterwards. Again, of course, the old well-known command: 'Leave' comes into the training, and by this time the dog should know that word means 'ignore everything and don't chase anything'.

It is in all these cases the attitude of the owner that matters. Occasionally I discover the owner is neurotic, and rather enjoys her dog disliking her husband's dog, though she wouldn't admit it. More troubles with dogs are caused because they are mirroring inhibitions with idiosyncrasies of their owners than we know about. That is why it is very difficult for me to diagnose what is wrong with a dog or owner when I only have a letter to read.

Although in the end one becomes like a psychologist and quickly sees under the veneer put on for one's benefit. Over-possessiveness on the part of the owner causes many dogs to do naughty things. The owner who never lets her dog romp with another for fear of picking up something, or the dog that is never allowed a good race over the fields because it gets it newly shampooed self dirty, is asking for trouble. Even toy dogs like Yorkshire terriers or Pekinese love a rat hunt. A dog becomes a dull creature with nothing but town walks and chauffeur-driven rides in the park. In my school, when the weather permits, we take all the so-called problem dogs into a field, and in spite of protests from owners who feel certain their dogs will fight or get eaten alive, or won't come when called, we let the whole lot go free at the same time. So far we have never had anything terrible happen. Sometimes a fight is imminent, but my voice can usually avert it, and soon the owners become confident and willing to trust their dogs, and that is the first step towards a happy dog and owner relationship. Good behaviour is undoubtedly infectious, and it is quite amazing to see how good these 'difficult dogs' are in school. If only one could instil the methods of control sufficiently into the owners they would be no trouble at home either. I think lack of time is the main enemy. Practice makes perfect. Working dogs only once a week is useless.

I think dog owners can be rash in the breed of dog they choose. I wish they would find out more about what the dogs were originally bred for, before they buy one. All the bull-breeds were for fighting in one way or another, also the Irish terriers and Kerry Blues. Why do weak little owners want this type of dog? Is it that they lack courage in their make-up and buy a courageous dog to compensate? If you are a flat dweller choose a dog that needs little exercise or work like the King Charles spaniel, whose ancestors are so often pictured in old oil paintings and whose lives in various courts of royalty were well known.

I have met a family who expected a Beagle to lead this sort of life and who complained when it became unmanageable. One Beagle in a family of children must be a misfit, they are hunting dogs, not playthings, and they have very stubborn natures. The choice of dog must of course rest with the buyer, but I do feel breeders could refuse to sell an old lady a Bloodhound, or a small child a big boisterous breed. I suppose those who breed dogs do so for profit, and few can afford to refuse a sale. I only wish they had the dogs to deal with when they become problem dogs, and it would then deter them from selling unsuitable dogs.

If a dog continues to fight at the slightest pretext after an owner has followed all my recommendations, I should say he was incurable, and the owner must decide whether to keep him, and always be on guard against a fight, and the risk of his causing harm which may end up in the law courts, or whether to have him put to sleep to end its unhappy existence. I hate to advocate putting a dog down at any time, and only the owner can decide on a matter of this kind.

Most fighters are what they are through bad handling by inexperienced owners. Once the habit is firmly established it takes an experienced handler to cure it, but a fighting dog is an unsafe dog at all times, even a partially 'cured' one.

CHAPTER EIGHT

DISTANT CONTROL AND ADVANCED TRAINING

I teach the handlers in my class distant control in a long line with their dogs at the end of the lead facing them. But it can be done alone at home just as easily. I give the command: 'Now' and the handlers give their dogs the same command as my next. Should I say: 'Down', the handlers must raise their right hands and bring them sharply to the ground with the command: 'Down'; the dogs must instantly drop to this position. They should do this without fuss if they have been trained step by step from this book. My next command may be: 'Sit'. The owners must repeat it to their dogs, and in doing so give the command by voice and the signal by raising their right hands from the ground to above the head. The command: 'Sit' should be given in a short quick word, not drawn-out like the command 'Down'. Change of tone of voice (I cannot say this too often) matters enormously in these exercises. If the dog does not go quickly to the 'sit', help him up by lifting him on the lead which should have been under his chin anyway, or by touching his front foot nails lightly with your foot so that he naturally breaks away into the 'sit'.

Next I shall give the command: 'Stand'. The owner repeats the command and the signal is a slap on the thigh of one leg, which encourages the dog to begin to come to you. As soon as the dog is standing, check him coming towards you with the command: 'Stay', which of course he should now know. Should the dog not stand, run your hand between his front legs along his chest to his tummy, and lift

ADVANCED WORK: (1) Leave the dog at stand. (2) Sit. (3) Down. (4) End the exercise with the dog at the sit.

DISTANT CONTROL: (1) Drop the hand and give the command 'Down'. (2) Raise hand and give the command 'Sit'.

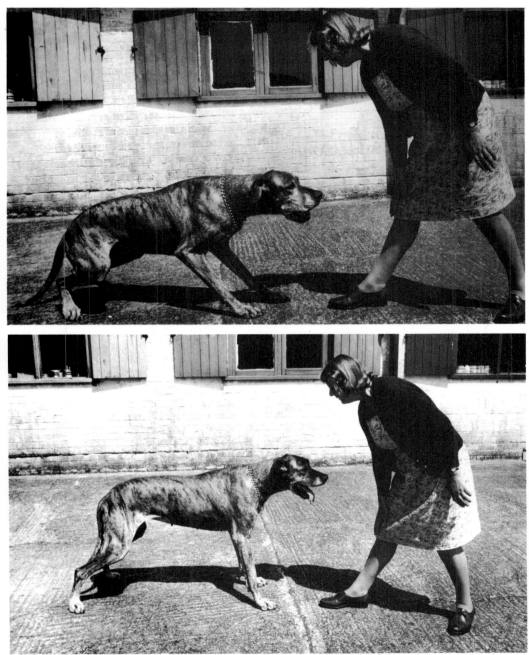

**DISTANT CONTROL: (1) Slap your leg for emphasis.
(2) Give the command for the dog to stand.**

him up on to his back legs. Alternatively, lift him up with both hands placed just inside his back legs at the thigh and stand him firmly on his legs. As your dog improves on the lead, put him on the cord and do the whole thing at a greater distance. He will at first try to advance towards you; this must be checked with the command: 'Stay', after the ordinary command. Even in competition work the dog is allowed six feet to move forward so don't worry too much at first if he can't stick to this; it is a goal to work for. If he came too far forward in the street he would get run over. I should teach a small dog on a table, a large one at the top of the stairs, so that they can't come forward. Eventually, when the dog does the exercise well, remove the cord and do it again with the dog free. We do six successive commands. Never repeat this exercise ad nauseam, for it is very tiring for the dog and requires great concentration on the part of the owner and dog. Once the dog has learnt it well, abandon it except for an occasional reminder. I hope you will never need to make much use of it.

Having accomplished the teaching of distant control, you want to practise it by leaving your dog at a distance, calling him, and when he's running quickly towards you, giving him the signal and command: 'Down'. If you have trained him properly he should drop instantly and wait for you to call him up when all is safe. In Obedience Trials this is called 'Drop on Recall'; it may be done there either by word or signal, but not both. I strongly disagree with this. I fail to see that in an emergency an owner wouldn't use a command and signal if the dog's or somebody's life depended on it, but then I am an outlaw where these fantastic rules are concerned. I love to see a dog working, but I like it only when it is a joint effort of understanding and brains on the part of both dog and owner. These silent masters and mistresses in the obedience ring can keep their dogs that way if they wish, but I defy anyone to say that the dog likes it. I believe that those dogs, bouncing about as if they were happy, are really a mass of nerves wondering whether they have done right. I am not a 'sour grapes'; my former dog won sixty-seven of these tests, but she and I hated every one of them. It was only that in order to be able to train other people and dogs, one had to prove that one could train one's own dog first. This is the only reason I took part in these tests. Some people think it is cruel to teach a dog tricks. My dog does endless tricks; and how she loves doing things for me! She arches her neck in pride when she has done something particularly clever, and wants to hear me say so. I love praise if I have done something well; so do children, and so do animals. If I am working her in a film she can't wait until after the Director has said: 'Cut' to dash round to everyone in the studio to hear how clever she has been. I can teach my dog anything new in a few minutes, and providing I can talk to her and praise her immediately after doing it, she adores it. Opinion is divided about teaching dogs tricks. Is it cruel, people ask? I fail to see that cruelty comes into it unless the tricks taught are for a circus or some such affair when the dog has to perform at a fixed time however little he may feel like doing so. Most dogs love the household tricks we all know, asking for food by begging or barking, playing hide and seek, trusting, etc. I think they join in the family spirit which encourages this harmless fun. A dog already trained in simple obedience is so very easily taught tricks, and I think likes 'being clever'. If he does not enjoy them, then I think it is cruel to force him to become a performer.

Training a dog to retrieve and seek back is another exercise which I think most dog owners should teach their dogs. Its practical advantage is that if you happen to be out walking and drop something, your dog will go back and look for it and retrieve it. Most of the dogs who come to my class and are given a dumb-bell for the first time, rush after it and joyfully pick it up. Some even bring it back to their owners. But it is these eager dogs who are the first to get tired of doing it, and who have to start all over again later. So we are going to teach our dogs the right way from the beginning and ignore their natural desire to retrieve, which may soon peter out if not properly directed.

First of all we use a dumb-bell, because it has big ends to make the centre bar stand up off the ground; this enables the dog to pick it up easily. The dog must never be allowed to pick it up by the ends or chew it. I keep my own high up on a shelf, and as I give it to my dog I use an excited tone of voice as if it were the greatest treat to be allowed to retrieve dumb-bells!

Now we begin with the dog on the lead at the 'sit'. Gently open the dog's mouth by inserting your finger into the side of the mouth where there are no teeth, immediately behind the large canine tooth, always keeping your hand on top of the dog's nose, not trying to pull down the bottom jaw. When the mouth is open pop the dumb-bell in with the other hand. *Don't push it back into the dog's mouth,* just balance it behind the canine teeth and allow the dog to close its mouth on it. If you shove it roughly into the mouth you will frighten and hurt the dog, and your task will become more difficult. Should the dog try to spit it out, as most of them do, put it firmly back with the command: 'Hold'; to help him do this, scratch his chest with the other hand, for dogs will hold dumb-bells for a long time so long as this pleasant scratching continues. Their docility enables you to say: 'Give' in a kind voice and take the dumb-bell away. Always take it out of the dog's mouth with two hands, holding the ends, never with one hand

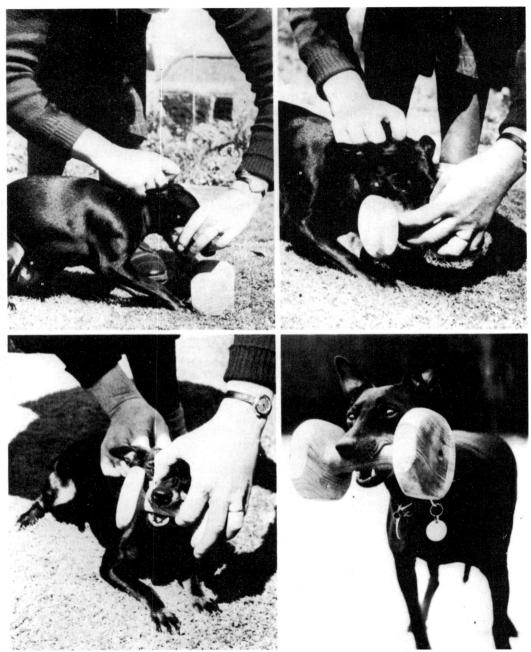

DUMB-BELL: (1) Place finger in dog's mouth and push head down. (2) Push dumb-bell into mouth with second finger. (3) Allow dog to close its mouth. (4) He's got it!

only. Repeat this, making the dog hold the object until he does so quite happily. I often advocate a titbit after he has held it well. The next step is to make him walk holding the dumb-bell. If you can get him to stay holding it when he is at the end of your long cord, and then make him bring it to you, you have surmounted a real difficulty. But if not, just be satisfied for the time being with getting him to walk beside you holding it, tell him to sit, still holding it, and then taking it away with the: 'Give' command. Praise him ardently if he has done it well.

Some dogs are unbelievably stubborn over this exercise, and will not hold the dumb-bell. They spit it out and fight to avoid holding it But dozens of times I have made a dog hold a dumb-bell when the owner has failed, and this is done only by showing the dog that your will is every bit as strong as his, and that if necessary you will go on until midnight if he means to defer holding it that long. In the end I always win, but that is more than I can say for many handlers with weaker wills and less determination than I have. Patience, firmness and love are the essentials.

We will presume you are a good handler and that your dog now holds the dumb-bell as soon as it is given to him. Next, you have to teach him to pick it up. This is done by standing beside your dog, with one hand holding the dog's scruff, or loose skin on the neck, while gently pushing his head down until his mouth is over the dumb-bell. Then, with the other hand, you open his mouth by inserting the first finger into the side of the mouth, and pop the dumb-bell into his mouth with the second finger. Let him close his mouth and tell him to 'hold'. Eventually your dog opens his own mouth as you push his head down, and later on, with infinite care and encouragement and practice, your dog will pick it up himself.

Once he has accomplished this, give the command: 'Hold' and run backwards; the dog will follow you, holding the dumb-bell. Turn round sharply and tell him to sit; push him down if he doesn't do it quickly enough, still telling him to 'Hold'. Then take the dumb-bell with the word: 'Give' and send your dog behind you to your usual left-hand side. Now you are getting on. There is one enormous fence still to get over, and that is the sending of your dog to fetch the dumb-bell. The best way I know is for you to get a friend to help. Ask your friend to hold on to the long cord on which you have put your dog; you must then make the dog sit by your side, throw your dumb-bell, and encourage the dog to go after it. If the dog won't do so, get your friend to pull the dog towards the dumb-bell on the cord. The dog should now, receiving much praise, pick up the dumb-bell and return to you, sitting in front holding it quietly until you take it, after which you will send the dog to heel on your left side. It doesn't usually take long for the dog to understand this 'going' part of the exercise. Lastly, you must teach it not to go after the dumb-bell: that they must not chase moving things without command. If this precaution is neglected, one day the children may be playing ball with the dog in the garden, and the ball may roll out into the road; and then, if the dog is untrained, it would rush after it. A trained dog waits for the command to get it. I usually recommend owners to hold their dogs by their collars and give the command: 'Wait' until the dog understands what is wanted of him, and will sit quietly after the dumb-bell has been thrown until given the command: 'Fetch'.

Before we can go any further with the 'seek-back' exercise, which consists of making your dog retrace your steps and find what you have dropped, you must teach it only to pick up your article carrying your scent; otherwise it may bring someone else's property, not yours. This exercise is called 'scent discrimination' in official circles, so I shall use this name. Most dogs enjoy this. The best way to teach a dog this exercise is once more to enlist other people to put articles on the floor, or on the grass. Use such things as purses, clothes pegs, match boxes, gloves, handkerchiefs, in fact anything the dog might come in contact with in everyday life. Next you decide what you wish the dog to find, let's say your glove. Place the glove, for a minute or two prior to doing the exercise, under your armpit, it will then pick up a good scent of you. Next, without letting the dog see it, place it among the other articles, not too closely jumbled at first. Then take the dog on its lead up to the articles, pointing to each one as you walk by it, saying, with some excitement, 'Seek', 'Good boy, seek'. Use a most inspiring tone, as though rats were his quarry. Usually when the dog reaches its owner's article he grabs it, and then you should praise him immediately; but should he pass it by, return to it, and show it to him, pick it up and use it to play with him. Then take him away, get it put down for you again, and try once more. This time he is almost certain to find the right article, so praise him and have a game with it.

Continue like this, with different articles all the time, until he knows that he must only find the one carrying your scent. Should he attempt to pick up the wrong article, say: 'No' crossly, take it away, and show him the right one. As soon as your dog has learnt thus to pick out your particular article only, teach him to bring it back to you as with the dumb-bell; and, as before, 'sit' in front and go round to heel to finish with. Now that we have taught the dog to find and retrieve any article, we are ready to teach him the 'seek back'. Go for a walk, and on your way drop something on the path that shows up well - for instance, a handkerchief. Walk on about twenty yards and in a very excited tone of voice tell the dog to 'seek back', pointing to where you have come from. The dog probably

ON THE SCENT: Teach discrimination between various objects.

won't understand, so run back, encouraging him to go away and seek all the time. Nine times out of ten he sees the handkerchief and picks it up. Then you must praise him with extravagant enthusiasm. Make him do this quite often on your walk; he will soon understand and enjoy the game. As he gets better at it, hide the article in grass near where you have been. That will teach him to cast round and look. Make it more difficult as the dog gets to understand, and you will soon have taught your dog something that may be very useful. One of my friends recently lost her house keys in a wood. She had trained her dog, and he went back over her tracks and found them. Needless to say, she was delighted.

The uses of the 'send away' exercise, in my opinion, are few. Perhaps it teaches your dog to go straight home should he insist on following you when you leave home and want him to stay behind. In Test C at shows the dog must go on a single command or signal in a dead straight line and continue going until you are told to drop him down. He must drop to the ground and stay there with you walking past him until you call him up. Marks are lost for a deviation from a straight line, no extra commands are allowed to change the dog's direction should he be going crooked, or you lose marks. This seems to me a pointless exercise. But as some of my readers enjoy competitions, I shall do my best to teach the necessary handling for this lesson.

I teach this on the long cord again if the dog shows no signs of leaving you when you say: 'Away' or 'Go'. Our dog has already learnt to go and fetch the dumb-bell, leaving you in order to do so, so it shouldn't be too difficult to go a step further and make them go and 'fetch' nothing. Let us assume that the dog will not budge at all. The trainer or helper must take the cord, as usual, some distance away from the dog. The dog is sitting quietly on the left-hand side of the owner and is given the command: 'Away' with the right arm pointing in the direction he is supposed to go; if he does not move, help him by repeating the command and giving him a simultaneous shove in the right direction. Keep repeating: 'Away', and stamp your foot as if you were going to chase him. He doesn't understand. Very well, ask your friend to pull him on in the cord, while you keep pointing and saying: 'Away'.

When he has gone a little distance, give him the command: 'Down'. He should know this, and drop; walk up to him, telling him to stay, walk round him and away, and then call him to heel. Praise him. Sometimes one can shortcut this method by another one. This is to put your dog at the 'sit', tell him to stay, and walk away some distance where he can see what you are doing, bend down and rub your hand vigorously on the ground, come back to your dog, and give him the: 'Away' command. Very often he will rush off to see what you did; you can then drop him and the exercise is begun. I find the other method better. This 'Away' exercise takes a long time to teach and reach perfection. Waiting on command is an advanced exercise used in Test C in competition work, when it is called: 'Advance Stand, Sit, and Down'. Here we are going to study it in relation to its usefulness to the ordinary dog owner. The idea is to make your dog stop instantly on command when you are in motion, either at the 'stand', 'sit' or 'down', so that you can run or walk on without it, and without worrying about its behaviour.

There may come an emergency in your life when this exercise might save someone's life. You might, for example, see a small child toddle into the street in the path of a car; with the command: 'Wait' your dog would instantly stand still, and unhampered you could rescue the child from its peril. On the other hand, you might just want to leave your dog in the drive for a second and run back to get something from the house without his coming; on the command: 'Wait' he would stay where he was until your return.

We teach this exercise in class by having helpers who walk behind the handler and dog, and on the trainer's command: 'Now' the handler drops the lead near the helper, who places a foot on it, and with a firm command: 'Wait', the dog is left in the standing position until the handler has made a circle and returned to the dog. He picks up the lead, and with the command: 'Heel' and a word of praise continues walking. On the next command, 'Now' from the trainer, the handler repeats the exercise with the dog this time put quickly to the 'Sit'. And so it is repeated, at the third time the dog being put to the 'down'. The idea is to teach your dog to stop instantly and to expect the owner back in a reasonably short time. It is quite amazing how quickly dogs learn this exercise. I find the 'stand' is the most difficult to teach them as they have learnt before this to sit at all times when not walking. If your dog sits when you wish him to stand, run your left hand quickly under his tummy and lift him to the 'stand' with a further command, 'Wait!' He won't mind this, and it soon teaches him. Don't forget to give the command: 'Wait' in a quick tone not a long drawn-out voice. Emphasize the 't' in the word 'Sit' and the 'D' in the command 'Down'.

When your dog has got used to being left with the helper, who must in no way touch your dog (he is only acting as an anchor), the next step is to leave your dog without a helper, but with the lead still on. You must practise alone in a room or your garden until the dog never moves until you come back. Next of course, you must take the lead off and repeat the exercise again. Practise it at a walking pace and then at a run. At the end of the three exercises give your dog a vast amount of praise. I use cheerful words in the middle of the exercise, like 'good boy' (or 'girl') so that the dog will realize he has not finished after one part of the exercise. But at the end of the three commands well carried out I bubble over with joy and praise!

I think that to teach this exercise correctly you must know how to teach your dog to stand, sit or lie down, at a distance. This exercise is most important to all dog owners, as sooner or later a time comes in all our lives when a loved dog races out to greet master or mistress on their return home, and this exuberance may be the death of the dog or of someone on the road, if the dog is so excited that it forgets to look before dashing across the road. But if the dog has been trained to drop into the sit or down position on a hand signal or by voice, you have a reasonable chance of stopping its rush to you when danger threatens.

CHAPTER NINE

INDULGENCES

To what extent does food govern a dog's mind? This is a question that most owners have had to face up to at one time or another, and many of them have told me they think food occupies most of the waking and thinking hours of their dogs. But I am quite sure that the people who own such dogs are very unlucky.

The hunting instinct is extremely strong in most dogs; therefore, with problem dogs that chase and kill chickens or other livestock, the act is only what nature taught them to do many thousands of years ago. Their noses were designed for the act of tracking down and killing and, although domesticity has vastly reduced the number of breeds who hunt to kill, Greyhounds, Foxhounds and like breeds still in fact have this instinct highly developed. Many other breeds would hardly know what to do with the prey they had killed as they no longer suffer from hunger and, without this urge to spur them on, the kill is not vital.

In the wild state dogs killed twice or three times a week and ate until they nearly burst, after which they were quite happy to laze between orgies. Nowadays from an early age our dogs' gastric juices have been trained to flow at fixed times each day and the desire to eat only becomes apparent normally at these times. It is true there are greedy dogs who will eat at all times of the day and night to the detriment of their figures and health, but these are the dogs that are easily trained by bribes. The dogs that are the most difficult to bribe are the naughtiest ones, because their minds are usually fixed on fighting another dog or running off into the distance, and I doubt if they think food will come from these escapades. The dogs who are most interested in food are the spoilt Poodles and Toy Dogs whose adoring owners give them snacks at all times. 'Just a leetle bitsie for Mitzie' has been known to do devastating things to Mitzie's mind and body. But here I blame the owner more than the dog. Thieving is a natural instinct in all dogs. From the earliest days in the nest he has had to fight for his existence. In the days of the wild pack his ancestors hunted and stole from those other animals not clever enough to guard their prey. The instinct to steal is strong in the dog. The dog's mind is cunning in stealing and hiding for future use either food or some article he fancies.

Much of it in the domestic dog today is done purely out of boredom. I have never known a well-trained dog, whose day is fully mapped out for it, steal. But the busy housewife, who owns a dog purely for the children to play with, often gets a thief as a result of lack of deep affection for anyone in particular by the dog, and from being bored with no work to do.

All dogs should have work to do, whether it be only tricks to learn from the children or obedience exercises or some real work like gun work, etc. Without this, their brains are wasted, their minds pretty empty and their cunning increases. Watch how a thief dog sleeps almost with one eye open to deceive its owner into thinking it is fast asleep when what it is really waiting for is the opportunity to slip into the chickens' yard and steal their food, or into the owner's kitchen to see 'what's cooking' and to take whatever has been carelessly left about. The obvious fear on the dog's part when caught makes us realise dogs do know the difference between right and wrong if caught in the act or even if heading for where the act is to take place. Obviously, to know they are doing wrong, they must at sometime or other have been scolded or punished for this self-same act.

Dogs aren't born knowing what or what not to do, they only learn like children. Having once been punished, dogs remember, but like children they hope they won't be caught in the act. Dogs can be so conscience-stricken that I have seen an innocent one creep and crawl away in shame when another dog has committed a crime, and the innocent dog has been punished in error.

I always remember as small children we had a big and a little dog. The big one had her puppies in the barn and rushed out when a tramp came too near, bit him, and streaked back before the tramp knew which dog had bitten him; the tiny one just stood there and watched. The tramp swore black and blue it was the little dog that had done the deed and if I had not seen the other one do it the little one would have been punished. Sometimes dogs steal for praiseworthy motives. Argus my Alsatian made a nest and when Andy, his mate, had her puppies. Argus, never having stolen before, went through a phase of thieving. One day I saw him steal some meat off the kitchen table and streak out to the orchard and drop it at the hole of the family and bark. I never scolded him for I knew in this case nature and the instinct to provide for his family was above all the training he had received. I think, therefore, owners should try to find the reason for the theft before correcting the dog. Sometimes worms produce a terrible hunger in dogs and a depraved appetite. When cured of these the dog no longer steals. Only punish when you are sure you as owner have not neglected your dog.

The teaching of food refusal in obedience tests was a very useful lesson to most dogs as people in shops often offer one's dog a titbit; when the dog turned his head away and refused to take it, it taught the shop-keeper not to repeat the offer. But it also had a disastrous effect on dogs sent to boarding kennels, as many refused to take food from the strange person who fed them and in one known case the dog nearly died. So now this test has been omitted from the schedule.

The diet of some dogs needs to be rigidly controlled. These include dogs that have been castrated, old dogs whose figures have already exceeded normal girth, and greedy dogs who would never be satisfied with the small amounts given to them and would therefore get more cunning in the hope of getting more food. Nervous dogs wouldn't take the food or, if they did take it, would probably be sick almost immediately because the nerves have an adverse effect on digestion; and to feed a dog suffering from nervous exhaustion does more harm than good. That is why I never allow the dogs to be fed during a day's training. I always tell the owners to wait an hour after training ceases and then give the dog one big meal and let it rest.

I am sure the most important thing about food in connection with the dog is to give a properly balanced diet with sufficient vitamins and iron, etc; for a dog to be intelligent it has to be sufficiently and adequately nourished. If a dog is lacking minerals it will eat rubbish and especially dung. How can one expect to train a dog to be a nice companion in the house if it forever rolls in nasty things, eats manure and has a depraved appetite? Again no mind-reader can fathom the depths of a dog's mind and find the answer to its apparently depraved nature. Only common sense and knowledge of the dietetic needs of a dog learnt from experience, books or your vet will help you. The question of indulgences needs much thought both from the point of view of the dog and that of the owner. I think more in the case of the latter. For is there one of us who at sometime or other in our lives cannot plead guilty to having indulged our dog? The mind of the dog tunes in very willingly to enjoy as many indulgences as it can persuade its owner to offer. Its brain is never slow to take advantage of every kink in the defence armour of its owner. The eyes of a dog, the expression of a dog, the warmly wagging tail of a dog and gloriously cold damp nose of a dog were in my opinion all God-given for one purpose only, to make complete fools of us human beings.

I write reams about over-sentimental dog owners spoiling their dogs, yet know in my inner heart that not to do so takes supreme will power. For dogs are champions at heart-stealing. Even the wickedest dog in my school who has severely bitten me makes me long to hug him close to me and force out his evil wickedness, and I love him. Dogs are not slow-witted. They know when to push the slightest advantage they gain over their owner. How many dogs do we know who have committed some sin and who have cleverly evaded punishment by bringing mistress something to play with and, with an innocent look of deep trust, waited for her to join in the game when at that very moment she should be stick in hand flaying the life out of him? But then that is the fascination of dogs.

Why do hundreds of us give up our holidays to stay with them, cry our eyes out when we lose them, defend them against all those horrid people who don't love them and on our death beds make provision for them in preference to our needy families? It is because there is something about a dog that gets you. Even if you own a problem one with all the evil the devil himself invented, you still know that, inside that dog, there is something very lovable - a dog that will never criticise you, a dog that doesn't care whether you are from the top or bottom drawer, who doesn't care whether you are clever or stupid, beautiful or hideous, rich or poor. He is yours and you are his.

At my residential training school in the past I am sure I have shocked pupils by feeding my dogs at meals. The dogs didn't ask, they just lay down waiting hopefully. My contention is, if my dogs don't annoy me and if I want to feed them, who is to say it is wrong? That is how I look upon all indulgences. If you like your dogs to sleep on your bed, putting up with the discomfort of not being able to turn over easily (especially if yours is a Great Dane) having a snoring bed companion, risking the hairs and dirt on the blankets and sheets, well, that is your business. What is my business, as a trainer, is to see these things don't happen if you wish otherwise.

This is where a dog needs firm training, for a multitude of dogs get on their owner's beds and refuse to get off without a struggle and often bite the owner in the process. This is where a psychiatrist would easily be able to help, for he would know that, in the past, the dog had got away with it and it needs no probing of the mind to know the dog much prefers a lovely warm bed with a warm owner in it, possibly a hot bottle, and certainly an eiderdown, to his own meagre offering of a basket and a blanket.

There is no doubt at all in his mind that dogs love luxury. 'Liver' instead of 'lights', beds instead of baskets, kisses instead of kicks and, if the owner doesn't want to bestow any of these luxuries on the dog, then the struggle to deny them to the dog must begin the moment the dog enters the house and must be carried on to its dying day.

My own dog, star of thirty-seven films, winner of sixty-seven obedience prizes, herself defeated rigid obedience at the ripe old age of ten and a half years. Never in her life had she been allowed to lie in front of the fire. The heat is not good for dogs. She was too big and took up too much room. Her digestion was not so good that Camay was her only scent. Nevertheless when we moved house she felt she would like a change and with audacious abandon lay full length in front of the fire.

At first we laughed. Then I said her name in a shocked voice. She smiled a sickly smile and the tip of her tail wagged, uncertainty backed by hope and then, sensing my sympathy for her aging self, downed her head and feigned sleep. I pulled myself together and one word, 'Sofa!' was enough to have her leap to her feet and climb on her own extremely comfortable sofa. You see her mind had picked up by telepathy that I didn't really mind her in front of the fire. In fact I thought she looked rather beautiful with her brindled body outstretched. My own mind was weak. The dog knew at once. You cannot train a dog if you are weak or over-sentimental. They know and you are lost.

Are indulgences wrong for dogs? I think, under certain circumstances, no. What does count is, can you give up indulging the dog without fights or disagreeable behaviour the very moment you wish? If you can't, don't indulge your dog until you have trained it sufficiently well to be able to do what you wish at any time. The day the dog takes over you are lost. I do think one indulgence is very wrong, that is when you cannot leave your dog alone without its screaming or barking; should anything vital happen so that you could not stay with it, the neighbours would have to suffer appalling noise and you and the dog would be utterly miserable.

I think dogs should always go with their owners whenever and wherever possible. Yet some places you go to don't admit dogs. Occasionally you are ill and may have to go to hospital or to a clinic. The dog can't go with you; it must stay at home or in your car. If neither of these things have been taught by previous training and endless tests, you won't know what to do. This sort of situation is bad. All dogs should be taught to stay quietly at home for some hours; as long as their routine is not broken too violently and they have been fed and exercised, there should be no hardship in staying at home for a dog.

We know titbits are bad for dogs; we know sleeping in owner's beds is inclined to overheat them and make them delicate; we know above all that giving a command and then not having it carried out is fatal to a happy relationship. We know over-indulgent owners get spoilt dogs, who are a joy to none and a nuisance to all. I suggest we have a happy medium. Let's spoil our dogs sometimes, then we shall all be happy. The happiest people in this world are those who are for ever giving and making others happy. I am sure our dogs are included in that.

CHAPTER TEN

NEUROTIC DOGS

Hysterical dogs, biting dogs, dogs that shriek if left alone, dogs that whine and bark or shriek in cars, dogs that apparently take leave of their senses when they see another dog, and dogs that tear up everything in the house, can all be dealt with under the above heading.

Hysterical dogs can be the result of inbreeding, or purely of mating together parents with the wrong temperaments. When the puppy first comes to its new owner it is probably a tiny mite and the mistress of its destiny pours out all her mother love, and sympathizes with its fears; it is taken everywhere with her, or someone stays at home to make it feel it is not deserted. Most probably it is allowed the luxury of sleeping under the eiderdown of its new owner's bed, because it is so tiny and helpless, and its cries are so pathetic.

If it is a small dog its fear of traffic is overcome by being carried in the town, its unwillingness to walk amongst big feet is sympathized with by the owner who uses endearing words of encouragement to help it take its first steps in this big terrifying world of traffic and feet. The result is the puppy gains no self-confidence, it is all boosted confidence given to it by the owner using comforting words and carrying it. Should one ever try to give the dog confidence by firm jerks and a confident happy voice, paying no attention to it, sitting down and refusing to walk, then one is bound to meet the over-sentimental, and ill-educated, so-called dog lover, who will in a loud voice accuse you of being cruel to a tiny puppy. Few owners can retaliate in public, so the best thing to do is to ignore such people and carry on with what you are doing, in the knowledge that only by ignoring the puppy's fears will you help it to overcome them. Walk firmly on, speaking happily to the puppy or nervous dog, making it come on with quick jerks, and very soon you will have helped it over its first hurdle - fear. I cure many dogs that will not show themselves at dog shows owing to nerves; dogs that will not be handled by men; dogs that are terrified of bangs and such-like noises.

The nervous show dog is easy. In most cases all it needs is a choke chain, a long lead, and a few quick sharp jerks when it sits back fearfully. That, coupled with a confident happy tone of voice and plenty of love when he comes on, soon does the trick. Being a show dog it has probably never worn a choke chain for fear of spoiling its ruff of hair round its neck, or some such beauty points; secondly the owner has never obedience-trained it for fear it will sit in the show ring instead of standing. But in omitting obedience training the owner has forgotten it is just as easy to teach a dog to stand, as it is to sit, and that is part of the training curriculum. Obedience training of some sort should be given to all dogs whether they be show dogs or just household pets.

When I get a nervous dog here that won't be handled by strangers or a judge, the first thing I do is to put a choke chain on it. This very often has a devastating effect on the owner, who immediately has visions of all her precious Afghan's hair being rubbed off, or her Samoyed's hair turning black where the choke chain meets the neck and it takes me a long time to convince owners that if the choke chain never closes on the neck, which is my method, how can it damage hair? I teach my owners to throw their hands forward, jerk and let go with the left hand, still keeping the right hand on the lead. In fact we almost have a ditty when everyone says: 'Throw the hands forward, jerk and let go' together before we start using the choke chain. Unless the hands are thrown forward you don't get the lead loose enough to allow the quick jerk. The dogs should not even see the jerk, it should be so quick.

The next excuse I get from nervous or disbelieving owners is that they haven't the strength to jerk a big dog. I point out that strength is not needed. I myself have an injured spine after a car accident, yet I can jerk a large St. Bernard and get the same result as I get with a tiny Papillon or Yorkie. It is a knack which is vital to learn. Sometimes I put the choke chain on my own wrist and act as the dog for the owner to practise on so that the poor dog should not suffer the incorrect jerks the owner gives until she has been really indoctrinated with the correct quick action. Let us take the cases of nervous dogs which won't allow the judge or stranger to approach them and open their mouths. My first instruction is for the owner to learn the correct tone of voice and the command: 'Talk', for it will be on this word 'Talk' that the whole training is based. This the dog must, if necessary, learn the hard way. If, on pointing to the person he is to allow to handle him, he backs away, he is jerked back into position, given a most loving tickle on the ribs at the side of the body which is kept up throughout the initial training, and again jerked back into position if he backs away. He soon gets tired of being jerked back and resignedly stands. Then he gets enormous praise in a fairly high pitched voice which is opposite to the low commanding tones of the order: 'Talk'.

It is quite essential for the owner to stand away from the dog. No show dog here is allowed to be strung up on its leash; they have to stay standing on the command: 'Wait,' then be placed, then the owner has a loose lead and stands at least eighteen inches. away from the dog. I loathe to see exhibitors forever placing their dogs. Place them, leave them, and relax. If you train a dog to do this stand every day for a few minutes—it will soon learn. I believe it is quite possible to get this behaviour in a few minutes with the right confidence from the trainer. People who come here with phobias about their dogs not liking men or not liking judges need to cast that idea out of their minds and believe the dogs will do as they are told.

Tickling tummies slowly and gently works wonders. Never use a rubbing motion, this makes dogs bad tempered. A gentle tickle with the tips of the fingers is all that is necessary to induce calm in a dog. I hate strangers who go up to dogs with their hands held to the dog's nose, usually palm towards themselves. How does the dog know with this action the hand doesn't hold something horrid? The palm should always be shown to the dog and should go straight down to between the dog's front legs and tickle gently with a soothing voice to accompany the action. Very often the dog raises its back leg in a scratching movement, it gets so much pleasure from it. The person acting as the judge in the training session must walk around the dog appraising it from all angles. Then he must go up to the dog, when the owner then gives the command: 'Talk' and points towards the judge with an upward swing of the finger. This usually raises the dog's head which improves the general outline. If the dog sits back, give the lead to the person doing the supposed judging and make him step back quickly giving quite sharp but small jerks on the lead with the word: 'Come'. The dog may play up; if so it is essential to continue this backward movement, often changing direction until the dog realises he has got to co-operate. Then the dog's head must be handled, the chest scratched and the teeth examined. Very seldom does the dog object to this after my instructions are carried out. If more owners handed the lead to their friends and helpers when the dog refuses to be handled, the trouble would be solved very quickly. I have often cured a nervous dog in less than thirty minutes by this firm compulsion method.

Why should dogs be allowed to dislike or be more frightened of men than of women or vice versa? This is the most peculiar form of instability in dogs. They seem to hate sex more than form and can be sweet and happy with a woman and nervous or vicious with the opposite sex. What form of neurosis causes this we don't know. What can an owner do to make a dog with this nature livable with? First, examine the owner's mind. Has she or he ever had a grudge against the opposite sex? Did an overpowering school mistress make the young boy or young girl's life a misery? Does she boast that she is a women's woman or does she only get on with men? 'I never get on with women, my dear,' is almost certainly said by the type of owner that makes a dog hate women.

Alsatians are peculiar in this way and will hate men or women instinctively if thought transference comes from an owner with a similar dislike. So many women own Alsatians to show their superiority over their fellow men or women. They like big guard dogs, and the big guard dog thrives under this state of affairs and develops easily a dislike of the sex the owner wishes to dominate. Corgis do the same. I have particularly noted it in these two breeds, partly because they are highly intelligent breeds and telepathy is very marked, and partly because the shepherding instinct is uppermost and they have a natural suspicion of strangers. Correct them firmly when young and one gets no further trouble. Revel in their suspicious natures and you will have dogs that hate men or women, usually women.

The first thing to do is to love and pet your dog, then hold it quite firmly by the choke chain, give the command: 'Talk', and ask the man to stroke its head and scratch its chest. Next give him the lead and ask him to take it for a short walk, jerking it on if it won't go, then when he returns praise it for all you are worth. I think it is rather cruel to force a dog to be sociable to someone it doesn't like, but all dogs should be taught to allow themselves to be handled on the command: 'Stand', in case the vet has to examine the dog. So the sooner it learns this exercise the better. But I fail to understand why people complain that their dog will not be friends with strangers. Who wants a dog to be friendly with strangers? As long as it is polite and well-behaved surely that is enough? If however you

FRIENDSHIP: Barbara surrounded by the dogs she loved.

ALLSORTS: Dogs of every kind—and not a bad one among them.

have a show dog the judge is always impressed by a nice happy friendly dog; he hates risking being bitten by a nervous one. In any case I think it quite wrong to show a very nervous dog. Bad temperament should be heavily penalized so that owners are not encouraged to breed with it and pass on this fault. If an adult dog shows nerves what good is he as a sire? However many beauty points he may possess, he can never be a first-class dog.

Some of the saddest letters I get come from wives with dogs that dislike their husbands; dogs that even go so far as to bite the husband apparently without any specific reason. The cause I think is jealousy. What would I do with them? I would train the dog and the husband to respect each other's likes and dislikes. I would train the dog to go instantly to its basket and stay there when the husband is about. I would never allow it to lie in front of the fire and bite the husband when he moves his feet, which is a very common complaint. I would ask the husband to feed the dog, and if possible never feed it myself; for most animals can be won over through their tummies. I would also ask the husband to ignore the dog's lack of affection and not try to force himself on the dog, however much it offends his dignity not to be liked. Very often when you ignore a dog it makes the first advances.

In many cases all these faults in dogs can be traced to some minor mental disturbance of the owner, though the owner may be unaware of it. I often ignore the dog, and ask the owner searching questions to probe why the dog is un-balanced. When I find out what is wrong with the owner the dog is automatically cured. Dogs mirror their owners' inner thoughts more than their looks, as some people say. A dog mirrors your soul, for you can't deceive animals even though you may think you can.

In some cases when dogs have been cruelly treated by men or women the resulting hate is purely and simply a natural fear. Then the only thing to do is train the dog firmly enough to make fear a thing of the past. Sympathy only makes things worse.

Take it to a club with the trainer of the hated sex. If the trainer is a real dog lover, get him or her to caress the dog and handle it as much as is possible in a training class. Once the dog has got confidence in a member of the hated sex you are half-way to curing it. The rest must come by constant mixing with people in crowded places where the dog hasn't time to distinguish men from women. Undoubtedly this sex hatred is not a breeding fault as so many mentally unstable faults are, so it should be easily curable with expert help. Never keep the dog away from the sex it hates, make it go amongst people all the time, especially if the dog hates children - another fault that comes from fear. Take the dog where children are coming out from school, playing fields, etc; daily doses of this will soon make familiarity breed contempt. Make sure first though that sub-consciously the owner doesn't also hate children. If this is the case get someone who loves children to take the dog out and amongst them for you, someone who trusts the dog and won't automatically tighten the lead when children approach. If there is any risk of the dog biting a child, muzzle it. I always fail to understand why people imagine muzzles are cruel; they are of the greatest help in training a dog, for when the dog is muzzled the owner's mind can be carefree. Time and time again I have met people who quake in their shoes and protest when I muzzle a dog, yet in a few minutes the dog pays no attention to the muzzle and plays happily in it; most unstable dogs would be happier with a muzzle and a less worried owner.

The best cure for a biting dog is to have a long piece of string attached to its choke chain. When it attempts to bite, the person it goes for should pick up the string and suspend the dog for a few seconds off its front legs, leaving its back feet on the ground, and at the same time by using a thunderous tone of voice should make it very clear to the dog that its actions are quite unwarranted, and in no way going to be tolerated. The dog while suspended thus will feel like choking and will quickly realize who is master of the situation. But how many children, or husbands for that matter, are capable of carrying out this unpleasant treatment? Very few.

Therefore, as the dog does not love or respect them, why keep it? I can never understand people who ring me up and ask my advice on what to do with a dog that has seriously bitten a child more than once. My answer must always be that that dog is a beastly minded dog, so why take the risk of injury to your family? Obviously the owner is incapable of training it or it would never have reached this state of retaliation. For dogs are only driven to bite under such circumstances because they despise people - the result of not having been trained by them to do anything interesting or useful.

But there is a worrying trend of dogs that suddenly and quite unexpectedly, turn on their owners. These are often dogs that have been faithful and contented companions for some time, and distraught owners phone me to know what to do. It is extremely difficult to help people over the phone, for it may be one of many things that makes a dog suddenly revert to this type of retaliation, but I am always suspicious that this is another case of schizophrenia.

The usual symptoms are a complete lack of warmth in the eye, as if the dog had a headache, the lower lids often become red and the eyes have no depth to them. The inside of the ears become red as if the dog had a toxaemia and a frightful headache. He may suddenly bite viciously the person he has previously loved most, and then some minutes later be perfectly normal; the ears return on the inside to a pale colour, the eyes get their depth and look of love back again, and I am sure the dog does not remember biting at all.

I myself had forty-six stitches in one arm and sixteen in another from a Bulldog which I'd been training. He did all the exercises to perfection and had been a very loving and lovable chap. I had him in a field on a lead, talking to his owner; he was behind me when suddenly I didn't know what had hit me. This animal leapt on to my right arm and bit right down to my tendons, a millimetre more and I would have been a cripple for life in that arm. I managed with superhuman effort to get his mouth open and he got me on the other hand and bit that to the bone. Then he dropped off, wagged his tail and obviously expected the loving treatment he had had throughout his training. It was only then that the owner told me he had bitten her five times. The vet agreed with me that this was schizophrenia and put the dog to sleep. I feel sure many of these unprovoked attacks which kill children or do some terrible damage to human beings are cases of schizophrenia. I once told the owner of a Labrador to put his dog to sleep when he described unprovoked aggression in the dog, and he said his wife would be heartbroken if he did that, and he was going to give it another chance. Ten days later the dog bit his small child, who was terribly injured in the face. The dog was put down. I often wonder why people phone me and don't take my advice. I have no axe to grind in saying put the dog to sleep, if I really feel the dog is not safe. My first idea always is to try and train the dog. My only other method of saving the dog's life is to have it sent to the vet and have all its teeth out. One dog who bit a child four times had this done on my advice and is now eleven years old; even if it made an attack it could do no damage.

Nobody knows the cause of schizophrenia. Many people say it is a hormone upset, many people think it a dietetic upset, but until the veterinary profession find some definite clues to its cause, whether hereditary or formed in the lifetime, no-one with a dog that behaves as I described should keep it unless muzzled, or with no teeth, for these dogs only have to get someone in an artery for that person perhaps to lose their life before help could be obtained. I am very shocked at the deterioration in dogs' temperament these days. At shows dogs should be disqualified at the slightest sign of bad temperament, but this does not happen. I've seen a bad tempered Dobermann win a challenge certificate. I've seen a very nervous Irish Wolfhound which would not stand up properly be placed over a beautiful dog with a wonderful temperament. I am not a show person so don't know what possible excuse the judge could have had for placing the dogs like this, but I think the judge should not be a judge and encourage the breeding of nervous or bad-tempered dogs. Very often the two run side by side.

Boredom is another problem I have to tackle in dogs. These days they have little to interest them, beyond the daily walks which are often only to the shops and back, not the woods and fields. Anyway the woods and fields are mostly empty of exciting smells and things to chase. The result is that dogs like Corgis and Spaniels with a background of useful work become neurotic, and as they can't hunt or chase anything they bite their owners. These self-same dogs, given a fixed schedule of obedience work or even just household tricks to perform, become different characters. Unfortunately these days owners are so busy that the time taken to train a dog can hardly be spared. They hope that the dog will fit in with their household arrangements without any special training, except house manners. They get annoyed or disappointed when this is not so. The result is that the dog becomes neurotic and sometimes vicious.

Every dog, like every child, should have some routine work given it to do every day, even if only for ten minutes a day. If the dog continues to be vicious after you have trained it, there is something lacking or abnormal in its make-up, and abnormal dogs cannot safely be kept. But this does not mean the dog should be given away to a so-called 'kind home in the country' to bite other un-suspecting people. I think the owner should face up to his or her responsibility and put it to sleep, and also face up to the fact that the owner has failed the dog, and vow to learn more about dogs before having another.

Bangs and noises that terrify dogs are a constant source of trouble to dog owners. Guy Fawkes' night is a night of terror for dog and owner. So may be a walk in the town or country when a backfire may make the dog slip its lead and disappear for hours or even for ever.

How is the owner to blame for this state of affairs? The answer is that familiarity breeds contempt, and if the owner takes the trouble to make these noises quite familiar to the dog during the day, the dog will soon ignore them, or even enjoy them. I trained Juno, my former Great Dane, who was a shivering mass of terrors when I bought her, to love gun-fire. I had a toy pistol with caps and played with it as a game, fired it and said: 'Attack' and had a rough and tumble game with her. Soon she connected the game with the bang and became used to it and enjoyed it. Then if anyone fired a gun she looked so beautiful, obviously longing to go and attack or have a game. I used also to drop heavy books unexpectedly, and then I praised her and laughed with her; dogs love laughter and smiles like children do. I always clapped my hands when she did right and she soon connected clapping with my happy voice and smiling face. If you make odd bangs and noises at intervals your dog will soon forget its fear. A phobia, usually suffered in smaller breeds, is the dog that won't go near another dog. The owners are usually of the shy type themselves and the dogs are only mirroring the owner's lack of really wishing to be gregarious. The best way to teach this type of dog to ignore other dogs, but to walk with them and past them without leaping away, is to use two dogs, put both on choke chains and just jerk them forward with small leaps at a very fast pace. They can't do otherwise than go together if this is done. Then drop the leads, give a thunderous command: 'Wait' and the dogs are usually so surprised at the tone of voice and backward hand signal over their heads that they stand quite still for a few seconds. With repeat performances of this, the dogs ignore each other and other dogs and are on the road to a cure.

I think the word 'won't' is the word I hate most in dealing with dogs with phobias. In my opinion there is no such thing as 'won't'. There may be an initial 'can't' in the early stages of training, but 'won't' is made up by the owner to cover a multitude of excuses, none of which I tolerate. In my opinion if the word 'won't' is allowed to excuse bad behaviour and nothing changes that attitude, the dog is not worth keeping, for the dog would be unhappy in the world of 'won't' and the owner ineffective and unlikely to get much joy from the dog. It is for this reason I always take the dog away from the owner for a few minutes on first meeting it, and show the owner it *will* do what is asked if the right tone of voice is used, the right happy attitude of mind cultivated, and above all the really happy praise that the dog gets when it does as is wanted.

In praising dogs I always use the words: 'What a good dog'. I have lined a class of dogs up and told the owners to praise them in their usual manner, then told them to prefix the praise with the word: 'What' and the effect on the dogs is undeniable. For some extraordinary reason the word: 'What' electrifies them and gives them so much more pleasure than ordinary praise. I have dozens of letters saying it really does work after I had told listeners in a broadcast to say this to their dogs.

One of the most difficult vices to overcome is that of the dog who will not be left alone. This takes longer to cure than most faults, because it is the owner who must be cured - of lack of firmness. Daily firmness is essential. The dog must be taught to lie down and stay down. When it gets up the owner must return to it and sound cross with it, and put it down again. There must be no let-up on this. It must be made to stay down in spite of piercing shrieks or whines. It may be necessary to give it a firm jerk as it is put 'down' on the choke chain. If it barks give the command: 'Cease' - and mean it. Tone of voice is everything in this case. Occasionally I have found the words: 'Shut up' extremely effective if snapped out. There must be no pleading with the dog to stay, for that won't help. But when it does stay, even for a few minutes, the praise must be terrific.

Always remember dogs cannot bark for long lying down, they get tired. Therefore whenever it makes a nuisance of itself by barking make it lie down. This is quite the most important exercise in dog training. If necessary you must sit down on a chair and put the dog with its lead on into the down position on the floor beside you. Then run the lead under the arch of your shoe. If the dog attempts to get up, give the command: 'Down' and tighten the lead by pulling it upwards from where it runs under your shoe. By this method the dog's head is pulled gently to the ground, and it must sooner or later lie down unless it wishes to choke itself. Try not to have to bend down yourself; it is better that the dog shouldn't connect you with what is going on. When it does lie down say something nice to it and show you are pleased, but not in an excited tone of voice or it will get up again. When the exercise is over then give it real petting.

Do this exercise for a few minutes to start with, eventually sitting the dog down for half an hour. Never relent whilst doing this exercise. Remember that if the dog obeys the pulling lead the choke chain will immediately release itself, so it is within the dog's power to be comfortable. I cannot repeat too often that to make a problem dog good you must have a strong will. Let the dog win and you are further back than when you started.

Leave the dog in the 'down' position for longer periods at a time each day. When he trusts that you are going to come back, the trouble of never being able to leave him alone in the house does not occur. Smacking is useless, scolding is only a little better. It is the quiet firmness that wins, never failing to put him back and down where he came from. Occasionally a 'put on' cross voice will steady a nervous dog, but never lose your temper. This exercise is just as much a test of the owner's character as the dog's. Weak people never win. Remember this trouble is probably your fault in the first place; it is up to you to put it right.

Always do everything you can to make the exercise liked by the dog. Give it its favourite blanket to lie on, especially in the car; if possible let it have its own chair in the sitting room. It is only when all these things fail that sterner measures have to be taken. And remember problem dogs need far sterner measures than puppies or normal nice dogs. Now let's deal with dogs that tear things up. In adult male dogs I have no hesitation in saying I believe it is sex trouble. Castrate the dog is my solution. It is useless letting him mate with an occasional bitch, that only makes him much worse. With Boxers in particular, many of those that tear things up will be found to be 'monorchids', which means they have only one testicle descended. This sexual abnormality makes them destructive. Castration is difficult in these cases and an operation to find the undescended testicle has to be carried out before castration can take place. Dachshunds also seem very prone to this trouble, but without exception I have found that castration will cure these destructive urges. But it takes two or three months for the operation to have full effect.

There is a prejudice against this operation in some circles, but I am sure that such people would change their minds if they followed the careers of difficult dogs which have been so treated. I have recommended castration for a vast number of dogs with certain vices, and in every case the owners have been most satisfied with the results. The dogs have in no way been spoilt nor run to fat, nor have they lost a lively character. It helps to stop a dog that fights. It makes the lamp post to lamp post trek a thing of the past, for the dog returns to the squatting position for passing urine. It stops that eternal search after the on-heat bitch. And it also stopped a Pekinese from lifting its leg over the wallpaper, the result of having been trained to use newspaper as a puppy!

Dogs only get fat through overfeeding. Undoubtedly castrated dogs need less food when so treated, as they worry less over distractions, and bitches. They are also much nicer companions out on a walk as they pay less attention to smells and they tolerate other dogs in the same house much better. It is an old wives' tale that other dogs attack them; you will find that other dogs ignore them. I can give the addresses of the many people who own these dogs, and if anyone has doubts I am sure these owners would be pleased to show you their dogs or write to you about them. I think far too many dogs are over-sexed, and would lead happier lives without the trouble of possessing the sex they are never going to use. If wandering mongrels were castrated there would be fewer of those poor little puppies sold in markets, which eventually end up in homes for lost dogs. The road accidents caused by dogs would also be greatly decreased, for it is the mongrels not the show dogs that are the chief cause.

Some vets won't castrate dogs. They can't in my opinion have had much experience of the results. I have had a great deal, and wouldn't dream of recommending it if I did not think it has been a good thing for the cases I mention. Before recommending that any male dog should be put to sleep for vice, I always try castration. In many cases it has saved the dog's life.

Despite the numerous remedies for dealing with neurotic dogs, I cannot stress often enough that, if you wish to keep a dog that is not normal, you must face up to living a slightly restricted existence. Although you may love a subnormal dog, other people must not be inconvenienced by it. If your dog pounces on little dogs for no other reason than wishing to see them helpless on the ground, it is useless to explain to the owner of the little dog that your dog won't really hurt it, for even being pounced on is quite enough to terrify a little dog though it doesn't get bitten.

It is your duty to keep your dog on a lead and away from other people's dogs until such a time as it is cured of its bad habits. If it is unlikely ever to be cured, you must at all times see that it causes annoyance to no one you meet. I don't think there is anything that produces deeper rage in me than to have my well-behaved dog attacked by someone else's untrained and uncontrolled animal. Much as I love dogs I feel hatred at those times, more for the owner than the dog.

One person I know can only exercise his dog after midnight because it is so vicious that he cannot hold it on a lead when approaching another dog or person. The dog goes completely berserk. I wonder whether an animal of this nature should be kept. Is it a dog's life only to go for walks when most animals naturally are asleep? I think not, but the owner thinks it worthwhile and that's all there is to it. This savage trait in dogs is terribly difficult to eradicate after the age of two. Up to that age there is a hope but, once a dog has got away with being savage for so long, the cure is usually only obtained by castration and rigorous training over a long period. To have allowed a dog to be savage for two years means the owner lacks responsibility in his or her duty towards her dog and the human race and is therefore unlikely to co-operate with either of the above cures.

Alas! The mind of a dog of this age is all-masterful. He has obtained supremacy over mankind and the canine race. As stags fight to the end, so will dogs and, if the dog is a big breed, the necessary strength needed to correct it is often absent in owner or trainer. It is for this reason alone that I think the dog should be put down. For there may come a day when the owner is ill and someone less efficient is left to cope with the dog. Then an accident may occur, perhaps even causing the death of another much-beloved dog.

People often mix up vices with unbalanced minds. The two things should never be confused. A dog that eats its own excreta or the droppings of farm animals hasn't an unbalanced mind. No training is likely to eradicate it completely, for this is a nutritional fault or an infestation by parasites. Given sufficient minerals the dog will often become completely normal. If punished for these things the dog loses faith in his owner, he is only doing what nature urges him to do to find the necessary minerals his body needs. Without training, a dog will cease this filthy habit when the mineral balance of its body is corrected.

Instinct is perhaps the greatest factor controlling the mind of a dog. Self-preservation, the urge to reproduce, the wish to follow a strong leader, the use of the senses to read the secrets of nature are inborn in all dogs.

No one in his sense would punish a bitch for tearing the sofa to bits when she is immersed in that queer state the 'pseudo pregnancy' and apparently about to give birth to phantom puppies. To her it is all very real, and even if you scold her for digging she will do it again when you are not there. If this does happen, the best thing to do is to keep her with you in these trying times. It only lasts about ten days and usually, if the bitch sleeps in your room, it doesn't seem to occur. But if left on her own, especially at night, she will make frantic efforts to make a nest with disastrous results to your furnishings. This is not a mental instability it is a hormone upset and will right itself. To be forewarned is to be forearmed. Either put her somewhere she can do no damage or keep her with you throughout her trying time. An indoor kennel is the best answer.

Only the owners of unbalanced dogs can really know where the line can be drawn between a dog that is sane or mentally unsound. No one can make up the owner's mind as to what to do with the last kind. I, as a great dog lover, feel it is kinder to put them to sleep. Surely, when all training and veterinary help has been exhausted and there is no hope of the dog living a reasonably normal existence, it is kinder to both to put the dog to sleep. There are so many nice dogs without vice or instability needing homes but with no hope of life because they are unwanted.

I believe that, if you understand how the mind of a dog works, you will not come up against many faults that cannot be cured or made livable with under certain conditions. I do not believe a dog can be cured by a psychiatrist, but think some owners could be helped that way.

CHAPTER ELEVEN

ROAMING DOGS

How irritating it must be never to know where your dog is! Or to own a dog that perpetually wishes to go off on its own pursuits. How does this happen? It comes about for many reasons. The first is that many people imagine it is cruel to confine a dog to the house with you, and that dogs can't be happy without their freedom. It comes about because people own dogs and haven't the time to exercise them, or the time to look after them, and they take the easiest way out by opening the front door and letting their dogs go out on their own, knowing they will return when tired or hungry.

These people lack imagination, they do not visualize what might happen in those hours the dog is running free on its own pursuits. They never think that their dog may cause a human being to die in a car accident, nor do they visualize the dog getting injured and lying uncared for on the road. They have never thought that their male dog may mate with some tiny little uncared for bitch on heat and cause her to suffer or die having puppies too big for her. They do not think of the risk of their dog picking up infection. All they like is to have a dog to bark at intruders at night and to play occasionally with the children. They have no idea what they miss. They do not know what heights of intelligence can be reached by a dog. They should never own a dog, a cat would suit them better, for cats prefer being allowed to roam when the spirit moves them, and most cat lovers agree that it is not kind to confine a cat too closely; although I think cats would also miss the deep affection this type of owner never bestows on an animal. How can one cure a roaming dog? First of all by training. Any sort of work makes a dog more interested in its owner. Having the dog with you when you shop, when you go in the car, when you are in the home, all tend to make the dog rely on you for all his needs. But there are some male dogs tortured by the sex urge and if there is a bitch on heat within five miles I have heard owners complain their dog knows and is a menace. My answer to that is, castrate him.

The roaming instinct is also the reason why the dogs do not come to their owners' call when out for exercise. This is a major problem and a large percentage of my correspondence is about it. The owners often say the dog is good and obedient in the house or garden, but get it outside where smells abound, or other dogs roam, and the dog becomes completely deaf to orders. What can they do?

They must put their dog on a long lead and a choke chain and take it where there are plenty of distractions, leave it at the sit and walk away from the dog to the fullest extent of the lead. Give the command: 'Come' prefacing all commands with the dog's name; if the dog looks about elsewhere or doesn't literally leap to its feet to obey, give it a very sharp jerk towards you and when it comes love it for all you are worth. The whole training depends on the way you jerk. The choke chain running end must be under the dog's chin, for in this way the jerk comes on the top of the neck—which is very muscular—and couldn't possibly cause any injury or pain to the dog; but it *does* give the dog a shock, and I have known Poodles and similar nervous dogs to give a squeal. This is not pain but shock, and you must carry on: the dog will soon learn that if it comes quickly it gets much love and praise, if it doesn't come quickly it gets an almighty jerk and has to come anyway. I reckon it only takes a few minutes to teach a dog to come when called.

Occasionally a very tough stubborn dog will not learn this way, and then once more you have to have co-operation from a friend who should if possible have a dog with her. She should have a spare long leather lead in her hand, and when your dog comes up to her dog and won't return to you when you call, she should give it a crack with the leather lead over its backside and say: 'Go Back' in a horrid tone of voice. The owner should meanwhile be calling in her most endearing tone of voice, and there is soon no doubt at all in the dog's mind which is the best place. I find this is easily taught in class in an enclosed field, because when there are twenty or more pupils all willing to help the owner whose dog won't come when called, by slapping it with a leather lead if it comes their way, the dog finds it most unpleasant to be away from its owner and safety. I hate having to do this to disobedient dogs, but these measures have to be meted out to dogs who don't love their owners. For make no mistake, if your dog doesn't come when called you take only second place in his mind to smells or other dogs. Otherwise the old trick of calling him and running away from him would be effective. He would think you were going to leave him and he would love you so much he would not want you out of his sight, and would run after you. You could then give the command: 'Sit' and catch him. No, if your dog does not come it means he doesn't respect you, and without respect you have no true love from your dog.

Force in any form is repulsive to many dog owners, and I heartily agree with them. I often have to use these more forceful measures to teach the dogs obedience to their unloved owners, and I also feel revolted at having to do it, but it is my duty to help to train these dogs, and if the dogs couldn't care less whether their owners jumped into the sea or not what can one do? I always find these dogs will come instantly to my call, which is very annoying for the owners, but then I am sending out by telepathy not only the 'or else' message, but my tremendous faith in them and my deep love for them when they behave well. Too many owners try to catch their dogs when they approach. I tell them to raise their hands up to their own chests and not use them menacingly to grab their dogs. Without the hands waving about the dogs will come right up close to the owners' knees and should sit on command, when the owners can drop down and kiss and love them for coming. I can't tell owners often enough that dogs love being kissed, they adore contact with the human face.

Should titbits ever be given to a dog on returning to its owner? With a puppy I think so, and occasionally with an adult dog, but not as a rule, or the dog may get fed up and go off again when you have nothing to give one day.

The right firm tone of voice when the command: 'Come' is given, the immense show of love when the dog comes, and the more severe measures recommended if the dog is a stubborn one - those are the only methods I use to teach countless dogs to return instantly to their owners.

Dogs that chase moving things are a menace and must be cured at all costs. Car-chasing is one of their worst crimes. When I was in Ireland recently I noticed all the dogs in country districts chased cars. Nobody seemed to do anything about it, and the dogs were incredibly clever at avoiding getting run over. I am glad to say the dogs in this country that chase cars are the exception rather than the rule. But when they do get this dangerous habit they undoubtedly cause many accidents. How can it be stopped? The quickest and most efficient way I know is to enlist the aid of a friend with a car. Ask him to drive you slowly past the dog that chases cars, and as the dog comes in to the attack throw out as hard as you possibly can any fat hard-covered book, and make certain that the book hits the dog. The shock it gives the dog so frightens it that I have never had to repeat the treatment more than twice, even though the dog may have chased cars for years. My favourite book is an old A.A. Handbook, it is just the right size. Try not to lean out of the car to throw it as then the dog may connect you with the throwing of the book, when you want him to connect the car with the shock he gets.

If the dog has only just developed the car or motor-bike chasing vice, a long cord on a choke chain and a terrific jerk as he goes to chase the vehicle works a cure, but an old hand at the game knows when he is on the cord and won't do it. Shepherds always say a sheep chaser is quickly taught to leave sheep alone by being penned with a fierce ram, and chicken chasers with a turkey cock, but I wouldn't like to bet on that. The old idea of giving the dog a kick was always stupid and cruel I thought. For one thing the dog quickly learnt to avoid the kick as the Irish dogs learnt to avoid being hit by a car. But a book thrown with skill can reach the dog every time, and frighten it without the risk of injuring it.

I recently cured a Corgi that chased motor-cycles by getting the motorcyclist to carry a jug of water in one hand and throw it over the dog as she came in to chase the motor-cycle. It took three dousings to cure her, but now she shrinks back into the ditch at the approach of a motor-cycle, and this may well have saved her life.

All chasing of vehicles and livestock can be stopped by proper training in the recall exercise. A dog should never be so far away from its owner that it cannot be recalled. No dog should be off the lead on the highway these days, there is too much traffic. If the dog shows the least excitement at the approach of a vehicle it should be given a sharp jerk and the command: 'Leave'.

No dog should ever be free where there is livestock unless the owner is absolutely certain his dog will stay to heel. Far too many owners look upon farmers' fields as their natural right of way and allow their dogs to wander out of hearing before they attempt to call them in to heel. If the dog is constantly taken amongst traffic and livestock on the lead the novelty soon wears off and the chasing does not occur. If only owners would think ahead and be alive to the risk that their dog may chase livestock, I feel sure it would never happen.

The fact remains that many people encourage their dogs to chase things, and the poor dog has to learn what he can chase and what he can't. Some dogs drive their owners mad by chasing birds on the lawn, some by running up and down the garden fence when people or dogs or vehicles go by. What is the cure? Keep the dog in away from temptation. I find a vast number of people whose dogs have many vices prefer to grumble rather than remove the source of vice. They obviously haven't the skill to train their dogs, so they must do the next best thing and keep the dog out of the way of temptation. Take for example the bitch that destroys everything in the house. Surely the best way to stop it is to confine her when you are not about in an indoor kennel lined with zinc. She can then do no damage. If she never has a chance to destroy things she forgets the vice, and it is a good bet that she will have grown tired of doing it when she is again given the run of the house.

I honestly believe some dogs that chase things and tear things up have a mental disease. If firm training does not stop them, and giving them plenty of interest in life has no effect, then I think there is no cure. I knew one Fox Terrier who used to chase his own tail like mad every morning. On his death he was found to have a tumour on the brain. There are 'mental' human beings and 'mental' dogs. Training must not be condemned as useless until the possibility of a mental disease in the dog has been eliminated, for however good you are at training dogs, a dog with a diseased brain will never respond.

CHAPTER TWELVE

A SUMMARY OF COMMON MISTAKES

Some owners are over-sentimental. Love is one thing, sentimentality to excess is another. Some dogs yelp when corrected when not in anyway hurt. I proved this to one dog owner by kissing her dog which yelped in exactly the same way as it did when corrected; I didn't think my kiss was that lethal! Dogs like firm commands and loving praise when they do right. Owners use unkind thin-linked choke chains and jerk them upwards instead of downwards to correct the dog, and forget to take the left hand off the lead immediately after the jerk to allow the choke chain to release itself. They also jerk the lead with the palm of the hand facing upwards instead of downwards; this closes the choke chain on the dog's neck, and this may spoil the hair and is not kind in my opinion. Choke chains of my pattern should never close on the neck. Owners forget to say 'what a good dog' when praising. The word 'what' has a magical effect on the dog and usually produces an instant happy rapport and obedience.

Owners' signals are ineffective or muddling; they give them bending forward so that the signal could be missed by the dog. Signals should be given firmly from the shoulder when standing upright. The hand giving the signal should be held away from the body so the dog can see the signal clearly. Owners often 'string up' show dogs on nylon leads; this must hurt the dog as nylon leads have sharp edges. Dogs should be trained to stand and look alert on the command 'talk' which in my school means allow the judge to handle the dog without it moving. If a dog can't hold it's head up naturally, in my opinion it is not worth an award. Owners fail to realise that with firm, confident, kind jerks and a happy tone of voice most dogs can be cured of nerves in a few hours. Never sympathise with a nervous dog, jerk it on gaily, speaking to it in a happy voice, using my thick-linked choke chain, and above all, have a four foot lead held loosely over the two middle fingers of the right hand. Never close the right hand on the lead. A tight lead makes a dog nervous and dependant on its owner's support. When showing a dog, stand at least eighteen inches away from it to give it confidence on being handled by a judge. Owners should move fast when running a nervous dog; it's tail then has to come up to balance it, and the habit grows and a natural tail carriage is established.

Owners fail when wishing a dog to be friendly, or be examined by a judge, to give the command 'go and talk', at the same time pointing at the person the dog has to acknowledge or be handled by. Without this training the nervous dog may be suspicious of anyone approaching it and back away. This especially applies to judges in the show ring who may be wary of approaching a dog who doesn't appear too friendly. The dog must be taught to stand still on the command 'stand' and look up wagging its tail if possible, at whoever is pointed at by the handler when given this 'talk' command. Owners have far too little range of voice tones. One needs low tones for commands given in a clear firm voice. Higher exuberant tones for praise when the dog has done well. A hard 'no nonsense' tone for wrong doing with deliberate disobedience.

Owners may still believe that a bitch's temperament is improved by having puppies; this is not so, she just passes on to her puppies bad temperament. They may also believe that to mate an over-sexed dog makes it better; this is also a fallacy, it makes it's behaviour much worse, and it may even become bad-tempered with other dogs into the bargain.

Owners often don't realise that male and female human beings each have a different scent to a dog's nose so that one often hears that dogs won't let men handle them. This may easily be true, as dogs know men from women by this different scent. A normal dog either likes or dislikes both men and women as a whole race not one sex of human being. Individual men and women are attractive to dogs - why we just don't know. I've often noticed that people who profess to be great dog lovers may not be liked by dogs, curious though it may be. I feel this is because they rush in too fast before the dog has time to sum them up. The holding out of one hand for the dog to smell in my opinion is the worst possible way to approach a dog, it shows the dog you do not feel confident that it will like you. I always approach a dog from the side if it is nervous and stand beside it, then take the lead and make it walk with me.

Dog owners often think that dog experts can solve their problems over the phone where temperament faults exist in the dog. This is rarely so, the owner has to be met and summed up. They also hope if they send their dog away to be trained it will return and obey them; in my opinion this is utterly wrong, for it is the owner who needs the training much more than the dog.

In the greater number of cases, a sensible attitude towards a dog's mind, not assuming it to be equal to that of a human being, is all that is necessary to insure that he will be throughout his life man's best friend, a joy to all and a nuisance to no one.

APPENDIX

BARBARA WOODHOUSE CHOKE CHAINS AND LEADS:

Choke Chains: Sizes at 2in Intervals: 12in to 18in £2.50
20in to 28in £2.75.

Leads Approx 4ft long in best quality bridle leather.
Large or small trigger hook: £5.50
(Please state breed when ordering chains and leads.)

*To obtain the correct choke chain, measure over the top of the dog's head, down over the ears and under the chin, then add 2in and round up or down to the nearest size.
(Please add 95p for carriage and packing on all orders for leads and choke chains.)

BARBARA WOODHOUSE AUDIO CASSETTE

Based on the series Training Dogs The Woodhouse Way.

Price: £4.75 inc P&P.

BARBARA WOODHOUSE VIDEO CASSETTE
QUICK DOG TRAINING
This video was recorded in he USA and is a short version of Training Dogs The Woodhouse Way. Price: £10.95 inc P&P.

INDOOR KENNELS

Designed by Barbara Woodhouse.

Sold under the Trade Mark BARJO, these kennels are made in all sizes from 20in long and 14in wide to 36in long and 25in wide.

Versions are made for all estate cars and hatchbacks and a full range of extras is available. Prices on application.

All these items are available from:

Ringpress Marketing,
Spirella House,
Bridge Road,
Letchworth,
Herts,
SG6 4ET

Phone (0462) 674177

Also available from Ringpress Books:

•Any of these books may be ordered direct from the publishers. Either send a cheque/postal order for the price, including postage and packing to: Ringpress Books Ltd, Spirella House, Bridge Road, Letchworth, Herts. SG6 4ET. **OR** just phone us on 0462 674177 and place an order by Access or Visa. Please have your card with you to quote the number and expiry date.

BOOKS OF THE BREED

Titles from this acclaimed series include:

SHETLAND SHEEPDOGS TODAY

by Maurice Baker

An excellent guide for everyone from the pet owner to the experienced showgoer.

More than 100 photographs. Price £12.95 plus £1.50 postage and packing.

"A best-seller if ever there was one. Of all the books I have ever read on dog care and management, I rate Shetland Sheepdogs Today one of, if not THE very best." – *Tom Horner, Dog World.*

THE SHOW BORDER COLLIE

by Joyce Collis

The first book ever written on the Border Collie as a show dog. Joyce Collis's blend of experience, common sense and humour make this book a must for all those who love this versatile breed.

Fully illustrated. Price £12.95 plus £1.50 postage and packing.

THE COMPLETE BERNESE MOUNTAIN DOG

by Jude Simonds

Following huge demand, top breeder and show championship judge Jude Simonds has written a highly informative book on the Bernese, now a firm favourite as a family pet and in the show ring.

Fully illustrated. Price £12.95 plus £1.50 postage and packing.

ROYAL TOY SPANIELS

by Alicia Pennington

At last there is a book that includes both the King Charles Spaniel and the Cavalier King Charles Spaniel. These delightful dogs have a unique Royal history and are a firm favourite with today's pet owners. International championship show judge Alicia Pennington, who is a top breeder of King Charles Spaniels and a Toy Dog specialist, brings her unrivalled knowledge to a memorable book.

Fully illustrated. Price £12.95 plus £1.50 postage and packing.

ALL ABOUT THE GREYHOUND

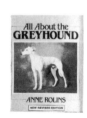

by Anne Rolins

A brand new revised edition of Anne Rolins's brilliant, comprehensive guide to the breed. Now in its third reprint, this book has been a huge seller all over the world.

Fully illustrated. Price £14.95 plus £2 postage and packing.

GER McKENNA
ON
GREYHOUNDS
by John Martin

At last the full story of Ger McKenna, the man they call the Maestro. Master trainer McKenna has won an incredible **32 CLASSICS**, including the 1989 Daily Mirror Greyhound Derby. John Martin's brilliant book gets to the heart of the most successful greyhound trainer of modern times.
Fully illustrated. Price £14.95 plus £1.50 postage and packing.

GEORGE CURTIS:
TRAINING
GREYHOUNDS
by Julia Barnes

The inside story of Britain's master trainer who took the great Ballyregan Bob to a world record of 32 consecutive wins. How did he do it? Read our best seller this year.
Fully illustrated. Price £14.95 plus £1.50 postage and packing.

THE DAILY
MIRROR
GREYHOUND
FACT FILE
Edited by Julia Barnes.

The most complete volume ever published on greyhound racing and coursing.
496 pages. Price £5.95 plus £1 postage and packing.

The
NURSE MANAGER'S
SURVIVAL GUIDE

Practical Answers to Everyday Problems

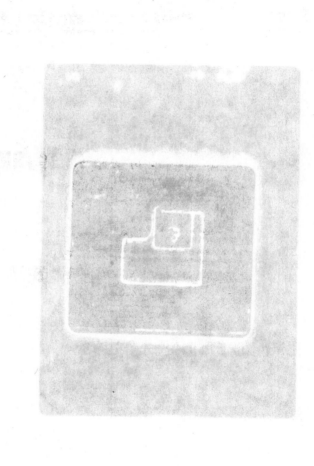

The
Nurse Manager's
Survival Guide
Practical Answers to Everyday Problems

T.M. Marrelli, MSN, MA, RN

Health Care Consultant
Boca Grande, Florida

With Assistance from
Lynda S. Hilliard, MBA, RN, CNAA

Third Edition

Mosby
An Affiliate of Elsevier

An Affiliate of Elsevier

11830 Westline Industrial Drive
St. Louis, MO 63123

The Nurse Manager's Survival Guide: Practical Answers to Everyday   ISBN 0-323-02329-0
  Problems, third edition

NOTICE

Library of Congress Cataloging-in-Publication Data

Marrelli, T. M.
    The nurse manager's survival guide: practical answers to everyday problems / T.M.
   Marrelli; with assistance from Lynda S. Hilliard. – 3rd ed.
      p.; cm.
   Includes bibliographical references and index.
   ISBN 0-323-02329-0
    1. Nursing services–Administration. I. Hilliard, Lynda S. II. Title.
   [DNLM: 1. Nursing, Supervisory. 2. Nursing Services–organization & administration.
   3. Personnel Management–methods. WY 105 M358n 2004]
   RT89.M389 2004
   362.17'3' 068–dc22   2003066607

Executive Editor: Loren Wilson
Managing Editor: Linda Thomas
Publishing Services Manager: Catherine Albright Jackson
Project Manager: Clay S. Broeker
Senior Designer: Amy Buxton

Printed in the United States of America

Last digit is the print number: 9 8 7 6 5 4 3 2 1

CONTRIBUTORS

Barbara Faruggio, RN, MS
Clinical Integration Specialists, LLC
Lavalette, New Jersey

Lynda S. Hilliard, MBA, RN, CNAA
Senior Manager
National Healthcare Regulatory Consulting Services
Deloitte & Touche
Oakland, California

Elizabeth E. Hogue, Esquire
Attorney in Private Practice
Burtonsville, Maryland

T.M. Marrelli, MSN, MA, RN
Health Care Consultant
Boca Grande, Florida

Margaret Sharp, RN, BSN
Clinician
Medical College of Virginia Hospitals
Division of Pediatric Oncology
Richmond, Virginia

Sandra Whittier, RNC, MSN
Case Coordinator
VNACare Network
Marblehead, Massachusetts

REVIEWERS

Dawn C. Barnes, RN, BSN
Chesapeake, Virginia

Paula Hutchinson, RN, BSN, MS, MBA, PHR
Nurse Recruiter/Senior Human Resources Generalist
Union Hospital, Cecil County
Elkton, Maryland

Christine Pierce, RN, CS, MSN
Senior Associate
Resource Group, Ltd.
Dallas, Texas

Nancy Valentine, RN, PhD, MSN, MPH, FAAN, FNAP
Vice President/National Nursing Executive
CIGNA Health Care
Hartford, Connecticut

Heather P. Wilson, PhD
President
Weatherbee Resources, Inc.
Centerville, Massachusetts

ABOUT THE AUTHOR

Tina M. Marrelli, MSN, MA, RN, is president of Marrelli and Associates, Inc., a health care consulting and publishing firm. Ms. Marrelli is the author of *The Handbook of Home Health Standards and Documentation Guidelines for Reimbursement* ("The Little Red Book") (fourth ed., Mosby, 2001), *The Nurse Manager's Survival Guide* (third ed., Mosby), *The Handbook of Home Health Orientation* (Mosby, 1997), *The Nursing Documentation Handbook* (third ed., Mosby, 1996), *The Hospice and Palliative Care Handbook* (Mosby, 1999), and *Mosby's Home Care & Hospice Drug Handbook* (Mosby, 1999). She is also the coauthor of *Home Health Aide: Guidelines for Care* (Marrelli, 1996), *Home Care and Clinical Paths: Effective Care Planning Across the Continuum* (Mosby, 1996), *Home Health Aide: Guidelines for Care Instructor Manual* (Marrelli, 1997), *The Manual of Home Health Practice* (Mosby, 1998), and *Home Care Therapy: Quality, Documentation, and Reimbursement* (Marrelli, 1999). Ms. Marrelli is also an editorial board member of *The Journal of Community Health Nursing* and *Geriatric Nursing* and contributes specialty articles for the monthly home health newsletter, *Clinical Supervisor Alert.*

Ms. Marrelli received a bachelor's degree in nursing from Duke University School of Nursing in 1975. She has directed various home care programs and has extensive experience in home care, hospice, and hospital settings. She has a master of arts in Management and Supervision, Health Care Administration, and a master's in Nursing. Ms. Marrelli worked at the central office of the Health Care Financing Administration (HCFA), now the Centers for Medicare and Medicaid (CMS), for 4 years in the areas of home care and hospice policy and operations, where she received the Bureau Director's Citation. Ms. Marrelli serves on the National Hospice and Palliative Care Organization's (NHPCO) Standards and Accreditation Committee, has been the recipient of the Arizona Association for Home Care's 1998 Genie Eide Award, and served as a member of the Hospice and Palliative Nurses Association's National Competency Project.

Marrelli and Associates, Inc. provides consultative services to hospitals, universities, publishers, home health agencies, hospice, and other programs in the areas of management, compliance, OASIS, accreditation, and other quality initiatives, daily operations, retention and recruitment initiatives, clinical documentation systems and written product development, case management models, and numerous other areas.

Ms. Marrelli can be contacted via e-mail at *news@marrelli.com* or through the website *www.marrelli.com.* Correspondence, including feedback or recommendations about this text, may be directed to the author at Marrelli and Associates, Inc. PO Box 629, Boca Grande, FL 33921.

When I first became a new manager, no one told me many of the things that, in retrospect, I needed to know. From the running of successful staff meetings to dealing with hospital administration, I learned to manage by trial and, many times, by error. To ease your journey and to refresh and reinforce management skills you already may have developed is the goal of this book. Staff nurses sometimes receive more extensive orientation and planned educational programs than the mangers who supervise them! As managers, we and our staffs deserve better. I hope this book fills the gap.

The Nurse Manager's Survival Guide is a practical guide to day-to-day operations for nurses who manage people, care plans, or groups of patients. This book is designed to assist nurses recently placed in management positions and serve as a refresher for more experienced nurse managers. As hospitals, home care organizations, and other patient care settings experience decreasing lengths of stay and increasing patient acuity, the professional nurse must manage more responsibilities in a shorter time frame.

It is unfortunate that some of us have encountered ineffective managers and unproductive or unpleasant management environments. My hope is that this book will help you become a competent, communicative manager and help you take the steps needed to improve your work circumstances, if necessary.

Some important information, usually not included in nursing books, has been incorporated, such as how to market yourself, how to honestly evaluate your own capabilities and needs, how to manage stress for both you and your staff, and how to know when it is time to move on. Many of the specific guidelines and descriptions included address nursing management in various practice settings. The general management principles and techniques described can be applied to any nursing care delivery setting, including the increasingly important areas of home care, ambulatory care, hospice, physician offices, and long-term care. For examples, principles of effective time management and communications are relevant regardless of the particular practice setting. Likewise, hiring and other human resource skills are needed and appropriate to all health settings. Because nursing management of the day-to-day operations in home care and in hospitals differs significantly, Chapter 12, titled The Nurse Manager in Home Care, Community Health, and Hospice, describes how to effectively manage daily nursing activities in these settings.

Some other special features have been included to make this revised edition easy to use. Helpful Manager's Tips, listed as behavioral strategies, are listed in every chapter. Glossaries to help you more easily understand unfamiliar terms are included for both Chapter 8, Resource Management and Budgeting Basics, and Chapter 9, Legal Issues and Risk Management. A summary concludes each chapter. Resources for further professional development, including lists of relevant organizations and certification programs, as well as a list of suggested readings, are provided at the end of each chapter.

Because contemporary health facilities are continuing to evolve at a rapid pace, this extensively revised third edition includes suggestions for coping with the changes and stresses brought about by restructuring, reorganization, and reengineering. It also addresses the major health care issues and concerns that have arisen as a result of the widespread adoption of managed care and case management. Rather than treat continuous quality improvement (CQI) in a separate chapter, this third edition carries the quality issues and processes incorporated throughout the book to reflect their importance as an integral part of all management functions and day-to-day operations.

Finally, because of the complexities of factors creating the nursing (and other care professionals) shortage, there is a new chapter in this edition. Chapter 4, Recruitment and Retention of Staff: A Strategic Overview, is devoted solely to improving retention of staff and addresses opportunities for recruitment. There is no question that the advanced technology and acuity levels of patients (particularly in hospitals) increases the needs for clinicians who are competent clinically and adept at problem solving. This chapter seeks to provide some practical tips for application in this long-term dilemma.

The process of becoming a competent and effective manager is a growth journey, unique to each nurse and to each specific work environment. This book was created to facilitate this process.

T.M. Marrelli

Contents

6   Effective Communication, 177
Margaret Sharp
T.M. Marrelli

13 Where to from Here?, 351
T.M. Marrelli

CHAPTER 1

THE NURSE MANAGER ROLE TODAY

T.M. MARRELLI

When the first edition of this book was published in the early 1990s, health care was starting its massive initial evolutionary process. Since then, the core of nursing management has remained the same; however, many more internal and external events are affecting the role of the nurse manager. External regulatory forces coupled with a severely constrained financial environment are refocusing the way in which house managers are trained, viewed, evaluated, and compensated for their endeavors to maintain stability in the face of change. This book seeks to provide the information needed to assist nurse managers in this tumultuous time in health care.

Congratulations! Because of your clinical expertise, education, and other valued traits, you were promoted to a management position. Yet the process of becoming an effective manager does not happen overnight. It is a growth process unique to each nurse and specific environment. The team members you will be managing are unique and are oftentimes the most positive part of this position. Manager and staff all work together to meet the organizational goals, as defined in your employer's mission statement and nursing philosophy. Any new role is exciting, but it can also be anxiety producing. Whether you are a new manager or new to a facility with a new team, you need to know you are not alone and you may need some insights to help you through this period of transition. The team members you will be managing are unique and are oftentimes the most positive part of the position. You can do it!

THE MIDDLE MANAGEMENT DILEMMA

The new nurse manager must remain flexible in order to survive in the health care industry, regardless of the specific setting, and the most valuable tool in her/his arsenal is the combination of clinical and business expertise. In addition, sharp clinical skills and a business acumen for financial, time, and other resource management make the experienced nurse manager a prime choice for promotion to middle and senior management positions.

In hospitals and other patient areas experiencing decreasing lengths of stay coupled with increased patient acuity and turnover, the professional nurse in a leadership role must manage more responsibilities in a shortened time frame. The learning needs of managers are varied and complex, covering various fields of study. In addition, as health care delivery has changed, so too has the diversity of settings in which nurses manage.

Nurses may practice in one or more of the following settings over the course of their careers: hospitals, community health programs, hospices, urgent care centers, outpatient surgical centers, subacute units, extended care facilities, home health agencies, specialized hospital centers, physician offices, long-term care, or other settings. Other areas include day care programs, office practices, health maintenance organizations (HMOs), occupational health, business settings, payer organizations, policy positions, as well as other sites.

With increased demands to improve quality, promote safety, decrease costs, and enhance customer service, it is sometimes difficult to aspire to a management role. Because staff nursing pay has increased over the years, the financial rewards of being a manager may sometimes not be as enticing as they once might have been. We sometimes wonder if it is worth the hassle to work extra hours (without additional overtime pay); to be the recipient of the grievances of patients, staff, physicians, and management; and to carry the burden of making sure a unit or other area functions smoothly with competent caregivers. Some nurses decline management positions because they desire continued patient contact and do not want the added responsibility of 24-hour accountability. However, for the nurse who truly desires to make a positive change in the care of patients and has the enthusiasm and motivation to continually challenge the status quo, as well as the ability to maintain excellent clinical skills, nursing management can be the perfect job.

ROLE TRANSITION

Too often, professional nurses in any health care setting receive little formal management training before being promoted to the management team. It is the nurse's education that ultimately facilitates the successful role transition to manager. Once a nurse is promoted, it is thought that some skills may have to be changed or even unlearned. The challenge is to provide new managers with the information and skills needed to develop fundamental and successful behaviors and thought processes that effectively contribute to work accomplishment.

Luckily, most new nurse managers bridge parts of this gap using the clinical and educational experiences they bring to the new position. These skills are what nurses do well every day, including communicating, planning, organizing, prioritizing, and documenting. All are talents that lend themselves well to the new role of nurse manager. Further expansion into the nurse manager role is based on learned management behaviors including planning, organizing, directing, controlling, and evaluating.

The nurse manager's orientation should follow a formal plan. It is important to note that no program, however well thought-out, can address all the issues that will confront the new nurse manager in any setting. Some skills develop fully only after a period of time with the integration of knowledge and practice. These good habits become "automatic" only with use.

All change is stressful, even though it may be experienced as good or bad. Some of the most frequently cited causes of stress include vague role descriptions and adapting to what may be perceived as continual change. We know that all nurses experience stress. The new nurse manager has the additional stress of changing roles and integrating herself/himself into the organization as a manager. It is important at the onset for the new manager to always look for opportunities in every problem. (For an in-depth discussion of stress and its management, see Chapter 10, Taking Care of Yourself and Your Staff.)

Example of a Position Description for a Nurse Manager

We have all seen position descriptions for a nurse manager that enumerate various responsibilities. The nurse manager is responsible for:

1. Staffing, organizing, and coordinating patient care 24 hours a day.
2. Developing, administering, and evaluating goals and objectives for the unit.
3. Providing for cost-effective use of human and material resources consistent with goals of cost containment and productivity, while providing outcome-oriented quality patient care.
4. Participating in the management process.
5. Problem-solving.
6. Directing the activities of subordinates.
7. Identifying systems problems.
8. Providing for the continuing education of staff.
9. Developing and evaluating staff.
10. Providing clinical assistance and consultation.
11. Developing, administering, and ensuring compliance with policies and procedures and any applicable governmental and accreditation regulations.
12. Assuming other responsibilities as assigned by the supervisor.
13. Role modeling and associated retention activities.

Appendix 1-1 presents an actual job description/competency review tool.

Reading this list and reflecting on what the nurse manager actually does on a daily basis can make the job seem overwhelming. The actual activities may include attending or chairing meetings, evaluating and counseling staff members, assigning or reassigning schedules, and myriad other functions. As we move toward a greater focus on outcomes or predetermined activity levels of patients at time of discharge (i.e., a satisfied patient whose needs have been met successfully by discharge), we see why this new role is stressful. Inpatient nursing staff comfort and care for patients 24 hours a day. The nursing staff coordinate all activities related to the patient. These activities are multifaceted and complex and range from clinical tests to therapeutic interventions.

Because of increased specialization of health care providers and complexity of patient problems and associated technology, multiple and varied services are provided to patients. Patients and their families and friends look to the professional nurse for quality care and the promotion of patient safety.

Health Care Changes Affecting Nursing Management

Four major factors contribute to the changes that are affecting nursing management.
1. The current economics of the health care system including managed care, capitation, and utilization management
    •   In response to spiraling health care costs, third-party payers (government, commercial, and business self-insurers) have increased their scrutiny of expensive hospital and other health services. Capitation, case management, and utilization management have all been influential in decreasing lengths of hospital stays.
    •   Decreased lengths of stay typically cause patients to have acute nursing care needs met in a shorter time frame. The phrase sometimes heard to describe this phenomenon is "quicker and sicker," referring to the patient's status at discharge. Ten years ago the same patient population would have been hospitalized for longer periods. Today much hospital care is provided on an outpatient-only basis.
    •   Clinical documentation often is the basis on which third-party payers make payment or denial decisions. Nursing documentation often becomes the core or foundation for providing substantiating documentation for a payment or denial determination.
2. The emphasis on quality, safety, and outcomes in health care
    •   As health care quality improvement and management programs have evolved, patient care outcomes are recognized as valid indicators of quality of care.
    •   The Joint Commission on Accreditation of Healthcare Organizations (JCAHO) has focused on interdisciplinary planning across a care continuum to create an atmosphere for the entire health care network to work together to achieve desirable patient outcomes.

        Depending on your work setting, there are other accreditation entities that may set or define the standards. Some of these include Commission on Accreditation of Rehabilitation Facilities (CARF), Community Health Accreditation Program (CHAP), and others. Regardless of the accreditation entity, the manager must be oriented to and have a baseline knowledge of the standards. JCAHO standards and an in-depth discussion of the outcome-oriented quality management and the improvement of organization performance processes are discussed throughout this text.

3. The emphasis on standardization of care, practices, protocol, and clinical pathways and the increasing recognition and empowerment of the nursing profession

   - All patients are entitled to a certain level, or standard, of nursing care. As patients become proactive consumers in the purchase of health care, patient satisfaction with care becomes key to a health care network's reputation and ultimate survival. Nurses, because of their healing skills and proficiency and the considerable amount of time spent with patients and families, are pivotal in achieving patient satisfaction. It is also known that, generally, satisfied patients are less likely to pursue legal methods to resolve disputes. The nursing roles of patient advocate, listener, and teacher have become even more significant in recent years.
   - All professions, including nursing, have recognized standards of care. As society has become more litigious, the professional nurse must be aware of State Nurse Practice Acts and other accepted standards of care. Other standards include health care institution policies and procedures, state and federal regulations, and the published standards of professional nursing organizations. It is important to keep current and informed of professional standards in nursing specialties or other groups and to be aware of the standards of professional nursing practice.
   - Health care settings, such as hospitals, also have their own nursing standards of care. Some examples are:
     - Every patient shall have a nursing assessment that is comprehensive, addresses specific patient needs, is performed by a registered nurse at least every _____ hours, and is documented in the patient's record.
     - Discharge planning will begin on admission and includes collaboration with other members of the health team and involves the patient, family, and caregivers.
   - Through complete and effective documentation, nursing demonstrates that the standard of care has been met.

4. The emphasis on effectiveness and efficiency in health care

   - As health care settings and hospitals continue to streamline, administrative tasks historically performed by nurses are being examined. Repetitive or duplicative activities, which can be found in some documentation systems, are inefficient. Better ways are being explored to meet patient needs while freeing nurses for other important activities. Patient care redesign, or reengineering, is one of many ways that patient care functions are being examined and reviewed for appropriate use of expensive staff resources.

- Considering these tumultuous changes in the current health care environment, we see why the nurse manager role is so important today. All these factors create an environment where the nurse has more responsibilities and less time in which to do them. Because of the many tasks that must be undertaken or delegated, flexibility is a necessity for effective nurse managers.
- The nursing (and other health care team member) shortage. This area is addressed in depth in Chapter 4, Recruitment and Retention of Staff: A Strategic Overview.

What Does the Nurse Manager Do?

Core duties that nurse managers assume, regardless of setting, include assignments, delegation, meetings, performance evaluations, budgets, writing and interpersonal skills, and 24-hour accountability for the area. All of these functions demand effective (and ongoing) communications. Nurse managers must blend business and clinical skills and perspectives. Because the bulk of the manager's education focused on clinical nursing, it is the business side that usually needs additional educational emphasis. The nurse manager, to be effective, also creates an environment that empowers staff to grow professionally. The staff are encouraged to identify problems, recommend and implement solutions, and evaluate outcomes. The staff "own" their issues and work as a group for resolution. Most importantly, the staff achieve patient goals while adhering to policies and the mission statement of the health care setting. The nurse manager is the key link between staff and upper management. This role, by definition alone, imparts significant influence and power.

The actual day-to-day operational duties of the nurse manager can be as varied as the practice area of responsibility. In a hospital or a home health agency, for example, the activities are focused on the patient, the consumer of the needed services. The nurse manager, by position and personality, sets the tone for the effective completion of numerous activities. In patient care settings, the goal of these activities is a satisfied customer.

Utilizing Power Effectively

Being new to management, the nurse manager needs to understand power and how to use it effectively. Leah Curtin, in her editorial *Power: The Trap of Trappings,* gives a very short but succinct definition of power: ". . . the ability to *do* something."[1] The corporate culture of an organization may be very subtle, but either through observation of formal structures (e.g., the organizational chart) or informal structures (e.g., seeing who really controls the place) the new manager should try to identify where the power is located and learn how to access that power to get the job done.

Just as important as gaining and developing power is the ability to do what is right with power—not only to use it for personal gain. As Curtin explained in the mentioned article, the concept of power includes action, knowledge, position, judgment, and perception. Power is not static; it is not a place. Power is intoxicating and its results can be devastating to staff and an organization if used in a nonproductive manner. It needs to be activated for the good of the group.

A new manager has the power that is associated with the hierarchy of position. However, that power can be eroded if not used effectively or if allowed to be usurped by another. Power becomes another tool for the manager to manage a department effectively. Even though it may appear superficial, it is important for nurse managers to look the part in order to receive the power that is due them. Dress as a manager, act as a manager—body language and communication styles exude power. That is not to say that aggressive behavior denotes power. Knowing when to use which behavioral style (e.g., aggressiveness, assertiveness, passivity, submission) is an important element of gaining a power base.

Power should never be used to dominate or totally control subordinates. Respect the individuality, responsibility, and creativity of staff and use power to develop and mentor them to be more involved in team efforts. Delegate, mentor, and manage through performance goals and expectations. Leadership (as described in depth in Chapter 2, Management: An Overview) is intertwined with effective use of power.

Just as important as communicating power to subordinates is the need to gain power with superiors. An old management saying goes, "the job of a manager is to make her/his boss look good." The purpose of a nursing middle management position is to manage a patient care department, meeting quality, regulatory/accreditation, safety, and financial objectives. The senior manager is responsible for a number of departments, overseeing the strategic direction and leadership of the organization. An effective manager is aware of the familial relationship and nurtures positive growth of that important relationship with a supervisor.

A senior manager can definitely give valuable feedback on various options to review the management of or answer to a specific problem. However, the responsibility of the middle manager is to operate the area, abiding by legal and accrediting standards and regulations without continually complaining to the senior manager about the job's difficulty or needing to discuss *every* operational decision that must be made. By having clearly stated strategic organizational goals and objectives that are filtered down to the appropriate departments, managers should have a general understanding of the status of the organization and receive the approval to operate within given parameters.

Senior management should be informed of the general direction of the unit and how it interacts and intersects with other departments. Problems that may affect another department or financially or legally affect the organization should be brought to the attention of the senior manager. It is the responsibility of the nurse manager always to inform her/his superior immediately of a potentially controversial or volatile situation, so that the senior manager isn't "broadsided" by an angry physician, family members, or other managers without having the appropriate information to respond or defuse the situation. Besides being frustrated, the senior manager faces embarrassment when caught unaware of a problem within the purview of a subordinate manager.

Be supportive of your supervisor; this, however, does not mean saying yes to everything. Rather, provide insightful, positive feedback and try to view situations as your manager would—see the forest, instead of only the trees. When time and responsibilities permit, request special projects to work on. Accept new responsibilities that are delegated as a professional. Provide your manager with both an analysis of what impact the new responsibilities will have on your ability to operate your area and possible solutions that will allow you to accomplish the new tasks.

The nurse manager may possess and use the following types of power to achieve her/his goals:

Coercive power As implied, this is the power to inflict some type of punishment. This is universally seen as the weakest type of power.

Expert power The power commanded by special knowledge or competence. This may include degrees, certification, publication, or other skills.

Legitimate power The power given to exert authority because of a position or title.

Referent power The personal power of the individual. An example is a person with a motivating personality.

Reward power The power to bestow or withhold something valued by another person.

The nurse manager's clinical skills may be used in the management role—if only as a resource for staff members (expert power). Some people theorize that a nurse manager, to be effective, must have strong clinical skills. This strong knowledge base may command immediate respect from staff and physicians. As health care becomes more specialized and the nursing shortage escalates, this may not be realistic.

The new nurse manager has tools available to appear powerful (see Manager's Tip 1-1). Initially, the manager's title alone will lend some legitimate power. Manager's Tips 1-2 and 1-3 on p. 9 present suggestions for maintaining personal power and making a successful transition to effective nurse manager.

CHANGE MANAGEMENT

Nurse managers are the "captain of the ship" in terms of assisting staff to view the positive element of change and leading staff toward their own positive growth. As the health care industry has grown and become a more competitive business, the public perception of the industry has changed from one of compassionate caring to a more profit-motivated enterprise. Whether this is true or not, consumers of health care want to be treated with respect and "get their money's worth." They want positive, quantifiable results to be achieved or maintained. However, it is not always easy to mesh positive outcomes, customer satisfaction, and cost reductions. The complexity of such a task can take its toll on managers, as well as frontline staff members.

MANAGER'S TIP 1-1

NINE WAYS TO APPEAR MORE POWERFUL

✔ Powerful people usually appear to be calm and unflappable.
✔ Powerful people feel comfortable saying, "Let's look into that further" (they know what they don't know).
✔ Powerful people usually speak less and listen more.
✔ Powerful people exude confidence in themselves and in their problem-solving abilities.
✔ Powerful people are usually optimistic.
✔ Powerful people set appropriate limits for themselves, their resources, and their staff.
✔ Powerful people may not always feel that way, but they have learned to act powerful and know the behaviors and feelings will follow.
✔ Powerful people dress for the role, modeling a potential mentor or successful manager in the organization.
✔ Powerful people are committed to their decisions and stay on course/remain focused.

MANAGER'S TIP 1-2

FOUR WAYS TO ACQUIRE POWER

✔ Ensure that an ongoing educational program is available and includes an orientation program for new staff RNs. Your attendance at this program accomplishes two goals: (1) you learn what new nurses are taught and (2) you learn more about the health system or institution.
✔ Participate in educational endeavors, such as pursuing an additional degree, certification, or learning in another area of interest.
✔ Network with other nurse managers on an ongoing basis. This peer support is invaluable for problem-solving support and builds morale.
✔ Acquire, develop, and maintain a mentor/mentee relationship.

MANAGER'S TIP 1-3

29 BEHAVIORS TO HELP YOU DURING THE TRANSITION

As a new nurse manager it is also important to recognize your own limitations while learning your new role. This can be accomplished initially with the following behaviors.
✔ Recognize and accept that, initially, it is okay to learn, listen, and observe.

Continued

29 BEHAVIORS TO HELP YOU DURING THE TRANSITION — cont'd

✔ Resist the urge to immediately intervene and change how things have been done in the past, unless patient or staff safety is in jeopardy. Change may be needed, but it may be more successful and acceptable to staff members if their input is sought after you have become the nurse manager in practice and perception. This will also allow for a thorough assessment of the problem and identification of possible solutions and implications.

✔ Remember that the nursing or scientific process is an effective tool for problem-solving and evaluation.

✔ Use the initial weeks as time to gather data and learn about the organization, daily routines, and your new staff.

✔ Remember that it is okay to NOT have an answer for all problems or issues that staff members may want to lay at your door. Direct the staff, because they are close to the problems and therefore are often the best source for effective solutions, to develop possible solutions for problems. This approach empowers the staff by valuing their input and may lead to team problem resolution. (They have more information!)

✔ Know that it is okay to ask your staff's input in the decision-making process whenever they are affected by or know the problem. Let them "own" problems and their solutions.

✔ Develop your own management style. You possess unique skills and traits that can be effectively used as a manager.

✔ Know that your unique individual presence will ultimately become your style. Observe managers you respect and add the behaviors you want to emulate to your repertoire. All managers have inherent personality traits. Make the best ones work for you.

✔ Seek ways to understand and motivate your staff. Dale Carnegie is credited with saying that there is only one way to get anybody to do anything—by making the other person want to do it. There is no other way. With this statement in mind, an effective manager learns what specifically motivates individual team members.

✔ Ask for feedback from peer managers or others you trust.

✔ Create an environment of cooperation through your example.

✔ Act and look like a manager. It has been said that perception looks like reality. If you make this leap of faith initially and successfully, so too will others. Observe the behaviors, dress, manners, and people skills of managers and past and present mentors you respect. Emulate those desired behaviors!

✔ Cultivate a positive relationship with your boss. Keep in mind that this important relationship may affect your overall success with the organization.

✔ Communicate clearly, both in writing and in speaking. Communications should be succinct and true. Always validate information before stating facts or committing them to paper. Use spell check on everything!

✔ Practice visualizing yourself as an effective manager. See yourself dealing effectively in a given situation. Practice this by trying it out behaviorally; then evaluate your actions, the process, and the outcome achieved.

✔ Recognize and accept that you cannot have all the right answers and knowledge all the time (and that is okay).

✔ Believe that you are the best person for this job.

✔ Give up on trying to initially address all identified problems.

29 BEHAVIORS TO HELP YOU DURING THE TRANSITION — cont'd

✔ Remember that, in time, role ambiguity will give way to role definition.

✔ Develop, maintain, and ultimately increase and use your sense of humor. All nurse managers must have a well-developed sense of humor as a stress management tool for self and staff and, where appropriate, for patients, families, and visitors. The inherent healing value of humor is finally being recognized.

✔ Prioritize and think through problems before acting. Some problems will resolve themselves; others may not be "yours." Those remaining need to be acted on.

✔ Remember that earning respect and credibility from your staff may take time.

✔ Understand that your staff looks to you as role model, teacher, and resource.

✔ Realize that sometimes you need to (diplomatically) rock the boat. Being a successful manager requires taking some risks.

✔ Remember that, although you may not think your boss is always right, she/he is still the boss and as such has inherent power.

✔ Accept that some of your decisions may not be popular. This does not mean that your decisions are wrong or that you are not a likable person.

✔ Recognize that during the role transition, one of the most difficult realizations is that you are no longer a staff nurse but a manager. Former peers, now staff members, may no longer confide in you and you may feel isolated. New peer networks and relationships need to be established.

✔ Remember that there is always more to learn.

✔ Realize that your staff is the key to getting all work accomplished.

As mentioned earlier in this chapter, hospitals are no longer the only place where health care is delivered to a large number of people. No longer can patient care or other health care staff go to school, graduate, be hired at a local hospital, and expect to remain there for the rest of their careers. In fact, some people believe that "job security" is an oxymoron in today's environment. Many health care organizations are large systems and as such will be affected by the fluctuation of supply and demand and cannot remain impervious to what is going on in the local and national economies.

The old saying, "the only constant is change," has never been more apparent than in health care. In order to survive this tumultuous time, nurse managers must have a clear sense of where they want to go with their careers, as well as where their organization is going. Strategic direction and leadership have never been more important. Managers must recognize all their personal skills and be able to translate their worth and areas of interest and knowledge to staff, superiors, mentors, and potential employers. Clinical expertise used to be the ticket to a management position. Now, in addition to maintaining clinical excellence, the nurse manager must exhibit financial acumen and human resource management and possess customer service as well as critical thinking skills. No one trait is more important than another, and the nurse manager must understand and translate into objective behaviors a balance between all the needed skills available in his/her own unique skill-set. Most important, the manager must understand and know at what time and in what situation certain skills are needed and should be employed.

It is important for the nurse manager to look beyond herself/himself to those on the patient care team for support and the inner resources to meet the challenge of operating on a daily basis in a positive, caring atmosphere. As Roberta Nicholson strategized in her article on developing managerial resources, ". . . tapping these strengths and developing them can help nurse executives facilitate a widespread increase in psychic energy, which can be channeled toward carrying out the goals and objectives of the organization."[2] Nicholson described the nine essential guidelines for successful nurse manager behavior as such:

1. Use mature defense mechanisms whenever possible:
    *   Sublimation
    *   Altruism
    *   Suppression
    *   Anticipation
    *   Sense of humor
2. Be able to give and receive love.
3. Exhibit a concern for the life and growth of those you love.
4. View responsibility as a voluntary act in response to your own needs.
5. Define respect as the ability to view the uniqueness of self and others.
6. Understand that knowledge of self and others is the cornerstone of respect.
7. Become committed—develop your mission statement in life.
8. Act with influence, or a sense of control through imagination, knowledge, skills, and choice.
9. View change as a stimulating challenge that enhances growth.[2]

Assuming the New Role

It is important from the onset that you firmly establish yourself as the new nurse manager. Hold a staff meeting as soon as possible after the announcement of your assumption of the position. Plan a meeting for each shift. For consistency, use the same agenda for all meetings. When in these meetings, keep in mind the nine ways to appear more powerful shown in Manager's Tip 1-1 on p. 9.

Your First Staff Meeting as New Nurse Manager

The meeting's goals are to formalize your new role with the staff members, introduce yourself, and begin meeting your staff. At this initial meeting:

*   Welcome everyone and introduce yourself
*   Have everyone introduce themselves
*   Speak briefly about your qualifications

An example would be, "As some of you know, I have my BSN and have worked at St. Elsewhere General for 7 years in cardiac rehab. I look forward to the challenge of being the nurse manager of your new cardiac step-down unit and to working with

MANAGER'S TIP 1-4

TIPS FOR CONDUCTING INITIAL STAFF MEETINGS

✔ Be aware that staff meetings and their management can be difficult even for experienced nurse managers.

✔ Reassure your staff that you will not be making any changes initially and that you will be observing and speaking to patients and staff members to learn the daily operational routines. This reassurance is needed at this time to decrease staff anxiety about a new manager and more changes.

✔ Share that you will be having similar meetings with the rest of the staff (if that's your plan) and will make rounds on all shifts with team leaders as part of your orientation.

✔ Do say that change is difficult for everyone and you are interested in their input.

✔ Reassure them you will not be changing representatives (again, if true) to the nursing practice council, the product selection committee, or other committees.

✔ Do not be offended if all staff members don't attend. Some staff members may act out or be complacent or appear uninterested. Change is difficult for all!

✔ Keep brief minutes, including attendance, topics discussed, and outcomes accomplished to share with staff members who were not able to attend the meeting. (Box 1-1 presents format for sample minutes).

✔ Always open with a welcome and state how long the meeting will last. Start on time and, when the end of the meeting is near, start wrapping up. An example of a closing statement might be, "We have a few minutes left, so we need to come to a conclusion."

✔ As nurse manager and often chairperson of the meeting, remember to plan for factors such as the logistics of time, place, and dates. Keep in mind also that the best attended and most successful meetings often include food. Some managers have luncheon meetings to capitalize on this fact.

you. Please let me know any recommendations you may have because I am open to better ways of doing things. Initially, I'll be in orientation and will be scheduling time on all shifts to get to know everyone and the patient routines." (See Manager's Tip 1-4 for suggestions about how to conduct the meeting.)

For a more in-depth discussion about conducting or leading meetings, please refer to Chapter 5, Day-to-Day Operations.

YOUR ORIENTATION

By title you are now a part of the management team and will be oriented to the organization (see Manager's Tip 1-5 on p. 14). Some power has been transferred to you by your new position and by your knowledge before the promotion. As professionals, all nurses perform some management functions. Staff nurses manage teams of patients, equipment, and clinical environments. They delegate as team leaders and assign duties. The leadership role inherent in RN education moves the

--------------------------------------- box 1-1 ---------------------------------------

SAMPLE MINUTES FORMAT

Items to include in minutes:
- Topic
- Discussion
- Recommendation
- Action(s)
- Who
- Due date

Sample agenda items include:
- Welcome and introductions of new staff members
- Update on performance improvement report
- Planning for upcoming holiday staffing
- Falls prevention program presentation
- Parking update
- In-house educational opportunity
- New computer system update, with schedule for inservices
- Next planned staff meeting date(s)

MANAGER'S TIP 1-5

AN ORIENTATION CHECKLIST

The following information and resources should be readily available to you as a new nurse manager. If not, you may need to tailor an orientation program for yourself with the help of your supervisor.
- ✔ Typical hours of the nurse managers in the setting
- ✔ Tour of the facility or other organization
- ✔ The shifts available to staff (e.g., 8, 10, 12 hours, or other options)
- ✔ Organizational chart specifying your position, your supervisor, and any direct reports
- ✔ Position descriptions for nurse manager, staff, and other care providers
- ✔ The organization's policy and procedure manuals (administrative and clinical)
- ✔ Human resource policy manuals
- ✔ Information regarding other policies (e.g., if, when, and where smoking is permitted)
- ✔ Location and hours of staff library, and types of material available
- ✔ Mentor, peer, or other manager orientation programs
- ✔ Information regarding continuing education and reimbursement policy
- ✔ Other, based on your specific learning needs

nurse to the head of the team. The successful nurse manager integrates these past roles with the knowledge base of sound principles in day-to-day operations. These behaviors coupled with learned skills make the nurse manager unique.

The new nurse manager has a special and well-known theory available throughout this transition. The nursing process can be readily applied to management in individual patient care scenarios and in the larger view of the health care or hospital system, which may span multiple departments, services, and across geographic areas.

MEETINGS WITH PEER MANAGERS

As a manager you need to understand the workings and specific functions of areas with which your unit or department frequently interacts. It is also helpful to get to know your peers, the managers of these areas. Setting up a meeting with these managers enables you to gather needed information and begin to network with your peers.

To be effective, a nurse manager needs information about the important services and departments listed in Appendix 1-2 at the end of this chapter. The suggestions presented in Manager's Tip 1-6 can help you maximize the value of your peer manager meetings. The peer managers you meet at these meetings may become part of your support group at work. They may become friends or important allies who can help you achieve your unit's and the organization's goals. They may have interpersonal, budgetary, or other skills you will want to learn (Box 1-2).

---

box 1-2

THE RIGHT STUFF: A SKILL-SET FOR SUCCESS

The following list of competencies is the skill-set that effective managers possess:
- Critical thinking skills
- Communication skills
- Negotiating skills
- Computer literacy skills
- The ability to embrace change and/or ambiguity and adapt
- Team-building skills
- Goal/outcome focused (can see the big picture through daily operations and details)
- Compassionate
- Respectful of diversity
- Optimistic with a sense of humor
- Interested in ongoing learning

As you can see from reviewing this list, many of these areas are improved with additional learning and your own motivation. As you go through your orientation period, when you identify a mentor, and throughout your career, keep these areas in mind for learning opportunities. In some of these listed areas, there is always more to learn. For example, with computer literacy, your organization may also support this area of knowledge for all of their managers, through ongoing classes and other mechanisms. When possible, take advantage of any of these offered opportunities to increase your knowledge base and the tools in your skill-set.

MANAGER'S TIP 1-6

EIGHT TIPS TO LEARN MORE FROM SCHEDULED ORIENTATION MEETINGS

✔ See these meetings as informational and networking sessions.
✔ Decide what information you want to learn.
✔ Think about the specific questions you want answered.
✔ From these meetings, consider possible actions to improve operations on the unit.
✔ Ask specific questions.
✔ Write clear, detailed notes for future reference; these notes can also serve as a source of information in the orientation of new nursing staff members.
✔ These meetings should be informational and only for meeting peers; withhold any criticisms at these introductory meetings.
✔ Remember, first impressions are important. Put your best foot forward.

TAKING TIME TO TAKE STOCK

During your learning and growth period it is appropriate and helpful to review your actions and accomplishments periodically. Questions may include:

• What did I accomplish or learn today?
• What did I learn from my staff, peer managers, and boss?
• On a scale of 1 to 10, how successful was I in achieving the goals I set for today? This week? This month?
• What did I do especially well that makes me feel proud?
• What can I do better the next time?
• What do I need help with and who can I ask for help?
• Did I visualize my success before I acted it out?

Most importantly, recognize that every issue and its resolution adds to your knowledge base of experience and leads to more successes in the future.

Nurse Manager Competencies

As a new nurse manager, you must measure your own competency as well as that of subordinate staff. Although the nurse manager is responsible for a wide range of activities, in frontline or first-line management, patient care competencies may be just as important as managerial competencies during this time of restructure and change. (For further explanation of competency-based achievement, see Chapter 3, Human Resource Management.)

According to a 1994 study of nurse managers by the American Organization of Nurse Executives (AONE), from rural to urban settings, ". . . human and leadership competencies are the most important for effectiveness in the nurse manager role." Effective communication and decision making were identified as the most significant skills necessary for nurse managers. Other strategies that ranked high included:

1. Effective staffing strategies
2. Counseling strategies
3. Performance evaluations
4. Team-building strategies
5. Delegation
6. Change process
7. Conflict resolution
8. Problem-solving[3]

Financial performance continues to be a major concern for new managers as they are confronted with increased pressure to adhere to tighter budgets. The ability to balance financial with quality and regulatory compliance goals becomes more of a challenge as health care moves into the future.

The Model of the Future: Patient-Centered Care

Patient-centered care is a term that has been used for a number of years in psychiatric treatment settings. However, during the past few years it has become a term synonymous with patient care planning in all types of health care settings. For the new nurse manager it is very important to understand the meaning of the term and how it is or has been applied in your unique work environment.

Patient care redesign is the process a group of patient care team members undertakes when analyzing the needs of patients and beginning the task of redesigning the implementation and flow of care a patient receives while in a particular setting. The implementation may include which team member does what, when, and where for the assigned patient. Patient-centered care is usually a goal of patient care redesign or reengineering and includes the integration of interdisciplinary care. Unfortunately, redesign, or reengineering, has gained a negative connotation because it was used in many health care settings as the primary tool to downsize or rightsize the number of care providers, particularly registered nurses, at the inpatient bedside.

Primary care, the nursing model of care from the mid-to-late 1970s until today, stressed the importance of the registered nurse in providing "total" care to an assigned group of patients, from giving bed baths, to providing medications and treatments; this allowed the RN to assess the needs of a patient and to problem-solve, as appropriate. The financial impact of managed care, decreased hospital census, and increased pay rates for registered nurses converged until a crisis point arose and the system needed a solution.

With public demands for more patient involvement, increased competition among care providers, tighter reimbursement regulations, and the need for quantifiable predetermined patient outcomes, patient-centered care was a model of care ripe for implementation. There are many ways to begin developing a patient-centered care model, but the most important element is placing the needs of the patient first. Quality of care and outcomes have to be the driver of this process because this undertaking is not just quick financial solutions for the health care entity.

The professional nurse is the ideal manager for patient care teams because her/his education and orientation are geared toward caring for the whole patient, physically, psychosocially, and spiritually. At the same time, the nurse manager must be constantly aware of the traditional "turf" issues surrounding other health care professionals, and disciplines who have worked "alone" in the past may resent being managed by a nurse. Reaching out and involving these staff members in the planning process as much as possible and having them interact with and get to know personally the other team members may often act as a catalyst in bringing the team together. Remember that all other members of the team have important contributions to make toward the patients achieving their goals.

The improvement of organizational performance (IOP) and the continuous quality improvement (CQI) processes are ideal ways to present patient care delivery processes for review. By having a multidisciplinary committee composed of both clinical and administrative staff systematically review current literature on practice patterns and standards of care, as well as analyze the customer service, quality outcomes, and financial resources at your organization required to attain a certain goal, diagnosis, or outcome of care, more rational decisions can be made. The process allows the staff members who know the most about the needs and desires of their patients to verbalize their concerns, present their ideas, and assist in deciding what will be the "best" model for this organization.

Marianne Dunn et al described the *Expert Panel Nursing Staffing and Resource Management Model* developed at the Veterans Administration to review the current nursing staffing model and revamp it for patient care in the future. As the authors explain, ". . . the expert panel method is based on the beliefs that the best decisions about staffing are made by knowledgeable nurses themselves . . . who are able to consider the many elements that go into providing patient care (and) can make fair and equitable decisions about nurse staffing requirements using their 'professional judgment'."[4] In this model, the panel systematically reviewed the structure, process, and outcomes of all areas providing either direct or indirect patient care; it began with the appointment of an implementation coordinator and went through the identification of final staffing recommendations. The outcome of the project included a shifting of nursing resources from one area to another as the data gathered indicated; in some cases, skill mix change or staff reduction in certain areas occurred. The changes were met with less resistance by staff because of the existence of data that supported either the staff reduction or addition.

For the new nurse manager, it is important to understand the process of project development and staff involvement (as much as possible) in the decision-making process. A thorough comprehension of change theory, as noted earlier in this chapter, is helpful in assisting staff to understand and work with the team on improvement of patient care systems. Change must be embraced as "the norm." Collaboration with other health care managers undergoing redesign is also helpful as a means to vent frustrations, commend successes, and learn by experience. It is imperative that the new nurse manager refrain from complaining about the process or any of the individuals, either peer managers, senior management, staff, or others involved in the process, to subordinates. It is counterproductive to inform staff of dissent within the planning group and ultimately lends itself to feelings of undue concern and fear of future outcomes.

It is imperative to have the team act as one, assisting each other when necessary and sometimes crossing traditional professional boundaries to care for the patient. This is not to say one professional can act in the scope of practice for another, such as a respiratory therapist (RT) medicating a patient for an RN; rather, the RT might assist the nurse in positioning the patient in bed (even though the patient is not receiving RT treatments at that time).

Using the management techniques described in this book will assist the new nurse manager in motivating and uniting her/his team to strive for improved patient care outcomes and any other goals and objectives directed toward patient care.

Important Realizations

The following realizations may be helpful during your transition to your new nursing management role. Often it takes new nurse managers many months to reach these important and perhaps surprising realizations.

- Resources (financial, personnel, and material) are limited and they will probably become more limited in the future as health care organizations continue to face fiscal constraints.
- There are rarely (if ever) enough hours in the workday.
- One new nurse manager cannot fix all the problems that have plagued a particular organization or area for years, perhaps even decades.
- People, including your staff, manager, and even those from other departments, will want more from you than you can reasonably give. Learning how and when to say no diplomatically is essential to your health and well-being as well as to your success.
- Your health care institution may not adapt well to change.
- There is a "good-old-boy/girl" network in many work environments. You may be faced with one at your organization. If you cannot or do not want to join it, you will need to learn to work around it. Chances are you will not be able to be effective by ignoring it.
- What the institution or your supervisor says may be different from the behaviors and rules implemented; when this occurs, remember that actions speak louder than words.

- You are not responsible for all of the problems at your workplace. Only "own" and work on those that are truly yours.
- Most nurses and nurse managers are women. If you are a woman, assumptions may be made that you will take care of and fix everything for everyone. It is up to nurse managers to be effective role models and to not reinforce the belief that women are selfless caretakers. This is not to say that you may not nurture when appropriate, but you must set limits for long-term success.

SUMMARY

Although management may have inherent pitfalls, effective nurse managers can make positive, lasting impressions on numerous patients, families, and staff. The new nurse manager may feel isolated and inadequate. Conversely, the successful resolution of problems and the delicate handling of personnel issues leave a feeling of accomplishment like no other. Nurses blend complex healing technology with nurturing care. This combination is why patients and their families marvel at the profession and those skills brought to the bedside as well as many other settings.

However, problems are inevitable, and some days the hassles may seem overwhelming. Yet problems present opportunities for personal growth and satisfaction in problem resolution. Use your orientation time to get to know others in your facility and to learn from their experience. They will be glad that someone values their knowledge and expertise.

The transition from staff nurse to a leadership position of nurse manager can be a difficult process. The initial enthusiasm, pride, and fantasies to "fix" the system must ultimately be tempered with a realistic role identification and realistic goal setting. You can do it!

QUESTIONS FOR CONSIDERATION

1. List three changes/factors in the external health care environment that are impacting nursing management.
2. Identify four ways or behaviors that describe how powerful people appear.
3. Describe five topic areas that your orientation will cover/address.
4. Define three attributes in a nurse manager's tool or skill-set for success.
5. Discuss the care model of the future—be as specific as you can.

References

1. Curtin LL: Power: the trap of trappings, *Nursing Management,* June 1989, p. 7.
2. Nicholson R: Manager's primer for developing inner resources, *Nursing Management: Management Briefs,* August 1989, pp. 17-19.
3. Chase L: Nurse manager competencies, *Journal of Nursing Administration* 24(4S): 63, 1994.
4. Dunn MG, et al: Expert panel method for nurse staffing and resource management, *Journal of Nursing Administration* 25(10): 62, 1995.

For Further Reading

Belasco JA, Strayer RC: *The flight of the buffalo: to excellence, learning to let employees lead*, New York, 1993, Waverly Books.

Blumenthal D: Health care reform—past and future. *New England Journal of Medicine*, 332(7):465-468, 1995.

Boll ML: Middle management in nursing. Notes from the field, *Nursing Management* 21(2),1990.

Carnegie D: *How to win friends and influence people*, New York, 1990, Pocket Books.

Clinical managers help agency staff cope with growth, stress, *Hospital Home Health*, August, 9(8):108, 1992.

Clinicians: manage your move to manager, Executive advancement, *Hospitals*, March 5, 1991; 60.

Curtin LL: Power: the trap of trappings, *Nursing Management* 20(6):7, 1989.

Dunn MG, et al: Expert panel method for nurse staffing and resource management, *Journal of Nursing Administration* 25(10): 35, 1995.

Gage M: The patient-driven interdisciplinary care plan, *Journal of Nursing Administration* 24(4):44, 1994.

Griest DL, Belles DR: Health care executives: a personality profile, *Hospitals* 64(3):74, 1990.

Hamilton JM, Kiefer ME: Personal power: your key to success, *Nursing 90*, October 1990, 146-148.

Hood JN, Smith HL: Quality of work life in home care: the contribution of leaders; personal concern for staff. *Journal of Nursing Administration* 24(1):40, 1994.

Janz M: Perception of knowledge—what administrators and assistants know. *Journal of Gerontological Nursing*, August 1992, 7-12.

Kaplan SM: The nurse as a change agent. Professional Perspectives, *Pediatric Nursing* 16(6):603, 1990.

Mason D, Leavitt J, Chaffee M: *Policy and politics in nursing and health care*, St Louis, 2002, Saunders.

Mills et al: *Nursing administration: scope and standards of practice*, Washington, DC, 2003, American Nurses Association.

Patz J, et al: Middle nurse manager effectiveness, *Journal of Nursing Administration* 21(1):15, 1991.

Rosener JB: The ways women lead. *Harvard Business Review*, November-December, 1990, 119-134.

Rutledge DN, Donaldson NE: Building organizational capacity to engage in research utilization, *Journal of Nursing Administration* 25(10), 1995.

Sherry D: Coping with staffing shortages: strategies for survival, *Home Healthcare Nurse* 12(1):38, 1994.

Smith TC: Management skills for directors of nursing, *Journal of Nursing Administration* 23(9):38, 1993.

Werkheiser L, et al: The nurse manager resource peer: part II. *Nursing Management* 21(12):30, 1990.

APPENDIX 1-1

JOB DESCRIPTION / COMPETENCY REVIEW

TITLE: PCS Nurse Manager
Department: Patient Care Services
Reports to: Director of Nursing Services

JOB CODE: 112
GRADE: N 14
EXEMPT STATUS: E
LAST UPDATED: 03/XX

- Position Summary: Responsible for 24-hour operation of an assigned patient care unit(s). This includes the assessment, planning, provision, and evaluation of patient care and nursing services for the assigned area of responsibility. Also participates in the assessment, planning, provision, and evaluation of overall nursing services within the Patient Care Services (PCS) department; provides on-call shift supervision coverage as assigned.
- Experience: 3 to 5 years' related nursing experience required; previous supervisory nursing experience preferred.
- Education: Bachelor's degree in nursing or related field required.
- Required License/Credentials: *State-specific nursing license,* BLS certification.
- Other Required Skills: Critical thinking, analytical thinking, interpersonal skills, basic computer skills.
- Contact with Others: Regular internal and external contacts involving tact, discretion, and persuasion in order to obtain information and/or willing action or consent.
- Supervision Given: Supervises all PCS employees on assigned unit. Has primary responsibility for assigning personnel and directing workflow.
- Supervision Received: Uses own initiative in handling the majority of intradepartmental matters, consulting with the director only in instances of policy changes.

GENERAL PERFORMANCE STANDARDS	BELOW STANDARD (Note Comment)	MEETS STANDARD	EXCEEDS STANDARD (Note Comment)
A. Addresses problems/concerns with the person directly (when appropriate), via departmental chain of command, in a professional manner and appropriate time and place. (E)	☐	☐	N/A
B. Consistently adheres to all hospital and departmental policies, procedures, and standards. Performs duties consistent with established Code of Ethics and Professional Conduct and the center's Corporate Compliance Program. (E)	☐	☐	N/A
C. Consistently uses time at work effectively and productively. (E)	☐	☐	N/A
D. Demonstrates effective working relationships with others, in own department and other departments. (E)	☐	☐	N/A
E. Dresses in a manner consistent with departmental standards. (E)	☐	☐	N/A
F. Follows proper safety policies and standards and maintains safe work area. (E)	☐	☐	N/A
G. Maintains privacy/confidentiality of patient/clinical and proprietary business information at all times. Adheres to confidentiality agreement, maintains information technology password in confidential manner, and protects against inappropriate access by other individuals. (E)	☐	☐	N/A

H. E Maintains and enhances skills and knowledge through continuing education or other means as necessary.

[ ] BELOW STANDARD

[ ] MEETS STANDARD
- Complete all required mandatory educational sessions for the review year.

[ ] EXCEEDS STANDARD
- Attends at least one nonmandatory continuing educational session, inservice, seminar, etc., approved to be job-related (inhouse or outside).

I. E Maintains attendance within defined acceptability ranges as dictated by center policy.

[ ] BELOW STANDARD

[ ] MEETS STANDARD
- *Unscheduled absent shifts* occur less than **3.5%** of scheduled shifts.
- *Unscheduled incomplete shifts* occur less than **4.5%** of scheduled shifts.

[ ] EXCEEDS STANDARD
- *Unscheduled absent shifts* occur less than **1.5%** of scheduled shifts.
- *Unscheduled incomplete shifts* occur less than **2%** of scheduled shifts.

J. E Maintains pleasant and courteous manner and projects a positive, helpful image to all customers, including patients, families, visitors, referring physicians, and coworkers.

[ ] BELOW STANDARD

[ ] MEETS STANDARD
- Consistently follows telephone protocols by answering phones within three rings, identifying self by name and department.
- Listens to others, asks appropriate questions, and provides accurate, timely information and assistance to all customers.
- Expresses enthusiasm, loyalty, and a positive demeanor with all customers. Trusts, respects, and supports coworkers.
- Assumes responsibility for own actions. Takes an active role in improving the department and center.
- Respects diversity of all customers.

[ ] EXCEEDS STANDARD
- Regularly goes out of the way to assist others without needing to be asked.
- Regularly takes an active role in correcting and/or redirecting misinformation.
- Regularly anticipates needs of customers and provides information and assistance to exceed their expectations.

Continued

K. E Participates in problem-solving and process improvement opportunities as appropriate.

[ ] BELOW STANDARD

_____
_____
_____
_____
_____

[ ] MEETS STANDARD

• Consistently and willingly participates in projects as assigned and demonstrates positive collaboration and competent performance.

[ ] EXCEEDS STANDARD

• Consistently shows initiative in identifying opportunities for improvement by offering viable suggestions and assisting with investigation of feasibility.
• Where appropriate, assumes leadership role in projects through positive support, data collection, and analysis and/or through managing project timelines.

L. E Performs other duties as requested.

[ ] BELOW STANDARD

_____
_____
_____

[ ] MEETS STANDARD

• Consistently and willingly assists with other duties as requested or assigned.

[ ] EXCEEDS STANDARD

• Consistently shows initiative in identifying areas of need and assisting others without compromising own duties.

LEADERSHIP-SPECIFIC PERFORMANCE STANDARDS

M. E Consistently demonstrates effective leadership skills.

[ ] BELOW STANDARD

_____
_____
_____
_____
_____

[ ] MEETS STANDARD

• Personally acts as a role model for Hospital Vision Statement. Reinforces vision with staff.
• Establishes vision for assigned department that supports and complements hospital's vision.
• Builds support to achieve willing "followership" for initiatives rather than "drive" or mandate compliance.
• Effectively leads change initiatives within department and hospital, garnering support of staff.

[ ] EXCEEDS STANDARD

• Serves as informal "resource" for other managers.
• Takes a leadership role in center initiatives to improve processes, outcomes, satisfaction, teamwork, morale, and/or cost-efficiency.
• Attends and actively participates in at least 90% of all assigned committees and leadership meetings. Where appropriate, takes leadership role in facilitation of meeting and/or projects.

- Empowers staff and teams by expanding responsibilities and giving assignments that increase range of influence, within clearly defined limits.
- Actively and willingly collaborates with other departments to improve processes, outcomes, satisfaction, teamwork, morale, and/or cost-efficiency.
- Effectively carries out planning and completion of projects.
- Makes effective use of time in carrying out. responsibilities and day-to-day operations.
- Accurately estimates and plans for the time necessary to complete projects.
- Attends and actively participates in at least 80% of all assigned committees and leadership meetings.
- Ensures department policies and protocols are up-to-date and comply with all applicable internal and external rules, regulations, and standards.

- Effectively manages complex cross-functional projects.
- Consistently demonstrates the ability to think conceptually and strategically as well as tactically and concretely.

Comments:

N. E Assesses customer satisfaction with departmental services and improves satisfaction levels.

[ ] **BELOW STANDARD**

[ ] **MEETS STANDARD**
- Personally acts as a role model to reinforce importance of customer satisfaction.
- Gathers valid data and/or utilizes existing measurements to establish and monitor specific departmental service standards.
- Initiates ongoing processes for the improvement of stated departmental service goals, utilizing staff in an active manner.

[ ] **EXCEEDS STANDARD**
- Takes leadership role to vigorously support hospital customer service initiatives.
- Collaborates with other departments to improve services across departments.

Continued

N. E Assesses customer satisfaction with departmental services and improves satisfaction levels.—cont'd

- Identifies and removes service barriers.
- Demonstrates the achievement of measurable meaningful service improvement in stated goal(s).
- Responds to all customer requests/complaints as soon as reasonable, personally whenever appropriate.

Comments:

_____
_____
_____

O. E Develops operating, capital, and information systems budgets that are necessary to achieve key departmental goals, and manages these in a responsible way with the center's best interests and cost savings in mind.

[ ] BELOW STANDARD

_____
_____
_____
_____
_____
_____
_____
_____
_____
_____
_____
_____
_____
_____
_____
_____
_____
_____
_____
_____
_____
_____

[ ] MEETS STANDARD

- Submits well-thought-out budget that is realistic and necessary to carry out ongoing departmental operations at expected levels and achieves stated departmental strategic goals.
- Understands and monitors monthly budget variance data, and manages operations accordingly. Responds to inquiries appropriately with meaningful data related to variances.
- Operates department within prescribed approved budgetary limits, taking into account actual activity/volume. Supports budget variances with valid and meaningful data.
- Supports efforts of other departments that improve efficiency with which hospital resources are utilized.
- Where applicable, identifies realistic ways to generate new revenue for the department/hospital.
- Investigates potential departmental cost-saving measure(s) to achieve meaningful cost reductions.
- Provides cost-efficient and customer-satisfying staffing patterns that are flexible enough to address variations in activity level.

[ ] EXCEEDS STANDARD

- Achieves expected departmental operations with an *overall* positive activity/volume-adjusted budget variance of 10% or greater.
- Proactively provides valid and meaningful budget variance data where line items exceed 5% of monthly and/or year-to-date (YTD) activity/volume-adjusted budget.
- Implements programs/services to generate meaningful new revenue.
- Implements departmental cost-savings measure(s) to achieve meaningful cost reductions.

Comments:

P. E   Develops department-specific strategic plan that supports the center's strategic initiatives (financial viability, customer satisfaction, quality outcomes) in both short-term tactical as well as long-term, future-oriented perspective.

[ ] BELOW STANDARD

[ ] MEETS STANDARD

- Identifies specific, well-documented departmental goals that are realistic, measurable, and complement the hospital's strategic initiatives and operating goals in a meaningful way. Communicates with others who may be impacted by the goals.
- Submits plan within prescribed time frame(s).
- Maintains open communication regarding status, obstacles, etc., and adjusts tactics or garners support necessary to stay on track for completion.
- Achieves stated goals within prescribed time frames, or when unable to do so, has done what is possible within scope of influence.
- Achieves stated goals within prescribed budgetary limits, or with reasonable variances.
- When appropriate, collaborates with other department(s) to facilitate their strategic goals.

[ ] EXCEEDS STANDARD

- Frequently achieves stated departmental goals ahead of expected time frames and shows initiative in taking on additional responsibilities.
- Achieves stated departmental goals under budgeted expectations.
- Utilizes current data to accurately forecast and plan for future trends and likely industry/professional changes that impact operations/services.
- Demonstrates flexibility to adapt to changes in goals, resources, activity, etc., by modifying plans based on these factors as appropriate.
- Proactively assists other department(s) in identifying and implementing specific and realistic strategic goals that contribute the hospital initiatives.
- Appropriately engages staff in development and achievement of departmental goals.

Continued

Comments:

Q. E Demonstrates effective written and verbal communication skills within and across departments.

[ ] BELOW STANDARD

_____
_____
_____
_____
_____
_____
_____
_____
_____
_____
_____
_____
_____
_____
_____
_____
_____

[ ] MEETS STANDARD

- Consistently disseminates information in an accurate, timely, and consistent manner.
- Provides regular monthly face-to-face staff meetings at least 10 times per year with all employees to convey department and hospital activity, initiatives, etc. Produces minutes within 10 working days of meeting. Engages in open two-way discussion.
- Asks for ideas, alternatives, and suggestions; listens and acknowledges individual ideas, keeping an open mind.
- Takes personal responsibility to seek information from reliable sources that affects departmental and/or center operations. Takes initiative to identify and correct misinformation.
- Participates in meetings, committees, etc., with pertinent input and feedback.
- All written correspondence is well thought out, easily understood, and appropriately timed.
- Adequately documents departmental procedures and protocols, ensuring they remain current and well understood.

[ ] EXCEEDS STANDARD

- Sees that change is effectively introduced and widely supported within the department.
- Reflects self-confidence and optimism with people inside and outside the center without being intimidating, superior, or cavalier.
- Effectively makes meaningful presentations, appropriately utilizing information technology as a means of improving understanding.
- Creates a climate of openness in which unpleasant and controversial topics can be discussed objectively.

Comments:

R. E Demonstrates effective problem-solving skills when dealing with analytical data, process issues and human resource/staff issues.

[ ] BELOW STANDARD

[ ] MEETS STANDARD

- Issues are addressed and systems/processes implemented in a manner so as to avoid the potential for problems to arise.
- Problems/trends are quickly identified and validated, separating perceptions from fact-based problems.
- All key parties are informed of problem/issue and the solution at the appropriate time.
- Relevant data and information are gathered in order to identify the root cause(s), consider alternatives, and utilize input where appropriate.
- Solutions address underlying causes (process, systems, etc.) and are implemented in a timely manner utilizing the input of appropriate parties. Buy-in achieved for long-lasting solutions.
- Conducts postimplementation assessment of solution to determine if the solution was effective in addressing the problem.
- Effectively delegates tasks or projects according to the individuals' skill, knowledge, and ability.

[ ] EXCEEDS STANDARD

- Demonstrates an ability to identify and implement solutions to challenges that others may have difficulty with.
- Demonstrates creativity in problem-solving by implementing nontraditional approaches that more effectively and/or most cost-efficiently resolve problems.
- Quickly identifies the root cause and explains the implications of a problem in a way that is insightful and easy to understand.
- Makes a good decision under pressure and tight deadlines when only incomplete information is available.
- Acts as a resource for peers within the organization.

Continued

Comments:

S. E Effectively manages performance of departmental employees.

[ ] BELOW STANDARD

[ ] MEETS STANDARD

- Acts as role model in demonstrating behaviors that reinforce hospital standards.
- Selects staff to introduce skills and experience that meet the department's needs.
- Effectively integrates new personnel into department team.
- Sets clear performance and behavioral expectations that are consistently reinforced and fairly managed for all staff.
- Provides supportive work environment. Is accessible to staff for problems, suggestions, and concerns.
- Frequently acknowledges and recognizes staff for their contributions, both formally and informally.
- Provides constructive feedback related to performance/goals in a timely manner, with direct, respectful, and confidential discussion of expectation and consequence. Provides personal support and encouragement for required improvement.
- Where formal performance counseling is indicated, follows hospital policy and provides specific feedback, including required outcomes and consequences of insufficient improvement. Documents employee counseling appropriately.
- Completes performance appraisals in a timely manner, with no evaluation more than 30 days past the scheduled date. Develops with the employee measurable goals and provides feedback consistently to employees.

[ ] EXCEEDS STANDARD

- Serves as an informal "resource" for other managers.
- Conducts 100% of performance appraisals by the scheduled "return" date.
- Utilizes self-assessment and/or peer input for performance appraisals.
- Effectively manages particularly difficult personnel issues in a timely and appropriate manner.
- Monitors staff turnover and implements interventions within the department's span of control, resulting in a reduction in "controllable" turnover.

Comments:

T. E Engages in ongoing process to improve effectiveness of departmental services.

[ ] BELOW STANDARD

[ ] MEETS STANDARD

- Provides staff education on principles of process improvement.
- Provides open environment where staff are encouraged to identify methods for improving departmental services.
- Encourages staff to challenge ideas and express themselves openly, professionally, and constructively.
- Submits well-thought-out and documented quality assurance reports by the prescribed deadline.

[ ] EXCEEDS STANDARD

- Develops and reinforces a culture of continual process improvement and appropriate risk-taking.
- Identifies realistic opportunities to collaborate across departments to improve services, delivery systems, and efficiency of resource utilization.
- Assumes leadership role in at least one departmental or cross-functional process improvement team.

Comments:

U. E Assesses and improves the competency of departmental staff.

[ ] BELOW STANDARD

[ ] MEETS STANDARD

- The initial assessment of staff competency is validated and documented on all new departmental employees by the completion of the introductory period.
- Ongoing systems effectively assess and improve the competency of staff through continuing education or other means as appropriate.
- Clinical care providers participate in specific targeted competency initiatives based on trending of performance data, observation, risk factors, etc. Staff competency is appropriately documented.

[ ] EXCEEDS STANDARD

- Attends greater than four hospital-sponsored management development programs each year.
- Identifies creative means to provide learning opportunities to staff to further their development.
- Keeps current with professional and industry trends.
- Takes leadership role in outside professional organizations.

Continued

U. E Assesses and improves the competency of departmental staff.—cont'd

- Using staff input, identifies learning needs and provides development opportunities to enable individuals to achieve personal growth.
- Ensures 100% compliance with all mandatory staff education/inservice.
- Personally attends at least four hospital-sponsored management development programs each year.

Comments:

JOB-SPECIFIC PERFORMANCE STANDARDS: Standards of Professional Nursing Administrative Practice

1. 20% E *Assessment:* Assesses the quality of nursing practice and patient care delivery within the primary unit of responsibility; collaborates with PCS leadership to develop, maintain, and evaluate assessment processes within the department.

[ ] BELOW STANDARD

[ ] MEETS STANDARD

- Uses valid and reliable data to assess patient care needs specific to target populations.
- Identifies, allocates, and efficiently utilizes resources required to meet patient care needs.
- Collaborates with the staffing coordinator in the daily assessment of staffing needs.
- Monitors and evaluates ongoing staffing trends, collecting and analyzing data to support unit staffing plans and budgeted full-time employees (FTEs).
- Identifies and uses nursing-sensitive indicators to monitor the quality of patient care and nursing practice.
- Collaborates with the director of nursing practice to coordinate activities related to continuing quality assessment, improvement analysis, and outcome evaluation of patient care delivery.

[ ] EXCEEDS STANDARD

- Consistently identifies and allocates the resources necessary to meet the patient care needs within the unit of primary responsibility in a timely and efficient manner.
- Consistently uses and analyzes staffing data to identify staffing needs appropriately and in a time frame that allows efficient utilization of nursing staff. Consistently plans and meets the patient care needs of the unit.
- Consistently collaborates with the staffing coordinator and director of nursing operations to ensure optimal utilization of nursing staff within the department, participating in assessing the need for and making provisions for staff reassignment.

- Supports the nurse practice council unit representative in coordinating all quality assessment (QA) monitoring activities within the unit.
- Collaborates with nursing education to provide ongoing competency assessment and professional development of nursing staff. Identifies staff needs for professional growth.
- Participates in the development, maintenance, and evaluation of data collection systems related to patient care and nursing practice.
- Facilitates the integration of unified patient care assessment processes developed in collaboration with other health disciplines and across the continuum of care.
- Participates in the development, monitoring, and evaluation of assessment processes that are sensitive to the unique and diverse needs of clients and staff.

- Consistently submits QA monitors and quarterly reports completed with all required data before established deadlines.
- Consistently identifies staff needs for professional growth and education, promoting and providing opportunities for staff continuing education.
- Assumes a leadership role in the development, maintenance, and evaluation of assessment processes and data collection systems related to patient care delivery and/or nursing practice.

2. 20% E *Planning/Goal Setting:* Develops, maintains, evaluates, and modifies unit and departmental plans to facilitate the delivery of nursing care.

[ ] BELOW STANDARD

[ ] MEETS STANDARD
- Participates in the identification of departmental strategic objectives and the development of the PCS strategic plan.
- Reviews and evaluates unit plan for utilization of staff at all levels of practice in accordance with PCS staffing policies, the State Nurse Practice Act, and practice standards.
- Integrates clinical, human resource, and financial data to facilitate decision-making and to appropriately plan for delivery of nursing services.
- Fosters interdisciplinary planning and collaboration in identifying and achieving desired, client-centered, cost-effective outcomes.

[ ] EXCEEDS STANDARD
- Assumes leadership role in developing, maintaining, evaluating, and/or modifying planning systems related to patient care delivery or nursing professional development.
- Develops, maintains, and evaluates a comprehensive written unit strategic plan based on data analysis and assessment findings.
- Promotes integration of contemporary management theories, nursing research, and practice guidelines into the nursing planning process.

Continued

2. 20% E *Planning/Goal Setting:* Develops, maintains, evaluates, and modifies unit and departmental plans to facilitate the delivery of nursing care. —cont'd

[ ] BELOW STANDARD

[ ] MEETS STANDARD

- Plans unit goals in accordance with departmental and hospital goals and objectives. Sets appropriate priorities in directing patient care delivery and nursing practice.
- Fosters staff participation in clinical decision-making and planning.

[ ] EXCEEDS STANDARD

- Fosters creative and innovative interdisciplinary planning and intervention for achievement of desired client-centered outcomes.

3. 20% E *Implementation:* Ensures safe, ethical, and competent delivery of nursing services.

[ ] BELOW STANDARD

[ ] MEETS STANDARD

- Provides and maintains current clinical resources and references within the unit.
- Promotes evidence-based practice, utilizing nursing research findings as the basis for decisions related to clinical and professional practice.
- Participates in the development, evaluation, and maintenance of departmental systems that integrate nursing policies and procedures with regulations, practice standards, and clinical guidelines.
- Implements unit staffing plan to ensure adequate numbers of qualified, competent staff are provided to meet patient care needs.
- Ensures appropriate and efficient documentation of nursing interventions. Completes and submits documentation reviews within specified time frames.
- Monitors quality of nursing care delivery within the unit of responsibility. Completes and submits quality indicator monitors of nursing practice within specified time frames. Ensures completion and submission of all QA monitors and quarterly reports.

[ ] EXCEEDS STANDARD

- Participates in the development, evaluation, and maintenance of organizational systems that integrate policies and procedures with JCAHO and DOH regulations, practice standards, and clinical guidelines.
- Implements creative and innovative plans for achieving desired outcomes. Fosters creativity and innovation in staff in achieving cost-effective, client-centered outcomes.

- Advocates for and provides educational opportunities for staff specific to current interventions, technologies, and other skills required to maintain competence and to enhance the quality of nursing care delivery.

4. 20% E *Evaluation*: Evaluates patient care and nursing practice in relation to attainment of identified goals and desired outcomes within the unit of primary responsibility. Participates in the departmental evaluation of delivery of nursing services within the organization.

[ ] BELOW STANDARD

_____
_____
_____
_____
_____
_____
_____

[ ] MEETS STANDARD

- Analyzes and uses QA data to evaluate progress toward attainment of unit goals and desired patient outcomes. Revises and modifies plans for patient care delivery based on QA data analysis.
- Analyzes patient satisfaction survey data and trends, identifies quality improvement areas, and initiates action plans for improving performance.
- Fosters staff participation and feedback in evaluating quality of nursing practice and in enhancing professional development.
- Facilitates the participation of staff in evaluation of patient care outcomes and new programs and/or processes.

[ ] EXCEEDS STANDARD

- Initiates a formal, dynamic process that encourages staff feedback and evaluation of clinical and professional nursing practice within the unit.
- Provides ongoing informal and formal recognition of staff achievements and contributions within the unit, department, organization, and professional community.

5. 20% E Provides on-call coverage for shift supervision as scheduled or assigned.

[ ] BELOW STANDARD

_____
_____
_____
_____
_____
_____
_____

[ ] MEETS STANDARD

- Fulfills or arranges coverage for all *scheduled* on-call shifts.
- Fulfills *unscheduled* on-call rotation requirements.
- Follows established protocols for coordinating the scheduling and assignment of staff during off-shift coverage.

[ ] EXCEEDS STANDARD

- Consistently is flexible in meeting scheduled and unscheduled on-call shift supervision requirements.
- Consistently arranges coverage if unable to meet on-call requirements.
- Consistently handles challenging shift

Continued

- Validates patient acuity and caregiver competencies prior to assignment of agency and per diem nurses, and reassignment of permanent staff.
- Follows administrative protocols to coordinate interdepartmental services and manage emergency operational procedures during off-shift supervision coverage.

supervisory situations efficiently and in accordance with departmental and hospital policies and procedures.

Comments:

This document is intended to describe the general nature and level of work being performed by staff assigned to this job classification. It is not intended to be a complete list of all responsibilities, duties, and skills required of personnel so classified. All employees are expected to perform all reasonable duties assigned.

E -ESSENTIAL JOB FUNCTION   M -MARGINAL JOB FUNCTION   ADS -AGE-DEPENDENT STANDARD

Working Conditions

None	Occasional (<20%)	Frequent (21%-50%)	Constant (more than 50%)	Physical Characteristic	Weight
	X			_Lifting_ objects from one level to another.	>50 lb
	X			_Carrying_ objects in your hands, arms, or on your shoulders.	>15 lb
	X			_Pushing_ an object so that it moves away from or stands in front of you.	
	X			_Pulling_ an object so that it moves toward you.	>25 lb
		X		_Standing_ on your feet without moving about.	>50 lb
		X		_Walking_ about on foot.	
		X		_Sitting_ in a normal seated position.	
	X			_Climbing,_ such as ascending or descending stairs, ramps, ladders, and the like.	
	X			_Stooping_ or _crouching_ by bending your legs and spine or by bending downward or forward at your waist.	
	X			_Kneeling_ by bending at your knees or coming to rest on your knees.	
X				_Crawling_ by moving about on hands and knees/feet.	

x   *Talking* to express or exchange ideas through the spoken word.

x   *Hearing* to perceive the nature of sounds by the ear.

x   *Far vision* to see objects clearly beyond 20 feet.

x   *Near vision* to see objects clearly within 20 inches.

x   *Depth perception* to judge distance and accurately see relationships between objects.

x   *Field of vision* to see an area up and down or right and left while eyes are fixed on one point.

x   *Sharp focus* to adjust vision when doing close work that changes in distance from your eyes.

x   *Color vision* to identify and distinguish colors.

Manual Skills:

[ ] Requires no more physical dexterity than that possessed by an able-bodied person.

[ ] Requires manipulative skills that require practice to perfect but that the majority of candidates will acquire during a training period.

[ ] Requires a special skill or knack that only certain individuals become proficient in after a training period.

Equipment Required for Position: Computers, cardiac monitors, patient care equipment

Other Comments: Effectively managing stressful situations is an essential feature of this position.

The signatures below indicate that this job description has been reviewed and approved as representative of the key elements of the position noted.

Signed: _____   Date: _____

   Department/Division Head / Medical Chair (if applicable)

Performance and Competency Review

- Note key accomplishments achieved within the prior review period. Note specifically any items identified as goals in the prior review period: _____

- Note educational programs completed in the prior review period, noting specifically attendance at mandatory programs and any other programs targeted in the last review period: _____

- Note educational programs targeted for the upcoming review year. Note specifically any learning needs identified through the review period: _____

- Note goals for upcoming review period: _____

- Note specific "action plan" for improving any items noted on this evaluation as Below Standard. Note specific measurable outcomes and time frames where possible: _____

- Based on this evaluation, day-to-day observations of performance, incident reports, QA monitors, and all other performance-monitoring activities throughout the review period, is this person deemed competent to perform her/his position? For staff who have regular clinical contact with patients, this would include performing duties in a way that considers the special needs (age-specific, physical, psychosocial, and cultural) of patients. [] Yes [] No

  If No, be sure action plan is completed (above) and formally reevaluate if required within no more than three (3) months.

- If applicable, have all required licenses, certifications, and/or credentials been kept current for the entire period being reviewed? [] Yes [] No

- Additional Comments: _____

Employee: This *Performance and Competency Assessment* has been reviewed with me. I have made my comments, if applicable, and I: ☐ Agree, ☐ Disagree with this evaluation. (Your signature only indicates that this has been reviewed with you, not that you agree with it.)

Employee's Signature _____   Date: _____

Comments: _____

_____

_____

_____

For *Introductory Employees:* Has the Departmental Orientation Checklist been completed? ☐ Yes ☐ No
If No, when will it be completed?

If Reevaluation or Extended Introductory Period Required, please note date: _____

Manager's Signature _____   Date: _____

Department Head Signature _____   Date: _____

HR Use—Do Not Write Below This Line

Date of Next Appraisal: _____   Evaluation Given on Time: ☐ Yes ☐ No

Overall Employee Rating: ☐ Below Standard   ☐ Meets Standard   ☐ Exceeds Standard

Signed: _____   Date: _____
   Director of Human Resources

Signed: _____   Date: _____
   Executive / Senior Manager

CHECKLIST OF KEY INFORMATION ABOUT IMPORTANT SERVICES AND DEPARTMENTS

CASE MANAGEMENT/DISCHARGE PLANNING

_____ Resources available to patients, families, and staff
_____ Policy of patients being evaluated on admission
_____ The referral process
_____ The schedule for discharge planning rounds held in the clinical area
_____ Other

CHAPLAINCY SERVICES

_____ Types of services (e.g., bereavement, remembrance, worship services, baptisms, other)
_____ Hours the chaplain or other representative chaplaincy staff is available
_____ How a referral is initiated
_____ Ethics
_____ Other

DATA PROCESSING AND INFORMATION SERVICES

_____ Orientation to nursing and other information systems (hardware and software)
_____ Video display terminal (VDT) password and confidentiality safeguards
_____ Management reports and their retrieval
_____ Other

DIETARY OR FOOD SERVICES

_____ Schedule of meal and snack delivery times
_____ Flexibility of menu based on specific patient needs (e.g., kosher, macrobiotic)
_____ Location and hours of restaurants, cafeterias, and snack bars
_____ Staff cafeteria hours
_____ Other

FINANCE

_____ How often the unit financial and other utilization reports are generated
_____ Your responsibilities regarding specific reports
_____ The budget processes and time frames
_____ The process for requesting new capital equipment
_____ Your role in the budget process

Continued

_____ The historic supply use baseline for the clinical area
_____ The current occupancy rate
_____ The facility's breakdown of types of payers
_____ Percentage of charity care the facility provides annually and the amount that gets written off
_____ The average length of stay
_____ Other

HOME HEALTH CARE

_____ The admission policies
_____ Which types (severity, diagnosis, specialty areas) of patients are appropriate for referral to the program
_____ The geographic boundaries
_____ The referral process
_____ Status of nurse-to-nurse communication for continuity of the plan of care before discharge
_____ Lists of supplies the in-patient nurse should send home with the patient for initial wound or other care
_____ How patients are admitted "after hours" or on the weekends
_____ Other services available to support patients and their families at home, such as personal emergency response systems or private duty care
_____ Areas of expertise offered, such as home IV administration or total parenteral nutrition (TPN)
_____ How the need for services at home is determined and who makes the determination
_____ How home medical equipment or other needs are addressed
_____ Status of the agency (e.g., licensed, Medicare-certified, JCAHO, CHAP, or other accreditation status)
_____ Other

HOSPICE

_____ The admission criteria
_____ How a referral is initiated and the admission policies
_____ Where the patient goes if inpatient care is necessary
_____ When the hospice nurse meets the patient and family before hospital discharge for continuity of care
_____ The geographic boundaries
_____ Acceptance of both pediatric and adult patients
_____ The bereavement support process
_____ Support groups for the family
_____ Other

HUMAN RESOURCES/PERSONNEL

_____ The process of nurse selection
_____ At what point the nurse manager's interview occurs after the nurse recruiter has validated licensure and references
_____ Nurse recruiter responsibilities
_____ Policies and procedures for counseling
_____ Status of union involvement
_____ Overtime and on-call salary guidelines
_____ Availability of a professional nursing pool, either in-house or through nursing agencies on a temporary basis
_____ Actions to take if you believe a nurse is impaired

_____ The standard policy for hiring, evaluation, and termination
_____ Grievance policy and process
_____ Location on the unit of the institution's personnel handbook
_____ Other

LABORATORY SERVICES

_____ Hours of service, pick-up schedule, stat bloods, prn delivery schedule
_____ Find out who is responsible for venipunctures, starting IV solutions, and maintaining IVs and other lines
_____ Other

MEDICAL RECORDS/HEALTH INFORMATION SERVICES

_____ Policy on patients accessing their clinical charts
_____ Protection of confidentiality if clinical records are data entered or keyed directly into a computerized system
_____ Services and results accessible
_____ Type of medical record system that is in place
_____ Types of charting that are the standard or acceptable
_____ Existence of an institution-wide charting process
_____ Role of nurses pertaining to documenting in the same clinical note areas as physicians and other professional team members
_____ The program's or hospital's use of problem-oriented medical record (POMR), SOAP, or focus charting
_____ Requirements for computerized documentation in lieu of clinical entries or narrative notes
_____ Other (e.g., HIPAA, other regulating standards)

RADIOLOGIC SERVICES

_____ Hours of services
_____ Availability of MRI
_____ Location of services
_____ The process for scheduling and transporting patients
_____ Availability and policy for portable X-ray examinations
_____ Ascertain who holds patients in position for X-ray examinations after hours
_____ Ascertain which X-ray examinations are not done after certain hours
_____ Other

REHABILITATION SERVICES

_____ Services available (e.g., physical, occupational, and respiratory therapies and speech-language pathology [SLP] services)
_____ How referrals are initiated
_____ Policy on all CVA patients receiving a swallowing evaluation on admission
_____ Ascertain which department does swallowing evaluations at the institution— occupational therapy (OT) or SLP
_____ Ascertain if the schedules for patient pick-up are posted for the nursing staff
_____ Learn who at the facility does chest PT (e.g., PT, RT, or RN)
_____ Length of time the patient is usually gone from the unit
_____ Accessibility of the charting entries by these professional associates
_____ The schedule for interdisciplinary team meetings
_____ Other

Continued

QUALITY IMPROVEMENT/RISK MANAGEMENT

_____ The roles of these departments in the facility
_____ The process and use of incident reports
_____ When to call the risk manager
_____ Status of studies under way (e.g., on patient falls, medication errors, or the use of restraints)
_____ How the nursing manager and staff members receive feedback on the findings
_____ Your areas of responsibility regarding quality improvement
_____ How nursing integrates with the overall quality improvement process of the hospital
_____ Other

STAFF EDUCATION

_____ The organizational structure for staff development
_____ The scheduled conferences or resources planned for the next two quarters (or other specified time frame)
_____ Availability of clinical preceptors, instructors, or specialists to the staff
_____ Research that is occurring in the clinical setting
_____ Ascertain if the orientation program is competency based and how competency is measured
_____ The needs assessment tools in use
_____ The mechanism for reevaluation and how often they are reevaluated
_____ Learn what program is employed to assist new graduates in their transitions to proficient, professional nurses
_____ The specific resources (e.g., human, fiscal, audiovisual) available to the nurse manager and her/his staff
_____ Ascertain if the manager of staff development is a peer resource for new nurse managers
_____ Ask if there is a peer support program for the staff development team
_____ Status of JCAHO or ANA Nursing Staff Development Standards in the program
_____ The resources available for specialty training (e.g., maternal/child, hospice, home care, operating room, or critical care staff)
_____ Other

Other areas could include housekeeping, facility management, development activities, and numerous specialty areas, depending on the size, resources, and structure of the organization.

CHAPTER 2

MANAGEMENT: AN OVERVIEW

SANDRA WHITTIER

MANAGEMENT: WHAT IS IT?

New nurse managers are experienced at nursing but may be new to management or in a new organization or a new role. Management is constantly working to define itself in a positive manner. For a new nurse manager, it means collaborating with clinicians from other disciplines and health care colleagues to accomplish outcome-oriented activities. A new nurse manager must:

- Define her/his unique management/leadership style.
- Assess the culture of the group and management environment.
- Master the organization's philosophy, as well as policies and procedures.
- Define knowledge deficits to pinpoint continuing education topics.

New managers initially may require guidance from their own manager and must be assertive enough to identify and operationalize behaviorally the expectations of the new position. It is for this reason that managers must have a clear understanding of the mission of the organization—in order to clearly communicate to subordinate staff and senior management. Initially, the new manager can focus on the following principles, outlined by McGregor[1]:

- Knowledge of organizational policies and management philosophy
- Knowledge of organizational standards, regulations, and procedures
- Knowledge of change theories
- An atmosphere of approval
- Subordinates' need for security
- Consistent behavior, including discipline

The purpose of the organization will enlighten the manager as to the management philosophy and reporting mechanisms of the organization or hospital. Departmental goals, documentation procedures, use of the nursing process, and any theoretic basis used for practice guidelines are communicated via the direct supervisor of the new manager.

Managers must have a clear understanding of the mission of the agency or organization and be able to communicate to staff in ways that promote understanding and adoption of that mission. Abilities and skills necessary for such communication are listed in Box 2-1.

WHAT IS LEADERSHIP?

Nurse managers are chosen for their leadership ability and demonstrated clinical competence. Earlier in their careers they performed well when "in charge," were complimented by staff or supervisors, and began to see themselves differently. At some point they discovered their innate leadership skills, a foundation on which to build and add new skills. Some believe that "leadership is viewed as larger and more important than management."[2,3]

Leadership is the key to management. According to Bethel,[4] a leader:

1. Has a mission that matters.
2. Is a big thinker.
3. Has high ethics.
4. Masters change.
5. Is sensitive.
6. Is a risk-taker.
7. Is a decision-maker.
8. Uses power wisely.
9. Communicates effectively.
10. Is courageous.
11. Is a team builder.
12. Is committed.

Leading is guiding and directing the skills of others toward positive outcomes. Leaders must continually examine and develop their own skills to remain confident in their abilities. Research studies defining desired nursing leadership qualities[5-8] by staff continue to illustrate the need for honesty, skilled communication, and team-building skills in addition to clinical knowledge.

Just as confidence and enthusiasm are contagious, insecurity can be sensed and targeted by some staff. Leaders must be perceptive and use their powers of observation when evaluating the group's cohesiveness. Divisive staff members challenge the manager to keep strengthening and reevaluating leadership skills. Leadership is essential to orderly direction in supporting the staff in quality patient care.

Types of Leaders

Excellent nursing leadership requires being action-, result-, or outcome-oriented.[8] Leading by example, being available to staff when needed, constantly sharpening skills, and having an earnest understanding of staff concerns are important to creating loyalty, respect, and empowerment between staff members and manager.

Leaders are problem-solvers who do not see a problem as an obstacle to *overcome* but as a puzzle requiring thought to *solve*.

box 2-1

ABILITIES AND SKILLS NEEDED BY NEW NURSE MANAGERS

ABILITIES

- Influence workers to believe in themselves
- Develop individual staff strengths
- Create a desire for excellence and loyalty
- Work with staff behaviorally to improve weaknesses
- Provide challenges in the context of a busy day
- Evaluate performance constructively using objective data/criteria
- Mentor both staff members who display leadership characteristics and those who require coaching
- Communicate with their managers and staff to outline responsibilities and decision-making
- Lead by example
- Demonstrate knowledge of human behavior and its motivation
- Motivate staff members to work together
- Administer departmental budgets
- Communicate clearly and nonjudgmentally
- Be consistent
- Be flexible
- Take risks
- Demonstrate concern for staff
- Be open and honest with staff

SKILLS

- Demonstrate clinical excellence
- Make effective decisions
- Evaluate the clinical knowledge and skills of individual staff members to match staff to patients
- Implement reasonable staffing schedules on a timely basis
- Have vision to plan for next week or month while getting through today
- Create a stimulating environment that encourages staff autonomy
- Develop short- and long-term goals with your staff's input
- Acknowledge that staff members need to ventilate emotions and allow this in the proper setting
- Display commitment
- Display effective team-building
- Make performance evaluations a positive experience
- Empower your staff
- Provide positive reinforcement—often and loudly
- Choose not to be intimidated by a "potential" or "de facto" manager
- Encourage professional growth of staff by exposure to clinical seminars or conferences
- Successfully incorporate change theory principles

Two leadership concepts, as defined by Burns,[9] can assist the new manager to establish a style of leading. A transformational leader has a vision that, when shared with the staff, creates motivation for working to accomplish the goal. A transformational leader is dynamic, can see the end result, and can incorporate staff input, thereby illustrating staff creativity. Once staff members see that their suggestions have value, more suggestions will follow, and they will begin to originate their own solutions to other problems.

The transformational leader gives responsibility to employees at all levels to make the most of their talents. The transformational leader encourages learning, exploration, and creativity.[10] This type of leader could be important for another reason—organizations cannot afford to support nonproductive employees. The transformational leader is able to take the employee beyond the level of performance achieved by the more traditional, transactional leader.[10,11]

Transformational leadership is perceived as essential for today's organization. Skills and motives necessary for transformational leaders are:
• A commitment to change as process
• A focus on relationships
• The ability to reconceptualize systems
• The ability to build networks and coalitions
• A tolerance for complexity

In contrast, the transactional leader is more involved with managing daily operations. The transactional leader negotiates with followers to meet immediate demands on a short-term basis. In transactional leadership, the exchange benefits both the leader and the follower but meets the immediate needs of the employee and management.

The transformational leader believes that cooperation, empowerment, vision, trust, and intuition are more valued than control, competition, and power wielding.[12]

THE MANAGEMENT ENVIRONMENT

All nurse managers face economic and professional influences that affect their work environment. These may be internal in the organization or external in the larger health care environments. Some of the most important contemporary influences are listed below.

Economic issues
• Increases in number of patients without health insurance coverage
• More acutely ill patients seeking care
• More pressure for staff members to work as more family members lose jobs in the current economic climate
• Third-party-payer restrictions on covered care
• Third-party-payer's increased expectation of patient participation in care
• Spiraling cost of health care

Professional issues

- Ethical dilemmas
- Values clarification
- Redesign of organizations with change in patient care delivery model
- Rotation and weekend work, overtime requests/demands, on call, other staffing needs
- "Quicker and sicker" syndrome causing the staff to respond by "doing the best they can"[11]
- Changes in testing/licensure shortening length of "GN" learning time
- Nursing shortage
- Computerized documentation
- Health care economics causing frequent changes in service lines, technology, and productivity
- Cultural diversity; all customers
- Managed care
- Customer service focus
- Outcomes management, CQI initiatives
- The need for more collaborative and interdisciplinary working relationships
- Professional development/continuing education
- Staff questioning of management decisions
- Staff, patient, and provider diversity issues
- Mergers creating work culture changes
- Multitasking

THE GROWTH OF A NEW MANAGER

Some new managers are fortunate enough to have worked for nurse managers who taught administrative as well as clinical skills. Those without this previous training or exposure will have to successfully develop these new skills.

Nurse managers report to managers themselves. Depending on the agency or organization, nurse managers are also influenced by layers of management and agendas, whose downward influence can determine a new manager's effectiveness and longevity. Good managers support, as well as develop, new managers and potential new managers.

Nursing management skills are vital to nursing's continued growth. Adverse economic and professional influences compound the difficulties seen by staff members as deterrents to managerial aspirations. The future of nursing management depends on the growth and positive leadership of staff. Nurse managers foster the development of future leaders by:

- Being managerially self-aware.
- Nurturing the staff's clinical and leadership potential.
- Leading by example and serving as a role model.

- Demystifying managerial concepts with the staff to increase mutual understanding.
- Mentoring other nurses.
- Becoming a role model by sharing a vision and strategy to support the culture of the organization.

As resources decrease and work stressors increase, nurse managers must use their individual strengths to promote loyalty in an atmosphere of trust. Creating a stable environment that promotes professional growth, excellence in patient care, and individual problem-solving and goal-setting is the role of the nurse manager.

The importance of effective nursing management must not be underestimated. New managers need guidelines and mentoring, especially through the classic management dilemmas, such as poor work performance or disruptive staff or behaviors. Without appropriate nursing direction, new managers will become discouraged and either return to patient care or leave nursing entirely. Nursing cannot afford to lose these potential managers who could have been effective leaders but who never fulfilled the manager role.

STYLES OF MANAGEMENT

Choosing one management style does not allow the nurse manager the flexibility required to meet her/his own needs or those of the staff. New managers will want to select a style that is satisfying and productive while continuously being developed (Manager's Tip 2-1).

All new managers may incorporate the positive and negative aspects of their own previous managers. Many managers can be categorized based on the management style characteristics displayed. It is important to note that staff members also function at varying levels, depending on the management style and expectations of their former nurse managers.

The tasks of the area, unit, or organization must be reviewed when considering management styles. For example, the immediacy of response to life-threatening events may require some autocracy in management. Imperative to management style development is the assessment of individual nurses' strengths and weaknesses. The same new critical care manager may have a disproportionate amount of new staff who require more supervision. Therefore a critique of staff performance can be a guide on which to base managerial style selection. In addition, the level of autonomy or professionalism in a particular staff member affects the choice of leadership style.

The concept of situational leadership can be used when considering which management style a group requires. All staff members and managers have various facets that influence their adaptability to change, new direction, or new management. Each staff member has strengths that rise to the surface, often based on clinical experience and problem-solving attributes, and these qualities can be matched by

MANAGER'S TIP 2-1

MANAGEMENT STYLES

Research and development to design strategies for managerial use have defined four management styles:

✔ *Autocratic managers*
- Do not delegate.
- Make all decisions.
- Have little or no use for staff input.
- Use authority to accomplish goals.
- Foster reliance on the manager.

✔ *Laissez-faire managers*
- Provide little direction.
- Perform without structure or organization.
- Do not provide guidance.
- Do not foster group cohesion.
- Abdicate decision-making.

✔ *Democratic managers*
- Initiate staff participation.
- Delegate with the purpose of staff development.
- Encourage staff toward goal-setting.
- Allow individuals a degree of control.
- Provide frequent positive feedback.

✔ *Participative managers*
- Make final decisions, but include staff input.
- Negotiate as well as direct.
- Enlist staff suggestions.
- Provide staff members with opportunities to develop their careers.
- Transcend the manager–staff gap.

the manager to foster growth in other staff members who need improvement in these areas.

To adapt leadership to the situation, the workers' needs, the leader's abilities, and the methods chosen to direct or supervise should be based on whether the required tasks are clear-cut or ambiguous, whether staff members desire structure or independence, and whether the leader is a skilled group worker or an autocrat.[6] Autocracy has its place at times, but no manager of today can use autocracy as a prominent style. Assertiveness of individuals, disappearance of the handmaiden concept of nursing, and changing medical/nursing relationships prohibit managers from directing without staff participation.

Management philosophies focus on the manager's ability to attain cost-effective and productive quality results. Therefore a laissez-faire style, with its lack of focus and direction, is not a useful style for the new nurse manager to develop. This is true in any nursing setting, where the new nurse manager must by her/his presence and personality lead the staff to work toward development of their potential, as well as positive patient outcomes.

The new nurse manager must have a working knowledge of all leadership styles for use in multiple situations. Communication with confidence is crucial when incorporating a style into the nurse manager's daily repertoire. Consistent behaviors by the manager will help staff members adopt a style to use themselves.

Autocratic and laissez-faire managers are extremes in management styles, the former manager making all decisions without staff input, and the latter being unable to make swift and decisive management decisions. More balanced management styles are democratic and participative. These styles allow the manager to develop staff members to a degree that they are often asked, and feel comfortable giving, their opinions for problem-solving. Remember, the staff are closest to the identified challenges and therefore may have the most workable or practical solutions. Short- or long-term goals generated by the staff are more likely to be successfully achieved when the manager leads democratically. Staff members led by a democratic leader who takes and uses their advice project a feeling of being part of an effective group process. A leader's use of a democratic style in management will not stifle or stagnate the staff. A true leader may find a few specific uses for the autocratic rule, but she/he will generally depend on democratic and participatory leadership styles that can be blended with transformational styles. The last two styles promote in staff members the ability and confidence to identify problems and solve them, while evaluating effects of both solutions and processes.

Participatory leadership varies from the democratic style of management in several ways. This leader presents the identified problem with potential solutions. Staff input is then invited, but the manager may ultimately decide on the specific implementation. Participatory leadership has its drawbacks. By creating an illusion of participation through feedback solicitation, but then not using the staff suggestions, the nurse manager may unknowingly sabotage future efforts to promote participation. Positive aspects of participatory management involve the commitment of sharing authority and responsibility throughout an agency or organization. This is most effectively ensured when the entire organization values participatory management as its philosophy. In fact, many believe that the sign of an effective manager is the organization's ability to function efficiently in her/his absence.

Participatory leadership creates a dependency on the leader to identify problems, unlike the democratic style, which encourages staff to initiate and develop ideas as well as solutions. An illustration of the various styles in response to a familiar scene might be:

The autocratic leader "I have completed the schedule for the holidays, using the policy of staff members working every other holiday. There will be no switching of time among staff members."

The laissez-faire leader "The holiday schedule is completed by the scheduling office; I can't think of a better way to do it."

The democratic leader "Mary has an idea to present at the staff meeting about coverage for the upcoming holidays."

The participatory leader "We will have a staff meeting and complete the holiday schedule as a group."

It may be appropriate, depending on the situation, to use any or all of these styles. This choice of leadership styles can be pivotal in being an effective nurse manager. It is important to be aware that staff members will respond negatively to styles and responses that are not consistent. Conversely, even when managers give predictable responses, the staff is at least aware of managerial expectations in given circumstances. *The test of managerial success in nursing is successfully developing a comfortable and consistent management style that facilitates growth and satisfaction for both the manager and the staff.*

The new manager, while studying management styles, may want to try out her/his initial responses to employees' performance and apply them to a behavior scale to characterize the style that surfaces. Several tools are available that categorize a manager's responses to the appropriate management style, such as Hersey,[13] Blanchard,[8] and Fiedler.[14] One classic example is Tannenbaum[15] (Fig. 2-1).

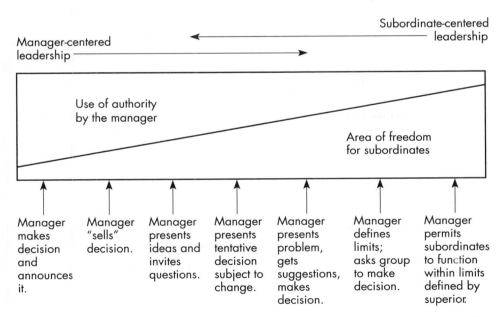

Fig. 2-1 Continuum of leadership behavior and participation. (From Tannenbaum R, Schmidt WH: How to choose a leadership pattern. *Harvard Business Review* 51:164, 1973.)

Figure 2-1 enables the new manager to problem-solve when dealing with various prospective solutions to practical situations. Making use of her/his knowledge of individual staff members and their needs, as well as her/his own, the new manager can anticipate new problems while solving others and analyze her/his own behavior at the same time. The new manager must have enough personal confidence to allow new and seasoned nurses to flourish without feeling that her/his power or knowledge is usurped or threatened. Nurse managers cannot control the environment by their presence alone and must be able to take a vacation with confidence that daily activities will continue smoothly. A key sign of an effective nurse manager is that the staff functions effectively whether or not the manager is present.

COMMUNICATION AND TEAM BUILDING

Communication, negotiation, the ability to understand the political process and economics, sensitivity to organizational process, knowledge of how to form alliances, critical thinking, and the ability to construct a solid case for a point of view are some of the skills nurse managers need.[16] Nurse managers can evaluate their communication skills by observing staff response when information is presented. An important aspect of communication is perception. One cannot assume that the staff will always understand and follow through with the agenda communicated by the manager. Verbal communication should be followed up in writing when appropriate. Written staff meeting minutes dispensed to all staff members unable to attend deflect the excuse, "No one ever told me." Clear communication leaves no room for conjecture, and all have an understanding of the material presented. With some staff members, this may require that the nurse manager request immediate feedback to validate the communication.

Five other aspects of communication vital for the new nurse manager are (1) negotiation, (2) the effective use of positive feedback, (3) conflict resolution skills, (4) working knowledge of the change process, and (5) team-building skills.

Negotiation

Negotiation can be useful as a tool to persuade even the most resistant staff member trying to exercise her/his power, which is a problem situation, directed toward the new manager. The new manager should assess whether this forcefulness results from insecurity of the staff person before using negotiation as a management tool. As an example, suppose a length of time has passed between managers, and this staff nurse has become an informal leader among the staff. This nurse probably needs some time to adjust to changing roles within the group. That power of the "de facto" leader can also be used to enable the staff as the new manager establishes her/his role.

Effective Use of Positive Feedback

If the new manager has evaluated the behavior and identifies it as insecurity, positive feedback may dispel any challenges to the manager's power. Positive feedback can be an icebreaker, is always necessary, and should be given sincerely in an atmosphere of team building. It can include any praise for any job well done:

- Strong assessment skills.
- Effective handling of an emergency.
- Working extra hours.
- Support during change.
- Support of another staff member—either emotional or physical.
- Handling a heavy assignment.
- Early detection of clinical signs requiring intervention.
- Working together as a team.
- Dealing with difficult physicians.
- Leadership skills demonstrated by staff.
- Dealing with supervisors.
- Maintaining consistency in management on a daily basis.

This list is by no means complete; please think of your own positive feedback and use it. At the end of each day, some managers thank staff members. Others get in the good habit of giving positive feedback daily. These are not empty words; they contribute positively to staff autonomy and self-esteem. For an in-depth discussion on communication, please see Chapter 6, Effective Communication.

Conflict Resolution

Conflict resolution must be addressed immediately and not be allowed to escalate. Personal and professional stressors are often a basis for conflicts between staff and will affect patient care if not resolved. The nurse manager must know all the staff well enough to ascertain whether negative comments or friction is situational or slowly festering personality conflicts. When counseling staff or patients, the behavior and its effects must be addressed without personal attacks. For example, if a staff member is creating tension with tardiness, the nurse manager should discuss the behavior (being late) and the consequences (not hearing a complete report at shift change) rather than being accusatory or attacking the person. Conflict between staff members can be defused by meeting with both staff together to find a common place to begin communication and design a plan to change behavior in a constructive, healthy, and positive way.

Change Process[17]

The nurse manager must become a master of managing change in today's dynamic health care environment. Mergers, acquisitions, fiscal restraint, and the technologic forces affecting nursing care delivery seem to be nearly a daily occurrence. Some changes are not seen as positive, and the nurse manager will be tested in the ability to present and assimilate change. Staff input in the steps toward adopting the change, whenever possible, will facilitate completion of this process.

Lewin (1971)[18] describes a three-step process of unfreezing, moving, and refreezing to control the forces rising during the change process.

Unfreezing describes the acknowledgment that a change must occur. The nurse leader change agent must be careful to assess resistance as it occurs[11]. Thoughtful description of the change, its purpose, and how quickly it must be instituted can defuse resistance and should be anticipated to promote the successful change.

The moving phase is the actual implementation of the change and strategy development, and problem-solving skills can smooth any transition period during the change.

Refreezing, the last phase, describes the adoption of the new process or behavior. This stage also requires continued evaluation to assess the consistency of the change adoption.

Team-Building Skills[18]

Team-building skills are mandatory in the current turbulent environment. The skills of the manager in developing the team and blending strengths and differences in meeting both staff and patient needs will determine the success of the organization. Team building tips:

- The manager must see that the work environment is fair, reasonable, and friendly.
- The manager must demonstrate an ability to see things from the worker's point of view.
- The manager must strive to gain acceptance as the group's leader and be seen as the champion for the work of the group.

The manager must encourage employees to work out problems, participate in decision-making and value all input, which boosts commitment and team spirit. The manager's leadership and role modeling can assist members to develop:

- Technical expertise.
- Problem-solving/critical-thinking skills.
- Interpersonal skills.
- An ability to identify skill gaps and self-development needs.
- Individual accountability.
- The ability to work as a group.
- A sense of satisfaction in the achievement of goals.
- Feedback for a job well done.

Positive and negative feedback, negotiation, communication skills, and choice of leadership style are the responsibility of new nurse managers. The methodical evaluation, choice, and development of managerial style and characteristics is never time wasted. It is easier for the manager and the staff as a group when the manager selects and implements a style that matches the manager's best skills and begins the process of fostering growth and unity among staff. The long-term effectiveness and excellence with which the organizational goals are attained are worth the effort because then patients' needs are met and professional nursing careers are fulfilled.

THE NURSING PROCESS

Nursing management involves nursing, general business, and management theories. Nursing theories abound and must be studied at greater length than is possible here. Nursing theory can lay the groundwork for nursing standards in any specialty. As an example, Orem's self-care theory[19] is adaptable to community health. Orem's emphasis is on health promotion and states that health information given to the consumer causes change in those behaviors that are deemed unhealthy, which is also the basis of community health nursing. Behavior change used as a demonstrated patient outcome can then be formulated into nursing standards of care. Nursing theory can be used when updating or creating nursing standards.

Regulations are promulgated by federal (e.g., Medicare, OSHA, CLIA, CDCP) and state Medicaid agencies or accreditation organizations such as JCAHO or CHAP. A heightened emphasis is on patients' rights and responsibilities, customer service, cost-effective care, and outcome achievement. The ongoing review of standards is a part of the responsibility of the nurse manager.

The new manager can use another theory that is very familiar when called on to problem-solve, evaluate nursing compliance to standards, or assess quality improvement or performance improvement processes.

Remember the nursing process:

Assessment
Planning
Implementation
Evaluation

The nursing or scientific problem-solving process helps the manager track or organize any issue objectively. Once potential solutions are identified, they can be categorized, studied, and (when managers are democratic or participatory in management style) shared with staff for their input and ideas. The manager projects an implementation time frame. Once the time frame is met, the evaluation process begins (or is initiated). The evaluation must continue to remain objective. Thus the cycle is complete and the next problem or issue can be confronted. The nursing process is one tool managers can use among other nursing and management theories.

RECORDS MANAGEMENT

The dynamic aspect of the manager role entails that even while planning for future needs, the staff's past cannot be forgotten. This historic overview is sometimes helpful to new managers. The long, sometimes tedious process of change and growth must be documented accurately to ensure that the process was true to objectives. A dependable method, which is needed when the manager must provide facts to defend positions, is written communication. Written communication, as an adjunct to the spoken word, can be difficult to incorporate into a busy day, but it is essential that the new nurse manager do so. The practice of committing to memory observations about behavior, good or bad, without actual notations is no longer feasible and is not responsible to the staff. Those preceptors or individuals guiding new managers must foster the use of anecdotal recording on a regular or as-needed basis as a management tool and assist new managers to develop strategies to meet this goal.

During meetings with the staff on a group or individual basis, the discussion should be summarized orally and then the plan of action summarized in writing. Short notes kept on the staff's performance can make evaluation time objective and full of examples, positive and negative, on which manager and staff goals are designed. All that must be noted are (1) the topics of discussion and (2) the outcomes or goals for either or both parties. Then the next meeting will first address the progress or steps being taken to meet the goals.

A manager owes the staff a meaningful performance evaluation, citing examples of behavior being reviewed. An example could be a review of the staff members' clinical documentation and a comparison to the organization's written documentation standards. This helps the manager be more realistic and fair, without being influenced by personality or popularity attributes. Some incidents will be remembered without hesitation; times of high emotion and tragedy, personal losses, and the legions of patients for whose lives the staff fought are emblazoned on everyone's mind. Time passes quickly between events that nurses remember, so notation of regular activity is a management obligation.

A new manager should begin by writing thoughts when evaluating the staff's performance of patient care, keeping in mind the objectives of the organization. Such documentation can be helpful in other situations; for example, the new manager might record that the staff members need more equipment or training, listing specific examples. She/he could then discuss this subject with her/his manager. The documentation then makes important information quickly available when needed. The ability to rapidly provide specific rationales supporting the manager's point is a key to the manager's credibility and ultimate effectiveness in an organization.

NURSING MANAGEMENT BY OBJECTIVES

Anecdotal comments, and their use as a daily chronicle, are beneficial as practice for working with management by objectives (MBO). These anecdotal notes reduce assumption and provide a foundation for evaluating staff performance. MBO for nurses uses the setting and meeting of goals, usually behavioral, that cause improvement in patient care and other valued outcomes. MBO causes one to strive to attain further goals within a specific period, and goals are designed at the individual's pace. The use of MBO provides focus and direction to both managerial and institutional goals. An objective of a new manager might be, "Evaluate all staff by observation of their work and documentation, among other factors, and conduct a personal review with each staff member by his/her annual anniversary date." This objective is measurable and has a specific time frame. Anecdotal documentation assists the manager in meeting this goal. MBO is for managers who want to create a new environment for progress and quality patient care. For the benefit of the new manager, MBO can be practiced whether or not the organization promotes it. Once the principles are understood, MBO can help in many ways as a step toward achievement of goals in any organization. Manager's Tip 2-2 presents MBO guidelines and characteristics.

MBO identifies where you fit in, organizationally or within the smaller group you manage. Expectations are put out for discussion and direction for the manager and her/his group or the manager's meeting with the nursing executive. Clear

MANAGER'S TIP 2-2

MBO GUIDELINES AND CHARACTERISTICS

GUIDELINES
All objectives must:
- ✔ Have a specific time frame.
- ✔ Be behaviorally stated.
- ✔ Be objectively evaluated.
- ✔ Identify positive rather than negative outcomes.
- ✔ Maintain and adhere to the organization's standards of practice and/or policies.

CHARACTERISTICS
A well-designed objective:
- ✔ Sets limits on the time for behavior to change.
- ✔ Uses negotiation.
- ✔ Is effective by making the point cumulatively.
- ✔ Is a clear and concise form of communication.
- ✔ Controls change.
- ✔ Can be used by any level of staff.
- ✔ Varies from the global to the very specific.
- ✔ Documents problems beyond the manager's control.
- ✔ Aids analytic thinking.
- ✔ Encourages staff development.
- ✔ Improves skill in planning.

expectations leave little room for misunderstanding, and individuals must improve or restate their objectives. The staff who do their best identify those objectives that are not effective.

Observation of staff performance, evaluation of written documentation, patient satisfaction or customer service surveys, and manager and staff position descriptions can be steps toward identifying realistic goals. Another example of an objective might be, "By June 30, 200_, the nurse manager will:

1. Set up June–December inservice topics as prioritized by the staff.
2. Accomplish all staff performance evaluations by a specified deadline.
3. Perform documentation reviews in view of agency/institutional standards.
4. Evaluate staffing patterns and rotate once to each shift every _____.
5. Schedule all registered nurses to have a minimum of 1 week in charge every _____ [defined by manager]."

An MBO Example

Practice of MBO is advantageous to the new manager. Much new information can be categorized and relegated to a step outlined in an objective. This allows the new manager to spend time prioritizing where attention is required first. MBO also lends the novice manager more objectivity, rather than "gut feelings," when learning and being challenged. For example, specific effects on the group by a staff member's tardiness can have extensive ramifications. The nurse manager, on identifying this problem, may create this objective, "By Friday:

•   Schedule and hold an individual meeting with the tardy staff member.
•   Negotiate a contract to stop tardiness. Check personnel policies, procedure manuals, and staff member's file to assess need for verbal warning.
•   List specific tasks done by others, in place of tardy nurse, and any other outcomes of the behavior (e.g., second report).
•   Document the meeting and agreed-upon goals and objectives.
•   Schedule next meeting to review goal achievement."

The new manager will be consistent with all team members using this method. Consistent behavior toward all staff members sends the message that criticism is constructive and fair. The manager's attitude should be positive, as much as possible.

Time can be spent on identified issues, improving operations, or patient care, as well as improving the staff's enjoyment of their work. Nurses can use objectives to require staff development in meeting individual and group goals. MBO encourages forward thinking by its use of setting objectives for the future.

The nurse manager can also use MBO to guide the staff toward larger, organizational targets. Dates for accomplishing objectives must be flexible, without negating the use of this tool. Thinking forward using goal-setting fosters continued personal growth and open communication.

MBO can be adapted to any work situation and, when gradually introduced, can be a positive growth experience for all. Control of growth by the staff can relieve some of the stressors of nursing in the 21st century. MBO for managers is an adjunct to improving:

- Interviewing
- Negotiating
- Delegating (and then leaving them alone!)
- Sharing power/authority
- Performance evaluation
- Managerial growth
- Development of leadership qualities and management style
- Budgetary responsibilities
- Problem-solving
- Building of credibility consistently
- Decision-making
- Listening
- Other skills

MANAGEMENT THEORIES

Management philosophy within the health care organization may encourage a specific style or theory utilization. Generally, if the organization values managers and encourages longevity, there is specific training directed toward leadership development and exposure to management theories. Several theories would be covered during the management's continuing education. The management philosophy of McGregor[20] is a good beginning:

Theory X The average human being has an inherent dislike of work and will avoid work when possible. This causes the need for direction and control in employee management.

Theory Y Physical and mental effort is as natural as play or rest. If employees are committed to organizational objectives, they will be self-directed and need fewer controls.[20]

These motivational theories can be likened to transactional (Theory X) and transformational (Theory Y) leadership styles. Blending the leadership style with the management theory can help the new nurse manager focus behavior toward staff for the best results. Management theory was further developed by Ouchi[21] in his Theory Z. Theory Z principles provided some of the basis for the concept of quality circles—a group process for improving quality through worker-management cooperation.[21]

An accepted concept being adopted as a management theory for organizations involves total quality management developed by Deming. Quality is achieved by:

- Encouraging problem-solving strategies as well as problem identification.
- Fostering cooperation/collaboration among staff, rather than competition.
- Identifying the customer, be it the patient, staff member, or physician.
- Empowering customers.

- Identifying flaws in the process or system rather than blaming staff.[22]

Increasingly, total quality management (TQM) is being adopted by institutions and organizations and is being woven into everyday operational practice. New nurse managers may have already been exposed to these principles during committee participation—whose mandate is to improve service delivery. TQM focuses on identifying problems within established systems and processes rather than with the people performing within the systems.

Simply put, data must be collected and compared to implement **quality assurance (QA)/performance improvement (PI)** in many high-priority areas. Examples abound in the literature of the use of continuous quality improvement (CQI) to generate ideas for improved patient care services. Some of the many issues addressed utilizing CQI concepts include:

- Adverse patient events
- Unusual occurrence reporting
- Meal service in nursing homes
- Emergency services
- Reduction of medication errors
- Industrial accidents
- Discharge planning
- Postanesthesia care
- Managed care in psychiatry
- Cardiopulmonary rehabilitation
- Fall prevention
- Infection-related sentinel event cases
- Clinical documentation
- Medication safety/prevention
- Pressure sore prevention
- Childbirth education
- Sentinel events
- Other safety-related initiatives

Participation as health care providers and consumers is key to improving health promotion behavior as well as systems and processes in care delivery for future viability and survival. Efforts to study systems within health care organizations must include the providers of care—the staff. Leaders in nursing management must establish trust between themselves and staff so that the processes to improve care and work situations will be followed. Participation in the education, support in allowing time for meeting attendance, and honest evaluation of results without repercussions will be beneficial in the long run for staff acceptance of TQM or quality improvement principles. These principles may be intertwined into patient teaching because they are not just designed for the management of people or the evaluation of current systems.

The use of TQM principles has been increasing in health care and has achieved support from the JCAHO and other accreditation and quality-related entities. However,

Smith et al[23] and McConnell[24] warn that without organizational commitment, TQM may be much less successful. Initial training can be supported by time and managerial coaching; however, in the long term, education and guidance are considered most important. The sometimes tedious need to examine every step in a process or system to extract unnecessary steps can be directed toward improving the work culture. Managers must remember that staff are very important as customers, as well.

Ultimately, management philosophy determines the growth and level of staff fulfillment. Guidance and direction should be provided by administration for all managers, giving them the responsibility to make decisions and control their work environment. Managers work best when they develop staff in a consistent and supportive manner and enjoy the same approach from their superior or senior manager.

The management team works most effectively when the environment is collegial, respectful, and nurturing. New managers should elicit advice about the level of support and managerial development systems from both peers and bosses. Gradually increasing responsibility while new managers expand their skills and are groomed in the management philosophy generates strong, decisive, and successful managers. The new nurse manager provides leadership to the staff while learning administrative skills.

An immediate source of information and guidance for the new nurse manager is her/his supervisor. Initially, the new nurse manager should expect frequent meetings, weekly perhaps, and should use this time with the supervisor wisely. Assessments of staff abilities and needs made by the new nurse manager can be reviewed with the supervisor, with problems and solutions identified. Explanation of channels of communication, rules, and etiquette expected of administration may be covered.

The new nurse manager should evaluate the level of support available from administration. Observing discussions and reactions of upper management with their managers and peers can give the new nurse manager insight into the hierarchy of the organization. The new manager determines whether the organizational philosophy is compatible with her/his own values. Ideally, the manager feels wanted, being part of an organization that historically promotes from within and rewards the progress and development of employees.

New nurse managers are thrust into a fast-paced job and so must rapidly determine how much authority is part of the position. If too many decisions are made above the nurse manager's level, she/he may feel stifled. The nurse manager must then decide whether the organizational goals permit some control and thus make the situation workable, or whether it would be better to move on to a new professional experience.

More often, nurse managers are allowed flexibility in such key tasks as hiring and scheduling. Building on these tools, new nurse managers develop their own style of leadership within the management group.

The nurse manager should strive for certain outcomes in the new role. As the new nurse manager tries to achieve these outcomes, she/he develops an ability to analyze the power structure of the organization. Box 2-2 on p. 66 lists role outcomes.[25]

---

box 2-2

NEW NURSE MANAGER ROLE OUTCOMES

POSTENTREPRENEURIAL STYLE

The ability to relinquish bureaucratic styles of leadership; more employee centered with core characteristics of innovation, efficiency, and reward of outcomes; authority derived from expertise and experimentation

EMPOWERMENT

Ability to empower self and staff for quality patient outcomes; ability to influence organizational policy development as related to patient care

VISION

Ability to foresee the growth and development of nursing and managerial practice and strategically plan to assist these processes

ENHANCEMENT OF IMAGE

Ability to identify self as a professional nurse and manager, perceiving self as a leader and enhancing the profession of nursing in the community and organization

FLEXIBILITY

Ability to adapt to turbulence in the organization and practice environment; ability to assess outcomes; ability to design better and newer processes in patient care and management to achieve quality service

CLINICAL EXPERTISE

Ability to identify with those who are managed; staying close to the client and the practice environment to manage the delivery of health care effectively

ANALYTIC THINKING

Ability to problem-solve effectively using logic and decision support systems and models; ability to conduct research in nursing management

LEADERSHIP ROLE IDENTITY

Ability to see self as a leader, mentor, and nurse or patient advocate; ability to assist in meeting institutional goals and objectives through effective performance; ability to get things accomplished

AUTONOMY

Ability to practice nursing and management in a highly decentralized environment without alienation of executive leadership

MASTERY OF CHANGE

Ability to identify, cope with, introduce, and assimilate change successfully in the practice environment

Source: Flarey DL: Redesigning management roles, *Journal of Nursing Administration* 21:44, 1991.

ORGANIZATIONAL CHART

Each organization has a formal and an informal communication system, also called a table of organization, and a chain of command that reflects the manager's base of power. Unofficial personal relationships may command more authority than the organizational chart structure, and all new managers should ascertain allies and adversaries. This will take longer for new managers who have just joined an organization but can also create an opportunity for improved communication among managers and administration. The middle manager is working from both sides, between staff and upper management and, as such, is vital to any organization.

Concepts to evaluate when beginning as a nurse manager are, as noted by Gillies[26]:

- Role
- Power
- Status
- Authority
- Centrality
- Communication

Studying these aspects of organizational hierarchy and using communication to validate perception make up an important exercise for new managers.

There will be occasions that test new managers. This is particularly true when management delivers an edict to the new nurse manager that is contrary to her/his principles. There are no rules as to which side wins, and this situation can cause both personal and professional stress. Sometimes the new nurse manager's loyalties will be with staff and in conflict with administration or vice versa, and managers need to know with whom conversation is confidential. New managers need to have a sounding board to assist in formulating answers, especially when directives appear to be unfair to staff.

The level of decentralization present in the management structure determines the autonomy allowed. Decentralization permits control or delegation by the nurse manager and the chance to develop and empower the staff. Decentralization promotes manager-manager communications and meetings and avails the nurse manager to other nurse managers or committee chairs of quality assurance, utilization review, continuing education, and infection control. Acknowledgment that highly educated or knowledgeable workers can evaluate, design, and implement the complex care required by nurses can be the attitude of an effective decentralized nursing department. Committee memberships add further to the amount of opinions generated and policies implemented on various issues that help establish management styles.

As a middle manager in nursing, the novice needs patience, advice, and a confidant with whom to debate strategy and concerns, pros and cons. Whether or not the manager's supervisor becomes the resource, that relationship is important to cultivate as well. Sometimes staff members become important as allies to the nurse manager. Their support during day-to-day operations and in crises is the real concern of the nurse manager. The manager acts as a filter through which administrative goals are communicated to staff and change directed. As it is possible to change a dressing differently, still using aseptic principles, the nurse manager can divert information not necessary for staff to know and still communicate necessary policy. Many times rationale is explained when change occurs. Administrative policies can be explained and practiced within the style of the nurse manager. As long as organizational principles are maintained, implementation can be staged by the manager.

Box 2-3 provides a case study that illustrates components of leadership and a management style example that lead to successful change in operations.

Through autonomy, independence, and decentralization come accountability and performance. Efforts at group cohesion and quality must be a result of the manager's ability to motivate and develop staff that is fulfilled and productive. Survival in

---

box 2-3

CASE STUDY OF COMPONENTS OF LEADERSHIP

SITUATION

Catherine has been a unit manager at Hardy Hospital for 3 years and has been recently promoted to a nursing director role. With the promotion has come expanded responsibilities that extend beyond the single unit on which she honed her managerial skills, and she is eagerly applying her proven techniques across a new span of control: cardiac services. Responsible for the staffing and operations of coronary care, cardiac step-down, and the telemetry unit, Catherine now oversees 73 FTEs (full-time equivalents), with a mix of 60% registered nurses, 20% licensed practical nurses, and 20% unlicensed assistive personnel. As an introduction of herself and her role, she has visited the units on all three shifts and spent some time speaking with staff at all levels. Additionally she has obtained, from human resources, finance, and senior administration, status reports regarding overall unit operations and performance.

PROBLEM

Catherine knows that she has inherited a noted "problem child," because her units have a history of poor intradepartmental relations, often affecting the smooth and effective transition of patients along the cardiac continuum of care. The length of stay (LOS) for a cardiac diagnosis has increased by 1.4 days, despite a decreasing acuity, and the productivity outcomes on all three units are below target. Interdepartmental relations have also been affected as the emergency department (ED) has recently logged complaints about transfer delays, resulting in ED backups and diversions. Additionally, the previous quarter's employee satisfaction survey indicated below-average scores in Catherine's areas for the following indicators: (1) I have adequate resources to get my work done, and (2) I would recommend this employer to others. The staff vacancy rate is currently 5%, significantly below the overall hospital rate of 11%, and the turnover has been minimal. Staff interviews reveal frustration with communication between the units and references to "they" or "them" when discussing employees of affiliated cardiac areas.

CASE STUDY OF COMPONENTS OF LEADERSHIP—cont'd

ANALYSIS

A low morale among staff seems readily apparent to Catherine, yet the turnover and vacancy statistics are better than for other areas of the hospital. Is this just a group of disgruntled individuals who, despite their unhappiness, will continue to work, therefore rendering their attitude irritating but harmless? Catherine's experience causes her to reject this hypothesis, aligning staff discontent with falling performance outcomes, and consider that the variables may be dependent. Improving the statistical and operational outcomes is imperative; however, Catherine understands that simply ordering the staff to "quit complaining and take care of patients" will not solve the problem. She describes her managerial imperatives as (1) to clearly identify the issues; (2) to uncover the root causes; (3) to coordinate the development of a plan for improvement; (4) to oversee implementation of the plan; (5) to evaluate the results; and (6) to administer a continuing monitoring function in order to avoid recurrence.

PLAN

Planning is the first activity that Catherine undertakes. She understands that gathering the facts, soliciting input from many sources, and taking time to analyze before acting are likely to prevent wasted resources and unreliable results. This first phase includes (1) scheduling open employee forums on all shifts; (2) presenting current outcome results with comparison to expected performance; (3) facilitating discussions regarding facilitators, motivators, obstacles, and barriers to performance; (4) holding director meetings with departments that interface with cardiac services; (5) performing walk-about visits with patients and families on the units; (6) holding focused discussions with involved medical staff; (7) undertaking a thorough review of all financial, statistical, and other outcome reports for the unit, carefully evaluating for trends; and (8) conferring with human resource specialists, and other experts for specialized advice. She also consults regularly with her mentor, from whom she derives professional support and encouragement.

Throughout this process, purposefully scheduled to unfold within a short time frame, Catherine has committed to clear, open, and frequent communication regarding the steps and rationales. She makes use of all available methodologies, including voice mail, bulletin boards, and meeting agendas, and she even develops a special employee newsletter. She engages a work team, composed of volunteers as well as appointed staff, carefully selecting across positions and attitudes, ensuring diverse representation. She provides an orientation to the team process and illustrates what being a "good team member" looks like. Together Catherine and the team members write a team charter containing the following critical elements: (1) statement of the problem; (2) list of members and contact numbers; (3) degree/limits of authority ascribed to team; (4) supports and resources available (people as well as materials); (5) frequency and type of meetings and communication; (6) budget (as related to team function); (7) time frame for completion; (8) goals/expected outcome; and (9) reward and recognition process for team members.

Catherine now positions herself as a resource and adviser to the team, role modeling problem-solving and analytical skills. She participates as a team member and facilitator, the group having selected a leader from their peers, and assists with goal-directed discussion. She also serves as a resource for accessing data and resources that may not be available through general channels. The team starts by identifying both the common and unique aspects of each cardiac unit and drafts a vision statement for their collective

Continued

CASE STUDY OF COMPONENTS OF LEADERSHIP — cont'd

service line. From there they move to data analysis, quantitative and qualitative, and the discussion of benchmarks for many aspects of their operation. Catherine guides and supports their work, acknowledging teamwork skills and developing the participants' abilities to draw conclusions. She employs standard performance improvement techniques, including brainstorming, cause-and-effect diagrams, force field analysis and statistics to assist the group in the development of an action plan, and provides the necessary routes and resources for approved implementation. Successful planning is rewarded and implementation celebrated. Milestones are set for outcomes and successful achievement, including timeliness, is showcased and celebrated.

GOALS/EXPECTED OUTCOMES

Catherine was not surprised to find that communication was at the root of this problem. The staffs of three of the units where physically isolated from each other, initially due to the physical limitations of the old hospital building. Over time the thinking and communication had become isolated as well, with each unit operating uniquely and independently of the other. Introduction of a team approach, facilitated by coaching and mentoring, developed autonomy, pride, and a little healthy competition among staffs who were now excited about change in which they had input and some control. As a result of the work team, the following recommendations were implemented: (1) monthly joint staff meetings; (2) cross-training, enabling flex-coverage for staffing; (3) self-scheduling with some limited flex-hour options; and (4) the willingness to solicit and apply departmental performance ratings from key customers, including the physicians and the ED.

---

middle management means success, with respect from both upper management and subordinate staff.

MENTORING

Mentoring is a subject not covered with any depth in traditional nursing school curricula. It is seen as a subject for those in business and management and can offer inspiration and real-world role-modeling to nurse managers.

A mentor should be an individual who:

- Demonstrates managerial and communication expertise.
- Inspires risk-taking and action.
- Constructively criticizes without overpowering.
- Allows freedom for growth.
- Assists with goal-setting.
- Provides guidance with problem-solving.
- Coaches the mentee through difficult situations (e.g., conflict resolution).
- Provides positive feedback.
- Serves as a role model.
- Supports the mentee.

Mentoring is an important skill to develop for those in management positions. Guiding a young or new nurse manager can be a growth experience for both the mentor and mentee. Seeking out a mentor role model as support for the new nurse manager should be a high priority while identifying other tasks already discussed.

The mentor acts as a nurturer who listens and guides the new nurse manager through dilemmas, with each encounter ultimately requiring less input from the mentor. The mentor-mentee relationship must not be a power struggle but rather a nonjudgmental, comfortable association. The capacity to have honest discussions without consequences can be enriching. The mentor must remain loyal through all phases of the new manager's growth. The new nurse manager must utilize newly learned strategies consistently until they are mastered. The mentor-mentee relationship is a dynamic one that goes through both periods of relative stability and times of higher need. A mentoring relationship may be the most important determinant for success in leadership roles (Box 2-4).

---

box 2-4

TIPS FOR MENTOR AND MENTEE

TIPS FOR MENTOR

Meetings outside the work environment are best, when possible.
Telephone consultation is a viable alternative.
Follow-up and/or feedback on previous concerns is a good starting point.
Anticipate common, difficult situations for discussions.
Suggest types of management conferences for the mentee to attend.
Respect confidentiality.

TIPS FOR MENTEE

Define and clarify professional and personal goals (e.g., improve knowledge, skills, and
    abilities in order to increase potential and identify opportunities).
Identify learning plans and objectives (e.g., self-development needs, which may be areas
    for improvement).
Verbalize what you want the mentor to assist you with.
Make time to receive and apply the mentoring information and output.
Undertake self-study in areas of defined need—books, articles, classes, etc.
The mentor need not be someone at your organization.
Organize your questions and concerns to maximize time allotment.
Take notes.
Ask your mentor if he/she can be called at home.
Regularly assess satisfaction with your mentor regarding experiences.
Utilize role-playing with the mentor to actualize learning.
Accept feedback in a positive manner.
Remember that mentors appreciate courtesies such as thank-you notes and other
    indicators of thoughtful consideration.

According to Holloran in her study of mentoring among nurse executives, "there were consistent differences between those who had a mentor versus those who had not."[27] She also found different levels of mentoring, depending on a participant's definition of the term. Role models may be guiding forces without the more personal commitment of the mentor. Those who have been mentored have experienced the following:

- Greater job satisfaction
- Higher productivity
- Increased professionalism
- Reduced turnover rates
- Greater organizational power
- Superior management skills

Mentoring is an interpersonal, nursing, and management tool to be used for decision-making, problem-solving, and planned change. Mentor connections may be long or short term but always should be gratifying and supportive. Confidence in one's abilities is a first step toward choosing to mentor new nurse managers or to develop the leadership potential of those we manage.

SUMMARY

New nurse managers may feel overwhelmed after the "honeymoon" period and as the realities and constraints of daily group management are identified. Early adoption of a leadership style that is effective for both staff and manager provides order and security in a highly stressful atmosphere. Consistency and objectivity with the staff create an environment of stability that can foster further growth and a higher level of professionalism.

The test of managerial success in nursing is developing a comfortable and consistent managerial style that facilitates growth and satisfaction for both the manager and staff. Professionalism includes experienced nurses and managers mentoring new nurses and new managers. Nursing may not have promoted this concept as well as has been documented in the business world, and despite the popular notion of nurses as nurturers, nurses have not always been supportive of or encouraging development of each other's leadership qualities. Nurses have a very important role in the positive nurturing of new managers and new nurses. Mentoring, whether formal or informal, must be considered, as is continuing education, a professional responsibility.

QUESTIONS FOR CONSIDERATION

1. List three attributes of a leader.
2. Describe three management styles and provide a practical example of each style.
3. Discuss the mentor/mentee relationship, the benefits of this relationship, and identify your own prospective mentor(s).

4. Create a case study that illustrates components of effective leadership. Try to make the case study as detailed as possible, incorporating aspects of MBO.

5. Review your organization's chart and describe the reporting mechanisms and other facets of the organizational hierarchy housed in that chart.

References

1. McGregor D: 1983, *Leadership and motivation*, Cambridge, MIT Press.
2. Mill M, Babcock D: *Critical thinking applied to nursing*, St Louis, 1996, Mosby.
3. Mathena K: Nursing leadership skills, *Journal of Nursing Administration* 32(3), 2002.
4. Bethel S: *Making a difference: 12 qualities that make you a leader*, New York, 1990, GP Putnam and Sons.
5. Dunham J, Fisher E: Nurse executive profile of excellent nursing leadership, *Nursing Administration Quarterly* 15:4, 1990.
6. Weick K, et al: What the emerging workforce wants in its leaders, *Image* 34(3), 2002.
7. Kawamoto K: Nursing leadership: to thrive in a world of change, *Nursing Administration Quarterly* 15(3), 1994.
8. Blanchard KB, Lorber R: *Putting the one minute manager to work*, New York, 1987, William Morrow.
9. Burns JM: *Leadership*, New York, 1978, Harper & Row.
10. Dunham J, Klafehn K: Transformational leadership and the nurse executive, *Journal of Nursing Administration* 20:28, 1990.
11. Bernard L, Walsh M: *Leadership: the key to the professionalism of nursing*, St Louis, 1995, p. 63.
12. Barker A, Young C: Transformational leadership—the feminist connection in postmodern organizations, *Holistic Nursing Practice* 9:1, 1994.
13. Hersey P, Blanchard K: *Management of organizational behavior: utilizing human resources*, ed 5 Englewood Cliffs, NJ, 1988, Prentice-Hall.
14. Fiedler F, Cherners M: *Improving leadership effectiveness*, New York, 1984, John Wiley & Sons.
15. Tannenbaum R, Schmidt W: How to choose a leadership pattern, *Harvard Business Review* 21:51, 1991.
16. Stivers C: Why can't a women be less like a man? *Journal of Nursing Administration* 21:51, 1991.
17. Whittier S: Effective team building; more important than ever, *Home Care Nurse News*, Marrelli and Associates 6(3):3, 1999.
18. Lewin K: *Field theory in social sciences*, New York, 1971, Harper.
19. Orem D: *Nursing concepts of practice*, New York, 1971, McGraw-Hill.
20. McGregor D: *The human side of enterprise*, New York, 1960, McGraw-Hill.
21. Ouchi WG; *Theory Z—how American business can meet the Japanese challenge*, Reading, MA, 1981, Addison-Wesley.
22. Deming W: *Out of crisis*, Cambridge, MA, 1986, MIT Press.
23. Smith B, Discenza R, Piland N: Reflections on total quality management and health care. In *Health care supervisor*, Gaithersburg, MD, 1995, Aspen.
24. McConnell C: Total quality and shifting management paradigm, *Health care supervisor*, Gaithersburg, MD, 1995, Aspen.
25. Flarey D: Redesigning management roles, *Journal of Nursing Administration* 21:44, 1991.
26. Gillies DA: *Nursing management: a system approach*, Philadelphia, 1989, WB Saunders.
27. Holloran S: Mentoring: the experience of nursing service executives, *Journal of Nursing Administration* 23:2, 1993.

For Further Reading

Brinkman R, Kirschner R: *Dealing with people you can't stand*, New York, 1994, McGraw-Hill.

Clinical managers help agency staff cope with growth, stress, *Hospital Home Health* 9(8), 1982.

Davidhizer R: Managerial credibility, *Nursing Administration Quarterly* 13(3), 1989.

Dixon D: Achieving results through transformational leadership, *Journal of Nursing Administration* 29(12), 1999.

Douglas L: *The effective nurse: leader and manager*, St Louis, 1984, Mosby.

Drucker P: *Managing for results*, New York, 1984, Harper & Row.

Dunham-Taylor J: Nurse executive transformational leadership found in participative organizations, *Journal of Nursing Administration* 30(5), 2000.

Etzioni A: Humble decision making, *Harvard Business Review* 21(2), 1989.

Fisher R, Ury W, Patton B: *Getting to yes: negotiating agreement without giving in, ed 2*, New York, 1992, Penguin.

Gillies D: *Nursing management: a system approach*, Philadelphia, 1982, WB Saunders.

Hackbarth D, Androwich F: Graduate nursing education for leadership in home care, *Caring* 8(2), 1989.

Harvey E, Ventura S: *Walk awhile in my shoes: gut-level, real-world messages from employees to managers*, Dallas, 2002, Walk the Talk Company, Performance Systems Corporation.

Hood J, Smith H: Quality of worklife in home: the contribution of leaders personal concern for staff, *Journal of Nursing Administration* 24(1), 1994.

Koslowski M, et al: An interactive model of leadership, *Nursing Administration Quarterly* 15(1), 1990.

Lasater M: Strategies for organizational change in home healthcare, *Home Healthcare Nurse* 11(2), 1993.

Leuesque R: *Business planning in home health agencies: a guide to nurse executives*, Columbia Teachers College, 1991, Ed.D.

Marquis B, Hurston C: *Management decision-making for nurses* (2nd ed), New York, JB Lippincott, 1994.

Matheny M: The art of management: three simple rules, *Nursing Management* 21(12), 1990.

Medley F, Larochelle D: Nursing management: transformational leadership and job satisfaction, *Journal of Nursing Administration* 9, 1996.

Moloney M: *Leadership in nursing: theory, strategies, action*, St Louis, 1979, Mosby.

Noone C, Szekely L: Working with consultants to achieve home health agency goals, *Journal of Nursing Administration* 21(10), 1991.

Orth C, et al: The manager's role as coach and mentor, *Journal of Nursing Administration* 20(9), 1991.

Phifer L: Managerial leaders and their influence in nursing, *Pediatric Nursing* 16(3), 1990.

Rosener JB: Ways women lead, *Harvard Business Review* 68(6), 1990.

Stachura L, Hoff J: Toward achievement of mentoring of nurses, *Nursing Administration Quarterly* 15(1), 1990.

Tappen RM: *Nursing leadership and management: concepts and practice*. Philadelphia, 2001, FA Davis.

Walton M: *The Deming management method*, New York, 1980, Dodd Mead.

Weick, Prydon, et al: What the emerging work force wants in its leaders, *Image* 34(3), 2002.

CHAPTER 3

HUMAN RESOURCE MANAGEMENT

T.M. MARRELLI

Personnel decisions and issues can be some of the most challenging episodes of any managerial career. Conversely, the effective use of human management skills can be the highlight of your professional career. With this in mind, this chapter emphasizes the latter. It is important to note that we all improve and grow through practice. This is especially true in personnel or human resource (HR) management functions. According to Patz and others,[1] a national survey of academic health chief nurse executives and nurse managers demonstrated that human management skills were considered the most important criterion of effectiveness. Flexibility, negotiation, and compromise were second. However, the management of human resources in a market exhibiting severe shortages includes flexibility, negotiation, and compromise, all while under great stress to manage the budget and meet the staffing effectiveness needs of the unit and the organization.

WHAT IS HUMAN RESOURCE MANAGEMENT?

Simply put, HR management can be defined as effective interpersonal communications among all levels of employees and staff. (Manager's Tip 3-1 on p. 76 summarizes some key issues in human resources.) This chapter is organized into the format followed in the employment process. Therefore the discussion begins with the recruitment process and proceeds to interviewing, hiring, orienting, coaching, counseling, training, motivating, and evaluating performance.

STAFF RECRUITMENT

If all managers were able to recruit the right staff for the right positions, their jobs would be tremendously easier. However, that is not the case, primarily because of human nature and the inability to discern the small seed of discontent that the candidate has with the organization or position during the interview process. There are methods to eliminate as many of the variables as possible in the new manager's search for the right candidate.

Recruitment in health care is a strong industry—it has been for the past 20 years. From the nursing, physical therapy, and pharmacist shortages of the 1980s and 1990s to the shortages of health care managers, recruitment has definitely been a major challenge to all levels of health care management. Unfortunately, the shortage of health care professionals in the first decade of the 21st century is far more severe than any of the prior shortages that we have seen in the 1960s, 1970s, and 1980s. This is a shortage that if not addressed aggressively may change the face of health care as no prior incident has. In addition we may not see the full effects until

MANAGER'S TIP 3-1

10 VITAL HR POINTS

✔ Clearly make your expectations known and hold employees accountable to them from the first day. Give lots of feedback, both formally and informally.

✔ Hiring and other personnel decisions are some of the most important decisions made as a manager.

✔ You make better, more informed decisions as you gain experience.

✔ HR issues must be addressed and dealt with effectively; usually they will not be solved without interpersonal action or intervention.

✔ You cannot communicate too often; convey unit and organizational goals, constructive or positive feedback (including a thank you for a job well done), or any issue affecting the staff's work.

✔ Remember that all work is done through the staff. This is the core of HR management.

✔ Familiarize yourself with your organization's policy and procedure manuals dealing with HR issues.

✔ Remember, you are not alone. The problems surfacing have occurred before and there is probably a standard procedure for you to follow. Integrate the knowledge from the manuals into daily practice.

✔ When making personnel decisions, particularly those involved with hiring, consider your needs (e.g., the organization, staffing patterns, care delivery system, types of patients or clients, shifts offered, benefit packages, tuition reimbursement for professional staff, and the type of nursing or administrative experience needed). Prioritize these needs.

✔ Use all resources and experts available to you for your growth as a manager in this important area. For example, if special HR department professionals or nurse recruiter professionals are available, use their services and expertise. This is especially true for areas where state or federal laws apply and you may not be aware or have the in-depth knowledge needed to interpret or implement these laws in your setting. Examples of these areas include equal opportunity employment concerns, Family and Medical Leave Act (FMLA), Americans with Disabilities Act (ADA), workers' compensation questions, benefit compensation issues, and other areas of a specialized nature.

well into the second decade. For an in-depth discussion related to recruitment and retention, see Chapter 4.

A necessity for the new nurse manager is retaining her/his existing staff. Another needed trait is proactivity. Not waiting until a staff member's final week before beginning the replacement process is the sign of a proactive manager. Historic unit-patient census trends over a period of time and anticipated openings of new units, beds, or services should give a manager a general idea of the amount and types of staff needed and when. Management by objective planning should occur, with the manager "mapping" out a strategy to get the needed staff according to the unit timeline. If the position is a critical one and historically has been hard to fill, the manager must have plans B, C, and D ready should plan A prove unsuccessful in identifying potential candidates.

First of all, even though it sounds so simple, develop a detailed outline of what traits and skills are being sought in this search. Understand all the requirements of the position and determine what the organization needs in this individual. Loyalty to the organization's staff should be a major initiative for the manager. Always look within your ranks for the new potential manager or candidate for another prime position. If you have been mentoring and developing staff, there may be individuals looking for an opportunity to expand his/her career horizons and move up in the organization. However, this type of recruitment should be done carefully and the position requirements should never be forgotten in an effort to "fit the job to the person."

The most common avenues to pursue when initiating the recruitment process (once the position and the hiring ability have been approved per organizational policy) are as follows:
- Internet posting
- Human resources department posting boards
- Local colleges or technical schools
- Local professional organizations
- Professional contacts
- Newspaper or professional journal classified sections
- Job fairs
- Specialty recruiting agencies (for the hard to place or specialty positions)
- Informal contacts/employee referrals (bonus programs)
- Web-based recruiting with hyperlinks to the hospital's Web page from postings on national specialty professional organizations

Reviewing Applications and Resumes

After the search has produced a number of applicants for the position, review the applications/resumes and rank each accordingly:
1. Inappropriate (candidates lack the required education, experience, and/or salary requirements)

2. Possible (second-tier candidates—skills/experience/education not exactly as requested)
3. Most likely (these candidates should be invited for the first interview)

Remember not to depend too heavily on what is written on an application or resume. It is the interview and reference checking process in which information is elicited about the skills a candidate will bring to the position. It is advisable to have at least five potential candidates to interview in the first round. As per organizational protocol, plan for the interview sessions.

INTERVIEWING

In planning the interview process, a succinct guide for the division of time has been developed by Donald Lombardi in his text, *Handbook for the New Health Care Manager*. Lombardi divides the interview time into three sections, stressing that the candidate should do most of the talking (about 80% to 85%) during the main part of the interview; 90% to 95% is too much, not affording the interviewer the chance to ask the leading or needed questions. The following list describes the three sections, the time usually allotted, and the percentage of time normally allotted to each participant:

*   Introduction/warm-up (3 to 5 minutes)
    Interviewer 75%
    Candidate 25%
*   Interview conducted (15 to 25 minutes)
    Interviewer 15% to 20%
    Candidate 80% to 85%
*   Interview questions and answers/wrap-up (4 to 5 minutes)
    Interviewer 75% to 80%
    Candidate 20% to 25%[2]

Manager's Tips 3-2 and 3-3 present some suggestions to help in preparing for and conducting an interview.

HIRING A NEW TEAM MEMBER

Congratulations! You successfully sold yourself and your organization and you now have a new staff member. Hopefully, your staff members were involved in the process and welcome this new nurse. There are steps you can take to ensure a smooth transition for new staff members (Manager's Tip 3-4).

Making a new staff member feel welcome and part of the group is the key to long-term employee satisfaction. The ideas in the tip list are simple yet important in making your practice setting a place where new staff feel comfortable and grow professionally.

MANAGER'S TIP 3-2

PREPARING FOR A SUCCESSFUL INTERVIEW

✔ Read any organization manuals available on the process. There may be factors unique to your setting.

✔ Identify the core requirements of the position and identify the traits that the most successful employees in this position have. Look for these same traits in the applicants.

✔ Plan for the interview. This is vital to an effective interview for both the interviewer and the applicant. Clearly define goals and needs before the actual interview. The applicant who cannot understand your needs may make incorrect assumptions and accept the position but leave shortly thereafter, disillusioned and angry. Clearly defining your needs includes answering the following questions: Do you need a nurse who has been or wants to be cross-trained in a particular specialty area? Do you need an experienced hospice nurse with specialized symptom management expertise? Try to define succinctly what your patient area needs to function more effectively.

✔ Plan your discussion with the specific questions and topics to be addressed, especially outlining behavior-based questions that test the applicant's ability to think on her/his feet.

✔ Use the same questions for all the candidates, so that the interview answers may be compared when making the hiring decision.

✔ Arrange to have your phone calls held and other interruptions deferred until the interview is complete. This demonstrates to applicants that you respect them and value their time.

✔ Schedule someone to be in charge during your interviews. This is particularly important if you schedule consecutive interviews.

MANAGER'S TIP 3-3

CONDUCTING A SUCCESSFUL INTERVIEW

In an effective interview the parties are allowed to clearly communicate and should be allotted enough uninterrupted time so that the interviewee is comfortable. Both parties should be allowed to meet their common objectives of exchanging information.

✔ Start on time. Do not keep the applicant waiting because this is not a sign of power, but of rudeness. If you are not punctual because of a unit emergency or other emergent concern, be professional and apologetic.

✔ Provide the applicant with a copy of the position description, if not already done.

✔ Describe the position to the applicant and delineate the responsibilities of the individual who will be chosen to fill the position.

✔ Remember how you felt when you were interviewed for your last position and what was said that put you at ease.

Continued

CONDUCTING A SUCCESSFUL INTERVIEW — cont'd

✔ Clearly outline at the onset the time allotted for the interview. For example, "I know personnel told you this interview would be approximately 1 hour. We need to cover the important information and wrap up by 2 PM because I have a meeting immediately following our interview."

✔ Have the applicant verbally verify what has been written on the application or resume.

✔ Protect yourself by avoiding statements or words that may lead to accusations of sexual or other types of discrimination. Common examples, very well known to most female nurses, include *honey*, *sweetie*, and *dear*.

✔ Do not inquire about spouses, children (or plans for children), day-care situations, or other sensitive areas.

✔ Treat everyone with the same respect, consideration, and professionalism.

✔ Be professional, kind, and a good listener. The better your active listening skills, the more information you receive from the applicant.

✔ When possible, use open-ended questions to elicit an open response. Ask about common problem situations and how the applicant would resolve them.

✔ Use silence; this allows the applicant to share more information.

✔ Remember first impressions do count, so make it a good one. You may want this applicant to also want to work on your team.

✔ Be enthusiastic and talk about the good things happening in your health care setting.

✔ Give a walking tour of the clinical area and of the institution, when appropriate.

✔ Provide a brochure on your program or health setting. Use the information listed as general information to relax the applicant initially or as points of discussion during the interview.

✔ Outline the health care organization's mission statement or values statement and how this position helps to achieve those goals.

✔ Dress professionally and neatly. If the interview is in your office, remember your office reflects you and the organization.

✔ Talk about the orientation program for new staff.

✔ Discuss the day-to-day operational aspects of the position.

✔ Elicit from the applicant why she/he is applying for this job. Though this sounds simple, the responses are rarely as simple.

✔ Ask, "If you are chosen for this position, what contributions will you make to the unit [hospital, organization] in the first year and where would you expect those to lead over the next 5 years?"[2] Most applicants are prepared with a canned answer to where would you like to be in 5 years—the more important question is what is the applicant going to do for us to earn that advancement?

✔ Ask the applicant to describe what her/his contribution would be to the department.

✔ Validate the applicant's understanding of the position.

✔ Repeat the applicant's response to make sure that what you understood to have been said is correct.

✔ Discuss the time frame in which you would like to fill the position.

✔ Have the applicant describe how her/his last manager and peers would describe her/his performance.

✔ Ask the applicant if she/he has any questions for you.

✔ Bring the applicant back for another interview if appropriate.

- ✔ Talk about the staff development program.
- ✔ Discuss the type of documentation used in your unit or area.
- ✔ Discuss the dress code requirements of the position.
- ✔ Summarize what will happen next at the conclusion. For example, "I have interviews scheduled through. . . . " or " I hope to have the process completed by . . ." (specify time frame or date).
- ✔ When appropriate, have the nurse recruiter or your staff interview your final candidate(s).
- ✔ For managerial candidates (e.g., assistant nurse manager), have members of your staff interview the final applicant(s).

MANAGER'S TIP 3-4

WELCOMING A NEW STAFF MEMBER

- ✔ Show the new staff member her/his personal space. This can include the locker, mailbox, phone message slot, or other areas. Make sure to clearly mark her/his name, spelled correctly, on such items.
- ✔ Schedule the new staff member to have lunch with those members of your staff who can be positive role models.
- ✔ Have the new staff nurse's identification badge, access/parking sticker, and security card completed as soon as possible.
- ✔ Schedule a lunch with all other new professional nursing staff. This peer camaraderie leads to job satisfaction. It also teaches the new staff members about other aspects of your facility or setting.
- ✔ Schedule and lead a personalized walking tour for the new nurse.
- ✔ Introduce the new nurse to key personnel and others encountered during the tour.
- ✔ Discuss the organization's buddy, preceptor, or mentor system.
- ✔ Allot time in your schedule at least three times a week (even if for a few minutes) for the first few months to check on the new staff member's progress. Delegate this responsibility to a trusted nurse leader on your staff if you will be unavailable. This is also a good time to ask if what you said in the interview holds true in practice. This will help you tailor comments to future applicants.
- ✔ Write a welcome note to the new staff member and have other staff members sign the note.
- ✔ Hold a breakfast or lunch meeting so all staff members can meet the new nurse. This is particularly important in practice areas where the staff members are rarely together, such as a home health agency or a community-based hospice.
- ✔ Personally spend time with the new staff nurse, especially introducing her/him to other team members in the organization at all levels.
- ✔ Create a phone list for new staff members. Alphabetize the list by first names. (Everyone else can remember the new nurse's first and last names, but it is unrealistic to expect the new nurse to remember all other staff members' last names immediately.)

ORIENTATION FOR NEW STAFF MEMBERS

Orientation is the most important time for a new employee. Starting a new job is both frightening and exhilarating, and the welcome and integration into the team is of prime concern. In nursing, orientation has not been given the respect and commitment that it deserves. This time period is useful in many ways:

- Orientation is the initial investment that we make in an employee, and the return on that investment will be repaid over the life of that employee's time with the organization. Orientation is also a critical JCAHO standard.
- It provides the employee with an overall perspective of the goals/mission of the organization.
- It familiarizes the new employee with organizational and clinical area–specific policies and procedures.
- It allows the new employee to interact with staff on a less stressful basis.
- It allows the employer to verify the competency and skills of the new employee.
- It allows both parties time to determine if this hiring decision was correct. Manager's Tip 3-5 on p. 83 provides a checklist for use in orienting a new staff member.

Remember, you get out of people, or staff, only what you expect. Studies have shown that the manager's expectations are the key to the staff's behavior and development. Livingston,[3] who has studied this "Pygmalion" performance, states, "The way managers treat their subordinates is subtly influenced by what they expect of them. If manager's expectations are high, productivity is likely to be excellent. If their expectations are low, productivity is likely to be poor. It is as though there were a law that caused subordinates' performance to rise or fall to meet managers' expectations."

With this information in mind, it is important to note that your enthusiasm (or apathy) is contagious, and work output is directly related to the level of managerial expectation. Use this important information to your advantage.

Nurse managers should make every effort to allow new employees the time to attend all elements of the orientation program—for both the unit and the organization—no matter how busy the patient area is. Allow new staff members to complete this process. They will respect you more as a manager and will be unable to claim that they were not exposed to needed information. It is very hard to catch up when these orientation programs are curtailed or deleted.

The clearer the instructions and direction provided in the orientation period, the fewer problems you will usually face in the future. Therefore the extra time you take in the beginning will pay off. You will not have to be continually clarifying rules. When you communicate rules or important information, use direct eye contact, be professional, and restate the specifics that need to be understood by both parties. There is nothing worse than a nurse saying, "I was never told that," when the subject relates to an important part of the job or could have caused a poor patient

MANAGER'S TIP 3-5

NEW STAFF MEMBER ORIENTATION CHECKLIST

Professional nurses practice in so many settings that it is not possible to list all areas that must be covered with the new nurse. This list contains the most common themes. Some items mentioned are clearly specialized areas of practice.

- ✔ Benefit; compensation packages, including medical and dental policies (including when coverage begins); malpractice; licensure; professional inservice credits; physical, overtime, and compensation time policies; other benefits.
- ✔ Leave allotments, including vacation, sick days, holidays, educational leave, other leave.
- ✔ Frequency and schedule of paydays.
- ✔ Savings plans available (e.g., thrift or credit union).
- ✔ Position description.
- ✔ Description of other team members' roles in patient care planning process.
- ✔ Hours of shifts, specific time to report, check-in procedures, break times.
- ✔ Uniform requirements and any associated compensation; name tag or access/security badge.
- ✔ Employee assistance program availability.
- ✔ Personalized orientation schedule, including clinical demonstrations, CPR, and other educational resources specific to clinical practice.
- ✔ An in-depth personalized tour.
- ✔ Availability and hours of organization's day-care facility and/or benefits, if applicable.
- ✔ Confidentiality policies and HIPAA training
- ✔ The health care facility's Nursing Plan for Care and philosophy.
- ✔ The state's Nurse Practice Act.
- ✔ The written standards of care.
- ✔ Schedule of introductory period and ongoing performance appraisal evaluation(s).
- ✔ On-call schedule and compensation process for on-call.
- ✔ Supply acquisition and process for charging to patient or unit account.
- ✔ The committees that the unit or staff are represented on and the process for input into change.
- ✔ Clinical and administrative policies and procedures.
- ✔ The program mission statement and objectives.
- ✔ Safety or risk management policies–include security (both patient and staff), Occupational Safety and Health Administration (OSHA), Centers for Disease Control and Prevention (CDC), or other safety concerns (e.g., fire or emergency preparedness plans, universal precautions, seat belt use for staff members driving in the community, violence in the workplace).
- ✔ Clinical documentation orientation, including forms, type and frequency of documentation required, paper flow, and an introduction to the nursing computer system.
- ✔ Quality improvement processes.
- ✔ Distribution and stocking of initial supplies for nurse bags in the community or other outreach setting (e.g., maps, resources available after office hours, report processes, use of pagers, cellular phones, and mileage reimbursement forms).
- ✔ Process review of how employee actions affect patient care and reimbursement systems.

outcome. For this reason, another nurse whose judgment and skills you trust should be "a buddy" with the new nurse during the formal orientation period. In some settings this person is called a preceptor. This delegation accomplishes three things: it (1) behaviorally demonstrates your trust in your staff; (2) frees you up from day-to-day operational orientation; and (3) develops the managerial skills of the staff nurse to whom you have delegated the preceptor responsibility. This type of delegation of responsibility empowers your staff and helps them to achieve more personally and professionally.

There are two main methods of ongoing communication once the official orientation or probationary period is completed. They are (1) counseling or coaching and (2) staff development. Both processes are equally important in different ways. These two major communication methods are discussed below.

Coaching

It would be ideal to work in a setting where everyone, once adequately oriented, functioned smoothly as if on automatic pilot. Unfortunately, this is not realistic. However, with careful planning, nurse managers have been able to choose, groom, and motivate a special group of nurses to work together, address issues, and reach consensus so effectively that it felt that way. This then can be a realistic goal.

Until that point is reached, ongoing training and reeducation must occur to attain professional and program goals. Counseling is often the vehicle used for this needed communication. Positive communication, such as that used in orientation and training sessions, is usually valued over corrective action, which is how counseling is sometimes perceived. Although it is often considered negative by some managers, counseling or coaching should be viewed as an opportunity for growth or to identify individual problem behaviors before they affect staff. Often, it is in the one-to-one encounters with staff members that the effective manager learns information informally that assists in unit or program planning. With this in mind, it is important that effective counseling skills be addressed (Manager's Tip 3-6).

An example of coaching documentation using SOAP. The following is a common example of unacceptable behavior that a nurse manager may encounter; it would affect other staff members and the smooth operation of your unit. A new staff nurse, 2 months out of formal orientation, spends the first 20 minutes of most mornings trying to change the unit's patient care assignment. She usually confronts you in front of the entire change-of-shift staff and, it always seems, on the mornings following an evening-shift crisis that needs to be immediately documented by you. Her behavior negatively impacts your unit, setting the stage for a stressful day. Even though she is relatively new, her clinical skills are strong, and she has already assumed the role of informal leader in the group.

As an effective manager, you (1) identify a problem behavior, (2) address it early and when you are not angry, and (3) ask her privately to stop by your office in 10 minutes (delayed counseling only adds to her worry and may cause the employee

MANAGER'S TIP 3-6

SUGGESTIONS FOR EFFECTIVE COACHING OR COUNSELING

✔ Look at counseling as positive and as a challenge.

✔ Visualize yourself as being good at it.

✔ Remember, expect the best and chances are your staff will live up to your expectations.

✔ Know and abide by contractual guidelines of union agreements, if applicable.

✔ Always address an identified behavior problem sooner rather than later.

✔ Do not attempt to counsel or reprimand staff in front of other people.

✔ Respect the staff's right to disagree with your assessment of the situation.

✔ Be objective. When discussing an incident use the factual *who, what, when,* and *where* queries that reporters use.

✔ Try to not allow your feelings to color your input or behavior. If you are very angry or irritated, it is usually better to talk at a later time when you have calmed down and can think and speak objectively and rationally.

✔ Do not overreact. Talk to a peer manager or a mentor for input before the session and imagine and act how that calm and effective role model would react in the same situation.

✔ Use organizational mandated formats. Document objectionable behavior in a factual, concise manner, listing the desired behaviors, policy or procedural reference(s), and time frame for adherence to a written action plan. If this is a written counseling statement, make sure that the employee acknowledges receipt of the information, in writing. Date and countersign the employee's signature, as appropriate.

✔ Discuss all written statements with the human resource department manager or designee to clarify that all organizational procedures (e.g., union contractual guidelines) are being met. This discussion should occur before the employee session.

✔ Set a time limit on the discussion. For example, "Lisa, as I said at the start of our meeting, we have 15 minutes, so now we need to wrap up in 5 minutes."

✔ Use listening skills and silence after you ask the employee to detail for you the events or incidents in question.

✔ Summarize the discussion and the outcomes or plan of action clearly and succinctly.

✔ Try to schedule the session at a time and in an environment free of interruptions.

✔ Conversely, if this employee has a long-standing pattern of behavioral infractions and does not listen to time or other limits you set, control your environment by setting up planned interruptions (e.g., have someone page you). Do not reinforce the employee's behavior by putting up with it.

✔ Always keep employee comments focused on behaviors, not personality or another employee's actions. Bring an employee back to the conversation at hand by saying, for example, "That may be true about John Doe, but today we are discussing your behavior and how it is impacting our unit's ability to accomplish our objectives."

✔ Treat all staff members the same; be consistent and thorough.

✔ Practice the skill of not being defensive and always try to see the other's point of view.

Continued

SUGGESTIONS FOR EFFECTIVE COACHING OR COUNSELING — cont'd

✔ Use the same documentation format for all staff members. Some health settings have their own counseling forms. Many use the SOAP format with very good results.

✔ Always counsel face to face. Do not use e-mail because the tone is not always clear.

✔ Do not address problematic behavior(s) with those employes who do not exhibit this problematic behavior. An example is holding a staff meeting with all staff, when the behavior only pertains to one or two of the team members.

✔ Determine what infractions at your place of employment are cause for verbal or written warnings.

✔ Seek guidance from the human resources department in order to avoid future litigation.

✔ Be a prudent nurse and document all coaching sessions. In addition, any written anecdotal notes or documentation of critical incidents will assist in your objective feedback and recall for performance appraisals. Use this written documentation as a reminder to yourself by keeping it in the staff member's personnel folder. Remember, awards, counseling, and other discussions are written objective reminders when it is performance evaluation time.

✔ Follow up counseling with another scheduled session as indicated in your disciplinary protocol. Hopefully, the problem is resolved and you will be giving positive feedback to the employee at the second meeting.

✔ Do not allow the employee to continue practicing unacceptable behavior. Instead, continue to the next step in the disciplinary process. If you do *not*, the resultant problem behavior will only increase and other staff members will lose respect for your managerial abilities and/or act inappropriately themselves.

✔ Remember that effective employee counseling does modify behavior (but the employee has to want to modify her/his behavior).

✔ Managerial avoidance of counseling employees who do not abide by organizational policies and/or procedures can result in the employee being allowed to continue such behaviors, based on "past practice." At that point, it becomes very difficult to discipline the employee and it may be demoralizing for other staff to work in such an environment.

✔ Always try to end these sessions on a positive note.

✔ Believe that all employees want to do a good job.

✔ Give feedback to all staff members on a regular, frequent basis.

to become defensive and upset). It is 7:40 AM and she comes into your office. The following is an example of the documentation that addresses what occurred in the meeting and the joint plan for resolution.

S(ubjective): Ms. Davis says, "I don't know why I do that every morning. I don't like my assignment. I still think though that Mrs. Smith should stay with Nurse Carter and I should get Mr. Jones, since he has cancer and you know I'm in school to become a clinical specialist in oncology."

O(bjective): 7:40 AM, 12/15/200_, Ms. Davis is in my office after two previous informal *(list dates, when known)* discussions with her about the same topic: wanting to revamp the patient assignments totally. Today specifically there were two nurses upset because they told me they were still not sure what their assignments were—and this was after report. Ms. Davis was calm and clearly stated that she transferred 2 months ago to care primarily for cancer patients.

A(ssessment): Situation leaves the staff feeling unsettled and compromises patient care by the nonproductive time spent haggling over assignments. After an open discussion with Ms. Davis, she believes I am not respecting her area of expertise and that she had the understanding when she transferred to this unit that she would care primarily for oncologic and hospice patients.

P(lan): Ms. Davis verbally validated that she understands how this behavior is not conductive to a team effort in caring for patients and why some of the nurses have discussed the problem with me. The plan we agreed on is as follows: when possible, I will assign her cancer patients. However, she verbalizes understanding of changing staffing needs and will accept assignments without comment or further discussion starting tomorrow at morning report. In addition, she asked that I investigate the possibility of her being cross-trained to the organization's affiliated hospice program. She stated that she believes this would allow more flexibility and perhaps continuity of care for some of our unit's inpatients. We will meet next Tuesday at this time to follow up on our plan and to validate that the complaining sessions have stopped as demonstrated by timely acceptance of assignments delegated.

The documentation of employee performance demonstrated specific, objective behaviors that necessitated the meeting. As shown in this example, training needs are often identified through effective counseling. Effective and timely feedback of clear expectations is critical in setting the employee up for success. The outcome of these sessions should leave both parties feeling better; the manager, who will see a positive behavior change because of the information learned in the session, and the employee, who sees that the effective manager identified training needs that will help the organization as well as the nurse's professional goals. These training needs are best met in ongoing staff development or educational programs.

Staff Development

An effective staff development program and expert patient care clinicians are vital to patient care, staff growth, satisfaction, and a quality care environment. Orientation, planned services, and continuing education programs all support an effective staff development program. With the constant development of myriad clinical breakthroughs, new technology, legislation, and other factors, professional nurses must be kept up-to-date. These educational encounters help ensure nursing maintains recognized standards of practice. In addition, a well-planned and executed staff development program is valued highly by staff. The effective new nurse manager recognizes that allowing staff specialization through continuing education is an adjunct to her/his role-modeling and facilitates staff attendance, thus behaviorally reinforcing the value of ongoing education and training in professional practice.

The role of the staff development department is one of support to the patient care staff of the health care organization. Its department structure and reporting mechanism are as varied as the different health care organizations and mission/ philosophy statements. It is becoming more common to see nursing education and/or staff development merged into the education departments serving the needs of other personnel in the facility in an effort to combine services and become more cost-efficient.

The nurse manager should have a basic understanding of the role of the staff development department and how each patient care unit interfaces with the department. Some of the more basic staff development responsibilities should include (but may not be limited to):

1. Age-specific competency-based orientation.
2. Competency program development and implementation.
3. Adjunct to health entity's improvement of organizational performance (IOP).
4. Planning, development, implementation, and evaluation of organizational education program.
5. Presentation of classes.
6. Maintenance of staff education records.
7. Community health education programs.
8. Consultative services to internal and external customers (department managers, local community health groups, others).

As employee monetary benefits start to plateau or decline, educational opportunities become more of a motivation and reward function. Continuing education classes, in addition to mandatory regulatory requirements, are always in demand by professional staff and positively reinforce the organization's commitment to staff growth and development.

COMPETENCY-BASED ACHIEVEMENT

Because of the very nature of health care services and the impact that one staff error can have on the well-being of a patient, competency-based achievement is extremely vital and important in the delivery of patient care. Over the past 20 years health care technology has progressed rapidly with new, complex treatment and diagnostic changes; new, more potent medications; and an increasing number of specialties within the nursing profession. The ability to keep abreast of all the new changes demands commitment on the part of nurses working with patients.

The viability of a health care setting depends on being able to accept patients for admission and care by having available and adequate staff. The nursing shortages of past decades forced health care institutions to recruit registered nursing staff whose competency was usually never questioned beyond the preemployment reference checks. Nurses were required to float from one patient care unit to another, no matter how the assessment and treatment needs of the patients differed. Nurses were uncomfortable with such practices and worked with their professional associations and unions to limit such practices in an effort to improve patient care.

Temporary nursing staffing services proliferated as the demands for licensed personnel increased. Unfortunately, not all nurses kept abreast of changes within their work environment and therefore may not have provided the highest quality service possible. In addition, as outcome-focused patient care becomes a reality, it is imperative for health care settings to establish standards of professional practice and institute protocols that will regulate how care is provided. It is a natural progression to have age-specific competency-based performance evaluation and achievement processes as indicators in the quest for the quantification of quality of care.

Competency assessment and evaluation should address the skills, knowledge, and abilities of staff required to promote safe outcome-oriented patient care. Competency assessment can include educational programs, simulation of actual care practices, and review of documentation, as well as other methods. The validity of the testing apparatus should be evaluated by personnel knowledgeable in education and performance assessment criteria measurement.

All staff should be measured for competency at the time of hire (during orientation), when taking on a new role or job (e.g., promotion or cross-training), when performance expectations change (new equipment or operating standards), when there is evidence of performance deficiencies, and at the annual performance appraisal/ review.[4] Competency testing is an integral part of the organization's plan for performance improvement and should include elements of validity and reliability in terms of assessment tools and evaluators. All contracts with staffing agencies should include a provision that their employees meet all JCAHO standards and allow for periodic random review of their employee personnel files to ensure that they are compliant with these requirements.

It is the health care organization's responsibility to designate the individuals who will administer the competency evaluation. Their specialized skills should be maintained and enhanced as needed to ensure objective and up-to-date testing ability. Staff who have been in the same or similar jobs may have competency gauged through the following methods:

1. Achievement of clinical or service outcomes
2. Processes by which they deliver care or services
3. Resource utilization
4. Satisfaction with performance by others, including patients, physicians, managers, and other staff[5]

Through the establishment of quantifiable management goals and objectives that are derived from the organization's strategic plan, a manager's competency can be measured. Quality of care (as evidenced by successful accreditation and positive patient outcomes), customer satisfaction (as documented through internal and external customer surveys), and financial performance (as evidenced by successfully meeting or exceeding budgetary goals) indicators are all measures of a manager's competency.

Competency-based achievement also becomes a basis to quantify compensation and other monetary awards. Objective criteria lend themselves to fairness in evaluating managers from various departments with different goals and objectives.

Some examples of competencies that have been developed for nurses and incorporated into job descriptions and performance appraisals may include:

1. Orients to care environment with collaborative practice and safety and security.
2. Provides nursing care to patients with alterations in pulmonary status.
3. Provides nursing care to patients experiencing pain and has understanding of pain management policy and provides nursing care in accordance with this policy to patients experiencing pain.
4. Identifies priority of actions for admissions/discharge, transfers/transport.
5. Provides nursing care based on a patient's developmental stage (pediatric).
6. Others.

Performance criteria associated with item 5 may include the following (with an area for the new orientee to self-assess and for the preceptor or manager [deemed competent to evaluate others] to document competency demonstration):

a. Reviews growth and development theories during orientation.
b. Accurately completes and documents developmental assessment on patient admission.
c. Care interventions reflect nursing care based on patient's developmental stage.

For an example of a criteria-based job description/performance evaluation, see Appendix 3-1 at the end of this chapter.

STAFF MOTIVATION AND RECOGNITION

Just as important as developing goals, objectives, and action plans for staff and your department is the attention a manager pays to staff, motivating and recognizing them for positive achievements and attainment of personal and unit goals. The rate of monetary gain for health service personnel has risen in the past two decades, but whether or not monetary gain occurs, managers must maintain a positive work environment, build team spirit, and motivate staff to continue to challenge and improve their performance. Management texts have described many different theories of human motivation and outlined strategies to improve productivity and morale within teams and organizations.

The most basic element for new nurse managers is the ability to lead staff and then thank them for their participation in organizational success. The success reflects the employee's personal actions as well as the organization's achievements. People generally want to perform to the best of their ability; they want to believe that the work they are doing is necessary for a greater good. From the administrator of the hospital to the housekeeping or security staff, each individual contributes as much to the goal of providing the best patient care as does the registered nurse, pharmacist, or physician. The ability to be part of a team, with a larger goal in mind, is the foundation for well-motivated staff.

Staff members also appreciate the efforts of their manager to understand and empathize with the job that has to be performed. They want to be able to depend on their managers to assist them in a crisis and they respect and will be led by managers they believe will stand by them. It is important for the new nurse manager to understand that the power of the new position does not preclude the manager from ever having to "answer a patient light" or "make a home care visit" again. It is during those busy times that the manager truly exhibits the mission of the organization or the department by showing staff that patient care comes first and that management is there to support and lead the frontline patient care staff.

Recognition needs to be regular, sincere, and from the "top down." Monthly recognition sessions lose their impact when staff members perceive the awards as shallow, insincere, and rotated among all staff regardless of actual input. On limited budgets, plan for special occasions, such as nurses' week, hospital day, or home care week, and recognize all appropriate staff. Make every effort to ensure that all staff who should be recognized are recognized! Printing the names of all the hospital nurses in a newspaper advertisement celebrating nurses' week and forgetting about the home care nurses or those working in the radiology department becomes a disaster. A rift widens between the staff themselves and the hospital that has publicly minimized their contribution. Also, the celebration of hospital week should include all staff, not just nursing, showing the staff that they are one team.

Examples of Recognition

Examples of positive and rewarding recognition can include:
1. Impact/on-the-spot awards (based on customer service/quality indicators).
2. Employee of the month/year (based on customer survey results).
3. Quality idea (based on contributions of staff that positively improve a process both qualitatively and quantitatively).

The awards could be monetary, gift certificates, points for future awards, choice parking, recognition at special functions, or as special and unique as you want to make them.

Team building can occur through both formal and informal efforts, from planned meetings and gatherings that effectively build consensus on your unit to informal, spontaneous potlucks or banding together during a crisis (e.g., keeping a unit open with 50% of the department out on sick leave).

TERMINATING OR LAYING OFF A STAFF MEMBER

Probably no management decision is as difficult to be involved in as the process of "involuntary end of employment," or laying off an employee. In most organizations, termination is the last resort. In rare instances, this process has been in the works for some time, but the infractions were not documented correctly or personnel's policies were not effective until the new nurse manager arrived. Should such a serious and ongoing problem be given to you, share this responsibility with both your immediate supervisor and the personnel manager. There are legal concerns, staff ramifications, confidentiality issues, and other areas that should be addressed by those with the qualified expertise in your organization. In most settings, these situations occur only with the concurrence and involvement of the HR manager. In all cases, it is a difficult process for those involved. Because of this, you should not handle this process without adequate support and direction, particularly in a situation that has been ongoing for some time and began before your tenure.

EVALUATING PERFORMANCE

Generally, no area creates more feelings between manager and staff members than the performance evaluation or appraisal process. Because it is often tied to money and self-esteem, it may become the focus of some disagreement between supervisor and employee. An effective performance evaluation is beneficial to both the manager and the staff member being evaluated. In addition, the performance evaluation should be a written validation of what the manager and employee have been discussing and documenting throughout the period before the formal process. Sadly, this is not always the case and so the employee feels and has a right to complain that the manager did not communicate problems to the employee before the meeting.

Usually there is a formal structure for the process and a time frame for appraising performance. Most settings also have a standard format and criteria on which to base the evaluation. It is very important that you learn the organization's evaluation process. Various evaluation tools are available, and you need to familiarize yourself with them. The purpose of this section is to prepare you for your first employee performance evaluation or to reinforce information if you have previously administered evaluations.

What Is a Performance Appraisal?

Performance appraisals occur to (1) give formal feedback on the current nursing performance and competency in the work setting and (2) determine the employee's development within the staff or other growth needs for the future. This is provided in a private discussion and can be a positive experience for both nurse manager and employee.

Though the process and time frames may vary, effective performance appraisals can accomplish several things:
- They provide needed recognition and structured feedback.
- They allow the manager and staff nurse time to reevaluate the bigger picture of organization, unit direction, or goals.

- They allow the nurse manager to clarify behavior or other expectations.
- They help identify a career path or dual career ladder for the employee and show that the nurse manager is interested in the future of the employee.
- They allow (or should allow) for the employee to self-assess and set goals and give feedback to the nurse manager on areas of concern or need as identified by the employee.
- They should always allow and encourage an open exchange of information.
- They allow the staff nurse a reading on her/his defined or written priorities, goals, and objectives.
- They permit the nurse manager another opportunity to create an environment that fosters personal and professional growth of staff nurses in an open environment that encourages risk-taking, where appropriate.
- They provide another time when the nurse manager can allow the exchange of creative ideas to accomplish work in a different or better way.
- They can provide the opportunity to coach the nurse employee to meet program or unit goals or objectives.
- Sometimes they are the environment for addressing the core of why we choose to be nurses. For example, discussions of effectiveness, professionalism, client relations, clinical expertise, and other factors all determine the level of the performance appraisal. All nurses and employees want to do a good job—this is a unique opportunity to find out what is impeding the employee's attainment of goals and what you can do as the manager to facilitate goal achievement. This role as coach and mentor solidifies your working relationship with your staff.
- They allow the quality of the work performance to be evaluated against specific predetermined standards that are correlated with the employee position description.

Legal and Risk Management Issues

As with all of health care, human resources are also affected by risk management and legal concerns that can prove frustrating and demoralizing for the new nurse manager trying to effectively manage a department. The most important point to remember is that as a middle manager, you are not alone. There is the expertise of your senior manager, legal counsel (inhouse or contracted services), and human resource department manager and staff. Strong policies, procedures, mission statements, and integrated values all add to a structure that protects both staff and management when making decisions that may be a potential for disagreement.

Risk management may be defined as the recognition that there is a potential for harm, risk, or loss. Where possible, it is the organization and manager's role to identify such risk areas as patient falls, medication errors, wrong-site surgeries, and others. The focus of the organization will be to identify risk areas and seek to prevent problems and loss by focusing on methods to control or minimize such episodes.

The organization will have risk management personnel who work with risk and prevention throughout the organization.

Some of the major human resource legal and risk management concerns affecting nurse managers today may include:

1. Delegation of patient care duties—from professional to unlicensed assistive staff.
2. Competency of staff.
3. Wrongful termination.
4. Unfair layoffs.
5. Substance abuse in the workplace.
6. Violence in the workplace.
7. Patient abuse by staff.
8. Nonreporting of child, adult, and elder abuse by patient care staff.
9. Pay practices including overtime issues such as mandatory overtime, which has been legislated against in many states.
10. Harassment.

Be aware of your institution's human resource policies and procedures and always adhere to them closely. Ask for input and support from your senior manager and human resource director when confronted with a nonfunctioning staff member who needs to begin the counseling process. Understand and abide by union contracts and work with the shop steward for your department in planning and implementing changes that affect staff. Always respect your staff. Never belittle or deride anyone in public. The best adage for a new manager is to *treat staff as you would like to be treated*. Readers are referred to Chapter 9 for a more in-depth review of legal concerns.

VIOLENCE IN THE WORKPLACE

Reports of workplace violence have increased tremendously during the past few years, the violence being especially due to increased pressure to improve productivity, layoffs, disagreements between management and staff, and disturbed relationships. Special training programs have now been established to assist managers in assessing and defusing potentially volatile situations. According to the Northwestern National Life Insurance study on nonfatal workplace violence, more than 2 million people were attacked on the job, 6 million were threatened with violence, 16 million suffered harassment, and 25% of all full-time workers were either harassed, threatened, or attacked on the job between July 1992 and July 1993.[6] Health care organizations have not been immune to violence. Emergency departments are prime areas for angry clients to express their hostility over the type or lack of treatment being afforded them or a significant other or, in most cases, the length of time waiting to be seen by a physician.

For the new manager, it is important to understand the buildup and progression of violent behavior. The checklists in Box 3-1 on p. 95 describe the various levels of violence and certain behaviors associated with them.

---

box 3-1

LEVELS OF VIOLENCE AND ASSOCIATED BEHAVIORS

FIRST LEVEL

❑ Sexual comments
❑ Noncooperation with supervisor
❑ Spreads rumors and gossip
❑ Argues with coworkers
❑ Belligerent toward customers
❑ Swears at everyone

SECOND LEVEL

❑ Argues with everyone
❑ Refuses to obey policies/procedures
❑ Steals for revenge
❑ Sabotages equipment
❑ Writes sexual/violent notes
❑ Makes verbal threats
❑ Feels victimized
❑ Sexually harasses others

THIRD LEVEL

❑ Frequently displays intense anger
❑ Often threatens suicide
❑ Frequent physical fights
❑ Destroys property
❑ Uses weapons to hurt others
❑ Commits murder, rape, or arson[7]

Adapted from Gilham DS, Schweitzer SM: *Workplace violence prevention*, Texas Association for Home Care 26th Annual Meeting and Exhibition, Dallas, September 1995.

In defusing a volatile situation or responding to aggression, either from a patient or a staff member, all staff should be aware of the signals they are sending the aggressor. Develop the following behaviors:

- Always actively listen to and focus on the individual.
- Show respect and concern for her/his issues.
- Control your body language and emotions during the conversation.
- Think twice before responding in anger, accusation, or humor.
- Remain calm and exude your authority and control of the situation.

Having a program in place is the first line of defense in dealing with workplace violence:

1. Know the signs to look for in a potentially violent individual.
2. Utilize criminal checks in preemployment procedures.
3. Have policies and procedures on:

    a. Acceptable employee behavior (no threats, violence).

    b. Possession of weapons.

    c. Duty of other employees to report suspicious behaviors.

4. Outline and use employee progressive discipline protocols.

5. Make sure that an employee assistance program is available.

6. Have a plan for violence management (similar to a fire/emergency-preparedness plan).

In the event of a potentially violent situation, notify your supervisor and human resource manager for additional assistance in dealing with the crisis. Do not act alone; there are experts in human behavior at your institution or, if not, consultants who can be brought in to help defuse the situation.

Conflict Resolution

Effective managers try to maintain a calm, objective work environment; stress may exist and conflicts may arise, but overall there is a general understanding by staff members that they are respected, their opinions are important, and resolution will be attempted in an objective but firm manner. Conflict resolution has four major points:

1. Clarification—the issues and the parties involved in the conflict.
2. Performance—identify with the involved parties the potential outcomes from the behaviors exhibited.
3. Question—what were the behaviors that initiated this conflict and how best to avoid them in the future.
4. Expectations—describe in detail (in writing if necessary) what the manager's expectations are, based on policies and procedures, and what will happen if these behaviors continue (further disciplinary actions).

This is the legal way of laying groundwork to accelerate the termination process without being penalized in the courts for failure to notify the employee of potential action.

Organizations with clear, concise, and complete policies and procedures have fewer opportunities for potential conflicts between interdepartmental and intradepartmental staff. By having objective and fair policies in place for reference, managers are not put into the unenviable position of having to decide who is "right" and who is "wrong." Employee behaviors and performance are dictated by organization-wide protocols. As in all personnel issues, it is important to notify your supervisor and the human resource department manager, either for assistance or notification of the situation and a review of your proposed actions. (For further discussion of conflict, refer to Chapter 6, Effective Communication.)

SUMMARY

The manager must effectively employ human management skills to achieve work objectives. The use of these skills, or their lack, is evident in any work environment.

As the role model for the staff, it is imperative that the new nurse manager have an open attitude that creates a workplace where staff nurses can grow professionally. An effective workplace has the following qualities:

1. It is an environment open to new ideas.
2. Staff members feel they can safely take risks, when appropriate.
3. Planning occurs for short-and long-term activities and the staff is involved and apprised.
4. Both management and the staff are working toward the same goals.
5. All levels of staff value human management skills and treat everyone, including peers, patients, and visitors, with kindness and respect.

As a nurse manager, these are the elements to strive for in your setting. The important human resource functions of interviewing, hiring, coaching, and evaluating performance are the hallmarks of the team's inception and structure.

Please see Chapter 6, Effective Communication, for a discussion of specific communication problems that may arise in HR management.

QUESTIONS FOR CONSIDERATION

1. Define "human resource management" and explain its importance.
2. Describe what a successful interview of a prospective team member looks like.
3. List five ways that you can welcome new team members into your organization that show them they are valued.
4. Discuss coaching, why it is important, and examples of successful coaching.
5. Identify two reasons why performance appraisals are so important.

References

1. Patz JM, Biordi DL, Holm K: Middle nurse manager effectiveness, *Journal of Nursing Administration* 21:15, 1991.
2. Lombardi DN: *Handbook for the new health care manager*, Chicago, 1993, AHA Publisher, p. 247.
3. Livingston J, Sterling HBR: Pygmalion in management, *Harvard Business Review* 66:121, 1988.
4. Rodriguez L, et al: *Manual of staff development*, St Louis, 1996, Mosby, p. 284.
5. Ibid, p. 281.
6. Gilham DS, Schweitzer SM: *Workplace violence prevention*, Texas Association for Home Care 26th Annual Meeting and Exhibition, Dallas, September 1995.
7. Ibid.

For Further Reading

Boyd C et al: Performance plan: a nursing management strategy to improve care delivery, *Journal of Healthcare Educ Train* 5(3):12, 1991.

Davidhizar R, Giger J: When subordinates go over your head—the manipulative employee, *Journal of Nursing Administration* 20(9);29, 1990.

Family-friendly: hospitals begin to modernize their time-off policies, *Hospitals*, January 20, 1992, p. 58.

Feldman R: Meeting the educational needs of home healthcare nurses, *Journal of Home Healthcare Practice* 5(4):12, 1994.

Finkler S, Kovner J, Hendrickson G: Innovation in nursing: a benefit/cost analysis, *Nursing Economics* 12(1):25-29, 1994.

Fulghum R: *All I really needed to know I learned in kindergarten*, Westminster, MD, 1988, Villard Books, Random House.

Hendricks W: *The manager's role as coach*, Shawnee Mission, KS, 1994, National Press Publications.

Hood JN, Smith HL: Quality of work life in home care: the contribution of leaders' personal concern for staff, *Journal of Nursing Administration* 24(1):40, 1994.

Huselid MA: The impact of human resource management practices on turnover and corporate financial performance, *Academy of Management Journal* 58(3):635, 1995.

Janz M: Perception of knowledge: what administrators and assistants know, *Journal of Gerontological Nursing* 18(8):7, 1992.

Mason D, Leavitt J, Chaffee M: *Policy and politics in nursing and healthcare*, St Louis, 2002, Saunders.

Ott MJ, et al: Peer interviewing: sharing the hiring process, *Nursing Management* 21(11):32, 1990.

Peters T: *Thriving on chaos; handbook for a management revolution*, New York, 1987, Harper & Row.

Pritchett P: *Firing up commitment during organizational change: a handbook for managers*, Dallas, 1999, Pritchett & Associates, Inc.

Pritchett P: *New work habits for a radically changing world*, Dallas, 1999, Pritchett & Associates, Inc.

Pritchett P, Pound R: *Business as unusual: the handbook for managing and supervising organizational change*, Dallas, 1999, Pritchett & Associates, Inc.

Shoemake A: Solutions to the home healthcare nursing shortage, *Home Healthcare Nurse* 12(4):35, 1994.

Trull S: Strategies of effective interviewing, *Harvard Business Review* 42(1):89, 1964.

Yochem B: Counseling: a "how-to" for new nurse managers, *Pediatric Nursing* 17(2):201, 1991.

Website Resources

"The Employer's Legal Handbook" NOLO, Fred S. Steingold; see *www.nolo.com* for specifics.

"Building a Framework for Workforce Solutions"; part of the Resource Collection available through ASHHRA (American Society for Healthcare Human Resources Administration of the American Hospital Association); *www.ashhra.org*.

Society for Healthcare Strategy and Market Development; *www.stratsociety.org*.

SAMPLE CRITERIA-BASED
POSITION DESCRIPTION/PERFORMANCE APPRAISAL

Position Description Data

TITLE OF POSITION: TEAM SECRETARY Name of Staff Member:_____	**REPORTS TO: PATIENT TEAM MANAGER** Performance Reviewer:_____

Status of Position: FT/Nonexempt
Type of Review:

Probation ___ Annual ___ Other ___

Date of Review:_____

Work Environment:

Noise level is usually moderate.
Employee may be required to assist in branch offices.
Employee must have vision capabilities to review and transcribe information from records to computer terminal and be able to work at CRT screen.

Position Description:

Under the direction of the patient team manager, provides all administrative support to patient care teams by setting up, tracking, filing, and maintaining all patient care records, per agency policy and applicable regulation. Also responsible for the preparation and tracking of all statistics utilized in billing process and report generation and/or verification as required. Provides support to receptionist staff by answering telephone calls and routing as appropriate utilizing customer service techniques.

Qualifications/Job Requirements:

High school graduate
Graduate of medical technical school desired
Familiarity with medical terminology
Ability to type at least 60 wpm
Data entry and word processing experience
Organizational and time management skills
Customer service orientation
Ability to work as a team in a fast-paced environment
Ability to lift up to 25 pounds

Performance Standards	Rating			
1. Maintains clinical record and billing information by accurately processing and filing all forms within specified deadline:	1	2	3	4
a. Plan of treatment is mailed out to appropriate physician within 5 days of admission and is noted on physician order log.				
b. Verbal/supplemental orders are processed and mailed out to physicians within 48 hours of receipt.				
c. Completed clinical forms are processed and filed in the appropriate part of the clinical record within 5 days of receipt.				
d. Discharge summaries are processed and mailed out to physicians within 30 days of discharge date.				
e. Closed records are audited and completed within 30 days of discharge.				
f. Prebilling invoice is audited and compared to clinical record for accuracy of date, bill for service, and signed physician order is on file.				
ETC				

CHAPTER 4

RECRUITMENT AND RETENTION OF STAFF:
A STRATEGIC OVERVIEW

BARBARA FARUGGIO

Ask "Them" to Help You Build It
and
"They" Will Stay and "They" Bring More!

This chapter will define, from an overall strategic viewpoint, the key strategies for success in team member recruitment and retention. Examples will be provided on how these strategies may be implemented in your organization. The end result of the implementation of these strategies will be an environment that achieves a valued relationship with staff—the cornerstone for staff retention.

Chapter 3, Human Resource Management, provides detail for successful management of the human resources (HR) component of a manager's role responsibilities. Human resource management at a unit level is defined as effective interpersonal communications among all level of employees and staff (see the section What Is Human Resource Management? in Chapter 3). Mastery of the skills of each employment process corresponds with the work environment components as outlined in Strategy 5: Become the Facility or Organization of Choice for Staff. Finding the resources to provide care in our organizations during the next several decades will be a challenge more formidable than any nursing shortage in the past. Shortage reasons are numerous, and a true understanding of the rationale behind each enables organizations to create a lasting success in procuring staff to provide patient care.

The American Hospital Association describes the current shortage as only the "first wave" of the nursing shortage and the future as a "looming crisis."[1] *What makes this shortage more formidable than other shortages?*

THE 12 CHALLENGING ISSUES

Let's consider the 12 challenging issues surrounding this shortage that depict the complexity of the situation.

Reason 1: Population Change—With Fewer Workers All Over, It Is Not Just a Nursing Shortage; This Has Global Implications

It is important to note at the onset of this discussion that the shortage does not apply only to nursing (Figs. 4-1 and 4-2). It also applies to numerous other health care professionals. Pharmacists, radiology technicians, and nuclear technicians are also in short supply. In some geographic locations, the lack of radiology technicians is more crucial than the nursing shortage. Geographically, some regions cannot recruit nursing aides, necessitating the closure of nursing units in the postacute setting.[2,3] In addition, the economic drivers of supply and demand are impacting this nursing shortage. This problem is not limited only to the United States. On an international basis, many countries that were once the source of foreign recruitment are now viewing foreign recruitment as one way to meet their own needs.

The shortage of registered nurses (RNs) is not distributed evenly among states. The reported range varies from 3% to 17%, with the greatest number of vacancies in the Midwest, western, and southwestern states.

The RN distribution by work setting remains about the same. Hospital usage is projected at 63%, with home health and nursing homes showing at least a 2% need increase by 2020.

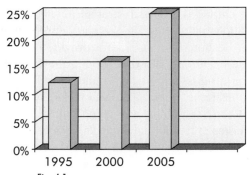

Fig. 4-1 Registered nurse turnover rate.

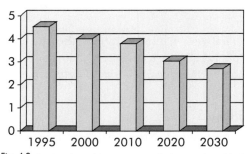

Fig. 4-2 Ratio of working age population to the elderly.

Reason 2: Increased Demand for Nurses Due to the Aging Population, Increasing Patient Acuity, Advanced Technology Requiring RN Skills, and Increasing Retirement of RNs

The aging patient population. An additional 50 million people will require health care by 2020. The greatest growth in acuity is in the population older than age 65 and then further seen in the 85 and older group. Multiple and more complex illnesses require more services and more nursing intervention.

Increasing utilization of services. Rather than being "over-bedded" as was thought to be the trend for the future, hospital activity has increased. This increase is reflected in shorter length of stays and an increase in the intensity of services for the shortened admissions. Simply put, this means there is more work to accomplish and in a shortened time frame. In addition, some parts of the country are projecting an increase in the number of hospital beds.

Postacute facilities continue to develop to meet the "output" needs of the acute-care facilities. From 1999 to 2000 there have been increases in:

- Inpatient admissions   3.4%
- Inpatient days   5%
- Outpatient encounters   11%

The aging nursing workforce. Although patients will require experienced professional nurses, the numbers of RNs are diminishing as the average age of the practicing nurse is 45 and continues to increase. Large numbers of RNs will be retiring in the next 10 years and new nurse school enrollment numbers have declined.[3] It was reported that the graduate nursing numbers were 26% lower in 2000 than in 1995 and the decline is distributed across all degree programs: diploma, associate, and baccalaureate.

Compounding the problem of the increasing average age of the nurse is that this trend is twice the rate of all other workers. By 2020, the average age of the nurse will be 50. The average age of the new associate degree nurse graduate is 33 years old, compared with 28 years old for those nurses who graduated in 1980.

The current deficit (6%) of not meeting *current demand* is directly impacting organizational operations. Table 4-1 shows the great variance that will exist between meeting demand and nurse availability.

The American Hospital Association reports the following[3]:

- Emergency department (ED) overcrowding—38%
- Diverted patients—25%
- Reduced number of open staffed beds—23%
- Cancellation of elective surgeries—10%
- Nurses feel it is more difficult to provide care today because of workforce shortages—60%
- Long-term care organizations lack sufficient nurse staffing to provide the most basic of care—90%
- Home health organizations and hospices are sometimes closing to new admissions

TABLE 4-1
Two Important Drivers: Supply and Demand

Year	2000	2010	2015	2020
RN demand not meeting supply—% variance	6%	12%	20%	29%
Demand	1,999,950	2,344,584	2,562,554	2,810,414
Supply	1,889,243	2,069,369	2,055,491	2,001,998

Source: U.S. Department of Health and Human Services, Health Resources and Services Administration: *Bureau of Health Professions, National Center: Health Workforce Analysis, Projected Supply, Demand, and Shortages of Registered Nurse, 2000-2020,* Washington, DC, 2000, Author.

- 126,000 hospital nursing positions are currently unfilled across the United States

Reason 3: Increased Career Opportunities—Nursing Salaries Not Remaining Competitive

During the past decade the career opportunity for women as physicians, engineers, and in the field of computers has skyrocketed. It could be said that the 1990s was a decade of career diversification for women. Enrollment in nurse practitioner programs increased from 4000 in 1992 to 20,000 in 1997. Nurse practitioners came from the ranks of the bedside nurse, further depleting the available supply to provide traditional or direct patient care.[3]

Unfortunately, nursing salaries have also not increased in comparison with other careers. For example, the increase in the average elementary teacher's salary in relationship to nursing salaries was $4000 more in 1983. By the year 2000, the difference of the increase percentage was $13,600 more than nurses.[3]

Reason 4: Increased Union and Coalition Activities

The health care working climate is also of great interest to unions who see the nursing profession as the final large nonunionized group and the way to increase their membership. The top reasons reported why nurses are unhappy are related to the work environment and manager capability. There are "isolated" instances in which facilities are decertifying from union membership. These are the organizations that are actively listening and responding to staff. Unfortunately some facilities are not focusing on changing the environment or workplace in which care is provided. In fact, this is a major frustration to staff. Some staff will look to unions for group resolution to their organization's operational issues.

Reason 5: Decreasing Nursing School Resources: From Shortage to Crisis

From an educational perspective, the crisis is already looming. The instructor's average age is 55 years old (as compared with the hospital staff nurse whose average age is 45 years old). This means that the educators will be retiring before the staff nurses. In addition, 5000 qualified baccalaureate program applicants in 2001 were turned away because of inadequate educator availability. *Who will be there to educate those recruited?*

Reason 6: Distribution of Government Dollars for Health Care Education

In 2001, *$78 million* was appropriated to fund *basic and advanced nursing education*, scholarships, or loans. In 2002, *$9 billion* was allocated toward direct and indirect *graduate medical education* payments to hospitals alone.[4] This discrepancy in the current nursing crisis must be addressed and resolved.

Reason 7: Students Graduating with Too Little Training

A division exists between nursing practice and nursing education. Patient acuity is increasing and there are no residency programs to support the transition of nurses into the reality of the facility or workplace. Instead orientation periods are decreased and ill-prepared preceptors may be preoccupied with the current patient load and "survival" for the day. Table 4-2 highlights the problem.

Reason 8: Increasing Involvement of Regulatory Agencies and Payers in Daily Operations

Some states already have or are considering regulating staffing and overtime. The issues of mandatory overtime and staffing ratios have resulted in state regulations. Some states, including Maine, Maryland, New Jersey, Minnesota, and Oregon, have passed legislation regarding mandatory overtime. California has taken the lead with mandated staffing ratios, and many other states are considering similar legislation.[3]

The Joint Commission on Accreditation of Healthcare Organizations (JCAHO) states that staffing levels have been a factor in 24% of 1609 sentinel events that have resulted in death, injury, or permanent loss of function as of March 2002. In addition, it has been stated that patient safety is threatened and health care quality is diminishing. Access to current care and the ability to respond to a mass casualty event are compromised.[3]

Reason 9: Increased Awareness, Concern, and Interest by the Public

The baby-boomer population wants to know who is going to care for them and that the staff is qualified. They are very knowledgeable consumers. Publicity on staffing

TABLE 4-2
Graduates' Rating of Their Supportive Experience from Unit Staff and Management

	Supportive (%)	Fairly Supportive (%)	Not Supportive (%)	Other (%)
Staff	23	48	22	7
Management	21	42	31	6

Source: Nurses: are we still eating our young? *Nursing 1999*, 29(10): 49-58, 1999.

and the shortage has increased the public's lack of confidence in the health care system.[3] A survey of the American public revealed the following:

81% know there is a shortage.

93% believe the shortage is threatening the quality of care.

65% see it as a problem.

Reason 10: Lack of a Systems Approach as an Industry to Resolving Operational Issues

The work environment continues to grow in complexity due to acuity, regulatory requirements, and information overload. The health care industry has lagged behind other industries in adopting information technology to improve workflow and improve the quality of life for health care providers. Documentation requirements are often redundant, unnecessarily taking the caregiver away from the patient.

Technologic supports such as wireless phones and point-of-care computer documentation are considered cost-prohibitive, and yet the lack of these technologies negatively impacts staff's productivity and the expediency of coordinating communications. Some health care organizations employ management engineers, because ineffective work processes still remain one of the major reasons why nurses leave (not just their place of employment, but also the profession). In fact, it is estimated there are usually nearly one-half million nurses not practicing in nursing.

Reason 11: The Multigenerational Workforce—Managers Need to Become Skilled in Developing the Optimal Working Team from a Very Diversified Staff[5]

Table 4-3 depicts workplace values and traits from a generational perspective. Table 4-4 presents the change in workplace motivators over 30 years.

Reason 12: Staff Satisfaction and Commitment Negatively Impacted from the "Turbulent '90s"

The "turbulent '90s" best describes health care in the past decade. We entered the decade with many organizations focused on total quality initiatives. In addition to the patient and physician who were our customers, staff were referred to as the customer and called "associates." Brainstorming sessions occurred routinely in which we asked our staff about the barriers that they were experiencing in providing patient care. Hospital management demonstrated a "caring" attitude. Then came the mid-'90s—the worst years of the decade—when organizations became reactive to the "threat" of living in a managed care environment. Consulting companies were utilized to redesign, restructure, or reorganize the way care was delivered.

Many work redesign initiatives resulted in organizations flexing and downsizing. The same employee who was our "associate" a few short years ago was being told, "If you don't like it here, you don't have to stay here." Graduating nurses (some with scholarship contracts) could not find jobs. Any potential interest in nursing was dampened by this negative climate. Many nurses left nursing during this

TABLE 4-3 **Workplace Values and Traits**	
Generation	**Traits and Attributes**
Baby-boomer (born mid-1940s to mid-1960s)	*Book smart *Willingness to go the "extra mile" *Interested in personal growth *Has a love-hate relationship with authority
GenXer (born mid 1960s to late 1970s)	*Pragmatic *Lack of commitment *Self-reliant *Risk-takers *Distrustful
Gen Yer/Nexter (Born late 1970s to mid-1990s)	*Short attention span *Sense of entitlement *Tenacious *Confident *Preference for collective action

Source: Health Care Advisory Board: *Managing a multigenerational RN work force,* Washington DC, 2002, The Advisory Board Company.

period, and many believe the current environment is the result of these "fixes" of the past.

The good news is that this is the decade to reestablish the trust factor, engaging staff in a valued relationship that benefits both the organization and the employee. There is no simple answer to how this relationship is achieved; it is a multifaceted approach. Start with the "end vision" of becoming an "eclectic organization," take the best of all that has been learned in the past decade, and mold it into a caring, sharing, inclusive, and rewarding environment for staff. Your organization will then become "the thriving work place," as termed by the American Hospital Association.[1] Characteristics of an eclectic organization are:

1. Establishing the vision for the organization.
2. Sharing the vision.
3. Including staff.
4. Developing staff.
5. Providing a barrier-free, hassle-free work environment.

TABLE 4-4 **Workplace Motivators Have Changed**		
Rating	**1970s**	**1999**
1	Respect for me as a person	Steady employment
2	Good pay	Respect for me as a person
3	Opportunity for interesting work	Good pay
4	Feeling job is important	Chance for promotion

FIVE KEY STRATEGIES FOR STAFF RETENTION

Five key strategies to achieve the valued relationship desired to ensure staff retention are[6]:

1. Have organizational commitment.
2. Promote the human resources department.
3. Recruit effectively.
4. Understand your target market.
5. Become the facility or organization of choice for staff.

These strategies are depicted in Fig. 4-3.

The systems approach to retention is an interconnected group of systems composed of many processes. Processes exist for recruiting strategies as well as implementing a satisfying work environment. A concurrent assessment and implementation of each process must occur for success. The strategy provides the infrastructure to make sure that all of the interconnected groups of systems are included in the assessment process.

Fig. 4-3 Five key strategies for ensuring staff retention.

Each of these five strategies are discussed in the remainder of this chapter, with operational examples for the department head/nurse manager.

STRATEGY 1: ORGANIZATIONAL COMMITMENT

> Example is not the main thing in influencing others.
> It is the only thing.
>
> Albert Schweitzer

The same principles employed in successful total quality management and case management programs need to be employed for successful staff retention. The philosophy of ownership for retention must start at the top using the following processes as a roadmap. For a visual reminder, imagine each employee in a T-shirt, with a dollar sign. Staff are resources comparable in importance to paper dollar resources. They are valuable and must be valued!

1. Administrative ownership and champion
2. Administrative visibility
3. Administrative support
4. Human resources as part of the organization's strategic plan
5. Utilize "the working triad"
6. Utilize an interactive planning model[6]

Administrative Ownership and Champion

The CEO/administrator must lead the charge for successful retention. Recruitment and retention are not the sole responsibility of the human resources department. Instead, the department serves as consultants to nurse managers and other department heads, facilitating the processes necessary for recruitment and retention. Effective demonstrated ownership at the top serves as a role model and will eventually reach the line staff—the people who bring in the new staff. Figure 4-4 is a visual model of this successful process.

Current employees are your most effective recruiting tool. As they go about their daily lives in the community setting, your employees speak about their work lives. It is an organization's responsibility to make work a meaningful experience in the employee's work life. Remember, this is the reason many people choose nursing as a profession.

Examples of how a CEO demonstrates this commitment are:

• Use department head meetings to:
  1. Set forth the "charge" that recruitment and retention is everyone's responsibility.
  2. Reinforce that the existing staff are your best recruiters. Say, "As department heads, you must be committed to establishing a work environment that creates that valued relationship with your staff."

People Leave Managers—Not Organizations!
Successful Retention Drives the Recruitment Process.

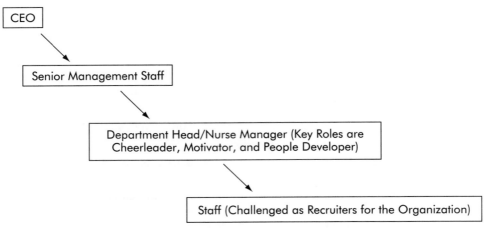

Fig. 4-4 CEO ownership drives staff ownership.

Visibility: Management by Walking Around

"Rounding" is done alone or with the senior manager for the area(s) being visited. The expectations for the rounds are that the CEO will view work processes in place so as to better understand staff needs and to develop relationships with staff. Manager's Tip 4-1 highlights steps for effective roundings.

Support Important Human Resources Functions

• Staff focus meetings facilitated by the human resources department.
• Dedicated resources for the function of recruiting and retaining. (Both of these items will be discussed in detail in the human resources section, Strategy 2.)

MANAGER'S TIP 4-1

QUALITY ROUNDING GUIDELINES

✔ Plan the itinerary so all areas are visited routinely.
✔ Do not "breeze through." Spend time with staff.
✔ Plan an agenda for the visit, such as a topic of the month, sharing new programs, etc.
✔ Bring rewards. For example, positive patient satisfaction comment forms: hand deliver to the staff member on the unit and give the staff person a fun gift, such as movie passes, a bag of candy for the unit, etc.
✔ Do your homework on the profile of the staff being visited.
✔ Do not make "instant of the moment" decisions. Take staff requests and discuss them with the senior management team with the necessary information to make appropriate and effective decisions.

Human Resources as Part of the Strategic Plan

Human resources usually establish the standard reports in collaboration with senior management. These are presented for review on a *monthly basis* (or more often if necessary) at the senior management meetings. It goes without saying that senior management should not wait for a crisis to occur for report review. These reports should be given the same "presence" as the financial statements.

In their book *First, Break All the Rules*[7], Buckingham and Coffman address their belief that the financial balance sheet is only 60% of an organization's true worth. The remaining 40% is "intellectual capital" and that is described as "what is between the ears of our employees." When people leave an organization they take this "working capital" with them. Particularly in health care, we seek "critical thinkers"—nursing specifically cannot continue to lose this capital.

In addition, there are other reasons to ensure that there is a comprehensive human resources strategic plan in place:

- The increased focus by regulatory agencies
- The impact on patient satisfaction (Fig. 4-5)
- The positive impact human resources management has on productivity and on the organization's culture

Human resources management policies and procedures have a positive impact.[8] The use of high-performance work practices such as:

- Comprehensive employee recruitment,
- Incentive compensation,
- Performance management systems,
- Maximizing employee involvement and training,
  improves employees' knowledge, skills, and abilities by:
- Increasing motivation.
- Reducing shrinkage.

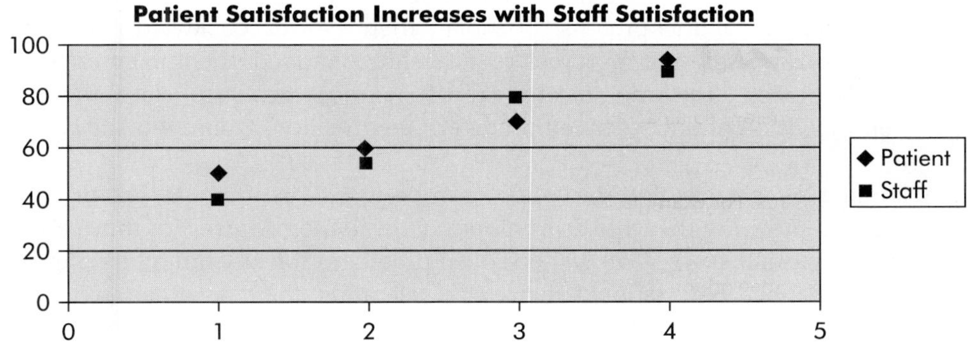

Fig. 4-5 Patient satisfaction increases with staff satisfaction. (Source: Press Ganey Associates: *Health care advisory board analysis.*)

- Increasing retention of quality employees.
- Encouraging separation of nonperforming employees.

Utilize the Triad Working Group to Develop and Maintain the Recruitment and Retention Plan

The "working triad" consists of patient care services (PCS), human resources, and finance. These three members of the senior management team have a responsibility for developing a collegial working relationship, which will result in a successful recruitment and retention plan. Human resources and PCS need to develop the plan based on research of market availability and the profile of the current staff. Meetings with finance occur before the senior management meetings to bring about a consensus of these three senior management leaders.

Each then takes a part in the presentation to the CEO and senior management team and subsequently to the board, depending on the organization's structure and reporting mechanisms.

Utilize an Interactive Planning Process[6]

Why an interactive planning process and what is it? An interactive planning process has as its main principles systems thinking, empowerment, and ends planning. Remember: **The future is largely subject to creation. No one can plan for someone else.**

Systems thinking involves people at all levels, both inside and outside an organization—all the stakeholders in the process. Coordination and integration are key in this process.

Empowerment demonstrates to staff that with their input, change is possible. Staff become energized and committed to the organization as they see evidence of their ability to influence. The challenge then becomes one of directing energies toward positive outcomes for the patient, staff, and organization.

Ends planning utilizes an interactive planning model that starts with an "end vision" in mind. This means that planning begins with where one wants to be— the end outcome of the process. The plan then evolves backward. After the strengths, weaknesses, and resources required are identified, the implementation plan is developed. This multifaceted approach must occur to close the gap between the vision and the desired predetermined reality.[9] Figure 4-6 shows this vision.

Examples of "establishing the vision" can be *global*, as in, "This organization will become known in the state as number 1 in customer service," or they can be *department specific,* as in, "We will establish processes for welcoming employees that exceed their expectations, thereby accelerating their acclimation to the department and increasing the department's retention. The sky's the limit!" Outcome measurements such as these examples are established as part of the process.

**THE INTERACTIVE PLANNING PROCESS
An Easy Sequence to Follow for Success**

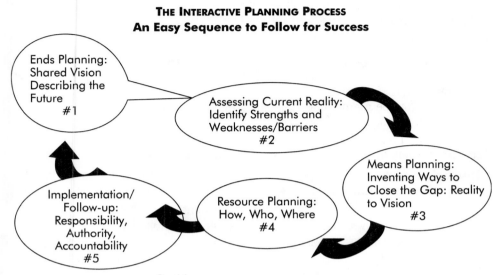

Fig. 4-6 The interactive planning process.

STRATEGY 2: PROMOTE THE HUMAN RESOURCES DEPARTMENT

It is well known that millions of dollars are lost in health care on turnover of staff. It is estimated that it costs approximately $42,000 to $65,000 (or more) to replace one RN, depending on the area worked. Comparable costs are mentioned for other professionals in the health care team. The impact of turnover on quality and patient satisfaction is seen repeatedly in literature. The major thrust of Strategy 2 is to promote human resources as the "employee's advocate." Staff need a frame of reference, just as the patient has, in knowing that their assigned staff take on the role of being their advocate as they journey through the health care system. The employee wants to know, "Who is my advocate?" If you do not position the human resources department effectively as the employee advocate, you open the door to continued or new union activity. To be an effective employee advocate, human resources must employ three key concepts:

1. Be visible to staff.
2. Be involved with staff.
3. Develop credibility with staff by employing and valuing measurable outcomes.

Be Visible to Staff

The human resources department should be easily accessible. It should not be located in the "trailer" two blocks away or in a basement that requires a yellow brick roadmap. It should be a service-oriented department. This means early morning and late evening hours at least once a week and responding quickly to employee queries and following up with prospective applicants.[9]

Be Involved with Staff

To be involved with staff, human resources should:
- Makes rounds with the senior management staff in their respective departments. Rounds are for all shifts. Follow the principles of quality rounding as defined in Strategy 1.
- Facilitate focus meetings. Guidelines for facilitating staff focus meetings are listed at the end of Strategy 2.

Develop Credibility by Employing and Valuing Measurable Outcomes

Measurable outcomes are the result of establishing a human resources strategic plan that speaks to relevant issues, is kept updated, speaks from fact, and justifies requests through showing a return on the investment.

An effective human resources strategic plan does the following:
- Recognizes the interdependence of recruitment and retention-related activities.
- Identifies all stakeholders and players.
- Defines accountability for the process.
- Promotes commitment to the process, plan, and outcomes.
- Demonstrates measurable outcomes.
- Shows a return on the investment.

Show a return on investment. Two examples of showing a return on investment are presented below:

Example 1: Areas to Include When Calculating Turnover Costs

Factors to include for replacement costs for staff are:
- Predeparture lost productivity.
- Separation pay-out or severance.
- Lost productivity of an open position.
- Differential costs of temporary replacement.
- Recruiting costs: staff time and advertising dollars.
- Increased workload (e.g., hours, overtime, etc., on remaining staff).
- Hiring costs.
- Orientation costs.

Result: $42,000 to replace a med-surg nurse—$60,000 for a critical care nurse.[11]

Example 2: How to Use Turnover Costs When Supporting a Scholarship Program

Cost of one agency nurse: $70.00/hr for 8-hr shift × 365 days = $204,400

Developing the scholarship plan:
- Night shift salary: average $46,000 + $10,000 scholarships costs = $56,000
  - Cost of one agency nurse: $204,400 − $66,000 for "hiring a scholarship nurse." Net result is a savings of $138,400 + stability and consistency in staffing. This same scholarship nurse will be on the night shift for 2 years.

MANAGER'S TIP 4-2

REPORTS TO REVIEW MONTHLY

✔ Turnover: overall, and by department, skill level, shift, and educational level
✔ Time to fill positions
✔ No shows
✔ Short stays
✔ Orientation time: against predefined time frames
✔ Absenteeism
✔ Number of positions filled against number of applications received
✔ Reasons for exiting: overall, by unit, and by reason
✔ Performance evaluation process: completed on time and staff feedback
✔ How long to receive termination paperwork from department
✔ Applicant source tracking: where do applicants come from?
✔ Department report card that tracks a manager's performance (known as a "dashboard")

Demonstrate measurable outcomes. Manager's Tip 4-2 presents a sample of the types of reports that should be reviewed monthly at senior management meetings.

Table 4-5 is an example of an applicant source tracking tool. An applicant source tracking report should be shared at the department head and recruitment and retention committee meetings as a means of educating staff on their impact on the recruitment process. The greatest source of referrals is from other satisfied employees!

Support structures for success. Effective recruitment activities are the key to success. All managers have heard stories of great staff who got away. You do not want to be one of those organizations.

• Recruitment function is clearly identified and functions are assigned according to organizational size and volume of recruiting taking place.

TABLE 4-5
Applicant Source Tracking Tool Sample

Applicant Source	January	February	March
Newspapers	1	0	1
Trade journals	0	0	0
Radio	0	1	0
Open house	2	N/A	N/A
Billboard	0	0	1
Employee referral	4	2	3
Referral program	1	0	2
Other (specify)	0	0	0

Though the number of RN recruiters may vary, usually in inpatient organizations of 300 beds or more, there is ample work for one or more full-time RN nursing recruiters who complete the entire hiring process. To facilitate these functions in smaller organizations, a collaborative relationship needs to be developed between human resources and all departments. Nursing in smaller organizations needs to identify one central contact for human resources for the more common issues that arise daily. Whatever the process, don't let qualified applicants slip through the cracks because of poor operations or an archaic structure. For example, make return and/or follow-up phone calls within 24 hours.

• Hire skilled recruiters. This is not the place or position for reassignment of the "sacred cows" or those who do not function effectively in another position in a given organization. Recruiters need to be personable, knowledgeable, and able to facilitate open-ended discussions that will result in the hiring of talented staff. In addition, there are times when the recruiter will need to be able to handle the difficult situation of convincing a department head that the "warm body" they are so interested in hiring may *not* be a good hire. They must have sales skill to succeed. Excellent communication and negotiation skills are a must!

Manager's Tip 4-3 is an example of a job summary for the role of nurse recruiter.

• Other supporting structures include policies for overtime, absenteeism, bonus programs, and others. One overall policy for an organization should exist, with departmental variation (addenda) as needed.

Focus Meetings: What Are They and How Does Human Resources Conduct Them?

The purpose of focus meetings is to provide a forum for staff interaction with members of the organization's operations group. The resulting exchange of information serves as an educational tool for both groups in improving the organization's performance and staff morale. Human resources is the usual department that facili-

MANAGER'S TIP 4-3

POSITION SUMMARY FOR NURSE RECRUITER

Coordinates the recruitment, interviewing, and hiring process for nursing staff inclusive of the RN, LPN, NA, and UA. Serves as the facilitator between the applicant and the nurse manager/department head.

Skill and talents necessary: excellent communication and organizational skills, a positive attitude, able to prioritize, a diverse clinical experience, and an ability to employ effective behavioral interviewing techniques.

tates the meetings due to their educational background, which focuses on being a "people advocate."

The objectives of a focus meeting are:

1. Obtain feedback from staff on opportunities to improve operations.
2. Hear the frustrations from staff that directly affect their morale.
3. Share the correct information to counteract the rumors.
4. Educate staff on the organization's mission and the relationship to current programs.

Though the format may differ across varying organizations, focus groups generally consist of:

- Interdisciplinary participation, unless there are discipline-specific or department-specific issues to be addressed.
- Implementation of "interactive planning concepts"—using a systems approach and staff empowerment as they see they make a difference.
- A workgroup of 10 to 12 (an appropriate size for effective discussions).
- Facilitation by human resources. Human resources is trained to answer the difficult questions and draw out information from staff, and they are seen (or should be seen) as nonbiased.
- Held to a maximum meeting length of 50 minutes.

A predictable schedule for meetings is usually monthly. In organizations of 100 beds or less, every 3 months may be sufficient.

- An agenda that is composed of several topics, and each topic is slated for 10 minutes of brainstorming participation and discussion. One suggested agenda includes the following topics:

    1. Barriers to workflow. Examples of barriers would be a long wait for a diet tray for new admissions, patients not ready for the OR at the scheduled time, or no nurse available for a timely home care or hospice admission.
    2. Improving the recruiting process.
    3. Feedback on retention/recognition programs in place.
    4. Feedback to the participants on issues addressed in the past 2 months, showing where administration has acted upon their ideas. This is also a good opportunity to see if the new programs or revised formats are working well for them as staff.

Keys issues to address when implementing effective focus or other group meetings: Must do's for success. The process and the meetings must be supported by administration and middle management. Administration commits to acting on information received in a timely manner. Acting does not always mean doing; it can also mean saying, "This why it cannot be done or operationalized now."

Middle management/department heads should arrange staff work schedules so that staff can attend the meeting. Create an environment where staff is comfortable sharing information in the meetings. For example, there should be no reprisals to staff for information discussed at the meeting.

Suggested topics for focus meetings are:

- What are the barriers to doing a good job?
- What are some ways to improve the recruiting process?
- What tools or support do you need to help in recruiting staff?
- What do you think of the current recognition programs in place? Should they be kept or done away with? Use a matrix to list three or four items each meeting and then solicit feedback. Some examples of recognition programs are employee of the month, birthday cards, and breakfast with the CEO.
- What are the characteristics of an effective department head? Keep this discussion generic.

Closing the loop. Getting back to the staff on issues raised can be done easily by human resources through a column in the organization's monthly newsletter. If the issues raised are controversial, it may be necessary to reconvene the group and present the feedback in person.

STRATEGY 3: RECRUIT EFFECTIVELY

Recruitment of staff has two major processes. The first process is that of advertising and getting the applicant *in the door* of the organization. The second major process is that of *selling* the organization once the applicant is inside. This section will focus on getting the applicant in the door. Selling the organization is addressed in Chapter 3, Human Resource Management, in the section on interviewing techniques.

There are two main considerations in recruitment:

- Successful recruiters define those who they are trying to recruit as those professionals not looking for a job.
- Universally, organizations agree that most new staff are referred from their own employees (and exclusive of offering a referral bonus).

Keeping these two important factors in mind, an organization needs to redefine its recruiting strategies in two directions.

- Advertise in places where those who are not interested in changing jobs will be looking, for example, the community section of the local paper and billboards.
- Establish an environment of reward, fun, and job satisfaction for the current staff. They are your walking billboards.

Short-Term Recruitment Initiatives

Some strategies that are working successfully and ways to consider realigning your current recruitment monies are newspapers, direct mail, radio, coupon inserts (in newspapers or by separate delivery), sign-on and referral bonuses, open houses, a professional recruiter, trade journals, the Internet, television, local theaters, job fairs, the organization's staff, and church and other community-based bulletins.

Newspaper advertising. Although newspapers consume a major part of the recruitment budget, there is consistent feedback that the main reason newspaper advertisements are done is so that department heads can see that human resources is doing something to recruit staff. Instead, the focus on staff retention and recruitment should be at the department head level. A manager's responsibility is to find ways to keep staff energized so that they are always "recruiting" for the unit. Keep in mind that recruitment is everyone's job, as outlined in Strategy 1.

Newspaper advertising does need to be done for visibility and for those looking for a job. Some of these same monies can be used for funding signature open houses and job fairs and creating a fun environment for staff.

One example of a fun activity is a quarterly drawing for 1 week of free child care, a day at a spa, two golf outing passes, or 2 days of maid cleaning services. Each employee gets a ballot and selects one of the four. These are comparable in cost and will have employees talking about the great things being done by their organization.

Many organizations are realigning advertising strategies to target those not looking for a job by advertising open houses and job fairs in the community activities section of the newspaper. Less advertising enables an organization to afford this more effective way of reaching its target market.

Signature events. Open houses and job fairs that produce positive outcomes become known as signature events. A signature event is a memorable experience and differs significantly from the open houses and job fairs of counterparts. They require extensive planning but are well worth the effort. They reach all target markets. A signature event has these major characteristics:

- Advertising in the community activities section of the newspaper.
- A theme that is carried throughout the program and in prizes.
- Door prizes and mini-raffles throughout the event.
- Short CEU session. An example of this is providing the latest information on cholesterol drugs from one of the drug companies or your organization's pharmacist.
- Participation by the medical staff.
- Presence of administration.

Some examples of signature events are:

- *Early Spring Open House—Come Join Us at Our Open House—Door Prize—5 days in New Orleans for Mardi Gras.*
- *Late Fall Open House—Come Join Us at Our Friday Open House—Door Prize—A paid hotel weekend at the adjacent outlet mall.* (This is especially good to do during the holidays.)
- *Job Fair at a Local Theater—Come Join Us for a Free Showing of* Star Trek *and Bring a Friend. Door Prize: $200 gift certificate to the mall.*

Many events such as these have had excellent attendance and have filled most of an organization's open positions. One organization tells the story of their door prize winner: "I had no intention of changing jobs . . . just went for the fun of it to see if I could win the trip . . . . Won the door prize . . . felt that I should at least go for the interview, and when I did . . . found out that I really did want to change jobs."

Some innovative organizations spend less money on agencies to write their advertisements by placing pictures of staff in the newspaper and have staff tell why they have remained at the facility for the past 10 to 15 years. This concept of including pictures and names of current staff and their quotes should be used in all media advertising. Some organizations have "fun quarterly drawings" (e.g., a weekend to Bermuda) for those who volunteer to have their names in print.

Other media approaches are:

- *Cable television* in most areas provides free community patient educational time. Using line staff for the educational presentations can be an effective approach.
- *Billboards* have excellent visibility, with staff providing the information on the clinical services being promoted or any awards received. For example, Magnet Status, when attained, shows the general public that your organization has received recognition for quality patient care and nursing excellence. It provides consumers with a benchmark for the care they can expect to receive.
- *Radio* results are best obtained in the morning because it seems that people become too busy by late afternoon to listen. They just have the radio on and are not listening to the messages.
- *Trade journals.* It is important to know when to use them and when not to. Several advertisements in a journal for "hard to recruit" positions might equal the costs of a professional recruiter, who usually has more expedient results. Organizations need to weigh the benefits of both approaches for each position.
- The *Internet* is growing in popularity. Again, it does not get to the person not looking for a job. Research shows that 66% of users new to the Internet are using it for shopping. If you do use the Internet, keep the process simple and easy. Do not have lengthy applications to complete. Instead, ask for the basics. The rest of the information can be obtained through follow-up phone calls.

Appendix 4-1, a departmental profile for Facility Anywhere USA, is a tool to look at trends across time to provide managers with a snapshot of successes and challenges related to retention and recruitment.

Other short-term initiatives. The use of bonuses has generated much discussion, and every effort should be made not to get into the "bonus war." This turns into a "bidding war" and creates a "can you top this?" environment. In some regions, nurses are moving from one hospital to another just for the bonus and are not thinking of the long-range implications, such as retirement benefits. Instead, initiatives should be taking place to create a practice environment, resulting in becoming the facility or organization of choice, which will be outlined in Strategy 5.

Long-Term Recruitment Initiatives

Examples of long-term recruitment initiatives are:

- Redesigning scheduling options to increase options for new target markets. For example, 4-hour slots—Monday to Friday—No weekends.

- Redesigning the patient care delivery system to be a multidisciplinary model in a barrier-free environment with staff members working together as a team. This will be discussed in more detail in the section about Strategy 5.
- Community organizations such as the Rotary Club or the Kiwanis.
- Foreign recruitment.
- Scholarships.
- Up-front tuition.
- Organization's staff.
- Implement the fun activity calendar, rounding, recognizing, and listening—ongoing.
- Teen volunteers within the organization.
- Alumni focus.
- Tuition forgiveness.
- Provide education about nursing to elementary, middle, and high school students.
- Develop programs to attract and support minorities. The health care workforce is 87% white, compared with 72% white in the overall population.

Community organizations. Some of the "newspaper monies" are better spent by having your facility represented in community organizations such as Rotary Club and the Kiwanis. This presence provides an opportunity to educate the public on the hospital's services, and you become a referral source for social work services, physician services, and outpatient programs as well as the recruitment of staff.

Scholarships and tuition reimbursement/forgiveness: Growing your own. Ensuring the succession line for your staff requires that your organization be involved in the three areas of scholarships, tuition reimbursement, and tuition forgiveness. This is called "growing your own."

An important part of this process is doing research and analysis trending. When developing the human resources plan, areas need to be identified where these programs can best provide support. Trending reports include an analysis of the "off-shift" core staff. The core staff is defined as those individuals that you know will be on nights until retirement or at least for the next several years for personal reasons. Targets should be established to decrease the off-shift vacancies and increase this "core staff." This is usually only accomplished through the two initiatives of scholarships and tuition forgiveness. Some hospitals will have night positions open for months or even years and expect that something will happen to change the situation. It won't without work.

If these positions are not being filled, a proactive approach must be taken to fill these positions because the chronic vacancies have a negative impact on the current staff's morale. The current staff is constantly being tapped on for overtime or orienting agency or other short-term staff. The following programs support the concept of growing your own.

Scholarships. One example of a scholarship contract is for a 2-year period and at the employer's choice of unit and shift. Scholarships should be open to the community with established criteria. Experience has shown positive outcomes with very few instances in which scholarship commitment has not been met.

Tuition Forgiveness. This is a short-range solution with a long-lasting effect. "Buying the clinician" enables an organization to plan ahead in supporting the scholarship and tuition up-front programs. During each school's graduation time, organizations need to be diligently recruiting staff to the off-shift and hard-to-fill positions through offers to pay back tuition costs. The set amount established would remain the same no matter which degree was attained, BSN or AD. The same concept should be applied to other hard-to-fill positions in health care such as pharmacists, radiology technicians, and others. Like scholarships, the reimbursement or "payback" commitment is usually a 2-year period and at the employer's choice of unit and shift.

Tuition Benefits. Many organizations provide tuition reimbursement, which enables their own staff to advance their careers and/or to attain a career in health care that benefits the organization. The challenge then is to develop the relationship with those employees so that they want to remain with the organization once they attain their career goals. Becoming the facility of choice helps to secure that commitment.

Tuition Advanced. Some employees who would be interested in a health care career, who are entry-level workers, do not have the monies for the first college course or the prerequisites that would make them eligible for their organization's usual tuition reimbursement program. These are the same individuals who many times must work as the sole supporter for their family and cannot take advantage of the scholarship program. Organizations can identify these future professionals through staff profiles and by paying for their first course up front; they are jumpstarting them on their educational journey. Criteria for this program may include:

- Participants must be employed at the organization for 2 years and free of disciplinary action.
- Participants must routinely collaborate with assigned mentors.
- Participants are allowed one non-passing grade with the requirement that they pay back the tuition costs over an extended period.
- Second nonpassing grade requires careful reassessment of person's career aspirations.
- Costs of books are included.

If there is reluctance to implement such a program in the organization, start small. Implement a pilot program for 1 year and offer it only to those interested in nursing, pharmacy, or radiology because these are usually the highest vacancy areas. Organizations need to think differently. *The kind of thinking that led to past success will not lead to future success.* Other opportunities to increase recruitment from community educational programs are:

- Encourage facility membership on educational advisory committees.
- Offer your site for clinical rotation.

- Consider offering internships.
- Develop mentoring programs.
- Create scholarships.
- Implement professional student nursing assistance work programs.
- Offer a nursing summer camp to provide on-site clinical experience.
- Consider a nursing educational liaison position with student recruitment as the sole focus for the role.
- Consider a formal student recruitment campaign composed of specific strategies with target dates and assigned areas of responsibility.

Teen volunteers. Most organizations have teen volunteers who are there because they have an interest in volunteering and health care or because the parents or school requires their participation. This is an untapped market and should become another "statistic" for the recruiters. How many of these teenagers became converted to a health care career because of this exposure in your organization? How many will return to your organization to work? A designated department head should be assigned to this group as the "professional liaison" to the director of volunteers.

Department head's role expectations are:

- Provide collaborative development of the job descriptions for the areas involved.
- Meet with the teenage volunteers monthly (and more often based on individual needs) to identify opportunities to improve their experience.
- Meet with department heads to educate and improve the teenagers' experience in their area.
- Meet with human resources for inclusion of this tactic in the overall human resources plan.

Shadow a Health Care Worker. This is another program designed to generate interest among the teen volunteers as well as an organization's administrative team and community leaders. The concept of the program is for a teen volunteer to shadow a health care worker, usually for a half-day, and then have a sharing of the reactions of the observer to the experience. The health care worker also views this as job recognition as others become more aware of the depth and complexity associated with a career in health care.

Alumni follow-up. Alumni follow-up focuses on following those who have left your organization with the expectation that some may want to return. People will leave an organization with the belief that the grass is greener on the other side. What often happens is that individuals find that the answer to their unrest is within themselves and some may want to return. The potential to re-recruit these individuals requires the following:

- Leaving the door open at the exit interview.
- Placing the departed employee on a mailing list for the monthly newsletter.
- Making contact with the employee 4 to 6 months after he/she has left the organization.
- Being able to offer a person full reinstatement on benefits if he/she returns within the first year.

STRATEGY 4: UNDERSTAND YOUR TARGET MARKET

A complex and diversified workforce challenges the manager of the 2010 decade. Understanding your target market is necessary from a recruitment perspective as well as for retention of staff. Where can recruiting monies be best used to attract new staff? Where should monies be spent for retention of current staff?

The challenge in managing today's workforce is to understand both the generational and personal needs of one's staff. The five main areas for focus are:

1. Generational differences
2. Expectations of the emerging workforce of today
3. Keys to staff empowerment
4. Current staff's career expectations
5. Reasons people leave an organization and during what time period

Generational Differences

Manager's Tip 4-4 delineates the categories by age of persons born since 1922. Ask where your staff fits within these categories. What will motivate them?

Emerging Workforce Expectations

Expectations of the emerging workforce include the following[9]:

- Believe rewards should be based on merit, not longevity.
- Want to take responsibility for their own careers.
- Recognize that the world is changing and are preparing themselves.
- Looking for training, mentoring, and responsibility.
- Want peer relationships.
- Prefer horizontally structured organizations with informal reporting lines.

When considering rewarding on merit and not longevity, consider the bell-shaped curve approach and the 80-20 rule in addressing the need to review at the compensation system in health care (Fig. 4-7).

MANAGER'S TIP 4-4

AGE CATEGORIES BY YEAR OF BIRTH

Veteran: Born 1922-1942. Dedicated, hard working, duty before pleasure
Baby-Boomer: Born 1940s-1960s. Optimistic, team-oriented, wants to be involved. Wants respect and attention.
GenXer: Born mid 1960s-late 1970s. Adaptable, independent, impatient, not intimidated by authority, poor people skills.
Nexter: Born 1986-1998. Multitasking, capable, optimistic, inexperienced, requires supervision and training. Has a sense of entitlement. Wants steady employment.

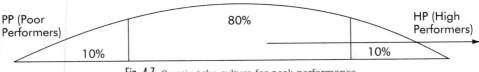

PP (Poor Performers)		80%		HP (High Performers)
	10%		10%	

Fig. 4-7 Creating the culture for peak performance.

A merit-based evaluation system has been a topic of research for years, when in fact there is a process in place that has been working well. This process is known in most organizations as a clinical ladder or professional grades.

Managers spend most of their time with the 10% of workers that are considered "problem employees." Managers should be focusing on the other end of the bell-shaped curve, creating the pull to shift more of the staff into the group of high performers. Nurse managers must then focus on recruiting and retaining the talented staff or high performers[8] (Manager's Tip 4-5).

Keys to Empowerment

Providing information to staff and seeking their input are the two driving factors in developing an environment of staff empowerment. This is accomplished through:

- Utilizing an interactive planning process, including all levels of staff in decisions on how their work will be accomplished.
- Conducting effective departmental staff meetings.
- Managers taking time for the "one-on-one" meetings.
- Holding focus meetings facilitated by the human resources department.
- Communicating through several ways on the positive changes made due to staff input—demonstrating that staff input is important.

Understanding Current Staff's Career Expectations

Staff profiles are completed on all employees and placed in an access database. Manager's Tip 4-6 presents the information that the profile should provide on all staff.

MANAGER'S TIP 4-5

RETAINING GENERATION X

X-tend yourself.
X-pectations need to be set.
X-plain not just the how, but the why (selling the problem with the solution).
X-press yourself.
X-pand the possibilities.

Source: Kaye B, Jordan-Evans S: Love 'em or lose 'em: getting good people to stay, San Francisco, 2002, Berrett-Koehler Publishers.

MANAGER'S TIP 4-6

INFORMATION FOR STAFF PROFILES

- Age
- Gender
- Educational level completed
- Schools attended; year graduated
- If matriculated, expected date of graduation
- Professional goals
- Years of service in the organization
- Units worked in the organization
- Certifications
- Community organization involvement
- Life interests
- Top three things the employee has liked about where previously employed
- Reasons the employee has stayed
- Top three things important to the employee in providing care
- Definition of what "input into decisions" means to them (will vary with age group)

Profiles are also used to identify the mentors for orientation and the advanced tuition participants. They also assist managers in identifying staff for projects that align with a person's "life interests." Asking staff how they like to receive communication is also an important part of this profile. This may vary with generations. For example, the baby boomer will read the detailed memo, whereas the GenXer wants his/her memos short and to the point.

Knowing the Reasons People Leave and When

Manager's Tip 4-7 presents the results of industry surveys about when people leave their place of work. How does your organization compare?

Data from health care surveys about why people leave are presented in Tables 4-6 and 4-7.

The reasons staff leave should become the basis for an organization's retention programs. As can be seen from the surveys, compensation is not what is primarily driving the exodus. Yes, money will motivate in the short run. Long-lasting results are obtained only from developing a professional work environment that has as its characteristics the retention suggestions presented in Table 4-8.

Input from major organizations substantiates the use of a structured process such as the ING Model to Improve the Organizational Work Place, which will be discussed in Strategy 5.

MANAGER'S TIP 4-7

WHEN PEOPLE LEAVE

Overall Nursing Staff

Years 2-4—64% think about leaving

Years 4-5—50% to 60% think about leaving. This is the group that needs to be included in focus meetings. Find out what they are thinking about their jobs—*before* they formally resign. Proactive retention!

New Graduates

Within the first 2 years 59% change hospitals. Inadequate orientations, poor reception by unit staff, and ineffective managers are the main reasons cited by many. This is a dismal number. As you manage your unit or area, keep this number in mind. Do your best to change the reasons.

TABLE 4-6
Things Nurses Are Not Happy within Their Jobs (in Order of Priority)

Priority	Work Situation
1	Intensity of Work
2	Recognition
3	Growth opportunities
4	Scheduling
5	Manager
6	Compensation
7	Decision-making
8	Clinical staff support services

Source: Health Care Advisory Board. *Nursing executive center national survey*, October 1999, Washington, DC, 1999, The Advisory Board Company.

TABLE 4-7
Reasons Nurses Leave

Percentage	Reason
68	Fair to poor morale
66	Patient load too large
65	Understaffing, coupled with sicker patients
64	Not enough time to spend with patients
53	Burden of excessive paperwork
35	Too stressful and physically demanding
35	Worsening work conditions
20	Irregular hours

Source: American Federation of Teachers: Nurse shortage will be worse than career estimates. Available online at *www.aft.org/press/2001/041901.html*.

TABLE 4-8
Suggestions for Retention

% Suggestion	% Suggestion
87—Better staffing ratios	71—Performance bonuses
87—More patient time	69—More flexible schedules
79—More input into decisions	63—More part-time options
76—Higher salaries	61—Continuing education funds
	60—Better health coverage

Source: American Federation of Teachers: Nurse shortage will be worse than career estimates. Available online at www.aft.org/press/2001/041901.html.

The Magnet recognition program, sponsored by the American Nurses Association (ANA), is based on quality indicators and standards of nursing practice as defined in the ANA's *Scope and Standards for Nurse Administrators*. Characteristics of Magnet hospitals[11] are the following:
- Strong support from the organization's leadership
- Nurses having control over support services and personnel
- Effective communications between nurses and physicians
- Lower levels of emotional exhaustion
- High nurse-to-patient ratios
- Substantial nurse autonomy
- Strong nursing leadership
- Nurse participation in the organization's policy decisions
- Shorter length of stays
- Better intensive care unit utilization

The JCAHO has offered strategies for addressing the nursing crisis. They are as follows[3]:
- Create a culture of retention for nursing staff.
- Provide management training for nurse executives and managers.
- Delegate authority to nurse executive managers and staff.
- Set staffing levels to meet patient mix and acuity.
- Measure, analyze, and improve staffing effectiveness.
- Adopt zero-tolerance polices for abusive behaviors of physicians and other health care practitioners.
- Minimize paperwork.
- Broaden base of potential workers.
- Adopt information and ergonomic and other technologies to improve workflow and reduce risks of error and injury.
- Adopt fair and competitive compensation and benefits packages for nursing staff.

Kaldenberg and Regret[12] offer the following concepts to transform the workplace and create an organizational culture of retention:

- Provide and/or seek management training.
- Implement supportive information systems and ergonomic technologies.
- Institute staffing levels based on nurse competency and skill mix relative to patient mix and acuity.
- Develop zero-tolerance policies for abusive behaviors by health care practitioners.
- Diversify the workforce to broaden the department/unit's base.
- Recognize that there is a correlation between hospital employee satisfaction and patient satisfaction when developing staff recognition programs.[13]

Other studies corroborate that nurses report that verbal abuse on the job and mandatory overtime are major reasons that they are dissatisfied with their work,[14] while still others report that the most enjoyable part of being a nurse is helping patients and their families.[3,13] All of these references indicate that developing the environment for staff satisfaction requires a multipronged approach, one of changing the environment and building satisfying relationships.

Since the intent-to-leave variables are many, the retention plan must have multiple initiatives addressing these variables. In addition to the external environment, staff motivation changes as their personal needs change due to their own personal environment. It is a variable phenomenon. What motivates them could change even within the same year. Strategy 5 provides an infrastructure to address all the areas cited as reasons nurses leave and provides steps that can be used to create an environment that will become known as a "great place to work" and "the facility of choice."

STRATEGY 5: BECOME THE FACILITY OR ORGANIZATION OF CHOICE FOR STAFF

Caring is a great business advantage.
Scott Johnson Canfield[15]

Becoming the facility of choice can pertain to the patients and staff. This strategy focuses on the staff. As health care promotes caring for the patient, each facility needs to adopt a culture of caring for the staff, which will then become the foundation upon which staff retention will be built.

Redesigning the professional practice environment means more than looking at a model for the delivery of care and flexible schedules. It is a complex issue and must be looked at from a systems approach. It requires a "metanoia" environment,[16] one in which there is a reawakening, a fundamental shift or change in how an organization looks at how work gets done and staff are treated.

The ING Model

The ING Model provides a systems approach for assessing the effectiveness in the work environment. The model consists of 12 components (Fig. 4-8). Each component mirrors one of the top reasons nurses leave organizations and may consist of several processes. Each of these processes must be assessed

THE ING MODEL

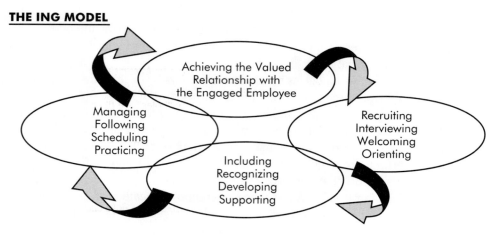

Fig. 4-8 The ING Model.

and *redesigned* if necessary for optimal effectiveness to produce the desired outcomes.

"ING" is a noun suffix and, when used with verbs, shows the end result of the actions connected to a component in the model. The redesign process becomes an evidenced-based approach, which ensures successful retention . . . the driving force for successful recruitment. The examples in Table 4-9 show, in part, how an outcomes-based model would address three of the components. Specific details and examples for operationalizing each component are addressed throughout the remainder of this book. Chapter 3, Human Resource Management, addresses recruiting, interviewing, welcoming and orienting staff, and completing performance evaluations. Scheduling and practical examples are located in the day-to-day operations chapter and role responsibilities of the manager are addressed throughout the book.

Implementation of the ING model. The following examples show some of the processes that could be implemented using the framework of the ING Model.

Following staff is supported by implementing a personalized interest plan (PIP) on each staff member. As nurses we implement a care plan on our patients. Are not our employees as important as the patient? Keeping the same concept in mind, managers should implement a personalized interest plan (employee interest plan) on each employee as part of developing the one-on-one relationship that is so necessary in building the team.

The PIP is not to be confused with a growth plan. Rather, the PIP addresses what self-interests staff have besides their actual work life. For years, great managers have

TABLE 4-9
Examples of ING Model Components

"ING" Component	Desired Outcome	Process for Assessment
Staffing	There is sufficient and well-educated staff to meet the needs of the patient. The staffing schedules have a variety of options to meet both the staff and patient needs.	Preparing the monthly schedule How "holes" are filled Absenteeism and vacation policies Staffing guidelines for census fluctuations
Practicing	The defined patient care delivery model meets the patient care needs of that unit's specific patient population through a process in which roles have been clearly identified. Barriers to providing the care have been eliminated through process-improvement techniques such as process flows and work analysis.	Determination of the model of care that best meets the needs of the unit Defining role responsibilities Processing of physicians' orders Discharge of patient—meeting all criteria for education and follow-up
Including	Established processes will provide opportunities for staff inclusion in decision-making for those areas impacting the staff members' work environment, educational needs, and self-fulfillment in their job role.	Monthly focus meetings by HR Inclusion in subcommittees of the recruitment and retention committee

intuitively discovered those personal interests of their staff and assigned them projects that would utilize these personal interests.

Recently, the term "job sculpting" has been used. It is derived from a concept developed for the work done by Waldroop, which he calls the psychology of job satisfaction. The concept states that employees become more committed to an organization when they can also become also involved in those life interest activities such as computers, mentoring, producing, and crafting.[17]

Examples of how the concept would be implemented:

- The person who loves to work on the computer could represent the department on the committee to select a computerized documentation system.
- The person who is talented in arts and crafts or producing could be assigned to job fairs and open houses.

How can the concept be implemented? Appendix 4-2 provides the structure for documentation and is symbolic for employees, who see a planned process is in place. It is a caring strategy. The process is what is most important. A manager taking time to meet with new staff within 2 weeks of orientation implements the PIP, and thereafter meets with the employee quarterly. The quarterly meetings provide a roll-up of information, making the annual performance evaluation process a more meaningful experience. (This is assuming the manager has responsibility over one unit and has an off-shift assistant manager in place.) Gallop's recommendation on meeting with staff on a quarterly basis to promote retention future supports the concept.[7]

Recognizing staff occurs through clinical ladder and/or performance reward programs. Those who kept *viable* clinical ladders in place for the past 10 years state that it promotes high staff satisfaction. Today's workforce wants to be rewarded for merit—work accomplished—and not just longevity. As a result, many organizations are reviewing the concept of a clinical ladder or a grading system versus an overall performance reward program. The concept is to reward those who are providing the care at the bedside, the hard-to-recruit staff.

Supporting staff includes providing programs that support personal lifestyle needs. Identified areas include quality child care facilities, a sick child care program, access to adult day care centers at reduced rates, and financial seminars given by women for women. These are just a few examples. Organization needs will vary. The process of surveying the staff to identify their need provides the information on what is needed. However, the process itself also promotes retention, because it is another "caring" strategy.

Each component in the ING Model must be studied to see what else can be added or what needs to be redesigned with input from your staff—every step of the way.

SUMMARY

This chapter focused on how an organization can be successful in retention and recruitment of staff. The key drivers for retaining staff are organizational commitment, having the human resources department seen as an employee advocate, knowing the targeted market, using recruitment monies effectively, and redesigning the work environment to become known as an "employer of choice."

Nursing shortages have been compared with cancer: it's there and everyone knows it's there, but administration tries to pretend it's not there and hopes no one will notice, or hopes it will get better. Acknowledging the issue, validating the concern, and letting staff know it is a priority can help a great deal. The process to address all these strategies must be implemented on concurrent tracks. Reviewing how work is done, staff inclusion, staff recognition, and effective communication tools all become a work in progress. The reward will be satisfied and energized staff, staff who will become your spokespersons as they go about their lives in the community. That is how recruitment is truly effective.

QUESTIONS FOR CONSIDERATION

1. List 3 of the 12 challenging issues surrounding the shortage of qualified team members.

2. Describe five key strategies to achieve a "valued relationship" to ensure staff retention.
3. Define what a focus meeting is and how one is accomplished.
4. Describe how generational differences may impact your team.
5. Create a plan for ongoing retention and recruitment for your area using the information in this chapter and other methods.

References

1. American Hospital Association Commission on Workforce for Hospitals: *In our hands—how hospitals can build a thriving workplace*, Chicago, 2002, American Hospital Association Publishing.
2. U.S. Department of Health and Human Services, Health Resources and Services Administration: Bureau of Health Professions, National Center: *Health workforce analysis: projected supply, demand, and shortages of registered nurses, 2000-2020*, Washington, DC, 2000, USDHHS.
3. Joint Commission on Accreditation of Healthcare Organizations: *White paper: health care at the crossroads; strategies for addressing the evolving nursing crisis*, Oakbrook Terrace, IL, 2002, Joint Commission on Accreditation of Healthcare Organizations Publishing.
4. Lovern E: Rx for nurses, *Modern Healthcare* 10:7, 2002.
5. Health Care Advisory Board: *Managing a multigenerational RN work force*, Washington, DC, 2002, The Advisory Board Company.
6. Ackoff R: *Creating the corporate future*, New York, 1981, John Wiley & Sons.
7. Buckingham M, Coffman C: *First, break all the rules*, New York, 1999, Simon & Schuster.
8. Huselid M: Study summary that describes the impact of human resources management practices on turnover, productivity and corporate financial performance, *Academy of Management Journal* 38(3):635-672, 1995.
9. *A special report: 31 strategies to recruit and retain nurses*, Management Briefings, Barrington, IL, 2000, Harling Communications, Inc.
10. Health Care Advisory Board, Nurse Executive Center: *Reversing the flight of talent*, Washington, DC, 2000, The Advisory Board Company.
11. Aiken L: *Superior outcomes for magnet hospitals: the evidence base*, Washington, DC, 2002, American Nurses Publishing.
12. Kaldenberg DO, Regret B: Do satisfied patients depend on satisfied employees? The Satisfaction Report, *QRC Advisor* 15(7): 9-12, 1999.
13. Institute of Medicine: *Improving the quality of long-term care*, Washington, DC, 2001, National Academy Press.
14. Aiken LA, Clarke SP, Sloan DM, et al: Nurses' reports of hospital quality of care and working conditions in five countries, *Health Affairs* 20(3):43-53, 2001.
15. Canfield J, et al: *Chicken soup for the soul at work*, Deerfield Beach, FL, 1996, Health Communications, Inc.
16. Senge, P: *The fifth discipline*, New York, 1990, Doubleday.
17. Butler, T Waldroop J: Job sculpting: the art of retaining your best people, *Harvard Business Review* 77(5):144-152, 1999.

For Further Reading

Blanchard K, Bowles S: *High five! The magic of working together*, New York, 2001, HarperCollins Publications.
Blanchard K, Carolos J, Randolph A: *Empowerment is more than a minute*, San Francisco, 1996, Berrett-Koehler.
Brady A: Recruiting, retention and returns, *CFO*, 65-76, 2000.
Bridges W: Managing transitions: making the most of change, Cambridge, MA, 1993, DaCapo Publishing.
Cohen RK: Mirror, mirror on the wall—who's the best employer? *Modern Healthcare* 10:12-14, 1999.

Connors R, Smith T, Hickman C: *The Oz principle*, New Jersey, 1994, Prentice-Hall.

Delassandro T: *Relationship strategies*, La Jolla, CA, 1990, Allessandro & Associates.

Denison DR: *Corporate culture and organizational effectiveness,* New York, 1990, Wiley & Sons.

Groomsman RJ: How recruiters woo high demand candidates, *HR Magazine* 43(3): 122-127, 1998.

Health Care Advisory Board: *Managing nurse overtime; strategies for reducing the burden on staff,* Washington, DC, 2001, The Advisory Board Company.

Health Care Financing Administration: *Report to Congress: appropriateness of minimum nurse staffing ratios in nursing homes,* Washington, DC, 2000, HCFA.

Harkins PJ: Why employees stay—or go, *Workforce* 17(10):74-79, 1998.

Hawke J: More good nurses needed by 2005, *Nursing Spectrum* 10A(2):14, 1998.

Institute for Nursing Healthcare Leadership: *Work force challenges in the 21st century: implications for health care and nursing,* April 2001, 15, Cambridge, MA.

Institute of Medicine: *Nursing staff in hospitals and nursing homes: is it adequate?* Washington, DC, 1996, National Academy Press.

Mezibov D: With demand for RN's climbing, and shortening supply, forecasters say what's ahead isn't typical "shortage cycle," *American Association of Colleges of Nursing Bulletin*, February 1998.

Nelson, B: *Ways to energize employees*, New York, 1997, Workman Publishing.

Pritchett, Price: *Fast growth: align, adapt, add value*, Plano, TX 1997, Pritchett & Associates, Inc.

Scott C, et al: The impact of communication and multiple identifications on intent to leave, *Management Quarterly* 12(3):400-435, 1999.

Solomon C: Workers want a life! Do managers care? *Workforce*, August:54-58, 1999.

Stewart M: New nursing shortage hits: causes are complex, *The American Nurse*, Washington, DC, March/April 1998.

FACILITY ANYWHERE, HAPPYTOWN, USA: DEPARTMENTAL PROFILE

Departmental Profile

MANAGER	DEPARTMENT					
Indicator	Qtr-1	Qtr-2	Mid-Year Average	Qtr-3	Qtr-4	Year-End Average
Turnover—Overall						
Turnover—RN						
Turnover—CNA						
Turnover—Other (specify)						
Grievances—Filed						
Costs—Overtime						
Costs—Agency						
Costs—Advertising (newspaper-other/ finders' fees)						
Patient Satisfaction						
Physician/Family Satisfaction*						
Staff Satisfaction*						
Quality						
Falls						
Medication Errors						
Pressure Ulcers						
Other						

*Define how your organization will measure this—focus groups, individual meetings, surveys.

FACILITY ANYWHERE, HAPPYTOWN, USA: EMPLOYEE CARE PLAN OR PERSONALIZED INTEREST PLAN

Employee Care Plan or Personalized Interest Plan

Employee Name: Jane Smith

SYSTEM/FACILITY EMPLOYMENT HISTORY

Date of Employment: _____   Department Assignment: _____

Transfers _____

Educational Background:

AD _____   BSN _____   BS _____   MSN _____   Other _____

Matriculated/or intentions:

Initial Interview
Rate **personal likes** in the following category list in descending order of interest
(10 = the most interest) (0 = no interest).

Technology _____   Working with numbers/math _____

Creative productions _____   Theory type issues/conceptual thinking _____

Mentoring/coaching _____   Influencing through ideas/language _____

Managing people/relationships _____   New program development _____

What does it take to keep you motivated, interested, and linked to an organization?

What has been your most significant and rewarding professional experience?

What has been your most significant and rewarding personal experience?

What are your goals for the next 3 months?

Date: _____   Manager's Signature: _____

Follow-up interviews on a quarterly basis:

Follow-up interview: Date: _____   Manager's Signature: _____

Review the above areas and note changes in interests or challenges that the employee would like to experience:

Results of review and discussion:

Goals for the next quarter:

CHAPTER 5

DAY-TO-DAY OPERATIONS

LYNDA S. HILLIARD

T.M. MARRELLI

I t has been said that "managing makes a manager." However, it does help to have some information about the nurse manager's day-to-day duties and responsibilities before being faced with carrying them out.

Supporting effective day-to-day operations is the core of the nurse manager's activities. Staffing and scheduling personnel, delivering patient care through an appropriate nursing care delivery model, and meetings (e.g., leading staff meetings, attending organizational planning meetings, supporting patient care conferences) are all activities vital to the day-to-day functioning of a patient care unit or area. Information about these subjects, as well as others relating to the day-to-day operations of a nursing unit or area, is discussed in this chapter.

Intertwined with these subjects are strategies for their implementation, as well as the quest for cost-effective quality patient outcomes, with a focus on customer service. These are considered while working to promote the professionalism and satisfaction of the patient care staff.

CONTINUOUS QUALITY IMPROVEMENT: THE FOUNDATION FOR EFFECTIVE DAILY MANAGEMENT OF OPERATIONS

In the first edition of this book, quality assessment and improvement were discussed in a separate chapter outlining the program that would be developed and implemented to determine the effectiveness of patient care and services. However, as an understanding of continuous quality improvement (CQI) processes evolved, it became more apparent that CQI was not an independent process, but one that must be intertwined in the daily operations of a department, as well as throughout the entire system. We have attempted to incorporate the elements of CQI throughout this book and will focus briefly on improving organizational performance (IOP) and its relationship to operational management.

Quality—More Important Than Ever

Quality is a very difficult term to define, especially in health care. However, for the new nurse manager it is important to understand and integrate quality management and the elements of measurement, assessment, and improvement into daily routine, as well as to understand how each area's performance is aggregated into a total organizational view of quality for internal and external customers. In the late 1980s, the National Association of Quality Assurance (NAQA) Professionals defined quality as, " . . . levels of excellence produced and documented in the process of patient care based upon the best knowledge available and achievable at a particular facility."[1] The definition of quality in health care has grown to include the documentation of those structures, processes, and outcomes necessary to replicate quality of care. Quality of care is predicated on positive outcomes, customer satisfaction, best practices, and cost-efficiency.

Each health care system has the opportunity to develop its own philosophy of patient care delivery, based on its mission statement, values, and the accepted standards of practice for medical, nursing, and other health care providers. The Joint Commission on Accreditation of Healthcare Organizations (JCAHO), in an effort to help health care organizations systematically improve organizational performance, has restructured its standards to focus on the functions involved in patient care delivery, for all those settings that have the opportunity to be accredited (Box 5-1).[2] The integration of the functions into the planning, delivery, evaluation, and revision process, all the while measuring outcomes against established benchmarks, is what constitutes an effective CQI program.

---

box 5-1

IMPORTANT FUNCTIONS ON WHICH JCAHO STANDARDS FOCUS

PATIENT-FOCUSED FUNCTIONS

1. Rights and ethics
2. Assessment
3. Care, treatment, services
4. Education
5. Continuum of care

ORGANIZATIONAL FUNCTIONS

6. Improving organizational performance
7. Leadership
8. Environmental safety
9. Management of human resources
10. Management of information
11. Surveillance, prevention, and control of infection

Adapted from *2002 Accreditation manual for home care*, Oakbrook Terrace, IL, 2002, JCAHO.

Effective managers are never satisfied with the status quo, especially if there are methods to improve the products or service that their department produces. Those health care managers who "rest on their laurels" or maintain the same clinical practice or administrative operations because of a fear of change will not survive. Administrative and clinical functioning of a patient care department should continually be reviewed for appropriateness and efficiency, with all staff involved in reviewing what is done, for what reasons, and whether it is being done "right the first time." Managers must also think strategically and plan for the inevitability of change. Continuing education seminars, networking, and literature review of pertinent subject matter are all important for a manager to both maintain a general view of the marketplace and enhance the knowledge base to plan for the future. Box 5-2 outlines ten steps to help achieve and improve quality.[3]

---

box 5-2

10 STEPS TO QUALITY TRANSFORMATION

- A quality organization begins by delighting customers and giving them more than they imagined possible.
- Remain close to your customer by knowing how customers use your products and services and any concerns or problems they have. Listen to customers and help them identify their needs.
- Lead customers into the future by anticipating their needs. Keep up-to-date on technologic advances that might prove useful to them.
- A flawless organizational system gives customers what they want, when they want it, with efficiency, precision, and consistency.
- The vision, values, and systems and process must be consistent with, and complementary to, each other. The vision answers the question, "What business are we in?" Values describe "how we conduct our business." Systems and processes are the sequence of activities by which all work gets done.
- Teamwork must pervade the organization and be based on commitment to customers and constant improvement. Teamwork results from a common understanding of the organization's vision and values, a dedication to delighting customers, a mutual respect for coworkers, and a shared commitment to the understanding and ongoing improvement of systems and processes.
- Everyone must know her/his job. This level of understanding requires both continuous education and regular feedback from each employee's customers. Employees must know how their work relates to the final product and ultimate user or consumer.
- Data and a scientific approach are used to plan work, solve problems, make decisions, and pursue improvement. All types of initiatives and activities are monitored to see how well they are working or can be improved.
- Select reputable companies from which to buy products or subcontract services, and develop working partnerships with these suppliers.
- Support and nourish improvement efforts of every group and individual in the company. Establish and maintain a spirit based on closeness with the customer, precise data, teamwork, constant improvement, and pride of work.

Adapted from Garland C, *Emporium medical supply,* Fullerton, CA.

NURSING CARE DELIVERY SYSTEMS

New nurse managers need to understand the various types of nursing care delivery systems (NCDSs), the strengths and weaknesses of each, and their unique value in their own setting. In fact, Manthey[4] believes that of all areas of technical knowledge required to understand unit functions, NCDS operations, including work structure, make up the most important area to know.

An NCDS is the way in which nursing care is provided to the patient or, according to Wake,[5] is "an interacting set of structural elements which control the way care is provided." Manthey[4] says that a delivery system has to answer five questions:

1. Who is responsible for making decisions about patient care?
2. How long do that person's decisions remain in effect?
3. How is the work distributed among staff members—by task or by patient?
4. How is patient care communication handled?
5. How is the whole unit managed?

Team Nursing

Team nursing is an NCDS that uses an RN as a team leader to lead a group of nursing staff, which may include other RNs, LPNs, and nursing or patient care assistants, to care for a group of patients together. Sherman[6] identifies a basic belief of team nursing—team members of varying skill levels can contribute to patient-centered nursing care if their activities are coordinated by a professional nurse.

The team leader is responsible for assessing the patients' needs, planning the care, and delegating tasks to the other members of the team based on their skills and abilities in relation to the assessed needs of the patients and within the scope of their job description. In addition, the team leader evaluates the care given and revises the plan of care as necessary.

The key to successful team nursing is communication among team members and with the patient and family. This is usually facilitated with the patient care conference or team conference, which is held to coordinate care and to gain input from all the team members. Care can be evaluated from everyone's perspective and care plans developed and modified if necessary.

Proposed strengths of the team nursing system are efficiency and lower costs as compared with the total patient care and primary nursing systems, as well as making use of varying levels of nursing personnel. Theoretically, an esprit de corps develops among team members as they work together.

Negatives include a lack of accountability (because everyone is accountable) and the costs associated with the need for daily conference time. From the patient's point of view, several caregivers are involved with care rather than just one person. This results in a task-orientation versus total patient care approach, which may increase fragmentation of care.

Total Patient Care

Total patient care is an NCDS in which the RN or LPN is given the assignment of planning, organizing, and providing care to a group of patients. The RN supervising the LPN may perform some assessment and planning activities on the LPN's assigned patients, but generally most care is performed by the nurse assigned.

Strengths of the total patient care system are fewer caregivers for the patient and theoretically a better knowledge of the patient by the assigned nurse because the numbers of assigned patients are less than with team nursing.

Weaknesses of the system are a greater cost as compared with the team nursing system, a possible lack of continuity, and care coordination and accountability, and some aspects of care for the patient may be overlooked or neglected.

Primary Nursing

Primary nursing is an NCDS in which the RN, called a primary nurse, is given an assignment of planning and organizing all care for a group of patients for the total hospitalization of those patients, 24 hours a day. The primary nurse may also give the care but may delegate particular aspects. When the primary nurse is not on duty, an associate nurse cares for patients using the plan set forth by the primary nurse.

Primary nursing provides a nurse who has accountability for outcomes of care and care planning and documentation. Usually there is high patient satisfaction, continuity of care, and care of a high quality. Of course primary nursing is only as good as the primary nurse, and it is considered more costly than team or functional nursing because it usually relies on a larger number of RNs.

Modular Nursing/Prime Team

Modular nursing is an NCDS in which an RN is assigned the nursing care for a group of patients, generally grouped geographically, along with another caregiver (either an LPN or an unlicensed staff member). It is a form of team nursing in principle but uses smaller teams. It provides closer monitoring of care than does team nursing and uses fewer RNs than the primary nursing system. It is less costly than primary nursing and can use other types of caregivers. It is, however, less efficient and costs more than team nursing.

Functional Nursing

Functional nursing is an NCDS in which each caregiver is given a task to perform within the scope of her/his abilities and job description for all the patients on a unit. The patient thus sees a number of caregivers, each an expert in her/his particular task (similar to an assembly line). One nurse gives medications and another gives treatments, an aide changes linen, and so on.

It is considered the most efficient and least costly form of care, requiring fewer RNs. It takes advantage of differing skill levels.

However, from the patient's perspective, functional nursing focuses more on tasks rather than meeting the patient's needs with multiple caregivers, who may not see the patient as a whole. From the staff's point of view, boredom may result from performing repetitive activities.

Case Management

Case management is a form of primary nursing whereby the RN who is the case manager is responsible for managing the nursing care of a group of patients across all units during that hospitalization. Protocols are developed by the health care team to achieve clinical outcomes within prescribed time frames.

The case management NCDS has all the advantages of primary nursing. Although primary nursing is considered costly, the emphasis on protocols and meeting outcomes within defined time frames may help to save money in the long run because of reduction in lengths of stay. It also promotes nursing professionalism and collegiality with other disciplines.

NCDS Considerations

Organizations across the country have adopted one or more of the NCDSs described. Most have modified the original system as proposed and tailored it to meet the needs of their settings and the availability of staff. Keep in mind that any NCDS can be used with any skill level and mix of staff. Factors that influence which model is chosen include:

- The values and philosophy of the organization, especially those of the nursing department.
- The numbers and quality of available nursing personnel.
- Consumer demands.
- Competition in the marketplace.
- The retention status of staff members.
- Financial status of the system or how much money is available to spend on salaries for staff members.

In 1989, a survey done by Wake[5] asked for the status of patient assignment in 1986 and 1989 and projections for 1992. Results showed that, although team nursing and primary nursing NCDSs increased from 1986 to 1989, the case management system was projected to be the NCDS of choice by 1992. In fact, case management is not yet the NCDS of choice, but it undoubtedly will be in the near future.

Since 1992, the need for a patient's total episode of hospitalization to be monitored for appropriateness and expediency of services has resulted in the implementation of a clinical case management model that interfaces with the nursing care delivery system at a unit level, with the physician and the payers. The patient's primary nurse in any model is the person responsible for ensuring that the plan of care is updated daily or more often if necessary and that all services necessary for timely treatment and discharge are taking place.

Because others, such as pharmacists and dietitians, provide elements of care to the patient, the process is actually of a multidisciplinary nature and can be termed a patient care delivery system. Close communications and good working relationships between the patient's primary nurse and the nursing case manager are major requirements for an effective patient care delivery system, and this is the one seen evolving most frequently.

Professionally Advanced Care Team Model

Several NCDSs have been successfully implemented that may be of some interest. The Professionally Advanced Care Team model (ProACT) was developed through the work redesign process. This NCDS delineates two RN roles, the primary nurse and the clinical care manager. The primary nurse manages primary patients and delegates caregiving to LPNs, associate nurses, and nursing assistants. The clinical care manager manages the entire hospital stay of a caseload of patients and ensures outcomes are met, much like the case manager. In addition, this model features unit-based nonclinical support personnel who function to relieve the nursing staff of nonnursing duties.

Partners in Practice

A form of primary nursing (or modular nursing) is partners in practice, which uses nurse extenders coupled with an RN to form a "partnership" to care for a group of patients together. The RN and nurse helper may or may not work the same schedule on the same shift to give care to patients. The RN assesses and plans care and delegates selected activities to the nurse extender.

Coprimary Nursing: Job Sharing

Coprimary nursing is an NCDS whereby two nurses function together as one to be the primary nurse. They work the same shift on differing days to provide continuity. This system was developed originally in the critical care setting to help deal with the fragmentation of 12-hour shifts.

Patient-Centered Care

Many hospitals across the country have begun to restructure delivery systems to become more patient-oriented as opposed to hospital-oriented. Services are being organized around meeting the individual needs of the patient. This change in focus involves an analysis and redefinition of all activities involved with patients, a work redesign. It involves all departments that deal with the patient, including the nursing department, and is truly multidisciplinary in approach.

After work redesign is implemented, often "multipurpose" roles are created to perform ancillary tasks and procedures for patients that were formerly done in other departments, such as the admission registration process in admissions, a phlebotomy in the laboratory, or an electrocardiogram (ECG) in the cardiology department. Often these activities are all carried out in the patient's room by one person, who may be teamed with an RN. Many systems have the nurse manager or staff nurses supervising these individuals.

Forces driving the restructuring efforts are customer service concerns and consumer demands, quality and efficiency needs, and the need to reduce costs.

As more and more institutions are restructuring care, we are likely to see other innovations in NCDSs emerge. Regardless of the specific patient care delivery system used, Fig. 5-1 delineates role responsibility and the relationship chart of the patient's primary nurse.

Home Care Patient-Centered Care Teams

Patient care delivery models in home care have traditionally surrounded the case management of a patient by an RN or physical therapist coordinating the care throughout the home care service, working with internal or external care

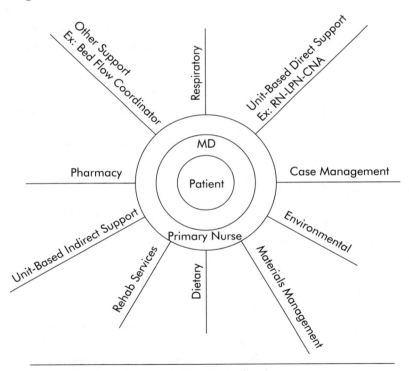

The Following Needs Must Be Defined
to Implement the above Relationship Chart:

    1. Role Expectations

    2. Educational Needs

    3. Structural Changes

Fig. 5-1 Role responsibility and relationship chart of the patient's primary nurse.

providers such as the home health aide, parenteral therapy staff from a pharmaceutical agency, and possibly, home medical equipment providers. However, in many home care organizations, case management was not truly implemented and care was not truly coordinated. A case manager may have been assigned, but nurses and other clinicians were assigned on a daily basis, based on scheduled availability of geographically assigned staff, as opposed to the assessed needs of the patient or an attempt to limit the number of different staff visiting a patient.

Home care organizations have received recommendations for improvement from the JCAHO or other accreditation bodies if it was found that care was being provided by a large number of nurses and not being coordinated by either a case manager or patient care coordinator. In an effort to improve patient outcomes, standardize some of the elements of the care process, and provide more cost-efficient care, patient-centered care teams have emerged in home care as well. Many different models exist; however, the core element of each includes one case manager who is responsible for developing, coordinating, assigning, and communicating with the care team (including the ordering physician) to make sure the patient is following an individualized care plan or clinical path that meets the goals as established, based upon assessed needs.

This type of model is becoming more of a necessity as managed care practices impact the productivity of home care staff in different ways. It is not uncommon for the number of visits per patient to decrease dramatically under managed care (both Medicare and general populations). It is the responsibility of the home care case manager to communicate regularly with the authorizing staff to update the patient's condition and request more visits or other types of supplies or services. Traditionally the case manager has worked with the physician in developing the frequency and duration of a plan of care based on assessed patient needs and communication focused on changes in the patient condition, not daily arguing or pleading for more services.

The typical home care patient-centered team may include an RN/CS case manager to admit and regularly assess the patient and, dependent on caseload size, additional RN and LPN team members (e.g., revisit nurses, home health care aides, therapists and appropriately credentialed assistant staff, and medical social workers). The case manager's productivity standards are less than the revisit nurses, since she/he is responsible for all the coordination and communication among managed care staff, physicians, and other team members, as well as the more labor-intensive admission and data collection and recertification visits.

Evaluation of the Nursing Care Delivery System

One role of the new nurse manager is to analyze the current NCDS for adequacy. The following questions should be posed:

- Are patient outcomes being achieved in a timely, cost-effective manner?
- Are patients and families satisfied with care?
- Are physicians and other health team members satisfied with the care?

Information on how to conduct an in-depth analysis of an NCDS is available in *Nursing Assignment Patterns User's Manual* by Munson et al.[7] Piltz-Kirkby[8] discusses her experience using the tool on a rehabilitation unit. How to gather information on patient characteristics, nursing resources, and organizational support is described, as well as a way to analyze the data gathered. An informed decision can then be made to keep or change the NCDS.

Accreditation standards do not specifically dictate which type of NCDS a facility should adopt, but instead focus on care coordination, assessment, skills of the clinician matching the needs of the patient, and other facets of care delivery.

PROFESSIONAL PRACTICE MODELS

Although the NCDSs previously described address assignment of patients and roles of nursing personnel, they do not identify underlying professional practice issues such as autonomy in professional decision-making, budgeting of time for care activities, and nursing practice growth and development. Professional practice models do address these issues.

Shared Governance

Many facilities have adopted some sort of shared governance model within nursing. Shared governance is an organizational model that gives staff the authority for decisions, autonomy to make those decisions, and control over the implementation and outcomes of the decisions. Authority and accountability are shared between and among all the staff and the organization as partners.[9] Various models are in practice, but generally councils or cabinets of staff nurses are developed, with staff members serving in leadership roles and management advising and supporting. Bylaws are developed that guide the function of the nursing department. Nursing practice is defined by the staff through their council, and they, not the nurse manager, are accountable for the level of that practice. Likewise, staff members are accountable for all quality improvement and related activities. Continuing development and competency are determined by the staff council as well.

PRACTICE STANDARDS AND PROTOCOLS

As outcomes management becomes more integrated into the daily operations of all health care settings, the need for reliable and valid data is essential. In order for data to be reliable and valid there needs to be uniformity in how the data are collected and what criteria are utilized in collecting the data. In health care, it is important to keep a focus on the patient as a person and not just as an element of data. However, in order to analyze outcomes and how they were achieved, as well as to try to quantify the cost of care in terms of monetary values, core standardization has to occur. Chapter 8, Resource Management and Budgeting Basics, discusses the financial implications of practice protocols.

Each health care setting has the ability to generate clinical practice standards or protocols based on acceptable medical, nursing, or other health care–related research data and standards of care. The Agency for Healthcare Research and Quality (AHRQ), a unit of the Department of Health and Human Services (DHHS), has developed a number of practice guidelines for various health conditions that are gaining much acceptance as the core foundation for development of specific practice parameters. Managed care organizations, as well as professional health care organizations, are accepting the validity of such practice standards, which, it is hoped, can decrease the legal liability of utilizing practice standards, once they are widely recognized and accepted by appropriate professional groups.

In the process of developing clinical practice guidelines (pathways) and/or protocols, planning staff need to be aware of the current scopes of practice of all licensed/credentialed staff, current regional or national published practice standards, and the desired outcomes of care. Many professional organizations have documented standards of practice for their individual profession outlining the scope of care that can be safely provided by competent, credentialed staff. However, as in all human-related endeavors, flexibility and the ability to apply appropriate medical, nursing, or other clinical judgment into practice standards or protocols are needed in any development and implementation of a prescribed plan of care based upon diagnoses and patient acuity levels. It is important to note that sound clinical judgment does not take the place of protocols as the health care industry moves toward standardization of care and care processes.

Compensation Innovation

Other concepts that have been integrated into some professional practice models are changes in compensation. Salaried nursing staff[9] and gain sharing[10] have been successfully implemented. The idea of "group practices" has emerged; it is similar to the physician model. A group of nurses contracts to care for a group of patients for a specified period.[11]

The role of the nurse manager in the new practice models changes dramatically from the traditional one of "supervisor." The manager role is one of support and facilitation, ensuring that proper resources are available to the staff of her/his unit or area so they can do their jobs. Although it takes time to change philosophy, the result is a staff who have control over their practice, practice in a professional manner, and are more fulfilled and satisfied.

PATIENT CLASSIFICATION

A comprehensive staffing system may comprise a patient classification system or acuity system, a master staffing plan, a scheduling plan, a position control plan, a budget, and reports that provide feedback to the manager on all components.

Patient classification is defined as "the categorization or grouping of patients according to an assessment of their nursing care requirements over a specified period of time."[12] It is seen as an objective and structured process to use in determining and allocating staff for patient care. In other words, patients are classified based on the projected number of nursing hours required to provide care. It can also be used as a measure of productivity and to help achieve compliance with accreditation standards. With increasing concerns about scarce resources, cost, and efficiency, patient classification systems can assist with appropriate allocation of resources to meet patient needs and provide justification as necessary for the decisions made. These standards imply the use of some type of patient classification system.[13] Patient classification can also be used to determine the cost of and bill for nursing services.

The patient classification process generally has two parts: (1) the actual classification procedure itself (using a tool), and (2) the quantification of the hours needed for the nursing care or staffing standards determined for each care category. In other words, for each category of care needed, from those patients needing the least amounts of nursing care to those requiring the most, an average number of nursing care hours is determined. Usually the tools are transferrable among facilities with similar groups of patients, but the staffing standards are not because of variations such as strength of support services, environmental factors such as unit or area layout, differences in philosophy including type of NCDS, differences in medical treatment, and levels and experience of nursing staff. Either work-sampling studies measuring indirect and direct care time or estimation procedures through trial and error can be performed to establish staffing standards for a tool borrowed from another facility.

Literally hundreds of patient classification systems are in use across the country. Some were developed specifically for a particular institution, and others were purchased from vendors. In a recent study, Nagaprasanna[14] found that a patient classification system is applicable to all types of nursing delivery systems. He also noted that internally developed systems were the most frequent type used, with four categories of patient acuity being the most common number of categories. Most facilities classify patients daily, and most systems are computerized, not manual. He found that the ease of classification is the highest rated factor in selecting a patient classification system.

The new nurse manager should become thoroughly familiar with the organization's system. Usually the system is managed by a person in the organization who assisted with its development and implementation; this is the person to seek out to explain the system. Questions to ask are outlined in Manager's Tip 5-1.

MANAGER'S TIP 5-1

QUESTIONS TO ASK ABOUT CLASSIFICATION SYSTEMS

✔ **Is the patient classification tool based on prototype evaluation or on factor-analysis evaluation?** Prototypes are broad descriptions of three or four levels, and the patient is compared to the levels and placed in the one that most closely matches her/his description. Factor analysis is based on a list of critical indicators that, when summed up, indicate a patient category.

✔ **What is the process by which the tool is used by the nursing staff?** It is essential to know each and every step. As issues arise, an awareness of where "things can go wrong" is helpful in solving problems with the system.

✔ **How is the system maintained and monitored? What is the role of the manager?** You need to know what orientation and ongoing educational programs for staff are available as relates to the system. Reliability checks are usually built into the system. Reliability means consistency between raters. Achieving agreement of at least 90% is generally considered acceptable. Validity monitoring refers to whether the system actually measures what it is supposed to measure. Sometimes surveys of the staff are done or actual time-motion studies are conducted to reaffirm the system.

✔ **How are data generated by the system interpreted? What should be done with data once they are interpreted?** Obviously the manager must understand what the data mean and then how they can be used as *aids* to staff the unit. Most systems compile and report an acuity number that is the sum of all patients' levels. They then predict the numbers of staff needed on the following shifts.

✔ **What exactly is patient classification used for in the organization?** Only for staffing on a daily basis? For the yearly budget? For productivity? For assignments? For placement of patients on units? For determining cost of patient services?

✔ **What are the current problems with the system?** The nurse manager should also ask this question of the staff. Sometimes there are problems with "acuity creep," or gradually rising acuity levels. It is a managerial responsibility to identify and work at resolving problems related to the system.

Two final points must be made concerning patient classification. First, the manager should understand that a high activity level in the unit or area and the acuity level of patients are not necessarily one and the same. Other causes exist that influence activity levels besides higher acuity levels, including factors such as experience and competency of the staff and presence and quality of support services at the unit level. Second, patient classification data are used as *supports* for decision-making. They never take the place of nurse manager judgment, nor should they ever be taken as facts not to be questioned. Despite millions of dollars expended to find the perfect system, no such thing exists. Keep that in mind.

SCHEDULING AND STAFFING

One of the activities that consumes the most time available to managers is scheduling and staffing. In a well-known 1990 survey of nurse managers by the American Organization of Nurse Executives (AONE),[15] it was found that 11.1% of their time was spent on this activity. Not only time but concern and worry also are often hallmarks of this activity because the manager is ultimately responsible to see that the facility is staffed appropriately. There can be legal ramifications if staffing is not appropriate.

Nursing staff are very concerned about scheduling and staffing. In fact, the *American Journal of Nursing*[16] conducted a survey of its readers in 1987 and found that a "desired work schedule" was number 1 of the 10 most important items that influenced decisions on whether to stay in nursing. Another top item was "having an adequate nurse/patient ratio," which again relates to scheduling and staffing. Clearly these two areas affect nurse retention, so sensibly, the new manager should be aware of scheduling and staffing practices and options. These continue to be important considerations for staff members.

As important as making sure that staff are scheduled and shifts or patient loads covered, it is also a managerial responsibility to assign patients to staff based on assessed patient needs, the patient's acuity levels, and the abilities and competencies of the staff members. Many hospitals and other types of health care settings have developed "cross-training" programs that assist in maintaining a stable staffing pool. Emergency department and critical care staff may be cross-trained, as may neonatal, labor and delivery, and pediatric nurses. With the emergence of more outpatient or ambulatory care areas, many nurses are cross-trained as "procedure" nurses to work in cardiac catheterization laboratories or the radiology departments for specialized angiography services. The core of a cross-training program lies in the regular testing of staff competencies to assess their abilities to work in those areas that they frequent less than their primary assignment.

Scheduling Patterns and Options

In the past 20 years, various types of scheduling practices and options have been developed over and above the traditional 8-hour-a-day, 5-day-a-week schedule. Several of the most prevalent patterns are noted in Table 5-1.

Almost every conceivable combination of shifts and days has been tried somewhere in the quest to find schedules that fit into every nurse's lifestyle, still meet patient care needs, and yet fit within the personnel budget and unit staffing model.

Cyclical schedules lend a degree of predictability to a staff member's schedule by using a pattern that is repeated consistently over a certain number of weeks.

TABLE 5-1
Types of Scheduling Patterns

Pattern	Comments
8-hour/5-day week	Still the predominant pattern. Allows for a 30-minute meal break and a 30-minute overlap time if used for 24 hours.
10-hour/4-day week	Gives an opportunity for longer overlaps during activity times, meetings, or educational sessions. Allows the staff an extra day off each week.
10-hour/7-day week	Staff works 7 days on and has 7 days off. Gives better continuity and periods of time off, but fatigue has been reported by the end of the work week.
Baylor plan	Staff member works only on weekends and either works 2 days with 12-hour shifts and is paid for 36 hours, or 2 nights and is paid for 40 hours.
12-hour/3-day week	Gives better continuity over the course of the shift but not over the week. Allows staff 4 days off during week.

Rotating shifts or permanent shifts for staff members are often an issue. Rotating shifts helps share the burden of the less popular shifts and increases cooperation between shifts, but it does cause stress, depending on how often the rotation is done. Permanent shifts better meet staff members' needs, but a problem usually arises because most nurses want the popular daytime shift. In that case, seniority often determines who gets which shift. Rifts between shifts may happen with greater frequency with permanent shifts than with rotation shifts.

Control of staffing can be highly centralized, which may be more efficient and fair, or it can be decentralized, to the manager level or even down to the staff level, better meeting staff members' own individual needs.

Centralized scheduling can apply facility staffing and scheduling policies fairly throughout nursing, so no one individual or group gets preferential treatment. It is easier to use float or per diem staff to fill in empty shift spots with centralization. Computerization can be used with centralized scheduling. Data are entered on staff members' preferences and on facility policies and procedures regarding staffing and scheduling. Unit staffing patterns are identified, and patient classification data is entered. No doubt the advantages of computer scheduling include an easy-to-read schedule, fairness and consistency, and less time spent by the manager doing the schedule. However, centralized scheduling does set up a "we" versus "they" situation. Staff members may not feel any obligation to solve problems in the process of staffing and scheduling because it is not their job, but the job of the central staffing and scheduling office. They may feel that centralized scheduling lacks individual attention and also feel that the schedule does not meet their needs.

Decentralized scheduling can be done by the manager or the staff. If the nurse manager does the schedule, she often becomes an expert very quickly. She best knows the needs of the unit and of the staff, if the staff communicate with her. It does take the manager large amounts of time to produce a schedule, especially if a variety of scheduling options are available to the staff. One significant problem with the manager creating the schedule is that some staff members may perceive that others get favored treatment. Although this may not be true, it is very easy for the manager to misguidedly use scheduling as a reward and punishment system.

Many organizations have implemented a staffing process that combines the best of centralized and decentralized. The nurse managers are still responsible for completing the unit schedule and communicating staffing expectations with their staff. However, centralized support for the many phone calls and clerical aspects of the staffing process have been implemented for better utilization of a nurse manager's time.

Self-scheduling by staff is described by Ringl and Dotson[17] as a "process by which nurses collectively develop and implement the monthly work schedule." Criteria are mutually agreed on by the work group and applied. Peers can negotiate and trade within the guidelines. Often an individual staff nurse or scheduling committee oversees the process, a position that may be rotated among every member of the work group. It works well with smaller units. The manager usually works with the group, especially when beginning the process. Although implementation of self-scheduling is not without problems, the process usually goes more smoothly the longer it is in place. Most staff members do not want to give it up once they have worked with it. It is said to increase job satisfaction, increase autonomy and control, and decrease turnover and absenteeism.[17]

When Staffing Problems Occur

Despite the best scheduling efforts, staffing disasters do occur. Nurse managers should be aware of the options available to deal with these crises and of the fact that everyone has them at one time or another, to a greater or lesser extent.

Sick calls are notorious for causing the manager headaches. They can be handled in a variety of ways, depending on the options available in your facility. Manager's Tip 5-2 outlines some of the methods that may be used.

There are pros and cons with each method used. One point to make about the final option in Manager's Tip 5-2 is that new managers particularly often work the shift themselves because it is the easiest solution. Although it may initially solve the problem, working as a staff member by necessity leaves other parts of the job undone and may set a precedent for what to do in a "crunch"—call the nurse manager. This may ultimately hurt the staff more than it helps. It is up to the manager to help the staff learn that each member has a job to do that is valuable and to get them to feel a responsibility to help with staffing as much as does the manager.

MANAGER'S TIP 5-2

HANDLING A SHIFT THAT IS NOT COVERED

- ✔ Use float or per diem, or ask a part-time staff member to work the extra shift.
- ✔ Ask a staff member to work for the person who is ill and take time off later in the week.
- ✔ Ask a staff member of the previous shift to stay over for either part of the shift or the whole shift.
- ✔ Ask a staff member on the shift following the shift in question to come in for the whole shift or part of the shift.
- ✔ Substitute one type of job classification for another, such as an LPN for an RN.
- ✔ Do without anyone.
- ✔ Work the shift yourself.
- ✔ Contract for an agency nurse. (Try all the alternatives first!)

Sometimes, if the supply of staff cannot be obtained, the manager can meet the need by working from the other side of the equation; that is, by reducing the need for staffing by transferring patients, screening types of patients that enter the system and thereby lowering acuity, or by "closing" beds.

Particularly during periods of nursing shortages, the manager might experience high vacancies on the unit. Although the solutions identified in Manager's Tip 5-2 for sick calls might help on an occasional basis, staff burnout will occur if they are used for prolonged periods. Using agency or traveling nurses has helped many facilities cope with vacancies until positions could be filled permanently. Closing, or "holding," beds also helps the situation. This practice, however, may decrease revenue for the facility if the patient goes elsewhere. The reasons for the vacancies and/or why positions cannot be filled should be thoroughly investigated and the causes fixed.

A master staffing plan (i.e., the guideline or plan by which the area is usually staffed) is usually developed for each area or unit. It is important for the manager to secure a copy of the plan and understand its components backward and forward. The components are the staffing pattern that gives the numbers and types of staff members to schedule on each shift and the numbers and types of staff members to hire to fulfill the pattern.

The design of the staffing pattern is based on a standard or statistic determined by the facility. That statistic will vary from facility to facility and might include factors such as patient acuity level and associated required hours of nursing care, census, numbers of procedures, and so on. Table 5-2 displays a staffing pattern for a 33-bed general surgical unit. The statistics that determined this pattern were patient acuity with associated hours of nursing care and patient census. Remember that this

TABLE 5-2
Example of Master Staffing Pattern

33-Bed Capacity	Su	M	Tu	W	Th	F	Sa	
DAY SHIFT								
RN	4	5	5	6	6	5	4	35
LPN	1	2	2	2	2	2	1	12
Aide	2	2	3	3	3	3	2	18
Total	7	9	10	11	11	10	7	65
EVENING SHIFT								
RN	4	5	5	5	5	5	4	33
LPN	1	1	1	1	1	1	1	7
Aide	1	1	1	1	1	1	1	7
Total	6	7	7	7	7	7	6	47
NIGHT SHIFT								
RN	3	4	4	4	4	4	3	26
LPN	0	0	0	0	0	0	0	0
Aide	1	1	1	1	1	1	1	7
Total	4	5	5	5	5	5	4	33
TOTAL NURSING HRS	136	168	176	184	184	176	136	165.7 (average)
AVERAGE CENSUS	25	30.5	32	32.8	32.8	32	25	30 (average)
HOURS OF CARE	5.40	5.50	5.50	5.60	5.60	5.50	5.40	5.5 (average)
AVERAGE ACUITY	2.20	2.30	2.40	2.45	2.45	2.40	2.30	2.36 (average)

pattern is built on *averages*, usually identified from historic data. As you know, anything can happen, in which case deviations will occur from the pattern.

The pattern displayed indicates the number and type of staff members that should be routinely scheduled based on an average daily census and acuity score, which dictates the hours of nursing care desired. Decisions were made about the distribution of staff members by job category based on patient needs and work requirements.

The pattern should be reviewed periodically to see if staffing practices need to be changed based on statistical increases or decreases or on other factors such as the strength of support departments or changes in patient mix or flow.

From such staffing pattern is built a full-time equivalent (FTE) budget to which nonproductive hours are added, such as vacation, holiday, and sick hours and staff development time. An FTE is equal to 2080 hours worked per year (i.e., what a person would work if 40 hours a week, 52 weeks a year were spent working). The budget is then translated into positions that are designated full-time or part-time, and it is used as a basis to hire personnel.

It is a good idea to share the staffing pattern with staff members so they understand how it was developed and can assist in supporting it.

LIABILITY CONCERNED WITH STAFFING

On a daily basis, the nurse manager often faces the problem of trying to staff the area or unit with dwindling resources while still maintaining a standard of nursing care. Indeed, the manager's job description usually states something like, "is accountable for staffing the unit on a 24-hour basis." Questions may arise as to the liability of the nurse manager in relation to unsafe staffing levels; to float, registry, or agency nurse errors; to staff refusal to accept a unit or float assignment; and possibly to nurses walking off the job. As background for addressing these issues, the nurse manager should become familiar with the facility's rules, regulations, policies, and procedures concerned with staffing, floating, and overtime. They will help direct decisions that must be made when problems arise. If the day comes when all options to cover an unsafe staffing situation have been tried to no avail, the next step is to communicate the inadequate staffing situation to the supervisor.[18] The guiding principle is that of reasonableness. If the nurse manager has done everything possible to solve the problem and has communicated that fact to the appropriate persons, then she/he is most likely absolved of liability for the situation. The situation should be documented in a report, dated and signed, and sent to the manager's supervisor. The write-up should be factual and describe what effect the situation may have on patient care.

The use of float, registry, or agency nurses is one way some facilities are coping with the nursing shortage in general or with occasional staffing deficiencies. Is the nurse manager liable for their actions? According to Fiesta,[19] the manager may be placed in secondary liability for these nurses. These nurses must be screened and oriented as are the regular staff. Baillie et al,[20] regarding float nurses, said, "Regardless, before floating any nurse, supervisors should determine her level of knowledge, the skills necessary, and functions required in the new assignment and provide adequate orientation."

With agency nurses, the manager should try to assign them to low-risk situations and ensure that the patients realize the nurse is an agency nurse. If any question arises as to competency, the manager has a duty to report that, in writing, back to the agency. Of course, the nurse manager should follow the facility's standard operating procedures regarding communication with the agency.

What if a staff nurse refuses an assignment or threatens to walk off the job? It is wise not to react too quickly to the situation. Often the refusal or threat results from fear or feeling unprepared. The manager should sit down and unemotionally discuss the situation with the nurse. Find out what would make the nurse accept the situation and then attempt to remedy the problem if it seems reasonable. If it does not seem reasonable and if, after talking, the situation is not resolved, the manager should be sure the nurse has been given a clear and direct order that is not misinterpreted as a suggestion or request or as advice. The nurse should be queried as to whether the order is understood and is clear and whether she/he is refusing to do the order. The manager may want to forewarn the nurse of possible consequences if the order is refused. These consequences could be disciplinary action and perhaps even being fired, depending on the facility's personnel policies and practices.

Delegation of Nursing Tasks

Delegation of nursing tasks has been a growing controversy during the past few years, as hospitals instituted nursing care models that included unlicensed assistive personnel, initially as a measure to meet the demands of the nursing shortage and then as a measure to control or cut the cost of providing primary care when nursing salaries rose and reimbursement dropped. With factors such as increasingly "sicker" patients being hospitalized for shorter lengths of time, the increased demand to cut the number of nurses at the patient's bedside and replace them with unlicensed personnel, and the downsizing or closing of acute care hospital beds, the loss of registered nursing positions has caused major rifts in patient care philosophy between nursing staff and nursing management in many areas of the country.

The new nurse manager must realize that there are different health care providers who can safely and effectively provide care to patients if they function within the constraints of their state or national scope of practice and protocols of care. The change from primary to patient-centered team nursing advocates using unlicensed personnel to assist with those elements of patient care (e.g., bed baths, feeding, venipuncture) that had been accomplished by nursing assistants in the past. The important elements for both nursing staff and management are the training and credentialing of the unlicensed staff member. These staff members, similar to the home health aide in home care, are integral and useful and can bring new perspectives to the care planning process. However, their practice needs to be structured, supervised, and delegated appropriately.

Delegation has been described as the ability to assign work to a subordinate. However, the most important element in delegation is the ability to assign to another the responsibility and authority to complete a task with the knowledge that the individual has the capability to accomplish the task successfully. According to nurse attorney Kathleen Flynn Peterson, ". . . the judgment one uses in the act of delegation, not one's accountability for the act performed, is essentially the issue."[21] All nurses, but especially the nurse manager, need to be aware of and trust the competencies of the staff members with whom they are working. The risk management of such a situation lies in whether the nurse making the assignment or delegating authority had reasonable knowledge that the delegatee had the competent ability to carry out the task. What better way to establish trust between team members than to have standardized protocols and competency levels that must be met by all staff members in particular job categories? Those competencies should be extended to all staff who either float or are hired temporarily from registries to provide safe, competent care on fast-paced patient care units.

Finally, nurses need to rid themselves of the widely held belief that they are the only ones who can provide the best care. They need to learn to view themselves as the *leaders* of the work group, rather than the work group itself, and focus on what they do best: assessing, planning, and evaluating the care that a patient receives. We cannot do it all alone—especially when caring for sick patients across the care continuum.

CREDENTIALING AND COMPETENCY

Credentialing continues to be a major issue for all professional and licensed or certified staff. Credentialing encompasses licensure, accreditation, certification, and academic degrees.[22] The nurse manager plays a major role in ensuring that the process is implemented and that the staff practicing in her/his area are competent to care for the assessed needs of the unit's patients. Credentialing came about because it benefits and protects the patient by ensuring that the nurse has certain minimum skills and abilities. A professional license may ensure skills and abilities on entry into practice, but it *does not guarantee ongoing competency*. With medical and nursing practice changing so rapidly, additional credentialing activities must be added to licensure to ensure ongoing competency.

During the interview, the nurse manager discusses degrees and experience with the potential new employee. Licensure is checked, and a copy is made (based on state law) and inserted into the personnel file if the nurse is hired. Other information on courses attended may be obtained.

Usually during an orientation period, performance standards are met by the orientee. A skills inventory is completed after satisfactory demonstration of skills such as patient assessment, care planning, or medication administration, and this is maintained in the personnel record of an individual nurse. This inventory needs to be dated and signed. The skills inventory, or orientation checklist, provides legal documentation of professional skills competency. Additional specialty courses may be completed and tests taken that show mastery of the material (e.g., fetal monitoring or group therapy facilitation). The nurse manager's role is to ensure that this process happens through to filing the results. Often the skills inventory will be distributed, explained, and even completed, but never make it to the personnel record. (For an in-depth discussion, please refer to Chapter 6, Effective Communication.)

Remedial study may need to be undertaken if deficiencies are identified through critical incidents. It may be up to the manager to see that a plan is formulated with the individual nurse to correct deficiencies and attain the necessary skills and knowledge to improve performance. As discussed in Chapter 3, Human Resource

Management, competency evaluation is an important tool in the CQI process. An ongoing program of education and evaluation of both the general and the specialized skills of staff is needed to ensure quality outcomes.

It is important that the nursing staff understand why their competence is being checked and that they participate in the determination and development of the plan for ensuring competency.

Another aspect of credentialing is external certification. Almost every nursing specialty organization has a mechanism for certification. A test is taken and, in some cases, proof is required for a certain amount and type of clinical experience. Attainment of certification ensures a certain level of knowledge. For more information on certification, please refer to Chapter 13, Where to from Here?

Many facilities promote external certification by reimbursing nurses or by making it part of the requirements for a higher level within a clinical ladder system. Review courses associated with particular tests may be given in the facility. Manager support of external certification helps the staff pursue this additional level of professional expertise.

MEETINGS

All organizations hold meetings of one type or another, health care systems being no exception. Indeed, because the nature of the business usually encompasses 24 hours a day, 7 days a week, with a multitude of various departments and disciplines participating, the need for meetings may be even higher than in the industrial or general business sector.

New nurse managers must acquire the skills for either leading or helping others to lead meetings if the managers are to function at an optimum level in today's modern health care organizations. Gone are the days when a manager issued a dictum without consulting others in the work group. Group problem-solving activities and planning for change with group consensus are common practices, and leaders are needed to make the meeting processes efficient and help ensure the best outcomes.

STAFF MEETINGS

In general, the most common meeting a new nurse manager will lead is the group staff meeting. Purposes of a staff meeting vary depending on the situation for which the meeting is called (Table 5-3). Identifying the purpose is important because that assists group members in knowing what is desired of them and gives the nurse manager some guidance on what leadership techniques to use.

Meetings are expensive when the salaries of all involved are analyzed. Thus some techniques can be used to make a meeting efficient and get its purpose accomplished. Box 5-3 on p. 161 describes behaviors for leading an effective meeting.

Attendees at the group staff meeting are usually chosen according to the philosophy of the organization and past practice. Options include meeting with just the members of a particular position (i.e., RNs or nursing assistants); all staff members from a particular shift; or the total staff. There are pros and cons for each grouping.

TABLE 5-3
Purposes of Staff Meetings and Leadership Techniques to Use

Pattern	Comments
Providing information (manager to group)	• Be sure the group understands what has been told to them by soliciting questions, approval, criticism, and so on.
Receiving information (group to manager)	• Ask clear questions and listen. • Use a "round robin" technique to solicit information from less verbal group members.
Interactional (group and manager) Problem-solving/decision-making	• Combination of above. • Help group identify real problem. • Use brainstorming techniques for alternatives. • Get consensus of solution. • Ensure actions are assigned.

---

box 5-3

12 BEHAVIORS FOR LEADING EFFECTIVE MEETINGS

1. Prepare by drawing up an agenda well before the meeting, posting it, and allowing addition of items by the staff. Identify the purpose of the meeting.
2. Be sure all agenda items are necessary. Some might be better addressed in a memo, posted on the bulletin board, or dealt with on a one-to-one basis.
3. Start and end promptly. Keep on schedule. Close the discussion if necessary but be prepared to readdress unfinished business later.
4. Clarify and summarize discussions and decisions so the group is clear on outcomes. Lend structure to the discussion.
5. Ask vocal members to allow others to contribute. Encourage the less vocal members to talk.
6. Keep a neutral, friendly, and respectful attitude while leading. Thank everyone for attending.
7. If necessary, request that arguments, criticisms, and side conversations be held until after the meeting.
8. Set up an environment conducive to the meeting, including adequate ventilation, room temperature, and seating. Interruptions should be kept to a minimum.
9. Have all handouts available, including agenda.
10. Ensure that minutes are taken.
11. Know that there may be more agenda items than time to discuss them all.
12. Prioritize agenda items and adhere to prepared agenda.

Small groups of 4 to 12 people seem to work best together. However, it is best to allow the group as a whole to decide who should attend the staff meetings. They should also determine the frequency, time of the day, day of the week, and length of the meeting.

It is through documentation of the staff meetings (minutes) that evidence can be found that accreditation standards are being met. Thus it is vitally important for the staff meeting minutes to be accurate, specific, and detailed as to discussions, decisions, action plans, and so on.

Minutes should be retained; however, the facility record retention policy should be followed in any case. The suggestions listed in Manager's Tip 5-3 describe important points to document in staff meeting minutes.

Two issues frequently arise in relation to staff meetings that the new nurse manager must often address: (1) the lack of attendance at staff meetings and (2) pay for attendance. In the former case, this is a problem the staff itself should address to determine the cause(s) and the solution. Absenteeism may be related to inconvenient times, inefficiently run meetings, or several other problems. Some organizations annually evaluate meeting structure to assist in meeting staff needs. Regarding the latter issue, most organizations have pay policies that outline whether staff members are paid for time spent at staff meetings when coming in on their own time. If not, a different policy would need to be developed by HR and/or nursing administration personnel because such a policy would affect the budget throughout the nursing department, if not the entire facility.

At times, the new nurse manager may lead other groups besides staff groups. These may include ad hoc groups formed to address issues or goals of the department or facility. The same principles identified earlier can be applied to leading these groups as well.

MANAGER'S TIP 5-3

IMPORTANT POINTS TO DOCUMENT
IN STAFF MEETING MINUTES

✔ Who did attend and who did not attend.
✔ Issues discussed and decisions regarding the issues, with an emphasis on those related to patient care.
✔ Quality improvement monitoring results should be presented with conclusions identified, recommendations by the group noted, and action plans listed. The process for evaluation should be identified by the group, highlighting the group's involvement in the process. When problems are corrected, this should be identified in the minutes.
✔ Any issues relating to patient care standards, standards of practice, or patient care delivery systems should be detailed, along with the resultant decisions and actions.
✔ Reports by staff representatives on committees should be documented.

CLINICAL CONFERENCES

In today's fast-paced, complex, highly regulated health care environment, it is essential that patient care be administered efficiently so patient outcomes can be achieved as rapidly as possible. Clinical conferences help in this process by assisting in the coordination of care for the patient among all the disciplines involved. Duplication of effort and unnecessary confusion and frustration for the patient, family, and health care team can often be eliminated by holding a clinical conference.

Although the primary nurse or the RN most closely associated with the patient usually leads the conference, the new nurse manager definitely has a role to play in the process. Mahan[23] believes that the nurse manager suggests, encourages, validates, role models, and educates and is a resource person and quality control agent.

Various members of the health care team may participate, including the physician, social worker, utilization review nurse, pastoral care staff, therapists, dietitian, home health nurse, and any others deemed necessary.

Often the family and the patient participate in the conference as well. Once someone on the team, the patient, or the family decides a clinical conference is necessary, a leader is chosen, persons who should attend are identified, and a mutually accepted date and time are chosen. A conference room is procured. Arrangements may need to be made to cover the RN's assignment while she/he attends the conference. At the beginning of the conference, attendees are introduced, the purpose is highlighted, and the leader gives a brief overview of the patient's status, encouraging others to add additional data. Issues are identified, alternatives are discussed, and an action plan is formulated. Consensus is reached on follow-up and evaluation plans and the need for further meetings. The whole plan should be in the patient's record for easy access by all health care team members.

Documentation of the clinical conference should go beyond writing the action plan in the patient's record. Consistent documentation of attendees and the process and outcome of the conference will help demonstrate meeting these accreditation standards on care coordination.

ROUNDS IN THE CLINICAL AREA

Rounds made by the nurse manager in the areas where care is given can accomplish several things in a relatively short period. Making rounds gives information as to the performance of the staff because nursing care can be observed in practice and be compared with standards. Patient satisfaction with care received can be assessed by conversing with patients. Checks of the environment in regards to compliance with public health and safety standards can be done, and the area can be surveyed for aesthetic or other problems.

Although there is no hard and fast rule, daily rounds are suggested. Observations thus occur over a long period, and erroneous conclusions based on just a few observations can be avoided. Times of rounds during the day or night can be varied. Making notes as rounds are done assists in following up on issues that are identified. Staff members see the nurse manager as they work and may be more prone to bring up new issues when they see the manager. Stevens[24] feels that the presence of the manager on the nursing unit has the effect of decreasing the perceived distance between the employees and the manager. Also, the nursing staff feels that the manager knows what is going on, and this communicates authority.

Rather than putting patients on the spot with pointed questions concerning their perceptions of the quality of care, it is better to ask open-ended questions that might be less threatening, such as, "How is everything going?" "What is going on?" or "How are you doing?" If a patient's answer indicates the possibility of a problem, the manager can then focus the questioning further to get to the problem. Public health and safety standards should be reviewed by the manager by meeting with the person in the facility who is the most knowledgeable about them. One suggestion is to make a checklist from the standards that can be used during rounds to assess compliance. Aesthetic issues such as worn, broken, or tattered furnishings and building materials can be noted during rounds. The manager should view the unit or area as a patient or family might view it (similar to a hotel) and pass on a list of the deficiencies to the responsible department. Also, consider bringing in an objective person and asking for her/his aesthetic assessment and feedback for improvement.

Usually the list taken on rounds will have several items on it that the manager should plan to follow up on.

PRIORITIZING DUTIES AND TIME MANAGEMENT

A manager's work is never done, and there is never enough time to do it all. Those concepts are difficult for a new nurse manager to accept. By the end of the day, as a staff nurse, most likely all one's tasks were finished. The nature of a manager's work is longer-term, and projects and activities may take more than just a day— often months, and occasionally years—to complete. On a daily basis, managers must decide what activity or project takes precedence over another as they are faced with multiple and sometimes conflicting demands. How does the new manager prioritize the schedule? Manager's Tip 5-4 presents some suggestions to help manage tasks and time.

Patients are important to a staff nurse, and they still are to a manager. Issues surrounding patients should be addressed promptly, such as patient complaints, staffing issues, or concerns related to supporting patient care. Top priority should be those issues that meet human needs.[25] In other words, patients, families, and staff concerns take priority over preparing for a meeting or justifying a budget variance.

At the beginning of each day, a "to do" list should be made in descending order of priority. Unanticipated problems may occur throughout the day, so priorities will

DEALING WITH THE WORKLOAD

- ✔ Make a "to do" list.
- ✔ Organize your office by labeling file folders for each staff member, for staff meeting agenda items, and for issues to discuss with your supervisor.
- ✔ Place agendas and minutes of all meetings you attend in folders.
- ✔ Delegate activities to others when possible.
- ✔ Always question whether a problem or an issue is yours to own or whether it is better handled by another person.
- ✔ Organize communication with staff members by using bulletin boards and communication books.
- ✔ Always carry a calendar and write down standing meetings, lunch, and other appointments.
- ✔ Schedule time in your calendar for planning and organizing.

need to be reset. This is common and really no different from when the manager was a staff nurse.

One trap new nurse managers fall into is that of trying to solve everything for everybody. In their eagerness to prove themselves to their subordinates, they take on the world. This does nothing more than frustrate the manager, if not immediately, then in time. Be very careful of reverse delegation by your staff. It is wise to adopt a coaching attitude, assisting them in solving the problem and implementing the solution, rather than ending up with all the problems heaped on your back. Solving problems can help the staff grow professionally as well as give them a different perspective.

Sooner or later the supervisor's priorities will clash with those of the manager. Rather than becoming frustrated, do not be afraid to negotiate a change in the project or the timeline.

DOCUMENTATION

Webster's New World Dictionary[26] defines documentation as "the supplying of documentary evidence . . . and the collecting, abstracting, and coding of printed or written information for future reference." This simple definition fits all of the varied and important roles that documentation, or the process of documenting and demonstrating delivery of patient care, assumes in health care. Nursing entries that appear in the medical or clinical record reflect the standard of nursing care, as well as the specific care provided to the patient. Other health care team members make decisions for further care based on the nursing entries. Also, today numerous third-party payers make legal and quality judgments, as well as administrative and payment decisions, based on the clinical record. Nurses have many responsibilities, all ultimately directed towards patient care. Because of these responsibilities, the actual task of documentation must sometimes be relegated to the end of the shift.

According to the AHA, patient charts now average 70 to 100 pages. This means that most midsized hospitals process 250,000 to 360,000 pieces of medical information each year.[27] The typical medical record may be read by a minimum of 10 people during a patient's initial 24 hours in a health facility. These may include the admitting or attending physician, three nurses on different shifts, the utilization review specialist, several nurse aides, and a dietitian. They may also include a surgeon, an anesthesiologist, and various technicians and therapists. With so many people depending on the medical record as a reliable and up-to-date source of patient information, the importance of the data contained in the record becomes evident. For an in-depth discussion of documentation, please see Marrelli's *Nursing Documentation Handbook* (St. Louis, 2000, Mosby).

THE PROFESSIONAL NURSE'S ROLE IN DOCUMENTATION

The professional nurse's entries in the patient's clinical record are recognized as a significant contribution documenting the standard of care provided to a patient. As the practice of nursing has become more complex, so too have the factors that influence the purposes of documentation. These factors include the requirements of regulatory agencies, health insurance payers, accreditation organizations, consumers of health care, and legal entities. The nurse must try to satisfy these various requirements all at once, often with precious few moments in which to accomplish this important task.

Any nurse writing a clinical entry today could be trying simultaneously to meet the standards of JCAHO, various insurers, state and federal laws and regulations, and other professional organizations. Fortunately, most hospitals have integrated many of these requirements, when possible, into hospital policy or procedure manuals.

The written clinical record is the professional nurse's best defense against litigation when malpractice or negligence is alleged. The increased specialization of health care providers and the complexity of patient problems and associated technology have contributed to multiple and varied services being provided to patients in a shortened time frame. The medical record is the only source of written communication, and sometimes the only source of any communication, for all team members. The members not only contribute their individual assessments of interventions and outcomes but actually base their subsequent actions on the record of events provided by other team members. As such, the actual entries must be recorded as soon as possible after a change in the patient's condition is noted, an intervention occurs, or the response to a treatment is observed. Nurses can have their practice well represented and quality demonstrated through thorough, effective documentation. Manager's Tip 5-5 explains the importance of outcome criteria, process, and standards of care to such documentation.

MANAGER'S TIP 5-5

KEY TERMS RELATED TO DOCUMENTATION

✔ **Outcome criteria**—Outcome criteria are the desired results on completion or the objective (or demonstrable) evidence observed at the end of care (e.g., a patient's anticipated knowledge or activity level on discharge). In a specific case, a patient with diabetes mellitus returned to self-care status. Outcome criteria would be that the patient demonstrated all activities noted on the diabetes mellitus checklist on discharge and patient verbalized that initial complaints were resolved and needs met.

✔ **Process**—A process is specifically how the care is provided. An example would be a standard that requires that all patients receive a complete assessment within so many (specify) hours of admission. The specific parameters that must be included in the assessment would also be identified.

✔ **Standards of care**—There is a growing emphasis on the standardization of care, policies, and procedures. All patients or clients are entitled to a certain level, or standard, of care. As patients become more proactive consumers in the purchase of needed health care services, patient satisfaction with care provided becomes the key to the facility's reputation and ultimate survival. Nurses, because of their healing skills and other areas of proficiency, are pivotal in fostering patient satisfaction. The roles of the nurse as patient advocate, listener, and teacher have become widely accepted in recent years. With these roles comes the responsibility of maintaining the hallmarks of any profession. These include licensure, education, certification or other credentialing processes, and other ongoing educational requirements. Standards of care in nursing today are varied and include nursing specialty association standards and ANA national, state, and local standards that define the acceptable level of practice. These standards are vital to the professional nurse's ongoing education. For this reason, it is important that the nurse remain informed on all areas of practice that affect the provision of care.

FUNCTION OF THE MEDICAL/CLINICAL RECORD

Clear documentation in the medical/clinical record is highly important because this record is:

- The only written source that chronicles a patient's stay from admission through discharge.
- The primary source for reference and communication among members of the health care team.
- The only documentation that supports insurance coverage (payment) or denial.
- The only evidence of the basis on which patient care decisions were made.
- The only legal record.
- The foundation for evaluation of the care provided.
- The basis for staff education or other study.
- The objective source for the facility's licensing and accreditation review (e.g., JCAHO, the American Osteopathic Association Standards).

The above factors have contributed to an environment in which the nurse has increased responsibilities for documentation and a shortened time frame for producing such documentation because of the decrease in patient lengths of stay. This written record is the only account of a patient's stay. Many processes involve the CQI/clinical record for these reasons. In addition, the Health Insurance Portability and Accountability Act (HIPAA) was signed into law and has implications for all health care managers.

HIPAA Considerations

The Health Insurance Portability and Accountability Act (HIPAA) was signed into law in 1996. The administrative simplification provisions of this legislation, including the transactions, privacy, and security rules, have a significant impact on the daily operations of most health care entities.

The Transactions Rule

The transactions rule is the driving force of the administrative simplification provisions. Its goal is to increase the efficiency of the health care industry by mandating standard formats and code sets for electronic transactions. By doing this, health care providers, health plans, and health care clearinghouses will be able to communicate with each other more effectively and utilize technology more efficiently. The requirements of the transactions rule mostly impact billing departments and software vendors.

Implementation of the transactions rule provides incentive for health care entities to move from paper-based systems to electronic medical records. This raises, however, many concerns about the privacy of a patient's health information and the security of information systems. The privacy and security rules address these concerns, and compliance with their requirements necessitates not only many operational issues but also the development of a culture within the organization of a commitment to the protection of the privacy and security of a patient's health information.

The Privacy Rule

The privacy rule delineates permitted and required uses and disclosures of patient health information and describes rights that patients have with respect to their health information. The following is a brief overview of some of the major components of the privacy rule that are evident in the daily operations of health care providers:

1. Information related to a person's health that could identify that individual is protected and may only be used or disclosed as permitted or required by the privacy rule.

2. Protected information includes information in written, electronic, or verbal forms.
3. A notice of privacy practices, a document describing how the provider uses and discloses a patient's health information and a description of patient privacy rights, must be provided to all patients at the start of care.
4. Every health care provider must appoint a privacy official, who is the focal point of accountability for all privacy-related matters.
5. All members of the provider's workforce (including volunteers) must use only the minimum amount of protected information needed to perform their job effectively.
6. All members of the provider's workforce (including volunteers) must receive privacy training soon after they begin working for the organization.

There are many other procedural requirements of the privacy rule that are designed to ensure that health care providers have systems in place to protect patient health information and accommodate patient privacy rights. The privacy rule also requires administrative, physical, and technical safeguards for the protection of health information. The security rule more fully describes these requirements.

The Security Rule

Privacy and security are very closely related. It is not possible to protect the privacy of health information if adequate security mechanisms are not in place. The purpose of the security rule is to safeguard the confidentiality (that it remains private), integrity (that it is not altered in an unauthorized way), and availability (that it is protected from loss or destruction) of electronic protected health information. Unlike the privacy rule, which applies to all forms of protected health information (written, electronic, verbal), the security rule applies only to protected health information that is stored or transmitted electronically.

The security rule requires that administrative, physical, and technical safeguards to protect electronic health information are implemented. The security mechanisms selected by health care providers must be based on a thorough assessment of vulnerabilities and careful decision-making related to how to minimize the potential for identified risks materializing.

The following is a brief overview of some aspects of the security rule that are evident on a daily basis:

1. A security officer is appointed who is the focal point of accountability for all matters related to the security of information systems and the safeguarding of electronic health information.
2. Access to controls are in place to ensure that only those who are authorized are able to access electronic health information.
3. Security awareness training is provided on an ongoing basis to ensure that members of the workforce understand password management, virus

protection, and policies and procedures related to work station use and security and reporting security incidents.

4. A contingency plan is in place and regularly tested to ensure the continued availability of electronic health information in the event of a natural disaster or other emergencies.

Summary of HIPAA

The administrative simplification provisions of HIPAA are laws. Compliance is not optional, and there are significant civil and criminal penalties for privacy or security violations. Nurse managers must do their part to ensure that those they supervise understand their responsibilities with respect to the privacy and security of patient health information. More important, the requirements of the privacy rule and the security rule are intended to restore public confidence in the privacy and security of health information, and it is the responsibility of nurse managers to contribute to the development of a culture of privacy and security within their organization.

COMPUTERIZATION/MANAGEMENT OF INFORMATION

Patient-centered, cost-effective care has driven another industry to the forefront of health care: information services. Manual, paper-heavy documentation systems are unwieldy in terms of getting information to where it is needed—the site of patient care. From the acute care setting to the outpatient facility to the physician's office to the patient's home, information is needed quickly and accurately. Adding to this burden is the specter of health organizations merging, affiliating, and growing by leaps and bounds. The use of computers with patient care databases is needed to move the patient safely and effectively along a care continuum, reducing unnecessary duplication of tasks and procedures, and quantifying appropriate outcomes and variance data in order to continually improve care processes.

Information systems for health care settings should include financial reporting as one element of the total product. Patient care planning and acuity systems, based on data generated and input from the patient assessment, will allow for more accurate scheduling and staffing systems. Data entry of physician orders (charge entry) should flow to all affected departments for appropriate service scheduling. As clinical protocols and outcome data are entered, appropriate variance collection and trending can be done, with resultant variance analysis as an integral part of a CQI system.

Health system information services staff and/or MIS vendors have developed, or are in the process of developing, interface capabilities between different computer software that will allow for the quick and efficient passage of information from one secured system to another. Thus selected patient information from an acute care setting can be downloaded to a home care setting at a scheduled time, so that patient demographic and clinical information will be readily available to home care staff, as opposed to requestioning the patient and wasting valuable time.

---

box 5-4

INFORMATION SYSTEM PLANNING/REVIEW CHECKLIST

❑ 1. Established goals, priorities, and outcomes of an information system—who will be end users?
❑ 2. Budget guidelines
❑ 3. Timelines for implementation
❑ 4. Future capabilities of system to expand or interface with alternate care sites
❑ 5. Impact on documentation of staff
❑ 6. Reduction of documentation—not duplicating information
❑ 7. Security/confidentiality features of system—HIPAA compliant
❑ 8. Acuity, patient care planning, clinical paths or protocols integration
❑ 9. Support of vendor and information services staff
❑ 10. Training needs of staff or end users
❑ 11. Commitment of resources for training and reinservicing of staff as needed
❑ 12. Ability to modify system for individual settings
❑ 13. Existence of ongoing information services committee and patient care staff involvement
❑ 14. Decrease in productivity (home visits) during implementation/learning phase
❑ 15. Names of other users of this system to use as references for quality, support, and practicality of the system

---

As a nurse manager in any health care setting, you may be asked to assist in the assessment of information systems for your organization. The checklist in Box 5-4, which can be used in any setting, includes some of the issues you should want addressed or have information about during these planning and review sessions. Box 5-5 is a summary of the daily operations of home care.

SUMMARY

Knowledge of current NCDSs being practiced can help the new nurse manager in evaluating her/his own system or model. Knowledge of more recent concepts of restructured patient-centered care, shared governance, and professional practice models is essential as the nurse manager leads his/her staff in providing quality cost-effective care to patients and families.

Understanding and using a patient classification system, together with a master staffing plan for the area, will help the new nurse manager to staff the area efficiently and effectively. There are always concerns about liability connected with staffing.

Issues concerning credentialing are important to learn, especially the issue of continued competency of the nursing staff.

Mastering the ability to lead efficient and effective meetings is of high priority, as is that of facilitating clinical conferences.

---

box 5-5

DAILY OPERATIONS IN HOME CARE

The daily operations of most nursing units, whether in the acute care or alternate patient care site area, are alike in many ways. The patients need to be cared for, following physician orders and utilizing competent, oriented staff who act within their individual practice guidelines. Home care operations are unique in that the practice setting for the clinicians is the patient's home, not an institution. The focus is, and always has been, on patient involvement and agreement on the plan of care.

Operationally, the home care manager must deal with the following issues:

1. Orientation and training of competent home care clinicians (generalist—Medicare visit staff versus IV, maternal-child, pediatric home care competency)
2. Maintaining personnel requirements that are not always synchronous with acute care requirements (e.g., education records of home health aides [12 hours per year, physical examinations, etc.])
3. Assignment of patients based on patient needs and geographic location
4. Scheduling of staff
5. Medicare Condition of Participation (COP) required team/case conferencing and staff meetings
6. Care coordination over a large geographic area and covering different vendors/providers of care
7. Physician orders need to be signed and on clinical records within specified time frames
8. Patient care records and security/confidentiality concerns (records taken out of office to patient's homes—HIPPA compliance considerations)
9. Patient care delivery models that meet patient needs and meet numerous regulatory payment requirements
10. Documentation requirements
11. Supervision of staff who are not visibly present in office
12. Medical emergencies in homes and staff members' "isolation" at those times
13. Need for collaboration with appropriate disciplines over patient care progress
14. Ongoing evaluation of staff safety driving to, and while in, patients' homes
15. Administrative functions that encompass total patient length of stay:
    a. Admission process—OASIS data collection, rights and responsibilities, etc.
    b. Data entry of daily visits, supplies, and other billable services
    c. Verification of insurance, billing information
    d. Billing routines to Medicare, other third-party payers
    e. Accounts receivable management
    f. Computerization and financial management
    g. Discharge of patients
    h. Annual reports of total organizational functioning to governing body
16. Risk management issues (staff awareness of potentially volatile situations)

Learning to prioritize duties, including time management, is a necessity for the nurse manager, whose work never seems to be done. Making rounds in the patient area assists in maintaining visibility as well as in accomplishing many other managerial tasks.

Finally, internalizing accreditation standards helps the nurse manager in decision-making, which helps the area achieve and maintain quality nursing care.

⟨?⟩ QUESTIONS FOR CONSIDERATION

1. Define the main purpose of the transaction rule.
2. Explain the main purpose of (1) the privacy rule and (2) the security rule.
3. To what form of protected health information does the security rule apply?
4. Define "protected health information."
5. Describe (1) what the nurse manager's responsibilities are with respect to HIPAA, and (2) what your staff's role is with respect to HIPAA.

References

1. Kibbie PE, editor: *Quality assurance, utilization and risk management: a study guide*, National Association of Quality Assurance Professionals, 1986.
2. *1995 Accreditation manual for home care*, Oakbrook Terrace, IL. 1994, The Joint Commission on Accreditation of Healthcare Organizations.
3. Garland C: *General manager*, Fullerton, CA, 1995, Emporium Medical Supply.
4. Manthey M: Structuring work around patients, *Nursing Management* 20(5):28, 1989.
5. Wake MM: Nursing care delivery systems: status and vision, *Journal of Nursing Administration* 20(5):47, 1990.
6. Sherman RO: Team nursing revisited, *Journal of Nursing Administration* 20(11):44, 1990.
7. Munson FC, et al: *Nursing assignment patterns user's manual*, Ann Arbor, MI, 1980, AUPHA Press.
8. Piltz-Kirkby M: The nursing assignment pattern study in practice, *Nursing Management* 22(5):96HH, 1991.
9. Porter-O'Grady T: Shared governance for nursing, *AORN J* 53(2):459, 1991.
10. Rose M, DiPasquale B: The Johns Hopkins professional practice model. In Mayer GG, Madden MJ, Lawrenz E, editors: *Patient care delivery models*, Rockville, MD, 1990, Aspen Publishers.
11. Lawrenz E, Mayer GG: Compensation for professional practice: an incentive model. In Mayer GG, Madden MJ, Lawrenz E, editors: *Patient care delivery models*, Rockville, MD, 1990, Aspen Publishers.
12. Perry L: Group practice model brings nursing unit's turnover to nil, *Modern Healthcare* 20:90, 1990.
13. Giovannetti P: *Patient classification for nurse staffing: criteria for selection and implementation*, Edmonton, Canada, 1983, Alberta Association of Registered Nurses.
14. Nagaprasanna BR: Patient classification systems: strategies for the 1990s, *Nursing Management* 19(3):105, 1988.
15. Barrett S: *Executive summary of 1990 National Nurse Manager Study by American Organization of Nurse Executives*, Chicago, 1991, American Hospital Association.
16. Huey FL, Hartley S: What keeps nurses in nursing—3,500 nurses tell their stories, *American Journal of Nursing* 88(2):181, 1988.
17. Ringl KK, Dotson L: Self scheduling for professional nurses, *Nursing Management* 20(2):42, 1989.
18. Fiesta J: The nursing shortage: whose liability problem, Part II, *Nursing Management* 21(2):22, 1990.
19. Fiesta J: Agency nurses—whose liability? *Nursing Management* 21(3):16, 1990.
20. Baillie VK, Trygstad L, Cordoni TI: *Effective nursing leadership—a practical guide*, Rockville, MD, 1989, Aspen Publishers.
21. Manthey M: Trust: essential for delegation, *Nursing Management* 21(11):28, 1990.
22. Lewis EM, Spicer JG: *Human resource management handbook—contemporary strategies for nursing managers*, Rockville, MD, 1987, Aspen Publishers.
23. Mahan F: Patient care conferences: a model, *Nursing Management* 19(7):60, 1988.

24. Stevens BJ: *The nurse as executive*, ed 3, Rockville, MD, 1985, Aspen Publishers.
25. Seven ways to sharpen your leadership skills, *Nursing '89* 19(10):130, 1989.
26. Guralnik DB, editor-in-chief: *Webster's new world dictionary*, college ed 2, 1982, Simon & Schuster.
27. American Hospital Association: Medical records: increasing importance, heavier workload. In *Side-by-side profiles*, Chicago, 1990, AHA.

For Further Reading

Adams C, Biggerstaff N: Reduced resource utilization through standardized outcome-focused care plans, *Journal of Nursing Administration*, 25(10), October 1995.

Bailet H, et al: Use of outcomes studies by a managed care organization: valuing measured treatment effects, *Medical Care* 33(4), 1995.

Batalden PB, Stolz P: A framework for the continual improvement of health care: building and applying professional and improvement knowledge to test changes in daily work, *Journal on Quality Improvement*, 19(10), October 1993.

Bayley BK, et al: Measuring the success of treatment in patient terms, *Medical Care* 33(4), 1995.

Bennett MK, Hylton JP: Modular nursing: partners in professional practice, *Nursing Management* 21(3):20, 1990.

Beyers M: Quality: the banner of the 1980's, *Nurs Clin North Am* 23(3):617-623, 1988.

Bossidy L, Charan R, Burck C: *Execution: the discipline of getting things done*, New York, 2002, Crown Publishing.

Bushy A: Quality assurance in rural hospitals, *Journal of Nursing Administration* 21(10):34, 1991.

Computers in home care *Caring Magazine* August 1995 (complete issue dedicated to computer issues in home care).

Dunn M, et al: Expert panel method for nurse staffing and resource management, *Journal of Nursing Administration*, 25(10), October 1995.

Gage M: The patient-driven interdisciplinary care plan, *Journal of Nursing Administration* 24(4), April, 1994.

Gillem TR: Deming's 14 points and hospital quality: responding to the consumer's demand for the best value health care, *Journal of Nursing Quality Assurance* 2(3):70, 1988.

Glazer SK, Gaintner JR: Hospital administrators: the challenge of living in a glass house, *The Journal on Quality Improvement* 20(7), July 1994.

Greer EG: The search for what works, *HealthCare Forum Journal*, July/August 1992.

Guadagnoli E, McNeil B: Outcomes research: hope for the future or the latest rage? *Inquiry*, Spring 1994.

Hansten R, Washburn M: Delegation: how to deliver care through others, *American Journal of Nursing* March 1992.

Harbin RE: Practicing effective delegation, *Pediatric Nursing* 16(1), January-February 1990.

Hengst WG: Outcomes—the cutting edge for improving care, *Advance/Rehabilitation*, July/August 1994.

Home care automation report . . . *home health line*, January 1996.

Hungate R: Purchase quality measures: progressing from wants to needs, *Journal on Quality Improvement* 20(7), July 1994.

Jencks S: The government's role in hospital accountability for quality of care, *Journal on Quality Improvement* 20(7) July 1994.

Katz J, Green E: *Managing quality—a guide to monitoring and evaluating nursing services*, St Louis, 1992, Mosby.

Leebov W, Scott G: The indispensable health care manager: success strategies for a changing environment, San Francisco, 2002, Jossey-Bass.

Lewis BE: HMO outcomes research: lessons from the field, *Journal of Ambulatory Care Management* 18(1), January 1995.

Manthey M: Structuring work around patients, *Nursing Management* 20(5):28, 1989.

Manthey M: Delivery systems and practice models: a dynamic balance, 22(1):28, 1991.

Marrelli TM: *Nursing documentation handbook*, St Louis, 2000, Mosby.

Marrelli TM: *The handbook of home health standards and documentation guidelines for reimbursement*, St Louis, 2001, Mosby.

Marrelli TM, Hilliard LS: *Home care and clinical pathways: effective care planning across the continuum*, St Louis, 1996, Mosby.

Marrelli TM, Whittier S: *Home health aide: guidelines for care*, Annapolis, MD, 2004, Marrelli & Associates.

Marriner-Tomey A: *Guide to nursing management*, ed 4, St Louis, 1992, Mosby.

Mayer GG, Madden MJ, Lawrenz E, editors: *Patient care delivery models*, Rockville, MD, 1990, Aspen.

Murray JA: Benchmarking: a tool for excellence in palliative care, *Journal of Palliative Care* 8(4), 1992.

Numeric R, Abrams MN: *Employee retention: solving the healthcare crisis*, Chicago, 2003, Health Administration Press.

O'Dell C: Building on received wisdom, *Healthcare Forum Journal,* January/February 1993.

Pace K: Data sets for home care organizations, *Caring Magazine,* March 1995.

Patterson P, et al: Nurse information needs for efficient care continuity across patient units, *Journal of Nursing Administration* 25(10), October 1995.

Perry L: Group-practice model brings nursing unit's turnover to nil, *Modern Healthcare* 20(36):90, 1990.

Porter-O'Grady T: Into the new age: the call for a new construct for nursing, *Geriatric Nursing* 22(1): 12-15, 2001.

Porter-O'Grady T, Finnigan S: *Shared governance for nursing—a creative approach to professional accountability*, Rockville, MD, 1984, Aspen.

Price CA, Southerland A: Rethinking staffing patterns in critical care nursing, *Nursing Management* 20(3):80Q, 1989.

Ringl KK, Dotson L: Self-scheduling for professional nurses, *Nursing Management* 20(2):42, 1989.

Teeter D, Johnson R: The roadmap for clinical quality, *HMO Practice* 8(1), March 1994.

Website Resources

For more information regarding HIPAA and the transactions, privacy, and security rules, see *www.hipaadvisory.com, www.hhs.gov/ocr/ hippa/,* and *www.nchcia.org.*

CHAPTER 6

EFFECTIVE COMMUNICATION

MARGARET SHARP

T.M. MARRELLI

Recognizing Your Inherent Interpersonal Skills

Managers can perform multitudes of tasks proficiently, effectively selecting and hiring staff, delegating appropriately, making sound decisions, and yet still not achieve maximal success. Strong, well-developed interpersonal skills are key to all management functions and are a large element of the art and science of effective management. These skills are necessary in the development of trust and mutual respect between manager and staff members. This trust and respect foster staff development and retention and can minimize the effect of negative events such as times of high stress or change.

Interpersonal skills can be learned, yet we all have "inherent" interpersonal abilities that affect our success as managers. Elements of personality and style are unique to each individual. Successful use of interpersonal skills is varied and adapted to the specific situation. Reading, noting instances of effective communication, and seeking feedback from supervisors and the staff are all methods nurse managers can use to analyze the impact and effectiveness of their "inherent" qualities.

Through thoughtful self-examination, it is possible to temper or emphasize personal characteristics to enhance your success and meet management goals. Some nurse managers naturally exhibit warmth and inspire liking and trust. Some have an innate ability to excite and inspire the staff and others to do well. Although these gifts assist managers, the gifts must be accompanied by learned interpersonal skills and sound managerial skills and abilities. We all have probably known ineffective managers with great charm.

Conversely, many of us do not have a personality or style that gives us rapid acceptance or strong impact. It is important to remember that long-term effectiveness need not be diminished in this situation. Fairness, good judgment, accomplishment, and communication will eventually establish a true foundation of the trust and respect needed by all nurse managers to succeed.

The analysis of personal skills and abilities allows one to use them to her/his advantage, develop complementary skills, and compensate for weaker areas. An example of this analysis and compensation was an experienced nurse manager with great organizational and systems skills who appeared cold and directive. In previous jobs, she had discovered that her perceived personality tended to shut her off from the staff. It took her years to win their trust, because she often experienced knee-jerk resistance to and suspicion of new ideas or recommendations. Over time, though, this behavior decreased as staff began to recognize the benefits and results of her abilities. In her next job she proactively compensated for such a reception by initially telling staff that she realized she was often perceived as difficult to approach and lacking in warmth. She asked them to look past this initial impression and give her time to demonstrate caring and open-mindedness through her actions and work. She worked hard to consistently reward those who approached her. She also hired an assistant head nurse with a warmer, more open attitude. These actions worked toward decreasing the negative impact her natural manner tended to create.

While recognizing the importance of building rapport, trust, and a support base, the nurse manager must realize that her/his goal is not to be universally liked or popular.

There are learnable techniques of communication, leadership, development, and motivation of staff that are components of interpersonal skills. These techniques are discussed in the remainder of the chapter.

How to Get What You Want

Interpersonal skills help you get what you want in order to achieve organizational work. This occurs directly, through clear communication, and indirectly, by creating an environment or unit culture that fosters open, trusting communication.

Know What You Want: Goals and Values

To get your desired outcome you and your staff must know specifically what you want. The first step is to establish clear, mutually accepted values. In most nursing settings, the focus of these values is directed toward providing quality patient care. It can be extremely useful to discuss and clarify with staff members what is valued and how those values are supported and demonstrated. A good place to begin this process is by reviewing your organization's mission statement or vision and values and philosophy. These should be frequently reviewed, even after consensus and clarity have been obtained. Most nurses are stimulated by this type of discussion. It causes them to remember why they became nurses and to examine their practice, work habits, and routines in a new light.

After values are clearly defined, future decisions and discussions of goals, standards, and performance should be guided by these values. Clearly stated goals for patient care, unit function, and individual staff members must be established. The goals should be behaviorally valued, measurable, and achievable. They should be developed using organizational, departmental, and regulatory guidelines, policies, and objectives. Staff members should always have ongoing input. Although goals should be achievable and realistic, they should also be challenging. Much productivity and pride in achievement is lost when goals are set at a low level. Relating unit goals to values concerning patient care is important. It is easier to set and strive for high-level goals when the effect on patients, if goals are not achieved, is clear and demonstrable.

The Nurse Manager Role

As the manager, your role in defining values and setting goals includes the following:
- Initiating and facilitating discussion to elicit clarification of values.
- Recording written value statements, seeking staff feedback, and incorporating revisions into the organizational review process.
- Initiating discussion of goals at the unit and individual levels with the staff you directly supervise.
- Bringing pertinent directives, regulations, accreditation standards, or other factors needing consideration to the discussion.
- Recording written goals and action plans for achieving them.
- Maintaining momentum of progress toward goals, giving positive and constructive feedback to promote progress toward meeting deadlines.
- Communicating to staff the progress toward goals through the use of Pareto charts or other visual tools.

Developing Resources

Clear goals and values assist the nurse manager and nursing staff in finding direction and setting priorities. To reach these goals, the nurse manager must develop, maintain, conserve, and wisely use both personnel and material resources. The development and retention of employees involve important interpersonal skills in any setting and time. They are crucial in nursing and any other health profession. Advanced, more complex practice requires experienced nurses. The demands for efficiency can only be met with a complement of staff members who are familiar with unit and ancillary systems. Nurses continue to be in high demand, and the turnover created as they seek new opportunities is expensive in dollars, productivity, and training.

Each staff member on any unit is a resource to be highly valued. The nurse manager must have individual knowledge of every employee directly supervised and ongoing communication with those indirectly supervised. There are several purposes of this communication and knowledge.

The first purpose is to identify the skill level and learning needs of the staff. Psychomotor skills, critical and evaluative thinking, and the ability to plan and deliver care should be assessed. Knowledge of individual learning styles should be incorporated into planning for the development of each individual. Professional staff members should be involved in developing their own plan and take responsibility for their continued learning.

The Importance of Job Satisfaction

Another key reason for the nurse manager to develop relationships with and knowledge of each staff member is that this increases the ability to maximize staff job satisfaction. Although the nurse manager must balance unit function against individual needs, there are many opportunities to assist staff in enjoying their work. Most nurses today balance family and individual demands against those of their career. A person who enjoys her/his work and workplace can be energized rather than drained by that work (on most days!). This allows the career person to carry energy rather than fatigue out of the workplace. It also leads to valuing that particular job setting enough to be less likely to leave it for other than serious career opportunities.

Mark Twain is reported to have defined the successful person as one who gets up in the morning and is excited to meet each day. When a job contributes to that feeling, one is not likely to move on. Many nurses today indicate that they leave their jobs because of poor work conditions, lack of opportunity, inability to advance, interpersonal conflicts, and conflict with personal needs.

The Nurse Manager's Role in Staff Retention

The nurse manager must understand the factors that satisfy or dissatisfy staff members in order to retain effective team members. Five examples of using this knowledge to retain your staff and create a healthier workplace follow. For an in-depth strategic view of recruitment and retention, see Chapter 4.

Example One

An assistant head nurse approached the nurse manager about a trio of staff members. She was concerned because they tended to work together and adjust their assignments and schedules to accommodate this goal. She was worried that this might adversely affect productivity. The three were skilled, competent, and experienced nurses. One historically had a problem with absenteeism and another was previously a loner. On further discussion with the manager, it became clear that these nurses were completing assignments, were not disruptive to others, were not cliquish, and were enjoying working together. They functioned as an effective, cooperative team. Their patients had good outcomes. The assistant head nurse was worried because of vague feelings that sociability at work should be limited and sensed some loss of control. She was encouraged by the manager to examine this situation for actual, objective, negative results and could identify none. They then explored possible positive effects such as increased collaboration, support, and affiliation. After further discussion, the assistant head nurse approached the three and remarked on their pattern. She verbalized appreciation of practice and collaboration, as well as support for its benefits (Box 6-1). She encouraged them to continue but discussed concerns about productivity. All agreed that patient care was the priority. Over time several benefits were seen: (1) the nurse with an absenteeism problem rarely called in sick because she did not want to let her friends down; (2) the three became very involved in unit orientation, and their skills and warmth were excellent for assimilating new staff members; and (3) the group also became a nucleus for social activities, as well as special projects—they worked so well together that they had very good ideas to share with others.

Example Two

A nurse manager met with an excellent RN who had been with the unit for 2 years. The nurse was clinically skilled but not very involved in unit issues outside of completing her work in a given shift. Historically, 2 years was the average turnover time for this particular unit. The manager and nurse explored the nurse's goals. The nurse liked the patient care setting but was in need of new stimulation and growth. They both agreed that she was not ready for a management position, nor was one available. After discussion, the nurse accepted an assignment to develop and implement patient teaching protocols for her area of clinical expertise. The manager met with her regularly to review progress, offer support, and assist her in obtaining needed resources (Box 6-2). The nurse was later selected for a hospital-wide committee, which furthered her growth and development. She became very active on the unit by sharing her new skills and acting as a resource to peers.

---

box 6-1

SKILLS USED BY THE NURSE MANAGER

- Recognized staff and what motivates them
- Reinforced positive behaviors
- Verbalized appreciation of practice and collaboration

---

box 6-2

SKILLS USED BY THE NURSE MANAGER

- Identified staff member's goals
- Listened and created an environment that allowed the nurse to grow professionally
- Scheduled regular meetings to review progress, offer support, and assist in obtaining resources

Example Three

The nurse manager met with a staff member who was going to school to advance from LPN to RN. She worked fulltime. They discussed ways to accommodate her class schedule without disrupting the staff schedule. She was given time frames for discussing scheduling needs in advance. At one point, it became clear that she would be 30 minutes late 2 days a week on the evening shift. She and the manager discussed options (Box 6-3). Because report was one-to-one on this unit, she was encouraged to approach others who might swap an hour during the week to be relieved 1 hour early on the weekend. This plan was successful for the nurse, the nurse manager, and the entire unit.

Example Four

The charge nurse on a step-down unit approached her nurse manager to discuss advancing her own critical care skills. The manager arranged for her to have access to an ICU preceptor. The charge nurse scheduled herself to spend time in the ICU when her shift was covered. She and the manager regularly discussed her progress and use of time (Box 6-4). At the end of 6 months, the charge nurse inserviced other staff on new procedures and began scheduling them for similar off-unit development.

Example Five

While meeting with a staff member, a manager discovered that an important part of her life was attending a Tuesday evening meeting. Without inconveniencing other staff, but with some effort on adjusting the schedule, the manager thereafter scheduled this nurse off on that evening whenever possible (Box 6-5). The manager later

---

box 6-3

SKILLS USED BY THE NURSE MANAGER

- Behaviorally supported a staff member's professional growth
- Listened and implemented a plan based on staff member's goal
- Discussed options for scheduling

---

box 6-4

SKILLS USED BY THE NURSE MANAGER

- Supported professional autonomy by having the nurse schedule herself
- Arranged access for the staff member to the ICU preceptor
- Discussed regularly progress and time use

---

box 6-5

SKILLS USED BY THE NURSE MANAGER

- Listened to and heard the staff nurse's need
- Altered the schedule to support the nurse's request
- Respected the staff member by implementing this change

---

discovered that of many more difficult tasks she performed on behalf of her staff this was one of the most appreciated.

In the previous examples the managers were successful in developing and retaining staff. The key to these simple but successful examples is that the managers' responses were individualized to the specific circumstances and individuals. Some management situations do not lend themselves to a single strategy and require ongoing evaluation and support for successful resolution. Most important, development and retention of staff can occur consistently only in an environment where each individual is valued and appreciated. This is demonstrated through action and verbalization by the effective nurse manager.

Using Resources: Motivation

We know that clarifying values, setting clear goals, and developing resources are important in a successful operation. Nurse managers must also use resources effectively. In the case of personnel resources, this requires motivation coupled with effective leadership. Remember, all work is done by the staff.

Lancaster[1] defines motivation as internal and unique to each employee. In other words, managers cannot motivate employees—they must be motivated from within, and what inspires motivation in one may not in another. Lancaster states that all employees are motivated, but those who appear to lack motivation are actually motivated in a direction different, or toward other outcomes, than a manager may desire. Because managers cannot directly motivate staff, they must work indirectly by creating an environment that tends to cause individual motivation toward the desired goals.

We have discussed several activities that are part of a motivating environment. The suggestions presented in Manager's Tip 6-1 on p. 184 will help the nurse manager create a positive environment.

The Work Environment

A healthy work environment, put simply, is one where all employees, managers and staff members alike, work toward common goals, receive feedback and communications on an ongoing basis, and meet the needs of their customers.

The presence or absence of some of the characteristics described above in an environment does not, in itself, determine a "good" or "bad" setting (Box 6-6). Some organizations may exhibit a blend of both in some situations, depending on times and areas observed. However, in a recent study of nurses and the culture of excellence in their hospitals, as defined by the attributes of excellence identified by Peters and Waterman in an article by Kramer and Schmalenberg, it was determined that "the presence of these attributes of excellence correlated with high job satisfaction and high self-esteem among the nurses."[2] In addition, when the authors looked at the data on the attributes of excellence, they saw "many more magnet hospital nurses indicated that their nursing leaders have power; that they're visionary; that they communicate and implement ideas, values, and goals; and that they function as a team."[3]

ABOUT FEEDBACK

The nurse manager should provide ongoing feedback and reinforcement concerning performance and achievement. Although feedback and reinforcement can be both positive and negative, Lancaster[1] suggests avoiding using threats and punishment as the predominating mode. Positive rewards and depersonalized, anticipated disciplinary action are more effective. Positive rewards should be individualized and can include raises, recognition, opportunities to participate in special activities, educational experiences, committee selection, and scheduling choices. Disciplinary action should be expected (i.e., a specific reaction to a specific behavior, consistent, timely, and focused on the behavior, not the person). It is important to remember that even discipline can occur in an atmosphere of approval and support.

COMMUNICATION PATTERNS

In any organization, both motivation and effectiveness are driven by the quality achieved and the patterns of communication. Without sound communication skills, the manager can be isolated and uninformed. Managers need to send and receive clear, well-understood messages. Communication patterns that affect their ability to do this are discussed below. Manager's Tip 6-2 on p. 186 presents some suggestions for effective communication.

The Communication Climate

In his book, Swansburg[3] discusses the importance of the overall tone of the environment in supporting clear communication, effective teamwork, and productivity. The supportive versus the defensive climate is discussed. The supportive climate is the goal of the manager who wants to encourage involvement and participation of staff at all levels. The manager must be open to disagreement, discussion, and input and use them constructively. Employees must feel they will be rewarded for speaking up, asking questions, and identifying problems. Individuality and spontaneity must be valued. Conflict should be seen as an opportunity for growth and learning. Empathy and support for and among staff should be evident. The only qualifier to these activities is that all should use them constructively to work toward unit goals.

---

box 6-6

ENVIRONMENT CHARACTERISTICS

CHARACTERISTICS OF A HEALTHY AND MOTIVATING ENVIRONMENT

Some work environments are healtheir than others. The following list outlines common elements of healthy work environments:

- People feel part of a team.
- There is ongoing clear communication up and down the organization hierarchy.
- Everyone is aware of and works toward defined goals.
- Good behavior is valued and reinforced.
- Staff development is ongoing.
- Employees have the authority to complete their work.
- The work and the people are respected.
- The staff feels generally positive about the work and other staff.

CHARACTERISTICS OF AN UNHEALTHY ENVIRONMENT

Similarly, unhealthy work environments share some common characteristics. They are listed below.

- Divisiveness is apparent among the staff, as in a dysfunctional family ("we versus they").
- People complain continually or do not communicate at all.
- People do not want to come to work.
- New members may feel isolated.
- "Top down" communication is rare or nonexistent.
- An open-door policy is espoused but in reality is rarely practiced.
- There are continually identified problems without attempts at resolution.
- Paralysis through continual analysis is apparent, and no or very little effective action is taken.

MANAGER'S TIP 6-2

BASIC TIPS FOR COMMUNICATING EFFECTIVELY

✔ Sharpen and use your listening skills to hear also the tone and intent of what is being communicated.

✔ Use appropriate eye contact during your conversations with staff.

✔ Validate what you thought you understood or heard by repeating the message in your own words, when necessary.

✔ If you find yourself in a situation where you know you are too busy to listen and address an issue, schedule time with the staff member to focus on the concern.

✔ Create an environment where the only dumb questions are the ones that do not get asked.

✔ Encourage feedback, recommendations, and "ways to make things better."

✔ Understand and effectively use the personality differences between your staff and the group you will be actively communicating with:

> *"Talker":* Do not give this individual continual openings by making eye contact. Defer to others in the group for a response to her/his comments.

> *"Recluse":* Draw this individual out by asking for opinions, comments, or questions on discussion at hand. Support this person by making environment as risk-free as possible.

> *"Arguer":* Do not act defensive when this individual questions or argues with each statement made. Respond to remarks with questions to clarify what is being said and steer or focus discussion back to desired areas.

> *"Expert":* Avoid having this individual monopolize discussion by directing conversation and having staff respond to comments with their impressions and interpretations.

✔ Smile when speaking with staff members whenever possible and appropriate.

✔ Summarize the conversation or discussion when finished.

✔ Ask for and thank staff and other team members for their ideas, input, and time.

✔ Be courteous and respectful of staff ideas and recommendations, even when they do not work out once implemented.

IMPEDIMENTS TO EFFECTIVE COMMUNICATION

Because of interference and noise, messages sent are frequently distorted before reception. Miscommunications can be caused by the sender, the listener, intermediaries, or the environment. The sender may clearly understand the message because of having had previous discussions and thoughts about the topic. The message may be poorly understood by the listener, who does not have the sender's frame of reference. The listener may produce interference simply by thinking about her/his response or another issue instead of listening carefully. A common example of intermediary interference is the parlor game in which a phrase is whispered from person to person and the first and final messages are compared. In the game, the disparity between the first and final messages can be very amusing, but in a work setting it is a serious problem. The nurse manager must consider possible sources of communication interference in advance and eliminate as many as possible (see Manager's Tip 6-3).

VERBAL VERSUS NONVERBAL COMMUNICATION

How something is said can be as important as what is said. Tone of voice, gestures, and posture greatly affect the listener. The nurse manager needs to appear assured, modify her/his feelings before speaking (or acknowledge rather than deny them), and maintain an open, attentive posture. The manager must also note body language in staff members that appears to be blocking communication. If an employee is turning away, or making a dismissive gesture, the manager must investigate or intervene at the appropriate time.

The nurse manager must always be aware of being a role model to the staff. The manager's example and behaviors must be consistent and professional. Communication should follow the formal chain of command. Nurse managers should be clear about the organization's expectations for intradepartmental and interdepartmental communications. They should make staff aware of these and their own expectations.

Inappropriate and negative forms of communication that the nurse manager should discourage in staff members, and must never personally demonstrate, include:

- Profanity, crudity, and personal criticisms. Professionals should express themselves professionally and demonstrate respect for others.
- Rumors and rumor spreading. Rumors can be destructive, divisive, and counterproductive.

The nurse manager serves as the vital link between the staff and the organization at large. The manager must accurately receive and transmit messages in both

MANAGER'S TIP 6-3

FOUR EXAMPLES OF WAYS TO AVOID MISCOMMUNICATION

✔ Communicate directly to groups.
✔ Hold meetings in a quiet setting.
✔ Encourage discussion of information given.
✔ Include a feedback loop in communication channels. After one-to-one, group, or written messages, the manager needs to ensure the message was understood as intended.

directions. Staff concerns, patient care issues, and system needs must be taken to administration or ancillary services. Imperatives, directives, objectives, procedures, and policies must be brought to staff. The manager uses writing, verbal, and listening skills to fulfill these linking functions. The nurse manager should review the institution's organizational chart with both supervisor and staff. The organizational chart delineates the chain of command and communication. It assists in clarifying direct, indirect, and collaborative relationships. Analysis of the chart can assist the nurse manager in ensuring that appropriate sources of information are fully used and that written and verbal communications are properly directed.

LISTENING SKILLS

It is important to remember that listening is an active process. It involves focusing, questioning, and validating, as well as allowing time to process the information gained. The listener who is judging the message or messenger, distracted, preparing a response, or not attentive cannot be listening effectively or gaining what is possible. Through meetings, nurse managers and their staffs maintain and work toward improving the function of their units. The new nurse manager needs to understand what information is important and must be noted and the process for recording such information. She/he needs to know how to obtain follow-up details and clarification, when needed. This clear, correct, timely information will then be communicated to all staff members. For an in-depth discussion of staff meetings, please refer to Chapter 5, Day-to-Day Operations.

VERBAL SKILLS

Nurse managers must always be prepared to represent or speak on behalf of their clinical areas. Although one does not want to be perceived as a squeaky wheel in an era of constrained resources, the unprepared and nonverbal may lose out. The successful manager can clearly articulate problems and quantify them, as well as suggest solutions. The manager should consult with supervisors, resource persons, and peers to develop the ability to speak in the language style understood and appreciated by administrators. The economic and patient outcome issues of a problem should be clearly defined. Knowing when to speak and being able to defer an answer are other important considerations. The manager does not want to be recognized for noise but for valued input. The points listed in Manager's Tip 6-4 are concepts to consider.

PUBLIC SPEAKING

The very thought of speaking in public brings fear to many who just think about it! Know that these feelings are not unusual; most public speakers have "butterflies" as they attempt to communicate verbally in front of a group. Public speaking skills are

MANAGER'S TIP 6-4

GUIDELINES TO CONSIDER WHEN REPRESENTING YOURSELF OR YOUR CLINICAL AREA

- ✔ If you do not have a complete answer for superiors or staff, say so, and commit to follow-up.
- ✔ Know your listener. Some people prefer a time-saving "bottom-line" response backed up by written reinforcement or discussion. Others need a progression of thought and time.
- ✔ Say less. If you are clear and concise, you need not say more except to be certain you were understood. Do not dilute the message by wandering or defending. Stay on the topic if a discussion ensues.
- ✔ If you are not sure that you have been understood, ask your listener for feedback.
- ✔ Be positive and constructive. Problems can be presented in terms of needs, goals, and possible solutions. Disagreement can be presented as an alternative view while acknowledging others and encouraging comparison.

important in our public, personal, and professional lives. The skills you learn and succeed here will also assist in other areas of your life. Remember you deserve to be "heard"—be it at a PTA meeting, when participating in town hall forums with elected officials, or at your health organization. Regardless of venue, the following tips will help you make the journey to experienced public speaker.

Seven Tips for Presentation Success

Believe you can be successful at this. Like any new skill, success comes with practice. Remember everyone has their "first few" presentations or speeches. Try to make these initial ones as comfortable for yourself as possible. This means bring more handouts than you think you need, wear comfortable clothes, and have friendly faces in the audience.

Know your topic and material. For example, if speaking to the management group about the new service your department is initiating, have the presentation answer all the questions they might have. What is this new service? Why is it needed? What specific patient populations is it designed to serve? How are referrals initiated from other areas within (and outside of) your organization? Illustrate with examples the types of patients and the process and the desired outcome of the new service. Bring flyers and other information to better explain the topic.

Change your nervous energy into enthusiasm. Everyone loves enthusiastic speakers and catches that positive energy. Particularly if you are an early morning or late evening presenter, involve the participants by asking questions such as a show of hands for "who is stressed about the changes in health care"?

Ask those you trust for evaluations. Frame the information in "what can I do to improve upon the presentation" terms. They will want you to succeed.

Use overheads, slides, and/or PowerPoint to your advantage. Technology is out there to assist in our communication. Just make sure to arrive at the meeting room early and check that the projector or computer or whatever else you need is there and that it works. Technical difficulties can happen, but try at the onset to prevent those you can!

Participate in a course specifically tailored to improve this communication skill. Sign up for a Dale Carnegie course or join the local Toastmaster's Club. Visit the website *www.toastmasters.org* to see where the closest meeting group is to you. Their members improve their skills weekly through participation and experience.

Watch public figures and others during presentations. Note what you wish to emulate and behaviors/actions that you do not want to incorporate into your presentations. For example, many speakers say "um" when there is a lull in their presentation or sway at the podium. Watch others and improve your own skills.

COMMUNICATING EFFECTIVELY ACROSS AN INTEGRATED NETWORK

Just as important as communicating up and down a chain of command in a hospital or other health care setting is the need for effective communication when actively involved in an integrated network. With the fast mergers and affiliations of large health systems, it is common to see a lack of organization and focus until the communication lines are well established and goals and objectives become aligned under strong leadership.

It is essential for the nurse manager of a patient care unit to understand the lines of communication and reporting mechanisms of the many departments on an organizational chart. The effectiveness of patient care planning needs to be emphasized from one setting to the next, and the relationship between each setting and the department that holds the groups together must ensure that the patient does not get lost in the system. In many instances, case management is the department that acts as the interface between different departments and different settings.

Regular written communication is needed between management and staff to enhance rumor control and keep staff informed of all appropriate changes. Management teams need to schedule, and keep, standing appointments with subordinates for discussions of ongoing happenings and the plans for upcoming events and projects. Many senior managers schedule routine meetings with their subordinate groups following their senior manager meetings. Department managers then follow suit and schedule departmental staff meetings within the next 24 hours to apprise staff of important items. This system is a viable adjunct to monthly department manager and divisional meetings. It keeps information fresh and timely and is a good deterrent to the rumor mill. One of the most frustrating, potentially volatile situations is when staff learn about events or happenings that will affect them from the media, such as television, radio, and newspapers.

E-MAIL AND THE INTERNET

Most large organizations with numerous departments or branch offices have established e-mail networks in an effort to promote paperless communication. In most cases, e-mail can successfully replace the written memorandum because the sender can keep a written or saved copy on file, and the recipient can produce a written copy for personal files. Most e-mail systems also verify to the sender when the recipient actually pulled the transmission up for reading, proof of receipt.

Basically, e-mail allows computers and their users to "speak" with each other as long as they are all on the same network or are interfaced with the communication network. Besides providing a medium for written communications to be sent instantaneously (without getting up and faxing a typed document), e-mail allows for quick notification of one or more parties who have been assigned stations or addresses on the system of official business.

E-mail allows a person to type a document once and send it on its way via modem. However, as with all computerized communications, there needs to be strict confidentiality and security precautions. There are few computerized communications systems that are impervious to hackers. Recent news stories have recounted the ability of international hackers, usually college students, to successfully breach government defense system computer networks and get access to top secret files. With that in mind, it is important to educate users to potential security breaches and what the organizational policies are in relation to confidentiality and the use of electronic mail.

The Internet is the latest tool in computer technology to make the world a smaller, more intimate place. With the appropriate computer hardware, software, server, and modem support, an individual can log into a multitude of websites that span a wide range of nations, lifestyles, businesses, and recreational activities. The controversial downside to this vast "information highway" is the ability to disseminate different types of information found to be morally or legally offensive. However, technology is being developed and implemented that will allow users better control of their systems, with more accountability and responsibility being forced on those traveling on this vast highway.

Currently, the Internet offers nurses and other managers access to on-line clinical and administrative management information, as well as the ability to "chat" with other managers for collaborative problem-solving without the expense of traveling and long-distance conversations. Bulletin boards exist in various nursing sites that allow the interchange of information between professionals. These sites become more specialized as they grow, targeting the interests and needs of their subscribers.

WRITTEN COMMUNICATION

The nurse manager cannot rely solely on verbal communication. Written communication provides important verification of verbal communication and discussion; access to those unavailable for meetings; documentation of standards, policies, issues, and goals; and time-saving transmittal of details and facts.

When communicating with administration and ancillary services, the manager should write a short, concise memo clearly stating the issue at hand. A memo is not the place to slowly build a case; there is too much risk of losing the reader's attention. Back-up data and explanations can be attached and referenced. The manager's supervisor should receive a copy of important memos and should be consulted about forwarding them to others.

Memo Example

In the example in Box 6-7, a specialty care unit was hampered by delayed transportation of patients. This had been discussed in many meetings, and both the manager's supervisor and the director of transportation were aware of the issues. The

---

box 6-7

MEMORANDUM

DATE: November 13, 200●
TO: Alice Johnson
           Transportation Supervisor
FROM: Jean Brown, Nurse Manager
           Cardiac Catheterization Laboratory
RE: Transportation of patients for cardiac catheterization

Since our last meeting on October 12, I have carefully monitored transportation data to assess its effect on our patient care services. During the past month, 30 of 50 patients were delivered to the unit more than 30 minutes late, and 22 were held on the unit for longer than 45 minutes awaiting transportation after the procedure was completed.

This caused six cancellations of procedures because of lost time slots and a significant amount of overtime paid to staff to stay beyond scheduled shifts.

Patient safety was maintained, but the patients were quite frustrated by long waits and especially by cancellations.

Although I appreciate your efforts to improve services and also the constraints on your department, I feel we must further consider alternatives if we are to meet our goals of quality patient care. Please contact me in the next week to arrange a meeting.

Thank you.
jb
cc: Jane Sessoms, Assistant Director
    Bill Elam, Director of Transportation

transportation supervisor had assured the nurse manager that problems were now corrected and insisted service was adequate. The manager and her supervisor agreed that the director of transportation should receive a copy of the memo, but that the transportation supervisor should review it with the director of nursing.

For an in-depth discussion of memos in daily practice, please refer to Chapter 5, Day-to-Day Operations.

Other Written Products

Staff meeting minutes, recording of unit and individual goals, and performance evaluations and feedback also require written skills. Goals and evaluations are usually recorded in an institution-wide format. The manager should work with her/his supervisor and employees to ensure goals and evaluations are measurable, accurate, constructive, and clear. Ongoing meetings with the staff to discuss goals and progress should occur. Documentation of these meetings should reflect achievement, need for growth, and plans (in specific terms) to meet goals. This documentation will then support and verify the formal evaluation.

Staff meeting minutes are recorded to (1) ensure verbal information was heard, (2) document that all staff members received consistent information, and (3) supply detail that need not be discussed. In addition to recording attendance, minutes should be placed in a communication book or other device and signed by those staff who were unable to attend the meeting and have read the written minutes of the meeting. Memos, new policies and procedures, and written announcements introduced in meetings should be referred to in the minutes and placed in the book for sign-off. The manager should ensure this feedback loop is completed by all staff members by periodically reviewing for completion and giving feedback and direction as needed. These meeting minutes can also be helpful when orienting new team members.

PROBLEM COMMUNICATIONS

The new nurse manager must bring or develop a wide range of skills needed for her/his new role. As any staff nurse or nurse manager knows, conflicts with physicians, other team members, or difficult patients and families can present their own unique problems and resolutions. Historically, nurses have been subordinate to physicians. In addition, because nursing is a predominantly female profession and medicine is a predominantly male profession, gender differences can contribute to physician-nurse problems. As the numbers of female physicians and male nurses increase, physician-nurse relationships may improve. But traditional male physician domination still sometimes sets the stage for power and control games between physicians and nurses. Because of these factors, you may need your supervisor's support in the management of these conflicts. Some systems are openly addressing these concerns by establishing nurse-physician committees. The JCAHO or other standards for multidisciplinary care can be the catalyst for needed changes in the relationships between health care professionals that would affect patient care positively and support increased nursing professionalism.

Communication problems are often heightened by the need for some reporting mechanism when a patient is placed at risk, for example, when a procedure is done incorrectly. A staff nurse describes the situation, "The hospital administration wants us to tell them anytime a physician contaminates a subclavian catheter during insertion. The physician knows when he's done a procedure incorrectly, and it's not my responsibility to monitor him." In this example the nurse is incorrect in her assertion. The law, including today's courts' interpretation of it, requires the nurse to pursue affirmative actions for patients and to safeguard them against incompetent health care providers. Such affirmative action—according to the courts—would, as a minimum, include monitoring the physician, even to the extent of confrontation. Otherwise, the nurse would be considered negligent.[4]

These examples and others like them bring home this difficult but ongoing problem. Like any other area in conflict resolution, the individuals involved in such a problem can usually identify and work out the most effective solutions. This is where your tact and communication skills can be put to the test. However, in those instances where the patient is jeopardized, there is only one solution. A nurse's primary duty is to the welfare of the patient, and the physician must be reported. Of course, the nurse must go through the appropriate channels in the chain of command to ensure protection of self and the patient. This is the level where the nurse manager most often becomes involved. Beyond you, the usual route is your nursing supervisor through to an administrative representative. Many times the nurse manager will clarify the situation with the physician directly. By asking the physician to explain and by getting input from others and following facility policies, particularly on the completion of incident reports, the nurse manager can follow up on known episodes where the patient was at risk.

It is important to note that some studies have demonstrated that positive professional relationships are reflected in lower patient mortality rates. Those who have been in nursing for some years know intuitively that this would be true. This concept is further explored later in this chapter.

There are positive, proactive steps the effective nurse manager can take to facilitate and maintain ongoing open communications between staff nurses and physicians. In addition, the collaboration between nurses and physicians is increasing. According to the National Joint Practice Commission,[5] "Collaborative or joint practice in hospitals is nurses and physicians collaborating as colleagues to provide patient care." Some of the ways to increase cooperation are listed in Manager's Tip 6-5 on p. 195.

There is no question that increased collaboration of physicians and nurses as well as other clinicians will become the standard in all health settings. This era of doing more with fewer resources ensures that we all must work effectively together to

MANAGER'S TIP 6-5

TECHNIQUES FOR IMPROVING NURSE-PHYSICIAN COOPERATION

- ✔ Establish a collaborative practice model.
- ✔ Provide assertiveness training for your staff, with an emphasis on clear communication skills.
- ✔ Be supportive by being an active listener for the nurses.
- ✔ Put the nursing or care philosophy and mission statement on the physician's bulletin board. This can help ensure that all are working toward the same goals.
- ✔ Develop and implement a buddy system to achieve these goals. Assign one nurse to one new resident or physician staff member. This will help increase the new physician's comfort level and ensure a complete orientation to your unit and to "how things are done." Most new physicians will welcome the opportunity for education rather than having to face learning by trial and error. In addition, such activities assist in the achievement of mutual respect and effective communications.
- ✔ Hear and understand both the physicians' and nurses' positions and roles.
- ✔ Develop and implement an integrated documentation system (if not currently available).
- ✔ Establish a physician-nurse committee for (1) collaboration (patient care review); (2) problem resolution, where indicated; and (3) continuing education.
- ✔ Provide ongoing education for nurses to ensure clinical expertise in care of patients. This promotes the nurses' self-esteem and is vital to effective communications or discussions with physicians about patient care.
- ✔ Schedule and maintain ongoing joint clinical care rounds for nurses and physicians. These are particularly important for planning care after discharge from your setting or program, considering increases in patient acuity, decreased lengths of stay, and increased patient turnover.
- ✔ Develop a communication process to keep physicians apprised of events, systems, or changes that affect patient care or their routines in your environment. For example, when you read your staff meeting minutes, look for these types of items. Then communicate them to the physician staff. Post a physicians' bulletin board on the unit. Information to post could include (1) new products selected and available for use; (2) staff changes and promotions; (3) QA/QI issues that affect your unit; (4) any research occurring; and (5) anything else that would give information to the physician that would facilitate being a part of the team.
- ✔ Involve physicians in new practice model development or in the planning of clinical pathways or other care protocols.
- ✔ Distribute communications about or from your area to physicians. It will help you and your staff by informing the physicians you work with in the facility. For example, accredited home health agencies or hospices are required to inform physicians of their responsibilities in the home care process. This is usually done at the time of first referral, by distributing a packet of agency information to respective physicians. This can include a welcome letter, signed jointly by the nursing and medical directors; the

Continued

TECHNIQUES FOR IMPROVING NURSE-PHYSICIAN COOPERATION — cont'd

philosophy; the patient admission criteria; the types of patients that would be appropriate; an example of the referral form; and a brochure on the program. Follow-up could also be arranged to personalize this interaction or to address any questions that may have been raised by the information sent.

✓ Provide ongoing physician and nurse educational sessions. For example, the hospice medical director, the pharmacist, and the hospice/home care nurse could provide a seminar on "effective pain relief." These clinical conferences are useful to both nurses and physicians and, as such, are important to patient care collaboration. Some other areas could be ethical dilemmas, available resources for discharge planning, and clinical updates. Be sure to evaluate these sessions to ensure that nurse and physician needs are being met. In addition, ask physicians what topics they would like addressed in the future.

✓ Post the next scheduled session and specific information on the bulletin board. Some hospitals host Grand Rounds and have well-known clinicians speak on a particular topic. They invite all physicians, nurse managers, and staff members and may have an evening meeting over dinner.

✓ Be a role model to your staff in your communications and interactions with physicians. This is particularly helpful with "difficult" physicians.

✓ Host get-togethers on a regular basis for new residents or staff physicians and nurses to begin this pattern of effective communication and role definition from the onset.

meet patient needs. Respect must be valued and mutual for communications to be effective among all team members. We know that increased morale and "making a difference" are important in nurse satisfaction and retention. The effective nurse manager can be successful as the catalyst to create this environment.

COORDINATION OF CARE ACROSS THE CONTINUUM

One of the positive outcomes of the managed care revolution has been the need to improve patient care coordination across the continuum. Not only is it beneficial for a patient to have her/his care coordinated and discussed at the different sites of care, it is also more cost-efficient in terms of resource utilization to make sure that all the health care practitioners involved in a plan of care are "speaking the same language."

In recent years, collaboration has increased between the different professional clinicians involved in a plan of care, from the acute to subacute to rehabilitation to home care to outpatient through to community services. This collaboration is necessary because of the need to standardize elements of the care process. In so doing, we are able to measure accurately the outcomes of care and compare that data from one site or patient to another. It is necessary to clarify terms and establish a consistent frame of reference between all parties planning the care. Definitions of terms between health care providers are not always the same and may cause confusion that negatively affects the patient and the planning process. For example, if a nurse defines functional status in purely nursing terms and a physical therapist uses another definition, miscommunication and poor planning may occur. It is essential that care be planned, coordinated, implemented, and evaluated and that a common language is maintained.

In an effort to improve communication and standardize patient care protocols within existing professional standards of care, many agencies and health care systems have instituted clinical paths on certain patient care medical diagnoses and conditions. According to Marrelli and Hilliard in their text, *Home Care and Clinical Paths—Effective Care Planning Across the Continuum*, to make clinical pathways more effective, all the providers on the care continuum need to be involved in the development or adaptation of the care protocols. Besides the departmental representatives from the acute care setting, all the alternate site settings need to be represented so that effective planning can occur and problem areas can be addressed before implementation. This involvement also helps to ensure buy-in from staff at the alternate site settings. It is interesting to discover how little staff from one setting understand the role of staff from another setting and how more cost-effectively one setting can accomplish the same goals as another. This collaboration and planning is definitely an example of performance improvement.[6]

Nurse managers again are the only professionals who can span the different sites and can be the advocates for both the patient and the institution. They need to include all appropriate setting representatives as needed on the planning committees, so that time and efforts can be maximized.

Managed care has also focused on the benefits of patient care provided at settings other than the acute care hospital. Ideally, patients are treated at the lowest level of care needed and will only utilize expensive, complex care settings as necessary. Home health care, subacute and skilled nursing facility care, and other forms of ambulatory and community care are becoming more involved in the patient care process. The hospital, no longer the only area where important care can be rendered, is simply another setting on the health care continuum.

THE WORK CULTURE

All work settings have a culture, which is the unique environment of the workplace. This culture includes the physical setting and layout, the management philosophy, and the written and unwritten rules for conduct and other activities. In nursing, the work of managing in this culture occurs in ongoing communications, usually with small groups, teams, or individual employees. A team is a group of people who perform the work of an organization to achieve that organization's goals.

Effective Team Building

Effective teams are the key to the accomplishment of all work. It has been projected that most organizations will be (more) decentralized and workers will be broken up into special work units, where they will have responsibility for all functions relating to their work.

These small teams will be autonomous for work products, including outcomes and even budget accountability. The cultures of some progressive companies are already structuring their work environments to facilitate this goal.

The Nurse Manager's Role with the Team

You manage a nursing unit where all work is accomplished by your team. Your team-building role provides a unique opportunity to develop staff, problem-solve, and meet the care needs of patients. The leader of any team determines the style of the team. Your most important and ongoing roles are those of communicator and role model. This is ensured through the activities in Manager's Tip 6-6 on p. 199.

Managers can create a motivating environment that empowers their nursing staffs. An environment where communications are open, where the manager listens, and where staff believe they have input and influence in decisions enables nurses to be committed. The team leader or manager must be trustworthy and honest, have good active listening skills, and communicate with the staff frequently about the achievement of the unit's and department's goals.

THE TEAM MEMBERS

Numerous categories have been used in labeling types of team members. Examples include natural leaders, initiators, motivators, loyalists, and other various types that contribute to a team's makeup. In fact, labeling team members as types may be counterproductive. However, each of us may exhibit these characteristics in different situations.

The best groups function effectively when they have input into the methods to be used in reaching the defined goal. It has been said that the true test of effective management is how well the group functions when the manager is not present. Therefore use your staff's natural skills and abilities. We all do best in tasks that we enjoy. So, when possible, let staff members choose assignments or tasks they want to perform. These roles can be clear at the onset. For example, delegate organizational responsibilities to a particularly well organized staff member, someone who can remind you of the time, take minutes of meetings, or reorganize an ineffective process through to resolution with input from other involved peer nurses.

Team Problems

All teams or staffs can have problems at one time or another. These problems can range in scope and significance and can affect the functioning of the unit as a whole. These problems can include the following symptoms:

- Cliques
- Increased errors or mistakes
- Isolation of new staff members

- Increased complaints
- "We" versus "they" feelings
- Scapegoating of specific staff members
- Negative comments from peers or your manager
- Decreased productivity
- Silence
- Failure to share needed information among team members

When problem trends are identified, self-evaluation is indicated. Is the manager doing anything to increase the conflict? An example could be a reward system that reinforces undesirable behaviors. Does the staff feel or perceive that there are favorites who get better assignments or more staff education days than do others? For example, if one staff member goes to lunch with you, rotate this opportunity with all your staff. Certain behaviors or personalities can sometimes lead to conflict. The effective resolution of conflict is one of the responsibilities of all managers.

CONFLICT

It is important that the nurse manager remember that not all conflict needs management intervention. Welcome the existence of differences in your work setting. Much has been written on conflict management and individual styles for conflict resolution. It is thought that we all use different styles in different situations, though we may have a favorite style. Use the presence of conflict as a possible indicator of the need for change or problem-solving. Conflict can be a strong motivator for change or growth.

Your Role in Conflict Resolution Between Staff Team Members

The suggestions shown in Manager's Tips 6-7 and 6-8 can help facilitate effective conflict resolution. Two traits are needed for effective conflict resolution—trust and rationality.

MANAGER'S TIP 6-6

MANAGING A SUCCESSFUL TEAM

✔ Manage in a way that demonstrates respect to staff, peers, and others.
✔ Remind staff of the task at hand.
✔ Respect the team for their professional skills and knowledge.
✔ Project self-confidence.
✔ Show enthusiasm.
✔ Listen and problem-solve.
✔ Be flexible.

Continued

MANAGING A SUCCESSFUL TEAM — cont'd

- ✔ Act as a role model.
- ✔ Provide support.
- ✔ Be organized.
- ✔ Continually use your human relations skills.
- ✔ Create an atmosphere of cooperation and collaboration.
- ✔ Keep the team on track and focused.
- ✔ Recognize staff.
- ✔ Give feedback.
- ✔ Share common goals.
- ✔ Give staff accountability and responsibility.
- ✔ Delegate effectively.
- ✔ Manage with a clear vision of where you are going; share it often.
- ✔ Allow staff to take risks.
- ✔ Provide encouragement and feedback.
- ✔ Clarify assignments when needed.
- ✔ Pilot staff-recommended changes.
- ✔ Listen to alternative solutions to daily challenges.
- ✔ Reward staff for work well done.
- ✔ Create and nurture rapport.
- ✔ Follow up on problems.
- ✔ Empower staff.
- ✔ Write about your team and their accomplishments in memos, newsletters, professional journals, and local papers.
- ✔ Be there to provide help when needed.
- ✔ Lead a well-balanced life.
- ✔ Create an ego-enhancing environment.
- ✔ Foster a cooperative environment.
- ✔ Demonstrate retention-directed management skills.
- ✔ Choose new team members effectively.
- ✔ Keep lines of communication open.
- ✔ Recognize individual nurses' contributions.
- ✔ Communicate to your supervisor the work accomplished by your team.
- ✔ Maintain and use your sense of humor.
- ✔ Share patient evaluation feedback with staff.
- ✔ Remove obstacles to work completion.
- ✔ Let go of owning all problems and solutions once you have delegated the work.
- ✔ Ask for suggestions on better ways to do things.
- ✔ Ask "What can I do to help you get your work done more effectively?"

SUMMARY

In conclusion, interpersonal skills important to the nurse manager include a variety of overlapping traits, activities, and attitudes.

The successful manager is open and supportive of staff, truly seeing them behaviorally as valuable resources. Constant communication, which is well planned,

MANAGER'S TIP 6-7

RESOLVING CONFLICTS

- ✔ Know that conflict is inevitable and not all conflict is destructive.
- ✔ Always work toward helping staff members settle differences themselves.
- ✔ View yourself not as a parent but as an objective observer only.
- ✔ Validate that you will not take sides.
- ✔ Be objective.
- ✔ Support harmony and resolution.
- ✔ Verbalize that staff members need to talk to each other and that you trust their problem-solving skills.
- ✔ Listen with understanding, not judgment.
- ✔ Clarify the issue only when necessary.
- ✔ Do not criticize or deny feelings such as anger or fear.
- ✔ Focus on maintaining the relationship between the conflicting parties.
- ✔ Create a problem-solving atmosphere.
- ✔ Offer your office space for a limited time for this discussion, when appropriate.
- ✔ Be able to identify a chronically complaining employee. This is important because such behavior can contribute to a depressing tone for the entire work environment.

MANAGER'S TIP 6-8

WHAT TO DO WHEN RESOLVING COMPLAINTS

- ✔ Listen to the complaint but set limits if it continues.
- ✔ Ask for the recommended solutions to the listed complaint.
- ✔ Work on the development of problem-solving skills for the staff members involved.

executed, and validated, combined with real caring and investment in staff, creates an environment that fosters motivation, retention, and success.

The successful use of problem-solving skills ensures that the feelings and energy generated by conflict are directed toward creative resolution. This approach welcomes the uniqueness of all individuals and is potentially growth enhancing for individuals and teams.

QUESTIONS FOR CONSIDERATION

1. Describe the nurse manager's role in creating a motivating environment.
2. List three characteristics of a healthy environment and three characteristics of an unhealthy environment.

3. Discuss verbal versus nonverbal communications and provide two examples of nonverbal communication.
4. Identify two resources to assist you to improve your presentation/public speaking skills.
5. Develop the following statement—"Never write an e-mail when you are angry"—and explain why this saying is true.

References

1. Lancaster J: Creating a climate for excellence, *Journal of Nursing Administration* 16, January 1985.
2. Kramer M, Schmalenberg C: Job satisfaction and retention, *Nursing 91* 21:51, 1991.
3. Swansburg RC: *Management and leadership for nurse managers*, Boston, 1990, Jones & Bartlett.
4. Horsley J: When to tattle on physician's misconduct, *RN* 4(12):17, 1978. In Luquire R: Nursing risk management, *Nursing Management* 20:56, 1989.
5. The National Joint Practice Commission: *The definition of joint or collaborative practice*, statement 4, September 1977.
6. Marrelli TM, Hilliard LS: *Home care and clinical paths—effective care planning across the continuum*, St Louis, 1995, Mosby.

For Further Reading

Barr and Barr: *Leadership development—maturity and power*, Austin, TX, 1994, Eakin Press.

Blanchard K, Bowles S: *High five! The magic of working together*, New York, 2001, HarperCollins Publications.

Blanchard K, Carolos J, Randolph A: *Empowerment is more than a minute*, San Francisco, 1996, Berrett-Koehler.

Bridges W: *Managing transitions: making the most of change*, MA, 1993, Wesley Publishing Company.

Cohen RK: *Mirror, mirror on the wall—who's the best employer? Modern Healthcare* 10:12-14, May 1999.

Connors R, Smith T, Hickman C: *The Oz principle*, NJ, 1994, Prentice-Hall.

Delassandro T: *Relationship strategies*, La Jolla, CA, 1990, Allessandro & Associates.

Drucker P: *The effective executive*, New York, 1967, Harper & Row.

Groomsman RJ: How recruiters woo high demand candidates, *HR Magazine* 43(13): 122-127, December 1998.

Harkins PJ: Why employees stay—or go, *Workforce*, October 17(10): 74–79, 1998.

Hawke J: More good nurses needed by 2005, *The Nursing Spectrum* I(2):14, January 1998.

HCAB: *Managing nurse overtime; strategies for reducing the burden on staff*, Washington, DC, 2001, The Advisory Board Company.

Hoff R, Maguire B. *I can see you naked: a new revised edition on making fearless presentations*, New York, 1992, Andrews McMeel Publishing.

Institute of Medicine: *Nursing staff in hospitals and nursing homes: is it adequate?* Washington, DC, 1996, National Academy Press.

Joiner and Associates, Inc: *The team handbook*, Madison, WI, 1996, Joiner and Associates.

Lombardi DM: *Handbook for the new health care manager*, Chicago, 1993, AHA Press.

Mackenzie A: *The time trap*, New York, 1990, Amacom.

Nierenberg A: *Nonstop networking: how to improve your life, luck and career*, Herndon, VA, 2002, Capital Books, Inc.

Patterson K: *Crucial conversations: tools for talking when stakes are high*, New York, 2002, McGraw-Hill.

Pritchett P: *Resistance: moving beyond the barriers to change*, Dallas, 1999, Pritchett and Associates, Inc.

Pritchett P: *Teamwork: the team member handbook: 16 steps to building a high-performance team*, Dallas, 1999, Pritchett and Associates, Inc.

Pritchett P, Pound R: *High-velocity culture change: a handbook for managers*, Dallas, 1999, Pritchett and Associates, Inc.

Taylor MW: Listening: a key management tool, *Pediatric Nursing* 17(4):390, 1991.

CHAPTER 7

EFFECTIVE TIME MANAGEMENT

T.M. MARRELLI

Effective time management is vital to accomplishing all work. Time management problems are easy to recognize; there is always too much pending work. The symptoms are papers piled high in baskets and stacks on your desk, notes attached to your office door, unread mail, notes framing your computer, and the inability to locate a specific piece of paper or document when you need it. The behavioral signs include thinking about the next project while discussing a current one, procrastinating about picking up the top piece of paper for fear of what's underneath, and forgetting appointments. These problems can be remedied. Effective time management, or habits that contribute to the effective use of this limited commodity, can be learned. More importantly, habits that are no longer efficient for you can be discarded. Working smarter, not harder, demands setting priorities, delegating effectively, and using other time management skills to achieve personal and organizational goals.

Effective time management has become even more important with the increased mergers, downsizing, and general increase of individual workloads over the past few years. In order to survive, management has had to restructure departments or positions so that middle managers may be wearing many different hats, picking up the job duties or managerial functions of individuals who have left or have been laid off. The important thing to remember during this stressful time is that one person may not be able to do it all or do it all as it has been done in the past.

Use your newfound skills as a manager to take stock of all the priorities and responsibilities of your position, work with your senior manager to define what needs to be done, delegate effectively, and do the best you can. As Chapter 10 will explain, balance is needed in everyone's life to prevent the negative outcomes related to increased pressure and stress.

THE THREE *PS* OF PROCRASTINATION

Three *Ps* may especially impede competent nurse managers from accomplishing dreaded work. These are:

1. Procrastination
2. Perfectionism
3. Prioritizing

Procrastination is generally defined as habitually postponing performance of burdensome tasks. Symptoms may include multiple stacks of paper on your desk overflowing onto credenzas, unopened mail, or the feeling of not wanting to go to work for fear of not meeting a deadline on a project. The problem with procrastination is that it is a learned habit. Like all habits, it can be unlearned and replaced with more successful behaviors. Examples of procrastination are delaying finalizing the minutes of the last product selection committee until the night before the next meeting or delaying performance evaluations because they are time consuming. When this occurs, the added stress and pressure become greater than if the minutes had been completed earlier or if one performance evaluation were completed every afternoon. All of a sudden, routine items take on immense importance and a dread of not meeting deadlines sets in.

It is interesting to note that in *Webster's New World Dictionary*,[1] the word *deadline* has its origins as a "line around a prison beyond which a prisoner could go only at the risk of being shot." It is no wonder that we take deadlines seriously and feel impending discomfort as they approach and we are not or perceive we are not ready. This feeling usually lasts until the work is accomplished, then tremendous relief is felt.

Also, while working, a realization usually is made—the task was not as bad as anticipated, or such a delay should not occur again because it takes too much energy. It is at this point that a conscious effort and decision must be made to change the habit of procrastination. Everyone endures certain job aspects that they do not enjoy. However, these dreaded duties grow in importance and cast a shadow on all other activities until completed. Just "doing it" results in incredible relief. In addition, it usually takes less time and energy than was anticipated. Most importantly, the feeling of accomplishment and satisfaction when done can reinforce the new just-do-it habit the next time. Therefore when you initially get these dreaded uncomfortable feelings, it usually means you should do this job first and stop procrastinating.

Perfectionism is known generally to mean that work is never perceived to be "good enough." Perfectionists usually procrastinate because at some level they believe that no product is better than a poor product. Although this is not true, we all have known successful, competent people who function with these beliefs. If this sounds familiar, it is important to realize that, generally, any work product is better than none, and you may never have the luxury of time or other resources to accomplish a given project in the manner you believe it should be accomplished. Trying to be perfect wastes time and is an unrealistic goal. In fact, this is perhaps one of the most frustrating aspects of being a manager; not only will your work product often be incorporated into your supervisor's project, but in the end it may not resemble the same product at all. In management, you must make it okay (to yourself) for your managers to "own" parts of your work and recognize that you cannot control your product once it is submitted to your manager.

Prioritizing is the decision-making process that results in a systematic order in which to accomplish identified tasks. Prioritizing leads to organization, which is vital to effective time management.

Prioritizing can be closely linked to perfectionism and procrastination in two ways: (1) putting off or delaying what you do not want to do (procrastination) can result in those tasks being relegated to the end of your list of priorities, and (2) avoidance of starting and completing a task moves other tasks toward the end of the priority list. As the dread of deadline looms, there are seemingly endless lists of newer items given higher priority. It is at this point that the perfectionist starts believing that it is just too late for an acceptable product to even be created.

Though it is hard, *do* the most difficult task first. Even a draft of the project will give you some sense of accomplishment and a feeling of control over your work environment. The difficult tasks we put off are what become bigger and cause stress in the workplace. Doing the dreaded task will give you a sense of relief, rejuvenation, and accomplishment.

The "Right Stuff" Attitudes

Kenneth Pelletier of the University of California San Francisco School of Medicine conducted an ongoing study of executives in the telecommunications industry, as reported by Olsen.[2] The telecommunications industry has been plagued by turmoil and changes. It was found through this study that the people who thrived on the continual fast-paced changes shared some common beliefs. Some of these lessons may be applicable to the health care setting because of the dynamic and ever-changing environment health care managers face. The suggestions for thriving on change in Manager's Tip 7-1 on p. 208 may help you be an effective manager in today's fast-paced health care environment.

If you believe that you are alone in struggling to effectively manage your time, consider this thought. Large[3] states, "More new information has been produced in the last 30 years than in the previous 5,000 . . . and the total of all printed knowledge doubles every 8 years." There is clearly too much information and not enough time to incorporate it. What is more, not all information received is relevant to the task at hand. The new term that has been created for this overwhelming amount of knowledge is *information anxiety*. In addition to this overload, you may have sales representatives and other vendors who wish to further increase your knowledge of the particular product or service they are selling. Finally, your life does not comprise only work (though in difficult times it can certainly *feel* that way), and you may receive additional information daily through your personal mail, home e-mail, and phone.

MANAGER'S TIP 7-1

THRIVING ON CHANGE

✔ **Challenge**—Do not view change as a threat. Perceive it as a challenge and the chance or opportunity to do something new and innovative.

✔ **Control**—Believe that you can make an impact or a difference. This is probably the most important trait for thriving in a changing environment.

✔ **Commitment**—Get involved and active in the new ideas and change. Do not deny the reality of the changing situation.

✔ **Social support**—Engage your friends, family, and colleagues for support. It helps to have a sense of working and pulling together. Your network does not have to be large, just established and used. Pelletier says, "It's enough that you have a supportive, trusting relationship with the person at the next desk."[2] (This reinforces the importance and need for peer support among nurse managers.)

✔ **Stress management**—Learn your own stress signals. Pelletier found that the healthiest executives all knew what to do when their stress levels got too high. He said methods for relief varied and the one chosen did not matter. For this group, methods included, among others, listening to music. Relieving stress is vital to reenergizing oneself.[2]

The good news is anyone can become organized. Contrary to belief, your desk does not need to be neat and clean to be organized. Tidiness works for some, whereas others can locate any needed piece of paper on what appears to be a messy desk. You can be more organized and use your limited time more effectively. The skills and time management suggestions recommended in Manager's Tips 7-2, 7-3, and 7-4 can also be extended into your home.

Handling Paper

Act-on-it items include action items such as memos needing response, confirmation of meeting attendance, scheduling changes, and other situations in which your immediate input is needed.

MANAGER'S TIP 7-2

FIVE WAYS TO HANDLE PAPER

✔ Act on it.
✔ File it.
✔ Discard it.
✔ Complete your part and forward it.
✔ Regardless of the chosen category, try to handle it only once.

26 WAYS TO HELP YOU MANAGE TIME

- ✔ Recognize that time is a scarce and nonrenewable resource.
- ✔ Remember that being organized is a key component of effective time management.
- ✔ Evaluate your own use of time. Keep a log for 2 weeks and note the activities and time allotted for them. Keep another log after implementing these suggestions to see if measurable improvements in your work output occur.
- ✔ Understand that everyone has her/his own organization style. You do not have to have a neat and spotless desk to be organized. Some very organized managers have messy desks but can put their hands on any piece of paper when needed.
- ✔ Know that successful, busy people usually have effective personal organizational skills.
- ✔ Schedule time to file or do paperwork *every* day. Start files for such ongoing business as leave requests, unit activity reports, or QA/QI minutes.
- ✔ Prioritize tasks on a daily basis.
- ✔ Schedule and meet deadlines.
- ✔ Formulate realistic goals and break them down into tasks by creating short-range goals. When all these tasks are completed, long-term objectives will have been achieved. Break down all large jobs into small pieces. Schedule time to do the small pieces.
- ✔ Maintain your flexibility. Reorder priorities whenever indicated based on organizational needs.
- ✔ Know that if something is not a priority or important, it may not need to be done.
- ✔ Visualize yourself learning to effectively cope with change, turmoil, and chaos. With this attitude, it will not unduly upset you when it happens.
- ✔ Managing your own time effectively will result in more efficient use of staff time as your actions are copied.
- ✔ Accept that your schedule may change based on many situations, such as your manager's needs, a clinical problem, or an unscheduled lengthy disaster drill.
- ✔ Maximize your use of time because this improves overall performance and contributes to cost containment goals.
- ✔ Know that planning and delegation are vital to organizational and personal goal achievement.
- ✔ Realize that an effective time manager gets more accomplished, has improved quality of work, meets deadlines and other commitments, and increases effectiveness overall.
- ✔ Make and use "to do" lists or planners whenever possible.
- ✔ Take the last few minutes of your workday to reflect on your accomplishments and to prioritize the tasks of the next day. Feel satisfied with those completed tasks and the job you are doing.
- ✔ You can have an open-door policy and attitude without the door always literally being open. Staff should have access, but you can control that access.
- ✔ Pick a regularly scheduled day (e.g., every third Tuesday) for clearing off your desk totally and reprioritizing big projects.
- ✔ Use the phone whenever possible—it may save you writing a memo and time-consuming communications.
- ✔ Check off tasks as completed—it feels great!
- ✔ Don't postpone any task that can be handled/completed immediately.
- ✔ Budget time for planning and thinking.
- ✔ Use a daytimer, PDA, or other technology to help organize your life.

MANAGER'S TIP 7-4

30 ACTIONS TO HELP YOU MANAGE YOUR ENVIRONMENT

✔ Hang a large calendar in an accessible area on which you and your staff can identify vacations, inservices, or scheduled absences. If feasible, it is particularly helpful if you are able to read this at a glance from you desk.

✔ Choose the style of "to do" list that works best for you. Try different ones until you decide which method suits you best.

✔ Identify your peak work time. Try to schedule the most intense or important tasks during this time.

✔ Concentrate on the task at hand by controlling distractions. It is okay to schedule time for you: close your office door.

✔ Leave the work area, when possible, for at least a few minutes a day. Take a lunch or other meal break, even if it means just shutting your door and eating an apple in peace.

✔ Place mailboxes for your staff in an easily accessible place for your use. Mailboxes can be used for scheduling, feedback, and delegated work.

✔ Schedule time for all routine duties; otherwise they probably will not get done. For example, schedule time to review performance evaluations and other ongoing area activity tasks. If it is not scheduled, it is not respected as a priority.

✔ Learn to use a computer for all written products. The editing, spelling checkers, and thesaurus tools are an immense help when memos or reports are due. When you use a computer, organize your disks in a manner effective for you. Remember to keep the phone, scissors, or other magnetic material away from your computer and the disks because such items may erase hours of hard work.

✔ Practice speedreading or proofreading skills if your position uses those special skills.

✔ Organize your phone numbers in a systematic way. This method should be whatever works and is easiest for you. Have the most frequently called numbers accessible and placed near your phone.

✔ Control interruptions for certain periods of each day. The ability to do this effectively will vary based on the work setting and other factors.

✔ Refer to a thesaurus and a recent edition dictionary whenever creating written products.

✔ Maintain and update a desk calendar or other organizer to determine your planned daily, weekly, and monthly schedules.

✔ Create an office environment that promotes work completion while also reflecting your personality.

✔ Organize and update your business phone numbers and addresses on a regularly scheduled basis.

✔ Make your environment work for you. Sometimes it may be appropriate to go to the hospital library to research a project for a presentation. Other times, just closing your office door and completing a literature search online may be sufficient.

✔ Remember that becoming and staying organized is a learned skill and that, with practice, good habits can replace bad ones.

✔ Believe that you cannot do everything for everyone else and still achieve your goals.

30 ACTIONS TO HELP YOU MANAGE YOUR ENVIRONMENT—cont'd

✔ Use your interpersonal skills to politely end conversations. When phoning people known to be long-winded, set up the conversation to be short. This can be achieved in a couple of ways: (1) "Dr. No, this is Nurse Manager, I have only a minute between meetings to return your call and tell you ..." or (2) "Well, I've got to go, I think my manager is on the other line" or "I have a call I've been expecting and have to go." Your pager can also be used for this purpose.

✔ Practice visualization daily, seeing yourself as a calm and effective manager.

✔ Begin every morning by taking 3 minutes to relax and focus on the day's tasks ahead. With practice, this exercise will keep you centered throughout the day on your priorities.

✔ Listen to *any* recommendations that have the possibility of being a more efficient and successful way of doing things. Stop yourself the moment your automatic response begins with, "But it's always been done this way." That alone is usually a good reason to reevaluate the way something is done.

✔ Learn to say "no" and mean it.

✔ Be flexible in the time parameters set in your schedule. If you overschedule your time and consistently run over, you will feel ever more harried and hassled. Allot sufficient time between scheduled activities.

✔ Accept that there will *always* be interruptions. This is part of being a manager. The key is controlling and balancing them. Evaluate your office space: is the furniture in a configuration that is conducive to decreasing or minimizing interruptions?

✔ Teach your staff that whenever a problem is brought to your attention, you will hear it only if a recommended solution accompanies the problem.

✔ Visualize yourself as an innovative, creative thinker and problem-solver.

✔ Practice relaxation techniques and deep breathing exercises on a regular basis.

✔ Take breaks. These are very important. Take them, do not feel guilty, and savor them. The restorative power of a break leaves you with more energy while increasing your productivity.

✔ Take great care of yourself. Get a massage, have manicures, exercise, read a book, eat well, play golf, or whatever you *like to do*. Effective time management will allow more time for those activities.

File-it items include items that may need retrieval in the future (e.g., communications from your manager, human resources (HR) issues, and other important documentation).

Discard-it items include advertisements for various services or products that are not appropriate for your area and memos sent to you as occupant nurse manager or confirmation memos that need no further action on your part.

Try to handle it only once, regardless of the chosen category.

The main difficulty in this process is deciding what to file and what to discard. You can learn a lot about the nurse manager who preceded you and the filing system that may be acceptable at your work setting by reviewing the remaining files. The core files may include HR files, copies of patient complaints that may or may not have been forwarded to the patient ombudsman and/or risk manager, clinical and management articles circulated to all managers from administration, and voluminous paper communications sent to or from the area.

You do not have to keep every piece of paper to be an effective manager. Ask your peers what information they keep and what they discard. Avoid the tendency to be a pack rat. Be aware of privacy and confidentiality considerations and laws. Complete your part and forward on.

THE IMPORTANCE OF DELEGATION

It has been said that the effective use of time, or time management, is more about management than about time. With this in mind, you will find that your staff is vital to accomplishing all work. Delegation is the tool that transfers the work to your subordinates, giving the staff the responsibility, which contributes to a sense of their belonging and accomplishment. Successful completion of the duties delegated empowers and develops the team member to whom the work was delegated. In decentralized organizations, delegation is key to work accomplishment. The nurse manager must achieve organizational and area goals, and the ordering of the priorities and the management of the time allotted in which to do them is of great importance. The more responsibilities a person assumes and the busier a person becomes, the more effective delegation becomes the essential tool to accomplish work and achieve goals (Manager's Tip 7-5).

RESOURCES FOR TIME MANAGEMENT

There are ways to improve time management. It is important to be open to new ideas. The resources discussed below are those that should be considered when possible.

Technology and Nursing

The time management implications of information systems for nurses and nurse managers are currently being operationalized in health settings and discussed in the literature. Automation in documentation should be fully explored because documentation continues to be an area of duplicative actions and inefficient use of the professional nurse's limited time. Computers are encouraging a shift toward standardized care plans, related processes, and other automated data trends. This needs to occur given the following information. The American Hospital Association[4] (AHA) says that patient charts now average 70 to 100 pages. Medical records departments in most midsized hospitals process some 250,000 to 360,000 pieces of information each year. Because a patient's medical record may be reviewed as many as 30 times and stored for up to 30 years, more than 90% of hospitals have turned to computers to manage the information.

MANAGER'S TIP 7-5

14 SUGGESTIONS TO DELEGATE EFFECTIVELY

✔ Believe it is *not* easier or quicker to do it yourself. (It is not!)

✔ Realize you must delegate to accomplish work.

✔ Learn to delegate wherever possible; it frees you up to manage and it develops your staff.

✔ Delegate by stating clearly the work and the product expected; specify deadlines, including a date on which you want a draft or the product; state that you be apprised of progress weekly in writing, and that you want immediate notification if a problem is impeding completion by the due date.

✔ Provide feedback, positive wherever possible, on the progress and on the final product. Share comments from others on the work product where possible. For example, if your manager compliments the work and writes you a note about it, share the note with the staff member who created the product. It also is helpful to keep such notes in the staff member's file so that during the performance evaluation, you remember work products accomplished and the feedback received.

✔ Teach and direct your staff to use each other as resources. This creates an atmosphere of autonomy and professionalism that keeps nurses satisfied with their jobs.

✔ Delegate initially to those who are assertive or have told you that they want more responsibility. At first it may be truly difficult to delegate, but give up this attitude. Believe that your staff will do a good job. Resist the temptation to meddle in delegated projects. They can do it—remember Pygmalion!

✔ Expect the best from your staff and chances are you will get it.

✔ Remember that working in an environment where autonomy and independence are valued is considered an asset by nurses and assists in nurse retention. Make that the environment where you are the nurse manager. You play a key role in retention!

✔ Staff members should know they can make mistakes and recommend solutions and improvements.

✔ Be professional. Do not denigrate your staff or their work to anyone; it comes back around and does not support an environment conducive to effective team-building.

✔ Remember the concepts of accountability, responsibility, and authority when delegating. Work may not be done the same way you would have done it, but it was completed and you did not have to do it personally.

✔ Offer a choice in the duties needing delegation when possible. This encourages staff growth and autonomy, and helps them develop their interests.

✔ Realize what should not be delegated. This may include HR issues, any confidential issues, delicate political problems with other departments or units, conflicts started by "he said/she said" scenarios, and complaints/communications with physicians or visitors that have risk management implications.

Computerized nursing documentation is becoming more common in health settings as applications for automation in nursing have increased. In some systems, the
nurse can identify those actions or findings appropriate to a specific patient to facilitate the clinical entry. Computerization, particularly at the patient's bedside, assists
in ensuring frequent, timely individualized nursing entries. Computerizing the
record and the nursing notes and other entries may ultimately save hospitals money
and increase the quality of care provided. Studies have shown that nursing costs can
account for 30% to 40% of a hospital's operational budget. It has been estimated
that 2 to 3 hours of a nursing shift are spent performing administrative tasks.[5]
Computer systems available today are integrating the different components of the
chart. For example, once the assessment is completed, an individualized care plan
is developed. From that point, a patient-specific flow chart can be generated, thus
decreasing the documentation process by 40% to 50% per nurse per shift. Kardexes
and other pieces of information can also be developed via the computer system.
Computerizing nursing and other documentation may be the next step in decreasing repetitive and duplicative administrative tasks. The confidentiality, security, and
HIPAA-related issues of information systems are important factors currently being
addressed by systems users and developers. The growing specialty of nursing infor-
matics is one resource available to nurse managers that facilitates the move toward
automation in the work setting.

Detail Management (Or, When You Cannot See the Forest for the Trees)

Undoubtedly, it is easy to be overwhelmed and burdened with details. Minutiae can
leave you exhausted before you even begin your first priority task. Details that
belong to a bigger project should be written down and placed in the folder for that
project. Other details should be judged as to whether they have true value or can be
thrown away.

Delegate the resolution of some of these details back to team members who
brought them to you. As with all duties delegated, provide a specific deadline for
when you want a report on the outcome. An example could be the completion of
meeting minutes that both you and a staff member attended. The staff member can
use your notes to effectively complete the assignment.

SUMMARY

Effective time management results in quality work produced by set deadlines. It also
develops staff initiative and personal growth through effective use of delegation by
the nurse manager. The nurse manager who practices effective time management
skills acts as a role model to both staff and peers. It has been said that, "Misuse of
time seldom involves an isolated incident. It is usually part of a well-established pattern of behavior." These patterns of behavior, or habits, can be changed.[6]

Greater job satisfaction is achieved through work being accomplished; all work entails time management skills. The improvement of these key skills will increase productivity, which in turn reinforces sound habits of time management. The nurse manager sees increased quality of care and improved morale in an atmosphere that fosters staff growth and autonomy. Time management is vital to the successful operation of any health care setting and to the personal health and professional growth of a manager.

QUESTIONS FOR CONSIDERATION

1. Explain why effective time management is the basis for getting all work accomplished.
2. List and explain the 3 *Ps* of procrastination and the way to overcome these barriers to work.
3. Describe the five ways to handle any paper.
4. Identify three technology tools that are available to help better manage time.
5. Define what effective delegation "looks like" in practice.

References

1. *Webster's New World Dictionary of the American Language*, college ed 3, New York, 1997, Simon and Schuster.
2. Olsen E: Beyond positive thinking, *Journal of Nursing Administration* 20(5):11, 1990.
3. Large P: *The micro revolution revisited*, Totowa, NJ, 1984, Rowman & Allenheld.
4. American Hospital Association: *Side-by-side profiles*, Medical records: increasing importance, heavier workload, Chicago, 1990, AHA.
5. Carter K: Computer technology advances will help hospitals to compete, *Modern Healthcare* 15(24):90, 1985.
6. Bliss EC: *Getting things done*, New York, 1978, Bantam Books.

For Further Reading

Covey S: *The 7 habits of highly effective people*, New York, 1990, Simon & Schuster.
Drucker P: *The effective executive*, New York, 1967, Harper & Row Management Library.

Mackenzie A: *The time trap*, New York, 1990, American Management Association Publishing.

CHAPTER 8

RESOURCE MANAGEMENT AND BUDGETING BASICS

LYNDA S. HILLIARD

Health care delivery managers need to intensely scrutinize the relationship between clinical and financial outcomes of care, whether that care is provided in the inpatient, outpatient, or community care setting. This intense analysis is needed to determine the point of intersection between the most clinically proficient method and the most reasonable cost of practice for a preestablished patient population. Not only must the finance department understand these data, but nurse managers also need a thorough understanding of budget and resource management processes to provide more cost-efficient management.

This chapter will explore the basic concepts of financial management for the new nurse manager, with a specific focus on the budget process—capital, personnel, and operations. The inclusion of definitions of commonly used financial or resource management terms will assist the nurse manager to better communicate the needs of the unit or facilitate area requests from the finance office staff, peer managers, or other management team members.

CONTINUOUS QUALITY IMPROVEMENT

Continuous quality improvement (CQI), with a basis in total quality management, consists of principles that have been derived from the business sector and applied to health care objectives. Competition, scarce economic resources, and societal demand for outcome-oriented quality care at a reasonable price are all factors forcing health care administrators to conserve limited resources by streamlining operations, while continuing to provide quality service to their customers. CQI is a process that focuses not only on fixing problems, but also on searching continually for methods to improve and make more cost-effective the delivery of services.[1]

This has provided the impetus for staff members from all segments of the health care environment to meet, prioritize goals, and cross traditional professional boundaries to develop and test methods for better serving their patients' needs and, usually, in a shorter period of time. Examples of quality work improvement teams that address patient customer service or clinical needs are:

- Outpatient service area wait times
- Coordinating care across the health continuum
- Patient/family education
- Patient care delivery models

All of the above quality teams may have staff members from various departments investigate and research the relevant issues and leave their territorial concerns behind as they search for solutions that enhance and improve the delivery of patient care. Patient satisfaction will ultimately be achieved. Also, this continuous review of operations will eventually make the organization more cost-effective—a needed ingredient in the health care arena of the 21st century.

Benchmarking

In order to focus CQI efforts in a health care setting to make the process more efficient, a goal must be established. Sometimes these goals, and the processes leading to them, are difficult for staff to visualize. For example, an attempt to decrease outpatient waiting time from 90 minutes to 5 minutes might seem admirable; however, on closer evaluation, it is too cost-prohibitive and unworkable in the available care environment. Benchmarking allows realistic goal setting because it compares a successful organization's processes and structures to the organization desiring a similar improvement.

Benchmarking can be defined as the structured process of taking practices of the best organizations anywhere in any industry, comparing those practices to your own, and adapting the best of them to your organization. As discussed by James Heidbreder, in *Looking for the Light—Not the Heat*, benchmarking is done ". . . to make a quantum improvement in your process effectiveness or efficiency. Appropriately practiced, benchmarking guards against jumping to quick conclusions or reaching for highly publicized results without understanding the driving forces behind those results."[2] It is important to understand the relationship between the process and the results and not to reach for unrealistic objectives—a clear frustration to staff, and clearly a detriment to the change process.

Data are not always readily available to groups wanting to initiate benchmarking. The health care industry has recognized the benefits of benchmarking after other major American industries have embraced it. The automobile industry, as well as other industries that have been tremendously affected by higher quality, cheaper imports, saw the need for a process to make itself more competitive. In order to identify correct data sources to successfully benchmark specific functions or processes, health care organizations must first understand *who they are, what they want, where they are going*, and *how to gauge when they get there*. It is a process that can be entered into only with commitment from the entire organization. There needs to be an identified need and a desired outcome. Nurse managers may recognize the problem-solving process that is applied to benchmarking: (1) planning; (2) collecting data; (3) analyzing data; and (4) adapting the practices.

CLINICAL PATHWAYS AND PROTOCOLS

An important element of resource management, especially in the health care setting, is the incorporation of practice protocols, case management, and clinical pathways into the care planning of a given patient population. It is important to note that clinical pathways or care protocols have financial implications because they dictate the types and amounts of care given.

In *Home Care and Clinical Paths—Effective Care Planning Across the Continuum*, Marrelli and Hilliard described clinical paths as ". . . clinical tools that organize, sequence, and time the major interventions of the nursing staff, physicians, . . . for a particular case type, condition, diagnostic category, or nursing diagnosis." They also explain that clinical paths ". . . may describe an institution's collective standard of practice, and are, in essence, a clinical 'budget' . . . they provide a direction and predictability to patient care and to the caregivers interacting in that case."[3] The Agency for Healthcare Research and Quality (AHRQ), funded by the Department of Health and Human Services (DHHS), has done a tremendous amount of research in the development of nationally accepted protocols for care of certain disease conditions. These protocols may be used in the development of individual institutional care practices or clinical paths as the foundation for different clinicians from the various health professions to begin the discussion of standardization of the many facets of health care. With increased and improved standardization, outcomes of care can be studied and scrutinized to determine the practices that will best lead to positive outcomes for all parties involved.

As a direct link to the controlling of costs, clinical paths are also integral to improving care processes, since variances gleaned from clinical path implementation should be reviewed and analyzed so improvements can be made to the care process. As explained in *Home Care and Clinical Paths*, clinical paths are not for all patients or conditions and need to be adjusted for complexity and acuity of patients.[3] Paths are a tool in the arsenal of health care providers to standardize, control, and ultimately improve care through scrutiny of measured outcomes. For more information on this subject, please see Chapter 5, Day-to-Day Operations.

DIAGNOSTIC-RELATED GROUPS

Nurse managers must understand the types and complexities of the resources needed to achieve patient care outcomes, and they also must be aware of the fiscal constraints placed on operations for the proper use of limited resources.

Diagnostic-related groups (DRGs) is a classification system that was developed in the 1980s and adapted by the Health Care Financing Administration (HCFA), now called the Centers for Medicare and Medicaid (CMS), to control the cost of health care to its Medicare beneficiaries by assigning a cost per diagnostic category to include all services provided. Because of this, nurse managers must be responsible for developing their area's budget and reducing or maintaining the cost of operations within the approved budget dependent on patient census.

Positive performance evaluations and career progression within the health care setting depend on a manager's fiscal knowledge and performance, as well as clinical expertise.

COST-BASED REIMBURSEMENT—A HISTORIC OVERVIEW

With the advent of the Medicare program in 1967 and prior to the 1980s, hospitals were reimbursed by the federal government on a "cost" basis. Basically, cost-based reimbursement for the Medicare program classified the various costs of operating a health care facility, noted the number of patients served, determined the average cost per patient, and then reimbursed the entity for all Medicare patients.

This generous but inefficient system, combined with the impact of Hill-Burton legislation after World War II (to expand hospitals into smaller communities) and expansion of medical technology and pharmacology, allowed hospitals to grow at a record pace and provide a wide array of very expensive, often duplicative, services without any incentive to economize.

Today, nurse executives, chief executive officers, chief operations officers, and chief financial officers review and analyze daily the financial operations of their institutions. Operational decisions are made quickly to react to adverse conditions (e.g., negative payer mix, low census, or rising staffing costs not related to increased volumes) that may endanger the financial viability of a hospital or other health care entity.

The nurse manager must continually view the patient care area as a viable business and be able to react to financial changes immediately. To do that, the effective nurse manager must understand the complexities and terminology of the fiscal process to be able to react quickly to change. A glossary of financial terms is available for review in Appendix 8-1.

FISCAL MANAGEMENT

Senior managerial staff are responsible to the governing body of a health care entity for the effective management of that organization. Proper financial management is just as important as the provision of quality patient care services. A hospital or other health program cannot survive without a fiscally astute management team. To understand fiscal management, a few basic concepts must be learned.

Fiscal or financial management is derived from basic accounting principles. According to Shillinglaw and Meyer,[4] "Accounting is the primary financial method of gathering, organizing and presenting information that can be utilized by management and outsiders in evaluating an organization." Manager's Tip 8-1 defines some fundamental accounting terms.

As with all professional disciplines, accounting uses methods or measurements that follow prescribed rules to provide standardized analysis when comparing one institution with another.[5]

Hospitals and other health care organizations follow the standards of the JCAHO or other quality entities to prove the quality of their services. Accounting practices are governed by the Financial Accounting Standards Board, which issues statements of financial accounting standards.

NONPROFIT VERSUS PROFIT STATUS

In the health care industry, hospitals historically have been nonprofit institutions, making them tax exempt. In years of efficient operations, hospitals list their excess revenues over expenses as a positive fund balance, or net worth.

In a for-profit business, a positive fund balance would be called profit and divided among stockholders in the form of a dividend, or it would be reinvested in the business. In a nonprofit hospital, excess money should thus be reinvested in the facility and/or in expanding services provided to the community it serves.

CAPITAL EXPANSION OR REINVESTMENT

Prudent business managers realize the need for a business to reinvest in its plant and facilities to maintain viable operations. Generally, health care institutions must

MANAGER'S TIP 8-1

ASSETS, LIABILITIES, AND NET WORTH

The most fundamental accounting maxim is:

Assets = Liabilities + Owner's equity (net worth)

✔ An **asset** is any property (tangible or intangible) that is owned by the institution (e.g., cash, accounts receivable, and property).
✔ A **liability** is a debt that the institution owes to other businesses or individuals, such as accounts payable and mortgages.
✔ **Net worth,** or **owner's equity,** constitutes worth in terms of money that would be divided among the owners if the institution were to go out of business.

realize an annual net gain of at least 5% (based on revenues over expenses) to replace assets as needed.

Many hospitals have historically derived a percentage of income from sources other than operations (e.g., fund-raising and interest or dividends on investments). However, utilizing such money as operating income is not a sound financial practice. The hospital budget should reflect expenses that can be covered by anticipated revenues from operations. It should not count on investment income to cover general expenses of daily operations. The situation is comparable to a family living beyond the earnings of its breadwinners and tapping savings accounts or investment accounts on a consistent basis. In such a case, annual family budgets are developed and include savings account income to cover expenses. After a short time, that source of income is depleted and the family has lost in two ways: (1) those emergency moneys or special project moneys are gone, and (2) the family has built a lifestyle that the annual earnings of the breadwinners cannot support.

PUBLIC PERCEPTION OF HEALTH CARE INSTITUTIONS

During the past decade, national controversy has arisen in the health care community regarding the public perception of hospitals being managed as a business while claiming tax-exempt status. Recent tax rulings by the Internal Revenue Service have pitted revenue-starved communities against major hospitals and medical centers. At stake are large amounts of property tax revenues being waived because of the nonprofit status of health care institutions. The tax-exempt status of such "profitable" institutions, which are perceived by the public as either limiting access or refusing health care to those community members without insurance or the financial resources to pay for their care, is under review.

The historic public view of hospitals as being charitable institutions providing care for all who come to their doors is being transformed into the view of a large, multifaceted corporation or integrated network system whose primary mission is to produce a positive bottom line, as evidenced by intense competition for pay patients. In the future, more institutions will be challenged about their tax-exempt status as local governing agencies examine the financial activities of their community-based health care providers against their mission statement.

Recent headlines outlining the profitability of health maintenance organizations (HMOs) and, specifically, the actual earnings of select senior managers of those plans have aroused the anger and suspicion of many Americans. In many cases, people accurately perceive the amount and quality of health care services as having deteriorated or having the potential to deteriorate under managed care delivery systems. News stories have pointed to anecdotal evidence of the "disasters" of managed care: the newborn sent home with undiagnosed jaundice or the patient whose cancer was overlooked until it was too late. In an effort to counteract what is seen to be unsafe patient care practices dictated by profit concerns, several state legislatures have passed, or are contemplating passage of, legislation that will dictate the types and amounts of care patients will receive while in the care of state-licensed health care facilities.

The successful health care management team will plan with their governing body to effectively recognize and integrate the health care needs of their community into their strategic plan, while conserving resources and maintaining a positive bottom line.

FINANCIAL PERFORMANCE REPORTS

The formal reports that measure a health care entity's financial performance are the *financial statements*, which include the income and expense statements and the balance sheet.

Income and Expense Statement

The income and expense statement lists all the revenues, expenses, and net income or loss for a given period, usually on a monthly or annual basis. Any type of revenue can constitute income (e.g., dividends or interest on investments). In a business, the entity should operate on the income generated from the service it provides. See Fig. 8-1 for a sample income and expense statement.

Balance Sheet

The balance sheet lists an institution's assets, liabilities, and net worth, as of a specific date. All an organization's assets must equal the total of the liabilities and net worth (fund balance) combined. To be in balance, the two totals must equal. Figure 8-2 is an example of a balance sheet.

Seaside Health Systems
Operating Income and Expense Statement
January 1–December 31, 200•
($000)

Gross revenues		$76,000
Deductions	$(25,000)	
Net revenue		$51,000
Operating expenses		
Salary costs	$25,000	
Other	15,000	
Bond expense	4,000	(44,000)
Net Income		$ 7,000

Fig. 8-1 An income and expense statement.

Seaside Health Systems
Balance Sheet
December 31, 200•
($000)

ASSETS

Current assets

Cash		$ 2
Accounts receivable*		6
Inventories		2
Total current assets		$10
Land, plant, and equipment	$20	
Less: accum depreciation	8	12
Total Assets		$22

LIABILITIES AND NET WORTH

Current liabilities

Accounts payable†		$ 4
Notes payable		1
Total current liabilities		$ 5
Bonds payable		3
Total liabilities		$ 8

Net worth

Retained earnings	$14
Total Liabilities and Net Worth	$22

*Accounts receivable is classified as assets because it is the amount of money owed to the hospital for the services already rendered (i.e., insurances billed, but money not yet received).

†Accounts payable is classified a liability because it is a cumulation of all the debts owed vendors for services already rendered to the hospital that will be paid for within the year

Fig. 8-2 A balance sheet.

INSURANCE OVERVIEW

As stated earlier, health care providers are generally paid for their services by third-party payers, as opposed to individual payers or self-pay. The process of indirect payment from individuals for their care has been part of the national debate over the rising costs of health care. In the past, consumers never felt the pinch of high health care costs because their insurance companies paid the bill and their employers paid the cost of the insurance premium.

With the rising cost of employee health care negatively affecting the competitiveness of American products as compared to their foreign counterparts, employers across the country have banded together in business coalitions to demand lower costs, improved quality and customer service, and quantifiable outcomes from their providers of health care services. In addition to the business sector's revolt against the status quo of health care, both federal and state governments are demanding increased access for all people, with less reimbursement available for providers. Health care reform, managed care, and the integration of health care providers into vertical or horizontal networks have all evolved to meet the demands of the buyers of health care services. In this section health care reimbursement models that have been developed to attract and secure contracts to provide beneficiary services are briefly described.

Types of Insurance Plans

Indemnity. Indemnity insurance is an insurance plan that allows members to choose their own health care providers, who are paid on a fee-for-service basis and are not usually controlled through prior authorization or utilization controls. Beneficiaries may have a deductible to meet annually and a co-pay with each encounter.

Fee-for-service benefit plan. Fee-for-service benefits are included in insurance plans that have generally paid for health care services on a full-charge basis. Historically, these plans have imposed few, if any, limitations on health care providers (hospitals, physicians or other providers). Reimbursement has been traditionally based on three factors, as follows:

1. Indemnity fee schedules/predetermined payments per procedure or service
2. Usual, customary, and reasonable fee schedule
3. Relative value units or the assignment of dollar values to a coded listing of services based on complexity of service

The two major categories of fee-for-service plans are as follows:

1. Basic hospitalization (with or without basic medical/surgical coverage)
2. Comprehensive hospitalization and medical/surgical coverage

Deductibles are usually associated with fee-for-service insurance arrangements; they are the amount of medical expenses that the individual must pay before a third-party payer will assume any liability for payment of benefits. The deductible can be either a fixed amount of money or the value of certain services over a given period (e.g., the deductible is equal to the charges for the first day of hospitalization).

As health care costs rose and insurance premiums followed, alternative delivery systems were developed to provide hospital and professional services on other than the charge, or fee-for-service, basis. Examples of alternative delivery systems include:

- Integrated delivery network
- Managed care organization

- Medicare health maintenance organization
- Health maintenance organization (HMO)
- Preferred provider organization (PPO)
- Individual provider arrangement (IPA)

Integrated delivery network. An integrated delivery network is a provider of a continuum of either horizontal or vertical health care services, including one or more acute care hospitals, skilled and intermediate care facilities, outpatient and ambulatory surgery centers, home care agencies, and physicians who either are employees of the group or are managed by utilization protocols, established to competitively negotiate for contracts to provide care to a given beneficiary population.

Managed care organization (plan). A managed care organization provides its beneficiaries with a network of patient care services (e.g., physician, inpatient and outpatient, ambulatory, hospice) for a set, agreed upon payment. This plan utilizes different types of control mechanisms to successfully manage the financial risk of providing health care services (e.g., case management, utilization control, other cost containment measures).

Medicare health maintenance organization (senior risk program). This is an alternative insurance product for Medicare beneficiaries that allows commercial insurers to contract with the CMS to provide similar Medicare-covered services. Providers must have a contract with such insurers to provide beneficiary care. The advantages of such a program are that beneficiaries do not have to submit paperwork for payment, do not have a co-payment or deductible, and may have a richer benefit package. However, beneficiaries are limited in the number of providers they may go to and the number or types of services allowed. Beneficiaries are able to opt in, return to Medicare fee-for-service, and go back on a defined basis.

Health maintenance organization. An HMO is a health care organization that provides comprehensive health service to its enrolled population for a fixed periodic payment.

Capitation is the term used to describe the fixed rate of payment (per member, per month) received by a health care provider on a periodic basis to cover a specified amount of health care services. All HMOs use a capitation rate when budgeting for their service area.

The ability to predict health plan premiums or costs based on the statistical analyses of financial, utilization, and demographic trends in a given area is found in actuarial services.

Preferred provider organization. A PPO is a health services organization of health care providers who have negotiated a special, usually reduced rate to attract insurance plan beneficiaries. Beneficiaries receive better cost coverage by using a contract provider; they can use a noncontracted provider but will be responsible for a co-payment or additional fee-for-service payment.

Individual provider arrangement. An IPA is an organization that contracts with health care providers for the provision of medical services in their own offices for prepaid or managed care plans. One of the first alternative delivery plans was the prepaid plan. This is an insurance plan that offers its enrollees a defined set of benefits provided by a panel of providers within a specified geographic area. Kaiser Permanente was one of the first employers on the West Coast that provided such a plan, starting about 50 years ago.

Managed Care or Discounted Services

All of the above plans have a common denominator—the demand for discounted services. Discounts or deductions from revenue are the contracted amounts deducted from patient care revenues that health care providers must write off. Any or all of the plans may also negotiate a daily rate for the delivery of all health care services or only selected services, regardless of the actual services provided.

For example, a hospital or a home care organization may have a discount arrangement with a local HMO that reimburses 80% of charges for the guarantee of all local enrollees to utilize the contract services. The 20% difference would be deducted from the gross revenue, as well as the actual expense of providing the services. Across the nation, third-party payers are actively negotiating preferential rates with health care providers to try and control health care costs to their beneficiaries.

It is very important for all managers and their staff to understand the concept of discounted services or managed care. Their health care facility may have a multitude of insurance providers demanding discounted services before allowing their enrollees to go to that facility. Each plan may have different preauthorization rules, lengths of stay, and types of service requirements that must be *observed, understood*, and *applied* appropriately to maintain financial viability.

Payer Mix

Payer mix is the distribution, usually expressed as a percentage, of all the sources of reimbursement for a health care provider. A typical example of a payer mix at a small urban hospital in the Northern California area is as follows:

40%	Medicare
17%	MediCal (Medicaid per diem or capitated)
5%	Commercial (100% of total charges paid)
33%	HMO/PPO (discounted contracts and Medicare Senior Risk)
5%	Self-pay/No-pay

As you can see, approximately 95% of anticipated revenues have been or will be discounted—Medicare through the prospective payment system for DRGs; MediCal with a structured rate system per diem or capitated; HMO/PPO through discounted arrangements; and, most probably, write offs for the self-pay/no-pay (usually working individuals without insurance who do not qualify for Medicaid funds).

When charges are revised reflecting the increased cost of providing a service, the average discount is added back in to reflect true costs. In this scenario it is easy to comprehend why charges are rising so fast—to react to the demands for increased discounts from the payers. Staff members and managers need to understand the correlation between the gross charge and the net charge. In some cases, health care facilities may be averaging $0.50 on each dollar of health care revenue because of discount arrangements.

CASE MANAGEMENT

Case management is a term that has developed a variety of meanings over the past few years, dependent on who was defining the term—the insurance carrier, the hospital, the home care organization—and from what perspective. There have been concerted efforts from both individual professionals and the national professional organizations for case managers to agree upon a common definition of case management that would span all patient care sites.

Case management has been defined by the Case Management Society of America (CMSA) ". . . as the collaborative process which assesses, plans, implements, coordinates, monitors and evaluates options and services to meet an individual's health needs through communication and available resources to promote quality cost-effective outcomes."[6]

With the emergence of integrated health care delivery systems, the ideal case management model should shift from the narrowly focused, institution-based one to a more wide-spectrum episode of illness-based, in order to more effectively coordinate patient care. Many health care facilities have enhanced and merged their discharge planning, utilization review, and in some cases social services departments into a more comprehensive case management staff. Those case managers are given the responsibility to plan for and monitor a patient's progress through the health care system, based on the patient's diagnoses, established treatment protocols and clinical paths, and utilization parameters. Working collaboratively with managed care plan representatives, physicians, and other health care professionals, case managers strive to provide the patient with the least disruptive care delivery system, with an efficient use of limited resources, while still striving to meet the assessed needs of the patient, both in the facility and back in the community.

Case management is important in the budget and resource management process within a health care setting. It allows for a reasonably accurate method to predict resource utilization of certain patients with given diagnoses, based on historic data, and it provides a foundation on which to gauge budget adherence when comparing actual expenses to budgeted expenses for certain patient categories.

THE BUDGET PROCESS

A budget is a document that outlines, for a specific period (usually 1 year), the plan an organization has developed for the consumption of resources. It involves the forecasting of revenue-generating activities and the resources used to achieve those goals. Nurse managers are usually involved in the development of three types of budgets:

1. Capital
2. Operating
3. Personnel

There are also different types of budgets, varying according to how they are generated and viewed during the budget cycle. A budget cycle is the period of time that the budget addresses—monthly, yearly, or multiple years. However, in most health care institutions, the budget cycle is on an annual basis following the fiscal year of the institution. Budgeting styles differ as well, as defined in Manager's Tip 8-2.

Capital Budget

A capital budget outlines the forecasted buying of large, fixed assets or types of equipment that depreciate (e.g., furniture, buildings, diagnostic imaging equipment). Usually the finance department will generate a payback analysis before approving the purchase of such budget items to ascertain whether the equipment can generate enough revenue to pay itself off over a given amount of time.

Depreciation is the amount/portion or cost of an asset that can be attributed to a certain operating period.

To meet Medicare regulations, capital budgets are forecasted over a 3-year period. However, they are reviewed and revised annually and as necessary as needs change. Figure 8-3 provides a sample capital acquisition summary.

Most payback analysis and net present value determinations can be generated with finance computer software. However, the nurse manager must supply the number of procedures and cost-related items that are estimated from the new piece of

MANAGER'S TIP 8-2

BUDGETING STYLES

✓ A **fixed budget** is a budget amount that does not fluctuate with volume or staffing levels.
✓ A **flexible budget** is a budget that can be adjusted either up or down depending on the volume of service, which gives a manager a more accurate accounting of the costs incurred during a certain time frame.
✓ **Zero-based budgeting** refers to the process of planning and reviewing operations from the bottom up. It is not just an add-on of a certain percentage each year to account for volume increases or other indicators. The manager must review the expected service, what resources that service will require, and the cost of each of the resources for inclusion on the requested budget.

Seaside Health Systems
Budget Calendar Year 200•
Capital Acquisition Summary
($500.00 or more per item and 3 or more years of useful life)

Dept. priority	Proposed buy date	Item description	Replace/ upgrade	Number needed	Estimated cost of each item	Estimated total cost (including tax)

Attach as much supporting data as possible for each item, along with Capital Budget Form C-1. Return to senior manager for review and approval by September 1, 200•.

_____

Manager Signature   Date

_____

Department Administrator Approval   Date

Fig. 8-3 A capital acquisition summary.

equipment, the amount of patient charge per procedure, and the total expense of operating the equipment. In that way, the finance department staff can determine whether the equipment can pay for itself within a stated period.

Not all capital expenditures should be analyzed on payback analysis or net present value. If equipment is needed for regulatory or safety reasons, those reasons should be documented first and receive a priority rating of #1. However, the above method is a good way to determine the allocation of limited capital money.

Operating Budget

An operating budget describes the day-to-day operational expenses of a unit (excluding personnel costs). These types of costs include, but are not limited to, medical and nonmedical supplies, electricity, small equipment items (usually less than $300 to $500 [i.e., stethoscope or sphygmomanometer]), and outside education expenses.

Ideally, all unit managers should create budgets using the zero-based method, which implies casting out all elements and components of all processes of care to be delivered (e.g., all alcohol swabs, Betadine swabs, and IV tubing needed for budgeted patient care). However, that is not always possible for all budget categories.

For this reason, it is important for the new nurse manager to review all the budget categories used for the past few years and determine appropriateness and continued applicability.

The categories that can be determined as direct costs and to which zero-based budgeting can be applied make the forecast more realistic and sustainable. An example of such a process includes the budgeting for an oncology unit with an estimated 100 admissions over the next 12 months. If the standard protocol called for IV lines for each patient and the lines were to be changed every 24 hours, and the length of stay was averaged at 3 days per patient, the manager could get an approximation of how many tubing lines to order.

$$100 \text{ patients} \times 3 \text{ lines per patient} = 300 \text{ tubing lines}$$
$$300 \text{ lines} \times \$25 \text{ each} = \$7500$$

Zero-based budgeting is very tedious, especially for a unit that uses a tremendous amount of supplies or other budgeted items. However, depending on the amount of time allotted to formulating budgets and the ability to control costs, it should be done at a minimum every few years to determine accuracy and serve as a monitoring system.

Understanding the mechanism of how costs have been applied to a budget and how the cost can be reduced from a budget provides the nurse manager with more fiscal control of the unit. It also makes reporting and understanding variances much easier to learn.

Personnel Budget

Finally, a personnel or full-time equivalent (FTE) budget is the document that forecasts the actual need for unit staff 24 hours per day, 365 days per year. Nursing personnel of FTE budgets differ from those of other hospital or health care setting departments in that, in addition to the estimated number of patient days being forecasted, the nurse manager must estimate the acuity level of the patients to more accurately determine the level, competency, number, and mix of nursing personnel needed to care for those patients.

The definition of an FTE is a personnel standard that allows for measuring and planning the staffing budgets. An FTE is equal to one person working 8 hours a day, 5 days a week, 52 weeks a year (2080 hours). It can be expressed in decimals as 1.0 (full-time) or 0.5 (half-time). An FTE does not necessarily mean one person; it can be two, three, or four workers providing enough hours to represent one person working a full-time shift. Figure 8-4 provides an example of a personnel budget form.

CLASSIFICATION OF COSTS

Costs incurred in the delivery of a service or the making of a product are called total costs and may be either direct or indirect, variable or fixed. A solid understanding

Staff	(Productive and Nonproductive, exclude relief) POSITION SHIFTS									
Position Description	Position Class	AM	PM	NIGHT	200• Total FTE	Annual holiday days accrual	Holiday percent replace	Average sick day usage	Sick percent	
Position Description	Position Class	Vacation FTE	Holiday FTE	Sick FTE		Non-productive FTE				

Fig. 8-4 A personnel budget form.

of the types of costs and how they relate to your unit will allow you to make more appropriate decisions on how to cut costs, determine break-even points, and measure the effectiveness of any action.

A **cost center** is any department or unit of the organization that has been designated as an area that accumulates costs. A nursing unit or area may have more than one cost center. More effective management can be accomplished by segregating costs and analyzing the benefits against the expenses in each center.

Fixed Costs

A fixed cost is a cost that does not change with the level of volume (e.g., the number of patients). Mortgage, loan, and bond payments are examples of fixed costs.

Educ/ orientation days usage	Educ/ orientation percent replace	Non- productive total days				Holiday over- time hours	Annual stand- by hours	Annual call- back hours
Relief FTE	Educ/ orientation FTE	Stand- by FTE	C/B FTE			Productive FTE	Total FTE	FTE Vari Productive STD

Fig. 8-4 cont'd.

Certain departments are considered fixed cost, or overhead, departments, such as health information management or medical records, admitting, the business office, and administration.

Variable Costs

A variable cost is a cost that is associated only with a specific activity (e.g., supply costs). Dressing supplies are considered a variable cost if a patient is being treated for a wound because the amount or type of supply utilized may vary. Variable costs may go either up or down with census shifts and are the first to be analyzed when operations are being reviewed.

Direct Costs

Direct costs can be allocated directly to the making or delivery of an item or service (e.g., nursing care hours in an intensive care unit or supply costs).

Indirect Costs

Those costs associated with the provision of services, but that cannot be directly linked to one specific area or service, are indirect costs. Generally, these costs are spread over the entire organization or areas of the organization based on some approved allocation method (e.g., number of FTEs or square footage of department prorated over total of classification). Some examples of these costs are security, housekeeping, and utilities.

Budgets can be defined as both planning documents and control documents—two methods of ensuring financial viability in this dynamic marketplace. The margin for error is decreasing because reimbursement tightens while the cost of providing services increases daily as a result of new technologies and equipment, as well as higher salary demands by all health care personnel.

THE ROLE OF THE NURSE MANAGER IN THE BUDGET PROCESS

Historically, nurse managers have not been perceived as astute financial managers. Their expertise was in the clinical area, and the expectation was that the finance department administration and management would worry about reimbursing the cost of providing nursing service. But for nurse managers to successfully participate in negotiations between all health care departments vying for decreasing budget moneys, they must speak the same language and understand fiscal processes. Nurse managers must also be able to enter into the budget process without personalizing any budgetary actions. Staff cutbacks are sometimes inevitable solutions to the daily decreases in reimbursement for care. Special programs or increases of staff members must sometimes wait until the financial outlook improves or revenues are generated to pay for those services.

To plan more realistically and effectively, a nurse manager must be organized and consistent during the budget planning process, anticipating all changes that may occur within the budgeted time frame.

Budget Assumptions: Getting Ready to Start

Initially, all departmental objectives and goals must be analyzed to give the nurse manager direction in allocating given resources.

New projects and added or deleted services must be taken into account, along with the ongoing service of the unit. Historic data about estimated patient days or encounters, levels of acuity, or types of patients are also needed to make a more educated budget estimate. Knowledge of equipment needs, physician requests,

MANAGER'S TIP 8-3

QUESTIONS TO ADDRESS
WHEN MAKING BUDGET DECISIONS

✔ Do the benefits justify the costs?
✔ Is the budget consistent with the health system's strategic goals and objectives?
✔ Is the budget reasonable and realistic?
✔ Will the organization be able to support the budget?

and regulatory requirements is also essential for proper budgeting. Manager's Tip 8-3 lists questions for the manager to address when making primary budget decisions.

It is important to note that *budgets as planning and controlling documents are only as reliable as the data that were used in the development of the plan.* Changing requirements, service levels, or charge structures may be revised, and the budget document may not be as relevant as it was when prepared. The nurse manager must be able to discern those changes that occur between development and implementation of the unit budget and reflect those changes once the budget period begins.

Recessionary cutbacks in tax revenues have forced certain state and local governments to reduce health care allocations immediately and across the board to all providers in their jurisdictions (e.g., the 1991 California MediCal cuts and state legislature's inability to pass a budget, thus resulting in the issuing of "warrants," or IOUs, for payment to health providers). Those health care entities with a large percentage of state Medicaid patients risk serious, if not fatal, financial duress if banking institutions refuse to accept the warrants as funds. Plans of action must be in place to meet such demands, including the issuance of loans or the reduction of services to stay financially viable.

The budget approval process is a dynamic function. Completed documents are submitted to higher management to be compiled and included in a larger document. For that reason, all department or service budgets are reviewed in relation to the prioritized needs of the organization.

Based on the organization's needs and financial abilities, a nurse manager may not receive all that has been requested during the budget process and thus must cut some costs from the budget. But the manager must be able to understand and distinguish the unit's core service and needs to more efficiently make the required cuts. Again, it is important that the new nurse manager not personalize any budget cuts because such behavior is counterproductive to successful management. Discussions should be ongoing between the unit managers and their senior management staff during the budget process to address the possibility of such problems.

BUDGETARY INDICATORS

Once settled in your new position as nurse manager with a basic understanding of the fiscal process, set up a financial report filing system that allows you the ability to monitor your unit's activities. Following is a list of financial reports that are used in various organizations:

Unit Reports

Payroll report	Employee earnings and hours worked by pay period classified by type of hour (e.g., education, productive, meeting time, vacation, sick, etc.)
Productivity report	Usually a percentage of total or productive hours worked for a given number of units of service (i.e., patient days as compared to budget)
Budget variance report	A listing of general ledger accounts, with monthly actual costs-to-budget amounts and cumulative year-to-date (CYTD) actual costs-to-budget amounts. Any deviance, whether positive or negative, is called a variance
Supply variance report	A listing by department of all supply costs and associated variances as compared with the budget amounts

All reports should be filed separately in chronologic order with the most recent on top. If your institution produces computerized ledger reports, there are expandable notebooks used to store these documents. These should be stored by fiscal year or fiscal period for easy retrieval and review.

Variances

Variances are the differences between the budgeted amounts and the actual amounts. Usually a negative (–) variance means a positive bottom line. In monitoring variances during periods of higher-than-budgeted volumes (e.g., numbers of patients), the manager must be aware of the forces of flexible versus fixed budgeting techniques. Variances may look askew, but when adjusted for volume, appear right on target.

Review all reports to ensure they are complete and correct; report discrepancies immediately to your supervisor or finance office (per organizational policy). Variances should be analyzed quickly and discussed with your supervisor. Abnormal or negative trends are insidious in nature, and you must closely oversee this aspect of your operations to analyze such occurrences and develop plans of action to correct identified negative trends.

Productivity and Variance Reporting

For an example of a productivity report showing a personnel usage variance, see Fig. 8-5. Different job classifications, as well as their corresponding productivity standards, are noted in the first two columns. The actual versus budgeted units of service for that pay period are noted in the third through the sixth columns. A negative number in the variance column notes less-than-anticipated units of service. The productive and nonproductive FTE blocks show the actual versus the budgeted amounts of personnel. However, these are fixed-budget figures and do not reflect the FTEs used as compared with the actual units of service.

In the total FTE block is a flexible budget figure. That figure determines the number of FTEs available based on the actual units of service. In other words, if your unit had budgeted 4 FTEs for 16 hours of service and only 12 hours of service were given, only 12 hours should have been used. If, in the above scenario, you had used only 3 FTEs, the productivity rating would have been 100%. If you used the full 4 FTEs (as your budget states), your productivity would be only 75%.

The two blocks in Figure 8-5 for productive and total hours per unit of service actually address the productivity standard used for your department. In the case of the ICU, the productive standard for ICU days would be 16.109 hours per day; the total standard would be 17.688 hours per day.

The salary variance of $3115 denotes a loss of $3115 during that pay period resulting from overstaffing the ICU by approximately 13% to 15%. The $3115 is an average amount of dollars for personnel costs across the board in the hospital. It is used as a guide to denote in dollar amounts the loss the hospital incurs from staffing overages. The positive amounts, such as are noted in the laboratory and pulmonary function columns, show the amount of moneys saved by increasing or decreasing staff.

Monitoring figures pay period by pay period allows the manager to review operations and identify negative trends. However, because of dramatic census shifts, labor contracts, and holiday and sick coverage, the manager must also look at the productivity rating over a longer period—either month to month or on a quarterly basis.

Ask Questions

Once you organize all the reports you have received to monitor the operations of your unit, set up a meeting with your fiscal representative. Ask questions and clarify statements or accounts at that time. Be clear as to the purpose of each report and what the data can tell you about the operations of your unit or area.

Productivity Measurement

Once approval has been given to the unit budget, the nurse manager must be able to abide by the financial constraints of that budget while still providing quality patient care services.

Productivity has been measured in many industries, and standards have been developed that enable a manager to quantify the effectiveness of any staff. For a long time, the production of only goods, not services, was felt to warrant productivity measure-

Seaside Hospital
Productivity Report PPE: 6/20/0•

Unit of Service						Productive FTE				Nonproductive FTE			Total FTEs	
Dept	Desc	Act	Bud	Var	Var%	Act	Bud	Var	Staff Var	Act	Bud	Var	Act	Fixed Budget
ICU	ICU DAYS	54	63	(9)	−15%	11.3	12.8	1.4	11%	2.4	1.3	−1.2	13.7	14.0
M/S	M/S DAYS	267	282	(15)	−5%	25.7	28.0	2.2	8%	3.9	3.1	−0.8	29.6	31.1
ER	ER VISITS	807	716	91	13%	14.0	13.3	−0.6	−5%	2.4	1.1	−1.3	16.4	14.4
OR	OR MINS	13,310	11,363	1947	17%	14.7	11.6	−3.1	−26%	2.5	1.4	−1.1	17.2	13.0
NSG ADM	ADJ PD	813	895	(81)	−9%	6.7	5.5	−1.2	−22%	0.4	0.9	0.5	7.1	6.4
Home Health	H.H. VISITS	444	577	(133)	−23%	14.2	15.7	1.6	10%	0.7	2.0	1.3	14.8	17.7
Lab	TESTS	8119	7898	221	3%	13.7	13.2	−0.5	−4%	1.6	1.9	0.3	15.3	15.0
Pulm Func.	CAP UNITS	9023	9750	(727)	−7%	1.0	1.4	0.4	29%	0.1	0.1	0.0	1.1	1.5
Medical Records	ADJUSTED PT DAYS	813	895	(81)	−9%	7.1	6.1	−0.9	−15%	0.4	0.8	0.4	7.5	6.9

Fig. 8-5 A productivity report.

ments. The introduction of time-and-motion engineers into patient care units was not accepted well by staff members. The staff felt that nursing care could not be measured and that any constraint would be detrimental to the quality of the service delivered.

But economic survival forced productivity standards into the forefront of operational management techniques in health care settings. All activities of patient care were thoroughly examined and dissected to determine the amount or consumption of labor hours needed to provide those services. The averages of all those hours were compiled to develop a patient care standard.

Total FTEs		Productive Hours/Unit of Service				Total Hours/Unit of Service					
Flex	Flex	Act	Bud	Var	Var%	Act	Bud	Var	Var	Salary	Pro%
Budget	Var								%	Var	
11.9	−1.8	16.755	16.109	−0.646	−4%	20.310	17.688	−2.622	−15%	($3115)	87%
29.5	−0.2	7.707	7.939	0.0232	3%	8.877	8.831	−0.046	−1%	($221)	99%
16.3	−0.1	1.387	1.490	0.104	7%	1.621	1.613	−0.008	−1%	($116)	99%
15.3	−1.9	0.088	0.082	−0.006	−8%	0.103	0.092	−0.012	−13%	($4357)	89%
5.8	−1.3	0.661	0.493	−0.168	−34%	0.696	0.572	−0.124	−22%	($2527)	82%
13.6	−1.2	2.551	2.179	−0.372	−17%	2.675	2.454	−0.220	−9%	($1663)	92%
15.4	0.1	0.135	0.133	−0.002	−1%	0.151	0.152	0.001	1%	$199	101%
1.4	0.31	0.009	0.012	0.003	27%	0.010	0.013	0.003	23%	$445	130%
6.3	−1.2	0.695	0.549	−0.146	−27%	0.734	0.618	−0.116	−19%	($1323)	84%

Fig. 8-5 cont'd.

PRODUCTIVITY RATINGS

Productivity rating is measured as a percentage:

$$\text{Standard} \div \text{actual} = \underline{\hspace{2cm}} \%$$

For example, if the standard for a home care nurse is 2 hours per visit, and the payroll records reflect that the average time spent per visit over a given time frame was 2.5 hours, the rating would be 80%. The usual variance is ±5%.

If the standard was 2 hours per visit and the nurse averaged 1.5 hours per visit, the rating would be 133%. That is a positive variance and reflects an overall savings to the home health agency.

FINANCIAL STANDARDS

There are many types of standards: national, industrial, local, and institutional. A standard is developed for use in a manager's facility, and the forecasting, budgeting, and actual review of operations must be consistent with the productivity standard that was designed to monitor the work of that individual department.

If a manager wants to develop a departmental standard, the following criteria need to be examined and then calculated into an amount of time per patient care service. First, a standard of quality must be agreed on for a given service, and then the average amount of time necessary to complete that service would constitute the production standard. Various methods can be used to gain that information: (1) an actual time-and-motion study, (2) an average formulated over a given period for the same type of services, (3) historic data, (4) benchmarking data from a similarly focused and sized facility, or (5) an educated guess if there are no data available.

BREAK-EVEN ANALYSIS

In learning how to be efficient in the management of your unit, you must develop the ability to determine a break-even analysis. Generally, all services or products offered by a business should be able to show a profit or should at least break even on costs.

However, breaking even is not possible in some health care situations, and the decision must be made whether to keep such services and balance their costs with other services. An example of such a costly service would be a trauma center or emergency service. Because of the specialized and expensive staff and equipment required to maintain the legal status of a trauma center on a 24-hour, 7-days-per-week basis, most facilities do not break even on this service. Most of the patients do not have sufficient insurance to cover all expenses, if they have insurance at all. However, it is a needed and vital service to the community.

Calculating Break-Even Points

The point at which the revenues equal the expenses is called the break-even point. A quick method to determine the break-even point is to divide the fixed cost of a service by the contribution margin per unit of service (see the definition of contribution margin on the next page). Break-even analysis is very important in health care facilities because hospital buildings generally have very high fixed costs.

Budgetary Example in a Home Health Agency

For example, in a home health agency, the following information is given:

Monthly fixed costs:	$10,000
Revenue per visit:	$100
Direct cost per visit:	$50
Contribution margin per visit	$50

Contribution margin = (Revenue per visit − Direct cost per visit)

The break-even point (or the point at which the next unit of service's contribution margin is considered profit) would be:

$$\$10,000 \div \$50 = 200 \text{ visits}$$

Contribution margin. The contribution margin is the amount of revenue left after the direct costs of providing the service are subtracted.

For example, the direct salary cost of a home health visit is $45 per visit, and the supply cost is $5, whereas the charge to the patient or payer is $100 per visit:

$$\text{Direct cost: } \$45 + \$5 = \$50$$

The contribution margin would be the difference between the revenue and the direct cost, or:

$$\$100 - \$50 = \$50$$

The contribution margin ($50) is then applied to the indirect, overhead, or administrative costs of doing business.

FUTURE TRENDS

As the health care industry continues its reforms and integrates CQI and fiscal responsibility into its case management structure, patient outcomes should improve and become more predictable.

Large employers, such as companies in the automobile industry, point out that they pay more than $500 of the revenue generated per new car for health care benefits for their employees. Just as consumers demand quality products off the automobile assembly line, health care consumers are demanding a standardized set of services that offers comparable outcomes.

This is a new concept to health providers—the argument has always been that health care is not quantifiable, as is the manufacturing sector of the economy. However, studies are showing that a wide divergence in standard practices for the same set of diagnoses or symptoms exists all across the country.

Large Business Groups on Health (LBGH, a lobbying group for business entities) is collecting and disseminating data on local hospitals and physician providers to the community denoting positive and adverse trends of service. LBGH is demanding that health care providers take a proactive stance for cost-effective, quality health care.

Once standards are clearly defined and routinely monitored, incentive systems can be put into place to reward those employees who use the best quality indicators, CQ/CQI, and patient satisfaction to turn their health care organization into a well-managed and effective organization.

Outcomes Management

Along with the demand for improved quality and decreased costs, health care buyers are demanding the quantification of what is being done to and for patients. They want to be able to compare patient care between similar settings to determine if the services are cost-effective. In the past, treatment varied with each practitioner and each setting in which it was delivered. However, with increased focus on patient satisfaction and the continual improvement of care processes, a need for the quantification of the results of such care arose.

Paul Ellwood, a leading futurist in outcomes management, described this emerging phenomenon as ". . . the technology of patient experiences designed to help patients, payers, and providers make more rational medical care–related choices based on better insight into the effect of these choices on the patient's life."[7] Outcomes research has proceeded in earnest in all patient care settings, especially in acute care hospitals.

Outcomes measurement is the ability to measure the progression of a patient from one point in time to another. In the past the traditional definition of outcomes included cost, mortality, and morbidity—data collected by the Health Care Financing Administration (HCFA), now the CMS. There are many different methods to quantify outcomes; however, the most common areas to measure are:

- Clinical (traditional medical outcomes)
- Functional (both physical and social functioning)
- Well-being (mental/emotional health—pain, energy)
- Satisfaction with care
- Cost (what the patient and the system can/will bear)

Patients must be quantifiably assessed before the beginning of the movement across a care or protocol regimen in order to validate progress. In order for the data to be valid and reliable, it is imperative that commonalties in care or protocols are established and well-documented so that variances can be noted and reviewed and systems revised to provide a more positive care outcome. The aligning of patient processes, related outcomes, and cost of care will provide valid budgetary guidelines, both for a broad universal basis for health care and for specific, area-based budget planning in a local health care setting.

SUMMARY

Health care finance is a complex and demanding field, and nurse managers are an essential link in maintaining cost-effective, quality-oriented care. By understanding the role of cost accounting in the planning, delivery, and evaluation of care, the nurse manager can provide the best advocacy for patient care services in health care.

Financial managers are usually trained in the accounting or finance fields and usually do not have the education or expertise to make patient care decisions that involve cutbacks or reductions in services. Their focus is on improving the hospital's bottom line and providing sound financial decisions.

Nurses with business acumen and finance knowledge blend the best of both worlds and provide the most equitable perception of the budgeting process. Always be aware of the forces that are affecting the delivery of your patient care and be able to adapt to new and challenging situations.

QUESTIONS FOR CONSIDERATION

1. Define the role of benchmarking and a possible example of its use, in relation to quality.
2. List four types of insurance plans that pay patient claims.
3. Describe why knowing your payer mix is important.
4. List and describe three budgeting styles used in health care.
5. Describe the important role of the nurse manager in the budgetary process at a health care organization.

References

1. Scholtes PR, et al: *The team handbook*, Madison, WI, 1989, Jointer Associates.
2. Heidbreder J: Looking for the light—not the heat, *Healthcare Forum Journal,* January/February 1993, p. 26.
3. Marrelli TM, Hilliard LS: *Home care and clinical paths: effective care planning across the continuum*, St Louis, 1995, Mosby.
4. Shillinglaw G, Meyer E: *Accounting: a management approach*, ed 7, Homewood, IL, 1983, Richard D Irwin.
5. Anthony N, Reece J: *Accounting texts and cases*, ed 7, Homewood, IL, 1983, Richard D Irwin.
6. Case Management Society of America: *Standards of practice*, Little Rock, AR, 1995, CMSA.
7. Ellwood PM: Outcomes management: a technology of experience, *New England Journal of Medicine* 318(23):1549, 1988.

For Further Reading

Felteau A: Budget variance analysis and justification, *Nursing Management* 23(2):40, 1992.
Loevinsohn HT: A new perspective on scheduling: freedom and cost control, *Nursing Management* 23(7):56, 1992.
Marrelli TM, Hilliard LS: *Home care and clinical paths: effective care planning across the continuum*, St Louis, 1995, Mosby.
Murray JA: Benchmarking: a tool for excellence in palliative care, *Journal of Palliative Care* 8(4):1992.
Shikiar MS, Warner P: Selecting financial indices to measure critical path outcomes, *Nursing Management* 25(9):58, 1994.
Tzirides E, Waterstraat V, Chamberlin W: Managing the budget with a fluctuating census, *Nursing Management* 22(3):80B, 1991.
Wilburn D: Budget response to volume variability, *Nursing Management* 23(2):42, 1992.

GLOSSARY OF FINANCIAL TERMS

The following is a list of key financial terms that can be very helpful to you while learning your way as a nurse manager.

Accounting The process of identifying and measuring an economic variable. Managerial accounting refers to the information that is prepared to assist managers in making decisions on how to use limited resources effectively and efficiently.

Acuity level A measured level that describes the severity of illness in patients by a weighted statistical method. Usually most acuity systems have four classifications of patients that describe the amount of time a nurse spends daily with each type of patient (i.e., ICU patients may have an acuity level of 4, denoting 1:1 RN:patient ratio). It was calculated using formulas that measured nursing functions in terms of actual time.

Adjusted average per capita cost (AAPCC) An estimate of the total payment for services a managed care payer would make for a unique category of services divided by the number of beneficiaries eligible for the services. This estimate is usually used in negotiating capitated agreements.

Aligned To be in accord with another similar management project or endeavor; working toward the same goal.

Arbitration A process of dispute resolution, principally employed by labor unions as a tactic to resolve a member's dispute with management, or a process to resolve perceived employee-related discrimination or termination.

Autocratic A style of management that does not allow others to make decisions and utilizes a rigid, structured style of leadership that does not include the input of others—a negative leadership style.

Bargaining unit A union group that is represented as a unified entity, usually made up of individuals who have related job titles or technical occupations within an organization.

Burnout The point at which an individual, usually a manager, becomes overstressed and ineffective in her/his job; can also describe work group or organization.

Buy-out Financial takeover of a health care organization or unit within an organization by a larger or financially more prosperous entity; also the termination of an established employment contract.

Capitated risk The financial risk involved in not being able to accurately estimate the cost of and appropriately contract for care or services to a capitated population.

Capitation A set dollar amount established to cover the cost of health care services delivered to an individual. The amount is based on the number of members in the plan, not the amount of services used.

Capitation management The process of gathering as much information on the population to be capitated and understanding the key characteristics of that population in order to manage the financial risk involved in providing care or services.

Card-signing Activity in which a union asks nonunion health care employees to sign cards requesting an organization-wide election that might vote a union into existence.

Certificate of need (CON) Document provided by a state governing body to a health care institution at the institution's request that allows the institution to build additional physical facilities or provide services to handle more customers.

Chain of command Term that reflects the lines of report and power structure within the health care organization, thus clarifying who reports to whom.

Chief executive officer (CEO) The main administrator of a hospital or health care organization; usually indicates that the administrator is also a member of the governing body.

Chief financial officer (CFO) A second-tier executive with comprehensive control of the financial systems; has responsibility for financial stability and compliance efforts.

Chief medical officer (CMO) A senior physician manager, usually reporting to the CEO of a health care organization with responsibilities over the medical functions and medical staff of the organization.

Chief nursing officer (CNO) A senior nurse executive (NE) who reports to the CEO with overall responsibility for the nursing services provided in the health care organization.

Chief operations officer (COO) Individual responsible for all critical operational facets of a health care organization; reports to the CEO.

Cost-based reimbursement Reimbursement to health care providers based on the aggregation of allowable costs, up to a certain limit (e.g., cost caps). This system of reimbursement was originally established for Medicare program providers and is quickly disappearing with the advent of capitation and managed care.

Cost control Management approach that encourages the insightful utilization of financial resources in the interest of getting maximum benefit from each dollar spent and effectively maintaining fiscal responsibility and budgetary integrity.

Cost shifting The act of increasing rates to one segment of the patient population to offset losses incurred by another segment, such as Medicaid or indigent patients.

Depreciation Erosion, over time, of the quality and effectiveness of certain resources within a health care institution, and the resultant financial practice of incorporating this erosion into fiscal and tax considerations.

Gross revenue/income The total amount charged for a service.

Hours per patient day (HPPD) The number of nursing care hours provided per patient per 24-hour day.

Liabilities The financial obligations of the hospital or other health care organization (i.e., accounts payable or loan amounts).

Medicaid program A state health insurance program for those individuals meeting certain financial guidelines that is supported by the federal government in association with funds from a given state. The programs and their coverage vary from state to state.

Medicare program The federally funded health insurance program for those individuals over the age of 65 or disabled. It was started in 1965 and totally revolutionized the delivery of health care in the United States. It initially reimbursed hospitals and other health care providers on a cost-based system. The health care system then experienced rapid growth because there were no incentives built into the program to conserve or properly use resources.

The Medicare program is undergoing extensive scrutiny and revision to meet the growing needs of the burgeoning older population. Most programs are now paid on a prospective payment system (PPS).

Net income The difference between the gross revenue and what remains after all expenses have been deducted.

Nonproductive hours Paid hours that are not associated with the provision of care or service (i.e., vacation, sick, and education leave).

Outliers Cases in which a patient's length of stay exceeds the national average by 20 days or a 1.94 % standard deviation, or in which the cost of treatment exceeds the national average diagnostic-related group rate by $12,000 or 150%, whichever is greater.

Patient classification system A system to classify patients using different criteria sets. The goal of the patient classification system is to allocate nursing personnel to specific units (i.e., staffing matrix).

Productive hours Paid hours that are associated with provision of care or service, including regular time, overtime, and holiday time.

Prospective payment system (PPS) The third party payment system that establishes certain payment rates for services regardless of the actual cost of care provided. The Medicare diagnostic-related group system for inpatient acute care services is the most widely known example of this type of payment. The prospective payment system was established in 1981 under the Tax Equity and Fiscal Responsibility Act (TEFRA).

Relative value units (RVUs) A numerical value that has been coded to reflect the relative complexity of a given service, such as time, skill, and overhead costs for a certain procedure. Many third-party payers attach a dollar value to these units in calculating reimbursement rates. An example of a service measured in RVUs is rehabilitation services (physical therapy).

Risk pool An incentive pool of moneys, over and above the direct payment made to a service provider, that is distributed to a determined number of providers if certain predetermined financial outcomes are met.

Staffing mix The type and ratio of professional personnel (RNs) to other patient care personnel. This mix varies from hospital to hospital and is gaining in popularity as the need to decrease personnel costs becomes more evident.

Nurse extenders or licensed vocational/practical nurses in tandem with an RN are two examples of using a varied staffing mix.

Subcapitation A subset of capitated moneys set aside for a particular group of services (e.g., home care services under a hospital-controlled plan or home medical equipment as a subcapitator to a home care organization).

CHAPTER 9

LEGAL ISSUES AND RISK MANAGEMENT

ELIZABETH E. HOGUE

This chapter focuses on significant legal issues. Discussion of legal issues in nursing management could fill *several* books, and it is often difficult for the new nurse manager to know where to focus attention in terms of legal issues. In addition, the new manager's difficulty in discerning significant legal issues may be further complicated by the staff's initial tendency to raise numerous questions or concerns about legal issues. In the absence of effective management, staff members may seek structure and stability in their work environment through the law. Once effective nursing leadership is in place, the tendency to see everything as a legal issue will disappear. Understanding the legal aspects of supervision can help the nurse manager provide such leadership and allay staff members' concerns.

LEGAL ASPECTS OF SUPERVISION

Nurses are generally responsible for the acts and omissions of all of the practitioners whom they supervise. Their liability is based on legal theory called *respondeat superior*, which literally means "let the master say." The theory is that because supervisors control what practitioners do, they are therefore legally responsible for their errors.

The only exception to this rule occurs when, despite appropriate supervision, practitioners take it upon themselves to do something that is entirely outside the scope of their job functions. A classic example of this conduct involves nurses who voluntarily provide care to patients in their homes after they have been discharged from the hospital, facility, or home health agency. As long as management is able to demonstrate that a policy was established that prohibited this conduct, liability for injuries to patients during such "detours" may rest solely with the practitioners.

Questions of appropriate delegation of allowable functions to certain types of practitioners are controlled almost exclusively by state laws. That is, state licensure statutes govern which functions related to patient care may be delegated to certain types of practitioners. Nurse managers must thoroughly understand these statutes in the states in which their organization provides services in order to ensure that functions are properly delegated. Any questions or areas of uncertainty should be referred to the appropriate state licensure boards for written clarification.

Many nurse managers are understandably concerned about the scope of their responsibilities for everyone who falls within their chain of command. They certainly cannot provide direct supervision to each practitioner whom they supervise on a daily basis. This valid concern serves to reinforce the importance of hiring and retaining practitioners who provide care to patients in an appropriate manner. It also underscores the need to take prompt disciplinary action with regard to practitioners who do not meet established standards.

Even though every practitioner's actions cannot be supervised directly, significant legal issues exist that always merit the attention of competent nurse managers. New managers should immediately focus their attention on these issues and continuously monitor developments in the following areas:
- Negligence
- Consent to treatment, including the patient's right to refuse treatment
- Employment issues

NEGLIGENCE

Health care providers often equate negligence with something going wrong. In fact, there are risks associated with treatment. Just because something goes wrong does not mean that any legal liability exists. Rather, there are four components that every patient must be able to prove were involved to show that nurses were negligent:
1. Duty
2. Breach
3. Causation
4. Injury

All four of these components must be involved to prove negligence. If patients fail to prove even one of these elements, they lose their cases. Thus these elements can serve as a checklist for the new nurse manager to use to manage risks and evaluate the likelihood of legal liability. If she/he can defeat even one of the components, no legal liability exists.

A determination that there is no legal liability is certainly not all that should concern the nurse manager. Managers may have significant ethical, quality assurance, employment, and licensure concerns that should be pursued even when no legal liability exists. However, it is helpful to eliminate concerns about legal liability even when other serious considerations require resolution.

It is also important to remember that involvement of these elements constitutes the definition of negligence that is actually used by the courts. That is, when courts attempt to determine whether providers are negligent, they consider these elements in relation to each case to determine liability. This is true regardless of the state in which nurses provide care. The definition of negligence in New York is the same as in California. The legal definitions of duty, breach, causation, and injury are discussed below.

Duty

Duty is the obligation owed by providers to their patients. Thus the existence of a provider-patient relationship is a prerequisite to liability.

The duty owed by nurses to their patients is a duty of reasonable care. Of course, the key question then becomes: What is reasonable? The law says that what is reasonable is what other reasonably prudent nurses do under the same or similar circumstances. Nurses know what other nurses do by examining standards of care. Standards of care define nurses' duties to their patients. Sources of such standards of care are listed in Box 9-1.

The Importance of Policies and Procedures

Policies and procedures constitute perhaps the most important source for standards of care. Developing appropriate standards of care through policies and procedures is certainly a double-edged sword for nurse managers. Although it provides an opportunity to establish standards that are appropriate for institutions and staff members, the law requires strict adherence to these standards once they have been developed.

In addition, developing policies and procedures is an exceptionally tedious task for several reasons. First, some nurses believe that policies and procedures should cover every possible contingency associated with the policy subject. Nurses who share this belief want such policies so that they feel they have clear guidance. Other nurses, however, believe that policies and procedures should provide only broad guidance, within which nurses should exercise appropriate professional judgment.

---

box 9-1

SOURCES OF STANDARDS OF CARE

- The employer's internal policies and procedures
- Court decisions
- Standards of professional nursing organizations such as the American Nurses Association (ANA) and the National League for Nursing (NLN)
- State licensure statutes
- Requirements of third-party payers
- Standards of accreditation organizations such as the Joint Commission on the Accreditation of Healthcare Organizations (JCAHO)

Obviously, finding a balance between these two competing goals is necessary. Policies that are too detailed often prove useless because staff members do not have the time or inclination to read through volumes to understand procedure. Conversely, promoting clarity of expectations of staff members is one of the basic tenets of effective nursing management.

Developing standards of care through policies and procedures is further complicated by the sheer number of individuals and committees that typically review a new or revised policy or procedure. Often, what goes into the process bears little resemblance to the final result.

Despite these obstacles, nurse managers must persist in developing and maintaining appropriate policies and procedures. A key to success is to avoid thinking that this process is ever complete. Nursing policies and procedures should be under almost constant review and scrutiny; they are not static. Rather, they change often because of experience, judgment, and new clinical developments. Manager's Tip 9-1 presents five key steps for developing policies and procedures as a means of risk management. If nurse managers follow these steps, they will have greater assurance that they appropriately manage risk by careful definition of duty in terms of policies and procedures.

Breach

Nurses may breach their duty to patients by doing something they should not do, which is commonly referred to as an *act*. They may also fail to do something that they should do, which is often referred to as an *omission*. In many malpractice cases, patients are able to prove that providers committed more than one act or omission. Yet, they *need* prove only *one* act or omission to prove a breach.

For example, in one recent court case, a man was brought to the emergency department with a chest wound. He was evaluated to see if he needed a thoracic surgeon. It was determined that he did not have such a need. He was reevaluated

MANAGER'S TIP 9-1

KEY STEPS TO MANAGING RISK
THROUGH POLICIES AND PROCEDURES

- ✔ Review policies and procedures at least annually.
- ✔ Involve different staff members in reviewing policies and procedures so that various points of view are obtained and the staff has an opportunity to review standards of care.
- ✔ Make needed changes promptly.
- ✔ Ensure that all staff members are informed of changes in policies and procedures.
- ✔ Ensure that all new staff members read and understand the policies and procedures.

an hour later, and it was determined that he, indeed, needed a thoracic surgeon. The surgeon was called but did not arrive for more than an hour. On the surgeon's arrival, the patient was rushed into the operating room, where he died. The family sued, claiming that if the surgeon had arrived earlier, the patient would not have died. During the course of discovery, the attorney for the patient's family found an emergency department policy that stated that if the thoracic surgeon was called and did not arrive within 30 minutes, the patient must be transferred to another hospital. The family won this case because the nursing staff breached its duty as established in emergency department policies and procedures.

Causation

A patient must show that the act or omission of the nurse caused injury or damage. The best way to define causation is in terms of "but for." That is, but for the action or inaction of the provider, the patient would not have been injured. Another way to consider causation is in terms of what courts call "foreseeability." That is if providers should have foreseen that their act(s) or omission(s) would cause injury or damage to a patient, the injury was foreseeable and therefore caused by providers. Conversely, if providers could not have foreseen that their act(s) or omission(s) would cause injury or damage to a patient, the injury was not foreseeable and therefore was not caused by providers.

Time is certainly a consideration with this requirement. For example, when a patient who is released from a mental health institution causes injury or damage to an individual after release, it is tempting to find a causal connection between the patient's release and the injuries sustained. Nurses recognize, however, that an individual's mental status may change very rapidly. Therefore no causal connection may exist whatsoever between release and the injuries.

Nurses sometimes ask how long a period must elapse before causation is no longer a concern. This period varies depending on the circumstances of individual cases. Providing specific rules is thus impossible. A good general rule is that the longer the period between the providers' action or inaction and the occurrence of the injury, the less likely that providers will be held liable.

Injury

To be held liable, nurses must injure or damage their patients. Most of the time the courts insist on a physical injury to establish liability. Courts require proof of physical injury for several reasons. First, if the alleged injury is not physical, patients may be faking their injuries. Courts have evidentiary requirements that must be met to prove injury. If the claimed injury is mental or emotional in nature, it is almost impossible to prove. Second, the courts recognize that a certain amount of irritation and inconvenience simply accompany being alive. It is not the job of the courts to address all of these inconsequential irritations and inconveniences. Rather, individuals are generally required to accept life's daily aggravations that are relatively insignificant. Unless patients can show a physical injury, their complaints may fall into the category of mere irritation and inconveniences, not legal liability. Finally, judges are increasingly distressed about their overcrowded dockets. In many jurisdictions there are so many cases pending that it takes several years for a civil, noncriminal case to come to trial. Courts recognize that caseloads will increase many times over if they start considering cases involving claims for emotional injuries only. They therefore normally insist the claimant have a physically injury before they will find providers liable.

Extreme and outrageous behavior. The one exception to this general rule occurs when the behavior of providers is what the courts call "extreme and outrageous." Extreme and outrageous behavior is outside of the acceptable bounds of civilized behavior. Extreme and outrageous conduct is illustrated by the case in which a woman was in the delivery room about to deliver a baby. Her husband was with her at her head. She died precipitously. The father rushed around to his deceased wife's side and put his hand on her abdomen. He could feel the infant still moving. He turned to the delivery room staff and asked them to perform an emergency cesarean section to save the life of the infant. The staff refused. He stood in the delivery room, begging and pleading with the staff, until the infant died.

In this case, there may have been liability for the death of the mother. Certainly there was liability for the death of the infant. But the court also acknowledged liability directly related to the father, even though his injuries were emotional only. The court did not require a physical injury because it was clear that the father was not faking emotional injury in view of the circumstances. The court was also certain that the father's injuries amounted to more than mere irritation and inconvenience. Finally, even though court dockets are crowded, the courts are extremely interested in hearing this type of case because of the egregious conduct of the providers.

Thus unless physical injury exists or extreme and outrageous conduct on the part of providers occurs, there is no legal liability. The focus of appropriate risk management is therefore on avoiding injuring patients. Good risk management truly amounts to damage control.

Nurst managers continually struggle to avoid certain common types of liability for negligence. They must work hard to control risk related to the types of negligence outlined in Manager's Tip 9-2.

Negligent Premature Discharge

Negligent premature discharge, a relatively new area of potential liability for negligence, merits special attention. Concerns about negligent premature discharge are directly related to changes in the activities of third-party payers. Third-party payers now command the authority of providers with their assumed decision-making authority regarding patient care. Whereas providers previously made decisions regarding patient care, payers are now the gatekeepers to the health care delivery

MANAGER'S TIP 9-2

FIVE COMMON TYPES OF NEGLIGENCE

✔ Failure to properly monitor and observe patients.
✔ Improper diagnosis, particularly meningitis in pediatric patients and myocardial infarctions.
✔ Falls.
✔ Foreign objects left in patients during surgery.
✔ Negligent premature discharge.

system. In view of this change, providers have begun to question why they may be held liable for the results of payment decisions of payers.

In response, payers argue that they do not write orders, including discharge orders. Providers are free to render as much care as they determine patients need. Payers are saying only that they will not pay for such care. Further, payers argue that, in many instances, they are simply enforcing a contract of insurance. Once benefits required by the contract have been provided, they are under no obligation to pay for additional care, regardless of the clinical condition of patients.

Providers, however, recognize the reality of the health care delivery system today, which is that payment decisions are, in essence, treatment decisions. Courts are considering the question raised by this reality to determine if payers should be held responsible for the injuries or damages that result from payers' adverse payment decisions. To date, three court decisions have addressed this issue.

Wickline Versus the State of California. In the 1986 case of *Wickline Versus the State of California,*[1] Mrs. Wickline had vascular disease. She had surgery, followed by a complicated recovery. Her physician wanted to keep her in the hospital to observe her for further complications. The Medicaid program, however, determined that no further payments would be made for acute care.

Mrs. Wickline's physician asked the Medicaid program for an additional extension of payment for acute care. Specifically, he asked the Medicaid program to pay for 8 additional days of care. Medicaid agreed to pay for 4 additional days.

At the end of the 4 days, the physician took no further action, and Mrs. Wickline went home. She developed further complications that ultimately resulted in the amputation of one of her legs. She then sued the Medicaid program. She claimed that the program had a duty to her to make payment for needed care that was breached when payment was refused for additional acute care. Medicaid's adverse payment decision, claimed Mrs. Wickline, caused injury to her in the form of the amputation of her leg.

It is important to note that there were alternatives that could have been used to limit risk in this case. For example, home care might have been an appropriate way to continue to monitor Mrs. Wickline for additional complications outside of the acute care setting. Even if nurse managers cannot ensure payment for the type or length of care that they regard as most desirable, it is important to arrange for other available care that may help to limit risk.

The court considered Mrs. Wickline's claim against the Medicaid program. It first recognized a so-called "changed reality" in the health care delivery system. That is, the court acknowledged that payers now make treatment decisions. Therefore, said the court, payers should be liable for adverse payment decisions that harm patients. The one condition placed on this shift of liability from providers to payers was that providers must satisfy what the court called "duty to protest." In other words, the court said that providers would not be liable for results of adverse payment decisions so long as they protest payment decisions that they think will injure patients.

Because the physician in Mrs. Wickline's case did not protest the decision to terminate payment after the additional 4 days, the court did not find the Medicaid program liable in this case. The physician was not liable either because he was not a defendant in the case. The court made it clear, however, that from then on it would hold payers liable if they persisted in adverse payment decisions in view of protests by providers.

Valro Versus Blue Cross and Blue Shield of Michigan. In the case of *Valro Versus Blue Cross and Blue Shield of Michigan,*[2] workers at General Motors (GM) Company decided that they wanted more mental health and substance abuse benefits. GM agreed to provide the additional benefits but wanted to self-insure for them because these benefits can be expensive to offer.

GM went to Blue Cross and Blue Shield of Michigan and asked Blue Cross to run a pilot program to assist in developing these benefits. Blue Cross agreed. Both parties signed an agreement that, among other factors, made it clear that the pilot program would include a rigorous utilization review (UR). It would include preauthorization, precertification, concurrent review, and prospective and retrospective review.

Blue Cross then signed agreements with individual mental health providers to treat patients in the pilot program. All of the participants were satisfied until the UR program became so rigorous that it interfered with the providers' ability to deliver patient care or receive payments for providing care. They thought that the activities of Blue Cross amounted to the practice of medicine and sued them.

The court considered the providers' claims. In the court's view, the providers were simply attempting to ensure payment for fulfilling their ethical and legal duty to provide care to patients. The court came very close to calling them greedy wimps and termed the basis of the providers' lawsuit "strange stuff" on which to base a claim.

Thus the decision in the *Valro* case is inconsistent with that in the *Wickline* case. Specifically, *Wickline* says that providers are not required to treat patients if payment is denied, and, when patients are injured as a result, payers, not providers, are liable if payment is denied despite the providers' protests. *Valro*, however, says that providers have a legal and ethical obligation to provide care whether or not they receive payment.

Wilson Versus Blue Cross and Blue Shield of Southern California, et al. In the case of *Wilson Versus Blue Cross and Blue Shield of Southern California, et al,*[3] decided in 1990, Mr. Wilson was hospitalized in Los Angeles for depression and anorexia. His physician, Dr. Taft, recommended inpatient care for 3 to 4 weeks. This recommendation was conveyed to Blue Cross.

Blue Cross contracted with a utilization review organization, Western Medical Review, to consider whether payment for claims such as Mr. Wilson's should be authorized. Dr. Wasserman at Western Medical Review considered Mr. Wilson's claim. He determined that he would authorize payment for the few days of inpatient care that Mr. Wilson had already received but would not authorize payment for any additional inpatient care.

This decision was relayed to Dr. Taft and Mr. Wilson. Mr. Wilson had no other way to pay for his care and was discharged from the hospital.

Within the period during which Mr. Wilson probably would have been hospitalized, if his request for inpatient care had been authorized, he committed suicide. His parents then sued Blue Cross, Western Medical Review, and Dr. Wasserman, claiming that Mr. Wilson was negligently prematurely discharged as a result of the adverse payment decision.

The case was dismissed at the trial level based partly on Dr. Taft's failure to protest the adverse payment decision. On appeal, the court said that the previous ruling in the *Wickline* case was wrong. That is, payers are liable for the adverse payment decisions made that injure patients, whether or not providers protest these adverse payment decisions. This determination may serve as a useful precedent, permitting courts in other jurisdictions to reach a similar conclusion that payers are now liable for injuries that occur because of failure to pay for needed care.

In view of these court decisions, which are clearly inconsistent in some respects, nurse managers may well ask how to take appropriate action. The best advice at this time is to fulfill the duty to protest adverse payment decisions. This recommendation is based on the conclusion that such protests are good risk management. It is also based on the importance of the nurse's role as a patient advocate. If nurses do not speak for patients in the face of adverse payment decisions, it is unlikely that anyone will do so. Most patients do not understand the complex health care delivery system well enough to be their own advocates.

Nurse managers must be prepared to monitor developments in the area of liability for premature discharge. The last word has by no means been spoken on this important issue by courts and legislatures.

INFORMED CONSENT

Informed consent is not required for routine or emergency treatment. Routine care often includes physical examinations and drawing blood. Emergency treatment usually occurs when danger to life or permanent injury to patients' limbs is threatened.

Informed consent is required for treatment that is neither routine nor provided in response to an emergency. Generally, the need for valid informed consent increases in direct proportion to the risk of the treatment.

Prerequisites

The following two prerequisites must be met to obtain valid informed consent:
1. The patient must have the capacity to give consent in terms of chronologic age and the ability to understand information.
2. The patient's consent must be voluntary.

Generally, patients must be of legal age before they can consent to treatment. The age at which an individual is legally considered to be an adult varies from state to state but is usually at either age 18 or 21. Exceptions to this requirement include:

- Minors who are emancipated because they are married, have borne a child, or are economically independent—the laws on this category vary from state to state.

- Minors who seek treatment for certain types of conditions such as sexually transmitted diseases, mental illness, or substance abuse—laws regarding these exceptions also vary from state to state.

Patients must also be able to understand information to give valid consent. Generally, this requirement means that they must be able to understand the consequences of their choices regarding treatment. Patients who have been found to be incompetent by the courts clearly lack capacity to understand information. Patients who have not been declared incompetent may, nonetheless, lack the necessary level of mental capacity. The best method for evaluating capacity is to use a mental status examination and to document the results in patients' records just before obtaining informed consent.

You should note that the law recognizes that capacity (the ability to understand information) may vary from moment to moment. Confused patients may suddenly seem much more lucid. It is appropriate to seek informed consent during such moments. Consent under such conditions is valid even after the patient becomes incapacitated once again.

A patient's consent must be voluntary (i.e., there can be no fraud or duress). Providers cannot tell patients that they are going to perform one treatment and actually perform an entirely different treatment. Providers walk a fine line between informing patients of the consequences of their refusal of treatment and threatening them. Manager's Tip 9-3 lists the information required for informed consent.

When obtaining informed consent, the provider must give a description of the proposed treatment because consent is valid only when a patient understands the treatment to be received. A patient cannot provide valid consent to a treatment that she/he does not understand.

Benefits of proposed treatment must never be described in absolute terms or as guarantees of results. If benefits are presented to patients as guarantees, a contract may be created that is breached by providers if they fail to deliver the promised result. Providers must speak of *possible* benefits from proposed treatment.

MANAGER'S TIP 9-3

INFORMATION NEEDED
FOR INFORMED CONSENT

Patients who satisfy the prerequisites for informed consent must receive the following information:

- ✔ Description of the proposed treatment.
- ✔ Possible benefits of the proposed treatment.
- ✔ Significant risks associated with the treatment.
- ✔ Description of alternative treatments.
- ✔ A clear acknowledgment of their right to refuse treatment.

A provider is not required to share *all* risks with patients. Rather, a provider is required to share those risks that are either statistically significant or are especially important to patients in the provider's opinion. For example, if proposed surgery involves even a slight possibility of injury to a violinist's hands, this risk must be disclosed.

Alternative treatments must also be described. These may include medications, physical therapy, surgery, diet and exercise, or whatever could be of benefit to the patient.

Finally, the unqualified right of patients to refuse any treatment must be acknowledged as part of the process of obtaining informed consent. Providers should make a clear statement to this effect, which should be specifically acknowledged by patients.

Patients who consent to treatment after the prerequisites have been met and the above information has been given have given valid informed consent. Verbal consent is acceptable.

It is important, however, to document the patient's consent. Providers use several methods to accomplish this goal. The most popular vehicle is undoubtedly a consent form, which is useful only when it documents the specific information given to the patient. Other providers use progress notes summarizing the consent process. Audio and video recordings are also acceptable means of documenting informed consent.

Nurse managers should understand that it is the physician's job to obtain valid informed consent. Nurses may ask patients to sign forms documenting that they have given informed consent. Their signature on such forms as witnesses means that they saw the patient sign the form; their signature does not verify that patients received appropriate information. But nurse managers must also realize that the nursing staff has a vested interest in making sure informed consent is obtained because health care is almost always provided as a team. When one member of the team fails to perform or to adequately protect the team, the whole team is at risk, not just one member.

Suppose, however, that patients cannot meet the prerequisites of informed consent because of their chronologic age or lack of ability to understand information. Who may give substitute consent on behalf of such patients? Manager's Tip 9-4 lists sources of substitute consent and presents additional information that nurse managers may find helpful.

WITHHOLDING AND WITHDRAWING TREATMENT
No Code Orders

"No code" or "Do not resuscitate" orders are a form of withholding treatment. It is important for nurse managers to understand, however, that these orders permit providers to withhold *only* treatment related to resuscitation if patients need such measures. Such orders do not apply to withholding nourishment, hydration, or IV fluids.

No code orders may be entered by physicians at their discretion for terminally ill patients after consultation with competent patients or family members. Physicians are required to provide these orders.

MANAGER'S TIP 9-4

THOSE WHO CAN GIVE SUBSTITUTE CONSENT ON BEHALF OF PATIENTS

✔ **Parents on behalf of minors.** In the case of separation or divorce, either the custodial or the noncustodial parent may consent unless she/he is prohibited from doing so in a separation agreement or a divorce decree. Nurse managers should educate staff to obtain copies of relevant documents and to place copies of these documents on patients' charts to certify that appropriate individuals gave consent on behalf of minors.

✔ **Courts.**

✔ **Guardians of the person.** Courts appoint two types of guardians or conservators: guardians of the property and guardians of the person. Only guardians of the person may consent to health care. Staff must obtain a copy of any decree of guardianship and place it on the patient's chart to document valid informed consent.

✔ **Attorneys-in-fact.** Attorneys-in-fact are appointed to act on behalf of patients in powers of attorney. Powers of attorney are very flexible instruments. Nurses must therefore obtain a copy of any power of attorney under which an individual claims authority to evaluate the scope of their powers. Powers of attorney may be executed only by patients who have mental capacity. When patients become permanently mentally incapacitated, it is too late to sign a power of attorney. Durable powers of attorney survive the incapacity of patients. The laws governing powers of attorney survive the incapacity of patients. The laws governing powers of attorney vary from state to state.

✔ **State statutes.** Some states have passed laws that permit individuals to make decisions regarding health care in the absence of a guardian or attorney-in-fact. There is significant variation among the state statutes.

No code orders may not be transferred between institutions. Patients who had no code orders in long-term care facilities must have a new order entered when admitted to a hospital.

Some institutions permit partial no code orders. Partial no code orders are undesirable from an administrative point of view. It is extremely difficult for staff members to remember what each patient's no code order permits.

Verbal no code orders. There is a clear difference of opinion regarding verbal no code orders. The best practice appears to permit them only under the following circumstances.

- They are given in the presence of two witnesses.
- They are valid for a very limited period before a written order is required, preferably 24 to 48 hours.

Withholding Other Forms of Treatment

Withholding or withdrawing other forms of treatment is always acceptable if the decision is made by competent adult patients. Difficulties arise, however, when family members or next of kin want to make decisions regarding withholding or withdrawing treatment. The question is: Under what circumstances may treatment be withheld from patients who lack capacity?

First, the providers must make a determination that the patient is either terminally ill or in a persistent vegetative state. This determination should be documented in the chart.

The question then becomes who can make decisions on behalf of the patient. The most important court decision that addressed this issue was *Cruzan Versus Director, Missouri Department of Health*,[4] a 1990 decision of the U.S. Supreme Court. In this case a young woman, Nancy Cruzan, was in an automobile accident. When rescue personnel reached the scene, Ms. Cruzan had no pulse or respiration. These two essential functions were restored at the scene of the accident, and she was transported to a local hospital. The initial diagnosis was cerebral contusions compounded by significant lack of oxygen. Neurologists determined that Ms. Cruzan had probably been deprived of oxygen for approximately 12 to 14 minutes.

She remained in a coma for several weeks and then progressed to a semiconscious state. She was able to take some nourishment. To ensure proper nourishment and hydration, however, physicians asked her husband for permission to insert a gastrostomy tube. Her husband gave consent and the tube was implanted.

Despite valiant efforts, Ms. Cruzan remained in a vegetative state. That is, her body functioned almost entirely by its internal controls. It was able to maintain temperature, heartbeat, pulmonary ventilation, digestive activity, and reflex activity of muscles and nerves, which permits low-level conditional responses. But she exhibited no behavioral evidence of self-awareness or awareness of her surroundings.

She remained in this state for several years. When it appeared unlikely that Ms. Cruzan would regain her mental capacity, her parents asked the hospital to remove the gastrostomy tube and to stop nourishment. Hospital personnel refused the request. Her parents filed suit and the case was eventually heard by the U.S. Supreme Court.

The Court said that each state has the right to safeguard the process for making decisions regarding withholding or withdrawing treatment. Each state is free to require whatever evidence it desires to accomplish this goal.

The Court recognized that family members do not always act in the best interest of patients. Therefore each state may decide to refuse to permit family members to make decisions on behalf of incompetent patients unless substantial proof shows that the decision made is one that the patient would also make. Substantial proof of patients' wishes may be expressed in durable powers of attorney or living wills.

Thus it is important for nurse managers to recognize that the requirements of the state in which they practice are paramount. At the extreme, states can refuse to permit withholding or withdrawing of treatment unless there is a clear statement from patients themselves about their wishes in the event of terminal illness or a persistent vegetative state.

To encourage clarity regarding patients' wishes, Congress passed the Patient Self-Determination Act, which became effective on December 1, 1991. This act requires providers to obtain information from patients about their wishes regarding future health care. Such information is commonly called an *advance directive*. Specifically, providers must:

- Develop written policies and procedures to implement patients' rights to make decisions concerning future health care through the use of durable powers of attorney or living wills (advance directives) as permitted by state laws.
- Provide all adult patients with written information about their rights under the laws of the state in which care is provided, including the right to consent to or refuse treatment, the right to sign advance directives, and a statement of the provider's policies governing implementation of patients' wishes.
- Document in patients' files whether they have executed advance directives.
- Provide education for all nursing staff members regarding advance directives.

Compliance with this statute will undoubtedly assist nurse managers in clarifying issues of withholding and withdrawing treatment.

EMPLOYMENT

Regardless of practice setting, health care is a labor-intensive business. New nurse managers may feel lost in a maze of employment-related laws and court decisions, particularly those relating to discrimination and termination of the employment relationship. Two key questions are as follows:

1. How can the new nurse manager avoid discrimination against workers?
2. Under what circumstances may workers be terminated?

Discrimination

As most nurse managers already know, both federal and state laws prohibit discrimination on the basis of race, sex, handicapping condition, and religion. The practical steps outlined in Manager's Tip 9-5 will help nurse managers ensure they do not violate these laws. New nurse managers who follow these guidelines will be successful at managing issues of employment discrimination.

Unlawful Termination

Similar steps may be taken to avoid liability for unlawful termination of workers who are not governed by a union contract (Manager's Tip 9-6). Generally, in the absence of any kind of contract, nurses can be hired and fired at will. Nurses

MANAGER'S TIP 9-5

STEPS TO AVOID DISCRIMINATION

✔ Identify the essential job functions of all positions for which individuals are responsible. "Essential job functions" is a technical term. New nurse managers may need assistance from their human resources (HR) departments to identify essential job functions and put them in writing in the form of job descriptions.

✔ Accept that reasonable accommodations are required so that individuals can perform essential job functions if the need for modifications is in any way related to a handicapping condition.

✔ Carefully follow the written essential job functions in carrying out all personnel activities, including hiring, evaluations, promotions, transfers, disciplinary actions, and terminations.

✔ Document all personnel actions in terms of the essential job functions.

MANAGER'S TIP 9-6

FIVE GUIDELINES TO HELP IN AVOIDING LIABILITY FOR UNLAWFUL TERMINATION OF EMPLOYEES

✔ Employee handbooks and policies and procedures must contain clear, unequivocal statements that they do not create a contract of employment.

✔ Managers must strictly adhere to their own policies and procedures, including definitions of circumstances that warrant immediate termination of employment.

✔ Except when immediate termination is warranted, managers must discipline workers progressively. They must first counsel workers, including development of specific corrective action, before taking more serious action.

✔ Managers must thoroughly document all disciplinary action, especially counseling and corrective action.

✔ Consistency in following procedures and applying rules to all employees is essential.

are generally so-called "at-will" employees. Employees' attorneys have tested the absolute nature of this doctrine in recent years. Nurse managers may unwittingly fall into the trap of taking action that amounts to the creation of a contract without realizing that they have done so, thereby destroying their ability to terminate employees. Although it is often difficult to find the time and energy to follow these steps, they are vital to avoiding personnel problems.

SUMMARY

The information in this chapter is by no means exhaustive. There is much more for the new nurse manager to learn in the area of legal issues, and readers are encouraged to seek further information when issues with legal implications arise. A glossary of legal terms is included in the appendix of this chapter for the reader's information.

New managers who arrive at their offices on the first day in their new positions with no more than the information provided in this chapter are well on their way to success in managing the various risks associated with managing nursing personnel. This can be accomplished by remembering to:

1. Continuously monitor the quality of patient care to limit legal liability.
2. Assist patients in giving valid informed consent and making decisions regarding withholding and withdrawal of treatment.
3. Identify essential job functions and apply them in relation to all personnel functions, discipline employees progressively, and avoid creating contractual obligations unless you intend to do so.

QUESTIONS FOR CONSIDERATION

1. List the four components that must be involved to prove negligence.
2. Describe three sources of accepted standards of care.
3. Explain why policies and procedures are important from a legal perspective.
4. Identify five common types of negligence.
5. Discuss risk areas related to employment from a management perspective and ways to avoid problems.

References

1. *Wickline v State of California,* 192 Cal App 3d 1630, 239 California Reporter 810, 1986.
2. *Valro v Blue Cross and Blue Shield,* 708 F Sup 826, ED Michigan, 1989.
3. *Wilson v Blue Cross and Blue Shield of Southern California et al,* Cal App 2d, 271 California Reporter 876, 1990.
4. *Cruzan v Harmon,* 760 S W 2d 408, Missouri 1988, en banc, *aff'd sub nom Cruzan v Director, Missouri Department of Health,* 110 S Ct 2841, 1990.

APPENDIX 9-1

GLOSSARY OF LEGAL TERMS

The author relied heavily on *Black's Law Dictionary*, ed 5, St. Paul, MN, 1979, West Publishing, to prepare this glossary. Readers should make further use of this excellent resource when necessary.

Actual damages Compensation for actual injuries or losses such as medical expenses or lost wages.

Affidavit A written statement of facts given voluntarily under oath.

Allegation The written statements by a party to a suit concerning what the party expects to prove.

Amended complaint A corrected or revised version of the document filed in court by the plaintiff to bring a suit.

Amicus curiae Literally, "friend of the court." Persons or organizations with a strong interest in or views on a suit may ask the court in which the suit is filed for permission to file a brief to suggest a resolution of the case consistent with their views. *Amicus curiae* briefs are often filed in appeals of cases involving a broad public interest such as civil rights cases.

Appellant The party who appeals the decision of one court to another court.

Appellate brief Written arguments by attorneys required to be filed with an appellate court stating the reasons why the trial court acted correctly (appellee's brief) or incorrectly (appellant's brief). The contents and form of appellate briefs are often prescribed by the rules of various court systems. Appellate briefs usually contain a statement of issues presented for review by the appellate court, a statement of the case, argument, and a conclusion stating the precise action sought by the party submitting the brief.

Appellate review Examination of a previous proceeding.

Appellee The party in a case against whom an appeal is brought. Sometimes also called the "respondent."

Assault Any conduct that creates a reasonable apprehension of being touched in an injurious manner. No actual touching is required to prove assault.

Assumption of the risk A defense to plaintiffs' claims based on the theory that plaintiffs may not recover for injuries to which they consent. To prove that the plaintiff assumed the risk, the defendant must show that (1) the plaintiff had knowledge of a dangerous condition, (2) the plaintiff appreciated the nature or extent of the danger, and (3) the plaintiff voluntarily exposed herself/himself to the danger.

Attorney-in-fact Any person authorized by another to act in her/his place either for a particular purpose or for the transaction of business affairs in general. This authority is conferred by a document called a power of attorney.

Battery An unconsented, actual touching that causes injury.

Borrowed servant rule A theory of liability or negligence that is used to extend liability beyond the person who actually committed negligent acts to include those who had the right of control over the negligent actions.

Brief A written statement prepared by an attorney arguing a case in court. A brief contains a summary of the facts of the case, the pertinent laws, and an argument of how the law applies to the facts supporting an attorney's position.

Burden of proof The requirement of proving facts in dispute on an issue raised between the parties in a case.

Captain of the ship doctrine This doctrine imposes liability on surgeons in charge of operations for negligence of assistants during periods when those assistants are under the surgeons' control, even though the assistants are also employees of a hospital. This doctrine extends the borrowed servant rule to hospital operating rooms.

Cause of action The fact or facts that give a person the right to begin a suit.

Common law As opposed to laws created by legislatures, the common law consists of legal principles based solely on usages and customs from time immemorial, particularly the ancient, unwritten laws of England.

Complaint The first document filed in court by the plaintiff to begin a suit.

Conservator Any individual appointed by a court to manage the affairs of an incompetent person.

Continuance Adjournment or postponement of a session, hearing, trial, or other proceedings to a subsequent day or time.

Contributory negligence A defense to a claim of negligence. Any act or omission on the part of the complaining party amounting to a breach of the duty the law imposes on everyone to protect themselves from injury that contributes to the injury complained of by the plaintiff.

Counterclaim Claim presented by a defendant in opposition to the claim of the plaintiff. If the defendant establishes her/his claim, it will defeat or diminish the plaintiff's claim.

Cross-complaint A defendant or cross-defendant (plaintiff) may file a cross-complaint based on (1) any claim against any of the parties who filed the complaint against her/him *or* (2) any claim against a person alleged to be liable whether or not the person is already a party to the suit. The claims in a cross-complaint must (1) arise out of the same transaction or occurrence as the original suit *and* (2) make a claim or assert a right or interest in the property or the controversy that is the basis for the claim already made.

Cross-defendants Plaintiffs who, subsequent to suing defendants, are then countersued by the defendants. Defendants in a suit brought by defendants.

Cross-examination The questioning of a witness by an adverse party to test the truth of her/his testimony or to further develop it.

Declaratory judgment Provided for in state and federal statutes. A person may seek a declaratory judgment from a court if there is an actual controversy among the parties, and the party asking for the declaratory judgment has some question or doubt about her/his legal rights. The judgment is binding on the parties both presently and in the future.

Defendant The person defending or denying; the party against whom a civil lawsuit is brought or the accused in a criminal case.

Defense A response to the claims of the other party stating the reasons why the claims should not be recognized.

Demurrer An argument in which the defendant admits the facts in the plaintiff's complaint but claims that the facts are insufficient to require a response.

Deposition Advice by which one party asks oral questions of the other party or of a witness for the other party before the trial begins. The person who answers questions is called a deponent. The deposition is conducted under oath outside the courtroom, usually in one of the lawyer's offices. A transcript, or word-for-word account, is made of the deposition.

Directed verdict When the party with the burden of proof fails to prove all necessary elements of the case, the trial judge may direct a verdict in favor of the other party because there can only be one result anyway.

Docket A list or calendar of cases to be tried during a particular period prepared by employees of the court for use by the court and attorneys.

Due process clause Two clauses in the U.S. Constitution, one in the Fifth Amendment applicable to the U.S. government, the other in the Fourteenth Amendment that protects persons from actions by the states. There are two aspects: (1) procedural, in which a person is guaranteed fair procedures, and (2) substantive, which protects a person's property from unfair governmental interference. Similarly, clauses are in most state constitutions.

Due process of law An orderly proceeding in which a person receives notice of the proceeding and the subject matter of the proceeding and is given an opportunity to be heard and to enforce and protect her/his rights before a court or person(s) with power to hear and determine the case.

Equal protection clause A provision in the Fourteenth Amendment to the U.S. Constitution that requires every state to treat individuals in similar circumstances the same in terms of rights and redress of improper actions against them.

Ex parte On one side only; by or for one party; done for, on behalf of, or on the application of one party only. A judicial proceeding, order, or injunction is *ex parte* when it is granted at the request of and for the benefit of one party only without notice to any person adversely interested.

False imprisonment A tort that consists of intentionally confining a person without her/his consent.

Felony A crime of a more serious nature. Under federal law and many state statutes, a felony is any offense punishable by imprisonment for a term exceeding 1 year or by death.

Guardian Any person responsible for managing the property of and protecting the rights of another person who, because of youth or lack of understanding, is incapable of managing her/his own affairs.

Guardian ad litem A special guardian appointed by a court to prosecute or defend, on behalf of a minor or incompetent person, a suit to which the minor or incompetent person is a party.

Harmless error Any trivial error or an error that is merely academic because it did not affect important rights of any party to a case and did not affect the final result of the case. Harmless error will not serve as a basis for changing a decision of the court.

Implied consent Signs, actions or facts, or inaction or silence that indicates that consent is given.

In loco parentis In the place of a parent; instead of a parent; charged with a parent's rights, duties, and responsibilities.

Infliction of emotional distress Conduct going beyond that usually tolerated by society that is calculated to cause mental distress *and* that actually causes severe mental distress.

Informed consent A person's agreement to allow something to happen that is based on a full disclosure of facts needed to make the decision intelligently.

Intent Design, resolve, or determination that serves as the basis for a person's actions. Intent can rarely be proven directly but may be inferred from the circumstances.

Interrogatories A tool to elicit information important to a case before trial. Interrogatories are written questions about the case submitted by one party to another party or witness. The answers to interrogatories are usually given under oath (i.e., the person answering the questions signs a sworn statement that the answers are true).

Judge a quo Literally, "from which." A judge of a court from which a case was taken before a decision is made.

Judgment of nonsuit A decision by a court against plaintiffs when they are unable to prove their cases or refuse or neglect to proceed to trial. A court decision that leaves the issues undetermined.

Judgment notwithstanding the verdict (inov) A judgment entered by order to the court for a party, even though the jury decided in favor of the other party. A motion for directed verdict must usually be made before a judgment, notwithstanding the verdict.

Jurisdiction The right and power of a court to decide a particular case.

Jury instructions Statements made by the judge to the jury regarding the law applicable to the case the jury is considering that the jury is required to accept and apply. Attorneys for both sides usually furnish the judge with suggested instructions.

Justiciable controversy Courts will decide only justiciable controversies. That is, courts will decide only cases in which there is a real, substantial difference of opinion between the parties as opposed to a hypothetical difference or dispute or one that is academic or moot.

Leave to amend Permission or authorization given by a judge to any party to a suit to correct or reverse any document filed by the party with the court.

Locality rule To show negligence according to the locality rule, a plaintiff must prove that the defendant practitioner failed to render care considered reasonable in the same or in a similar geographic location.

Misdemeanor Criminal offense less serious than a felony and usually punished by a fine or imprisonment in other than a penitentiary. Any criminal offense other than a felony.

Motion for a new trial Request to a judge to set aside a decision already made in a case and to order a new trial on the basis that the first decision was improper or unfair.

Motion for summary judgment An application made to a court or judge to obtain a ruling or order that all or part of the other party's claim or defense should be eliminated from further consideration. This motion is made when a party believes there is no significant disagreement concerning important facts among the parties *and* the law supports the position of the party making the motion. A motion for summary judgment may be directed toward all or part of a claim or defense. It may be made on the basis of the pleadings or other portions of the record in the case, or it may be supported by affidavits and a variety of outside material.

Motion to dismiss An application made to a court or judge to order that the plaintiff's suit be eliminated from further consideration by the court or judge. This motion is usually made before a trial is held and may be based on a variety of reasons: for example, insufficiency of the plaintiff's claims or improper service of process of the plaintiff's suit on the defendant.

Motion to intervene/Plea in intervention A written request to a court to become a party to a case field in the court based on an interest in the results of the case.

Negligence The failure to do something a reasonable person would do or doing something a reasonable person would not do.

Nominal damages A very small amount of money awarded to plaintiffs in cases in which there is no substantial injury. Nominal damages are awarded to recognize technical invasions of rights or breaches of duty or in cases in which the injury is more substantial but the plaintiff fails to prove the amount.

Parens patriae Literally, "parent of the country." Refers to the role of each state as sovereign and guardian of persons under legal disability. This concept is the basis for activity by states to protect interests such as the health, comfort, and welfare of the people.

Per quod Literally, "whereby." A phrase used to designate facts concerning the consequences of a defendant's actions on the plaintiff that serve as the basis for an award of special damages to the plaintiff.

Petition A formal, written request to a court asking the court to take certain action regarding a particular matter.

Physician-patient privilege The right of patients not to reveal or have revealed by their physicians the communications made between patients and physicians. The privilege is established in most states and therefore varies from state to state. The privilege belongs only to the patient and may be waived by the patient.

Plaintiff A person who sues in a civil case.

Pleading The formal, written statements by the parties to a suit of their respective claims and defenses.

Power of attorney A document authorizing another person to act on one's behalf. The other person is called the attorney-in-fact. The power of the attorney-in-fact is revoked on the death of the person who signed the power of attorney. The powers given to the attorney-in-fact may be general or for special purposes.

Prejudicial error Any error that substantially affects the legal rights and obligations of a party. A prejudicial error may result in a new trial and the reversal of a decision by the court.

Pretrial conference A meeting between opposing attorneys and the judge in a particular case. The purpose of the meeting is to define the key issues of the case, to secure stipulations, and to take all other steps necessary to aid in the disposition of the case. Such conferences are called at the discretion of the court. The decisions made at the conference are included in a written order that controls the future course of the case.

Pretrial discovery Any device used by parties before trial to obtain evidence for use at trial such as interrogatories, depositions, or requests for admission of facts.

Prima facie case Sufficient evidence presented by the plaintiff on which a decision that the plaintiff's claims are valid can reasonably be made.

Proximate cause The dominant cause or the cause producing injury. Any action producing injury, unbroken by any efficient intervening cause, and without which the injury would not have occurred.

Punitive damages Money awarded to the plaintiff over and above compensation for actual losses. Punitive damages are awarded in cases in which the wrongdoing was aggravated by violence, oppression, malice, fraud, or wickedness. They are intended to compensate for mental anguish, shame, or degradation or to punish or make an example of the defendant.

Remand To send back. The sending back of a case by an appellate court to the court in which it was previously considered to have some further action taken on it.

Request for admissions Written statements of fact concerning a case that are submitted by the attorney for a party to a suit to the attorney for another party to the suit. The attorney who receives the request is required to either admit or deny each of the statements of fact submitted. Those statements that are admitted will be treated by the court as established and need not be proved at trial.

Res ipsa loquitur Literally, "the thing speaks for itself." Although the plaintiffs cannot testify to the exact cause of injury, they can prove (1) that the instrument causing injury was in defendants' exclusive control and (2) that the injury they sustained does not normally occur in the absence of negligence. Plaintiffs who prove both of these things can recover damages for negligence even though the exact circumstances of injury are known.

Res judicata A legal principle that says that once a *final* decision is made on a matter, the same question may not be raised at a later date.

Respondeat superior Literally, "let the master say." A basis for extending liability to include the employer for the wrongful acts of an employee. The doctrine is inapplicable where injury occurs when the employee is acting outside the legitimate scope of employment.

Retrial A new trial of a case that has already been tried at least once.

Stare decisis Literally, "to abide by or adhere to decided cases." The policy of courts in the United States to apply previously established principles of law to all future cases in which the facts are substantially the same, even though the parties to the suit are not the same.

State action Activity of a state necessary to trigger the protection of the Fourteenth Amendment of the U.S. Constitution for private citizens.

Statute of limitations Legislative enactments establishing limits on the right to sue. Statutes of limitations declare that no one may sue unless the suit is filed within a specified period after the occurrence or injury that is the basis for the suit.

Stay A stopping by order of a court. A suspension of the case or some designated proceedings in it. A stay is a type of injunction with which a court freezes its proceedings at a particular point. It can be used to stop the case altogether or hold up only some phase of it.

Stipulation A voluntary agreement between opposing attorneys concerning disposition of a point that alleviates the need for proof of this point or for consideration, signed by the attorneys for all of the parties and placed on file as part of the court record.

Third-party defendant A party brought into a suit by the defendant who was not a party to the transaction on which the suit is based, but whose rights and liabilities may be affected by the suit.

Tort A private or civil wrong or injury for which a court may award damages. Any civil suit except a suit for breach of contract. Three elements of every tort claim are (1) existence of a legal duty by the defendant to the plaintiff, (2) breach of this duty, *and* (3) resulting damage to the plaintiff.

Transcript A word-for-word written record of a trial, hearing, or other proceeding.

Trial An examination and determination of issues between the parties to a case by a court.

Trial by court Judicial examination and determination of issues between the parties in a case.

Trial by court or judge A trial before a judge only, in contrast to a trial before a judge *and* jury.

Vicarious liability Indirect legal responsibility.

Voir dire Literally, "to speak the truth." Refers to the preliminary questioning that the court or attorneys conduct to determine the qualifications of a person to serve as a juror in a particular case.

Writ of certiorari An order of an appellate court used when the court exercises discretion about whether to hear an appeal. If the writ is denied, the court refuses to hear the appeal, and the decision of the court that previously heard the case remains in effect. If the writ is granted, the appellate court will reconsider the case and perhaps change the decision of the lower court.

Writ of error A writ issued from an appeals court to a trial court requiring the trial court to send the record of a case to the appeals court for reconsideration. The writ is based on errors of law apparent from the record. It is the beginning of a new suit to reverse a decision of a lower court and is not a continuation of any suit in a lower court.

Writ of habeas corpus Literally, "you have the body." The primary function of this writ is to force the release of a person from unlawful imprisonment.

CHAPTER 10

Taking Care of Yourself and Your Staff

T.M. Marrelli

Maintaining Balance under Stress

Nicholson, a registered nurse and certified stress management program director through the American Institute of Preventive Medicine, proposed a definition of stress as it applies to the nursing profession. After reviewing the work of Hans Selye and many others, Nicholson suggested that stress in nursing is

> . . . a phenomenon that is characterized by a response to a certain occurrence. This response may be interpreted as positive or negative by the individual and can affect biologic processes, which may result eventually in wear or tear on one's physical, psychologic, behavioral, and/or emotional well-being.[1]

Stress in the Nursing Profession

Careers in nursing and nursing management bring with them careers in managing stress. It is important to your personal and professional long-term success as a nurse and nurse manager to integrate effective stress management skills into your life.

A critical element in managing stress in the nursing profession is accepting that stress does and always will exist. Some of these stresses are unique to our profession. Foxall and others[2] compared the frequency and sources of nursing job stress perceived by intensive care, hospice, and medical-surgical nurses. Although the groups assigned different degrees of stress to various aspects of their work, the overall frequency of job stress was similar among the three groups.

Numerous studies detail the sources of stress experienced by nurses. Although many of these stresses may be identified in non–health care settings, many stresses found in the nursing profession are products of the environment. Examples include dying patients, cardiac arrest, communicable disease, and upset families.

Stresses in the nursing workplace that also are identified in non–health care settings, such as increased workload and conflicts with staff members, can be intensified

The author wishes to acknowledge the work of Patricia M. Feeney for this chapter in previous editions of this book.

in the health care setting. These common or universal job stresses affect nurses more because they can directly affect patients and their care.

Nurse Managers: A Twofold Responsibility

As a nurse manager, you accept a twofold responsibility in stress management: (1) guiding and supporting your staff as they experience stress and (2) coping with stress as it affects you. Although these responsibilities seem self-evident, many managers are not successful in supporting their staff, themselves, or both. Sadly, a failure to support one or the other generally results in a failure to support both.

For example, if your concern rests primarily with your own stress and coping mechanisms, your staff will recognize this fact. Eventually, they will resent your lack of support and may begin to experience excessive stress themselves. Over time, these feelings may result in high staff turnover, decreased staff performance, and unhappy patients and physicians. These factors in turn lead to excessive stress for you.

Conversely, if your concern is exclusively for your staff, eventually you will become emotionally drained, resentful, and overly stressed. As these feelings take their toll on your well-being, your ability to manage and support your staff will diminish. This diminishing performance in turn will lead to excessive stress for your staff.

It is imperative that you understand the importance of attending to the needs of your staff, as well as to your own needs—consistently and simultaneously.

Stress Evaluation Exercises: Introduction

This chapter contains stress evaluation exercises. These exercises are designed to help you identify and evaluate stress in your work environment. The exercises include stress self-knowledge, stress coping mechanisms, and signs of unmanaged stress. You may use these exercises alone or in brainstorming sessions with your peers. The exercises may also be used in staff support groups that are conducted by a professional facilitator.

The stress evaluation exercises are tools to help you identify stress and its accompanying problems. In most cases, you and your staff will be able to respond to stress effectively. However, you may find that you, an individual on your staff, or your staff as a group is experiencing stress beyond normal levels or is developing a serious problem in response to stress. If so, seek professional support for yourself or the employees experiencing the problem. Please refer to the section When You Identify a Serious Staff Problem on p. 296 of this chapter for further discussion.

SOURCES OF STRESS IN THE PATIENT CARE ENVIRONMENT

Once you are committed to monitoring and managing stress in the workplace, a clear understanding of the sources of stress is critical. Undoubtedly, you have a good sense of the types of events or situations that create stress for you. Most nurse managers have spent a considerable part of their career in staff level positions and are well acquainted with the rigors and challenges of the profession.

It is important to note that the areas of stress that affect you may not be the same as those that most affect the members of your staff. For example, off-shift scheduling affects people differently and may affect them differently at various points in their lives. Working the night shift profoundly affects some people's sense of emotional equilibrium and their sleep patterns. Yet some nurses enjoy an occasional rotation to nights and some happily choose to work nights full-time.

Caring for dying patients is stressful. Yet for some nurses, caring for a dying patient is not experienced as a negative stress. These nurses may exercise hidden strengths and qualities and be deeply satisfied by the experience. For other nurses, caring for a dying patient may be deeply depressing.

It is helpful to review an inventory of the sources of stress in the patient care workplace so that you can be sensitive to the differences among your staff members and guard against generalizing your experiences to them.

Lees and Ellis investigated a variety of common stresses in their study of nursing staff, nursing students, and students who left nurse training.[3] The stresses they identified are listed in Box 10-1, with the stresses most frequently cited appearing at the top of the list.

Simms and others investigated some of these same stresses in their study[4] of nursing burnout. Box 10-2 on p. 280 lists the exhausting activities cited by nurses in their study. The activities at the top of the list are those most frequently cited.

Staff may experience additional stresses when they care for patients with specialized needs or with an illness such as AIDS or hepatitis, which can be threatening to one's own health. Although caring for a patient with a communicable disease

---

box 10-1

COMMONLY OCCURRING STRESSES

- Understaffing
- Dealing with death and dying
- Conflict with nurses
- Overwork
- Conflict with doctors
- Hours
- Cardiac arrests
- Responsibility/accountability
- Training junior staff
- Dealing with relatives
- Lack of resources (beds/equipment)
- Aggressive patients
- Study/examinations

- Carrying out certain nursing procedures
- Feeling inadequate to carry out procedures
- Seeing patients in distress
- Staff rough with patients
- Conflict with others (administrators, dietitians)
- Child abuse
- Dealing with overdose patients
- Living in nurses' home
- Open visiting
- Working off-shifts
- Disorganization of workloads
- Being in a new situation for the first time
- Heat in the hospital

Lees S, Ellis N: The design of a stress-management programme for nursing personnel, J Adv Nurs 15:946, 1990.

---

box 10-2

EXHAUSTING ACTIVITIES

- Decreased staffing
- Negativism on part of staff
- Demanding families
- No time for breaks or lunches
- Increased patient load
- Too many patients
- Dealing with difficult people
- Being on feet all day
- Routine patient care
- Transferring patients in beds
- Mandatory overtime
- Running errands
- Problems with other departments
- Dealing with staff conflict

- Patients and families unwilling to accept diagnosis
- Patients who are self-abusing
- Paperwork
- Cardiac arrests
- Caring for debilitated patients
- Meetings in other buildings
- Not being busy
- Being on call
- Orienting new staff
- Repetitive teaching
- Scheduling and staffing
- Responding to alarms
- Trying to alleviate patient's pain

Adapted from Simms L, et al: Breaking the burnout barrier: resurrecting work excitement in nursing, *Nurs Economics* 8(3):185, 1990.

may cause anxiety for nurses, there are several other, less visible, special-care situations that may concern nurses.

Some of these situations are those that pose a real or imagined threat to the health of the nurse or the nurse's family. For example, nursing personnel in neonatal intensive care units may be called on to hold or otherwise manage infants during X-ray procedures. If the infant is in isolation, does the nurse contaminate a lead apron (creating the need for time-consuming decontamination), put on and cover the apron, or simply hold the infant without protecting herself/himself from the radiation? This kind of decision, invariably made in a split second, may create stress for the nurse making the decision.

Nurses on oncology units regularly manage chemotherapy agents and waste products of patients receiving these agents. The threat of possible exposure to mutagenic chemicals may bring considerable stress to the nurses managing these patients. Nurses who plan to have children, particularly those who are pregnant or actively trying to become pregnant or father a child, may experience additional stress in care settings where they may be exposed to mutagenic chemotherapy agents, communicable diseases, radiation, and other threats to their ability to bear or father a healthy child.

In addition to the stresses intrinsic to the workplace, nurses, like all people, may experience personal problems that magnify the stress at work.

STRESS EVALUATION EXERCISE: STRESS SELF-KNOWLEDGE

Develop a list of all possible sources of stress in your workplace. Recognize that there are no "rights" or "wrongs" in your evaluation and that not every stress identified will apply directly to you or to every nurse on your staff. The purpose of your evaluation is simply to identify sources of stress, not to assign blame for the stress or to provide solutions.

By limiting the first task at hand to a simple process of identification, the pressure to solve—or deny—problems is eliminated.

STRESS FOR NURSE MANAGERS

The nurse manager is vulnerable to stresses that are inherent to the twofold role of nurse and manager (Box 10-3).

One source of stress is a result of the nurse manager's position in the organization. New managers typically are first-line supervisors and must report to a supervisor above them. In fact, there may be several layers of personnel between the nurse manager and top management. This "layering" of management can be a significant source of stress.

---

box 10-3

OTHER SOURCES OF STRESS FOR THE NURSE MANAGER

- Feeling "sandwiched" between your staff and your supervisor.
- Being responsible for patient care/client services delivered by each member of your staff.
- Accepting fiscal responsibility for your area of supervision.
- Being responsible for staff turnover in your area of supervision.
- Serving as liaison in physician-nurse relationships.
- Serving as liaison in staff–upper management relationships.
- Having responsibility for staff education and training.
- Handling conflicts with role expectations from your staff and your supervisor.
- Handling internal role conflicts concerning your responsibilities as a nurse and as a manager.
- Scheduling staffing for your area of supervision.
- Making unpopular decisions.
- Facilitating communications between your staff and upper management, especially when faced with implementing unpopular decisions.
- Evaluating staff.
- Setting reasonable, objective goals for your staff and monitoring performance.
- Taking disciplinary action against a staff member.
- Terminating a staff member.
- Hiring a staff member.
- Responding constructively to unmanaged stress among your staff.
- Recognizing the signs of unmanaged stress among your staff.
- Working with staff who refuse to be accountable for self and professional behavior.
- Recognizing signs and symptoms of unmanaged stress within yourself.
- Facilitating open communication among your staff with each other and with you.
- Conducting staff meetings.
- Accepting criticism from your supervisor and from your staff.

Continued

OTHER SOURCES OF STRESS FOR THE NURSE MANAGER — cont'd

- Taking a vacation from your job.
- Learning to delegate appropriately.
- Being seen as the "bad guy" by your staff.
- Being regarded as "omnipotent" by your staff.
- Having little orientation for your management role.
- Dealing with employees who merely want a "job" and are not committed to their profession or career.
- Keeping a balance at work when your personal problems seem to be following you to work.
- Managing an employee who brings her/his personal problems to work.
- Other stresses you have identified.

For example, when you receive top management's communications through your supervisor, she/he may alter the positioning or emphasis of the communication to motivate you to act positively. This is not necessarily a problem. In fact, you will find yourself doing the same in your communications with your staff. As you become an effective manager who is more acquainted with the staff, you will learn how to report information so that the staff members understand the content and are motivated to take the desired positive action.

However, this filtering of information can become a problem for you when your supervisor, committed to her/his own agenda, misinterprets information and communicates misinterpretations to you. You then receive communication that is inconsistent with top management's message and possibly inconsistent with the organization's objectives. You, in turn, communicate this misinformation to your staff, who ultimately may experience their own stress related to this situation.

Managing an employee with a personal problem warrants a brief discussion. Employees' personal problems are just that—*their* personal problems. Nonetheless, if one of your employees is experiencing difficulty in her/his personal life, be it financial, marital, child-related, or so forth, it is not uncommon for the employee to bring the problem to work. Sometimes an employee may be so stressed and distracted by personal concerns that her/his job performance is affected. Although you must address the employee's performance deficits, it is especially important in these circumstances to do so with compassion.

If an employee confides a personal problem to you, it will be important to keep a balance between showing concern and caring and trying to correct the problem. Keep in mind that you are not a therapist and are not equipped to psychologically counsel your staff. You cannot remedy your staff's personal problems. Sometimes the greatest support you can offer is to suggest that the employee seek guidance from an employee assistance program (EAP), community resource, or trained professional. Examples of resources are discussed in the section When You Identify a Serious Staff Problem on p. 296.

You have probably become acquainted with many of the sources of stress on the nurse manager's stress list. It may also be helpful to brainstorm sources of stress with your peer group. Discussing sources of stress with other first-line managers can help validate your perceptions. This process also can strengthen your peer relationships.

THE MANAGER-STAFF RELATIONSHIP

To understand the stress you experience as a nurse manager, it is helpful to examine the nature of your relationships with your staff and with your supervisor.

A guiding principle behind successfully managing your staff is a clear understanding of the psychology at work. As simplistic as this sounds, this psychology often is neglected when a nurse manager is caught up in day-to-day operational management responsibilities.

How the Staff View the Manager

Regardless of your age, experience, and education, generally your staff will view you as an authority figure. This authority is vested in you because you have a supervisory job title.

Your staff will expect you to respond to their needs, alleviate the stress of their job, and guide them through troubled times. Over time, the authority your staff vests in you must be proven, or the staff will lose the respect for you that is important to successful manager-staff relationships. Nonetheless, knowing that you arrive on the job with a certain measure of authority can boost your confidence as you face the challenges ahead.

But what does this authority mean? At first glance, it seems great. People will listen when you speak. People will work harder and do their best if they believe you are aware of their performance. You have at your disposal several ways to motivate your staff: pats on the back, performance reviews, certificates of merit, continuing education days, and other perks you can provide.

However, your position of authority brings with it some other, less desirable, effects. People will listen when you speak, but they may criticize you for what you say, regardless of whether the blame is accurately assigned. For example, if you have to report staff cutbacks that have been formulated by upper management, *you* may be blamed for the cutbacks. If you correct someone's nursing technique, you may be considered "too hard," "unrealistic," or "out of touch with the real world."

Staff cutbacks and correcting a nurse's technique may be necessary, but they will still create stress for you and your staff. As the manager, you must be aware of this inherent stress so that you communicate with your staff in a positive way, without placing undue stress on them or on yourself.

Open Communication

Effective communication as a nurse manager is not measured by how much your staff likes you. Rather, it is measured by how well you relate verbally and nonverbally in a clear, respectful manner, listening to your staff, encouraging comments and constructive criticism, and creating an environment in which each individual's opinions are respected. As the manager, you ultimately must make decisions on matters related to personnel and operations in your area of responsibility. These decisions—although not always popular—must be respected.

A manager who has created an environment of open communication may experience what appears to be a lack of support in the face of an unpopular decision. Staff members who feel comfortable expressing disagreement and concerns will be more apt to criticize—and sometimes do so unfairly. It will be important to remember that the staff are simply expressing openly what they would think covertly in a less communicative environment. Even if you are unable or unwilling to alter your decision, listening attentively to your staff's dissatisfaction will provide a degree of relief from the stress brought on by your decision.

Do not underestimate your staff and expect that unpopular decisins will necessarily make you unpopular. Sometimes a manager finds unexpected support in the face of a tough decision. This support may not be apparent until the staff has had the opportunity to assimilate the decision. In most cases, your staff will recognize a fair or necessary decision for what it is and respect you for making it.

Regardless of your staff's response to an unpopular decision, you must bear in mind your first priority: to live up to your job responsibilities to the best of your abilities. This generally means doing what is best for the patients/clients first, and then for your staff.

Balancing Your Emotional Needs and Your Job Responsibilities

Because your job can be draining, take care to see that your emotional needs are met in constructive ways. Avoid using your staff as the key source of your emotional support. This does not mean you must tense up if one of your staff extends a helping hand or offers a kind or caring remark. (This would be wonderful!) However, keep in perspective how much you can expect of your staff. Although you may come to enjoy being with and care about many of your staff members, relying on them to support you emotionally is not fair. If you become dependent on one or more of your staff members for support, your judgment will be clouded and it will be difficult for you to do your job.

Although most nurse managers want their staffs to like and care about them, focusing on this desire can create serious problems. Most experienced nurse managers know that it is difficult to do a good job *and* be liked all of the time. Some nurse managers—just like some of the population at large—have a strong emotional need to be liked. If this is true of you, it is important that you continually assess your performance to be sure you are doing your job, not running for office. In fact, even experienced managers may be vulnerable to the desire to "run for office" when things seem particularly tough in running their department, clinic, or home health agency.

Conversely, some managers, in an attempt to establish their authority, tend to go overboard and create an environment akin to a police state. This pitfall, as well as running for office, seems particularly common with first-time managers and is an understandable mistake. It's difficult to gauge how to present oneself, or how strong to come on with the staff, when the nurse manager has had no previous management experience.

Inventory of Your Management Practices

You may want to take a mental inventory of your management practices. The quiz in Box 10-4 presents questions designed as triggers to help you evaluate your behavior and to build a healthy work environment—an environment in which your staff feels able to communicate with you and contribute to decision-making, but is

---

box 10-4

MANAGEMENT PRACTICE QUIZ—QUESTIONS TO ASK YOURSELF

	YES	NO
1. Before I report a management decision to my staff, do I worry about what the staff will think and say about me (more than what they will think and say about the decision)?	____	____
2. When I report an unpopular decision, do I usually say, "I didn't have anything to do with this," "It's not my fault," or make another "Don't get mad at me" statement?	____	____
3. Do I back down from enforcing policies because I do not want to deal with the resentment of the staff?	____	____
4. When I make the work schedule, am I guided first by my interest in serving the needs of my staff (rather than my commitment to serving our patients/clients)?	____	____
5. Do I subtly try to align my staff with me against my supervisor?	____	____
6. Do I speak negatively about my supervisor to my staff?	____	____
7. Do I find myself trying to do my staff's work to gain their acceptance/approval?	____	____
8. Are my efforts to help my staff with their work impeding my ability to meet the requirements of *my* job?	____	____
9. Do I avoid terminating an employee when it is necessary?	____	____
10. Do I show favoritism to any member of my staff?	____	____
11. Do I give good performance evaluations to all my staff regardless of performance?	____	____
12. Is it clear to my staff how they can earn "perks," such as extra education days, bonuses, or other privileges?	____	____

Continued

MANAGEMENT PRACTICE QUIZ — QUESTIONS TO ASK YOURSELF — cont'd

	YES	NO
13. Do I strike a balance between lending hands-on assistance to my staff and managing my department so that my staff do not routinely need this assistance?	____	____
14. Do I provide ample opportunity for my staff to express their concerns and needs?	____	____
15. Whenever possible, do I request input from my staff in making decisions that affect our department?	____	____
16. Do I ask for input from my staff on things they would like to see change in our department?	____	____
17. Do I clearly explain how much change I can and cannot effect?	____	____
18. Whenever possible, do I request input from my staff in determining how to execute management decisions?	____	____
19. Do I set clear verbal and written expectations and goals for my staff?	____	____
20. When an employee does not meet expectations, do I provide clear verbal and written guidelines and expectations for improvement?	____	____
21. Do I understand and follow human resource guidelines in taking disciplinary action with members of my staff?	____	____
22. If I take disciplinary action against an employee, is it the same action I would take against *any* employee with the same record?	____	____

---

respectful of your responsibilities as a manager. The questions also will help you measure your management "comfort level" (i.e., how well you are accepting the nurse manager's responsibilities). Following the questions are guidelines to evaluate your responses.

The first 11 questions address fundamentals of your responsibility as a nurse manager and your ability to execute these basics effectively. If you responded "yes" to any of these questions, you may be resisting the psychologic jump from staff nurse to nurse manager or you may need additional guidance or training in effective management. Take a serious look at your thinking and your management practices. You probably need to adjust both. If you answered "no" to these questions, you have a good start in defining your role as a nurse manager.

The rest of the questions address your ability to (1) facilitate open communication with your staff and (2) create a fair, supportive work environment. A "yes" response to these questions indicates a commitment to these goals. If you answered "no" to any of these questions, consider the consequences of your management practice in question. For example, if you fail to set clear guidelines for performance improvement, it will be difficult for an employee to meet your expectations. You will create a stressful work environment—one in which an employee may never really understand what you expect. Or, if you fail to follow human resource guidelines for disciplinary action, you will create an unpredictable and stressful work environment. In addition, your disciplinary actions may be overturned in grievance procedures, greatly weakening your credibility. As you examine the consequences of your management practices, you will probably realize that the energy you invest to create a predictable, positive workplace will pay great dividends.

How the Manager Views the Staff

The way the manager views the staff is generally given less attention than the way the staff views the manager. Just as a certain authority is vested in the manager, the manager enters this role with beliefs about employees. These beliefs vary, depending on the manager.

For example, some managers may view their employees as children to be cajoled, scolded, rescued, and praised. Some managers may view their employees as a group of potential friends and supporters who will meet their emotional needs for love and acceptance.

Ideally, a manager will view employees as valuable members of the team—a group of people who can cooperate in creating a successful work environment. Although the manager must provide guidance, leadership, and support, her/his self-respect and respect for the employees will not falter.

How a manager views her/his staff generally depends more on the psychologic makeup of the manager and less on the actual history or potential of the staff. Because of this, it is important to assess your beliefs before you get too far into your job. The more you understand about how you view your staff, the easier it will be for you to avoid intensifying stress and creating problems with your staff. Also, this understanding will help you identify problems for what they really are, not for what you may believe them to be.

For example, if you are the type of manager who tends to view your staff as children, you may unknowingly create stress and resentment among the ranks. Few adults want to be treated like a child.

If you feel threatened by your staff, not only will this be evident to the staff, your management judgment will be impaired. It's difficult to make fair decisions and carry out your responsibilities if you are preoccupied with protecting your own interests.

If you view your staff as potential friends, you may create an adolescent environment with an "in crowd" and an "out crowd." This is not effective in the adult world of providing services to patients, carrying out responsibilities, and building careers.

Although these examples of manager beliefs may be ineffective and sometimes even destructive, most managers enter their roles with a little of each of these, as well as other points of view. What is important is that you understand how you actually *do* see your staff—before you determine how you think you *should* see your staff.

As you determine how you actually see your employees, you are in a better position to change your point of view, if necessary, and to develop effective management practices.

Ideally you come to your manager role with a healthy respect for your staff and yourself—a respect that all human beings deserve, whether they are one of the best nurses in town or one of those who needs help developing. On this premise you can build a realistic and effective view of your staff—one in which stress is manageable and all are able to thrive.

Inventory of Your Beliefs About Your Staff

Box 10-5 presents a quiz to help you clarify your management practices regarding your beliefs about or preconceived notions of your staff. The questions are designed as triggers to help you think about and develop or change your beliefs.

Following the inventory are guidelines for you to evaluate your responses to the first eight questions. The rest of the questions will help you reflect on how comfort-

---

box 10-5

BELIEFS ABOUT YOUR STAFF—QUESTIONS TO ASK YOURSELF

	YES	NO
1. Do I invite feedback from my staff?		
2. Do I invite constructive criticism of management policies or practices, including my own?		
3. Do I communicate my staff's concerns to my supervisor?		
4. Do I discuss star performers with my supervisor? Do I discuss problem employees with my supervisor?		
5. Do I communicate openly with my staff about the overall operations and goals of the institution or business? Whenever possible, do I inform them of any information handed down to me?		
6. Am I easily irritated when my staff expresses dissatisfaction with a policy or management practice? Why?		
7. Do I discuss staff members' personal or work-related problems with other staff members? Why?		
8. Are there staff members to whom I give preferential treatment? Why?		
9. Do I think someone on my staff wants my job? Why do I think this? Would this person or someone else on my staff be able to do my job? What have I done to explore her/his professional growth objectives? What have I done to encourage capable staff members to consider a management job in this institution or elsewhere?		
10. What do I think of my previous managers? Was anyone exceptionally good? Exceptionally poor? Why?		

BELIEFS ABOUT YOUR STAFF—cont'd

		YES	NO
11.	How did my previous managers view their staffs? Do I share any of these views? How did their opinions of their staffs affect the staffs? Were the managers' opinions of their staffs justified? Why do I think this? Did their opinions of their staffs become self-fulfilling prophesies? Why do I think this?	_____	_____
12.	What are the positive lessons I have learned from my previous managers? How can I incorporate these lessons into my management style?	_____	_____
13.	What aspects of my previous managers' styles do I want to avoid? Why? How can I avoid repeating management practices that could be mistakes?	_____	_____
14.	How do I think my present supervisor views me? Is this justified? Why? Is this effective and productive? Why?	_____	_____
15.	Do I want to pass on this view of subordinates to my staff? Why? How can I do or not do this?	_____	_____

---

able and confident you are in your role and in "what makes you tick" as a nurse manager.

"Yes" responses to the first five questions generally indicate a positive, respectful attitude toward your staff.

If you respond "yes" to any of the next three questions, you may be experiencing problems with your management role (i.e., recognizing the boundaries between you and your staff, as well as recognizing your responsibility to be objective and fair). For example, if you find you are generally irritated when your staff is dissatisfied, you may be personalizing their reactions. Your irritation may stem from your own difficulties in recognizing boundaries.

COPING MECHANISMS

Although many sources of stress are in the nursing workplace, individual nurses cope differently with these stresses.

In their study of critical care nurses, Robinson and Lewis[5] reviewed various coping mechanisms, including adaptive and maladaptive mechanisms (Box 10-6). Adaptive coping mechanisms are positive responses to stress and require no intervention. Maladaptive coping mechanisms indicate a negative response to stress and call for stress management intervention.

As you can see, this list includes adaptive and maladaptive coping mechanisms. Although the study characterized various mechanisms as either adaptive or maladaptive, some of these coping mechanisms could fall into either category. For

---

box 10-6

COPING MECHANISMS

- Take vacation.
- Watch television or read.
- Problem-solving.
- Hobbies.
- Discuss problems with family.
- Caffeine (coffee, tea, or soft drinks).
- Exercise.
- Consider changing jobs.
- Work harder and enjoy less.
- Overeating.

- Progressive relaxation techniques.
- Deny problems.
- Alcohol.
- Absenteeism.
- Imagery.
- Meditation.
- Smoking.
- Self-hypnosis.
- Drugs to relax.
- Discuss problems with coworkers.

Robinson JA, Lewis DJ: Coping with ICU work-related stressors: a study, *Crit Care Nurs* 10(5):86, 1990.

---

example, discussing problems with one's family may prove to be adaptive for one individual but maladaptive for another.

The way a nurse copes with stress in the workplace is highly individualized. Coping mechanisms that work for one may not work for another. In addition, a coping mechanism that works for a nurse under low-level stress may not work for that same nurse under higher levels of stress.

For the purposes of this discussion, those coping mechanisms that cause additional, albeit different, physical or emotional stress in a nurse are maladaptive coping mechanisms. Generally, behaviors such as overeating, undereating, overworking, drinking alcohol, smoking, and so forth eventually cause additional stress in the nurse.

Stress Evaluation Exercise: Coping Mechanisms

Earlier in this chapter you were asked to list as many sources of stress in your work environment as you could identify. As a follow-up to this exercise, now list all coping mechanisms you can imagine. Do not exclude those coping mechanisms you consider to be maladaptive. After generating your coping mechanisms list, consider those coping mechanisms that may be helpful and those that may not be helpful. Identify reasons some coping mechanisms may be adaptive and some maladaptive. You may further define coping mechanisms in terms of their usefulness for various levels of stress (e.g., taking a vacation may be appropriate as temporary relief from long-term stress, and reading or watching television may be effective as relief from short-term stress brought on by a rough day).

If you are doing this exercise with some of your peers, take ample time for discussion. Resist the temptation to push your personal agenda. Rather, learn from each other and broaden your understanding of how people cope with stress.

UNMANAGED STRESS IN THE PATIENT CARE WORKPLACE

Recognizing the signs of unmanaged stress in the workplace is critical to the nurse manager's ability to respond constructively to her/his own and the staff's needs.

Understanding the sources of stress in the patient care workplace and the accompanying coping mechanisms is a prerequisite to understanding what you and your staff are experiencing. When a stressful situation continues for an extended period, or when coping mechanisms are maladaptive or are failing, stress may become unmanageable.

Unfortunately, early signs—and even later signs—of unmanaged stress often go unnoticed. In fact, some managers first recognize that stress is spiraling out of control when staff members resign in legion numbers. Staff members themselves may not even recognize the early signs.

For various reasons, nurse managers often fail to recognize early stress signals. Most managers have risen through the nursing ranks. They have often been conditioned by their supervisors to ignore stress until it reaches mountainous proportions. Thus "It's always been like this" becomes a way to minimize the seriousness of stressful situations. Some nurse managers bring to their jobs a history of ignoring their own signs and symptoms of unmanaged stress, as well as inexperience in recognizing others' signs of unmanaged stress. In addition, the new nurse manager has not had the experience of viewing stress from the vantage point of a manager and claiming responsibility for helping the staff to manage it.

Breakwell,[6] in analyzing the stresses experienced by those in the health care profession, discusses the effects of stress as being both psychologic and behavioral (Box 10-7). The psychologic effects are seen in changes in one's thinking, as well as in one's emotions.

---

box 10-7

EFFECTS OF UNMANAGED STRESS

SOME CHANGES IN THINKING AS DESCRIBED BY BREAKWELL[6]

- Deteriorating memory.
- Declining concentration and attention span.
- Dissipating powers of organization and long-term planning.

SOME EMOTIONAL CHANGES

- Depression.
- Hostility.
- Defensiveness.
- Feelings of powerlessness and worthlessness.
- Cynicism.
- Mood swings.
- Hypochondria.
- Personality changes (e.g., a shy person becomes gregarious or vice versa).

Continued

EFFECTS OF UNMANAGED STRESS — cont'd

SOME BEHAVIORAL EFFECTS OF STRESS

- Decreased energy level.
- Disrupted sleep.
- Increased drinking and/or smoking.
- Absenteeism from work.
- Diminished sex drive.
- Lack of enthusiasm
- Lack of interest in activities and hobbies that once were satisfying.

SOME CHANGES BROUGHT ON BY CHRONIC, UNRELIEVED STRESS (MAY BE SUBTLE)[7]

- Feeling overwhelmed.
- Fatigue, angry outbursts, depression.
- Forgetfulness and disorganization.
- Guilt and self-sacrifice.
- Feeling disillusioned.
- Passivity.
- Distancing yourself from your patients.
- Letting yourself go.
- Substance abuse.
- Physical illness.

Stress Evaluation Exercise: Signs of Unmanaged Stress

Nurse managers would do well to monitor themselves and their staffs for the changes brought on by unmanaged stress. Because many of these changes are subjective symptoms, astute nurse managers must learn to observe staff members for the objective signs that usually accompany these subjective symptoms. Box 10-8 on p. 293 presents a stress inventory checklist.

FAILING TO MANAGE STRESS: A COMMON PITFALL

Once a nurse manager learns to identify signs of stress in the workplace, the next step is problem-solving and responding to this stress. Failing to respond constructively to stress in the workplace is a common pitfall for nurse managers.

Often managers minimize the toll stress can take on themselves and their staffs, ignoring even late warning signs of stress's wear and tear. There are many reasons for this failing. For example, a nurse manager may ignore the effects of stress because of a fear of impotence (e.g., "There's nothing I can do about it, so I'll ignore it"). Unfortunately, this attitude of impotence—no matter how toughly exhibited— is communicated to the staff. When one experiences impotence in the face of stress, the stress is magnified, creating an even more strained environment. On the

---

····· box 10-8 ·····

STAFF STRESS INVENTORY CHECKLIST

As a manager, you can take stock of what you are seeing in your staff's behavior by asking yourself questions that address Wilson's[7] list of symptoms. You may ask yourself the questions in reference to an individual on the staff or in regard to the staff as a whole. For the purposes of this discussion, assume that you are considering one individual.

FEELING OVERWHELMED

Is she slow to start at the beginning of the workday? _____

Does she "jump right in," before having had the chance to organize the workday? _____

Does she dart from task to task without a clear sense of purpose or control? _____

Does she seem to respond mostly to the "squeaky wheel" (or patient), rather than acting on priorities? _____

Does she express a fatalistic attitude about the workload (e.g., "Oh well, it's not going to get done anyway")? _____

Does she consistently have to work overtime to complete assignments? _____

Has she failed to complete assignments? _____

FATIGUE, ANGRY OUTBURSTS, AND DEPRESSION

Does he lose his temper at the slightest provocation? _____

Does he respond rudely or abruptly to patients? _____

Is he rough with patients? _____

Has he become quiet or unusually reserved? _____

Has he lost his sense of humor? _____

Does he get tearful with little provocation? _____

Does he remark that the job is "getting to him"? _____

Has he been absent from work more often than is considered average absenteeism? _____

Does he say he is depressed? _____

Has he shown personality changes? _____

Has he become disinterested or apathetic about work? _____

Has he become disinterested or apathetic about other aspects of his life? _____

FORGETFULNESS AND DISORGANIZATION

Is she making more than the normal amount of mistakes? _____

Are you seeing an increase in her incident reports? _____

Does she forget aspects of patient care? _____

Does she forget to report patient problems appropriately? _____

Is she failing to recognize patient problems or make logical deductions about patient problems? _____

Are her usual thinking abilities impaired? _____

Does she seem distracted? _____

When you address her, does she sometimes seem not to hear you? _____

Adapted from Wilson LK: High-gear nursing: how it can run you down and what you can do about it, *Nursing '89* 19(21):81, 1989.

Continued

STAFF STRESS INVENTORY CHECKLIST—cont'd

GUILT AND SELF-SACRIFICE

Is he coming to work when he is ill? _____

Is he consistently skipping lunch or work breaks to catch up on work? _____

Is he consistently working overtime? _____

Does he consistently volunteer for distasteful tasks, overtime assignments, and holiday shifts? _____

FEELING DISILLUSIONED

Does she express resentment about the nursing profession? _____

Does she express envy of people in other professions or regret that she became a nurse? _____

Does she remark that the actual practice of nursing is much different from what she learned in school? _____

Does she express regret that she can never deliver the type of care she would like to deliver? _____

Does she express feelings of hopelessness about nursing (e.g., "It will never change")? _____

PASSIVITY

Does he take abuse from coworkers or physicians? _____

Does he remark that "it's not worth" disagreeing with difficult individuals? _____

Does he seem indifferent about problem-solving? _____

Is he among the first people you consider when you must assign a distasteful task (because you know there will be no resistance)? _____

Is he described as a wimp by coworkers? _____

DISTANCING ONESELF FROM PATIENTS

Does she refer to patients as disease entities, rather than as people (e.g., "the hepatitis in 22")? _____

Does she respond irritably to patients who "interrupt" tasks with questions or requests? _____

Does she limit conversation with patients by speaking only when absolutely necessary? _____

Does she ask patients to make their requests all at once so she can limit interactions with them? _____

Does she focus almost exclusively on the physical aspects of caring for patients, rather than also considering the psychologic aspects? _____

Does she make remarks about family members who "interfere" with patient care by asking questions or making requests? _____

Is she "cold" or "cool" to patients? _____

LETTING ONESELF GO

Has he gained or lost weight recently? _____

Is his appearance sloppy or haphazard? _____

STAFF STRESS INVENTORY CHECKLIST—cont'd

SUBSTANCE ABUSE

Is she drinking more coffee or smoking more cigarettes? _____

Has she said she is taking something to sleep? _____

Has she been late to work? _____

Has she been absent from work more often than is considered average? _____

Has she joked or commented about excessive "partying"? _____

Is she showing any of the physical or psychologic signs of chemical dependency?
_____ (Refer to the later section When You Identify a Serious Staff Problem.)

PHYSICAL ILLNESS

Has he had excessive absenteeism because of illness? _____

Does he seem to have an inordinate number of colds, headaches, or gastrointestinal problems? _____

---

contrary, the sense that one can effect change, regardless of degree, provides a feeling of hope and empowerment.

A second reason nurse managers may fail to respond constructively to stress is a false sense of their own invulnerability. This sense of invulnerability—"That doesn't bother me," "I've been in nursing 10 years [or 3 or 5 years]; I'm used to that"—often is no more than a way of building up to the burnout so many nurses experience. A nurse who appears immune to the emotional roller coaster of nursing may in fact be closer to burnout than suspected.

For example, distancing oneself from and depersonalizing patients (e.g., "the colon cancer in 13-A" or "the three 'total-cares' I had today") help a nurse avoid feelings of frustration, fear, or grief but are poor substitutes for accepting and sharing these feelings with others.

In the long run, trying to be invulnerable leaves one vulnerable to frustration, depression, and burnout. And a nurse manager who, by example, fosters such invulnerability in her/his staff also fosters burnout in her/his staff.

A third reason nurse managers may fail to respond constructively to stress is a misguided belief that managers are expected to "roll with"—rather than respond to—stressful situations. Often managers are concerned that acknowledgment of the stress level in their area may indicate a deficiency in their management skills. This concern is heightened when a manager's own supervisor appears unaware of or invulnerable to stress.

You may be able to identify other reasons nurses and nurse managers fail to respond constructively to stress. Regardless of the explanation, the result is the same: failure to respond constructively to stress leads to increased stress. When you are able to recognize unmanaged stress, you are better able to respond to stress in the workplace with effective coping mechanisms. You will also be better equipped to respond to the needs of your staff and help them in enhancing their adaptive coping mechanisms.

When You Identify a Serious Staff Problem

Occasionally you will identify an employee who has a serious problem. This problem may be caused by job stress, personal difficulties, or a combination of factors.

If you are concerned that an employee's performance may be impaired because of chemical dependence, or that she/he may be experiencing serious emotional problems or depression, you need to request guidance. You can speak with your EAP counselor, the staff social worker or psychologist, the psychiatric nurse specialist, or a professional outside your organization.

It generally is best to use your organization's resources first. People within your organization may know the employee, or your organization may have resources or policies to respond to these types of problems.

If you do seek assistance from an outside professional to guide you in your dealings with an employee, resources are usually available. Most cities have emergency or crisis hotlines for referrals to appropriate organizations, many of which will discuss your concerns about your employee free of charge. Hospital emergency departments frequently keep hotline and other organization listings.

Discuss your concerns with your supervisor and determine a course of action. If your supervisor is not responsive, these cases—because of their serious nature and possible consequences—obligate you to take your concerns up your organization's chain of command or to HR, the EAP counselor, or other professional until you get assistance.

The Chemically Dependent Employee

It is important for nurse managers to be aware of the problems of alcohol and other chemical dependencies in the health professions. Bissell,[8] a nationally recognized expert on addicted health care professionals, and Jones[8] conducted research indicating the severity of chemical dependency in the nursing profession. Their research suggests that approximately 5% of the 1.5 million registered nurses in the United States are dependent on alcohol or drugs.

Selbach[9] cites job strain—including factors such as the nursing shortage, work overload, and dealing with illness and death—as a traditional source of the frustration and stress contributing to a nurse becoming chemically dependent. She cites rotating shifts, night duty, chronic stress, tension, fatigue, and anxiety as factors that can lead to insomnia and the initial use of chemicals to unwind, relax, and sleep. In addition, most nurses are women, and many actually have two full-time jobs, nurse and mother, and try to be "superwoman" at both.

A word of caution: the chemically dependent nurse, like many others dependent on drugs or alcohol, often does not embody the stereotype of the debilitated addict.

In fact, some chemically dependent nurses are excellent workers who show no sign of their dependency until late in the disease. The chemically dependent nurse may be a high achiever, an individual who has done well in school and in past jobs and may have been the model employee/spouse/friend/parent before the dependency. She/he often is a compulsive individual, which is a trait that can lend itself to good patient care but which can also cause the nurse to create unrealistic expectations of herself/himself at work and in other areas of life. These expectations can produce the stress overload the nurse believes is alleviated by using drugs or alcohol. Box 10-9 lists signs of the chemically dependent nurse.

Many health care facilities have policies concerning the chemically dependent employee, including policies to assist the employee in seeking treatment. Although terminating a chemically dependent employee may appear to be a quick fix, the

---

box 10-9

SIGNS OF THE CHEMICALLY DEPENDENT NURSE

Numbers 1 through 7 are signs identified by Patton, an occupational health nurse and EAP coordinator. Other common signs follow.

1. Too many medication errors.
2. Frequent absences from the nursing unit.
3. Too many controlled substances wasted and/or spilled.
4. Consistently incorrect narcotics count.
5. Signs out more controlled substances than do others.
6. Rapid, extreme, and inappropriate mood changes.
7. Patient complaints of the ineffectiveness of pain medication when administered by individual. (This could be a sign that the nurse is substituting saline or sterile water, emptying capsules, or substituting nonnarcotic tablets.)
8. Excessive absenteeism.
9. Tardiness.
10. Getting by at work, but not performing beyond the bare minimum needed.
11. Failure to complete assignments.
12. Leaving responsibilities to other staff.
13. Sloppy, illogical, nonexistent, or meaningless charting (often by rote and could apply to any patient).
14. Excessive incident reports and/or failure to file incident reports.
15. Excessive mistakes.
16. Abnormal physiologic reactions resulting from drug or alcohol use, such as headaches, diarrhea, lack of sleep, and withdrawal symptoms.
17. Inappropriate behavior or quick flashes of temper.
18. Personality changes.
19. Obvious physical signs of drug use, such as slurring speech, rapid speech, smell of alcohol, confusion, or weight loss.
20. Accusations that people are "out to get" or are against her/him.
21. Blaming others and refusal to take responsibility for actions.

From Patton J: Addicted nurses, *J Pract Nurs* 37(4):40, 1987.

terminated employee probably will not seek treatment. In fact, she/he will probably move onto another job—the "geographic cure"—taking the chemical dependency into another workplace.

As a nurse manager facing the possibility of a chemically dependent employee, your responsibilities are twofold: (1) to see that your patients are receiving proper care from responsible employees and (2) to address the needs of the chemically dependent employee, including the right to privacy and the opportunity to seek help.

If you believe you have a chemically dependent employee on your staff, discuss the matter with your supervisor to determine a course of action (i.e., what policies your organization has in place, what professional person will guide you). If your supervisor is not responsive, continue to seek guidance.

The Employee with Emotional Difficulties

If you are concerned that an employee is severely depressed, disturbed, or suicidal, seek guidance immediately to determine how to handle the situation. If you have fears or concerns that an employee is "not right," these feelings are probably well founded. In these cases, you must provide for the safety of your patients and determine, with the help of your supervisor and a trained professional, how to support your employee. Again, if your supervisor is not responsive to your concern, seek guidance from others.

Other Serious Problems

Aside from chemical dependency and emotional difficulties, other serious problems that warrant attention may manifest themselves in your department as a whole or in a member or members of your staff. For instance, sometimes a staff member copes with stress by blaming you, another individual on the staff, or a small group of individuals for the stress. This scapegoating can become a way of life in the department and can devastate the person or persons being scapegoated. In addition, it never alleviates the stress in the department because it does not solve the problem.

Other problems that may arise in your department could affect almost everyone on your staff. The situation may be the result of long-term problems within your organization or department, such as excessive turnover, or it may be a problem that is clearly time-limited—whether it be 1 month or 1 year in duration. Examples of these situations include major management changes (e.g., a new CEO who effects many changes), a large construction or renovation project that disrupts daily activities, a flu epidemic that depletes the staff, or the introduction of computerized scheduling, which requires a period of adjustment while the "bugs" are worked out.

In some instances, you may recognize that many of your staff are experiencing a great deal of stress, but you cannot identify the source. If you think your staff as a group is feeling the strain of unmanaged stress, regardless of the source, it may be helpful to invite a professional to facilitate an ongoing staff support group. It is not recommended that a nurse manager try to lead these group meetings. The support group should allow for the sharing of feelings and personal interpretations, which only a trained professional should direct. In addition, if there are communication gaps between you and any of your staff members, a professional can help in closing these gaps. Discuss your options with your supervisor.

UNMANAGEABLE ENVIRONMENTS

Although most problems can be solved with time and the proper guidance and intervention, you may find yourself in a work environment in which the problems are so many or so deeply rooted that you are unable to be an effective manager. In this instance, it is generally best for you to leave the position.

There are many understandable reasons why you may leave a job. Some examples include a poor job match for you, a disagreement with the values or policies of a supervisor or organization, a realization that you prefer not to be a manager, or a realization that you are not ready to be a manager. Another understandable reason for leaving a job is the recognition that you are attempting to manage an unmanageable environment.

Generally, an unmanageable environment is characterized by two components: (1) a serious problem exists in the department or organization, and (2) you have little or ineffective management support in solving it. If your immediate supervisor shows little support or if the support is ineffective, you may be able to find help from someone else within your organization. Some problems, because of their serious nature, require you to seek this help when your immediate supervisor is not responsive. Some of these situations were discussed earlier in this chapter, under "When You Identify a Serious Staff Problem."

You may identify other serious problems that call for immediate attention. For instance, staffing that is so lean that patient care is threatened would require you to seek help beyond a nonresponsive supervisor.

A word of caution: when you secure problem-solving assistance or intervention from someone in your organization other than your supervisor, the immediate problem may be resolved, but you have not changed your environment. Although your first responsibility must be to solve the immediate problem, you must then evaluate your options and the viability of continuing as a manager with an ineffective supervisor.

Ineffective Management Support

A supervisor may demonstrate ineffective management support or a lack of management support to the nurse manager in many ways. For example, the nurse manager may be restricted from taking corrective action against employees who defy the policies of the organization or department. The manager may be prevented from taking disciplinary action against an employee who is rough with a patient. The supervisor may listen sympathetically to the nurse manager's concerns about the department but offer no advice or direction. The nurse manager may be consistently scapegoated by the staff, and the supervisor may offer no guidance for dealing with this situation.

These are a few examples of how a supervisor may fail to support a nurse manager. In each case, the manager's inability to take action, to correct a problem, or to establish leadership authority will affect the morale of the staff, the quality of patient care, and the manager's ability to manage the department.

Sometimes a new nurse manager enters a job without knowledge of the department's history and resulting problems. Perhaps the staff members believe the previous manager was unfairly dismissed from the position. Or they may have experienced a long period without leadership and resent the arrival of the new manager. These factors alone do not necessarily create an unmanageable environment. However, if the new nurse manager receives little support and guidance from her/his supervisor, effective management could be difficult.

Box 10-10 presents a list of conditions that, when combined with ineffective support or a lack of support from management above you, could signal an unmanage-

---

box 10-10

SIGNS OF AN UNMANAGEABLE ENVIRONMENT

- An individual or group (or clique) of nurses holding the unspoken power in the division.
- Understaffing, with no plan or hope for improvement.
- Poor patient care.
- Staff scapegoating of you or a member of your staff.
- A chemically dependent employee.
- An employee stealing drugs, narcotics, or supplies.
- Widespread absenteeism.
- An employee coming in late to work, leaving early, or disappearing during the workday.
- An employee who physically or emotionally abuses patients.
- An employee who defies the policies of the organization.
- An employee who shows you no respect (e.g., walking away from you when you talk, shouting at you, ignoring you).
- A staff that is divided along lines of race, gender, professional status, levels of competence, tenure, or other factors.
- A supervisor who makes management decisions based on any of the factors cited in the preceding point.
- A supervisor who maintains friendships with one or more staff members who do not support you or who undermine your authority.

SIGNS OF AN UNMANAGEABLE ENVIRONMENT — cont'd

- A supervisor who misrepresents you to upper management (e.g., lying about you, taking credit for your work).
- A supervisor who listens to the complaints of the staff (about you, your management, or other matters related to your department) without encouraging the staff to talk to you or without informing you of the conversations.
- An apathetic staff.
- An employee who defies your instructions, policies, and so forth.
- An employee who seems seriously depressed, disturbed, or suicidal.
- Other conditions you have identified.

---

able environment. You may be able to add items to this list. Included in the list are some additional destructive behaviors your supervisor could exhibit—behaviors that go beyond not showing support and are more actively destructive.

If you determine that you are in an unmanageable environment, it is important that you give yourself permission to resign your position. Sometimes nurse managers are reluctant to give up on a job, believing if they only try harder, conditions will improve. In an unmanageable environment, unfortunately, this often is not the case. By definition, this type of environment cannot be improved without radical changes in the leadership above.

If you resign a position because you believe the work environment to be unmanageable, you may want to request an exit interview with an objective nurse recruiter, personnel director, or other individual in an influential position who may be receptive to listening. Each organization is different, and you will have to determine your best course. Because patient care may be at stake, it is important to share your perceptions of the environment in the hope that the situation will be addressed. As you relate your perceptions, take care to provide only the facts, not your subjective feelings or intuitions about the situation. For example, relate problematic events in your department and how you attempted to get help to solve them.

Sometimes it is best to schedule an exit interview for a time after you have recovered from the immediate stress of your resignation. If you choose to pursue an exit interview, it will be important for you to conduct the interview calmly, presenting your information in a rational manner.

TAKING ACTION TO SUPPORT YOUR STAFF

Fortunately, most nurse managers do not find themselves in unmanageable environments. And in most cases, there are many steps a nurse manager can take to alleviate routine stress in the department. Everyone agrees that a nurse manager's support is critical to the staff's successful management of stress. Albrecht and Halsey[10] suggest that we consider "social support as verbal and nonverbal communication between recipients and providers, which reduces uncertainty about the situation, the self, and others . . . to enhance personal control."

Albrecht and Halsey Study on Support to Staff Nurses

Albrecht and Halsey[10] discuss the types of messages that are most helpful to a distressed nurse (Manager's Tip 10-1).

Their study of staff nurses' stress and how their managers support them was very revealing. The nurses' perceptions of a manager's supportive behaviors were measured separately in four hypothetical stress situations. The combined results show that the manager's listening, offering reassurance, and giving advice were supportive behaviors that were valued by many of the nurses. Although the manager's taking action to solve the problem also was viewed as supportive, the results showed that this behavior was not valued by as many nurses as were the manager's communication and advising behaviors.

However, one stress situation in which many of the nurses viewed the manager's action as supportive was when the staff nurses were working in an understaffed situation. Here, the manager's helping with the work was particularly valued. This makes sense because understaffing threatens the nurses' ability to provide good patient care, the driving desire of most nurses. However, even in this situation, many nurses also valued the manager's listening skills.

As a nurse manager, you must weigh each stressful situation and determine the steps you can take to support your staff. In some instances, active, as well as communicative, support is imperative, lest you become known for "all talk and no action." In the case of understaffing, it may be important to help in the immediate situation, then take action to see that understaffing does not become a chronic problem.

The lesson to be learned from Albrecht and Halsey's study[10] is not to underestimate the value of each of a manager's methods of offering support to the staff:

MANAGER'S TIP 10-1

HELPFUL MESSAGES FOR THE DISTRESSED NURSE

✔ Reduce uncertainty by offering a new perspective on the problem (e.g., "Why don't you think about this?").
✔ Help increase feelings of control over the problem by allowing education days or teaching new skills.
✔ Help enhance a sense of control over the problem by providing tangible assistance (in a friendly, noncondescending manner).
✔ Offer acceptance and reassurance.

Modified from Albrecht TL, Halsey J: Supporting the staff nurse under stress, *Nursing Management* 22(7):60, 1991.

listening, offering reassurance, giving advice, taking action, validating your staff's feelings, and helping your staff understand the perspective of other employees and of physicians.

In some cases, good communication skills or concrete suggestions will greatly alleviate staff nurses' stress. In others, you will need to combine this support with action.

To address some forms of stress, you may need to make changes in how your department operates. Be mindful of ways you can alter your work environment to alleviate stress. Include your staff in discussions of ways to modify operations for a smoother, less stressful workday. Enlist the guidance and support of your supervisor. Work with your supervisor to determine what changes you can and cannot effect and why. For example, if you have been unable to fill some vacant positions, what alternatives do you have to tide the staff over until the positions are filled? Is there a way to get more secretarial support? Can you employ temporary nurses? Can you draw more help from the float pool? Are there some nonpatient care activities that can be suspended until your positions are filled?

Drawing on the Work and Experience of Other Nurse Managers

Many nurse managers fall into the trap of thinking they are alone in dealing with staff stress. In addition to your supervisor and a myriad of other resource people within and outside your organization, consider the experience of your peers. Ask them how they support their staffs and consider if these techniques would work for your staff. Be sensitive to the differences in departments, personnel, and your personality versus the personalities of your peers. What works for them may not work for you. Also, you may find that you simply do not agree with the approaches of some of your peers. Nonetheless, your peer group may offer new ways of looking at conditions and new ideas for supporting your staff.

Another resource to consider is the nursing literature. Much has been written about stress in nursing and the allied health care professions. A trip to a nursing or medical library can result in a lot of new information. If you have specific concerns, such as the impaired nurse or the stress of dealing with death and dying, you can easily find articles on these topics. If there is no nursing or health services library in your facility or where you live, contact your local library to see if they carry any appropriate journals. Also, if your organization has an education or training department, consult with the director.

Subscribing to one or more of the nursing professional journals is a good idea, both for the clinical and management information. You may want to share subscriptions with some of your peers to cut costs and increase your access to various publications.

Communicating with Upper Management

An important way to support your staff is to communicate their concerns to your supervisor. By working with your supervisor, you may be able to generate additional ways to demonstrate support to your staff. Manager's Tip 10-2 provides further suggestions.

If your department is experiencing a particularly stressful situation, be certain to let them know that you and your supervisor are concerned. Tell the staff what you and your supervisor are able to do to support them. Often, your staff's knowing that you recognize their stress is the first step in alleviating it. Also, their knowing that you consider their feelings important enough to discuss with your supervisor lets them know that you care.

MANAGER'S TIP 10-2

LENDING SUPPORT TO YOUR STAFF

- ✔ Encourage camaraderie among your staff. Provide the opportunity for them to know each other as people, not just as nurses. Whenever possible, schedule breaks and meals for at least two nurses at a time.
- ✔ Sponsor a staff party away from the workplace a few times a year. A potluck dinner is an inexpensive way to get together and will encourage staff participation.
- ✔ Take time to know your staff. Ask about their families, friends, and school experiences. Take some of your breaks and meals with them.
- ✔ Let your staff know you. Do not discourage casual conversation. Let them know it is okay to ask you about yourself by volunteering information about your life and interests away from the job. However, do not overdo it by talking about yourself in a one-sided conversation.
- ✔ Allow time at regular staff meetings for your employees to ask questions and voice concerns. You can invite this communication broadly (e.g., "Is there anything anyone would like to discuss?") and specifically (e.g., "Does anyone have any questions or concerns about our new admissions policy?"). A combination of both techniques is most effective.
- ✔ Recognize unmanaged stress (e.g., "It seems this is a difficult time," "Are you okay?" "It would make sense that you would be stressed out today.").
- ✔ Listen. Listen. And listen again.
- ✔ If you are concerned that someone may be experiencing stress, talk to the person and offer reassurance and support with constructive problem-solving. In cases of severe stress, look to your supervisor and a trained professional for guidance.
- ✔ Provide time in the workday for your staff to think and reflect on the best way to organize and deliver patient care.
- ✔ Provide regular staff inservices and updating of skills.
- ✔ Allow for education days for your staff to encourage them to develop professionally.
- ✔ Use your supervisor for assistance in supporting your staff.
- ✔ Help your staff learn to manage their time.
- ✔ Arrange staff coverage so that your employees are able to take vacation breaks on a regular basis.
- ✔ Offer words of support, recognizing your staff's good work and giving positive feedback frequently and freely.

Humor

Humor can break the tension in even the most stressful situation. If you are attuned to the sensitivities of your staff and have a good sense of timing, you can use humor very effectively to make a tough day a little less stressful.

As wonderful as humor can be, there are some basic guidelines concerning its use. For example, never make a joke at the expense of another person—present or absent—or at the expense of a group of people based on their gender, race, sexual orientation, and so on, regardless of whether a member of the group is on your staff. Hostile, bigoted, or demeaning humor may lead to feelings of insecurity among your staff (e.g., "When will she/he come after me or someone like me?").

In addition, it is important not to use humor at an inappropriate time, such as in a serious patient-care situation that requires concentration. Laughter at this time could have serious consequences for the patient. Also, do not use any form of humor that would show disrespect for a patient or the patient's family.

Particularly effective is lighthearted humor poking fun at yourself (however, not at your gender, race, sexual orientation, and so forth). If you are comfortable with self-deprecating humor, you can give your staff the chance to relax a little, as well as to see you in a more personal light, thus strengthening the bonds between you. According to Smith,[11] "Team spirit and improved staff morale are benefits reaped by the nurse manager who knows how to take her job seriously while taking herself lightly."

Smith[11] notes that it is difficult for most people to tell a scripted joke and get the desired effect, particularly to a group or to people with whom relationships are not well developed. For spontaneous situations, Lee[12] suggests that a comical remark about a personal event or predicament generally works best.

SUPPORTING YOURSELF

As was discussed at the beginning of this chapter, it is critical that you support yourself as you simultaneously support your staff from the effects of stress. Listed later are various ways to help you manage long-term and short-term job stress. However, there are individuals for whom these and other methods may not work. The following discussion addresses these individuals.

If you believe your environment is basically manageable, but you are having difficulty coping with the stress of your job, give yourself permission to get professional help, either from your EAP counselor, another in-house professional, or a professional counselor or therapist outside your organization. Remember, you are new to your job and to the stresses of being a manager. Even when you are an experienced nurse manager, there may come a time when you feel your coping mechanisms are failing you. Do not consider yourself inadequate if you are having problems dealing

with the stress of your job. Discussing your situation with an impartial professional can help you to problem-solve, strengthen your coping mechanisms, or
develop new ones.

If There Is (You Feel) No Hope in Sight

You may reach a point where you cannot handle the stresses of your job, despite
the fact that the environment may be manageable (when viewed objectively),
despite your best efforts to problem-solve and seek help, and despite your belief
that you should be able to handle the stress. Or you simply may know it is best for
you to leave your position because you are not able or do not want to invest the
energy necessary to cope with the stress. If you have no reason to believe your situation will improve, give yourself permission to leave your job. Many nurses are
drawn to their profession because of their gifts and inner needs to care for others.
Although these qualities are admirable and serve others well, they do not always
serve the caretaker well. Resigning a position does not mean you are a failure. It
could be a way to take control of your life and afford yourself the type of care and
attention you are so good at giving to others.

In most instances, your work environment will be manageable and you will be able
to support yourself and your staff. Below are recommendations for supporting yourself.

MANAGER'S TIP 10-3

SUPPORTING YOURSELF

✔ Develop a "can do" attitude. Consider the problems you *can* solve and focus on these,
rather than all the problems you *cannot* solve. These successes will help you feel
capable, stronger, and more able to take on the next problem.

✔ Become more assertive. Feeling powerless in your relationships is a great source of job
stress. Learn constructive ways to solve problems and communicate effectively with
others—not aggressively, but calmly, directly, and with respect for yourself and others.
Take a class or workshop in communications or assertiveness.

✔ Make overwhelming tasks manageable. Break down big tasks into their component
parts. Then concentrate on completing each part. At the beginning of the day, instead
of feeling powerless in the face of the next 8 to 10 hours of work, prioritize and write
down your tasks for the next 30 minutes, 2 hours, 4 hours, and so on. Then take them
a step at a time.

✔ Manage your time better. Combine tasks when you can. If you have to make a call,
before you pick up the phone, consider if you have other matters to discuss with the
same person or department. If you take a patient admission history, write it directly
onto the form. Do not write it on scratch paper and copy it later onto the form. Learn
to delegate when appropriate. Do not think you have to do *everything*. Learn what you
must do to take care of yourself and what can be expected of others.

SUPPORTING YOURSELF—cont'd

✔ Accept your failures, and do not take yourself so seriously. When you fail, look at what went wrong and why, and consider whether you could have done something differently. Learn from your mistakes and resolve to put this learning to use. Accept that you are human and that you will make mistakes. Learn to laugh at yourself sometimes and appreciate the good things around you.

✔ Nurture each other. Use your caretaking skills with one another. Cultivate friendships with people you trust.

✔ Nurture yourself. Learn to relax, listen to your body's needs for caretaking, exercise, and do something fun for yourself at least once a week.

Adapted from Wilson LK: High-gear nursing : how it can run you down and what you can do about it, *Nursing '89* 19(12):81, 1989.

Wilson[7] recommends the strategies in Manager's Tip 10-3 for nurses dealing with the stress of their profession. These tips apply to staff nurses as well as to nurse managers.

More Tips for Taking Care of Yourself

Manager's Tips 10-4 and 10-5 offer other ways to support yourself and alleviate the effects of routine stress on a short-term and long-term basis. Work to stop a mole-hill of stress from building to a mountain. Many of these suggestions also could be helpful for your staff. We saved the best lists for last.

MANAGER'S TIP 10-4

SHORT-TERM STRESS: TIPS IF YOU ARE FEELING TENSE AT WORK

✔ Ask a coworker to relieve you for a few moments so you can adjust your thinking and put things in perspective.

✔ Take a few minutes to sit down, take some deep breaths, and relax.

✔ Step away from the work environment and stretch your arms and legs, touch your toes, and open and close your fists to release tension.

✔ Take a moment to think of an enjoyable time you had with a friend or family member. Let yourself smile.

✔ Take a moment to visualize yourself as a relaxed, capable individual who *can* solve problems.

✔ Take a few minutes to consult with a peer, ventilate, and perhaps get a different perspective.

✔ Make up your mind that the stressful situation at hand will not get the better of you.

MANAGER'S TIP 10-5

EFFECTIVE STRESS MANAGEMENT: TIPS FOR THE REST OF YOUR LIFE

✔ Take time to "smell the roses" every day. Do something just for you, no matter how small. Watch a favorite television program, talk to a friend on the phone, take a walk, give yourself a pedicure, or curl up in bed an hour early and catch up on your reading.

✔ Get a manicure, facial, or a new haircut.

✔ Get regular physical exercise, such as walking, jogging, swimming, or gardening.

✔ Eat healthful foods. Limit caffeine and alcoholic beverages.

✔ Ventilate tension from work by talking for 5 or 10 minutes to a sympathetic listener— a spouse, friend, or coworker. Talk in general terms—"Two people died today," or "We had to work short today." Avoid detailed discussions or blow-by-blow accounts of your day, which only serve to make you relive the stress a second time, instead of relieving it. The object is simply to feel the support of someone who cares about you.

✔ Learn to meditate. Meditation is a good way to focus yourself and to relax. Fifteen to thirty minutes of meditation in the morning or evening will go a long way toward helping you keep perspective for the rest of your day.

✔ Build your relationships with your peer group. Sharing concerns, considering solutions to routine problems, and enjoying one another's company all are good ways to give and receive support.

✔ Schedule regular vacations, usually at 3-month or 4-month intervals. In the interim, a 3-day weekend can provide a great deal of relaxation.

✔ Leave work at work. Plan so that you are not taking home work on a regular basis.

✔ Cultivate outside interests that are unrelated to your work. Include individuals who are not in the health care field in your circle of friends.

✔ Ask your supervisor to set up time with you to brainstorm solutions to particularly stressful situations.

✔ Stay tuned to the stress level of your staff. The more quickly you address their stress, the less likely serious problems will develop.

✔ Participate in professional development, quality control, or other committees in your work setting. This involvement will help you become more familiar with your institution, help you to network, provide different perspectives on situations and problems in your job, and give you exposure for recognition for your good ideas and work.

✔ Be active in your professional organizations. Through this participation, you will learn nursing and management skills, as well as increase networking and strengthen peer relationships. As a result, you will feel stronger, smarter, and less stressed.

✔ Be realistic about the problems on your job. Not every problem is your responsibility, and you cannot solve the world's problems. Take responsibility for only those problems that are yours.

✔ Have realistic expectations of others. Eliminate the stress of being frustrated by inconsequential shortcomings of others.

✔ Keep a positive attitude. Bad attitudes are contagious and breed additional stress.

✔ Address and correct mistakes. Then forgive yourself and others for making mistakes.

SUMMARY

This chapter reviewed stress in the nursing workplace and how it can manifest itself, stress-coping mechanisms, and signs of unmanaged stress. Examples of serious staff problems and recommended actions were discussed. Also, the unmanageable environment was explored, as were points on how to recognize this "no-win" situation.

Many suggestions were made about supporting yourself and your staff. Undoubtedly you can think of additional ways—ways that apply specifically to you or to your staff.

No single reference, person, or resource contains all the answers to a given situation or problem. Talk to your supervisor and your peers. Read professional journals. Continue your efforts to seek information and develop your own solutions to take care of yourself and your staff. Develop and use your sense of humor! The return on your investment will be great.

QUESTIONS FOR CONSIDERATION

1. Describe three sources of stress in the patient care environment.
2. Identify five stressors specific to the nurse manager's management responsibilities.
3. List three positive (adaptive) coping mechanisms and three negative (maladaptive) coping mechanisms.
4. Describe ten possible signs of a chemically dependent team member.
5. Discuss ten positive stress management tips "for the rest of your life."

References

1. Nicholson L: Stress management in nursing, *Nursing Management* 21(4):53, 1990.
2. Foxall MJ, et al: A comparison of frequency and sources of nursing job stress perceived by intensive care, hospice and medical-surgical nurses, *Journal of Advanced Nursing* 15(5):577, 1990.
3. Lees S, Ellis N: The design of a stress-management programme for nursing personnel, *Journal of Advanced Nursing* 15:946, 1990.
4. Simms L, et al: Breaking the burnout barrier: resurrecting work excitement in nursing," *Nursing Economics* 8(3):185, 1990.
5. Robinson JA, Lewis DJ: Coping with ICU work-related stressors: a study, *Critical Care Nurse* 10(5):86, 1990.
6. Breakwell GM: Are you stressed out?, *American Journal of Nursing* 90(8):31, 1990. Article abstracted from Breakwell GM: *Facing physical violence*, first published in London, 1990, The British Psychological Society in association with Routledge Ltd, and 1990, New York, Chapman & Hall.
7. Wilson LK: High-gear nursing: how it can run you down and what you can do about it, *Nursing '89* 19(12):81, 1989.
8. Bissell L, Jones D: The alcoholic nurse, *Nursing Outlook* 29:96, 1981.
9. Selbach KH: Chemical dependency in nursing, *AORN J* 52(3):531, 1990.
10. Albrecht TL, Halsey J: Supporting the staff nurse under stress, *Nursing Management* 22(7):60, 1991.
11. Smith LB: Humor relations for nurse managers, *Nursing Management* 21(5):86, 1990.
12. Lee BS: Humor relations for nurse managers, *Nursing Management* 21(5):86, 88, 90, 1990.

For Further Reading

Albrecht TL, Halsey J: Supporting the staff nurse under stress, *Nursing Management* 22(7):60-61, 64, 1991.

Bennett S, Robertson R, Moss P: Education: learning the pitfalls of codependency, *Nursing Management* 23(2):80B, 1992.

Cauthorne-Lindstrom C, Hrabe D: Codependent behaviors in managers: a script for failure, *Nursing Management* 21(2):34, 1990.

Fortman R: Staff support groups: what works, what doesn't, *Hospice* 1(1):23, 1990.

Guntzelman J: Making frustration work for you, *Nursing 90* 20(12):85, 1990.

Kaplan SM: The nurse as change agent, *Pediatric Nursing* 16(6):603, 1990.

Nicholson L: Stress management in nursing, *Nursing Management* 21(4):53, 1990.

Selbach KH: Chemical dependency in nursing, *AORN J* 52(3):531, 1990.

CHAPTER 11

WHEN BAD THINGS HAPPEN TO GOOD MANAGERS

T.M. MARRELLI

Certain problems commonly faced in management are unpleasant or difficult for many managers. Hopefully you will not experience many of them. However, they do occur and should be addressed. These problems can be as simple as feeling vulnerable during the transition from nurse to manager and wanting to stay in the former role. You must put these problems into perspective. Although they alone are not usually good reasons for leaving a position that you otherwise would enjoy, they can make you feel like resigning. Some of the most common problems faced by new managers are discussed in this chapter.

SPECIAL PROBLEMS
When You Are Promoted and Your Friend Is Not

When you are chosen for a management position, a friend or close colleague who also applied for the position may feel hurt, disappointed, or resentful. Your friend's reaction may, in turn, make you feel sad, disappointed, or even guilty. These feelings can be incredibly uncomfortable and usually do not go away overnight. You must remember that you are now the manager and were chosen over your friend for a reason, although you probably should not verbalize this to your friend. In addition, no matter how happy your friend may appear for you, hurt feelings will probably arise. You cannot pretend that the relationship has not changed; it has by the nature of the hierarchy in the workplace. The change can be particularly difficult if you have been long-term peers and have experienced parallel careers and a close friendship. Although your goal may be to stay close friends, this may be difficult. It depends on you and your friend. The new manager must realize that favorites or perceived favorites cannot exist on a cohesive team. Therefore follow the suggestions in Manager's Tip 11-1 on p. 312 to ease the transition.

MANAGER'S TIP 11-1

DEALING WITH A CLOSE FRIEND AFTER YOUR PROMOTION

✔ Do not apologize even if you feel somewhat guilty about receiving the promotion.

✔ Do not give your friend favorable treatment. Your guilt may cause you to want to "protect" your friend, which will cause problems with other staff members.

✔ Try to ignore the situation if your friend teases you verbally about the position (e.g., referring to you as the big honcho). However, you will have to set limits on this behavior if it continues.

✔ You can try to maintain your social relationship, but you must accept that it will change. Obviously, your social relationship must be kept outside the work setting. Sometimes the relationship will deteriorate, and you may have to accept this loss.

✔ Work on achieving mutual respect. Bringing professional behaviors and effective interpersonal skills to these uncomfortable situations can help. The effort expended to maintain the friendship can be draining, and the transition period can be disheartening for new managers.

✔ Give this process time. Your friend may need space initially while getting used to the change. Eventually you and your friend may be able to resume the friendship.

✔ Discuss with other nurse managers how they have addressed and solved this problem. Such support can be beneficial to you in this uncomfortable situation.

Discomfort in an Unfamiliar Environment

As health care settings must be financially conservative in order to survive, some changes are being felt in the patient care environment. The new nurse manager can be easily overwhelmed by the red tape, politics, and sabotage that sometimes occur if she/he is not prepared to deal with them. The suggestions in Manager's Tip 11-2 can help you adjust.

Terminating or Letting Go of a Staff Member

Probably no management process is as difficult to be involved in as terminating a staff member. This process can be especially challenging for new managers. When there are serious and ongoing problems with a staff member, discuss the situation with both your immediate supervisor and the human resources (HR) manager. You should not attempt to handle this process without adequate support, particularly if the staff member's problems precede your tenure. For a more in-depth discussion of this process, please refer to Chapter 3, Human Resource Management.

Times of High Stress or Anxiety

Maclaren said, "What does anxiety do? It does not empty tomorrow of its sorrow; rather it empties today of its strength" (Jan Maclaren, 1920). As nurses, we all know

MANAGER'S TIP 11-2

TIPS ON ADJUSTING TO A NEW ENVIRONMENT

✔ Talk to trusted peer nurse managers and on an ongoing basis.

✔ Introduce yourself to everyone you can. Ask people to lunch or to tell you about their role in the organization. People love to talk about themselves and their accomplishments, and these meetings can give you the needed insight into the corporate culture that you would not find on the organizational chart or in the recruitment brochure.

✔ Watch how people communicate with each other (formal, informal, e-mails, memos) and observe nuances that are unique to your work setting.

✔ Rely on both the grapevine and feedback. Unfortunately, in some environments, there is poor communication from the top levels to the ranks below. If you are in this type of environment, the grapevine may often provide more information than do formal communications.

✔ Try to remain objective. If your current setting operates differently from the last setting you worked in, give your new organization time to demonstrate how it works before judging and trying to implement major changes.

the symptoms of anxiety and stress. Probably few, if any, management positions exist in which stress is not a hallmark of daily life. You must remember that some stress is good and that the way you view your relationship to stress can help you master it. You must take steps to control stress or channel it into productive activities.

You can use the uncomfortable feelings stress creates as catalysts for needed change and to learn new or more effective behaviors. Yet, when you are stressed, you may not feel like doing anything that affects or solves the problem. At these times, you may want to meet with peers, your mentor, or other appropriate staff members such as the social worker or the psychiatric liaison nurse. Some organizations provide nurse managers with counseling to assist them through change and crisis and also to help them support their own staff. J.L. Casey, a nurse, said the following about this positive process:

> Through the counseling sessions, the clinician helped me to understand group dynamics and to learn how to support the staff effectively in times of stress or change. Also, she enabled me to gain an awareness of my own personal management style and of how others react to me. Indeed, the clinician's support has alleviated much of the stress of my new job. She has given me the courage to meet new challenges and to continue to grow and develop both professionally and personally.[1]

Please refer to Chapter 10, Taking Care of Yourself and Your Staff, for an in-depth discussion on stress and stress management. The following are some of the most common dilemmas that can be difficult.

Unfulfilled Promises by Management

It can be disheartening when your supervisor makes promises that are simply not kept. This is why many employment counselors suggest obtaining a written job offer with all details specified before accepting a position. Unfulfilled promises can also occur with bonuses, promotions, or other aspects of your employment. Broken promises erode trust and can be damaging to morale and productivity. It is best to avoid making promises, either actual or implied, to your staff unless you are certain that you can fulfill the promises.

REORGANIZATION

As mentioned throughout this book, health care is in a tumultuous state. Downsizing, reorganizing, facility closings, merging, and disengaging are just a few of the many changes occurring to organizations across the country. What can a patient care manager do to survive the stress of such times?

First of all, realize that the downsizing of health care facilities is due to an increase in empty beds, as the paradigm of health care completes its massive shift from inpatient to outpatient settings. Patient care units are being merged with other units and staff are being relocated to other more flourishing departments, such as outpatient or ambulatory care services and community health care (home care) programs. As mergers and acquisitions occur, one facility and its staff may take precedence over the facility being bought out or merged with. Besides trying to increase market share and revenue opportunities, such mergers usually are aimed at increasing cost-effectiveness through the combination of support functions and other commonalities. Job loss is a threat to management staff as well as to clinicians.

There may be major management shifts in organizations that have not been achieving projected revenue or expense projections. It is not uncommon for middle management to witness the complete change in senior management staff over a short period of time when a new CEO/administrator is brought in because she/he may recruit her/his own management team. Especially hard for new nurse managers is the possible loss of the person who recruited them for their management position and/or who has been their personal mentor. In addition, she/he may be perceived as a member of the "old order" and will be watched for signs of counterproductive behavior or attitude. Focus your attention on assisting your new supervisors, peers, and subordinate staff in the transition.

Because the philosophy of the organization and the corporate culture may change with the new management team, the nurse manager must step back, observe, and evaluate the new changes before taking any drastic steps. Give the new management team your support during this time, because it will probably be fraught with disorganization, conflict, and high tension. Encourage, motivate, and support staff during this time, protecting them from the bureaucratic and nonproductive tensions that might arise. However, keep them informed of the pertinent factual items that are necessary to accomplish the goals of the department. In their best-selling handbook, *Business as unUsual*, Pritchett and Pound, of Dallas-based Pritchett & Associates, Inc., delineate 27 tactics for managing and surviving organizational change (Manager's Tip 11-3). Readers are referred to Chapter 1 for more information on change in management.

Corporate management tactics in an unstable economic environment may cause great stress and turmoil, testing the personal mettle of managers and staff alike. No matter what is occurring in your institution, do not allow yourself to get caught up in the negative side of power politics, such as backstabbing, backbiting, whining,

MANAGER'S TIP 11-3

MANAGING AND SURVIVING ORGANIZATIONAL CHANGES

✔ Be a change agent.
✔ Keep a positive attitude.
✔ Give your troops clear-cut marching orders.
✔ Nail down each person's job.
✔ Promise change ... and sell it (carefully).
✔ Don't give away your power.
✔ Focus on short-range objectives.
✔ Establish clear priorities.
✔ Raise the (performance) bar.
✔ Motivate to the hilt.
✔ Get resistance to change out in the open.
✔ Don't try to cover all the bases yourself.
✔ Create a supportive work environment.
✔ Provide additional job know-how.
✔ "Beef up" communication efforts.
✔ Protect quality and customer service.
✔ Take care of the "me" issues in a hurry.
✔ Reduce the level of job stress.
✔ Encourage risk-taking and initiative.
✔ Rebuild morale.
✔ "Ride close herd" on transition and change.
✔ Pass out more "psychologic paychecks."
✔ Go looking for good news.
✔ Re-recruit your good people.
✔ Play the role of managerial therapist.
✔ Be supportive of higher management.
✔ Be more than a manager or supervisor . . . be a LEADER.[2]

From Pritchett P, Pound R: *Business as unUsual*, Dallas, 1999, Pritchett Publishing.

and sabotage. Instead, be professional and humanistic at all times, focusing on your true objectives—enhancing the quality of service to the patients/clients entrusted to your care and developing your staff.

YOUR POSITION IS ELIMINATED

In the unlikely event your position is eliminated as a result of unit mergers, a reduction in force (RIF), or downsizing, hopefully you will have nurtured a positive relationship with senior management or with a network of health care professionals. Senior managers are continually searching for good managers to run patient care departments. By carefully using the skills outlined in this text, your chances of quickly being recruited for the new merged position, or a new, more exciting position borne out of the paradigm shift, is likely. Positive attitudes, "can-do" spirits, and the ability to successfully manage people are traits always in demand. Manager's Tip 11-4 provides suggestions for helping yourself and your staff through the change.

MANAGER'S TIP 11-4

TAKING CARE OF YOURSELF

Once it has been determined that your managerial options at this health care setting are nonexistent, plan for your departure, both personally and for the staff you may leave behind:

✓ Ascertain what severance options you might have with your employer:
  • Management severance pay options vary among employers; however, a good rule of thumb is to provide 1 week of pay for each year of employment, with a minimum base of 4 weeks for middle management.
  • Health insurance coverage for the length of severance period if not longer (COBRA benefits are available per legislation).
  • Outplacement services:
    ▪ Assistance with resume preparation (you should always keep up-to-date).
    ▪ Assistance with learning interview and job search techniques.
    ▪ Assistance with career counseling (if new career direction desired).
    ▪ Put in contact with professional recruiters.
  • Assistance with job search—networking within organization or health care community.

✓ Do not speak negatively about the organization or management staff (the health care world is ever shrinking and you might "burn your bridges").

✓ Prepare staff and unit for changes (as much as possible with time allotted).

✓ Write letters of recommendation for staff and request letters of recommendation for yourself from senior management.

Unreasonable or Bad Managers

"In a recent study of 73 managers conducted by the University of Southern California, nearly 75% of the participants reported having had difficulty with a superior. Moreover, bad-boss behavior appears to be on the rise."[3] It is hoped that you never work for someone who expects more every day when you have no hope of getting the staff or other resources needed to do the tasks. The continual feeling that you can never do enough can lead to burnout. The successful nurse manager must set limits and know what can be accomplished effectively and realistically in what time frames and with what resources. Network with your peers to validate your perceptions. You may find that you are not alone and that they may have developed coping skills to assist them in remaining fairly content in their positions. Their advice and insight may help you to cope with your situation.

Little or No Management Training

Perhaps your "management training" consisted of the regular staff nurse orientation accompanied by a videotape on assertive behavior and a 2-hour session on HR management! Then you were left to sink or swim. This is a problem. To successfully make the transition to management and function as an effective manager, the new nurse manager should receive structured training related to management issues, concepts, skills, and techniques. If you do not feel that you received the orientation you need, talk to your supervisor about your specific needs. Do not be embarrassed—you are entitled to an orientation commensurate with your responsibilities. To supplement formal educational offerings, you can also offer to lead a peer nurse manager workshop and have the new group define the topics on which orientation is needed. Responsibility for running these meetings can be rotated among the members. It might be helpful to invite and involve your facility's staff development coordinator. Reading the numerous books and journals available can also help you develop your management expertise. Educational offerings such as workshops, courses, and conferences can further enhance your understanding and mastery of management. The resources listed at the end of this and other chapters (see For Further Reading) may be helpful in facilitating development of your management expertise.

Following in the Footsteps of Multiple and Short-Term Managers

When you inherit staff members who have been through a lot of change, problems may abound. Initially, it may be best to observe before making changes of your own. In addition, the staff may feel you will be another short-term manager and may be skeptical. Considering the numerous changes, the setting may need some structure. One way to provide structure is to improve the organization of the unit. Look at your office and talk to peer nurse managers to determine which files are truly needed. Use aids such as accordion binders or a scheduling board to help you feel more organized. The simple acts of organizing the mess may help you and your staff feel less overwhelmed. Get vertical files, bookcases, and whatever else is needed to gain some control over your new environment. Remember and practice organizational skills. Integrating these skills into your daily work life will result in the following:

1. A sense of accomplishment.
2. A feeling of control over your space.
3. More time to do the task at hand; namely managing the area or unit.
4. Demonstrating organization for your staff.
5. Role modeling your expectations.

It may take your staff time to believe that you will be the manager for an extended period if they have "been through" numerous managers. Sometimes such frequent changes create strong and effective staff members because they have functioned as the leaders for their areas throughout the gaps and turnover of managers. This staff may also have had to adjust to very different management styles and expectations over time and may know what works best for their area. Because of these factors, the staff members can be knowledgeable resources about their area. They may have good ideas about the stability and direction needed on the area and contribute positively to these goals. Encourage staff members to share their ideas. For a more in-depth discussion on organizational skills, see Chapter 7, Effective Time Management.

Your Supervisor's Negative Evaluation of You

Performance evaluations can be difficult for both the evaluator and the employee being evaluated. If your supervisor gives you a poor or average evaluation, you must, with her/his help, determine the cause or causes. Try to be objective and put yourself in the evaluator's position. Does your supervisor feel uninformed? Are you generally late with work projects? Are you loyal? Do you follow through when your supervisor delegates work to you? Does your supervisor feel respected by you?

Sometimes it is hard to remember that your supervisor is your supervisor and, as such, must be considered correct. If you are surprised by your supervisor's negative evaluation, you can ask for additional feedback on an ongoing basis to gauge your progress. Ask what specific behaviors are problems and how you can demonstrate improvement to your supervisor. If you are in a new position, it is important to remember that you probably will not perform exceptionally from the start. Stress your interest in learning and improving and ask for your supervisor's help.

A disappointing performance evaluation can be particularly frustrating in those instances where the supervisor promoted you into the position or recruited you for the job. You may feel misled or even betrayed. If you feel that you did not receive an adequate management orientation, you may wish to request additional training. Look objectively at your job description and objectively demonstrate, in writing if need be, the ways you feel you meet the position standards. Whatever you do, especially in the current economic climate, do not tell your supervisor that she/he is wrong. Other mistakes to avoid are blaming others and constantly complaining (especially about issues over which your supervisor has no control).

Also, consider how your supervisor deals with other nurse managers she/he supervises. If she/he frequently praises a peer nurse manager, observe what your peer does differently from or better than you. Perhaps you have not gained recognition for your accomplishments. We all would like to believe that good work gets recognized and reinforced, but, in reality, sometimes the squeaky wheel gets the attention. In this case, the squeaky wheel also gets the positive strokes and evaluations. Some people have a knack for pointing out to their supervisors just what they are doing that is wonderful, helps the organization look good, and most important, makes the supervisor look great. No one likes to be self-congratulatory, but sometimes you may need to bring your achievements to your supervisor's attention.

When You Do Not Get the Recognition You Deserve

The questions in Box 11-1 may help you identify whether you are getting the recognition you deserve. Your supervisor may not know what you are doing, and it may appear that the work you are accomplishing is minimal. This situation particularly can be seen in some settings where there are bonuses. Workers who toot their own horns and come out ahead are not necessarily better workers; they may simply be better at public relations and at communicating to their managers what the managers want and need to hear.

---

box 11-1

DOING YOUR PART TO RECEIVE RECOGNITION

The following questions can help you determine if you are doing your part to receive the recognition you deserve.
- Do people at different levels of the organization know who you are?
- Do you volunteer for assignments or opportunities to increase your visibility?
- Do you routinely tell your supervisor about your accomplishments?
- Sometimes we may be hassled or nervous when we meet with our supervisors, and we may neglect to refer to our accomplishments. Try to make it a point to always have three accomplishments to tell your supervisor about at the onset of your meetings. The supervisor wants to see objective results too, so in turn your boss's boss may hear those same items. This positive action reflects on your boss and can only help you.
- Do you share your unit's accomplishments with your staff and encourage them to share their individual accomplishments with you?
- Have your staff enumerate three accomplishments every week that you can then present to your supervisor. It will help your staff feel a part of the team. In addition, the knowledge that you share this information with your boss will increase their feeling that you are all working together.

WHEN YOU IDENTIFY THE NEED FOR A CHANGE IN YOUR JOB

Occasionally, your work situation may be so uncomfortable or stressful that you want to leave your position. When you are unhappy at work, you must try to determine specifically why you feel that way. Such information will help you identify the actions you need to take to improve the situation. All jobs have inherent pros and cons. The important issue is that the position meets your unique needs. The decision to leave is usually reached when all other available actions taken fail. Many skills are available to try to affect a negative work situation.

Problem-solving, conflict resolution, and other avenues toward finding solutions should be attempted when possible. However, note that sometimes, even when your job is fulfilling, it simply may be time for a change. At some point, people consider changing careers entirely. Knowing when to leave can sometimes result from intuition and honest discussions with trusted friends or colleagues.

Many businesses will welcome an RN on their staff's roster. Nurses have many job opportunities that tie together health interests and other activities. Some of these include health care–related sales such as computers, medical equipment, or supplies; programs for the aging; nursing staffing companies; medicolegal consulting; research; health or hospital administration; liaison between facilities; teaching; insurance utilization review; case management services; private practice; lobbying; and occupational health and wellness programs. For an in-depth discussion about other opportunities and marketing yourself and your skills, refer to Chapter 13, which specifies steps that may help you find the right position or identify the next professional stage in your career.

THE BOTTOM LINE

"It was much pleasanter at home, thought poor Alice, when one wasn't always growing larger and smaller, and being ordered around by mice and rabbits. I almost wish I hadn't gone down that rabbit hole. . .!"

The thoughts and experiences of Lewis Carroll's Alice are an eloquent parallel to those of nurses in middle management roles. Many wish to go "home" to bedside nursing, where one is not accountable to, and responsible for, everyone above and below (all those mice and rabbits!), besides being responsible for quality patient care. The step into management, be it prompted by curiosity, ambition, or a desire to contribute, can mimic Alice's dreamlike fall down the rabbit hole, complete with changes in size and form, and encounters with all kinds of mysterious characters.[4]

Determine if your current position has the critical elements needed to make you happy and allow you to effectively use your special skills and abilities. It is important that you spend some time considering those aspects of the position that are satisfying as well as those that are not. Weighing these criteria will assist you in deciding whether to move on. This is also the time to reflect on your perception of problems. Those who frame problems as challenges and find solutions seem to enjoy their work more. In addition, although every setting has different problems, some types of problems are inherent in management and may follow you regardless of the setting or organization in which you work.

SUMMARY

Problems appear in many facets of our worklives. It is important to realize and sometimes remind ourselves that we are not alone. The good point about addressing problems is that once we problem-solve or identify the action needed for resolution, we have one less problem to address. In addition, some problems, after initially being addressed, serve as precedents for our way of effectively handling similar problems. With these facts in mind, problem-solving becomes easier. For example, human relation problems are varied and can be addressed in many ways. However, your organization's policy manuals and your supervisor are resources for guidance or responses needed during the period of transition to experienced nurse manager. Your peer nurse managers can be a source of support and of information about "how do you handle" issues. A peer manager meeting on problem-solving and conflict resolution may be a particularly effective method of increasing your comfort level, obtaining support, and increasing your job knowledge.

We learn from our experiences, and the problems become easier to solve with time and experience. Addressing the problems is what is important. We cannot have all the right answers all the time. There are resources in your chain of command to help you during this time, and it is important that you use them when needed. You must realize that being a manager is a continual growth process. This process can be facilitated through the reading of professional books or journals and participating in workshops or attending courses.

In your capacity as manager, you are the role model for your staff. This cyclical process of training members of your staff through delegation, empowerment, and their assumption of accountability develops their skills to professionally grow and perhaps become managers themselves.

QUESTIONS FOR CONSIDERATION

1. Describe how to best address the following situation: "I got promoted and my friend did not."
2. List three positive ways to adjust to a new management environment.
3. Identify 10 ways to manage and survive during organizational change.
4. Create a plan that takes care of you as you plan a departure from a work setting.
5. Discuss how you can improve your recognition and value at an organization.

References

1. Casey JL: Counseling nurse managers, *Nursing Management* 20(9):53, 1989.
2. Pritchett P, Pound R: *Business as unUsual*, Dallas, 1999, Pritchett Publishing.
3. Lopez JA: The boss from hell, *Working Woman* p. 69, December 1991.
4. Boll ML: Middle management in nursing, *Nursing Management* 21(2):54, 1990.

For Further Reading

Betancourt EK: Job sharing in nursing management: it can work, *Nursing Management* 21(1):47, 1990.

Bramson RM: *Coping with difficult people*, New York, 1981, Ballantine Books.

Covey SR: *The seven habits of highly effective people: powerful lessons in personal change*. New York, 1989, Simon & Schuster.

King P: *Never work for a jerk*, New York, 1987, Dell.

Perlman D, Takacs G: The 10 stages of change, *Nursing Management* 21(4):33, 1990.

Pritchett P, Pound R: *The employee handbook for organizational change*. Dallas, 1999, Pritchett & Associates.

Pritchett P, Pound R: *A survival guide to the stress of organizational change*, Dallas, 1999, Pritchett & Associates.

CHAPTER 12

THE NURSE MANAGER IN HOME CARE, COMMUNITY HEALTH, AND HOSPICE

T.M. MARRELLI

HOW HOME CARE, COMMUNITY HEALTH, AND HOSPICE ARE UNIQUE: MORE THAN THE CARE SETTING

This chapter is directed toward managers whose staff members work "out" or "in" the community and whose team members; are not "down the hall" or even onsite within a building or facility on a regular basis. Examples may be managers who supervise or direct visiting nurses; managers who have operational responsibilities for a home health agency (HHA) or a hospice; and those who manage community health centers and/or public health nurses, direct and coordinate WIC or other food delivery programs, are responsible for satellite offices, and manage assisted living centers, group homes, and other sites too numerous to list. Nearly 50% of patient care is delivered outside the acute care setting, and this trend is projected to continue. In fact, this list should only get longer as more health care continues to move outside the realm of the direct, face-to-face onsite management and into community health settings. "Home care" will be used to refer to managers in this section, rather than listing all possible examples of where managers may practice.

Whatever your management title or role, whatever the specific practice area, nurses who are responsible for "distance" management must add additional, unique tools to their skill-set in order to effectively manage team members that are "out there". From the onset it can be surmised that directing team members that you may not see daily (or even weekly!) creates a different relationship that is based on trust and experience. This chapter explores this growing management perspective in which the span extends beyond proximate staff, sites, and operations.

Home care itself is different for many reasons. The reasons center primarily around the fact that health care or service providers are guests in their patients' homes. Unlike the inpatient setting, visiting hours are not set, and patients have control over their environment as well as numerous other choices within their homes, including their clothing, food, visitors, and lifestyles. The care provider or visiting team member must be the one to adjust whenever accommodation is necessary. This customer-oriented or service-driven philosophy is what makes the home setting so different from other care environments. To support this structure we need to see how nurses who make visits or provide care at home must bring special skills to the position. This is not to say that nurses in inpatient areas do not have some or even all of these traits. Rather, this chapter concerns the attributes that must be developed by effective home care managers for nurses and other clinicians to be retained in home care and addresses the specifics of home care management that are not integrated into other chapters.

UNIQUE OPERATIONAL CONSIDERATIONS

The multifaceted administrative and clinical operations that must be maintained to provide patient care in the community setting are the core of the home care manager's responsibilities. Be aware that all the chapters (e.g., Chapter 8, Resource Management and Budgeting Basics; Chapter 10, Taking Care of Yourself and Your Staff; and particularly Chapter 4, Recruitment and Retention of Staff) are relevant to home care managers. Stress management skills are needed by all managers, and the budgeting discussions are particularly relevant in home care.

The management skills needed in home health, community health, and hospice are many and varied. They range from effective recruiting and hiring of skilled and interpersonally effective clinicians to the ongoing duties needed to achieve timely and correct billing submissions. Regardless of the type of care or service program provided at home, the manager's duties and responsibilities are directed toward the maintenance of effective daily operations to provide high-quality patient care.

This chapter is organized with an overview of the hallmarks that make up the professional practice of home care, the regulatory aspects and requirements, and patient care considerations. The overview includes important issues such as how patient/nurse assignments are made, the practice models used, documentation considerations, and the unique billing, data collection, and related administrative functions that the manager directs on a daily basis.

HOW HOME CARE MANAGEMENT IS UNIQUE

You may have been promoted from being a staff nurse in home care to being a manager because of your clinical competence, expertise, and other valued skills. However, in addition, the new home care manager must be willing to achieve or possess the following skill set and knowledge:

- An in-depth knowledge of the current regulatory environment, including the Medicare Conditions of Participation (COPs) and state surveyor interpretative guidelines for compliance, the state Certificate of Need (CON), and licensure laws, where applicable. Also, the manager must know the status and source of accreditation and the complex multifaceted "rules" that are synonymous with home care, including the HHA *Health Insurance Manual-11 (HIM-11)*, the specific provisions for eligibility coverage, and the documentation requirements.

- Knowledge of the billing procedures and rules that dictate the administrative structures and processes necessary to support timely and accurate billing. The administrative skills needed to orchestrate the many steps that must occur require flexibility. A structure that moves the process forward regardless of staffing problems or other operational problems is demanded. This is part of the manager's responsibility for being accountable for the fiscal health of the organization. Please refer to Chapter 7 for an in-depth discussion about effective time management.

- A repertoire of service-driven and patient-oriented interpersonal skills. Unlike inpatient facilities, where the structure defines the services, in home care, because the patient is at home, the patient's needs are the criteria that drive the program. These skills are also highly valued in the manager's role in public relations or community liaison activities, which are a part of effective external operations.

- The experience base and knowledge to successfully and credibly deal with complex situations that may be addressed exclusively over the phone and through documentation. In the inpatient setting, nurses are down the hall or physically in proximity for consultation or direct supervision. In home care, delegation, communication, or follow-up interventions are with staff members who may be four counties away, an hour's drive away, or even across state lines. This is why there is such an emphasis on continual quality improvement in home care, including the ongoing and systematic process of data review related to outcomes and other quality initiatives.

- Possession of an incredible attention to detail. This is necessary in the daily operation related to (1) billing and (2) documentation, especially related to outcome and assessment information set (OASIS) data collections. Because these components go hand in hand, they are equally important. An HHA manager who does not have necessary documentation to support the bills faces problems not only from a risk-management standpoint but also from the payer's viewpoint. The payer may view problems like this situation as overutilization, a gray zone that may sometimes indicate abuse or even fraud. The documentation in billing and the clinical records must be correct for any audit trail.

HOME CARE REIMBURSEMENT

Beneficiaries who qualify for Medicare coverage are eligible for home health services if they have a need for either skilled nursing or physical, occupational, or speech therapy; require intermittent or part-time services; are under the care of a physician; and are homebound. An understanding of these rules and any changes is key to managerial success.

Home care, like other Medicare-reimbursed programs including hospitals and hospices, is paid in a managed care model. Home care agencies changed to a prospective payment system (PPS) model as of October 1, 2000. The PPS in home care is based on a group of home health resources groups (HHRGs). Set dollar amounts for 80 HHRGs are determined by numerous factors including the data documented upon assessment at ongoing intervals—the OASIS—which evaluates home care patients on specific data items that assist in determining their projected resource utilization. Like hospitals, with their PPS system based on diagnosis-related groups (DRGs), a dollar amount is determined. Similarly, there are outliers or unusual cases in which patients do not fit the norm, and the HHA may receive additional reimbursement with appropriate documentation and patient findings. Similarly, readers that are from a nursing home background may think of OASIS as analogous to the minimum data set (MDS), which also mandates assessment information and specifies time frames for recapturing nursing home data.

In the same way that the change to PPS was a challenge for hospitals in the 1980s, home care programs are developing innovative ways to care for patients and their families more efficiently. Out of this change have come the following trends: increased use of clinical paths or protocols, review of case management models and roles, an increased focus on the importance of the interdisciplinary team, improved knowledge of the actual costs of care and related activities (e.g., wound care products, specialty visits, etc.), an emphasis on decreased duplication and increased efficiencies as agencies seek to standardize care and related processes where possible, and HHAs specializing when possible on certain or higher-risk patients. In addition, administrative automated systems are being improved to track, control, and manage the care of patients and the resource usage associated with a particular episode of care.

How Home Care Nurses Are Unique

Box 12-1 lists some of the unique characteristics of nurses and other team members in the home care setting. Obviously, the management skills needed for success in home care are many and varied. The range includes effective hiring of skilled and interpersonally strong clinicians to ongoing orchestration of duties to achieve timely data collection, billing submissions, and a strong grasp of the PPS reimbursement methodology.

Nurses who choose home care must be able to function somewhat autonomously. Consider the inpatient critical care nurse who goes into home care thinking it will be less stressful and finds the culture so different that she/he cannot successfully make the transition to independent and successful home care nurse. With this in mind,

---

box 12-1

UNIQUE CHARACTERISTICS OF NURSES AND THESE SETTINGS

1. The staff must be flexible. It is home care staff members who must bend or renegotiate, not the patient, as members are guests in the patient's home. This usually includes visit times but can include aspects of the plan of care as well.

2. The staff member must not mind driving, even in inclement weather; have a good sense of direction; and be willing to take risks (e.g., get lost).

3. Staff members assume responsibility for the patient's plan of care. True case management occurs in home care. From the initial assessment visit with OASIS data collection to identifying and prioritizing needed care, the nurse in home care assumes the planning and follow-through of care. Possibly only one or maybe a limited number of team members are involved in the care, depending on the patient's needs. These team members directly affect the care and see the results of care provided. Because of this, the outcomes may be more directly attributable to care provided. This total patient management function, with its associated prioritizing and complex decision-making, renders this field unique. Note that in practice, simple, positive patient and family outcomes and feedback are where many home care nurses receive a great deal of personal and job satisfaction—which supports retention. Because of this factor, this feedback also needs to be highly valued by all members of the management team.

4. Staff members must be generalists and specialists. This means that, although clinically the RNs may be able to competently and proficiently handle a wide range of patients and clinical problems, they usually have an area of expertise that can be called on for specialized clinical problems, for orientation of new staff, or as a resource for information (IV, pediatrics, oncology, wound care, etc.).

5. The staff must be autonomous and able to function in a nonstructured atmosphere.

6. The staff must have effective time management skills regarding both visits scheduled and documentation/administrative duties required. The amount of detail management that must be mastered is key to long-term success for many nurses in home care. Accurate data collection and visit schedules demand nurses who are detail-oriented and even value that detail. In addition, plans made between the nurse and patient must be followed up in actuality and on paper.

7. The staff must be open and accepting of people's unique and chosen lifestyles and the associated effects on their health. Judgments about lifestyle, the presence or absence of family support, and the choices patients make with which nurses do not agree must be diplomatically and carefully voiced when appropriate.

8. The staff must like to interact with patients and their families and caregivers. This teaching or consulting role also brings job satisfaction to nurses in home health.

9. The staff must be aware that a constant balance exists between the clinical and administrative demands and that they are equally important, but in different ways and for different reasons.

10. The staff must be aware that successful mastery of time management and delegation skills is essential to effective daily operations.

plan orientation periods with the goal of the participant's having long-term success in the role. We know change is difficult, and the home care nurse culture and setting are very different from the structure and onsite camaraderie, supervision, and peer consultation available from the structure of an inpatient facility. Similarly, your orientation as a new manager must be effective for you to efficiently carry out your new management responsibilities.

THE NEW MANAGER'S ORIENTATION TO HOME CARE

There are too many stories of home care managers who receive almost no orientation and, not surprisingly, get burned out or disillusioned and leave their position, home care, or even nursing. Do not let this "revolving door" phenomenon happen to you. All managers are entitled to an appropriate orientation period. No matter how understaffed the administrator says the agency is, protect yourself from being put in that position from the start. Try to define or address your orientation, including time span and content, before accepting the position. The following discussion addresses what areas your orientation should address.

YOUR ORIENTATION: TIPS FOR SUCCESS

The items in Box 12-2 are the *minimal* topics that can be considered to provide an effective orientation to home care. Obviously, if you have been in home care for some time, some of these may not be appropriate or needed, but all managers

---

box 12-2

HALLMARKS OF ORIENTATION

1. The HHA's or other orientation manual.
2. The conditions of participation and state licensing regulations, as appropriate.
3. The organization's continuous quality reports. This will help you to follow up on areas or data that needed improvement before your tenure began. If no report exists or one was not done last quarter, this could indicate why the agency needs your skills. Obviously, this can be a good or a bad sign!
4. The *Health Insurance Manual-11*,[1] including the HHA coverage requirements section.
5. The clinical policy and procedure manuals.
6. The human resource policy manual, including position descriptions.
7. Organization chart and current staffing needs. This includes who you report to and who has true (not just on paper) responsibilities for specific areas.
8. The staff education and inservice training log.
9. An overview of the clinical records and documentation systems.
10. An overview of the clinical/billing/administrative information system.

HALLMARKS OF ORIENTATION — cont'd

11. A schematic diagram of the paper flow process from patient intake/admission through to discharge and billing at this organization.
12. The HHA's fiscal statements and accounts pending.
13. The caseload of the previous months/year.
14. The HHA's annual report.
15. Their accreditation and most recent report (e.g., JCAHO, CHAP, ACHC).
16. The HHA's strategic plan.
17. Community linkage and involvement.
18. The HHA's denial rate; monthly number of requests for additional documentation (ADR).
19. The HHA's participation in state and national industry organizations.
20. Other regulatory information including Health Insurance Portability and Accountability Act (HIPAA), CMS, medical leave act, the state Medicaid program, etc.
21. Other information as needed.

---

should have these "hallmarks" of home care as a base of information. In addition, these items will provide you information about the HHA's internal operations.

Orienting a new manager should take at least as long as it does for a new clinical nurse in home care. Much of the above information is also appropriate for the new nurse in home care. Remember, the more managers communicate the program's goals or visions, the more staff members feel a part of the team and are thereby more effective.

It goes without saying that your staff members cannot be held accountable for what they do not or could not know if they did not get an effective orientation. With this in mind, and from your perspective as the risk manager and person responsible for implementing continuous quality improvement (CQI) or performance improvement, adequately train your home care clinical staff. Like you, their manager, they need to know the cornerstones of information about home care. These should **always** include such basic topics as making home visits and what they entail, including buddying with an experienced, positive role model nurse; visit utilization and projecting patient needs for the plan of care (POC); orientation to the OASIS and forms used; infection control and surveillance activities; and coverage and associated documentation requirements of home care services and CQI processes. The manager cannot be effective if she/he does not know the program, the key players, and the expected performance goals. Similarly, it is difficult and usually unfair to hold staff members accountable for information of which they were unaware. Be a prudent manager; orient your team effectively.

IF YOU HAVE TO NEGOTIATE FOR AN ORIENTATION

If you are in the unfortunate position of bargaining for an adequate orientation, there is a problem. Most nurses want to be affiliated with high-quality programs.

However, believing that all home care programs are functioning at the same (high-quality) level would be naïve. There may be instances when your supervisor's actions concern you. Trust your nursing knowledge and experience. Look to the professional standards of care for guidance and more information.

If you are always needing information to do your job, if you cannot do your job effectively because of no orientation or support, or if you are a manager in "title" but are continually in the field seeing patients because of incredible turnover, you are experiencing problems that may not be resolved by your current management. Note that you cannot be expected to be continually in the community making vis-its and also be in the office supervising agency operations. This could be a pre-scription for failure in a busy HHA setting. Clinical and administrative demands are so different that to attempt both for any length of time is ineffective.

Another uncomfortable position that a manager can be involved in entails the admission of patients clearly needing home care services and not having the person-nel resources available to provide them. For example, the admitting nurse appropri-ately identifies a patient's need for skilled intermittent services and, because of extensive personal care needs, frequent home health aide visits. Your agency does not have the aides (or the speech/language pathologists or the physical or occupational therapists) to adequately meet the patient's care needs. Admit only those patients whose care needs can safely and adequately be met. It is most unfortunate, and cer-tainly not fair to the patients or their families, if patients do not receive the services they need because of HHA's administrative problems. The necessity of demonstrating quality outcomes in patient care delivery must not be underestimated.

THE MANAGER'S EVOLVING ROLE: DETERMINING COMPETENCY AND MENTORING

The role of the home care nurse manager continues to evolve as does her/his coun-terpart in the other health care settings. The most important elements that may affect that role are:

- The change to a PPS
- Transition nurses new to home health care
- Intense scrutiny of the industry by government and consumers
- Increased community violence and safety issues surrounding home care personnel
- Increased computerization of home care and improved linkage with other health care settings
- Need for quantifiable, reliable, and valid home care outcomes
- Risk management and safety/security concerns unique to home care
- The shortage of nursing and other staff in certain parts of the United States (e.g. OT, PTs, SLP etc.)

Home care managers must be creative and think globally when strategically plan-ning the future because they may be the type of individuals who understand the needs of the community and must take the lead in collecting data and developing programs that will address the community health needs of the 21st century.

Competency Issues

It is important for home care managers to set up systems and processes to orient, train, and educate staff on new or revamped home care protocols. The determination of staff competency in home care is more important because staff members are usually in the home alone and do not have the backup of other staff in the same vicinity if a problem arises. As agencies grow, the tendency to hire quickly to meet referral needs must be weighed by the value of having qualified, competent, and oriented staff to provide safe, quality care.

Mentoring

Home care managers, like in other sites, are clinicians who have been promoted from the staff ranks. The education and nurturing of good managers must begin before the individual is promoted. It is very important for nurse managers, especially for women managers, to commit to providing leadership and mentoring services to those promising staff members who have the ability, ambition, and courage to pursue management. Even as the workday never seems to end, it is vital that we train the new, next generation of managers to successfully take charge.

Seek out opportunities to mentor—either at your own workplace or through professional, business, and clinical service organizations. A mentor can be of either sex and need not be in your direct chain of command. What is important is the dedication of time, energy, and commitment toward assisting a "budding" manager in developing the maturity, problem-solving skills, and networking abilities to successfully tackle projects and potentially challenging positions. Having a "sounding board" or someone you can "run ideas by" is invaluable.

MEASURING OPERATIONAL QUALITY: VARYING FACETS

There are varying facets of quality in home care and hospice. Achievement of accomplishments is one part and may be confirmed or awarded by CHAP, JCAHO, or ACHC. The design and implementation of a continuous quality or performance improvement program in your organization must meet your agency's unique clinical focuses. Organizations incorporate CQI operational aspects into their daily operations. The CMS defines the quality indicators that must be collected and analyzed. All Medicare-certified HHAs receive their home health outcome reports, which are saved on their reported OASIS data. CMS continues to focus on varying components of quality home care. These quality initiatives must be embraced by managers to best improve the value of home care. It may include patient, physician, and referral source satisfaction surveys. The manager in home care must be very involved in the organization's CQI program. In addition, as with other sites, home care staff need to have a voice in operations for improved performance.

The educational preparation and clinical knowledge and experience of home care staff can be another measure of quality. Certification in home care is offered by the American Nurses' Association Credentialing Center for home care nurses. Similarly, there are certifications for nurses practicing in hospice and palliative care, certified hospice and palliative care nurse (CHPN) and certified registered nurse hospice (CRNH). This certification is obtained through the Hospice and Palliative Nurse Association. There is also a certification for managers in home care and hospice and a certified home care executive (CHCE), which are available through the National Association for Home Care and Hospice. In addition there are numerous specialty certifications and credentials for nurse clinicians, including IV certifications, wound specialist certifications, pediatrics, and many others. These are either through varying professional associations or the American Nurses Association's Credentialing Center. Credentialing brings an additional level of expertise to an organization and assists in developing a specialized body of knowledge for a given area of practice.

The nursing care delivery model used by an HHA can also affect the quality of care provided by affecting patient outcomes.

Legal/Risk Management Issues for Home Care Managers

Nurse managers who are responsible for home care services should take special note of the following issues:

- Exercise care with regard to hiring and retaining staff members. Remember, supervision in home care is less intense than in institutional settings, so only practitioners who can operate effectively with a relatively great degree of independence should work in home care.
- All patients admitted or readmitted to the agency should be appropriate for home care services. Staff must perform a global assessment of appropriateness that includes evaluation of care needed, whether the patient can care for self or a reliable primary caregiver is available to assist patients, and whether the environment of patients' homes will support home care services.
- Staff must accomplish appropriate follow-up on their communications with physicians. That is, staff must report all changes in signs and symptoms to physicians. They must then obtain a response from physicians' offices regarding the changes that they have reported. When physicians order changes in plans of care, those changes must be implemented promptly.
- Staff must refuse to implement inappropriate orders from physicians. An area of particular concern in this regard is wound care. Physicians may not be familiar with relatively recent changes in standards of care and may continue to order care that has become obsolete. Nurses are responsible for making certain that they do not act on physicians' orders that result in inappropriate care.

Legal Considerations: Delegating Nursing Tasks*

Delegation of nursing tasks to unlicensed individuals carries serious patient care and legal implications. Nurses practicing in a home care setting must be concerned especially about the nursing tasks they delegate to the unlicensed individuals who provide care in the home under the nurse's supervision. If care is improperly provided and harm results to the patient, the nurse will be held responsible. More and more frequently in malpractice lawsuits, licensed nurses are held liable for improper delegation or inadequate supervision of delegated tasks. Also, actions taken by state boards of nursing against a nurse's license based on delegation issues have been increasing.

To avoid liability for the delegated acts of others, the following considerations are recommended:

- *Recognize when you are delegating* a nursing task. Any action that falls within your state's definition of nursing practice may be performed only by an unlicensed individual under delegation by a licensed nurse.
- *Check your state's Nurse Practice Act* and regulations on which nursing acts may be delegated to a nonlicensed individual, and which nursing acts may not be delegated.
- *Check your home health agency's policies and procedures* on delegation of nursing tasks and on requirements for supervision of unlicensed individuals.
- *Delegate only those nursing tasks that are within the area of your responsibility* as a licensed nurse.
- *Evaluate* whether, in your opinion, the delegated task can safely be performed by an unlicensed individual.
- Prior to delegating a task, *assess the client's nursing care needs* to ensure that the delegated task can be appropriately performed by an unlicensed individual for that particular client.
- Prior to delegating a nursing task, *verify the competence* of the unlicensed individual to whom you are delegating.
- If you are in a situation *in which you determine that delegation may not appropriately or safely take place, do not delegate* the task, but rather perform it yourself.
- *Instruct* the unlicensed person in performance of the task and verify that the unlicensed person is competent to perform the task. Return demonstrations are recommended.
- *Direct or supervise the performance of the nursing task* by regularly evaluating the nursing tasks performed by the unlicensed personnel.
- *Assess the client* to ensure the nursing tasks performed by the unlicensed individual are effective in the care of the client.

*From Guarino KS: Legal considerations: delegating nursing tasks, *Home Care Nurse News* 2(7):5, 1995.

- *Ensure accurate documentation* of all tasks performed in the patient care setting.
- *Correct* any situation in which an individual under your supervision is performing nursing acts incompetently. Once you know, or should have known, that an unlicensed individual is unsafe, you are under a duty to ensure that the individual is removed from the patient care setting.

Even if you are not sued as a result of delegated nursing tasks, your license may be at risk for acts improperly delegated or improperly supervised. To defend either a legal claim or an action against your license by the board of nursing, you must be able to show that you took all of the steps itemized above and that you established effective mechanisms for monitoring the unlicensed individuals under your supervision. It is essential that you create a process whereby the unlicensed individuals are provided with well-defined expectations and reporting requirements, and that you have a consistent means of ensuring they were meeting those expectations. Be able to show that you trained the unlicensed individuals well (or ensure that they have been well trained), that you were available to them, and that you were consistently aware of how they performed the nursing tasks you delegated to them.

Remember that the licensed nurse is ultimately responsible for making the decision whether to delegate and under what circumstances the delegation is appropriate. Agencies cannot delegate nursing tasks. Even if your employer has protocols that require unlicensed individuals to perform nursing tasks, an individual with a nursing license will be held responsible if the unlicensed individual performs the task improperly.

MODELS OF NURSING CARE DELIVERY SYSTEMS IN HOME CARE

Various models in home care describe how care is delivered to HHA patients. Case management (CM) is a model frequently seen in home care. It is recognized that continuity of the same staff visiting patients, regardless of the care model, promotes accountability and increased effectiveness in care communications and patient outcomes. The manager's knowledge of each staff member's preparation, experience, and capabilities promotes the fullest use of skills and provides a basis for continued growth.

Regardless of the model used, assigning a nurse who has the overall responsibility for assessing, data collection, planning, implementing, and evaluating the ordered plan of care is key to positive patient outcomes. The purpose of assigning one nurse or case manager to this responsibility is to help ensure the quality of the care by providing a mechanism for consistent rapport and communications between patient and caregivers. Clearly, this is not to say that additional nursing staff such as "associate or revisit nurses" are not also involved in the care of the patient. In fact, involving another nurse can be helpful. For example, a nurse specialist, such as a wound ostomy specialist, may consult on appropriate cases, thus ensuring quality while providing patient care in a consultative role. Assigning home care nurses to patients, in keeping with your organizational philosophy, also supports patient care assignments that are directed toward meeting the specific physical, psychologic, cultural, social, and other defined needs of patients.

This assignment is most effectively accomplished by the case manager evaluating the projected assessed needs of patients as soon as possible after the referral process has occurred. The effective case manager accomplishes this by gathering all the available and pertinent information about the patient and her/his care needs.

This is accomplished through a comprehensive assessment, of which the OASIS data collection is a part. In addition, such continuity may also positively affect retention. The manager then assesses the availability of RN resources. This includes the number of staff members and their clinical expertise, educational preparation, experience, and demonstrated capabilities. Matching of patients and nurses is sometimes referred to as "skill matching" or "care matching." In addition, the manager should also consider the individual preferences of staff members while evaluating the complexity or extent of patient needs. Consideration for the preferences of patient care staff members needs to be kept in mind and valued, since this positively influences the morale of the group.

Information concerning preferences needs to be acquired in a systematic way, such as regular individual staff meetings with the manager, to ensure all staff members are given equal consideration. The assignment process is also made with the primary nurse's current patient caseload in mind. Geographic location and equitable work distribution are two additional factors to consider. In addition, matching assignments to the abilities and growth potential of the professional staff member enhances the quality of care, is cost-effective, increases productivity, and promotes staff member satisfaction. Effective managers work with their staff to assist them, when needed, in understanding the rationale of assignments.

Depending on your chosen nursing or patient care model, the delegation of responsibility for planning, supervising, and evaluating the care of the patient occurs when the patient is assigned to the nurse or case manager.

Communication with staff on an ongoing basis is the key to a successful operation where all efforts are directed toward common goals. Although the bulk of daily communications with clinical staff may be over the phone, it is important that you interact with staff on a regular basis. Box 12-3 addresses the important role of staff meetings in home care and hospice.

STAFF MEETING EVALUATIONS

Regularly evaluate the staff meetings. On a written evaluation form, ask open-ended questions to elicit if staff needs are being met by the current forum. Some HHAs have only the nurses and home health aides at the meetings, others involve the medical social workers (MSWs) and other team members as well. These choices and

---

box 12-3

THE IMPORTANCE OF STAFF MEETINGS IN HOME CARE AND HOSPICE

The importance of regularly scheduled staff meetings in the home care or hospice office cannot be understated. Because the very nature and definition of the care provision are external, the staff members need to be, and feel like, a part of the group. Staff meetings assist in meeting both the staff and manager's goals. Although you may define the agenda, ask your staff members for issues or concerns they want addressed and incorporate these items whenever possible. Make the staff meetings and their agenda items and ensuing discussions meaningful and valuable. Sometimes there is not enough time to address all the staff items. As the manager, you may need to prioritize requests, but you should communicate your shared concern about the item and ensure staff members it will be on the next agenda. These items are sometimes refered to as "parking lot" items.

Staff meetings are an appropriate forum for team members to share clinical information or "better ways of doing things," or to evaluate any process that affects their patient care or work life. For example, a typical staff meeting may consist of administrative agenda items: addressing the fact that the MSW is on vacation on such dates and naming the MSW who will be covering the clients and available for new referrals, the new home health aide assignment form (the nurses and aides should see drafts first), and any problems that need resolution or clarification. Standing agenda items should also include safety, CQI activities, and educational opportunities.

These meetings can also foster camaraderie and trust among members. Any manager in home care or hospice knows that the nurses must feel that other staff members are clinical peer professionals, or problems can arise with long-term coverage or on-call or other assignments. In addition, some nurses, if they are sick or on vacation, have other nurses they usually want to cover their patients. As long as the patients are cared for appropriately and cliques do not develop, nothing is inherently wrong with this practice.

These meetings can also influence positive morale as the nurses in the community realize they are not alone and that the other home care nurses share the same concerns. Some HHAs hold their meetings at lunchtime and have food there for their staff, or the staff brings their own lunch. Others hold meetings in the morning. The common complaint about early morning meetings in home care is that patients with IVs or receiving insulin must be seen in the morning. Schedule meetings at whatever time seems best for the consensus of the staff. It is difficult, if not impossible, to listen and **hear** what is being said in a staff meeting if the nurse is worried about her/his next three patients. Always include evening and weekend staff. This allows them a forum for issues even if they are unable to attend.

The manager must value the meetings and thus make them mandatory. Again, it is difficult to hold staff members accountable for what they were not told in the interviewing, hiring, and orientation processes. If a requirement for your program is that staff meetings are mandatory, this needs to be communicated clearly to all. However, the manager must be realistic about such a decision. Obviously, with an extensive traffic backup or if a patient problem in the community needs resolution, the actions of the home care nurse are clear. However, the nurse should call the manager as soon as possible and explain her/his absence. Minutes from these meetings should be typed and distributed to staff. This process reinforces items presented and resolves the "I wasn't at the staff meeting" comments and resulting problems.

THE IMPORTANCE OF STAFF MEETINGS IN HOME CARE AND HOSPICE — cont'd

Again, allow the home care staff input into the time and, if appropriate, place of the meetings. Try to make these meetings informative and valued. The meetings should start promptly and end at the designated time. If you note many absences, this may be a sign that the staff does not value the time and content of the meetings.

decisions are all based on your program's unique history and needs. Some HHAs do an annual (or more frequently if needed) evaluation of the staff meeting structure, agenda contents, physical space, and so on, to ensure, as part of the CQI process, that meetings are meaningful to all involved.

MULTIDISCIPLINARY TEAM CONFERENCES

Some HHAs schedule their multidisciplinary team conferences immediately following staff meetings. For example, if the staff meeting is held every other Wednesday at 11:30 AM and the meeting is conducted during lunch, the clinical case conferences begin promptly at 12:30 PM, when the other service representatives appear for these meetings. Again, staff meetings must end promptly. The rationale for scheduling such conferences in this way is (1) there may be new referrals for these colleagues, and the nurses can expect that they will be able to discuss these new patients with the appropriate colleague after the staff meeting, and (2) the staff members are already out of the field. Always try to get "the most mileage" out of an idea or process. In the above example, the nurses are already at the office. To bring them in another day and disrupt their schedule may not be cost-effective because it pulls the nurse out of the community again.

HOSPICE STAFF SUPPORT MEETINGS

Similarly, hospices may have the ongoing staff support sessions scheduled immediately following hospice staff meetings. The meeting with the facilitator is scheduled in this way for a few reasons. First, the staff is already onsite, having just attended the staff meeting. Second, the clinical and administrative issues that needed to be addressed were usually taken care of in the staff meeting. The resolution of the problems and the end of the staff meeting helped the staff members let go of those immediate concerns as they were completed. Third, the staff members may be in a more relaxed frame of mind than if they had just driven to the office, run up the stairs, and sat down for staff support or were late or feel hassled on a particularly busy day. This also helps ensure that the group is all present at the onset of the support meeting, which decreases or minimizes the interruptions or disruptions.

It is important in staff support meetings that the facilitator, the format and process, and the associated environment also be regularly evaluated by the manager and the hospice team participating in hospice support. In home care and hospice, it is of utmost importance that we care for the caregivers. The stress of the care provided must be identified and dealt with effectively and appropriately. The managers in home care and hospice must be aware and attuned to the stress levels and any overextension of involvement by the nurse with the patients and their families. For an in-depth review of stress of both manager and staff members, please refer to Chapter 10, Taking Care of Yourself and Your Staff.

STAFF MEETINGS WITH ADMINISTRATIVE STAFF MEMBERS

In home care or hospice you may also have accountability for administration and operations subordinates who report to you. This can include clerical, secretarial staff, coders, scheduling and intake staff, and billing/data entry accounting personnel. Others may include patient coordinators, private pay schedulers, and miscellaneous staff members. It is important to hold meetings with this staff. Initially, meetings should be held weekly until you understand the paper flow and work process across the organization. It is important that the staff who represent the agency or program on the phone (as well as in person) be articulate, helpful, and professional. Administrative functions should be included in the organization's CQI program. An example would be a policy of all phones being answered by the third ring. Referral sources want to call these types of service-driven organizations. Remember, how you sound on the phone forms an outsider's first impression of you. Clearly, a case manager who wants effective care, usually at the "best" price, will call a service-oriented organization. The perception here is that how things "look" is often times how they are.

All parts of your team must work together. Do not make references to outside (field, visiting) staff and inside (administrative) staff. The team works together. It goes without saying that all team members should be "equally" busy. In addition, the office administrative staff reporting to you should be cross-trained whenever possible. Always keep this in mind when bringing in new administrative staff members. For example, the clerical staff should be able to enter data on patients as a backup to the billing staff. Remember, many vacations, holidays, and/or other unplanned days away (e.g., sick, emergency) must be covered. Do not put yourself in the position of having only one person who can accomplish a given function accurately and competently (e.g., data entry, intake, statistical report collation, phones, reception, aide scheduling, record review).

Have your administrative staff function as small teams broken down into similar functions. Cross-train them all to know at least one other position. Do not wait until a crisis to discover the effectiveness of a staff member's cross-training. Plan for practice days and stagger the days so there is backup. These efforts will pay off significantly. It is also a way to develop your staff and see and value them for their range of skills.

Remember, part of your job as manager (and in home care this is a large part) is to help make the clinical staff members' jobs "easier" by the successful resolution of administrative problems. For example, if your home care field staff are being hassled by an archaic or duplicative documentation or operational system, address this concern. Have the administrative and clinical staffs work together with you to determine a more successful way to handle the process.

FISCAL RESPONSIBILITIES IN HOME CARE

Billing functions are closely integrated with the clinical information in home care. Because the HHA must have the physician's POC on the clinical record before billing for the care provided, this discussion begins with documentation.

Although not all patients are Medicare patients, Medicare sets the standard for documentation, and sometimes coverage, offered by other payers. Because documentation in home care can comprise an entire book, the following discussion is an overview of the topic to assist the home care manager develop the staff's documentation skills. In addition, the PPS HHRG is based primarily on the data assessed and documented on the OASIS in the comprehensive assessment and noted in other components of the clinical records. This documentation must accurately reflect patient findings as it drives the HHA payment for the care.

AN OVERVIEW OF THE CENTERS FOR MEDICARE AND MEDICAID SERVICES (CMS)

The CMS has responsibility for the Medicare and Medicaid programs. Remember that Medicare is a medical insurance program and, like all medical insurers, there are exclusions to coverage for services and specific coverage criteria. CMS is administratively under the Secretary of Health and Human Services. CMS contracts with insurance companies to process and adjudicate (make a payment determination or decision) Medicare claims. There are specialized regional home health intermediaries (RHHIs); these process all the HHA and hospice claims nationally. These RHHIs are generally given the HHAs in certain geographic areas as their service area. (However, chain HHAs usually have one RHHI because these HHAs may have centralized billing.)

In addition, the COPs are also part of Medicare requirements for HHAs. With this information in mind, be aware that CMS, by law, can pay only for necessary and covered care. When admitting patients to your program, ensure that they meet all the criteria. For example, they must *meet* the homebound criteria, the skilled care criteria, and the intermittent/part-time criteria to be covered under the Medicare program. These criteria must be reflected in the clinical documentation.

The COPs define what home care and hospice "look like"—they create the framework for care, service, and coverage.

Documentation Considerations

All efficient HHAs must have their nurses and other care providers generate documentation that simultaneously does the following:

1. Demonstrates in the documentation the patient care provided and the patient's response to that care.
2. Shows that current standards of care are maintained.
3. Meets documentation requirements for Medicare and other payers.

The nurse's entries in the patient's clinical record are recognized as a significant contribution that documents the standards of care provided to a patient. As the practice of nursing has become more complex, so, too, have the factors that influence the roles of documentation. Some of these factors include requirements of regulatory agencies (e.g., the state health department), health insurance payers (e.g., Medicare), accreditation organizations (e.g., JCAHO, CHAP, ACHC), and consumers of health care and legal entities.

In home care, the nurse must try to satisfy these various requirements all at once, often with precious few moments in which to accomplish this important task. The *Handbook of Home Health Standards and Documentation Guidelines for Reimbursement*[2] was written expressly to show how to ensure meeting the various requirements simultaneously. The manager should have these standards and guidelines available to the home care and discharge planning staff members. This will help ensure an understanding of the level and clarification of specific documentation required by any payer.

As manager, a system should be created to review a percentage of documentation on an ongoing basis to monitor the quality of care as demonstrated in the documentation, and to ensure that other, particularly reimbursement, requirements are being met. This review can also be incorporated into your CQI or PI program, and clinical factors may be identified through the review process that can become the subject of further analysis for a PI initiative. In addition, areas for further education may be identified through this process.

In your sample review, ask the questions in Manager's Tip 12-1 on p. 341 to assess the quality of the home care medical record. Manager's Tip 12-2 on p. 342 presents some suggestions to help you help your staff improve their documentation.

The Importance of Management and Other Reports

Reports present information that is useful and objective for any manager. They track what is happening with the HHA or program. Many types of report tools are available. Following is a discussion of the report tools the new manager should find

MANAGER'S TIP 12-1

NURSE MANAGER'S CHECKLIST FOR DOCUMENTATION

✓ Are the OASIS, admitting forms, and other required documentation completed accurately and on time (per HHA policy)?

✓ Try to look at the documentation objectively: does it tell the story of the patient's progress (or lack of progress) and the interventions implemented based on the initial assessment and plan of care?

✓ Are telephone calls and other communications with physicians and other team members documented? Do they explain what occurred with the patient; what actions were ordered, modified, and implemented; and the patient's response to these interventions?

✓ Is the nursing process demonstrated in the record? Look for the nursing diagnoses, the assessment, evidence of care planning, implementation or ordered interventions and actions, assessment of the patient's response, and continued evaluation.

✓ Is there documentation of goal achievement or progress toward predetermined, mutually set goals and outcomes? Are the goals realistic, quantifiable, and patient-centered?

✓ If progress has not occurred as planned, are the reasons explained in the documentation?

✓ Is the patient's/caregiver's response to care interventions or actions documented?

✓ Are the interventions modified, based on the patient's response, where appropriate?

✓ Is there evidence of intradisciplinary team conferences and discussions?

✓ Does the chart show continuity of care planning goals and consistent movement toward goal achievement?

✓ Generally, does the record tell the story of the patient's care and progress while receiving home care services?

✓ Do the entries and overall information reflect care of the level expected by today's health care consumers and their families?

✓ Does the clinical documentation demonstrate compliance with regulatory, licensure, and quality standards?

helpful. A prudent manager is up-to-date on the status or health of the HHA. Keeping current helps ensure the early and easy identification of problems or trends that should be watched closely before they become risk management problems or financial disasters. The CMS mandated home health outcome reports must be reviewed as soon as they are available, and on an ongoing basis. Reports ensure objective findings of different components of the operations in an HHA. This helps the manager by showing information in an organized format that assists and improves managerial effectiveness. Reports can help quantify information you may need at a glance. For example, if you believe that the nursing visits are up significantly over the last 2 weeks (e.g., by viewing the nurse visit logs or the number of referrals), the actual

MANAGER'S TIP 12-2

SUGGESTIONS TO HELP YOU HELP YOUR STAFF IMPROVE DOCUMENTATION

✔ As a manager, show by your actions that you value effective documentation. This attitude will be conveyed to staff and become the standard of the performance expected.

✔ Remember that writing effective documentation is a learned skill and, as with any skill, improvement comes only with practice.

✔ Recognize that in home care, at the first visit the nurse usually begins the process of claims payment (or denial) with the initial 485, OASIS data, and other supporting documentation.

✔ Have your nurses read their own documentation objectively. They should ask themselves, "Does this visit record say why the patient is homebound [if Medicare or another insurer has that criterion]?" and "How or why are the skills of a nurse or therapist needed?" Involve your staff in peer review of clinical charts. This will significantly help develop their documentation skills, and they will be able to objectively read their own documentation.

✔ As a manager, look at who is admitted to the home care program. Do the patients meet your admission criteria? If the nurse cannot clearly identify the skilled, covered service needed but does know the requirements, the patient may not be appropriate for insurance coverage.

✔ Have your staff focus on the patient's problems in their documentation. That is why home care is being provided, and it is what the payers must see to justify reimbursement.

✔ Have your nurses demonstrate through their documentation that the care provided is patient-centered. Make the patient goals clear and desired outcomes specific to the patient's unique problems and needs. Whenever possible, the patient should help set goals.

✔ Emphasize to the nurses that anyone else who picks up their patient's chart does not have the information they have from actually being there and seeing the patient in her/his own home setting. Encourage your staff to write information that is objective and clearly paints a picture of the patient, the problems, the needs, and where the care is directed for goal achievement and discharge.

✔ Have the clinical records reviewed overall when the initial admitting information has been completed. Use a checklist form to make it easier. This is the best time to check that all identifying information is completed, accurate, and consistent across the various admission forms.

✔ Remember to tell your staff that effective documentation does not have to be lengthy or wordy. However, it should convey to any reader the status of your patient, the plan for care, and the consistent movement towards predetermined patient-centered goals.

✔ Have the nurses check that the information on the record flows well and that you can tell by objective evidence what is happening with the patient. This includes the problems, projected plans, and the skilled services that are needed, based on the clear picture presented in the documentation.

SUGGESTIONS TO HELP YOU HELP YOUR STAFF IMPROVE DOCUMENTATION — cont'd

✔ Emphasize that paperwork needs to be legible, neat (if handwritten), and organized consistently.

✔ Remind your staff that the payers generally only know as much as is communicated from the data submitted. They are painting a picture for the payer/reviewer of why the patient needs nursing or other skilled services. Emphasize that the forms must document why the care was initiated, the problem to be addressed, what the clinician is doing (i.e., what the skilled interventions are), where the patient's plan is going (patient-centered goals), and the plans for discharge and why the case should continue.

✔ Encourage and appoint a staff nurse representative to your HHA's regularly scheduled CQI or PI committee meetings. This nurse can communicate to peers the important role of documentation and bring forward ideas to the group.

✔ Instruct your home care nurses to complete admissions and most of the documentation in the patient's home, when possible. This is particularly true for new admissions to home care or hospice care. Patients clearly know that third-party payers (except in private pay service home care) generally pay for the care the HHA is providing. Complete the visit record and all the initial admitting forms. The nurse should not rely on memory to complete needed documentation. In addition, tell your nurses to explain on the initial visit that requirements must be met for the payers and that the last few minutes of the visit are for the nurse to complete these requirements. Some agencies have implemented this standard very successfully, and it is reflected in the quality of the detailed documentation. If your HHA is automated, complete the documentation as per the policy.

✔ Emphasize that the POC and the OASIS are the most important parts of the home care clinical record. All other information flows from the identified skilled needs ordered on the plan and supported by the documented clinical findings.

report that integrates the information by nurse, by week, and by total visits by day or week would validate that finding. This report and the rationale would then help justify an increase in FTEs to your supervisor. The ability to use data to be flexible and respond to meet the patient's needs is a key to successful HHA operations.

Management Reporting Tools for New Managers

1. Regardless of site, use your referral logs as an important source of information at least weekly. The weekly information may be tabulated by your staff for monthly or cumulative reports. Look at:

   • Who and where your referrals are coming from. Are there trends in the diagnoses, types of patients, payer sources, or other information (i.e., visits per referral may indicate level of acuity)?

   • Who are the specific hospitals, physicians, discharge planners, and inpatient nurses? Compare this current information to that of the previous period. If a change exists, try to determine its cause. Have your own HHA coordinator involved in the causes.

- The referral log's information should not be underestimated. Use this as a working management tool to track your referrals or nurse care manager caseloads or to project future work assignments. In addition, it is the one place, at a glance, to see your payer mix or geographic spread or to identify trends.

2. Readmissions to the hospital.
3. Complaint logs.
4. Accident/incident or safety logs.
5. Requests for additional data or documentation (ADRs). These forms generated by the RHHI request more clinical information. They should include the date received and the date the information is requested. In addition, look at the entire process: locating, copying, and collating the information. Analyze these findings on a quarterly basis because these requests for information cost time and money. In addition, share the request with the primary nurse, not in a negative or punitive way, but as an educational opportunity and as a way to perhaps avoid such information requests in the future.

    Clearly, an increase in ADRs may signify the need for inservice training on documentation and/or a query into the reason for the increase.
6. Reports generated from automated systems. HHAs have specialized software systems to assist them in their daily operations in such important and time-consuming data-tracking areas as intake/referrals or billing data entry. Many of these systems are capable of generating useful information for managers. An example is categorizing patients by diagnosis, geographic area, or primary nurse. In addition, nurse productivity reports or financial reports (e.g., status and aging of accounts) assist the manager in planning daily and future operations. Still others include status of budgeted versus actual expenditures and numerous fiscal information. Such reports can be generated for your weekly or monthly review to assist in making decisions.
7. Monthly or quarterly quality report/update/activities. This report should include all continuing education sessions held since the last report and all ongoing research or special-focus studies. These findings, or a synopsis of the findings, may be appropriate for inclusion in the utilization review committee meeting report or in the HHA annual report.
8. Referral source; patient and family satisfaction surveys.

    The information to be found in reports is important. An effective automated system that meets your HHA's needs can prove invaluable once you and the staff have learned to use it.
9. Others, including infection surveillance or other areas so chosen or mandated for accreditation.

Special Programs
Hospice and Other Palliative Care Programs

Hospice care is a very special type of care and is receiving deserved recognition. The nurses, social workers, chaplain, volunteers, and other hospice team members all bring their unique skills to assist patients and their families at the end of life. This discussion focuses on the special needs unique to hospice management.

Managers in hospice are unique for several reasons:

1. They provide direction and support to a staff whose patient population, by definition, has an illness of a terminal nature.
2. They interface daily with the processes of dying and death. Therefore the feedback about feelings of anger, denial, and sadness is incorporated into their management role.
3. They must have specialized skills to work successfully with volunteers.
4. They must have training skills to train and successfully maintain volunteers.
5. They must have specialized knowledge of hospice reimbursement systems (e.g., the Medicare hospice program and all its specific nuances).
6. All these functions demand effective interpersonal communication skills and the ability to talk and teach about hospice factually and sensitively.

In addition, because of the nature of hospice care, funding has historically been problematic. Many hospices are involved in fund-raising to support their continued services in communities. The manager in hospice must have or develop the skills to work with fund-raising committee representatives or other associated entities that do this important work for the hospice. There is an ongoing need to be able to articulate clearly the special needs and costs of hospice care. Readers may want to review the public speaking tips addressed in Chapter 6, Effective Communication.

Hospices must have systems capable of tracking needed information for such important components of hospice care as bereavement counseling and the associated anniversary or remembrance information. In addition, many hospices keep detailed statistics about their programs and the patients and families served in the community. These functions also generate the need for effective tracking through automated systems.

Personal Emergency Response System Programs

Some HHAs also have another special program that is a part of their organization and that the HHA manager may also have responsibility for—the personal emergency response system (PERS) program.

Such PERS systems are a unique application of technology that allow some patients the ability to remain in their home alone or give them a heightened sense of security. Most nurses in home care are familiar with this technology, because most have the subscriber (patient) wear the PERS button around the neck or on a belt clip. This technology is tied into the phone system and, once activated, contacts one or more preselected family members or friends of the subscriber to come over immediately. The responders then go to the home, because they have access, and address the problem. Sometimes the responders are municipal services—the fire department or ambulance service. Generally, falls cause the most calls for help to be initated in this patient population.

Many of these programs have volunteers who may provide some of the actual installation and explanation of this important service and technology. Reports should be available to you, as the manager, about the number of subscriber calls, equipment inventory, current or projected purchase needs, public relations associated with the service, costs, and other factors that ensure a safe and responsive program for subscribers and their families and friends.

In addition, most PERS programs have (at least) quarterly meetings that are advisory in nature. They may include the manager, the operators who receive the calls (the response center), a representative of the company that sells and services your PERS equipment, a representative consumer of the service (if possible), the volunteers who assist with the program, and others in the program who are key factors in the effective functioning of this 24-hour service. Some programs have hundreds of these PERS units in the community because the programs allow some frail or elderly people to remain at home. Otherwise, they could not be at home and alone.

The HHA manager may have responsibility for numerous other programs (e.g., Meals on Wheels, private duty services, or home medical equipment and supply services) in day-to-day operations. With the increasing population of the older elderly (over 85 years), and as community service becomes more the pattern of care, these and other kinds of monitoring programs can be expected to grow.

COMMUNICATION: MORE IMPORTANT THAN EVER

In home care, as in other health care delivery sites, effective communication is very important, both when working with clinical team members and when teaching patients and their families how to provide effective care at home. Due to the unique environment of home care, in which staff are in patients' homes most of the workday and available to office staff only by beeper and telephone, communication becomes more involved as well as more important.

All patient care managers need to understand how and what to communicate to the audience they are trying to reach:
• Peers (want to be included): Tactical communication
• Subordinates (need to be instructed): Technical communication
• Supervisor (expects to be informed): Strategic communication

Home care managers are also faced with regulatory and accrediting standards that focus on the effective communication and coordination of care across many professional disciplines, as well as between different providers of care (e.g., the home parenteral infusion pharmacy with an intermittent nursing visit agency, and home medical equipment company). Effective communication and timely documentation of communications between the service vendors and the patient care team led by the ordering or attending physician are needed both to achieve positive patient outcomes and to meet regulatory standards.

Case coordination, or team conferencing, as it is frequently called, is essential to effective care communication. It should occur at least twice a month, with all care providers attending, including the home health aide. Goals or outcomes of care that have been established need to be reviewed and revised based on the patient's progress, revised assessments, and identified new problems. The input of all team members should be respected and included in the planning process. The effectiveness of the care and the appropriateness of ordered services (or those services that should be ordered) need to be reviewed. Home care managers must ascertain that team conferences are productive and involve all team members. One or two problem patients and/or staff should not be allowed to monopolize the discussion, and efforts should be made to adhere to an established agenda and include all staff.

Home care communication relies greatly on policies and procedures regarding staff members' notifying the office about patient care schedules, new admissions or changed assessments, and new or revised orders. A major problem in home care involves the timely assessment and other documentation and submission of supplemental orders. Clinicians are required to update the physician on any significant changes in patient status and note new orders. The ability of the home care nurse or therapist to reach the physician on the first call is limited, and the exchange of telephone messages is common. Many agencies utilize staff voice mail/beeper or cellular phone communication systems so that clinicians can leave messages and receive direct answers that they can access from the field.

With the emergence of laptop computer documentation systems, modems, and cellular phones, communication has become more technologically complex but also more streamlined, making staff more accessible. However, confidentiality remains a major concern, especially for the staff member who receives or returns a call to the physician or office regarding another patient. The potential for confidentiality breach is enormous and the home care manager must ensure that the policies and procedures are present to cover these occurrences and staff are adequately oriented, trained, and supervised to minimize the chance of these breaches occurring.

SUMMARY

The successful home care manager must be flexible, have vision, and be committed to a service-oriented management style. This manager will use newer technologies with the staff to ensure increased communications and safety for the staff. Even 5 years ago, who would have imagined the number of cellular phones, laptops, voice mail, and beepers in use as there are today for home care staff?

Home care and hospice has an important niche in the health care continuum. As patients become more proactive consumers of care, they will continue to demand care in their own home setting. However, as PPS continues to sometime appear to rachet down the number of patient visits, the home care manager must be able to articulate the clinical needs of the patient for that patient to receive quality care while remaining at home. Complex patient problems will increase as the health care technology explosion continues. The effective home care manager is poised to respond to the challenge!

The proactive manager who can quantify and communicate staff needs and explain to superiors the needs based on objective information will be successful in home care. This chapter is a brief overview of what you need to know to manage a quality program. Many good resources are available to the new manager in home care. The hope is that you will locate or create them.

QUESTIONS FOR CONSIDERATION

1. Discuss how managing staff that is not nearby is unique and requires a specific skill-set and processes to best manage.
2. Briefly discuss the changes brought to home care pursuant to the PPS.
3. Discuss three facets of legal/risk management issues that are unique to home care.
4. Identify five reasons why staff meetings are very important.
5. Describe the interface of documentation in home care to reimbursement.

References

1. *Health Insurance Manual-11,* Washington, DC, 1995, Government Printing Office.

2. Marrelli TM: *Handbook of home health standards and documentation guidelines for reimbursement,* St Louis, 2001, Mosby.

For Further Reading

American Nurses Association: *Scope and standards of home health nursing practice,* Washington, DC, 1999, ANA.

Benner B: *From novice to expert,* Menlo Park, CA, 1984, Addison-Wesley Publishing Company.

City of Hope National Medical Center: *HOPE: Homecare Outreach for Palliative Care Education,* Duarte, CA, 2001, City of Hope National Medical Center. Available online at *http://coh.org.*

Finkelman, Anita: *Psychiatric home care,* Gaithersburg, MD, 1997, Aspen Publishers, Inc

Fitchett G: *Assessing spiritual needs: a guide for caregivers,* Minneapolis, 1993, Augsburg.

Hospice and Palliative Nursing Association: *Hospice and palliative nursing practice review,* Dubuque, IA, 1997, Kendall/Hunt, HPNA.

Hospice and Palliative Nursing Association: *Statement on the scope and standards of hospice and palliative nursing practice,* Dubuque, IA, 2000, Kendall/Hunt, HPNA.

Lynn, Schuster, Kabcenell: *Improving care for the end of life,* New York, 2000, Oxford University Press.

Marrelli T: *Hospice and palliative care handbook: quality, compliance and reimbursement,* St Louis, 1999, Mosby.

Marrelli T: *Mosby's home care and hospice drug handbook,* St Louis, 1999, Mosby.

Marrelli T: *Handbook of home health standards and documentation: guidelines for reimbursement,* ed 4, St Louis, 2001, Mosby.

Marrelli T, Friend L: *Home health aide guidelines for care: instructor manual*, Englewood, FL, 1997, Marrelli and Associates, Inc.

Marrelli T, Hilliard L: *Home care and clinical paths: effective care planning across the continuum*, St Louis, 1998, Mosby.

Marrelli T, Hilliard L: *Manual of home health practice: guidance for effective clinical operations*, St Louis, 1998, Mosby.

Marrelli T, Krulish L: *Home care therapy: quality, documentation, and reimburse-* ment, Englewood, FL, 1999, Marrelli and Associates, Inc.

National Hospice and Palliative Care Organization: *Standards of practice for hospice programs*, Arlington, VA, 2000, NHPCO.

Stanhope M, Knollmueller R: *Handbook of community-based and home health nursing practice*, ed 3, St Louis, 2000, Mosby.

CHAPTER 13

WHERE TO FROM HERE?

T.M. MARRELLI

During the course of your career, there may be times when you question your level of job satisfaction. Your questioning might begin in the form of occasional nagging doubts such as, "Why did I ever accept this position?" or "Management is nothing like the recruiter told me it would be." Maybe you find yourself not laughing as much, dwelling on work problems when at home, or answering the phone at home with the name of your work organization. All of these are clues that it may be time to reevaluate your job satisfaction. If, like many workers today, you are seeking personal fulfillment, this introspective evaluation may be a difficult process. However, you should start the process when you want to, not when you are stressed out and are forced to address the issue. So where do you start?

Nurses, by nature and education, have a strong tendency to take care of others. However, this chapter's focus is on you and your needs and goals. You must realize that the perfect job does not exist. All positions have their own unique strengths and drawbacks. This review includes what your aspirations were when you accepted your current position, your dreams of being a nurse when you were a student, and your perspectives on the realities of nursing now. Put simply, are your professional and self-fulfillment needs being met in your current position and environment? Are your expectations realistic? Is it time for a change?

ASSESSING JOB SATISFACTION

The types of questions to ask to assess your satisfaction with your job may be broken down into two areas: (1) the work and the associated environment or culture of the setting in which you manage, and (2) your professional and personal needs and where these fit in your life in relation to other responsibilities. These questions are best answered initially with a quick "yes" or "no" without much thought (this is your "gut" feeling). You can then go back and reconsider your answers after the overall evaluation is complete.

Asking yourself the questions in Manager's Tip 13-1 may help you assess your position and determine if management and this particular position are suitable for you.

It is important to note that some of us have a tendency to give and take care of everyone and everything except ourselves. This can lead to exhaustion and burnout. Our work life must be successfully integrated into other parts of our lives.

Part of the personal growth process is the identification of problem areas in our lives and the identification of actions for resolution. Maslow's needs identify the basic needs that must initially be attained before self-actualization can be achieved. The setting, evaluation, and reevaluation of personal and professional goals on a regular basis can be an effective tool in achieving what we want.

Focusing on the answers to the questions in Manager's Tip 13-2 can help you decide how well a management position fits with your personal needs. The direction your career takes is up to you. It is always okay to reconsider and ultimately readjust career goals to meet your unique needs. After a thorough review of your answers, your next step is to reaffirm or reevaluate your stated goals. In this way you can begin implementing changes to work toward achieving them. Only you know what will contribute to the feeling of self-fulfillment in your life. It has been

MANAGER'S TIP 13-1

THE WORK AND ITS ENVIRONMENT

Ask yourself these questions to help you determine whether management and your present position are suitable for you:

✔ Do you enjoy the actual work tasks? In management this includes the human management activities of dealing with difficult personalities, conflict resolution, and having the position of power (whether or not you want it). This also includes the satisfaction of being part of a special team providing care to patients and being able to effect needed change or being appreciated by patient's families.

✔ Overall, do you like going to your job every day?

✔ Do you feel you have some control over outcomes and the tasks accomplished?

✔ Generally, are the obstacles to completion outweighed by the work accomplished?

✔ Generally, do you feel that you have the support you need to accomplish your work? If you decide that you enjoy the actual work responsibilities but still are not happy at work, consider whether your supervisor provides sufficient support for your team to get tasks accomplished. Continual frustration of goal achievement is very disheartening and leads to nurse manager and staff turnover. You may wonder, "Who else cares, so why should I?"

✔ Does your job leave you feeling energized or drained? Does your family see you enough? When they do, are you emotionally available, or are you redoing the staffing schedule in your head while having dinner?

MANAGER'S TIP 13-2

YOUR PERSONAL NEEDS

To help you decide how well a management position fits with your personal goals, ask yourself these questions:

✔ Do you find the actual activities of the manager stimulating while being able to integrate the rest of your responsibilities into your life (e.g., your family and friends)?

✔ Are the rewards appropriate to the energy expended?

✔ Are you able to fulfill your own personal goals in this position (e.g., go back to school, have a family, complete certification, teach Sunday school class, or be a volunteer fire-fighter or paramedic in your community)?

said that, "Nurses leave the profession because they experience a lack of personal fulfillment, stemming from their inability to meet the unrealistic expectations imposed by this ever-changing environment."[1] Nurse managers do not always have to leave their current work environment to feel more fulfilled in their professional roles. Skills that nurses use daily outside the work realm lend themselves to other potentially fulfilling professional or personal activities. The following are examples of such endeavors:

1. *Organizational skills*—Are you the family member who is, by nature, the organizer? You can use these skills in professional association activities in various administrative capacities.

2. *Writting skills*—Do you edit the community newsletter or contribute to the local newspaper? This can be developed into a resource for the nursing news at your facility or for publication in a professional nursing journal.

3. *Public speaking skills*—This needed communication skill can be used by speakers' bureaus, the local community college for health classes, support groups, or for speeches to elementary school students on subjects such as "Why I Like Being a Nurse."

4. *Persuasive skills*—Consider running for office or campaigning for the candidate of your choice.

Any of these special skills can be effective in assisting you in meeting your goals and helping you match them with your unique talents.

In the beginning of this chapter, you evaluated your satisfaction with your current work position and where it fits in your life. This chapter also discusses the importance of recognizing available employment choices. Specific ways to succeed and make yourself uniquely qualified for a position are addressed, and examples of choices and qualifications that may be helpful to you are included.

CHOICES

Choices are options that you give yourself. People tend not to give themselves the luxury of choices. In addition, even when we know that we may be unhappy in our work environment, we may procrastinate about taking the steps needed to change and grow. You are not alone. (The Procrastinator's Club has approximately 10,000 members!)

Once you recognize that professional nurses have numerous choices for employment, you can begin to explore your many options. Even if you have a satisfying job, considering your options can provide growth opportunities important to your professional career in the future. This is also a way to help market yourself and your skills. Being open to and considering your choices enables you to (1) keep some perspective on your current job (this is particularly important when you are unhappy in your position), (2) receive objective feedback about yourself and the external professional environment, and (3) receive information on possibilities for the future. This feedback can be received through the interview process, through networking with professional associates, and through other methods of communication.

MARKETING YOURSELF

Marketing is broadly defined as the theory and practice of selling. In reality, we market ourselves in any interpersonal or written encounter. However, when we consciously market ourselves, we focus on the unique skills that we bring to a work environment and offer to a prospective employer, enhancing our desirability to that employer. Examples of assets that make a nurse uniquely qualified include advanced degrees or certification in a specialty area. Still other examples include awards, experience, and other types of recognition in a chosen field. We sometimes tend to underestimate our own unique skills. The credit and acknowledgement of others can be of important benefit in achieving your long-term professional goals.

A large part of successfully marketing yourself is your projection of your belief in yourself. This is your self-confidence. We know that feelings follow thoughts. Therefore even if on a bad day you are not feeling self-assured, your acting that way may contribute to your feeling more confident. Use available resources to develop or improve such self-promoting skills. Look at role models who seem self-assured; watch how they act, dress, and behave. It is important that you recognize your strengths and areas for improvement. This level of self-knowledge leads to an increased self-assurance that is communicated as belief in yourself.

IDENTIFYING YOUR UNIQUE OR SPECIAL SKILLS—AREAS FOR CONSIDERATION

Although professional RNs must pass nursing boards for licensure, and thus meet specific standards, the following section addresses additional ways to help you grow professionally.

Certification

In the 1940s, nurse anesthetists were the first nurses required to meet specific standards to enter professional practice. Since then, certification has grown to encompass those nurses who meet high standards through experience and expertise in nursing practice. Certification is a validation of clinical or administrative skill. The process of certification generally requires an RN license, a set amount of years or hours in practice in a specific specialty, and documented continuing education credit hours. A major benefit of professional certification is the recognition that sets certified nurses apart. Several nursing organizations have boards for certifying nurses. These boards set the criteria, determine scoring, validate credentials, and confer certification in more than 50 nursing specialties. Examples of organizations that certify nurses include the American Nurses Association (ANA), the American Association of Critical Care Nurses, and the National Certification Corporation. These and other unique credentials you have as a nurse contribute to your power base as a nurse, specialty clinician, and/or nurse manager.

Professional Associations

Membership and active involvement in professional associations provide many benefits to nurse managers. Serving on committees, organizing educational programs, and assisting in creating standards for your specialty area are all important contributions that membership allows. Volunteering on committees and assisting in the work of the organization provide a platform for growth as well as opportunities for networking and solidifying professional relationships.

Writing for Professional Publications

Because of their clinical expertise and communication skills, all nurses, particularly those in management, have something important to share with other nurses and nurse managers. In addition, the initiative and perseverance necessary to research and develop an idea and then create and submit a completed manuscript reflect other desirable traits to a prospective employer. Publication in a nursing or health journal, for example, sets you apart from other candidates who may be similarly qualified. This has been particularly true for some time in the academic environment.

Workshops, Seminars, and Other Development Activities

Some people attend classes and expect to absorb all the information by listening quietly. Yet, it has been demonstrated that we forget most of what we learn within days, particularly when there is no active participation on our part. The 10 suggestions in Manager's Tip 13-3 on p. 356 can help you make the most of learning and networking opportunities at professional workshops or seminars.

MANAGER'S TIP 13-3

10 TIPS FOR ONGOING LEARNING

✔ Set three learning goals. Develop a list of three to six overall goals in attending the educational session. This will help you focus your thinking. Your goals generally will be oriented toward getting specific questions answered or utilization or practical application of skills or theory.

✔ Think about specific questions you want answered. Develop a list of 10 to 15 specific questions. (Consider giving this list to the seminar leaders in advance.)

✔ Meet other participants at the program. Network with them. Each attendee has a specific area of expertise. Make a note of it. Start your own network. Exchange cards (bring along plenty). Go to breakfast, lunch, and dinner with those with whom you can share information and learn. Send notes to those participants that you would like to keep in touch with.

✔ Develop a plan of action. Make a list of anything you want to consider doing differently when you get back on the job. This will help you apply what you learned and help you achieve objective benefits.

✔ Participate. Ask questions and make contributions. Comment. Be visible. You will benefit in two ways. First, your mind will almost automatically start working on information, problems, and solutions. Second, the speaker and other attendees will also contribute by finding answers for you.

✔ Make contact with the seminar leader personally (and early) when possible. She/he will think more of and about you. It will also be easier to follow up with questions and problems after the program.

✔ Take clear, detailed notes. Not only will this be helpful for future reference, but the very act of taking good notes and organizing your thoughts will keep you more involved. Take notes legibly and coherently the first time to eliminate any need for rewriting them later.

✔ Write a brief report—one to three pages—based on your plan of action and notes. Consider sharing your report with your supervisor.

✔ Hold a staff meeting when you get back and share the useful information you have gained. Implement a plan of action using your new ideas.

✔ Enjoy yourself—we all learn more when we are having a good time.

Networking

The contacts made and developed through professional organizations can be very advantageous. In time, these professional colleagues may become your peer support group, your friends, and sources of information on viable job alternatives when you want to move on professionally.

Working with Recruiters

As your management expertise and your networking contacts grow, your name will inevitably be given to a health care recruiter who is assisting an organization in locating potential candidates for middle to senior management positions. There are recruiters who specialize in physician, senior management, middle management, and hard-to-recruit staff positions. There are as many different types of recruiters as there are nurse managers, each with varying styles of accomplishing goals.

Recruiters are inherently interested in whether you would like your resume presented to a search committee or manager and, if not, if you are aware of any similarly qualified professionals who may be in the market for a change or new position. Recruiters should be treated with the same respect as any vendor or other professional that you deal with. Even though you may not be job-hunting at this time, you may need assistance in the near future. Recruiters are a potential resource in your job hunt. Manager's Tip 13-4 offers some pointers for working with recruiters.

RESUMES AND CURRICULUM VITAE

Resumes, curriculum vitae, and associated cover letters or other written products all represent you. Remember, they are sometimes the only communication about you that a prospective employer receives. These first impressions do count. Resumes are used in most business settings, whereas curriculum vitae are used primarily in the educational and teaching realms. Always type your resume or curriculum vitae, and print the document on the best quality paper available. It is a good idea to have someone proofread your resume or curriculum vitae and cover letter for content, implications, format, clarity, and typographic errors. If no one is available to provide

MANAGER'S TIP 13-4

POINTERS FOR WORKING WITH RECRUITERS

✔ Be open and honest about whether you are interested in pursuing a position.
✔ If no position is available now, ask them to hold your resume and assist them if you know of other possible candidates.
✔ Do your homework and research the reputation of the recruiter or parent firm.
✔ Treat the recruiter with respect and professionalism.
✔ Recruiters usually are paid on a commission or retainer basis, dependent on the amount of business done with a client; they need to be assertive but not aggressive.
✔ The recruiter is "working for the employer." The goals will be aligned as such and you are under no obligation to take a job that does not interest or will not compensate you as you desire. Remember, they called you for your expertise.
✔ Outline your salary and benefit requirements early in initial negotiations, based on skills, job requirements, market demand, and personal desires.
✔ Get a clear description of job responsibilities before the interview.
✔ Do not try to negotiate with a potential employer without the consent or knowledge of the recruiter.

objective comments, put your materials aside for a day or two and then reread them. You may be amazed at the findings. Most print or copy shops will print your resume or curriculum vitae on quality paper fairly inexpensively. The outcome may be worth the cost if it results in additional interviews scheduled. About now, you might be saying, "I do not have the time to do all this and pay attention to such details." Remember the resumes and cover letters that have come across your desk? You have probably been drawn to those that are short and neat and that communicate clearly. Use your time management skills to ensure that the documents you provide any prospective employer are clear, complete, accurate, and professional.

Resume Preparation

A resume is a well-organized synopsis of an individual's educational and career experiences. Its purpose is to give enough information to the potential employer to initiate a first interview; therefore it must be concise, factual, and targeted to the position being sought. With the availability of word processing, resumes should be reviewed and revised based on the focus of the position in question. This is not to imply that one should document untrue statements on a resume but rather target or customize specific career and educational achievements to what is potentially needed in a desired position. In fact, that way the resume can be accessible and e-mailed as an attachment.

Resumes should be no longer than three pages, unless there are extensive professional experiences and accomplishments. They can be organized in a number of different manners; however, it is best to organize positions, experiences, and accomplishments chronologically. This is a professional tool; do not list hobbies. For the individual who is contemplating a career change, or who has been out of the job market for an extended time, the resume should focus on functionality, listing the skills possessed that can transcend different industries.

Resume Dos and Don'ts. Do not list any salary information or reasons for leaving any positions. It is not a good idea to list family, gender, or other personal information. And NEVER, NEVER stretch the truth, lie, or fabricate information on your resume— at some point, it will come back to haunt you. Manager's Tip 13-5 lists the basic elements to include in a resume.

Your resume, particularly for management positions, should indicate the number and types of staffs you have been responsible for in your current and previous positions. Be clear about your level of responsibility (e.g., "24-hour responsibility for more than 50 nurses and for over 25 professional associates [speech-language pathologists, occupational therapists, medical social workers, physical therapists, etc.] who cared for more than 400 patients in the home setting"). When writing your resume, always use verbs that express management in action. Appropriate verbs include *created, developed, initiated, chaired, implemented, evaluated, supervised, problem-solved,* and *analyzed.* Examples of a resume and cover letter, the introductory letter about you and your skills that accompanies your resume or curriculum vitae, are given in Boxes 13-1 and 13-2.

MANAGER'S TIP 13-5

BASIC ELEMENTS TO INCLUDE IN A RESUME

When preparing a resume, be sure to include the following basic information:
- ✔ Identifying information: name, address, home and work phone numbers.
- ✔ Career objectives (aligned with the specific position requested).
- ✔ Academic degrees and honors; applicable credentials.
- ✔ Pertinent education (do not list high school if college degree is noted) and skills.
- ✔ Progressive career experience, with both accomplishments and job functions listed.
- ✔ Publications, awards, and presentations as applicable.
- ✔ Professional affiliations.

---

box 13-1

EXAMPLE OF A RESUME

Name and Credentials
Address
Phone Number
Professional-Sounding E-Mail Address

Career Objectives:

Professional Experience:
Dates: Most Current Position, Employer Name, City, State (Continue for all positions—up through 10 years)

Major Accomplishments:
List major accomplishments of career (e.g., expense control, revenue growth, development of service line or program, etc.). Use verbs when possible.

Education:

Professional Affiliations:

Awards, Presentations, Publications, etc.

References (upon request)

---

box 13-2

EXAMPLE OF A COVER LETTER

June 14, 200–
Alice Campbell, RN, MSN   1212 Mockingbird Lane
Recruitment Office   Anytown, Maryland 11111-2222
St. Elsewhere General Hospital
Anytown, Maryland 11111-2222

Dear Ms. Campbell,

I am writing in response to your ad for a nurse manager in the Sunday Anywhere Paper
of June 12, 200-. I believe my 4 years of experience in the St. Elsewhere General Hospital
telemetry unit as evening shift coordinator, as well as other accomplishments, make me
uniquely qualified for this position.

I have attached my resume, which highlights my experience, for your confidential
review. I look forward to hearing from you. I can be reached at (410) 222-1234 or by
e-mail at _____.

Sincerely,

Jennifer Brown, RN

Curriculum Vitae

A curriculum vitae (CV) differs from a resume in that it is a written progression of
your career that is used primarily for academic purposes or in such settings. A CV
outlines in more detail than a resume and includes all educational opportunities that
have affected your career positively, as well as a listing and description of all positions you have held.

BEFORE THE INTERVIEW

Consider *any* communication that occurs with a prospective employer as an opportunity to shine and market yourself. Even if you suspect that the employer may not
be considering you or have a position available for someone with your unique qualifications, remember that this person might consider you in the future or knows
of another or other positions. What you do and say today can position you for a
future job. Your interactions can influence early deliberations about such future
opportunities.

At the beginning of this chapter you considered and identified what is important in order for you to meet your unique needs in a nursing management position. The following sections will discuss the active process of the job search and offer tips for finding and getting the job you want. Manager's Tip 13-6 offers suggestions to help you prepare for the interview.

Your responses should reflect your professionalism, job knowledge, management skills, and goals. Being well prepared will also help decrease most interview jitters or nervousness.

THE INTERVIEW

The interview process is appropriately valued as the most important factor in getting a job. In addition, the interview is an important step in the information-gathering process about the prospective employer. Through actively listening to someone who knows the system and manages there, you can learn needed information about the

MANAGER'S TIP 13-6

PREPARING FOR THE INTERVIEW

✔ Find out all you can about your prospective employer. Many organizations have websites that are full of information, including the vision, mission, and other areas for review.

✔ Talk to employees, including nurses you know who no longer work there.

✔ Recognize that the advertisements in the newspaper communicate important information about the position and the facility. For example, does the ad describe where you would live and work geographically (urban, rural, etc.)? Does the employer sound progressive? Does the ad mention clinical ladders, collaborative practice models, or other progressive nurse-oriented activities that are important to you? Ads sometimes communicate the management philosophy. Ads may provide information that can help you determine whether or not you would fit in as a team member in a particular setting.

✔ Obtain written materials. Most health care facilities produce flyers or brochures, available to the community, about their services. Read the factual information listed. This may include the size of the facility or program, the number of beds (if an inpatient setting), the mission statement or goals, the specific services or programs provided (e.g., maternity care, ambulatory care, hospice, home health), and the geographic area they serve.

✔ Write and send a cover letter with your resume to the person identified in the newspaper ad. This may be the nurse recruiter, the nursing office supervisor, or an administrator for the clinical area. In the letter clearly request consideration and an interview at this person's earliest convenience. Set the tone to sound professional and enthusiastic.

Continued

PREPARING FOR THE INTERVIEW — cont'd

✔ Think about and prepare a written list of questions for the interview. Your questions might relate to the nursing philosophy, the mission statement of the program, the average staffing ratios on the unit you would be managing, the kind of documentation system used, computerization status, the average length of stay for the hospital or for the specific unit, or information about the nursing newsletter.

✔ Make a list of questions you think you might be asked and practice answering them. Think of those questions that you ask prospective applicants. Practice before the interview so that you will not need to have your notes with you. Questions commonly asked in interviews include:

　✔ Where do you want to be professionally in 5 to 10 years?

　✔ What are your strengths and weaknesses?

　✔ Give an example of a particularly difficult management situation and how you addressed the problem.

　✔ Why are you looking for another position?

　✔ Tell me about your nursing management style.

　✔ Why do you want to work here?

　✔ What is your background?

　✔ Why do you believe you are the best person for this job?

---

actual nursing and management philosophy. Manager's Tips 13-7, 13-8, and 13-9 on pp. 363 and 364 provide general suggestions for interviewing, taking advantage of opportunities that the interview offers, and concluding the interview.

THE INTERVIEW WITH YOUR PROSPECTIVE NEW STAFF

Many employers now schedule the nurse manager candidate finalists to meet with and be interviewed by representatives of the staff they may be managing on accepting the position. Usually the staff chooses representatives. The number may vary based on the facility's philosophy. This can be a very useful opportunity for the prospective nurse manager to determine more about the actual day-to-day operations and culture of the clinical area. Usually the nurses chosen are leaders in the staff hierarchy. The interview with representatives of your prospective staff will also give you needed information about the staff and should be looked on as a positive and information-finding meeting. This is your time to be professional, positive, and persuasive. Smile! You might practice with a trusted friend the speech about why you are the best candidate for the job and about your style of management.

FOLLOWING UP ON THE INTERVIEW

If the interviewer or the nurse recruiter does not call by the discussed date, call her/him to determine whether a decision has been made and, if not, when you

MANAGER'S TIP 13-7

GENERAL TIPS FOR INTERVIEWING

✔ The more prepared you are, the more self-assured you will be, and this information will be projected to any prospective employer.

✔ It is a good idea to bring along an extra resume should the interviewer not be able to locate her/his copy. (If this happens, it may give you important insight into the work environment, such as disorganization, tight resources, or poor communication between human resources and nursing [or it may be that this is just a bad day].)

✔ It is okay to ask for a copy of the specific position description should one not be offered. Because usually more functions are required than those listed on the position description, consider asking the interviewer to describe the daily routine of the area.

✔ As part of your preparation, bring a typed list of professional and personal references. List the names, professional degrees, addresses, and telephone numbers of your references. The three professional references should be people your have worked with and/or who have supervised your work. Be sure to notify your references that you will be actively interviewing and that they may receive a call. Of course, you should ask if they are willing to serve as references before you list them.

✔ It is important that you appear as calm and composed as you can for an interview. This gets harder the more you want a specific job. Therefore plan to arrive at the setting at least 20 minutes ahead of time, assume you will not find a parking place anywhere near the facility, and plan to complete some paperwork, such as an application, before the actual interview begins. Take some deep breaths and try to relax.

✔ Be punctual, dress professionally in a suit that you feel good in, get a good night's sleep the night before, and tell yourself that you will have a successful interview. Visualize yourself being calm and smiling.

✔ Use your interpersonal skills and good judgment throughout the process. Allot plenty of time; some interviews can be lengthy depending on who else the interviewer wants you to meet with or on whether the interviewer gives you a tour of the clinical setting.

✔ Many interviews with potential employers include a variety of interview panels (e.g., peer managers, subordinates, managers, or select group of senior managers). Be prepared to speak before a small group of people with different information needs and interview focus. You can get this job! Try to enjoy the process.

should call back. When you call, be brief and pleasant. Communicate that you are still interested in the position and want to know if a candidate has been selected. Offer to call back the following week. Remember that if you really want the job, be assertive and let the interviewer know that you are available for a second interview if she/he so desires. It is important to be patient. Getting the position you want may take time but will be well worth the wait if the position meets your identified needs.

MANAGER'S TIP 13-8

MAKING THE MOST OF THE INTERVIEW

✔ Use your active listening skills.
✔ If you determine that the interviewer is having a bad day and seems very hassled (e.g., there may be numerous interruptions), know that this could be indicative of the interviewer's personality or of the setting. Try to use your intuitive skills during the encounter to know the difference between a bad day and what is "normal" for the functioning of the setting (e.g., crisis management).
✔ Do not smoke (even if the option is offered).
✔ Try to bring the conversation to the style of management practiced (e.g., "Are the staff nurses involved in shared governance or other aspects of departmental decision-making?").
✔ Do not share negative feelings or experiences about your current or past work settings. Although these occur to all of us, discussing them, particularly during a first meeting, may be perceived as indicating failure to appropriately address and handle identified problems.
✔ Act enthusiastic and you will feel that way. This will be communicated.
✔ Smile, use eye contact appropriately, take some deep breaths, try to relax, and listen.
✔ Communicate to the interviewer that you want this job (if indeed you want it) and that you are right for it.

MANAGER'S TIP 13-9

CONCLUDING THE INTERVIEW

✔ Allow the interviewer to wrap up the interview.
✔ Make sure that your correct phone number is on your resume and application.
✔ Have your questions ready when the interviewer asks, "Do you have any questions for me that I have not covered?"
✔ Thank the interviewer for the time and information.
✔ Ask how soon a decision will be made or what the next step will be (e.g., how soon the interviewer plans to fill the position and when you will be hearing about the decision or a second interview). In addition, ask who you will be hearing from (e.g., the interviewer or the nurse recruiter).
✔ Offer a verbal affirmation of wanting the job at the end of the interview (if you do, or think you do).

THANK-YOU LETTERS

Always send a thank-you letter to the interviewer within a week after the interview. Even when you call and speak to the interviewer, it is courteous to follow up with a thank-you note or letter. Two sample thank-you letters are provided in Box 13-3. The second letter gives you an idea of what to say if you are certain you are not interested in the position.

KEEPING A RECORD OF YOUR JOB SEARCH AND INTERVIEW INFORMATION

In your search, you may be in contact with and interviewed by various prospective employers. While you are trying to determine why you prefer one position or setting over another, it can be difficult to remember your thoughts and impressions without a written record. A notebook or log can be an easy way to help you remember details and your overall reactions to a specific facility.

Columns can be drawn vertically down a page with the following kinds of overhead information across the top horizontally. An example is:

NAME OF FACILITY   INTERVIEWER   BENEFITS   FOLLOW-UP   OUTCOME

Other variables that may be tracked in the log or notebook include dates (or copies) of letters, positions interviewed for, parking problems, commute time, the actual physical plant, other perceptions, and the interviewer's management or organizational style. Your record could also include your perceptions of such things as the level of cooperation when you called the facility, the human resources office, the security guards, the interviewer's receptionist, and how long you were kept waiting. Overall, did you feel like an intruder or that they were glad to have a promising candidate and communicated that to you? It is hard to go back and recreate details, so keeping the log in the car with you enables you to write your perceptions and objective facts immediately following the interview.

AFTER THE INTERVIEW

Identify whether this position has the critical job elements needed to make you happy and feel as if your best skills are being used. Brainstorm those factors you identified in your self-evaluation process that would help you achieve your professional goals. These may include the location (state, city, rural, urban, etc.), staff development program, professional growth opportunities, specialty areas, and any other factors, such as shared governance or nursing representation at the board level, that you value as criteria preferred in a prospective work setting.

box 13-3

SAMPLE THANK-YOU LETTERS

LETTER 1:

June 21, 200-

Alice Campbell, RN, MSN
Recruitment Office
St. Elsewhere General Hospital
Anytown, Maryland 11111-2222

1212 Mockingbird Lane
Anytown, Maryland 11111-2222

Dear Ms. Campbell:

Thank you for interviewing me yesterday for the position of nurse manager on the B-4 telemetry unit. As you know, I am very interested in assuming this position. I believe I have the skills and experience to be a great asset to St. Elsewhere General Hospital and would welcome the opportunity to join the management team.

I look forward to hearing from you; I can be reached at (410) 222-1234.

Sincerely,

Jennifer Brown, RN

LETTER 2:

June 21, 200-

Alice Campbell, RN, MSN
Recruitment Office
St. Elsewhere General Hospital
Anytown, Maryland 11111-2222

1212 Mockingbird Lane
Anytown, Maryland 11111-2222

Dear Ms. Campbell:

As I said in today's phone conversation, and after further thoughtful consideration, I realize that the nurse manager position is not the job I am seeking at this time. It sounds as if you have a great team working on the B-4 telemetry unit. Thank you for your time. I wish you success in filling your open position and in your other professional endeavors.

Sincerely,

Jennifer Brown, RN

NEGOTIATING

Salary is not the determinant of the best job, but in nursing, as in other fields, it sometimes can be a harbinger of the amount of work you will be responsible for. In addition, although starting nurses' salaries are usually fixed, experienced nurses, particularly managers, may consider negotiating for more based on their unique qualifications. Remember that you may never get what you do not request. Assessing a prospective employer's needs gives you information on which skills to emphasize. Remember:

1. You both want something. You want a fulfilling position that uses your talents effectively, and they want a competent manager who has the skills needed to accomplish the work at hand.
2. You are a competent manager who brings experience to this position. Be positive and enthusiastic about the position, and stress what you can do for them.
3. Know their specific needs. Often in an interview, the interviewer will share information about where the unit or organization is going. In fact, if this information is not shared, this is a good question to ask when the interviewer asks if you have any questions. The actual question could be phrased as, "What is St. Elsewhere General Hospital's vision for the future?" Many times you can use this information to promote your qualifications that make you the best candidate for the position. Examples are described in Manager's Tip 13-10.

Before you accept a position, know what you need to be happy and to meet your goals. You may need to negotiate for what you want. People do respect people who negotiate for what they believe they deserve. Many settings now offer "cafeteria style" benefit packages to more successfully meet an individual's needs. This contributes to position retention. Some of these items may be the salary, tuition reimbursement, professional workshops and development, or flexibility in your work hours. Remember that successful negotiations are truly "win-win" (i.e., you both get what you want).

WHEN YOU RECEIVE AN OFFER

Listen to what is said, and know that you do not have to make a decision immediately. In fact, it may be helpful to "try on" what it would feel like to work at the facility for a few days before giving them an answer. This could include driving 20 miles to the prospective setting for a few consecutive days to see if the commute would be a problem or other behaviors that might help you in your decision-making process.

ACCEPTING THE OFFER

The job acceptance process can be as individual as the work setting. However, to protect yourself, as a general rule, ask to receive the offer in writing and wait until

MANAGER'S TIP 13-10

HOW ASKING ABOUT THE ORGANIZATION MAY HELP YOU WIN THE JOB

✔ *Recognize and take advantage of unique opportunities.* The interviewer states that the facility is currently completing long-term plans for one of its medical-surgical units to become a designated hospice unit. She/he goes on to say that it looks as if the state planning process is almost completed and that conversion could occur as soon as 3 months from now. If you have the skills or experience and express the desire to be of assistance, this could place you at an advantage over other candidates. In addition, in this current era of working to increase effectiveness with fewer resources, you could offer this prospective employer the needed flexibility and options.

✔ *Offer any relevant special knowledge that you might have.* The interviewer shares the information that the facility is undergoing a transition to make all the units more decentralized and autonomous. If you have experienced a similar process at another setting, your special knowledge could be valuable to a new employer to help ensure a successful change.

✔ *Do not be afraid to share your accomplishments.* Remember that the resume is only the introduction that gets your foot in the door. There is much more that must be communicated. Identify your special skills and accomplishments, such as serving on the local health department board, being a member of a speaking organization or a speaker's bureau, attaining certification, and publishing. (These special skills and accomplishments should be listed on your resume.)

you receive a written validation of your job offer from your new employer before giving notice to your current employer. This should be done even in instances when the position has been offered verbally and you have verbally accepted. It has happened in some settings that because of disorganization or a miscommunication, it was said that the offer never was extended. If this occurs, it does not matter why it happened; you still do not have the job and will not be working there.

GIVING NOTICE

Read your organization's policy about the procedure for giving notice of resignation in your particular setting. This usually ranges from 2 to 4 weeks depending on the setting and culture. If you have signed a contract, consult your contract. In addition, some nursing agencies, particularly in the sales or community health setting, may have noncompete clauses as part of the nurse's contract or as a separate agreement that was signed on employment. You must address these and other unique situations for your own protection and for professional integrity.

SAMPLE RESIGNATION LETTER

The actual resignation letter can be brief and to the point. Your letter should be directed to your immediate supervisor. The following is an example of the language that should be clearly stated:

"It is with regret that I inform you that effective [specify date], I will be resigning from my position as [position, area]."

Some people also state that they have enjoyed working in their position, when this is appropriate. It may not be appropriate if your supervisor knows that you have been stressed out and looking for a position for some time.

ABOUT "NOT BURNING BRIDGES"

All managers grow and change and sometimes need to move on, but we have all heard the saying "never burn bridges." This is true in all industries but particularly in the nursing profession. Health care is a small world. The cohesiveness of the nursing profession, particularly in one specialty or state, ensures that in the future there will be interaction with past employers. For these reasons, and for your own professional growth, always try to leave the area for which you were responsible in better shape than when you first took the position. This will help you be successful in your future professional endeavors.

GUILT AND GROOMING YOUR SUCCESSOR

Supervisors may try to make you feel guilty once you have made the decision to leave official. You have been in their shoes as a manager, so you already bring insight into this common phenomenon. One way to assuage any guilty feelings you may have is to have already begun the process of developing skills in a few nurses who will be ready to assume your role. When your manager says, "You know I can't fill your position for at least [hyperinflated] weeks and besides . . ." you can offer a suggestion for an appropriate successor. If you have used effective team-building and participatory management skills, your group is sure to have a few staff members qualified to act in your position should there be a delay in replacing you. Remember that you have a choice about whether to accept guilt about leaving a job.

SUMMARY

Changes and choices can be difficult but do present new and positive opportunities for growth. Personal and professional development, active involvement in professional nursing associations, and networking with leaders in your specialty field all can be occasions for growth. The process of learning, integrating new behaviors, and changing positions can be difficult. Once the choice has been made to accept a new opportunity, you have the challenge of creating a special environment for your team where your management style blends with your employer's organizational goals. Remember that effective nurse managers have been described as a "wonder in action." Being a nurse manager can be very fulfilling and exciting. You may have the good fortune of working with a highly competent and sensitive team.

There is no perfect job, only jobs that meet your needs and aspirations at particular times in your life. Only you can evaluate your unique needs, goals, and dreams and work toward achieving them. You can do it!

QUESTIONS FOR CONSIDERATION

1. Support the statement: I market myself every day by _____.
2. List three tips for your ongoing learning.
3. Create a resume or curriculum vitae that highlights your work experience, credentials, and accomplishments.
4. Discuss components of a successful interview and how to best prepare for your interview.
5. Identify three ways you groom staff to become managers and list three team members who you believe would make good managers at your organization. Create an action plan to assist them.

Reference

1. Butler J, Parsons RJ: Hospital perceptions of job satisfaction, *Nursing Management* 20(8):46, 1989.

For Further Reading

Bolles RN: *What color is your parachute?* Berkeley, CA, 1992, Ten Speed Press.

Butler J, Parsons RJ: Hospital perceptions of job satisfaction, *Nursing Management* 20(8):45, 1989.

Fisher P, Vry W: *Getting to yes: negotiating agreement without giving in*, New York, 1981, Penguin Books.

Flores DW: Marketing yourself in an interview, *Nursing 92* 22(8):100, 1992.

Kaplan SM: The nurse as change agent, *Pediatric Nursing* 16(6):603, 1990.

Krouse HJ, Holleran SD: Nurse managers and clinical nursing research, *Nursing Management* 23(7):62, 1992.

Pearlman D, Takacs GJ: The 10 stages of change, *Nursing Management* 21(4):33, 1990.

Perry L: Nursing supervisors continue to lead climb up the ladder, *Modern Healthcare* 21(21):27, 1991.

Sher B: *Wishcraft*, New York, 1983, Random House.

Taylor T: Healthcare marketing and the nurse manager, *Nursing Management* 2(15):84, 1990.

INDEX

Page numbers followed by *b*, *t*, or *f* indicate boxes, tables or figures, respectively.